List of Illustrations

List of Tables

Acknowledgments

Soviet-style regimes officially encouraged all sorts of communal endeavors, including the writing of books. In East Germany, however, "collective authorship" rarely translated into real cooperation or intellectual exchange, constricted as the work was by the compulsion to ideological precision, the lingering hierarchies of German academic traditions, and the power relations that pervaded the dictatorship. In contrast, this book is in many ways truly the product of a collective enterprise. I feel fortunate to have benefited from a remarkable combination of institutional and intellectual support during the time that it has taken to write it.

I am grateful to the many organizations that have supported my research over the years. A Fulbright Research Grant brought me to Germany in 1994, and the Social Science Research Council–Berlin Program for Advanced Studies kept me there for another year. The Institute for the Study of World Politics provided me with the opportunity to conclude my research and begin writing. The University of California at Berkeley furnished me with the financial means to finish writing. During my time at Berkeley, I had the good fortune to enjoy a Chancellor's Dissertation-Year Fellowship, a Hans Rosenberg Fellowship twice, a John L. Simpson Memorial Research Fellowship, a Reinhard Bendix Memorial Research Fellowship, and a Fellowship at the Doreen B. Townsend Center for the Humanities.

In 2001, the dissertation out of which this book emerged won the Fritz Stern Prize. I am grateful to James Brophy, Lisa Heinemann, and Jonathan Petropoulos of the Stern Prize Committee and to the German Historical Institute for its continuing and generous support of my work. My thanks to Boston University for granting me a release from teaching to revise the manuscript. *German History*, the Klartext Verlag, and *Zeitschrift für Geschichtswissenschaften* have kindly granted me permission to reproduce portions of articles that they previously published ("The Vehicle of Desire: The

Trabant, the Wartburg, and the End of the GDR," in *German History* 3:15 (1997), pp. 358–80; "Consuming Ideology: Socialist Consumerism and the Intershops, 1970–1989," in Peter Hübner and Klaus Tenfelde (eds.), *Arbeiter in der SBZ-DDR* (Essen, 1999), pp. 555–72; "Eingaben und Ausgaben: Das Petitionsrecht und der Untergang der DDR," in *Zeitschrift für Geschichtswissenschaft* 45:10 (1997), pp. 902–17).

I am deeply indebted to the many people who facilitated my research. Agnes Petersen at the Hoover Institution was instrumental in helping me find sources. The archivists and librarians at SAPMO, and especially Solveig Nestler, Carola Aehlich, Frau Müller, and the late Volker Lange, were most generous with their knowledge of the party archives and enlivened many a gloomy Berlin day with their humor. Frau Bossier at the Bundesarchiv in Berlin and Frau Gruenspek in Coswig gave me excellent advice. Kurt Schober at the Gauck-Behörde and Berit Pistora at the Bildarchiv in Koblenz were wonderful to work with. Richard Lindenlaub and Manfred Körber at the Deutsche Bundesbank were kind enough to help me obtain interviews with past central bank presidents. The imperturbable Henryk Skrypzcak helped me gain access to East German politicians and provided me with much-needed encouragement. I am grateful to the late Gerhard Rambow for educating me about Germany and sharing his experiences at the West German Economics Ministry over the years, and to Hans Koschnick for assisting me at the beginning of my career. I would also like to thank the many East and West German officials who spent hours educating me and supplementing the archival record.

This book has greatly benefited from the encouragement and constructive criticism of many friends and scholars. In Berlin, Wolfram Fischer, Carl-Ludwig Holtfrerich, and Heinrich August Winkler were kind enough to let me sit in on their doctoral seminars and present portions of my work. Hartmut Kaelble took the time to guide me through questions of social history, and Klaus Tenfelde provided me with several opportunities to test my ideas. Wolfgang Seibel's thoughtful restatements of my central argument made me aware of the importance of this project and gave me the courage to continue with it. I am grateful to Richard Bessel, Warren Breckman, Lord Ralf Dahrendorf, Bernhard Debatin, Christhard Hoffmann, Hans-Hermann Hertle, Wolfram Kaiser, Anthony Kauders, Mary Sarotte, and Patricia Stokes, who took the time to make valuable criticisms of my work. Jonathan Wiesen and Katherine Pence have provided me with insightful analysis and stimulating friendship over the years.

I am greatly indebted to all of those who have commented on portions of the manuscript, and especially Tom Brady, John Connelly, Barry

Eichengreen, Amy Leonard, Carina Johnson, Alf Lüdtke, Elliot Neaman, Heath Pearson, Norma von Ragenfeld-Feldman, James Sheehan, and David Woodruff. Corey Ross's sophisticated assessment of my use of economic and cultural analysis proved invaluable when it came to reorganizing the book. Jonathan Steinberg's brilliant observations helped me understand once again what it is that I am attempting. Hans-Helmut Kotz, whom I have known since my days as a journalist in Frankfurt, took the time to comment in great and useful detail on the manuscript. Margaret Anderson, whose unerring sense of style has rescued many a weak paragraph, helped me understand the historiographic contexts in which my arguments matter. Carla Hesse managed to sum up the entire book in one word on the way to lunch one sunny Berkeley day; I only wish I could be as concise. Jason Scott Smith and Monica Rico suffered through various iterations of numerous chapters and helped clarify my arguments. Scott Tang has allowed me to bounce ideas off him, both on and off the squash court.

My colleagues in the history department at Boston University, especially Barbara Diefendorf, Charles Dellheim, Fred Leventhal, Ezra Mendelsohn, Jon Roberts, and Julian Zelizer, have been exceedingly generous with their advice and help. Lou Ferleger sacrificed the better part of a summer helping me tighten the book, for which I will be eternally grateful. Jeffrey Kopstein and Harold James, who read the manuscript for Cambridge, made suggestions that have greatly improved the book. I would also like to express my thanks to David Lazar of the German Historical Institute for his advice and encouragement and to Lew Bateman at Cambridge for supporting the book in every way. To all my colleagues and friends, who are too numerous to name, my sincere thanks.

This book has been deeply influenced by two brilliant and generous but very different teachers. I have profited greatly from Martin Jay's ability to infuse the most static of arguments with life, to uncover the intellectual lineage of the most recondite positions, and to reembed the academic in the private. Working with Marty has greatly expanded the intellectual horizons of my work. My relationship with Gerry Feldman has been a constant source of professional enlightenment and personal joy. His tremendous generosity, intellectual encouragement, sense of humor, keen historical instincts, and even his daunting productivity have made me a better historian.

There are many others without whom this book would not have been possible. Gerd-Rüdiger Stephan introduced me not only to books and people, but also rescued me many a time from Berlin's worst weather. I am especially grateful to Catherine Epstein and Andrew Zimmerman for their intellectual rigor as well as their friendship. Peter Blitstein's analytical precision and steadfast friendship have helped me understand why anyone bothers to write books. Laurie Case and Tim Davis helped me finish this book and enjoy it, too. I want to thank my brother Andrew and my mother Linda for their love and support. My mother, whose love of words is what convinced me to write, spent hours editing this manuscript – a true labor of love for which I am grateful. Finally, I could not have invented better companions with whom to share this journey than my wife Katharina who has made my East her West, and my children Max and Leora, who quite correctly believe books without pictures are uninteresting: They have all become adept at reminding me that the present can never be recovered, not even as the past.

While I do imagine this book as a collective enterprise, the liberal emphasis on the individual must nevertheless have the last word: Despite the kind assistance of these scholars and friends, I alone am responsible for the views expressed in this book.

List of Abbreviations

AHB	Foreign Trade Enterprises (*Außenhandelsbetriebe*)
BArchB	Federal Archives in Berlin (*Bundesarchiv Berlin*)
BStU	Federal Representative for the Materials of the State Security Service of the Former German Democratic Republic (*Bundesbeauftragter für die Unterlagen des Staastsicherheitsdienstes der ehemaligen Deutschen Demokratischen Republik*)
CDU	Christian Democratic Union of Germany (*Christlich-Demokratische Union Deutschlands*)
CoCom	Committee for Coordinating East–West Trade
Comecon	Council for Mutual Economic Assistance
DIW	German Institute for Economic Research (*Deutsches Institut für Wirtschaftsforschung*)
DM	West German mark (*Deutsche Mark*)
ESS	Economic System of Socialism (*Ökonomisches System des Sozialismus*)
GDR	German Democratic Republic
Genex	Gift Service and Small Export Company (*Geschenkdienst und Kleinexport GmbH*)
FDGB	Free German Trade Union (*Freier Deutscher Gewerkschaftsbund*)
FRG	Federal Republic of Germany
HA XVIII	Economic desk at the Ministry for State Security (*Hauptabteilung XVIII*)
HO	Retail Organization (*Handelsorganisation*)
IFA	Industrial Association for Automotive Construction (*Industrieverband Fahrzeugbau*)

KoKo   Commercial Coordination Area (*Bereich Kommerzielle*
                              Koordinierung)
MEW   Marx-Engels Collected Works (*Marx-Engels Werke*)
MfS   Ministry for State Security (*Ministerium für*
                              Staatssicherheit)
Ministry for ALF Ministry for General Machine, Agricultural Machine,
                              and Automobile Construction (*Ministerium für*
                              Allgemeinen Maschinen-, Landwirtschaftlichen
                              Maschinen- und Fahrzeugbau)
NATO   North Atlantic Treaty Organization
NEP   New Economic Policy
NES   New Economic System (*Neues Ökonomisches System*)
OibE   Stasi Officer on Special Assignment (*Offizier im*
                              besonderen Einsatz)
OPEC   Organization of Petroleum Exporting Countries
Politburo   Political Bureau of the Central Committee (*Politisches*
                              Büro des Zentralkomitees)
Riko   directional coefficient used in calculating the value of
                              the East German to the West German mark
                              (*Richtungskoeffizient*)
SAPMO-BA   Foundation Archive of the Parties and Mass
                              Organizations of the GDR in the Federal Archives
                              (*Stiftung Archiv der Parteien und Massenorganisationen*
                              der DDR im Bundesarchiv)
SBZ   Soviet Zone of Occupation (*Sowjetische Besatzungszone*)
SED   Socialist Unity Party of Germany (*Sozialistische*
                              Einheitspartei Deutschlands)
SMAD   Soviet Military Administration
SPD   Social Democratic Party of Germany
                              (*Sozialdemokratische Partei Deutschlands*)
Stasi   Ministry for State Security (*Ministerium für*
                              Staatssicherheit)
USSR   Union of Soviet Socialist Republics
VEB   People's Own Factory (*Volkseigener Betrieb*)
ZK   Central Committee (*Zentralkomitee*)

Introduction

The condition of a society's money is a symptom of all of its conditions.[1]

In August 1988, an 84-year-old working-class resident of Leipzig named Erich K. wrote to the Central Committee (Zentralkomitee, ZK) of the East German communist party to complain about money. Ironically, he was less concerned about not having enough money than he was that the German Democratic Republic (GDR) had too much of it. Because of money, K. argued, socialism had so far been unable to create the economic conditions necessary for the liberation of humanity. Instead, "socialist states with their bank notes are enmeshed in the capitalist network of bank notes, and for this reason the socialist economies in all socialist states do not make much headway."[2] The problem with money, according to K., was that it derived its value from human suffering. In a reference to his experience of the First World War and his service in Hitler's army during the Second, K. contended that "the trail of capitalism leads over the war dead and much other human misery, and capitalism turned all of this into money, minted increasingly from the suffering of humanity."[3] Not only had the GDR's entanglement with capitalist money impeded the economic progress of socialism, but the use of money itself had also compromised socialism's moral superiority. To restore ethical and economic autonomy to the project of socialism, K. urged the ruling Socialist Unity Party (SED) to abolish money.

Officials at the ZK were greatly disturbed by K.'s letter. Despite the fact that the party officially encouraged East Germans to communicate their concerns by writing letters of grievance, ZK officials were taken aback by

---

1 Joseph A. Schumpeter, *Das Wesen des Geldes* (Göttingen, 1970), p. 1.
2 Bundesarchiv Berlin (BArchB), DN10, 3287, petition from 23.8.88, p. 1. The names of petitioners have been rendered anonymous to protect their privacy.
3 Ibid. See also BArchB, DN10, 3287, petitions from 10.11.85 and 20.6.77.

1

the challenge to their authority contained in K.'s letter. They arranged for local representatives of the party and state to visit the elderly man in his home and "discuss" his ideas. Although the delegation clearly sought to intimidate K. into retracting his letter, it nonetheless took pains to create the semblance of a dialogue between an attentive state and a concerned citizen. K., at any rate, appears to have taken this pretense of debate for the real thing. After a brief exchange of views, the elderly man declared himself satisfied by the delegation's explanation of socialist monetary policy. To the relief of the ZK, he withdrew his letter. Not two weeks later, however, in a second letter, K. recanted, complaining that his guests had not really engaged him in conversation but had instead put words into his mouth.[4]

SED leaders were incensed by K.'s new letter. Not only had he demonstrated open disregard for the coercive etiquette of letter writing in the GDR, but he persisted in willfully misunderstanding a fundamental aspect of SED policy. Furious at the inability of their subordinates to silence K., officials at the ZK shifted responsibility for the fiasco onto the East German central bank. In a scathing letter to the Staatsbank, Günther Ehrensperger, head of the powerful Department of Planning and Finance at the ZK, implied that the bank was unable to control the circulation of ideas in the area of its own expertise – the circulation of money. Ehrensperger then demanded that the central bank coerce K. into rescinding the retraction of his withdrawal.[5]

Faced with intense political pressure from the SED leadership to silence K. on the one hand and an avalanche of cantankerous letters from the elderly man on the other, Gerhard Serick, Deputy President of the Staatsbank, tried to depoliticize the affair by attributing K.'s recalcitrance to his advanced age rather than some heretical obstinacy. Noting that K.'s ideas were "totally confused and ludicrous," Serick suggested that he was simply senile. In a report to the Politburo, Serick concluded that "Herr K. is no longer able intellectually to comprehend our arguments regarding the theory and praxis of money under socialist conditions. Further conversations are futile – his last letter is renewed demonstration of that."[6]

Even if K. was merely muddled and ornery, however, he had succeeded in agitating the communist party leadership with his suggestion that a profound discrepancy between theory and praxis existed in the GDR. Not only had K. pointed out that the party had yet to implement its egalitarian promise of a moneyless society, but he also suggested that the GDR's entanglement

4 BArchB, DN10, 3287, petition to Herzog, Staatsbank Leipzig, 25.11.85.
5 BArchB, DN10, 3287, Ehrensperger to Meier, 7.9.88. See also BArchB, DN10, 3287, Serick to Wackernagel, 20.11.85.
6 BArchB, DN10, 3287, Serick to Ehrensperger, 9.9.88.

with capitalism had compromised the "better" German state financially and morally. And he had done so in defiance of the SED's otherwise tight control over the circulation of ideas.

This book is about the East German attempt to create a society of inexhaustible plenty and limitless good by eliminating money. Like communist parties elsewhere, the SED sought to reverse what Karl Polyani called the "great transformation" and reembed economic activity in social relations.[7] By unmaking money, the party believed it could turn private into common wealth and eventually realize the promise of Edenic riches.

The East German heirs of Marx and Lenin failed, however, to devise a genuine alternative to capitalism, much less put an end to social injustice. Though there were many reasons for this failure, this book argues that the most important involved a confusion of money with the market. In their quest to subordinate the instrumental reason inherent in economic calculation to ethical principles, East German communists tried to preempt capitalist exchange by creating extramonetary relationships between producers and consumers. As Marx himself noted, however, merely reforming the system for allocating resources would not alter social relations under capitalism because it could effect no change in the methods of production. Far from reordering trade along nonmarket lines, the SED's partial elimination of money only aggravated existing asymmetries between supply and demand, unleashing increasingly bitter distributional conflicts that eventually discredited central planning.

If the shortcomings of economic planning were broadly similar across Eastern Europe, what distinguished the GDR from other Soviet-style regimes was the division of Germany. Unlike its communist allies, East Germany was forced to compete with a hostile capitalist state in the same national space. This geographical and cultural proximity involved the GDR with the capitalist West to a degree not experienced by other Eastern European states. The SED's decision in the 1970s to introduce capitalist currency and commodities into the GDR, for example, initially stabilized the planned economy. But this economic reliance on the West undermined the political authority of socialism. Not only did borrowing money from the class enemy constitute a tacit admission that capitalism was the superior system, but the official promotion of West German money and merchandise supplanted the East German currency and commodities, reinforcing the sense of ordinary East Germans that they were second-class citizens in a capitalist world. Despite the SED's commitment to fashioning a society that would

---

7 Karl Polyani, *The Great Transformation: The Political and Economic Origins of Our Time* (Boston, 2001).

suspend the "laws" of capitalism by transforming the function of money, the GDR's entanglement with the West ultimately devalued the meaning of socialism by undermining the actual currency itself.

At least initially, however, the philosophical anticapitalism of Marx and Engels, as interpreted by Lenin, resonated powerfully with the anticapitalist traditions of German history. In particular, the portrayal of money as a source of social injustice animated East German communists, who agreed that money could have no place in the future of the socialist state. To some extent, their mistrust of money had been shaped by the peculiarities of German history. The traumatic experiences of the hyperinflation during 1922–3, when Germans had too much money, and the radical deflation of the Great Depression, when it seemed as if they had too little, turned a majority of Germans away from liberal democratic solutions to the challenges of modernity. While the Nazis linked the circulation of money to the expansion of "Jewish" values, denouncing interest rates as a form of servitude that obstructed racial solidarity, the German left sought to expose the uneven distribution of power and privilege masked by money.[8] As the playwright Bertolt Brecht, who would settle in East Berlin after 1945, put it, "What is robbing a bank compared to founding one?"[9]

After World War II and the defeat of German fascism, the renewed threat of hyperinflation heightened the determination of many Germans to organize economic activity according to the principle of social justice. The role of money as a causal factor in German history took on new meaning in 1948, however, when the *Deutsche Mark* replaced the *Reichsmark* in the Western zone of occupation and precipitated the partition of Germany into a capitalist West and a communist East. For forty years, the two German states sought to link national identity with economic organization – the social market economy in the Federal Republic and the planned economy in the GDR. In 1989–90, the systemic competition between capitalism and communism would once again thrust money onto center stage, as East German demand for West German marks paved the way for German–German reconciliation after the collapse of the Berlin Wall.[10] For the first time in German

8 On the hyperinflation, see Gerald D. Feldman, *The Great Disorder: Politics, Economics, and Society in the German Inflation, 1914–1924* (New York and Oxford, 1993). On the Depression, see Harold James, *The German Slump: Politics and Economics, 1924–1936* (Oxford, 1986); Richard Evans and Dick Geary, *The German Unemployed: Experiences and Consequences of Mass Unemployment from the Weimar Republic to the Third Reich* (London, 1987). On the Nazis, see Avraham Barkai, *Nazi Economics: Ideology, Theory, and Policy*, trans. Ruth Hadass-Vashitz (New Haven, Conn., 1990); Richard J. Overy, *War and Economy in the Third Reich* (Oxford, 1994).
9 Bertolt Brecht, *The Threepenny Opera*, Act , scene i.
10 For more on the social market economy in the Federal Republic, see Anthony James Nicholls, *Freedom with Responsibility: The Social Market Economy in Germany, 1918–1963* (Oxford and New York,

history, money played a unifying, rather than a divisive, role: German unification was preceded and made possible by German monetary union, which replaced the East with the West German mark in the summer of 1990. In the meantime, however, K. and millions of other Germans like him experienced money as a medium for creating and intensifying social stratification.

In addition to this historical equation of money with social inequality, East German communism inherited a philosophical antipathy toward money from the Soviet Union. Like the utopian socialists before them, the Bolsheviks identified money with economic exploitation – as the instrument employed by capital to dispossess labor of its value. Marxism-Leninism presented capitalist exchange not as the mutually beneficial and therefore welfare-enhancing activity of liberal economic theory, but rather as a zero-sum game in which one party necessarily exploits the other. The asymmetrical structure of power intrinsic to market relations favors those who possess capital over those who must sell their labor power or risk destitution.

Not only do workers suffer from material oppression, but their apparent freedom to alienate their labor by selling it for money also leads to a form of spiritual alienation. Capitalism's elevation of economic rationality over ethical concerns, the SED claimed, encourages people to treat their lives as if they were a means to an end, rather than an end in themselves. The liberal celebration of private vice as advancing public good further confuses the purpose of human economic production – the sustenance of life – with the instrument people employ to sustain that life – the pursuit of money. As a result, people end up living to work, rather than working to live. For this reason, East German communists perceived in money both the starting point and the ever-receding horizon of people's enslavement to this confusion of ends and means.

In addition, the party argued that capitalism produces a form of alienation Marx termed commodity fetishism, or the false attribution to products of the power to gratify human needs. According to Marx, money is the quintessential commodity fetish because it "debases all the gods of man

1994). For the Soviet zone of occupation, see Mary Fulbrook, *Anatomy of a Dictatorship: Inside the GDR, 1949–1989* (Oxford, 1995); Christoph Kleßmann, *Die doppelte Staatsgründung: Deutsche Geschichte, 1945–1955* (Bonn, 1991); Norman Naimark, *The Russians in Germany: A History of the Soviet Zone of Occupation, 1945–1949* (Cambridge, Mass., 1995); Hermann Weber, *Geschichte der DDR* (Munich, 1989). For more on the East German planned economy, see Jeffrey Kopstein, *The Politics of Economic Decline in East Germany, 1945–1989* (Chapel Hill, N.C., and London, 1997); André Steiner, *Die DDR-Wirtschaftsreform der sechziger Jahre: Konflikt zwischen Effizienz- und Machtkalkül* (Berlin, 1999). For more on the collapse of the GDR, see Hans-Hermann Hertle, *Der Fall der Mauer. Die unbeabsichtigte Auflösung des SED-Staates* (Opladen, 1996); Konrad Jarausch, *The Rush to German Unity* (New York, 1994); Charles S. Maier, *Dissolution: The Crisis of Communism and the End of East Germany* (Princeton, N.J., 1997).

and turns them into commodities. Money is the universal, self-constituting value of all things. It has therefore robbed the whole world, human as well as natural, of its own values."[11] Everything can be had for money, yet only money is completely fungible; it stands in for every value, but none in particular.

Building on these insights into capitalism, the SED sought to distinguish between "real" and "false" needs. According to the party, the needs of an individual, whether physiological or spiritual, are shaped by social relations in a given society. In capitalist societies, a person's real needs are manipulated and falsified by the exploitative constraints of market forces. Through this dichotomy, the SED established an equivalency between false needs and commodity fetishism, between desire and money.

The planned economy, or so the SED alleged, was superior to capitalism because it removed the grounds for desire by creating social conditions in which only real needs exist. Although money continued to circulate in socialist society, it existed only in vestigial form, as a medium for the satisfaction of real needs, and would become entirely redundant once the GDR was transformed into a communist society.[12] Where capitalist currency functioned as an agent of economic scarcity and social alienation, the currency of socialism offered the opportunity to apportion the wealth of society along egalitarian lines – "from each according to his ability, to each according to his needs."[13] For factories, the stimulus to production was no longer profit, but rather a matrix of economic targets formulated by the party according to its political preferences. Unable to command resources, socialist money circulated as an accounting unit that recorded centrally authorized transactions, such as the payment of wages. Nor did acquiring money for its own sake hold much attraction for private economic actors. The SED's decision to subsidize the basic needs of consumers, from food to housing, helped uncouple wealth from money. In this manner, the SED hoped, the currency of socialism would recast the relation between economy and society, between desire and need.

Making money worth less, however, was not the same as making it worthless. The social construction of value in the GDR was mediated not

---

11 My translation of Karl Marx, "Zur Judenfrage," in *Marx-Engels Werke* (*MEW*), vol. 1 (East Berlin, 1981), p. 374 (Karl Marx, "On the Jewish Question," in *Karl Marx and Friedrich Engels: Collected Works*, vol. 3, p. 172).

12 In communist parlance, "socialism" is an intermediary stage in the transition from capitalism to communism. While most socialists believe in the organic historical development of socialism out of capitalism, communists are socialists who advocate the violent overthrow of capitalism and its replacement with a centralized economy supervised by a one-party dictatorship.

13 Karl Marx, "Critique of the Gotha Program," in *Marx/Engels Selected Works*, vol. 3 (Moscow, 1970), p. 19.

by a utopian transparency of need, but by shortages of economic and ethical goods. Replacing money with planning indicators permitted the party to emphasize its production priorities. Yet the system of apportioning resources from the center led to the uneven distribution and waste of resources. Freed from the threat of bankruptcy, East German factories were no longer guided by cost constraints, but were responsible instead for fulfilling the plan. Ignoring costs, however, made for increasing inefficiency, low levels of productivity, and waste, all of which eventually overwhelmed the productive capacities of the GDR.

In the consumer sector, moreover, the chronic shortages of consumer goods afflicting the planned economy further undermined the value and function of socialist money. Although the East German mark sufficed to complete purchases of the basic necessities of life, such as bread and the rent, it could not overcome shortages or the unofficial forms of rationing typical of the planned economy, such as exorbitantly high prices for consumer durable goods or exceedingly long lines. To ensure the prompt delivery of washing machines, reduce the long wait for cars, or purchase stockings, not to mention Western consumer goods, West German currency came to play an increasingly prominent role. As a result, the GDR's monetary regime fragmented into two competing modes of exchange: Socialist money was used to satisfy basic needs, while capitalist money was used to fulfill the desires of East German consumers for convenience, creature comforts, and social status. The SED sought to construct political authority through economic practice, but its attempt to govern an industrial – and divided – nation by force fostered instead the creation of political identity through national currency. By 1989 at the latest, it was clear that the party's attempt to control what money can buy, as well as what purchase it has on human imagination, had failed.

The SED's attempt to subordinate economy to society had not always met with such rejection, however. In the immediate postwar period, for example, the economic reorganization of society along socialist lines enjoyed considerable support, not least because many Germans perceived the "Third Reich" as the logical outcome of capitalist excess.[14] The party also benefited from the political topography that coalesced out of the Cold War. In

---

14 For the communist view, see Gunther Kohlmey, *Das Geldsystem der Deutschen Demokratischen Republik* (East Berlin, 1956), pp. 19–32. Even many Christian Democrats initially expressed sympathy with socialism, as in the Ahlener Program (Weber, *Geschichte der DDR*, pp. 78–9, 136–8). The reputation of West German industry continued to suffer from its association – both real and imagined – with National Socialism. On the ties of industry to the Nazis, see Reinhard Neebe, *Großindustrie, Staat und NSDAP 1930–1933: Paul Silverberg und der Reichsverband der Deutschen Industrie in der Krise der Weimarer Republik* (Göttingen, 1981). On the postwar image of industrialists, see S. Jonathan Wiesen, *West German Industry and the Challenge of the Nazi Past, 1945–1955* (Chapel Hill, N.C., 2001).

particular, the territorial and ideological division of Germany facilitated the SED's efforts to establish its moral superiority over its capitalist cousins. The fact, for example, that prominent Nazis continued to wield influence in West German public life – from Hans Globke, coauthor of the Nuremberg racial laws and Chancellor Konrad Adenauer's top aide, to Kurt Georg Kiesinger, a Nazi expert in radio propaganda who became chancellor in 1966 – lent the SED's tireless efforts to conflate capitalism with fascism more credibility than they merited.[15] Nevertheless, the party's skilled representation of the GDR as a bastion of antifascism, along with its promises of social equality and solidarity, ensured it a measure of loyalty, especially among intellectuals.[16] The commitment to socialism, moreover, entailed the concomitant belief that political freedoms are derived from the economic organization of society. Thus, the SED's ideological justifications for its despotism, and for its subjugation of civil to economic rights in particular, resonated with many other interpretations of Weimar's collapse and the rise of National Socialism.[17]

Competition with West German economic success dogged the East German regime from the start. Especially after the violent suppression of the popular uprising of 1953, when the SED relied on Soviet tanks to quell a workers' revolt, many who were unwilling to serve the regime or suffer its repression braved the growing obstacles and emigrated to West Germany. The result was a more homogeneous and pliant population, as open dissent was diminished by a combination of material blandishment, administrative coercion, and sheer attrition. But whatever advantage the SED might have gained from the exodus of "undesirables" was offset by the yawning economic gap the émigrés left behind them. In particular, the flight of skilled

---

15 In addition, "examples of right-wing extremism or meetings of former Nazis in the Federal Republic offered the argumentation of the GDR important assistance" (Weber, *Geschichte der DDR*, p. 373). Of course, a number of former Nazis also exercised key functions in the GDR, such as State Prosecutor Ernst Melsheimer, who had been a prominent Nazi legal advisor; Herbert Kröger, a high-ranking SS officer who would become the SED's most important jurist; and State Planning Commissioner Erich Apel, who helped organize slave labor to produce V2 rockets for Wernher von Braun. Nor did the Nazi past of the GDR's central bank president, Horst Kaminsky, prevent his rise through the ranks of the East German economic bureaucracy. On the high numbers of ex-Nazis in the ranks of the East German professoriate, see John Connelly, *Captive University: The Sovietization of East German, Czech, and Polish Higher Education, 1945–1956* (Chapel Hill, N.C., 2000), pp. 134, 158.

16 Jeffrey Herf, *Divided Memory: The Nazi Past in the Two Germanys* (Cambridge, Mass., 1997); Sigrid Meuschel, *Legitimation und Parteiherrschaft in der DDR* (Frankfurt/Main, 1992); Vladimir Tismaneanu, *Reinventing Politics: Eastern Europe from Stalin to Havel* (New York, 1992), p. 210; John C. Torpey, *Intellectuals, Socialism, and Dissent: The East German Opposition, and Its Legacy* (Minneapolis, Minn., and London, 1995).

17 As Ralf Dahrendorf has pointed out, this subordination of civil to economic rights is present in Marx's use of the phrase *bürgerliche Gesellschaft* – a term referring both to the bourgeoisie and to civil society – to disparage liberal democracy as a social order that serves the economic interests of capitalists (Ralf Dahrendorf, *Der moderne soziale Konflikt. Essay zur Politik der Freiheit* [Stuttgart, 1992], p. 15).

labor, attracted away by the "magnet" of growing West German affluence, threatened to destabilize the socialist state during the late 1950s.[18] When the seven-year plan ran into difficulties and the rhetoric directed at stanching the outflow of emigrants backfired, the SED responded by sealing off the country with the Berlin Wall.[19] The construction of the Wall on 13 August 1961 removed any lingering doubts regarding the nature of the East German state, revealing that communist party rule rested primarily upon the threat of violence.

The relation between theory and practice in the GDR became increasingly clear during the 1960s. Under pressure from the USSR and his own party, SED chief Walter Ulbricht put an abrupt end to the regime's brief attempt to reform itself from within in 1965, then responded to the more sustained reformist efforts in Czechoslovakia by advocating the use of force against Prague in 1968.[20] While Marxist-Leninist ideology continued to be an important factor in East German life, especially among SED members, the party's ability to manage popular dissent was on the wane. Its decline as an effective tool of political integration was hastened by the ascendancy of Erich Honecker.

Honecker's assumption of power in 1971 heralded a significant change in the party's stance toward many of the GDR's most pressing problems. His most immediate and significant accomplishment consisted of leading the GDR out of the wilderness of diplomatic isolation. After signing treaties with the United States and West Germany in 1972, the GDR's international position improved dramatically. By 1978, the GDR entertained diplomatic relations with 123 countries and could claim membership in major international organizations, including the United Nations.[21] These

18 The flow of skilled laborers westward continued to be a source of concern to economic experts well after the construction of the Wall. See, for example, Alexander Schalck-Golodkowski and Heinz Volpert, "Zur Vermeldung ökonomische Verluste und zur Erwirtschaftung zusätzlicher Devisen im Bereich Kommerzielle Koordinierung des Ministeriums für Außenwirtschaft der Deutschen Demokratischen Republik" (Ph.D. dissertation, Potsdam, 1970), Anlage 10. I am thankful to Rainer Karlsch for permitting me to read the copy in his possession.

19 Hertle, *Der Fall der Mauer*, pp. 17 ff.; Christoph Kleßmann, *Zwei Staaten, eine Nation* (Göttingen, 1988), pp. 303–24. For an evaluation of the party's perspective, see Andreas Malycha, "Von der Gründung 1945/46 bis zum Mauerbau 1961," and Gerd-Rüdiger Stephan, "Vom Mauerbau 1961 bis zur Wende 1989," in Andreas Herbst, Gerd-Rüdiger Stephan, and Jürgen Winkler (eds.), *Die SED: Geschichte – Organisation – Politik. Ein Handbuch* (Berlin, 1997), pp. 53–8. For a typical account of the "antifascist protective barrier" during the Honecker period, see Akademie für Gesellschaftswissenschaften beim ZK der SED (ed.), *Die Volkswirtschaft der DDR* (East Berlin, 1979), pp. 125–6.

20 Kopstein, *The Politics of Economic Decline*, pp. 41–72; Steiner, *Die DDR-Wirtschaftsreform*; Stephan, "Vom Mauerbau," pp. 59–68.

21 Before the Basic Treaty was signed with Bonn on 21 December 1972, the GDR had formal diplomatic relations with thirty-eight states (Weber, *Geschichte der DDR* [Munich, 1989], pp. 432–3; M. E. Sarotte, *Dealing with the Devil: East Germany, Détente and Ostpolitik, 1969–1973* [Chapel Hill, N.C., 2001]).

foreign political successes contributed to a "normalization" of relations for the GDR that enhanced Honecker's status at home and abroad. In addition, Honecker relaxed domestic political constraints and introduced a new economic course that would fundamentally alter the structure of the East German economy.[22] According to the party, the GDR was now entering the phase of "real-existing socialism," a slogan reflecting the new policy of shifting resources to meet consumer demands. Initially, Honecker's economic policies, enshrined in the slogan of the "Principal Task" (*Hauptaufgabe*), succeeded in producing tangible improvements in the East German standard of living. Soon, however, the political climate began to change. The liberalization of cultural policy initiated in 1971 had been languishing for some time but was completely repudiated in 1976 with the expatriation of the folksinger Wolf Biermann.[23] In its place, an unabashedly neo-Stalinist approach to cultural politics flourished under the watchful eyes of Kurt Hager, Cultural Secretary of the ZK.

More fateful than the political crackdown, however, was Honecker's economic program. The Principal Task had introduced imbalances into the GDR's economy that were to worsen with time. These failures might not have been so grave had the gap between East German shortcomings and West German achievements not become so clear to East Germans by the late 1970s.[24] Nowhere was the asymmetry in wealth more apparent than in the supply of consumer goods, from cars to coffee, and in the money necessary to purchase them. At the same time, the ideological justifications the party deployed to obscure its dictatorial methods proved increasingly unable to manage material dissatisfaction. The nimbus of antifascism, whose almost talismanic qualities had once possessed an integrative force, had congealed into an obscurantist fog by the 1980s. By renouncing future utopias in favor

22 Stephan, "Vom Mauerbau," pp. 76–8; Jürgen Winkler, "Kulturpolitik," in Herbst et al., *Die SED*, pp. 399–400; Rüdiger Thomas, "Kulturpolitik und Künstlerbewußtsein seit dem VIII. Parteitag der SED," in Gert-Joachim Glaeßner (ed.), *Die DDR in der Ära Honecker: Politik, Kultur, Gesellschaft* (Opladen, 1988); Weber, *Geschichte der DDR*, pp. 451–5.

23 Winkler, "Kulturpolitik," pp. 400–3; Weber, *Geschichte der DDR*, pp. 452–3. For the growing disillusionment among intellectuals caused by the expatriation of Wolfgang Biermann, see Manfred Krug, *Abgehauen: Ein Mitschnitt und ein Tagebuch* (Düsseldorf, 1997). Rüdiger Thomas and Heinrich Mohr imply that this disenchantment with the GDR also entailed a generation gap defined by receding memories of the "Third Reich" (Thomas, "Kulturpolitik und Künstlerbewußtsein seit dem VIII. Parteitag der SED," pp. 605–7; Heinrich Mohr, "'Das gebeutelte Hätschelkind': Literatur und Literaten in der Ära Honecker," in Glaeßner [ed.], *Die DDR in der Ära Honecker*, pp. 627–9). See also the work of the East German poet Uwe Kolbe, who coined the term *hineingeboren* to describe those who had no other experience outside the GDR (Uwe Kolbe, *Hineingeboren: Gedichte 1975–1979* [East Berlin, 1980]).

24 Except for those living in the so-called valley of the clueless (*Tal der Ahnungslosen*) near Dresden, East Germans were able to receive West German television and radio. Copies of West German periodicals also found their way into the GDR.

of present prosperity, moreover, Honecker had opened the door to criticism of the real-existing here and now. In particular, the increasingly stark contrast between western plenty and eastern penury undermined the regime's most effective arguments regarding its own legitimacy. The party's cherished visions of egalitarian freedom had given way to nightmares of administrative harassment and social inequality.

The regime's shrinking political capital was reflected most notably in the diminishing desirability of its currency. East Germans referred derisively to their coins as "aluminum chips" (*Aluchips*), for example, reducing them to the metal that deprived socialist money of its heft. This popular expression of the asymmetrical relation between weight and value was not, however, merely the residue of an earlier time when the material of money possessed a value independent of the currency itself.[25] The unbearable lightness of East German money stood in stark contrast to the weighty claims that the regime inscribed on its currency, not the least because the East German mark gradually ceased to function as money. The SED's tireless invocation of the Marxian labor theory of value had taught East Germans to understand the money in which they were paid as the unmediated equivalent of the work they had done. Even as the party alleged that this money, unsullied by capitalist exploitation, was the substance of their labor, however, the everyday experience of economic shortage illustrated to East Germans how little their labor was worth. The shortages generated by economic planning partially demonetized the economy by resurrecting the practice of barter and permitting the use of Western currency. Because not every good or service could be had for it, East German money quickly became a sometimes necessary, but not always sufficient, aspect of economic transactions. In fact, commodities were often a more valuable source of exchange than money. People often hoarded spare parts for automobiles, for example, against the potential of future necessity or a trade for something else they required. Timely delivery of consumer durable goods could also be encouraged by providing salespeople with scarce goods such as Western coffee, which was not brewed, but circulated instead like money – its use suspended by an abstraction of its value. The scarcity of key consumer goods, moreover, increased the power of the institutions and individuals entrusted with the distribution of those goods. Proximity to the party leadership, or to the local distribution nexus – such as ties of family or friendship to the salesperson

---

25 Mercantilism, for example, with its concentration on bullion and specie, confused wealth with money for political reasons. See Eric Roll, *A History of Economic Thought* (London, 1992), pp. 48–71; Eli F. Heckscher, *Mercantilism*, vol. 2 (London and New York, 1955), p. 202 ff.

behind the meat counter at the neighborhood grocery store – often guaranteed better and more reliable choices. In this manner, the shortages forced the East German mark into the role of a partially, rather than universally, exchangeable good, thereby robbing it of its quality as money. Privilege and corruption began to replace the *Ostmark* as the coin of the realm.

Worse still, the SED under Honecker institutionalized the devaluation of its own currency. In its pursuit of new sources of foreign currency to alleviate the shortages, the party dramatically expanded the number of hard-currency stores (*Intershops*). By permitting East Germans to hold Western currency and encouraging them to purchase Western consumer goods with it, the party hoped to increase its foreign currency revenues while making the thriving black market less attractive. By sanctioning a sphere of the economy in which the West German mark was legal tender, however, the party weakened the purchasing power of wages paid in *Mark der DDR*, which could not be used in the Intershops and had little value on the black market. At the same time, the socialist state's official use of capitalist currency came close to an open disavowal of East German money. Expanded use of Western currency, moreover, rewarded people with ties to the "class enemy" in West Germany, rather than those loyal to the regime, or even the working class as a group. By the late 1970s, proximity to West Germany, together with privilege and corruption, were supplanting East German money and institutionalizing the material inequalities that the regime was ostensibly devoted to eradicating. Ironically, the very social injustices against which the GDR officially defined itself – commodity fetishism, social hierarchies based on the acquisition of material goods, the inequitable distribution of wealth, and a lack of economic freedom – became the substance of everyday experience.

By the 1980s, Honecker's refusal to alter his economic policies had effectively bankrupted the GDR. With the help of Günter Mittag, his tyrannical yet talented aide, Honecker embarked on a series of risky projects whose short-term success only delayed the necessary introduction of austerity measures for consumers and a shift in production priorities. The revenue generated from Honecker's schemes, which included a gamble on oil prices, the cannibalization of East German capital stock, and the dramatic expansion of Intershop operations, helped reduce the GDR's hard-currency debt. It did so, however, by intensifying the administrative irrationalities inherent in the planned economy and exhausting the GDR's future productive capacities. By 1986, a combination of bureaucratic over-centralization and the deterioration of industrial plant produced increasingly acute shortages of consumer goods. The tangible decrease in living standards, along with Honecker's vehement rejection of the economic and political reforms instituted in the Soviet Union by Mikhail Gorbachev, encouraged popular unrest. At the same time, Honecker's economic policies and intolerance of criticism weakened the ability of the socialist state to neutralize political discontent. The circulation of Western money and merchandise, caused by the shortages and expanded by Honecker's policies, contributed to the ideological and material delegitimation of the socialist economy. It was these shortages of economic and ethical goods – the absence of key commodities and social equality – that fueled the political unrest that breached the Berlin Wall on 9 November 1989.

Once the SED's power had been broken, many East Germans turned from reform of socialism to its elimination. The diminished legitimacy of socialism, along with the popular equation of West German money with prosperity, put the GDR's future into question, as the perceived power of the Deutsche Mark (DM) to provide access to a world of consumer plenty functioned as a bridge to German unification during the winter of 1989–90. Thus, the fragmentation of money as a medium of exchange not only hastened the collapse of the GDR, but also determined the pace and mode of German unification.

In its stress on the economic and cultural meanings of money, this book diverges from most accounts of economic planning, which identify price distortion as the source of scarcity in planned economies.[26] The interwar debate between Ludwig von Mises, who argued that industrial production requires rational economic calculation to function efficiently and that the ex ante valuations of socialist planners were not a sufficiently rational substitute for market relations, and Oskar Lange, who insisted that the rational allocation of resources by a central entity was theoretically possible given the right incentives, greatly shaped the reception of economic planning in the West.[27] Especially influential has been Friedrich von Hayek's sophisticated development of Mises's ideas, particularly his objection that centrally determined prices do not capture subjective valuations, do not rely on the dispersed knowledge of individual economic actors, and therefore cannot aggregate

---

26 Scholars as diverse as Peter Rutland, who relies greatly on Hayek, and Alec Nove, who was unsympathetic to the neoclassical project, ground their assessments of economic planning in problems of price formation. Two notable exceptions include the work of Gregory Grossman and Hajo Riese, *Geld im Sozialismus. Zur theoretischen Fundierung von Konzeptionen des Sozialismus* (Regensburg, 1990). For a concise review of this debate, see Gavin Peebles, *A Short History of Socialist Money* (Sydney, London, and Boston, 1991).

27 Ludwig von Mises, "Die Wirtschaftsrechnung im sozialistischen Gemeinwesen," *Archiv für Sozialwissenschaften und Sozialpolitik* 47 (1920), pp. 86–121; Oskar Lange, "On the Economic Theory of Socialism, Part ," *Review of Economic Studies* 4 (1936), pp. 53–71.

information cheaply, much less provide knowledge about local conditions and special circumstances.[28] Most of the literature on Soviet-style regimes explains both production shortfalls and chronic excess demand as consequences of rigid pricing policies, with excellent results.

This book offers an alternate route to similar conclusions, arguing that an antipathy toward money rooted in non-Marxian socialism was a constituent element of economic planning. The central determination of prices has rightfully attracted scholarly attention because it offers a compelling explanation for the pathologies of economic planning while providing insight into the transmission of communist power. But hostility toward money was both logically anterior to price control and more basic to the socialist project. Thus, an exclusive concentration on price formation can offer a powerful analysis of the immediate causes of economic scarcity in Soviet-style regimes, but it obscures the theoretical justifications for central planning and neglects the mechanisms by which prices came to express politicized value hierarchies. It also forecloses a key question that socialists believed they had resolved – that there is an alternative to the categories of liberal economic theory, such as supply and demand, in assessing economic performance.

Perhaps more importantly, the language of economics captures the socialist attempt to reorder the relationship between economy and society only in part. Like many on the left, the Bolsheviks and their Eastern European heirs viewed money as a metonymy for capitalism, a dubious part standing in for the damnable whole. The belief that by gaining control over money the planned economy could improve efficiency in production and eliminate economic amorality in consumption was not simply a technical question SED leaders left to financial experts. The prejudice against money also shaped the approach of East German politicians to basic questions of economic autarky and political independence. As the Roman politician and orator Cicero famously remarked, money forms "the sinews of war."[29] In their battle against capitalism, SED leaders were hamstrung from the start.

Reintegrating ideological objections to money into accounts of the planned economy, moreover, is vital to understanding the peculiarity of the GDR's situation. Poland, for example, benefited from hard-currency remittances sent by Poles living abroad. But communist Poland was never forced to vie directly with a hostile capitalist state that lay claim to the same

28 Friedrich von Hayek, "Socialist Calculation: The Competitive Solution," in *Economica* 7 (1940), pp. 125–49, and "The Use of Knowledge in Society," in *American Economic Review* 35 (1945), pp. 519–30.
29 Marcus Tullius Cicero, *Philippics*, trans. D. R. Shackleton Bailey (Chapel Hill, N.C., 1986), pp. 150–1.

political legitimacy in the same language. In contrast, currency became a battleground for the political and economic loyalties of the East German populace. After all, it was in money rather than prices that the systemic competition between the capitalist West and the socialist East was experienced most palpably by East Germans.

All Soviet-style regimes experienced some degree of monetary collapse, but the GDR's proximity to the West provides an unusual opportunity to observe the economy and culture of socialist consumerism. In contrast to market economies, economic planning created a bifurcated experience of money. Employees were paid a sum of money for their work, but when they tried to spend that money as consumers, it often failed to secure the products they desired – that is, the limited purchasing power of socialist money disrupted the consumer economy, which required a strong and stable currency to function. The exceptional fragmentation of the East German monetary regime further undermined the purchasing power of the East German mark. As a result, the SED found itself not only without a reliable instrument for imposing its policy of enforced underconsumption, but was also increasingly vulnerable to the West German model of consumerism, with its strong mark and panoply of abundance. By the 1980s, the relation between the two marks increasingly determined the relation between the two Germanys. As East Germans gravitated toward the Deutsche Mark because of its greater purchasing power, they began attributing a metaphoric power to it that shaped their economic behavior, social practices, and, ultimately, their political loyalties.

For all of these reasons, this book seeks to restore money to its place as a central theoretical category and an object of utopian passions. By showing how an institutionalized mistrust of money contributed to the GDR's economic problems, from production failures to its foreign debt, this book is intended to supplement rather than supplant traditional price-oriented accounts. Where possible and appropriate, it reconstructs production problems not simply in terms of politically induced price distortions, but also as a function of the GDR's inadequate allocative framework. By interpreting the cultural meaning of money as it was understood by SED officials as well as ordinary East Germans, it also tries to reunite the sphere of production with that of consumption, which are often divided in traditional accounts. Nevertheless, the book's focus on the power of the state to shape economic behavior is not intended to promote clichés about "free markets." In contrast to neoclassical theorists, who pretend that perfect competition unfolds only when free of state control, and communist theoreticians, who pretended that state power could banish market forces from economic activity, this book assumes that markets exist wherever there is trade, which itself is constituted by the interplay between individual utility maximizers and the legal and cultural frameworks in which they move.

The first half of the book attempts to construct an economic and political history of the Honecker period. It makes use of money in the form of its scarcity – debt – to discuss the relationship between the capitalist West and the communist East. The first chapter traces the intellectual debt of the planned economy to classical liberal theory, arguing that the SED's perception of money as the locus of immoral economic behavior – as encouraging the desire for social status – was a constituent element in the structure of the East German economy. The next three chapters analyze the material debt of the GDR to the West. Chapter 2 explores the problem of economic accountability, which persisted despite the party's reduction of money to an accounting unit. It argues that, once liberated from monetary constraints, the use of planning indicators proved insufficient to hold producers responsible for their actions. The resulting decline in productivity rates led the SED leadership to borrow money from the capitalist West.

If the SED could denigrate money at home, however, it was forced to treat its hard-currency debts as real constraints on the GDR's resources. Chapter 3 analyzes the crisis of liquidity that nearly led the GDR to default on its loans. It suggests that the West German decision to bail out the SED rescued Honecker's career, while the constant threat of bankruptcy enabled Günter Mittag to amass almost unchecked power. Chapter 4 examines the risky solutions adopted by the SED leadership to liberate the GDR from its reliance on Western capital. Mittag's efforts to pay down the debt generated administrative disarray, as the center increasingly intervened with rapidly diminishing resources to alleviate production bottlenecks. As the importance of exports in the struggle to earn hard currency eclipsed the East German mark in economic relevance, so too did the center's control over economic life diminish.

The second half of the book employs money as a cultural category to analyze the formation of social identity and national allegiance. Drawing on the examples of the automobile industry and the Intershops, Chapters 5 and 6 argue that value in the GDR was mediated not by labor, as the SED hoped, but instead by shortages of economic and ethical goods. The chronic shortages of consumer goods afflicting the planned economy exposed everyone to the experience that money was a substance of limited exchangeability, and that West German money was more effective in obtaining popular consumer goods. Such attitudes toward money are evident not only in aggregate economic behavior such as trade on the black market, which functioned as a site of an alternative value system at odds with the regime, but also in the citizens' petitions (*Eingaben der Bürger*) – the letters of complaint that the population was encouraged to write to party leaders and government institutions. Chapter 7 employs the petitions, which are a rich but neglected source, to disclose the growing inclination of the populace to link economic performance to the SED's moral claim to political leadership. It argues that the emergence of the petitions as a check on the SED's power was critical to the development of the East German revolution, just as the gradual marginalization of this nascent public sphere by the West German media helped pave the way for German unification.

Finally, the epilogue suggests that socialist ideas about money, conditioned by the experience of real-existing socialism, overdetermined the East German decision to relinquish monetary, and therefore political, sovereignty of the GDR. The chapter argues that popular demand for an extension of the Deutsche Mark eastward made political sense, since it also entailed bringing East Germans into the institutional embrace of the West German state. Yet it made little economic sense for East Germans. Despite Marx's critique, then, money exercised a totemic allure on East Germans. That money took on fetishistic qualities in the GDR, and that it did so because of the SED's own policies, is the subject of this book.

PART I

Production

1

Making and Unmaking Money

Monetary Theory and Economic Planning in East Germany

Money is the purest reification of means, a concrete instrument that is absolutely identical with its abstract concept; it is the embodiment of pure function.[1]

Money is the pimp between human need and its object, between life and the means of life.[2]

During Erich Honecker's tenure as General Secretary, a joke circulated that deftly paraphrases the peculiar position of money in Soviet-style regimes. Two men, eager to enrich themselves by producing counterfeit bank notes, mistakenly print 70-mark bills. To improve their chances of unloading the fake notes without getting caught, they decide to travel to the provinces. Sure enough, they find a sleepy state-run retail outlet in a remote East German village. The first forger turns to his colleague and says, "Maybe you should try to buy a pack of cigarettes with the 70-mark bill first." The second counterfeiter agrees, and disappears into the store. When he returns a few minutes later, the first man asks him how it went. "Great," says the second man, "They didn't notice anything at all. Here are the cigarettes, and here's our change: two 30-mark bills and two 4-mark bills."[3]

Like much of the black humor inspired by authoritarian rule, the joke makes use of irony to render unlike things commensurate. This particular joke acquires a subversive edge from its equation of communism with forgery. The two men successfully dupe the state-run store into accepting

---

1 Georg Simmel, *Philosophie des Geldes* (Frankfurt/Main, [1900]1989), p. 265.
2 My translation of Karl Marx, "Ökonomisch-Philosophische Manuskripte (1844)," in *Ergänzungsband Schriften bis 1844, Erster Teil – Karl Marx* (East Berlin, 1968), p. 563 (Karl Marx, "Economic and Philosophical Manuscripts of 1844," in *Karl Marx and Friedrich Engels: Collected Works*, vol. 3 [New York, 1975], p. 322).
3 A version of this joke can be found in Reinhard Wagner, *DDR-Witze: Walter Schützt vor Torheit nicht, Erich währt am längsten* (Berlin, 1995), p. 82.

their phony bills, but the socialist state replies in kind by passing on equally fake money. The joke does not exhaust itself, however, in an attack on the moral integrity of communism, which responds to one crime with another, or even with the powerful suggestion that any regime that counterfeits its own currency must be a sham. What is unusual about the joke – and most likely responsible for blunting its satiric edge – is that it preserves the socialist yearning for a society in which money has no meaning. After all, the transaction is successful despite the fraud: The two men are able to purchase the cigarettes with the most inept of fictions. At least in the counterfeit world of the joke, then, the organization of the economy along socialist lines has reduced money to the paradoxical status of a necessary, yet somehow insufficient, condition of exchange. The resulting liberation of economic activity from monetary constraints makes possible a world of consumer plenty, where moral and industrial goods abound – where people can counterfeit their money and smoke their cigarettes, too.

At the heart of the joke resides a fable about how the planned economy was supposed to work: To eradicate poverty, unemployment, and exploitation, Marxism-Leninism sought to free economic activity from the shackles of pecuniary mediation. Denied value in exchange, money would no longer prove an obstacle to the satisfaction of consumer demands, much less an object of desire and envy. Nor could it be misused to gain political power. Reducing money to a partial expression of comparative value constituted not by market forces, but instead by Marxist-Leninist theory, would, so the SED hoped, transform money into a purely notational device, a marker balancing production against consumption. The disciplinary powers of money were transferred to planning indicators, which pointed toward the future production of specific physical values in line with the party's political priorities – creating what János Kornai aptly termed "soft budget constraints," since they were seldom binding.[4] Money became an instrument for allocating wages and procuring consumer goods – that is, for redistributing social wealth for consumption along egalitarian lines. Unlike capitalist money, which served as an agent of social alienation and injustice, socialist money would never prevent consumers from buying what they needed. Instead of mediating exchange, the East German mark would circulate as the official embodiment of an egalitarian consumerism and a ceremonial reminder of socialist legitimacy.

Of course, the reality of production and consumption in the GDR was more prosaic than the fabulous world of the joke or the utopian reveries

---

4 János Kornai, *The Socialist System: The Political Economy of Communism* (Princeton, N.J., 1992), pp. 273, 294–301.

of communist party members. The inability of the planned economy to deliver prosperity, much less the moral emancipation from economic constraint envisioned in the joke, made the elimination of money impossible. Instead, the SED's attempt to order economic interaction along extramonetary lines disrupted production and consumption: That is, the party's efforts to suppress the formation of prices according to supply and demand and their expression in monetary terms were the main reason for the GDR's large-scale waste of resources. Although releasing companies from the threat of bankruptcy ensured that workers never had to fear unemployment, rescinding the disciplinary powers of money permitted an inattention to cost constraints that generated inefficiency and waste. The resulting economy of shortage undermined the currency of socialism by depreciating socialist money, as East Germans increasingly discovered that they could not acquire the goods they desired with the East German mark.

In explaining the failures of Soviet-style economies, most Western scholarship focuses on the role of politically induced price distortions in creating inefficiency and waste. Using the analytic tools of neoclassical economics, price-oriented approaches have demonstrated how the continued existence of markets under socialism defied the best efforts of economic planners to substitute bureaucratic control for economic exchange. Despite the invaluable contributions of this literature, however, it leaves unexplored the fundamental misapprehension on which Marxist-Leninist economic theory rests: a confusion of money with the market. As a supplement to the analysis of the relation between price and power, this chapter restores money to the position of theoretical prominence it originally claimed in socialist thought. In particular, it contends that a deep-seated hostility toward money animated Marxist-Leninist economic theory. Although Karl Marx had been outspoken in his criticism of this attitude, his heirs continued to view money as the locus of social inequality, and the elimination of money as central to the task of subordinating economics to ethics. Rather than suggesting a genuinely different relation between value and exchange, however, Marxist-Leninist economic theory foreclosed a serious engagement with alternatives to the market. Instead, communist regimes contented themselves with a partial adoption of the financial framework developed by market economies. Merely restricting the function of money did not reduce its meaning, however, just as substituting administrative "distribution" for buying and selling did not resolve the problem of how best to allocate limited resources.[5]

5 Franklyn D. Holzman, "Some Theories of the Hard Currency Shortages of Centrally Planned Economies," U.S. Congress, JEC (1979), p. 300, cited in Iliana Zloch-Christy, *Debt Problems of Eastern Europe* (Cambridge, 1987), p. 4.

If usurping money's power to dispose of scarce resources did not liberate the planned economy from the underlying constellation of supply and demand, it did offer political advantages. The partial elimination of money furnished communist leaders with an economic lever that consolidated their power. By determining production priorities centrally, the party could substitute its own control over economic resources, which it allocated through the use of administrative directives such as planning targets or prices, for the rent-seeking behavior of capitalists, who invest without regard to the needs of the rest of society. Without independent economic variables such as money, the party could more effectively control the circulation of goods, the ideas that are embodied by those goods, and ultimately the people engaged in producing and consuming them.

Nevertheless, conflating economics with politics and morality with money could not rescue the planned economy from the necessity of honoring its intellectual debts. The failure of Marxism-Leninism to provide a viable alternative to capitalism, and more specifically to the money that mediates commercial activity, was central to the collapse of European communism. This is all the more true for the GDR, which unlike its socialist allies was forced to contend with a hostile capitalist state competing for legitimacy in the same national space. Increasingly exposed to the very market forces it had failed to eliminate, the SED turned to the West German mark, whose power it foolishly tried to harness. The resulting fragmentation of the East German economy into competing monetary spheres undermined the currency of socialism by making plain the second-class stature of the socialist currency.

THE SOURCES OF SOCIALIST MONETARY THEORY

From the biblical story of the golden calf to Thomas More's work of Christian egalitarianism, religious critics in the Western tradition have long singled out money as a source of envy and deceit.[6] Given the relative insignificance of the cash nexus in precapitalist societies, where most sectors were not commodified, it is not surprising that money did not occupy a central place in social criticism until the Industrial Revolution. Early socialists such as Robert Owen, indignant at the rise of poverty and unemployment in early

---

6 Exodus, chapter 32; Thomas More, *Utopia. A New Translation. Backgrounds. Criticism* (New York and London, 1975), pp. 49–52. On the tradition out of which More writes, see Timothy Kenyon, *Utopian Communism and Political Thought in Early Modern England* (London, 1989), pp. 74–82. On the Platonic skepticism toward money, see Kirill Postoutenko, "Die Geburt des Rubels aus dem Geist des Platonismus (Zur Entstehungsgeschichte des sowjetischen Geld- und Wertesystems)" in *Zeit-Räume (Wiener Slawistischer Almanach)* 49 (2003), pp. 75–91.

nineteenth-century Britain, attributed the social injustice they observed to the inequitable structure of economic exchange, which they believed permitted the capitalist to appropriate the worker's labor. Since labor for them, as for most observers of the time, was the source of all value, they were outraged by the ability of market forces to determine the value of a commodity to the disadvantage of workers.[7] Some Owenites responded to the asymmetry of power inherent in industrial relations by adopting cooperative measures, from trade unions to banks, as a means of leveling the playing field against expropriating capitalists. Others took aim at the medium of exchange itself. To render exchange more equitable, Owen's followers "proposed schemes of labour notes based on labour time, thus institutionalising Owen's demand that human labour, not money, be made the standard of value."[8] If all value derived from labor, and labor was commensurable with itself, so the argument ran, then society could abolish pecuniary mediation and its evils, and exchange commodities instead based on the labor-time it took to produce them.

On the strength of these arguments, Owen and his adherents set about trying to redress the social wrongs wrought by capitalism. In early 1832, two banks using labor notes were established, the First Western Union Exchange Bank and the Gothic Hall Labour Bank. Later that year, Owen founded the National Equitable Labour Exchange in London, followed by a branch in Birmingham in 1833, which created a market for the purchase and sale of goods among craftsmen using labor-time as a medium of exchange, in the form of labor notes denominated in units of one labor hour.

Despite initial success, these artisanal bazaars closed in 1834. Although their failure had many sources, the most important reasons involved the labor notes, which simply did not provide a satisfactory alternative to the British pound.[9] Owen's notes were unable to compete with the pound in part because they were not recognized by enough economic actors. Those who did use the labor notes found them wanting as a means of payment because

---

7 The British socialists William Thompson, Thomas Hodgskin, John Gray, and John Francis Bray are sometimes called Ricardian socialists because they adopted the economist David Ricardo's formulation of the labor theory of value (George Lichtheim, *A Short History of Socialism* [New York, 1970], pp. 39–42; Mark Blaug, *Ricardian Economics: A Historical Study* [New Haven, Conn. 1958], pp. 140–50).

8 John F. C. Harrison, *Quest for the New Moral World: Robert Owen and the Owenites in Britain and America* (New York, 1969), p. 72.

9 Ibid., pp. 202–7; Frank Podmore, *Robert Owen: A Biography*, vol. 2 (London, 1906), pp. 402–22; Keith Taylor, *The Political Ideas of the Utopian Socialists* (London, 1982), pp. 77–8; Polanyi, *The Great Transformation*, pp. 176–8; Edward Palmer Thompson, *The Making of the English Working Class* (New York, 1963), pp. 790–2. Similarly, the Owenite community of New Harmony, Indiana, in the United States began using labor notes in 1842, but ultimately found it impossible to sustain the value of the currency (Harrison, *Quest for the New Moral World*, pp. 189, 202).

they were relegated to specific economic sectors: Because the exchanges largely comprised craftsmen, the market they established could not supply all of their needs. There was, for example, little food traded, which limited the scope of the notes' usefulness. Moreover, some claimed that the bazaars quickly became "a dumping ground for unsaleable items," which further depreciated the value of the labor notes.[10] Finally, the notes' acceptance was hindered by legitimate concerns about their future usability.

But Owen's attempt to circumvent money did not fail simply because the supply of attractive goods at the bazaars was inadequate. Rather, the labor exchanges did not succeed precisely because they incorporated money into their workings. Owen's scheme did not obviate the need for money; absent a system of barter, the transaction between buyer and seller required some medium through which the exchange of labor could take place. Nor was substituting one medium of exchange for another the same as eliminating money. In fact, Owen's device was but a different form serving the same function − the function of a generalized good of exchange. Indeed, the problem with the labor notes was not that they replaced money, but that they were money − and bad money at that. Without organizing trade on lines different from the market model, the labor exchanges found themselves in the awkward position of having to assign a value to the labor backing the paper they issued. But this labor was obviously not homogeneous. Unable to determine on their own how to measure the heterogeneous labor that went into producing different articles, Owen's exchanges simply adopted the valuation of labor set by the very markets they abhorred − the standard rate of sixpence for an hour's work. Thus, the labor notes constituted a less widely accepted and consequently less efficient translation of the decisions made to buy and sell labor on British markets using the pound. The inability of Owen and his followers to generate a genuine alternative to capitalist money reflects their lack of understanding of money and markets. The labor theory of value, which was attractive to socialists because it privileged labor as the sole source of value in a way that fit in well with their heroization of the working classes, encouraged them to confuse money with exchange.

Nevertheless, the failure of the Owenites' project did little to diminish the utopian yearnings of European socialists for an end to the despotism they perceived in money.[11] In 1849, the French socialist Pierre-Joseph Proudhon

---

10 Harrison, *Quest for the New Moral World*, p. 207.
11 For more on the various socialist schemes to eliminate money, see Leszek Kolakowski, *Main Currents of Marxism: Its Rise, Growth, and Dissolution*, vol. 1 (Oxford, 1978), pp. 194, 208, 212–13, 225; Taylor,

sought to emancipate workers from monetary constraints by constructing a national bank. The *Banque du peuple*, which was to issue labor notes on easy terms, bore strong resemblances to the British labor exchanges. Proudhon's bank was, however, even more short-lived, lasting little more than three months.[12] Although the immediate reason for its demise was political – Proudhon was charged with sedition for having criticized Louis Napoleon Bonaparte – the *Banque du peuple* was "never more than a project in search of finances."[13]

The only distinctive effort among nineteenth-century socialists to understand money belongs to Karl Marx. Beginning in 1847 with his sarcastic rebuke to Proudhon, entitled *The Poverty of Philosophy: Answer to the Philosophy of Poverty of M. Proudhon*, Marx ridiculed his predecessors for permitting moral outrage to cloud economic judgment. Marx's main objection to the labor-note schemes of Owen, Proudhon, and other socialists is that they represent an effort to preempt the market. Imagining that labor notes could become legal tender on the basis of the commensurability of labor assumes that the notes could acquire value before they are used merely because they are denominated in units of labor-time: That is, the utopian socialists "wanted to transform labor into money by having labor acquire exchange value before it was exchanged."[14] Since there is no way of escaping the necessity of trade in a society composed of interdependent, rather than self-sufficient, individuals, and since exchange, in contrast to barter, requires some sort of fungible medium, it is clear the labor notes do not exit the circle of capitalist relations. They are, in fact, contingent upon capitalism in the same way that alternate or "near" monies are, such as frequent flier miles or gift certificates. For this reason, Marx dismisses Owen's attempt to replace money with labor notes, scoffing that they are "no more 'money' than a ticket for the theatre."[15]

Implied in Marx's sometimes gleeful scorn for the shaky grasp of economics exhibited by early socialists is a far more important charge, namely, that doing away with money would not do away with the contradictions

The Political Ideas of the Utopian Socialists, pp. 155–6, 176, 202; Nicholas V. Riasanovsky, *The Teaching of Charles Fourier* (Berkeley and Los Angeles, Calif., 1969), pp. 136–7.

12 Pierre-Joseph Proudhon, *Organisation du crédit et de la circulation et solution du problème sociale*, in *Oeuvres complètes*, vol. 6 (Paris, 1868), pp. 259–85; George Woodcock, *Pierre-Joseph Proudhon: A Biography* (Montreal and New York, 1987), pp. 122–3, 142–9, 173; Kolakowski, *Main Currents of Marxism*, vol. 1, p. 206.

13 Woodcock, *Pierre-Joseph Proudhon*, p. 144.

14 Paul Craig Roberts and Matthew A. Stephenson, *Marx's Theory of Exchange, Alienation and Crisis* (Stanford, Calif., 1973), p. 67.

15 Karl Marx, *Capital*, in *Karl Marx and Friedrich Engels: Collected Works*, vol. 35 (New York, 1997), p. 105, fn. 1.

of capitalism. Marx argued consistently throughout his life that "money is not a thing, it is a social relation."[16] On his interpretation, money is not the root of all evil; since it is not an independent force in human relationships, it cannot be the locus of social injustice. It simply permits economic actors to engage in the exchange of goods and ideas. Money does not cause the asymmetry of power that characterizes social relations between economic actors in capitalist society; it reflects that asymmetry. Marx registers his disbelief that other socialists confuse money with capitalism, submitting with a characteristic reference to religion that "we might just as well try to retain Catholicism without the pope."[17] For Marx, a genuine transformation of society will come about only when private property is abolished, not the currency that embodies this particular mode of production.

The difference between Marx and other socialists regarding money is but one manifestation of a more fundamental disagreement over the meaning of economic modernization. The early socialists insisted that money is a causal relation in economic activity, a view rooted in their indignation at the extremes of penury and plenty created by capitalism. For Marx, however, the problems afflicting industrial society are not the result of destitution, but rather of alienation. In Leszek Kolakowski's elegant formulation, "Marx's starting point . . . is not poverty but dehumanization – the fact that individuals are alienated from their own labour and its material, spiritual, and social consequences in the form of goods, ideas, and political institutions, and not only from these but from their fellow human beings and, ultimately, from themselves."[18] By linking economic alienation, or the act of selling property or labor, with its social consequences, Marx presents capitalism as a profound confusion of means and ends. The reversal of the goal of human existence with the method we employ to sustain ourselves robs our lives of meaning; instead of working to enjoy life, we are reduced to living for our work. By confusing the purpose of life, the exchange economy impoverishes some of us materially and all of us spiritually.[19]

Nowhere is the conflation of means and ends wrought by capitalism more apparent than with money. The money form is for Marx a physical

---

16 Karl Marx, *The Poverty of Philosophy: Answer to the Philosophy of Poverty by M. Proudhon*, in *Karl Marx and Friedrich Engels: Collected Works*, vol. 6 (New York, 1976), p. 145. See also the discussion in *Capital*, vol. 35, pp. 86, 97, 107.

17 Marx, *Capital*, vol. 35, p. 97, fn. 1. For an East German rendering of Marx's critique, see Paul Danek, "Der Warencharakter des Geldes," in Hannelore Riedel (ed.), *Das Geld im gegenwärtigen Kapitalismus* (East Berlin, 1989), pp. 46–8.

18 Kolakowski, *Main Currents of Marxism*, vol. 1, p. 222.

19 That the capitalist is also enmeshed in the web of alienation – and not merely through the act of consumption – is central to Marx's concept of freedom.

expression of alienation that casts a veil over the real relations of production that structure exchange. For this reason, we are often blind to the causal inversions generated by money, as were the early socialists. In explaining "the magic of money,"[20] Marx mocks its ability to generate boundless fictions: "My power is as great as the power of money. The properties of money are my – (its owner's) – properties and faculties. What I *am* and what I am *capable of* is therefore by no means determined by my individuality. I *am* ugly, but I can buy myself the most *beautiful* woman. Consequently I am not *ugly*, for the effect of *ugliness*, its power of repulsion, is revoked by money.... Does not my money thus change all of my incapacities into their opposite?"[21] The fact that anything can be had for money bestows upon it the apparent ability to negate reality. The appeal of its commensurability leads people to read the general measure of value as if it were value itself, and so "this estranged essence dominates people, and they worship it."[22] In industrial society, money becomes the repository of our displaced, alienated desires.

In his later work, Marx presents the "distorting power of money" as a form of commodity fetishism. People, who have become estranged from themselves and others, believe that inanimate objects can alleviate their sense of alienation.[23] As he explains it, "the specific social relation between people ... assumes in their eyes the fantastic form of a relation between things.... [T]he products of the human brain appear as independent beings endowed with life in relation to each other and to people."[24] Not only does the "expression of human creativity [appear] to be a natural object," but this disruption in people's perception of their own agency leads them to imbue their inanimate creations with human subjectivity.[25] Money appears to acquire supernatural powers because of its ability to resolve harsh realities into their opposite.

Marx's critique of the illusions by which economic exchange turns the world upside down remains one of the most compelling – and in its vulgar

20 Marx, *Capital*, vol. 35, p. 103.
21 My translation of Marx, "Ökonomisch-Philosophische Manuskripte," p. 564 (Marx, "Economic and Philosophical Manuscripts," p. 324).
22 My translation of Marx, "Zur Judenfrage," p. 375 (Marx, "On the Jewish Question," p. 172). According to Anitra Nelson, his mature theory of money relies on Hegelian distinctions between appearance and reality (Anitra Nelson, *Marx's Concept of Money: The God of Commodities* [London and New York, 1999], pp. 183–6).
23 Marx, "Economic and Philosophical Manuscripts," p. 326. According to Marx, "the riddle of money fetishism is but the riddle of commodity fetishism, which formerly blinded us and has now become visible" (my translation of Karl Marx, *Das Kapital*, in *Marx-Engels Werke*, vol. 23 [East Berlin, 1970], p. 108; Marx, *Capital*, vol. 35, p. 103).
24 My translation of Marx, *Das Kapital*, vol. 23, p. 86 (Marx, *Capital*, vol. 35, p. 83).
25 Schlomo Avineri, *The Social and Political Thought of Karl Marx* (Cambridge, 1988), p. 118.

form one of the most durable – challenges to capitalism. In twentieth-century Germany, where successive economic crises immiserated so many, protests against the moral indifference of the market resonated deeply. Liberal economists have defended the apparently immoral behavior of the individual economic agent by arguing that it benefits society as a whole – that private vice engenders public virtue,[26] or in today's terms, "principles must often take a back seat to principal."[27] Ethical plenty was to flow from economic bounty; an increase in the wealth of nations would hasten the reduction of private social ills, especially the moral penury contemporaries associated with economic want. In this manner, liberal economists removed moral calculations from the marketplace and entrusted them to a system of fiscal checks and balances guided by the profit motive. As Marx pointed out, however, the increasing subordination of ethical to economic value represented by the market only permitted financial concerns to dominate our lives more completely.

Despite his sharp reproach of other socialists, however, Marx's account of money is most insightful as social analysis, not economic theory. As we have seen, Marx does not locate money's role as a medium of exchange in the rational criteria intrinsic to exchange relations, such as the institutions that frame economic behavior or the drive toward efficiency that eventually eliminates barter in favor of the cash economy. Like other socialists, he pays little heed to structural factors beyond the division of labor in creating the conditions for the widespread monetization of economic life. As a result, he denies the state a role in determining the value of money.[28] He even castigates Proudhon for daring to imply that the value of money might possess a fiduciary character.[29]

Contrary to Marx's assertion, however, the credibility of the issuer is crucial to the adoption of money as a medium of exchange, for the value of a currency is related to the state's ability to determine its use and to honor its attendant obligations. As Max Weber remarks, "the modern state has seized for itself the monopoly over the monetary system."[30] On the one

26 Bernard Mandeville, *A Fable of the Bees, or Private Vices, Publick Benefits* (London, 1714), Remarks H and I; Adam Smith, *Wealth of Nations* [1976] (Amherst, N.Y., 1991), pp. 351–2; Albert O. Hirschman, *The Passions and the Interests: Political Arguments for Capitalism before Its Triumph* (Princeton, N.J., 1981).

27 Alan S. Blinder, *Hard Heads, Soft Hearts: Tough-Minded Economics for a Just Society* (Reading, Mass., 1987), p. 198.

28 Although de Brunhoff argues that Marx does concede a regulatory role to the state, this role is clearly incidental to his definition of money (Suzanne de Brunhoff, *Marx on Money* [Paris, 1973], p. 46; Nelson, *Marx's Concept of Money*, p. 25).

29 Marx, *The Poverty of Philosophy*, pp. 147–9.

30 Max Weber, *Wirtschaft und Gesellschaft: Grundriß der verstehenden Soziologie* (Tübingen, 1972), p. 97. For a contemporary assessment of the nominalist position, see Nigel Dodd, *The Sociology of Money: Economics, Reason and Contemporary Society* (Cambridge, 1994), pp. 24–40.

hand, the legal monopoly over the emission of money presents the state with important fiscal benefits, such as seignorage. Occasionally termed an emissions tax, seignorage consists of the profit derived from the difference between the cost of printing the currency and its value in circulation. In addition, control over the quantity of money permits the state to help itself to excellent credit conditions, while furnishing it with a policy instrument for affecting investment and employment levels by influencing real interest rates. On the other hand, issuing currency provides the state with an important device for enhancing its power. Because the state is the largest payer and receiver of money in the economy, it is able by virtue of its economic weight to compel other economic actors to play on its terms and use its money.[31] Money is an indispensable lever of state power because the circulation of money enables the state to extend its reach into the most remote areas and integrate them into its rule. In contrast, the more the currencies that circulate, the more restricted the state's power to shape economic behavior is. In the East German example, the SED's decision to institutionalize the use of West German marks in the Intershops did not merely represent a symbolic surrender to the value of capitalist money or a tacit concession to the superiority of the West German consumer model. By the late 1970s, capitalist money had displaced socialist money as a store of value and a medium of exchange. As a result, the East German state found its ability to shape commerce according to Marxist-Leninist principles severely constrained.

Because his monetary theory understands demand as a function of alienation, Marx dismisses economic rationality as a factor in the spread of monetary systems. An alternative explanation of the function of money views efficiency as an end in itself, and thus the driving force behind the expansion of money as a medium of exchange. Barter, for example, requires a "double coincidence of wants" for its success, or the relatively rare instance in which both trade partners possess precisely the same object that the other is seeking. Money, in contrast, greatly increases the flexibility and frequency of trade by permitting transactions to occur even when there is no coincidence of want; because all prices are denominated in money, its use diminishes the number of possible price formations, which in turn reduces the costs of obtaining information and carrying out the transaction. To explain this gain in efficiency, Weber imagines money as a kind of abstracted confidence in the future stabilized over time by the legal guarantees of the state. The result is a legal and mathematical rationality that increases the calculability

---

31 Not only can the state oblige economic actors to pay taxes in money, rather than in kind, but it can also raise the transaction costs for alternate or "near" monies, or simply ban them (Simmel, *Philosophie des Geldes*, p. 398; Weber, *Wirtschaft und Gesellschaft*, p. 97; Thráinn Eggertsson, *Economic Behavior and Institutions* [Cambridge, 1990], pp. 231–44).

of trade while diminishing the risks and uncertainties involved.[32] Thus, the
return to barter, such as that forced by production shortfalls generated by
the East German planned economy, also entails a concomitant diminution
in the state's power to regulate trade.

Like most classical economists, moreover, Marx focuses on money's properties as a medium of exchange to the neglect of its other functions,[33]
including its roles as "a measure of value, a standard for deferred payments, and a store of wealth."[34] These functions are related to questions
of demand – for Keynesians in the choices made to hold money or capital,
which along with the marginal efficiency of capital determine interest rates
and hence investment; and for quantity theorists following Milton Friedman,
the demand for wealth as distinguished from income and interest income,
which determines the purchasing power of money. In other words, money
acts as both a bearer of news and a bearer of options, providing information
about the allocation of resources in the past and the opportunity costs of
future allocations.

All of this is a technical way of saying that money is intimately bound up
with the process of modernization. While Marx may not have fully appreciated the variety of economic functions carried out by money, he certainly
understood its social meaning better than did his contemporaries. Above all,
Marx correctly accused his rivals of confusing cause with effect, and therefore
of fundamentally misapprehending how capitalism works. Ironically, however, his censure failed to reconstitute the hostility toward money among
his heirs. Instead, a deep-seated antipathy to money, rooted in non–Marxian
traditions of socialism, continued to inform socialist attitudes toward the
economy.

In their confusion, his successors were assisted by Marx himself. Despite
his otherwise trenchant critiques of fantastical schemes, Marx was not
entirely immune to the utopian allure of a moneyless society. At one point in
the sprawling second volume of *Capital*, for example, Marx speculates that
workers in a socialist society will be issued labor vouchers, which will entitle
them "to withdraw from the social supplies of consumer goods a quantity
corresponding to their labor-time. These vouchers are not money. They
do not circulate."[35] As the economic historian Alec Nove rightly observes,

---

32 Weber, *Wirtschaft und Gesellschaft*, pp. 38–9. For a discussion of the cultural challenge to the rational
    model, see Glyn Davies, *History of Money: From Ancient Times to the Present Day* (Cardiff, 2002),
    pp. 12–17.
33 This is Polanyi's central argument regarding Marx (Polanyi, *The Great Transformation*, p. 205). Blaug
    reads the price-value controversy as evidence of Marxian indifference to money's function as a store
    of value (Mark Blaug, *Economic Theory in Retrospect* [Cambridge, 1996], pp. 148, 215–49, 257).
34 Harry G. Johnson, *Macroeconomics and Monetary Theory* (Chicago, 1977), p. 55.
35 Karl Marx, *Capital*, in *Collected Works*, vol. 36 (New York, 1997), p. 358.

Marx may not imagine the vouchers to be money, but for all intents and purposes they are.[36] This key inconsistency in Marx's thought no doubt confused the issue further, encouraging socialists to ignore Marx's caveats against conflating money with the motive force of capitalism.

Despite Marx's critique, then, European socialists continued to believe that money was the source of social evil and see in its elimination the realization of social justice. Thus, Karl Kautsky – whom the Russian revolutionary Leon Trotskii labeled "without doubt the most outstanding theoretician of the Second International" – could argue in 1902 that "many of its functions, especially that of the measure of value, will disappear" under socialist conditions.[37] Similarly, Kautsky's most vitriolic opponent, Vladimir Il'ich Lenin, found it possible to ignore Marx's caveat against conflating money with the market. Money, Lenin declared, was the mechanism by which capitalists exploit the working class, "a token which enables its owner to take tribute from all working people."[38] The durability of this hostility to money was due in no small part to its great moral appeal, which was not confined to left-wing critics of capitalism. In the years immediately after Marx's death, moreover, socialist theoreticians were consumed by the need to explain the most important flaw in their economic model – how the value of labor determines prices – and this task distracted them from remarking on Marx's concept of money.[39] For all of these reasons, the future of money under socialism was confined to theoretical obscurity – until 7 November 1917, when an avowedly communist party seized power in Russia.

COMMUNIST THEORY AND PRACTICE

As Gregory Grossman observed, "an ambivalent and at times hostile attitude towards money runs vividly through all of Soviet history."[40] Although the Bolsheviks do not appear to have believed that eliminating money was "the

---

36 Alec Nove, *The Economics of Feasible Socialism* (London, 1983), pp. 53–4.
37 Leon Trotsky, *War and Revolution*, vol. 1 (Moscow, 1919), in Leon Trotsky, *Political Profiles*, trans. R. Chappell (London, 1972), p. 65; Karl Kautsky, *The Social Revolution*, trans. A. M. and May Wood Simons (Chicago, 1910), p. 129.
38 V. I. Lenin, "Seventh Moscow Gubernia Conference of the Russian Communist Party, October 19–21, 1921," in *Collected Works*, vol. 33 (Moscow, 1966), p. 358; Nelson, *Marx's Concept of Money*, pp. 77–8.
39 The two most important works on economic questions from this period undertook only modest revisions aimed at reconciling Marx's sociological account of money with the rapid evolution of financial markets before World War I: Rudolf Hilferding's *Finance Capital* (1910) and Rosa Luxemburg's *The Accumulation of Capital* (1913). See Kolakowski, *Main Currents of Marxism*, vol. 2, pp. 64–76, 290–7; Nelson, *Marx's Concept of Money*, pp. 188–92.
40 Gregory Grossman, "Gold and the Sword: Money in the Soviet Command Economy," in Henry Rosovsky (ed.), *Industrialization in Two Systems: Essays in Honor of Alexander Gerschenkron* (New York, London, and Sydney, 1966), pp. 205–6.

way to attain socialism,"[41] they clearly believed its abolition was a necessary precursor to a socially just commercial order.[42] Upon coming to power in 1917, the Soviet leadership used its control over the state to demonetize the economy. The new Soviet power eliminated money in its transactions with economic actors, supplying firms freely with resources, paying its workers and demanding taxes in kind, and encouraging a barter economy.[43] Plans were even drawn up in 1920 to replace money entirely with a unit of labor-time (the *tred*). Although they were never realized, the proposals bore a striking resemblance to the impractical schemes of non–Marxist socialists and made use of the same flawed logic.

But abolishing money was not merely an ideological predilection for the Bolsheviks; it also coincided with their political goals. They welcomed the effects of the inflation generated by their fiscal policies, for example, because the collapse of the ruble acted as a confiscatory tax on the wealthy in the towns and countryside – precisely the group the Soviets wanted to evict from positions of power. As the economist Evgenii Preobrazhenskii described the Bolsheviks' fiscal strategy, "the printing press [is] the machine gun of the Commissariat of Finance that poured fire into the rear of the bourgeois system and that made use of the laws of currency circulation of that regime for the purpose of destroying it and of financing the revolu-tion."[44] In the chaotic environment of the civil war, however, this con-tempt for monetary institutions made it difficult to control the inflationary beast. As in Germany in 1922–23, the state-sanctioned monetary expansion soon broke out into a hyperinflationary sweat. The rapid depreciation of the ruble, combined with the state-sponsored attempt to eliminate mone-tary transactions, thoroughly disrupted production and trade. By 1921, the Bolsheviks had vanquished the Whites and their Western allies, but eco-nomic disruption and food shortages provoked peasant rebellions and led

41 Commissar of Finance Grigorii Sokolnikov, cited in Arthur Z. Arnold, *Banks, Credit, and Money in Soviet Russia* (New York, 1937), p. 103.
42 The following account is based on Arnold, *Banks, Credit, and Money in Soviet Russia*; S. S. Katzenel-lenbaum, *Russian Currency and Banking, 1914–1924* (London, 1925); O. Kuschpèta, *The Banking and Credit System of the USSR* (Leiden and Boston, 1978); Marie Lavigne, *The Socialist Economies of the Soviet Union and Europe*, trans. T. G. Waywell (White Plains, N.Y., 1974); Alec Nove, *An Economic History of the U.S.S.R.* (London, 1989); David Marshall Woodruff, "The Making of Money: Media of Exchange and Politics in Post-Soviet Russia" (Ph.D. dissertation, University of California at Berkeley, 1996); David Marshall Woodruff, *Money Unmade: Barter and the Fate of Russian Capitalism* (Ithaca, N.Y., 2000).
43 By 1921, only 7 percent of all wages were paid in money, while 93 percent were paid in kind (Kuschpèta, *The Banking and Credit System of the USSR*, p. 28).
44 E. Preobrazhensky, *Paper Money during the Epoch of the Dictatorship of the Proletariat* (Moscow, 1920), p. 4, cited in Arnold, *Banks, Credit, and Money in Soviet Russia*, pp. 95–6.

to the Kronstadt uprising of February 1921. Not for the last time would economic mismanagement pose a threat to communist power.

The economic chaos resulting from wartime dislocation and the partial abolition of money put an end to hopes among Russian communists that the new society could do without money right away. In their celebrated *ABC of Communism*, for example, Nikolai Bukharin and Evgenii Preobrazhenskii simply defer that dream until the future: "Communist Society will know nothing of money. Every worker will produce goods for the general welfare. He will not receive any certificate to the effect that he has delivered the product to society. He will receive no money . . . in like manner he will pay no money to society when he receives whatever he requires from the common store."[45] In the meantime, Lenin argued that the communist party was forced by the practical exigencies of maintaining power to "retreat" from the abolition of money "to the state regulation of trade and the money system."[46] If the party could not immediately create the foundations for a new form of economic behavior, at least it could subordinate existing capitalist structures such as the banking system "to the proletarian Soviets."[47] Drawing on Marx's comment in *Critique of the Gotha Programme* that "between capitalism and communism lies a period of the revolutionary transformation of the one into the other,"[48] Lenin suggested that this transitional phase of socialism would last for some time.[49]

Marx, however, provided no map for making the transition from capitalism to socialism, much less from socialism to communism. This is not surprising, since his relative silence regarding the specifics of the future socialist society is entirely in keeping with his insistence on the historical evolution of the mode of production. He does assure his readers that capitalist production will "not cast off its mystical veil until it is consciously regulated by freely associated men in accordance with a plan." But he says precious little about the form production will assume in his free society, other than to comment that "the socially planned distribution" of labor-time will regulate

45 N. Bukharin and E. Preobrazhensky, *ABC of Communism*, cited in Alan H. Smith, *The Planned Economies of Eastern Europe* (New York, 1983), p. 83. They continue by noting that "a very different state of affairs prevails under Socialism."
46 Lenin, "Seventh Moscow Gubernia Conference," p. 100. See also Lenin's explanation that "for the time being money will remain and remain for a fairly long time in the transition period from the old capitalist system to the new socialist system" (V. I. Lenin, "First All-Russia Congress on Adult Education," in *Collected Works* [Moscow, 1965], vol. 29, p. 358).
47 V. I. Lenin, "Can the Bolsheviks Retain State Power," in *Collected Works*, vol. 26 (Moscow, 1964), p. 106.
48 Karl Marx, "Critique of the Gotha Programme," in *Collected Works*, vol. 24 (New York, 1989), p. 95.
49 V. I. Lenin, "Greetings to the Hungarian Workers," in *Collected Works*, vol. 29, p. 388.

"the correct proportion of various labor functions according to their various needs."[50] Presumably, once capitalism has been superseded by socialism and labor is no longer alienated, labor power will not be allocated through money. Like the state, money will wither away under socialism until it ceases to exist under communism.

To stabilize the economy without relinquishing control over it, Lenin advocated a series of reforms called the New Economic Policy (NEP), which provided for reestablishing private markets for commodities such as grain under strict state supervision. Because these markets needed money to function, the Bolsheviks were forced to halt the depreciation of the ruble. They refrained at first, however, from completely overhauling the monetary system or replacing the old with a new currency, as the Germans would do in 1923. Instead, they introduced a new currency – the *chervonets* – alongside the ruble in October 1921. But the creation of a dual currency system only exacerbated the ruble's weakness. Backed by gold and in heavy demand, the chervonets disappeared from circulation, which only helped depreciate the ruble further. With the ruble in danger of collapse, the Bolsheviks were forced to take more aggressive measures to support the money economy. In late 1923, they permitted peasants to pay their taxes in money rather than in kind and replaced the dual currency system with a new ruble in early 1924. Confidence in the currency rose, inflation temporarily subsided, and NEP functioned more smoothly.

The Bolsheviks' lack of commitment to monetary policy as an instrument for regulating price levels and allocating resources, however, would eventually contribute to the collapse of NEP. By 1927, inflation was resurgent and actively undermining the *smychka*, or political alliance with the peasants, on which NEP was based. Despite price controls for industrial goods, an expansive monetary policy pushed up effective prices for manufactured items. Meanwhile, prices for grain had not kept pace, and this, combined with the shortage of industrial goods, decreased the incentive to grow and sell agricultural products.[51] As one peasant remarked, "If I sell my grain, what will I do with the money, since there is nothing to buy? It's better to hold onto the grain."[52] The combination of easy money and fixed prices disrupted relations between town and countryside, imperiling NEP. Under the leadership of Bukharin, the right wing of the Bolshevik party continued

---

50 My translation of Marx, *Das Kapital*, vol. 23, pp. 94, 93 (Marx, *Capital*, vol. 35, p. 90).

51 Simon Johnson and Peter Temin, "The Macroeconomics of NEP," *Economic History Review* 46 (November, 1993), pp. 757–62.

52 Cited in Elena Osokina, *Our Daily Bread: Socialist Distribution and the Art of Survival in Stalin's Russia, 1927–1941* (Armonk, N.Y., and London, 2001), p. 20.

to seek improvement in the terms of trade for the peasants in price controls for industrial goods and markets for grain. In contrast, Joseph Stalin viewed falling grain output in 1927–28 as cause for ending the alliance with the peasants. Exploiting Bukharin's incautious support for market mechanisms to discredit the right, Stalin adopted a political solution to the economic problem and applied state power to "squeeze" savings from the peasantry by forcibly collectivizing it.

After his victory over the right, Stalin authorized a reform of the credit system aimed at "taming" money without entirely doing away with it. The new measures effectively rendered the production sphere moneyless by eliminating the use of commercial credit (and with it capital markets) and transferring the power of money to allocate resources to a series of centrally determined planning indicators.[53] If factories now operated under soft budget constraints, however, private households did not. Despite the state subsidization of some consumer goods, individual economic actors still had to make ends meet, balancing the token money wages they received from work with their real expenditures on consumer goods they urgently needed.[54] At the "Congress of Victors" in 1934, Stalin defended this system of "partitioning" money by labeling all talk of eliminating money "anti-Bolshevik."[55] "We shall continue," he declared, "to have money for a long time until we achieve the first stage of communism. . . . [M]oney is an instrument of bourgeois economy which the Soviet government has taken into its hands and adapted to the interests of socialism in order to give full vent to the development of Soviet trade and thereby prepare the conditions for direct exchange of products."[56]

It is tempting to conclude from the early history of the USSR that the Bolsheviks "did not understand basic monetary economics."[57] While there is much truth to this claim, it nevertheless overlooks how central the aversion

---

53 Grossman, "Gold and the Sword," p. 234; Kornai, *The Socialist System*, pp. 404–7.

54 The partial neutralization of money did not always map precisely onto a division between production and consumption. Some factory activity, such as foreign trade, required careful attention to monetary considerations, while the subsidization of certain consumer goods, such as housing costs, rendered pecuniary concerns marginal. For more on the travails of consumers in the Soviet Union under Stalin, see Osokina, *Our Daily Bread*; Julie M. Hessler, "Cultured Trade: The Stalinist Turn towards Consumerism," in Sheila Fitzpatrick (ed.), *Stalinism: New Directions* (London and New York, 2000); Sheila Fitzpatrick, *Everyday Stalinism: Ordinary Life in Extraordinary Times. Soviet Russia in the 1930s* (New York, 1999), pp. 89–114.

55 Woodruff employs this term to describe the division in mature Stalinist economies between trade that requires money for the successful completion of transactions and economic activity that does not require money, but that is triggered by centrally determined directives (Woodruff, *Money Unmade*, pp. 24–5).

56 Cited in Arnold, *Banks, Credit, and Money in Soviet Russia*, p. 446.

57 Johnson and Temin, "The Macroeconomics of NEP," p. 758.

to money was to Marxist–Leninist thinking. Despite the practical setbacks experienced by the Bolsheviks and despite Stalin's political approach to economic policy, the distinction Marxist–Leninists drew between communism and socialism helped link the tasks of the present with the goals of the future, nourishing the illusion that the need for money would eventually be overcome.

Stalin held fast to this formula, which suspended the currency of socialism between the exploitative capitalist past and an egalitarian communist future, even after he oversaw the transfer of Soviet economic institutions to Eastern Europe after 1945.[58] Several factors, including the legacy of Stalinism, the dependence of local rulers on Soviet patronage, and the opportunity for ideological reinforcement via schooling in Moscow, helped ensure that economic planning in Eastern Europe partook of shared theoretical premises and common practices. Behind a façade of institutional uniformity, however, a variety of indigenous traditions flourished, reinforced by the local conditions within which policy makers operated. While Romania and Hungary made the most of their relative autonomy, for example, the GDR quickly distinguished itself by an almost slavish devotion to Soviet precedent.

To some extent, the path to ideological conformity had been paved by the Stalinization of German communism after World War I. After the murders of Rosa Luxemburg and Karl Liebknecht in 1919, German communism possessed few figures of the intellectual caliber or organizational talent capable of formulating a politically viable alternative to Bolshevism. By 1925, German communism enjoyed little intellectual or political autonomy from Moscow; by 1929, the party had become entirely dependent on Stalin for its political direction. Whatever alternative conceptions of communism survived the Stalinization of the German party were marginalized during the struggle against the Nazi dictatorship, then shunted aside after 1945, when the Soviet Military Administration (SMAD) reorganized the eastern zone of defeated Germany.[59] In addition to this doctrinal constancy, the peculiarities of the East German situation reinforced the SED's orthodox approach to economic policy. Forced to compete with West Germany in a shared national space, the GDR was more reliant on Soviet protection than its Eastern European allies. That direct confrontation with capitalism, moreover, encouraged the SED to emphasize the GDR's integration into the Soviet bloc.

---

58 Joseph Stalin, *Economic Problems of Socialism in the USSR* (New York, 1952), pp. 16–17, 70.
59 Hermann Weber, *Die Wandlungen des deutschen Kommunismus*, vol. 1 (Frankfurt/Main, 1969); Ossip Flechtheim, *Die Kommunistische Partei Deutschlands in der Weimarer Republik* (Offenbach/Main, 1948); Naimark, *The Russians in Germany*, pp. 251–317.

The contours of economic debate in the GDR reflected these pressures. Although the most important contributions to socialist economic theory before World War I had appeared in German-language publications, the center of Marxist-Leninist debate quickly shifted eastward. In contrast to their Eastern European allies, East Germans produced little work in economic theory of distinction.[60] Nor did the discipline generate the kind of reformist impulses that were to transform countries like Hungary, where the field of economics was instrumental in the transition from communism to capitalism in the 1980s. With the important exceptions of the early 1960s and the Gorbachev period, East German economic policy was remarkably responsive to Soviet dictates.

MONEY IN THE GDR

In 1945, the leaders of the German communist party, most of whom had spent the Nazi period in exile in Moscow, returned to Germany to find a country materially and psychologically exhausted by the war.[61] Extensive Allied bombing had destroyed a large portion of the capital and housing stock in what was now the Soviet zone of occupation (SBZ). Despite the SED's later claims, war-related economic damage was greater in what would become West Germany than in the SBZ.[62] The regions that would become the GDR, however, were forced to shoulder the burden of Soviet claims on Germany in compensation for the criminal behavior of German troops on the eastern front.[63] In addition to dismantling over 2,000 factories and shipping them off to the Soviet Union, Stalin extracted reparations in the form of people, products, and profits. Between 1945 and 1953, the SBZ/GDR indemnified the USSR to the tune of $14 billion (in 1938

---

60 Important exceptions include Fritz Behrens, Arne Benary, and the economic historian Jürgen Kuczynski. The lack of distinction is particularly striking when compared with Poland, which produced theorists such as Oskar Lange, Michal Kalecki, and Włodzimierz Brus; Hungary, which produced János Kornai; or the USSR, which produced thinkers such as Grigorii Fel'dman, Nicolai Voznesenskii, and the Nobel Prize winner Leonid Kantorovich. Because they often dissented from the party line, however, their audience was mainly Western.

61 For more on the role of exile in the political rivalries of the 1950s, see Catherine Epstein, *The Last Revolutionaries: German Communists and Their Century* (Cambridge, Mass., 2003); Peter Grieder, *The East German Leadership, 1946–1973: Conflict and Crisis* (Manchester and New York, 1999), pp. 8–107; Herf, *Divided Memories*, pp. 106–61.

62 Raymond G. Stokes, *Constructing Socialism: Technology and Change in East Germany, 1945–1990* (Baltimore, Md., 2000), pp. 19–21.

63 Only 3 percent of the industrial capacity of the FRG was dismantled, compared to nearly 30 percent of the GDR's fixed capital (Rainer Karlsch, *Allein bezahlt? Die Reparationsleistungen der SBZ/DDR 1945–53* [Berlin, 1993], pp. 46, 233). For more on Soviet economic goals in Germany, see Naimark, *The Russians in Germany*, pp. 150–93; Stokes, *Constructing Socialism*, pp. 21–35.

prices). In addition, it sent some 3,000 East German engineers and scientists to the USSR to improve the Soviet economy.[64] The imposition of such onerous reparations on an economy already devastated by the war was only somewhat mitigated by other factors. On the one hand, payments in kind to the Soviet Union replenished East German fixed capital by creating a demand-pull that stimulated production.[65] On the other hand, the GDR, in marked contrast to the Federal Republic, rejected any suggestion that it might bear responsibility for trying to make redress for the crimes of the Nazis and refused to offer compensation to surviving victims of Nazi persecution or aid to the state of Israel.[66]

It is clear that the reparations significantly retarded the GDR's economic development. But as Rainer Karlsch has taken great pains to demonstrate, it is "not possible to hold the reparations for the only cause of the SBZ/GDR's backwardness."[67] The most important constraint on economic growth in the GDR was Marxism-Leninism, beginning with the SMAD's decision to transform the SBZ into a planned economy starting in 1948 and continuing with the consistently poor economic judgment of the SED leadership. Chapters 2, 3, and 4 explore the SED's mismanagement of the economy during Honecker's rule; the remainder of this chapter is devoted to explaining the official role accorded to money in the GDR before Honecker came to power in 1971.

Like the Bolsheviks, the SED evinced a desire to restrain the spontaneity of money, or its ability to express in aggregate terms the myriad economic decisions taken by individual economic actors.[68] Throughout their rule, East German communists remained confident that the "transition to communist

---

64 Although the USSR formally ended reparations payments in 1953, the GDR continued to deliver uranium and pay for the cost of stationing the Red Army until 1990 (Karlsch, *Allein bezahlt*, pp. 230–1; Stokes, *Constructing Socialism*, p. 26).

65 Christoph Buchheim, "Kriegsfolgen und Wirtschaftswachstum in der SBZ/DDR," *Geschichte und Gesellschaft* 25 (1999), pp. 515–29; Stokes, *Constructing Socialism*, p. 23. The USSR also supplied natural resources to the GDR at substantially discounted prices, a fact easily forgotten in the debate over Soviet influence.

66 The cost of compensation to the victims of Nazi crimes and of liquidating prewar German debt amounted to 91.1 billion West German marks (Karlsch, *Allein bezahlt*, p. 235). To this sum, we could also add the burden of housing and caring for the expellees, the vast majority of whom settled in West Germany. For more on the SED's policy toward Jewish and Romany survivors of the genocide, see Angelika Timm, *Hammer, Zirkel, Davidstern: das gestörte Verhältnis der DDR zum Zionismus und Staat Israel* (Bonn, 1997), pp. 51–80, 127–46. For more on the Federal Republic's policies, see Herf, *Divided Memory*, pp. 267–333.

67 Karlsch, *Allein bezahlt*, p. 240.

68 As Nove remarks, "the word 'spontaneity' was never close to Bolshevik hearts" (Nove, *An Economic History of the USSR*, p. 360).

production and distribution" would eventually render money obsolete.[69] Toward this end, East German economic planners circumvented the use of money in their own work by calculating labor productivity according to units in time – just as the utopian socialists had.[70] Given their suspicion of money, neither the SED nor the SMAD set much store by introducing a new currency as a method of reinvigorating trade after 1945. In contrast, the Western Allies recognized that the *Reichsmark* had collapsed. Yet replacing it with a new pan-German currency would have given the Soviet Union undue influence over German economic development. For this reason, the Allies introduced the Deutsche Mark without Soviet participation. Only once it was clear in April 1948 that the Allies were intent on proceeding unilaterally did the SMAD permit the introduction of a new communist currency into the SBZ.[71] Initially, this new money issued on 24 June 1948 – the *Klebemark* – was nothing more than the old Nazi paper with a new stamp, although the glue was so bad that the stamps often fell off. A month later, the SMAD introduced entirely new banknotes.[72] The SED took advantage of currency reform – as had the Bolsheviks before them – to consolidate its political power. By setting different rates at which the old Nazi mark could be exchanged for the new communist mark, the party redistributed the assets of Germans living in the SBZ away from those who had flourished under the "Third Reich" and toward less prosperous inhabitants and communist coffers.[73]

The introduction of two different currencies in Germany presaged the country's division into a capitalist West and a communist East. But the city of Berlin continued to be jointly administered, which meant that it remained the only open frontier in Europe. As long as the division of Berlin was imperfect, the two German states remained linked. To complete the separation of East from West, the Soviets tried to unify the city under

69 Willi Ehlert, Diethelm Hunstock, and Karlheinz Tannert (eds.), *Geldzirkulation und Kredit in der sozialistischen Planwirtschaft* (East Berlin, 1976), p. 19.
70 Werner Obst, *DDR-Wirtschaft. Modell und Wirklichkeit* (Hamburg, 1973), pp. 218–19. For an overview of debates regarding money in the Soviet Bloc after 1945, see Smith, *The Planned Economies*, pp. 3–7, 15–16, 83–98.
71 Christoph Buchheim, "The Establishment of the Bank deutscher Länder and the West German Currency Reform," in Deutsche Bundesbank (ed.), *Fifty Years of the Deutsche Mark*; Frank Zschaler, *Öffentliche Finanzen und Finanzpolitik in Berlin 1945–1961* (Berlin and New York, 1995), pp. 75–7.
72 Rittmann, *Deutsche Geldgeschichte seit 1914* (Munich, 1986), pp. 365–6.
73 Klaus Bolz, "Währung/Währungspolitik," in Hartmut Zimmermann (ed.), *DDR Handbuch*, vol. 2 (Cologne, 1985), p. 1449; Rittmann, *Deutsche Geldgeschichte seit 1914*, pp. 363–7; H. Jörg Thieme, "The Central Bank and Money in the GDR," in Deutsche Bundesbank (ed.), *Fifty Years of the Deutsche Mark*, pp. 580–4.

communist rule by force. But the United States was committed to retaining
a Western presence in Berlin, a city deep in the heart of the GDR and not
sixty kilometers from the border with Poland, and the Soviet blockade of
Berlin in 1948–49 failed.

For a closed society competing with a larger and more powerful neighbor,
the open border was destabilizing. The mobility of labor, merchandise, and
money consistently undermined the SED's control over trade, disrupted the
East German labor market, and provided an embarrassingly public index of
the popular preference for things Western. The uprising of 17 June 1953,
when wage reductions triggered spontaneous walkouts by workers in East
Berlin that quickly spread to the rest of the country, only accelerated the
flight of labor and capital from the GDR.

Desperate to sever the connection between East and West, the SED
turned to money as a political weapon against its adversaries. On 13 October 1957, the party abruptly announced a currency reform that mandated
the substitution of banknotes issued after 1948 with new bills. The purpose of "Operation Death to Black Marketeers" (*Aktion Schiebertod*), as the
communist press dubbed it, was to strike "a serious, enduring blow" at
those who were profiting from the economic division of Germany.[74] As
the official announcement put it, "these measures are being taken because
the monopolists and militarists in West Germany have come into possession
of certain sums of banknotes with the aim of speculating, disrupting our
economy, and financing spies and intelligence services. It is therefore in the
interest of the citizens of the German Democratic Republic and the democratic sector of Berlin to render the banknotes held by capitalist circles and
spy rings in West Germany and West Berlin worthless."[75] The asymmetry
of supply and demand due to the shortages of consumer goods in the GDR
had made the illegal transport of West German products across the border
quite remunerative. In addition, the communist state's policy of subsidizing
goods rather than people attracted a stream of West Germans looking to
take advantage of the comparatively low prices for basic necessities, such as
food. Finally, West Germans visiting friends or family or simply on business bought East German marks to bankroll their trips.[76] Although the East
German mark was not a convertible currency, a vibrant market in socialist

---

74 *Neues Deutschland*, 14.10.57.
75 Cited in Rittmann, *Deutsche Geldgeschichte seit 1914*, p. 424. See also SED leader Otto Grotewohl's
    address in *Neues Deutschland*, 14.10.57; Stiftung Archiv der Parteien und Massenorganisationen der
    DDR im Bundesarchiv (SAPMO-BA), DY30, 3702.
76 We might add those who worked in one part of the city but lived in another, and the retailers who
    did business with them. See Erika M. Hoernung, *Zwischen den Fronten: Berliner Grenzgänger und
    Grenzhändler 1948–1961* (Cologne, Weimar, and Vienna, 1992).

money had sprung up to lubricate the flow of goods and people between the two hostile German states. The main actors were small entrepreneurs located at the Berlin Zoo train station, but major West German banks were also willing to sell East German marks.

Outraged by the fact that capitalist money changers were profiting from trading socialist money – and this at "fraudulent rates" – SED leaders hoped to beggar them by rendering the notes they held worthless overnight.[77] The party announced the switch without warning on a Sunday, informing the populace via radio broadcasts and loudspeakers mounted on trucks.[78] It took Western intelligence services entirely by surprise – a triumph that communist officials openly savored. Caught unprepared, West German "monopolists and speculators" were stuck with 267.5 million East German marks that were now worthless.[79] In addition, the Ostmark reserves held by the city of West Berlin, the "bridgehead of the global imperialists," were destroyed.[80] Even West Berlin retailers suffered, losing the East German cash they had on hand and experiencing a decline in sales as buyers stayed home. Communist retailers registered a temporary decrease in sales of subsidized goods, from meat to coffee.[81] In addition, the East German police arrested 261 black marketeers, snaring a total of 973,568 socialist marks.[82] The surprise measure served as a painful reminder of the risks of trading in socialist money. A cartoon from *Neues Deutschland* illustrates the SED's glee, depicting a worker kicking over a bag of worthless bills onto West German capitalists who resemble Chancellor Konrad Adenauer and Economics Minister Ludwig Erhard. As if to remind readers of the purported connection between capitalism and fascism, one of the Western businessmen wears a dark suit whose outlines recall a swastika.

Despite communist propaganda, however, the primary purpose of the currency reform was not to bankrupt capitalists in the West. As with the Soviet currency exchange of 1947, the East German banknote substitution was designed to increase the party's control over people at home, and in

77 *Neues Deutschland*, 14.10.57 and 16.10.57.
78 Those unable to exchange their bills on Sunday were required to present credible excuses at an office near their residence, which had the effect of filtering out those who were not East German citizens (*Neues Deutschland*, 14.10.57; Rittmann, *Deutsche Geldgeschichte seit 1914*, pp. 424–5).
79 Thieme, "The Central Bank and Money in the GDR," p. 588. The SED claimed that West Germans had lost over 600 million East German marks (SAPMO-BA, DY30, 3702, "Bericht über die Durchführung des Umtausches der Banknoten in der Deutschen Demokratischen Republik und in dem Sektor von Groß–Berlin am 13. Oktober 1957," November 1957, p. 48; *Neues Deutschland*, 16.10.57).
80 *Neues Deutschland*, 14.10.57.
81 SAPMO-BA, DY30, 3702, "Bericht über die Durchführung," November 1957, p. 109.
82 Ibid., pp. 106–7; *Neues Deutschland*, 14.10.57.

„Zweifeln Sie immer noch an der Existenz der DDR?"
Zeichnung: Beier-Red

Figure 1. "Do you still doubt the existence of the GDR?" (Courtesy of *Neues Deutschland*, 15.10.57.)

this regard, the SED deemed it "unexpectedly successful."[83] The operation provided the party with a snapshot of the demand for money according to social group. Although party officials apparently believed legends about peasants squirreling away vast sums of money, the banknote swap revealed that small farmers were not "hoarding" cash. In contrast, the party discovered that members of the intelligentsia did have large sums of cash at home – a portfolio choice that communist officials ascribed to "an old and traditional attitude" toward money.[84] Particularly valuable was information regarding the assets of East German churches, which maintained personal and financial ties to their West German counterparts. Religious institutions

83 SAPMO-BA, DY30, 3702, "Bericht über die Durchführung," November 1957, p. 48. For more on the Soviet measure, see Peebles, *A Short History of Socialist Money*, pp. 15–17.
84 SAPMO-BA, DY30, 3702, "Bericht über die Durchführung," November 1957, pp. 75–6. More plausibly, higher-income households are generally wont to hold more cash, even when monetary transactions are cumbersome.

were especially loathe to place their worldly belongings in the hands of the avowedly atheist communist party, not the least out of fear that their access to funds would be restricted by bureaucratic chicanery. The famous Ursuline convent in Erfurt, for example, tried to disguise its considerable wealth by distributing its money among its residents. But party officials were not fooled when ninety-seven nuns descended on the exchange offices, each pretending that large sums of money were her own – despite their religious vow to foreswear temporal things.[85] Ironically, the SED had forced women living in a truly moneyless living arrangement to lie and claim a fictitious attachment to money.

In addition to providing information about the East German populace, the currency reform increased the communist state's power and wealth. For example, the switch forced people hiding money under their mattresses to deposit it with the state bank. Not only did this greatly increase the SED's control over the volume of money in circulation, it also placed some 800 million marks at its disposal.[86] Furthermore, the operation allowed communist authorities to confiscate any cash they suspected of stemming from "speculation," a slippery proviso that made it possible for the party to seize anyone's money.[87] Perhaps most importantly, however, the measure provided the party with an opportunity to use its monopoly over the emission of money to discredit its political adversaries and circulate its distaste for money among the populace. In particular, the SED went out of its way to humiliate East Germans who had lots of cash by compelling them to display it in plain view of their neighbors, a practice calculated to stir up envy and hatred. As a report drawn up by ZK officials noted approvingly, "it was often embarrassing for the members of the middle class to appear at the exchange outlets with their bundles of banknotes."[88]

If the banknote swap was a "black Sunday for speculators" and strengthened the SED's control over East German finances, it nevertheless fell short of the total success claimed by communist propaganda.[89] As it turned out, the element of surprise was as disruptive for East German officials as it

85 SAPMO-BA, DY30, 3702, Org.-Abteilung beim ZK der SED, Sektor Parteiinformation, "Einschätzung des Verlaufes der Umtauschaktion des Geldes der Deutschen Notenbank in der DDR," 16.10.57, p. 33.
86 SAPMO-BA, DY30, 3702, "Bericht über die Durchführung," November 1957, p. 48.
87 *Neues Deutschland*, 14.10.57.
88 SAPMO-BA, DY30, 3702, Org.-Abteilung beim ZK der SED, Sektor Parteiinformation, "Einschätzung des Verlaufes," 16.10.57, p. 31.
89 *Neues Deutschland*, 14.10.57. The following details are taken from SAPMO-BA, DY30, 3702, Org.-Abteilung beim ZK der SED, Sektor Parteiinformation, "Einschätzung des Verlaufes," 16.10.57, pp. 28–30, and "Bericht über die Durchführung," November 1957, p. 61.

was for West German money changers. The substitution of old for new
banknotes was poorly organized. Tracking down mayors and town council members on a Sunday proved difficult, and no one was in possession
of the right information. "In many instances, our financial experts showed
nervousness," ZK representatives observed. State and party officials issued
contradictory decisions, and when they were not bickering, they dupli-
cated each other's work. Some local officials even resisted the measure. The
mayor of Gera, for example, refused to set up enough exchange outlets
or accept outside assistance. Worse still, administrators in Leipzig demonstrated "ideological-educational inadequacies," a coded way of saying that
these civil servants did not display the proper antipathy toward money or
support for the measure. Most importantly, the currency exchange fright-
ened ordinary East Germans. In a self-critical comment – something that
would virtually disappear from official reports after Honecker's takeover –
ZK representatives conceded that "among older citizens who had lost their
money two or three times there were signs of fear." Using money to solidify
the SED's political control had understandably stirred up memories of the
hyperinflation of 1923 and the collapse of the Reichsmark after 1945, provoking anxieties about the economic hardship and political instability that
accompanied them.

Not only had the banknote swap revealed organizational inadequacies and
weakened support for the SED at home, it provided no lasting relief from
pressure abroad. Confiscating socialist property held by the "class enemy"
proved no more than a temporary solution to black market trade. Its deterrent effect was limited, since the SED could not undertake such drastic
measures with great frequency for fear of destabilizing its own financial system and disorienting its citizens. Raising the cost of trading in East German
marks hardly addressed the principal source of Western demand for the
socialist currency, which was not directed at the Ostmark as such, but linked
instead to substantial imbalances between supply and demand and price distortions. Nor did introducing new notes stem the exodus to West Germany,
which continued apace.

What the banknote exchange had demonstrated was that money alone
did not suffice to separate the GDR from the Federal Republic. Ordinary
East Germans like the elderly K., whom we encountered in the introduction, correctly perceived that communism remained far too dependent on
capitalism. Even the more modest goal of severing the connection between
capitalist and socialist money, as the elderly K. advocated, proved increasingly
impossible. Ultimately, preserving the integrity of the East German mark

necessitated a commitment to meaningful economic reform – or, failing that, an effective political barrier dividing the two German states.

In the end, East Germans got both, but in the wrong order. SED strong-man Walter Ulbricht's rejection of reform during the 1950s only aggravated the GDR's economic difficulties. Despite the end of rationing in 1958 (eight years after its end in West Germany), the planned economy performed basic tasks poorly. The shortage of consumer goods and deteriorating housing stock compared unfavorably with what East Germans knew of the Federal Republic's accomplishments. Weak economic performance combined with political coercion only spurred migration to the West. The exodus of skilled and young workers, moreover, provoked new bottlenecks, often in key sectors such as medicine and civil engineering, creating fresh incentives for people to squeeze through Berlin into West Germany.[90] The failure to reform the economy necessitated an extreme political solution – a pattern that would follow European communism to its grave. In 1961, Ulbricht received Soviet leader Nikita Khrushchev's support for sealing off egress to the West; on 13 August 1961, construction on the Berlin Wall began, overseen by Ulbricht's aide Erich Honecker.[91]

Ironically, the respite from economic turmoil provided by the "antifascist protective wall," as the party called it, freed up the SED to embark on a series of reforms to the planned economy. Faced with a growing gap between labor productivity and wages, the East German leadership solicited the Soviet Union for the massive financial assistance it needed to modernize the GDR's industry. When Khrushchev demurred because of the cost, it became clear that the path toward economic growth required meaningful changes in the East German manufacturing process. Yet Ulbricht's adoption of technocratic solutions to inefficiency and waste hardly amounted to the thorough-going overhaul required to stimulate economic growth. Once again, Marxist-Leninist economic theory had failed to produce an economic system that did not depend on market mechanisms for assessing economic performance.

Insofar as they sought to rehabilitate financial instruments and cede some independence to factories, however, Ulbricht's reforms were bold.

---

90 Patrick Major, "Going West: The Open Border and the Problem of *Republikflucht*," in Patrick Major and Jonathan Osmond (eds.), *The Workers' and Peasants' State: Communism and Society in East Germany under Ulbricht, 1945–1971* (Manchester and New York, 2002); Steiner, *Die DDR-Wirtschaftsreform*, pp. 38–44.
91 Hope M. Harrison, *Ulbricht and the Concrete "Rose": New Archival Evidence on the Dynamics of Soviet–East German Relations and the Berlin Crisis, 1958–1961* (Washington, D.C., 1993).

The New Economic System (NES) drew upon the work of two East German economists, Fritz Behrens and Arne Benary. Although Ulbricht had denounced both men in 1957 as deviationists and hounded them out of academia, their advocacy of a more decentralized economic decision-making process remained influential with a generation of economic planners. Without rehabilitating either man, Ulbricht began implementing their ideas starting in 1962. Around the same time, a discussion arose in Eastern Europe around the work of Soviet economist Evsei Liberman, who recommended a partial restoration of the meaning of money as a method of containing costs.[92] Ulbricht seized upon the Soviet promotion of Liberman's work to provide political cover for his own goals. But the Soviet leadership eventually decided against pursuing thorough-going reform. As a result, Ulbricht and his aides – Economic Secretary Günter Mittag and State Planning Commissioner Erich Apel – failed to secure more than begrudging support from Moscow for their economic experiment. As the economic historian André Steiner has written, "the lack of support from Moscow was motivation for many in the SED leadership to remain skeptical about the reforms."[93]

Ulbricht's reforms were designed to increase the efficiency of East German production by introducing cost and profit as meaningful measures of success at the factory level. In the context of the Soviet bloc, the NES constituted a relatively aggressive attempt to use "financial levers" to create a system of incentives that would make the costs of production more transparent while penalizing waste and mismanagement. Walter Halbritter, who was briefly Deputy Minister of Finance and an architect of the NES, even entitled an early article on the reforms, "Profit Should Be the Measure of Performance."[94] To East German reformers, reinstating the importance of monetary values in a limited manner was essential to revivifying the GDR's economy.

Despite initial successes, however, the efficiencies anticipated by Ulbricht failed to materialize. The partial remonetization did not put the planned economy on sounder footing, but instead created serious dislocations as

---

92 The publication of Liberman's article in *Pravda* on 9.9.62, which sought among other things to elevate the category of profit to the status of a planning indicator, aroused a flurry of interest throughout the Soviet bloc. See Thomas A. Baylis, *The East German Elite and the Technocratic Intelligentsia: Legitimacy and Social Change in Mature Communism* (Berkeley and Los Angeles, Calif., 1974), pp. 221–5; Grieder, *The East German Leadership*, p. 161; Kopstein, *The Politics of Economic Decline*, pp. 45–6, 50; Lavigne, *The Socialist Economies*, pp. 57–8, 223–90; Smith, *The Planned Economies*, pp. 54–80; Steiner, *Die DDR-Wirtschaftsreform*, pp. 52–5.
93 Steiner, *Die DDR-Wirtschaftsreform*, p. 55.
94 Walter Halbritter, "Der Gewinn soll Gradmesser der Leistung sein," *Die Wirtschaft*, 31.10.62.

producers and suppliers tried to adjust to a new but incoherent system of production signals. Together with Ulbricht's pursuit of risky agricultural projects, the NES created an economic environment characterized by many planners as strained and chaotic. In addition, replacing administrative with market instruments entailed a decentralization of economic power that alarmed many party members, who were fearful of relinquishing their control over the economy.[95] Given the enduring antipathy toward money in communist thought, it is not surprising that opposition to the NES in the Politburo coalesced around the use of profit as a planning indicator.[96] Outside the party, Ulbricht's neglect of consumers, exacerbated by the bottlenecks the NES created, intensified popular discontent with the SED. Most importantly, Ulbricht's aggressive reforms alarmed the new Soviet leadership under Leonid Brezhnev, who demanded an end to the NES in 1965. The suicide of Apel, who had become its greatest exponent, heralded the end of Ulbricht's flirtation with reform from within.[97]

To placate his critics, Ulbricht introduced the Economic System of Socialism (ESS) in 1967. Although the ESS served largely to roll back previous reforms, it failed to alleviate serious imbalances in the economy, which were exacerbated by the severe winters of 1968–69 and 1969–70. Nor did Ulbricht's retreat defuse the anxieties of planners concerned with economic stability, such as Gerhard Schürer, who had replaced Apel as State Planning Commissioner. In his efforts to unseat Ulbricht, Honecker drew quite skillfully on his colleagues' frustration over the failed reforms, their fear of Ulbricht's penchant for ill-advised economic experimentation, and their irritation at his increasingly brusque manner and inflated ego. When he finally moved against Ulbricht in 1970–71, Honecker made certain he also enjoyed the support of Brezhnev and other Soviet leaders, who felt that Ulbricht's hectoring condescension, rash economic ventures, and opposition to détente with the West had made him unpredictable and a liability.[98] Honecker's own economic program, which he introduced at the Eighth

---

95 SAPMO-BA, DY30, JIV 2/2A 3196; Steiner, *Die DDR-Wirtschaftsreform*, pp. 520–59. In contrast, Kopstein suggests that political rivalries, intensified by Leonid Brezhnev's ouster of Khrushchev, doomed economic reform in the GDR (Kopstein, *The Politics of Economic Decline*, pp. 47–60).

96 Ulbricht even appears to have proposed introducing the possibility of bankruptcy for enterprises (Grieder, *The East German Leadership*, pp. 163, 166).

97 Despite continued speculation that Apel's suicide was triggered by guilt over his Nazi past, it is more likely that the political defeat handed to NES by the Soviet trade delegation in the fall of 1965 combined with a history of depression led him to take his life.

98 Grieder, *The East German Leadership*, pp. 171–93; Norbert Podewin, *Walter Ulbricht. Eine neue Biographie* (Berlin, 1995); Sarotte, *Dealing with the Devil*; Jochen Staadt, "Walter Ulbrichts letzter Machtkampf," *Deutschland Archiv* 29 (1996), pp. 686–700; Jochen Stelkens, "Machtwechsel in Ost-Berlin," *Vierteljahreshefte für Zeitgeschichte* 45 (1997), pp. 503–33.

Party Congress of the SED in June 1971, consisted of returning to a more conservative approach to economic planning.

MONEY UNDER HONECKER

What, then, was the official role accorded to money in the GDR by the time Honecker came to power? Despite Ulbricht's reforms and Honecker's return to orthodoxy, monetary theory changed surprisingly little in East Germany's forty-year history. Minor emendations were always justified with reference to official affirmation of the GDR's alleged progress toward the goal of establishing a nonalienated, classless society.[99] The organization of society along socialist lines meant that "every kind of exploitation of people by people is eliminated."[100] Public ownership of the means of production had allegedly created a nonfetishized society in which "human labor power is no longer a commodity."[101] If labor is not alienated and its abstract incarnation, money, is a commodity of a "special type" by virtue of its integration into the process of planning, then money is, in a certain sense, superfluous. The result is that the fetishization of money ceases to exist. Appearance (money) and reality (labor) take on a new relationship to each other, characterized by their identity.[102] The identity of money and labor is ensured by adjusting the relationship between production and consumption to obviate the mediation of the market. Money surrenders both its informational and allocative functions to the work of planning; it is "the object and instrument of societal management and planning."[103] The market in socialism, so the theory went, "is not an autonomous sphere that spontaneously regulates production, as it does in capitalism. As an integral part of the process of social reproduction, the market in socialism is planned. . . . The market functions as an indicator of the socially necessary labor specified by the plan. This indicator function is realized by planning."[104]

---

99 Compare Kohlmey, *Das Geldsystem*, pp. 74, 78–81, 93–100, with Georg Ebert, Fred Matho, and Harry Milke, *Ökonomische Gesetze in der entwickelten sozialistischen Gesellschaft* (East Berlin, 1973), p. 202.

100 Akademie für Gesellschaftswissenschaften, *Die Volkswirtschaft der DDR*, p. 15.

101 Ebert et al., *Ökonomische Gesetze*, p. 203. See also Willi Ehlert, Diethelm Hunstock, and Karlheinz Tannert (eds.), *Geld und Kredit in der Deutschen Demokratischen Republik* (East Berlin, 1985), pp. 26–7.

102 As the Academy of Sciences of the GDR proclaimed, money's "substance is the socialist labor of society" (Akademie der Wissenschaften der DDR, *Zur aktiven Rolle der Finanzen* [East Berlin, 1980], p. 9).

103 Ibid. See also Ehlert et al., *Geldzirkulation und Kredit*, pp. 41–2.

104 Ebert et al., *Ökonomische Gesetze*, p. 192. A similar version of the same idea can be found in Willi Ehlert, Heinz Joswig, Willi Luchterhand, and Karl-Heinz Stiemerling (eds.), *Wörterbuch der Ökonomie Sozialismus* (East Berlin, 1984), p. 30.

Economic planning itself derived its legitimacy from Marx's criticism of the inherently irrational nature of capitalist production. In Marx's writings, production in capitalist economic orders is presented as excessive and therefore morally compromised, while the logic internal to the subsystems upon which classical liberal theory is based, such as efficiency or supply and demand, is exposed as proceeding from irrational, and therefore unpredictable, sources.[105] In particular, Marx argues that the profit motive and the time lag in producers' response to market signals are responsible for the crises of over- and underproduction periodically experienced by capitalist economies. This irrational allocation of resources leads in turn to material waste and the attempt, via advertising, to manufacture desire for the surplus produced and sell it as a need.

Following Marx, the SED distinguished between the rational and irrational, between "real" and "false" needs. "Real" needs, whether of physical or spiritual nature, are generated by the material conditions of a given society in history.[106] In contrast, "destructive, parasitical, and false (illusory) needs" consist of "needs [that] are deformed, manipulated, and in part artificially manufactured to suggest illusions to working people about their real situation in society."[107] Through this dichotomy, the SED conflated desire with commodity fetishism. A powerful confluence of Marxian criticism of the desire to accumulate material things and traditional German working-class resentment of the status hierarchies entailed by consumerism thus found expression, albeit in distorted fashion, in economic planning.

The planned economy, or so the SED alleged, is superior to capitalism in part because it creates social conditions in which only real needs exist while permitting a logical balance between supply and demand to facilitate their satisfaction. Not only had the public ownership of the means of production eliminated the morally reprehensible aspects of capitalist exploitation and rid the world of commodity fetishism, but it had also opened up the possibility for the rational allocation of resources that could prevent capitalist excesses.

---

105 Karl Marx to Ludwig Kugelmann, 11 July 1868, in *Karl Marx and Friedrich Engels: Collected Works*, vol. 43 (New York, 1988), p. 69; Karl Marx, *Capital*, in *Karl Marx and Friedrich Engels: Collected Works*, vol. 37 (New York, 1997), pp. 866–7.

106 Marx, *Capital*, vol. 35, p. 181; Ehlert et al., *Wörterbuch der Ökonomie Sozialismus*, pp. 136–7.

107 Horst Seeger (ed.), *Lexikon der Wirtschaft: Volkswirtschaftsplanung* (East Berlin, 1980), pp. 86–7. For more on Marx's conceptualization of need, see Agnes Heller, *The Theory of Need in Marx* (Nottingham, 1976). For more on the SED's application of the category of need to the production and distribution of consumer goods, see Dorothea Hilgenberg, *Bedarfs-und Marktforschung in der DDR. Anspruch und Wirklichkeit* (Cologne, 1979). For more on consumerism during the 1950s and 1960s, see Ina Merkel, *Utopie und Bedürfnis: Die Geschichte der Konsumkultur in der DDR* (Cologne, Weimar, and Vienna, 1999); Patrice G. Poutrus, *Die Erfindung des Goldbroilers. Über den Zusammenhang zwischen Herrschaftssicherung und Konsumentwicklung in der DDR* (Weimar and Vienna, 2002).

As the Leipzig Institute for Market Research explained it, "rational standards of consumption" would eliminate "tendencies toward waste as well as elements of prestige and the desire for status through consumption."[108] In other words, ideologically directed production offered the opportunity to increase social equality by removing the grounds for desire, which was demoted to the ethically dubious need to enhance individual identity by buying into the social hierarchies often attached to consumer goods. To eradicate these false needs, the party sought to inhibit the temptation toward social differentiation through a didactic restriction of the objects of desire. In a society where desire did not exist, so the argument ran, there was no need to manufacture and sell people goods they did not require. Instead, the SED was able to plan correctly to satisfy people's real needs, which the party was able to recognize because it enjoyed a privileged position to the truth in its capacity as the vanguard of the working class.[109]

In this scheme, liberal norms such as supply and demand did not cease to exist as indicators of consumer behavior. They were, however, robbed of their autonomy and subordinated to needs that the party, in its role as the arbiter of production, determined according to moral criteria. Following the abstemious maxims central to Marxism-Leninism, the SED proclaimed that everyone had the right to essential material goods at just prices, which led to the policy of subsidizing employment, housing, and basic foodstuffs. As the quintessential expression of "false" needs, money was assigned a severely restricted role; it became a necessary, but insufficient, element of economic transactions. Planning targets usurped money's function as a measure of value related to supply and demand. Instead of an invisible and irrational hand, the all-too-visible hands of planners apportioned resources according to preestablished production priorities. In turn, money's allocative properties were transferred to planning indicators, numerical signs that instructed producers how much of what product to produce and when.[110] As Helmut Koziolek, the Director of the Central Institute for Socialist Economic Planning at the ZK from 1965 to 1990, put it, "value and the forms it takes in

---

108 BArchB, DL1, 23780, Institut für Marktforschung, "Prognose der Entwicklung des Konsumgüterverbrauchs der Bevölkerung der DDR bis zum Jahr 1990," 1973, p. 3.
109 Compare Nove, *An Economic History of the U.S.S.R*, pp. 20–36, 109–25; Thomas T. Hammond, "Leninist Authoritarianism before the Revolution," in Ernest J. Simmons (ed.), *Continuity and Change in Russian and Soviet Thought* (Cambridge, Mass., 1955), pp. 144–56.
110 In line with a general reassertion of central control during the 1980s, the number of planning indicators was increased in 1984/85 to 214 from 156, rising to 225 by the late 1980s (BArchB, DE1, 56323, "Welche Kennziffern werden jetzt als staatliche Orientierungsgrössen herausgegeben," no date, p. 573; Phillip J. Bryson and Manfred Melzer, *The End of the East German Economy: From Honecker to Reunification* [New York, 1991], p. 38).

the socialist planned economy, particularly money and prices, . . . represent objective economic categories that are shaped consciously and according to plan by socialist society."[111] Money and prices possessed only the values assigned to them by those in charge of economic planning; they were little more than ciphers for the political agenda pursued by the ruling party. Depriving money of its informational content would help prevent status seeking and social envy by stripping money of its "spontaneity" and independence as a variable in economic choice. Where once the uncontrolled desire of the consumer stood, now stood the egalitarian intentions of the party.

In addition to establishing social need rather than profit as the standard for production, the SED looked to liberate labor from the punitive constraints of money. Just as the threat of bankruptcy shapes corporate behavior by forcing companies to keep costs down, so too the fear of poverty governs the actions of individual economic agents by forcing them to live within their means. But workers in capitalist societies are not only bound by the same hard budget constraints that apply to other economic actors. In addition to its marginal access to capital, the proletariat is unable to prevent other economic actors from passing costs onto it. Through the mechanism of unemployment – what Marx called the "reserve army of labor" – employers can place downward pressure on wages.[112] The organization of workers into trade unions offers partial protection from fluctuations in the labor market because unions can negotiate collective wage agreements and assist those members who are dismissed with funds and services from the membership dues they collect. As the German experience during the Depression demonstrated, however, unions provide the most support for skilled workers, that is, for those whose labor is in greater demand.[113] On this view, trade unions fail to counterbalance financial coercion because they address the effects, rather than the causes, of what liberal economists have termed the natural rate of unemployment and perpetuate social stratification.

Like other communist parties, the SED pursued three strategies designed to neutralize the coercive power of money for individual economic actors. First, it guaranteed everyone a job. Full employment was made possible by

---

111 Helmut Koziolek, "Schlußwort," in Akademie der Wissenschaften, *Zur aktiven Rolle der Finanzen*, p. 130.
112 Marx, *Capital*, vol. 35, p. 384.
113 Richard Evans and Dick Geary (eds.), *The German Unemployed: Experiences and Consequences of Mass Unemployment from the Weimar Republic to the Third Reich* (London, 1987); James, *The German Slump*; Peter D. Stachura (ed.), *Unemployment and the Great Depression in Weimar Germany* (London, 1986); Heinrich A. Winkler, *Der Weg in die Katastrophe: Arbeiter und Arbeiterbewegung in der Weimarer Republik 1930 bis 1933* (Berlin, 1987).

the rational supervision of production. Central direction of the distribution of labor would eliminate not only the business cycle, but also concomitant fluctuations in labor markets. As one group of East German economists put it, abolishing money in the manufacturing process would end "the spontaneous regulation of production behind the back and against the will of the producer and at a great loss of labor available to society."[114] To highlight its commitment to full employment, moreover, the party established one unified trade union, the Free German Trade Union (FDGB), in lieu of the competing organizations that had fragmented working-class power during Weimar. Like many communist institutions, however, the FDGB's mission sounded more emancipatory than it actually was. Although the union was nominally committed to representing workers' interests against managers, it served in fact to discipline workers. Because the regime denied workers the right to strike, the FDGB could not protect them. Instead the party used the organization to tame workers, distributing rewards such as vacations on the Baltic according to political loyalty.

Second, the SED used the power of the state to protect individuals against the perils of poverty. The party dedicated massive resources to welfare expenditure, constructing a comprehensive social net for every East German citizen from cradle to grave. In this sense, the GDR was a welfare dictatorship. Ironically, however, the SED's economic paternalism increased its control over the economy without increasing popular support for communism. Through its policies, the party encouraged East Germans to view its welfare statism as an entitlement rather than an achievement. Successive East German constitutions, for example, described a variety of social services, from medical care and residential housing to "rest and relaxation," as legal rights.[115] Nor did the SED develop a participatory procedure that might have made East Germans feel responsible for the services they used. As a result, East Germans took this impressive array of state-funded benefits for granted.

Finally, the SED tried to ensure a high social wage by fixing prices. Large subsidies for those consumer goods identified by the regime as "necessary" further reduced the usefulness of money as a transmitter of information about value. Together, low prices, stable wages, and job security went a long way toward neutralizing money's disciplinary force by uncoupling it from

---

114 Ehlert et al., *Geldzirkulation und Kredit*, p. 26. The citation makes questionable use of a famous passage found in Marx, *Capital*, vol. 35, p. 117.

115 Articles 15, 16, 22, 26, and 32 of the constitution of 7 October 1949, and articles 34–38 of the constitution of 6 April 1968 and the constitution of 7 October 1974 (*Gesetzesblatt der DDR*, Teil I, pp. 5 ff., 199 ff., 425 ff.).

the task of sustaining life. As we shall see, however, these policies actively undermined fulfillment of the very goals they were intended to achieve. Fixed prices dissociated costs from revenue streams, permitting a creeping inflation while eliminating the main mechanism for rationing scarce goods – higher relative prices. The ensuing shortages of various consumer goods – and surfeit of undesirable products – limited the usefulness of socialist money.

For consumers, the East German mark was increasingly reduced to a necessary but insufficient ingredient of successful purchases. Confronted with a distribution system insensitive to money, consumers were forced to make use of money substitutes, such as time (standing in line). The long delays, however, increased the willingness of most East Germans to shorten the line by turning to illegal substitutes for the Ostmark, including personal ties, barter, and capitalist money, to obtain the goods they desired. As we shall see, the resulting competition for money substitutes rewarded East Germans unevenly, which worked against the SED's egalitarian designs. Even the policy of subsidizing goods (rather than people) furthered social differentiation because it benefited individuals with higher incomes, who paid the same prices as those with lower disposable incomes.

The SED's attempt to minimize money resulted in a two-tiered system similar to that in other communist regimes. Money played no significant role in production, where the party substituted its political priorities for the profit motive, but retained a distributive function in consumption, where it remained an important conduit for underwriting social equality in the form of material benefits awarded to private citizens. As Heinz Klopfer, who was State Secretary at the State Planning Commission from 1969 to 1990, characterized the party's "partitioning" of money between production and consumption, "we simply ignored financial questions. We paid pretty well. Money simply did not have any function for enterprises."[116] In other words, the party created soft budget constraints for producers but relaxed those constraints for consumers only somewhat. This dual approach to money created serious impediments to economic growth. Like some of its Eastern European neighbors, the GDR turned to the West to modernize its economy. Unlike its communist allies, however, the SED's attempts to restrict the usefulness of money were undermined by Honecker's decision to yoke the planned economy to the West German mark. It was a

---

116 Interview, Heinz Klopfer, Deputy State Planning Commissioner (1963–6), State Secretary, State Planning Commission (1969–90), ZK candidate member (1976–89), Chairman, Working Group on Automobiles (1980s), Berlin, 4.10.95. As Klopfer noted, money's lack of importance was illustrated by the fact that no financial experts sat in the Politburo.

competition conducted in the same political space for economic currency –
a competition the GDR could not win.

If the SED was to retain money even in this marginal form, it required
a central bank to oversee the circulation of the Ostmark. In contrast to
its aggressively independent West German counterpart, however, the East
German central bank, the Staatsbank, existed only to realize the political dictates of the SED. Indeed, its primary responsibility was entirely unrelated to
monetary policy, charged as it was with upholding socialism. Since planning
targets obviated the need for capital markets, moreover, interest rate policy
was irrelevant. Outside of printing and distributing the Ostmark, then the
Staatsbank's jurisdiction was relegated to minor accounting responsibilities
toward enterprises.[117]

Only in two respects can one detect anything peculiarly German about
East German financial institutions. Even though the money supply could,
according to Marxist-Leninist theory, have no function independent of the
plan, East German bankers and economists discussed it in terms reminiscent
of their West German colleagues. The Staatsbank was often called upon for
example, to maintain "a tight control over monetary and credit policy."[118]
The experience of inflation during Weimar, the "Third Reich," and the
immediate postwar period, as well as the institutional memories inherited
from the Reichsbank, led officials at the Staatsbank to share the bias toward a
restrictive monetary policy championed by the West German Bundesbank.
It is no accident that the East German mark was the strongest currency in
the Soviet bloc, paralleling the achievements of the D-Mark in the West.[119]

Because monetary policy for all intents and purposes no longer existed,
the commercial lending structure was deprived of its independence and
reduced to carrying on as the party's fiscal amanuensis. To meet the needs
of private individuals, town or county councils administered the savings-
and-loan institutions traditional to Germany (*Sparkassen*). Primarily, the
Sparkassen acted as clearinghouses for the financial transactions of East
German households, although they did grant loans on a limited basis for
"private needs." Recently married couples, for example, could obtain small
interest-free credits, a policy that reflected the SED's hopes of boosting
the birthrate as a method of increasing the workforce and so economic

---

117 BArchB, DN10, 3119, Hauptabteilung Volkswirtschaft, "Vermittlung von Erfahrungen der DDR
auf folgenden Gebieten lt. Fragespiegel," 3.9.86, and Staatsbank der DDR, "Wie ist die Struktur
des Banksystems und welche Funktionen haben die einzelnen Banken," 1.4.87; Ehlert et al., *Geld
und Kredit*, p. 85; Thieme, "The Central Bank and Money in the GDR," pp. 599–603.
118 Ehlert et al., *Geld und Kredit*, p. 92.
119 SAPMO-BA, DY30, IV 2/2.039/60, Politburo meeting from 19.4.88; BArchB, DN10, 3329;
SAPMO-BA, DY30, Vorläufige SED 41757.

Figure 2. Ironically, the SED was headquartered in the old Reichsbank building in Berlin, a monument to capitalism built by the Nazis. The "Big House," as East German officials called it, was built under Hilter's direction during the 1930s. The banner reads "Long live May 1 – the fighting day of the international working class!" (Courtesy of Bundesarchiv Koblenz, Bildarchiv, 183/FO427/202/001.)

power.[120] Rather than doing away with the instruments of financial policy, then, the party merely adopted capitalist institutions and subordinated them to its control.

If the SED employed the "partitioning" of money to organize its power in the domestic economy, the party maintained a monopoly over foreign trade by making its currency nonconvertible. Legally, the *Mark der DDR* was a "domestic currency" that possessed a value limited by geography, a tacit recognition that the currency was backed by the Wall and of little value in international trade. To calculate the volume of foreign trade, the SED created another currency, the *Valutamark*, or foreign currency mark. The Valutamark did not actually exist; it was nothing more than a notational device established by bureaucrats as a quantitative guide to evaluating trade with the West. The Valutamark was pegged to the value of the West German mark before its revaluation in 1961. The conversion rate from hard currencies to domestic marks was not made public, although most managers had access to it.[121] Likewise, the unit of value employed by socialist countries for

120 Ehlert et al., *Geld und Kredit*, p. 95; Lavigne, *The Socialist Economies*, p. 257. It also provided small loans earmarked for improvements in residential housing.
121 Interviews with Peter Jacob, Economic Director, IFA Combine, and Wolfgang Sachs, Director of Production and Planning, IFA Combine, Chemnitz, 26.2.96; Klopfer, Berlin, 4.10.95; Gerhard

trade with each other was the transfer ruble, which was tied to the USSR's valuta ruble.[122]

Given that very few countries are in a position to float their currencies, the GDR was not unusual in its attempt to protect the Ostmark – and its economy – from international markets.[123] The difference was that the SED sought for ideological reasons to devalue the role of money domestically while protecting the GDR from the international division of labor so that it could pursue economic autarky within the Council for Mutual Economic Assistance (Comecon), which was established in 1949 to coordinate economic trade within the Soviet bloc. Through the partial elimination of money at home and the device of a nonconvertible currency abroad, the SED could claim to have reversed the subordination of ethical behavior to economic rationality effected by the market while in reality tightening its control over the circulation of money, ideas, and people.

The planned economy sought to reconfigure the social constitution of value by replacing principal with principles – doing away with the profit motive and organizing economic production along communitarian ideals instead. For all of its anticapitalist rhetoric, however, the SED's emphasis on the rational allocation of resources as the criterion for economic decision making illustrates precisely how much the planned economy had in common with liberal capitalism. Replacing supply and demand with the category of need constituted an important criticism of capitalist production, but it ultimately failed to alter the pattern of production that created markets. Efficiency, cost reduction, and material incentives remained categories of analysis fundamental to communist economic theory, even if it sought to subordinate them to ethical considerations. Indeed, many official statements made by Marxist-Leninist regimes contain exhortations toward greater efficiency and cost reduction. To underline their importance, the parties invented concepts such as "socialist competition" and the "self-assessment of costs." Despite their rhetoric, however, communist parties ultimately sacrificed independent measurements of economic performance,

Schürer, State Planning Commissioner (1965–89), candidate member, Politburo (1973–89), Berlin, 20.6.95; Lothar de Maizière, GDR Minister-President (March–December 1990), Berlin, 8.5.96. The conversion rate from hard currency to East German marks was calculated using a "directional coefficient" (*Richtungskoeffizient*, or Riko), which reflected "the average economic costs expressed in [domestic] marks required for our exports to the nonsocialist economic region" (BArchB, DE1, 56285, "Zum Umrechnungsverhältnis der Mark der DDR zu kapitalistischen Währungen," no date, p. 3).

122 Kornai, *The Socialist System*, pp. 358–9.

123 In 1991, thirty-six countries floated their currencies (Stanley Fischer, "Distinguished Lecture on Economics in Government: Exchange Rate Regimes: Is the Bipolar View Correct?" *Journal of Economic Perspectives* 15 [Spring, 2001], p. 4).

such as efficiency or cost reduction, to political control. Yet the intellectual debt of Marxism–Leninism to capitalism was not restricted to liberal economic theory. It can also be detected in the institutional landscape of the planned economy. In order to distribute goods and services, the East German state continued to require the services of money to pay wages and salaries and express the relative value of consumer goods.

This intellectual and institutional debt was to have serious consequences for any economy that sought to enthrone a suspicion of money as the regulative instance for the allocation of resources. Despite the regime's insistence on constructing an economic sphere in which value was predicated on the moral identity of money and labor, depriving money of its ability to direct the distribution of resources did not free production from the constraints of financial rationality. Without the threat of insolvency to guide production, producers and distributors had no incentive to worry about costs or customers. Disregarding costs made for waste and inefficiency, which eventually overwhelmed the productive capacities of the East German economy. The regime put a higher priority on the fulfillment of its social goals, such as full employment and a socially just distribution of consumer goods, than on instrumental rationality in the economic sphere, a choice that entailed the gradual decay of the East German industrial base. The SED tried to compensate for the irrationality of economic planning – the chronic asymmetry between supply and demand created by the partial suspension of market forces – by micromanaging the production process after the fact and making ad hoc adjustments to its policy of enforced underconsumption. The rigidly hierarchical transmission of power in Honecker's East Germany ensured that interventions by the center were quickly realized. The difficulty was that the center proposed solutions that often created new problems for the periphery, plugging one hole by opening up another.

For consumers as well as producers, the waste and inefficiency related to socialist money most often expressed itself as a problem of complementarity, or the dependence of one commodity on another for it to function.[124] To give just one example, in the summer of 1979, East Germans experienced a severe shortage of ketchup, a scarce and highly desirable commodity.[125]

---

124 The problem of complementarity achieved popular notoriety in the GDR in the early 1980s through East German pop star Nina Hagen's song "Michael, du hast den Farbfilm vergessen" (Michael, you forgot the color film), which contrasts the colorfulness of the singer's experience with the frustrating black-and-white record her lover will leave her.

125 The following account is based on BArchB, DE1, 53092, Komitee der Arbeiter-und-Bauern-Inspektion (ABI), 29.4.80, pp. 63–9, and Klopfer, "Stellungnahme zur Information über Kontrollergebnisse des Komitees der Arbeiter-und-Bauern-Inspektion zu Ursachen von Verstörungen bei Senf vom 29.4.1980," 9.5.80, pp. 46–7.

The shortage of ketchup induced consumers to shift to mustard as a sub-stitute. The mustard plan for 1980, however, had not accounted for such an increase in demand. The responsible factory had no difficulty producing the mustard but discovered that it did not have enough jars. The production bottleneck created a minor political crisis, as East Germans were forced to eat without condiments. By April 1980, the Politburo found it necessary to intervene by conscripting the Schmölln glass factory of the VEB Preßwerk Ottendorf-Okrilla to produce more jars. Schmölln had no problems meeting this revision in its plan and was able to produce several million containers. It did so, however, only by ignoring another task: producing marmalade jars.

In the absence of cost constraints to induce rationing or "active" money to provide an incentive for expanded production, supply in the GDR could be influenced only by the written directives of the center. Despite the bravest attempts of East German planners to constrain it, however, money did not surrender its importance to economic activity. Rather, the Ostmark con-tinued a schizophrenic existence as a marker for pent-up consumer desires whose practical use was increasingly restricted. In attempting to thwart the penetration of the monetary paradigm, with its alienating effects, into every sphere of life, the party had not nullified the role of finance in the eco-nomic sphere, but only confused it. As we shall see, casting out the logic of accounting resulted not in greater social equality, but rather in the disap-pearance of accountability for the social inequality that the SED created. It was this discrepancy between theory and practice – the SED's own reversal of means and ends – that was embodied in the currency of socialism.

2

Accounting and Accountability

Financing the Planned Economy under Honecker, 1971–1980

They pretend to pay us, and we pretend to work.[1]

The story of the East German planned economy during Erich Honecker's rule is the story of two kinds of debt. Above all, it is a cautionary tale about the perils of intellectual debt. As we saw in Chapter 1, Marxist-Leninist economic theory proved unable to fashion a genuine alternative to market relations. Rather than devising a framework for economic activity that would not require a medium of exchange, the SED relied on anticapitalist rhetoric and the partial elimination of money to suspend the "laws" of capitalism. Although making money passive helped consolidate the communist party's power, it did not liberate economic exchange from market forces. In fact, the party's abolition of financial constraints for manufacturers created a more wasteful and inefficient yet less innovative caricature of capitalism.

By 1970, Walter Ulbricht's last year in power, this intellectual debt had begun to translate into a financial obligation to the West, as East German industry started relying on Western money to overcome what economic planning could not. After the failures of Ulbricht's reforms, SED leaders concluded that the key to economic growth lay outside the planned economy – in technology transfers from the West. With Soviet acquiescence, the GDR embarked on large-scale purchases of Western machines and equipment on the assumption that short-term indebtedness to the West would make possible long-term autarky. They were wrong. Under Honecker's leadership, the GDR took on Western loans at a rate that soon endangered its stability. Despite the SED's attempt to fashion an economy in which the meaning and function of money would be different than under capitalism,

---

1 Common joke told in Soviet bloc states.

61

the party found itself increasingly dependent on the West and subject to the very market forces it abjured.

To some extent, the GDR's experience in the 1970s was shared by other Eastern European countries. Soviet-style regimes organized their economies around similar premises about money and the market, which limited their economic performance for comparable reasons. In addition to domestic sources of economic stagnation, the Soviet bloc was shaken by the very same external shocks that slowed growth throughout the world. In particular, the oil crises of 1973 and 1979 dealt a crushing blow to communist development strategies. On the one hand, the saltations in the price of oil curtailed the USSR's ability to provide energy at low cost to its Eastern European allies, a subsidy that formed the pillar of economic cooperation among Comecon members. On the other hand, skyrocketing prices for natural resources made the cost of Western imports prohibitive, which upended plans to modernize industry by importing Western machines and equipment. Because of the shared intellectual and institutional landscapes, similar development strategies, and a common vulnerability to international events, the story of the GDR's growing debt to the West has important parallels with other Soviet bloc countries.

Despite comparable obstacles to economic growth, however, local economic conditions and national traditions resulted in differing paths to economic development. Some Eastern European nations adopted import-led growth strategies similar to the SED's. Hungary, Poland, and Romania, for example, were particularly aggressive about taking on Western debt in the hopes of replenishing their capital stock. In contrast, the Soviet Union, Bulgaria, and Czechoslovakia decided against using Western capital to stimulate economic growth. Even among those countries pursuing import-led growth strategies, moreover, differences quickly arose over how to proceed after the first oil crisis. For example, rising prices prompted Hungary to experiment with localized markets and Romania to crack down on consumption, while Poland and the GDR began using the Western loans to fund the importation of consumer goods rather than economic reform or capital investment.[2]

---

2 Ivan T. Berend, *The Hungarian Economic Reforms, 1953–1988* (Cambridge, 1990); Christoph Boyer, "Sozialgeschichte der Arbeiterschaft und staatssozialistische Entwicklungspfade: konzeptionelle Überlegungen und eine Erklärungsskizze," in Peter Hübner, Christoph Kleßmann, and Klaus Tenfelde (eds.), *Arbeiter im Staatssozialismus: Ideologischer Anspruch und soziale Wirklichkeit* (Cologne, Weimar, and Vienna, 2005), pp. 71–86; Michael Shafir, *Romania: Politics, Economics, and Society* (London, 1985); Batara Simatupang, *The Polish Economic Crisis: Background, Causes, Aftermath* (London, 1994); Ben Slay, *The Polish Economy: Crisis, Reform, and Transformation* (Princeton, N.J., 1994); Nigel Swain, *Hungary: The Rise and Fall of Feasible Socialism* (London and New York, 1992); Iliana Zloch-Christy, *Debt Problems of Eastern Europe* (Cambridge, 1987). For a comparative overview, see Smith, *The Planned Economies*.

What made the GDR's development exceptional within the Soviet bloc was the division of Germany. If Marxist-Leninist theory and Soviet power established the framework within which the SED formulated economic policy, the competition for political legitimacy in a shared national space informed the East German party's decisions. The SED's economic strategy was shaped by two opposing forces that emerged out of national division: Although the hostilities generated by the Cold War necessitated that the SED keep its political distance from West Germany, West German capital and consumerism offered a path to economic growth. These two contradictory imperatives converged with two challenges confronting Honecker upon his accession to power, the one political, the other economic. On the one hand, the SED's antifascist ideology became increasingly ineffective during the 1970s as a method of reconciling young Germans, who had no direct experience of Nazism, to communist rule. Merely equating West German capitalism with fascism no longer sufficed to create political sympathy for socialism or at least sow confusion about the reality of life under Honecker's GDR. On the other hand, East German industry desperately needed to replace moribund plant with new technology and equipment, much of which dated to the Nazi period.

To balance these countervailing forces, Honecker sought to subordinate the GDR's systemic competition with the FRG to the calculation that higher living standards would bring domestic stability. At least for a while, easy access to cheap money made Honecker's reliance on Western capital appear less irresponsible than it was. Eventually, however, exploiting the financial advantages of German–German trade risked making the GDR economically and politically vulnerable to West German capitalists. In the long term, moreover, taking on too much debt threatened to provoke domestic unrest if SED leaders were forced to adopt austerity measures to pay off capitalist creditors. Most paradoxically, Honecker's economic policy required closer relations with the Federal Republic for its success. But this proximity to the class enemy blurred the differences between capitalism and socialism, as the GDR increasingly adopted Western economic ideas.

The peculiarity of East Germany's position in the Soviet bloc, moreover, also helps explain why there was no serious challenge to Honecker's leadership even though his policies provoked dissent in the Politburo. Like other Soviet-style regimes, his critics were hamstrung by the intellectual limitations of economic planning and the stifling obedience commanded by party leaders. In addition, the systemic competition with West German capitalism inhibited a more imaginative understanding of the GDR's economic needs. Thus, there was little experimentation along Hungarian lines, while the fear of West German intervention prevented the adoption of austerity measures periodically attempted by Poland or imposed in such a draconian manner by Romania. The main reason Honecker successfully fended off criticism of his economic illiteracy, however, was Germany's fascist past. As an old communist who had been jailed by the Nazis, he possessed a political authority with which few SED leaders could compete. Together with his authority as General Secretary, Honecker used his antifascist credentials to squelch challenges to his leadership. Thus, the division of Germany not only reinforced the illusions about money under which SED leaders labored, but mortgaged the GDR's financial future to Erich Honecker's political welfare as well.

This chapter analyzes the political context in which the GDR came to live beyond its means – how the Marxist-Leninist denigration of money led the SED to become dangerously indebted to its capitalist enemies. It argues that the peculiarities of economic policy making in the GDR reinforced Honecker's economic adventurism. After assessing the sea change in economic policy that Honecker instituted after taking power in 1971, it shows how Honecker's charisma, which had less to do with his physical person than his political biography, helped ensure that economic rationality was increasingly subordinated to political concerns. Finally, the chapter investigates the often absurd attempts of economic planners to mend the growing rift between the GDR's increasingly modest economic means and Honecker's unrealistic political ends.

Informing these arguments is the idea that the elimination of money in the sphere of production institutionalized a preference for accounting over accountability, and that the incentives to ignore financial constraints on the microeconomic level were reflected in Honecker's pursuit of reckless fiscal policies. Demonetizing commercial activity had uncoupled production from economy, removing cost constraints and disrupting financial communication. Released from the tyranny of hard budgetary constraints, factories were free to meet other obligations, from full employment to the provision of social services. No longer inhibited by the profit motive, enterprises discharged their responsibilities with little attention to costs. Because economic planners were forced nevertheless to work with finite resources, the tendency of factories to focus on quantity rather than quality undermined the effectiveness of the plan. Yet no amount of rhetorical exhortation or structural tinkering could transform soft into hard budgetary constraints. Without money to supervise the gap between production goals and factory performance, the central directives communicated by the plan lacked coercive power. Thus, the plan was binding not in an economic but in a legal sense. Without active money and hard budget constraints to close the gap between reality and its representation, breakdowns in production could literally be papered over.

And they often were. Under Honecker's rule, conflicts between the production results demanded by the SED leadership and the enterprise's actual performance were frequently concealed by fictional accounts of factory activities.[3] Producers employed a variety of methods to compensate for the fact that materials were limited, but planning targets were not. Some falsified their plans, holding back resources so that they could meet the unrealistic goals set by the center in future plans. One factory director, for example, rigged his production records to create a "planning cushion" to help his enterprise meet increases in their planning targets. Over a three-year period, he and his staff managed to sock away 29 percent of total production before being caught.[4] Other enterprises simply neglected to report bad news.[5] As Willi Stoph, who chaired the Council of Ministers from 1964 to 1973 and again from 1976 to 1989, lamented, "there are factory directors, general directors, and ministers who already know that they will not fulfill the plan this year and [simply] do not tell us."[6] When they did not lie outright, managers prevaricated. Factory directors knew, for example, that Economic Secretary Günter Mittag went on vacation in August, so they often submitted records of production shortfalls while he was away.[7]

Nor were communist party leaders above confusing appearance with reality. For example, Honecker was distressed by the sight of East Germans standing in line for oranges – which were in short supply like most tropical fruits – along the stretch of road he took to his office every day. Honecker demanded that Berlin's leaders attend to these signs of economic

3 SAPMO-BA, DY30, Vorläufige SED 35649, Kruse, "Standpunkt des Direktors für Produktionsdurchführung zu falschen Angaben im operativen Meldesystem und in den Dekadenmeldungen im Jahre 1985," 23.2.85; BArchB, DE1, 55834, Ministerrat Beschluß vom 13.4.89, Anlage, "Information über die Industrie und des Handels über die Vertragserfüllung im Rahmen der monatlichen Abrechnung des zentralen Versorgungsplanes," p. 6.

4 BArchB, DL2, 995, *Liberaldemokratische Zeitung*, no date, and unidentified newspaper reports from early September 1978.

5 For example, some factories falsely reported that they had made deliveries to wholesalers (BArchB, DE1, 55834, Ministerrat Beschluß vom 13.4.89, Ministerium für Handel und Versorgung, "Stellungnahme zur Vorlage 'Information über die Untersuchung der Ursachen für Differenzen zwischen der Abrechnung der Vertragserfüllung der Industrie und der im Handel noch nicht eingegangenen Waren,'" no date, and Stoschus, Komitee der ABI, "Stellungnahme zu den Ereignissen und Schlußfolgerungen der Untersuchungen in Handel und Produktion zum Problem der im Handel nicht eingegangenen Waren," 22.6.89).

6 BArchB, DE1, 55384, Klopfer, "Persönliche Notizen über eine Beratung beim Vorsitzenden des Ministerrates am 17.11.1988," 18.11.88, p. 19.

7 Interview, Jacob and Sachs, Chemnitz, 26.2.96. Furious, Mittag thundered in 1988 that "whoever takes on a plan is responsible for it. They simply leave and we are left standing there" (BArchB, DE1, 56285, Klopfer, "Persönliche Notizen aus einer Beratung beim Mitglied des Politbüros und Sekretär des ZK der SED, Genossen Günter Mittag," 10.11.88, p. 12).

insufficiency. Rather than proposing an increase in the supply of oranges or changing how they were doled out, however, Günter Schabowski, the party boss who ran East Berlin, and Erhard Krack, the mayor of East Berlin, simply changed the point of sale to prevent lines forming within sight of Honecker's route.[8] The shortcomings of central planning, characterized by its confusion of planning with money and accountability with accounting, together with Honecker's economic irresponsibility, would soon transform the GDR's claims of intellectual and financial autarky into a crushing debt to the capitalist West.

THE PRINCIPAL TASK

The economic policy introduced by Erich Honecker upon his ouster of Walter Ulbricht in June 1971 was officially touted as a fundamental departure from the SED's previous approach to the problem of consumer sovereignty in the GDR. The SED's new economic strategy was derived from a similar program presented by Soviet leader Leonid Brezhnev at the Twenty-Fourth Party Congress of the Communist Party of the Soviet Union earlier that March.[9] Honecker, who time and again demonstrated a canny ability for manipulating political constraints to his advantage, proved extraordinarily adroit at adapting to East German conditions the new emphasis on consumer goods emanating from Moscow. By committing the SED to furnishing the population with more residential housing and a more continuous and broad supply of consumer goods, Honecker aimed to distinguish himself from his predecessor in the popular imagination, reassert the SED's fealty to Moscow, and reap the political benefits of an increase in the standard of living. Ironically, however, Honecker's Principal Task would eventually put the SED leadership at odds with Moscow, fail to create an enduring improvement in living standards for most East Germans, and nearly bankrupt the GDR.

At least as far as East German producers were concerned, what was new about Honecker's economic policy was its reinstatement of the old: The Principal Task put an end to the experimentation of the 1960s and signaled a return to the Stalinism of the 1950s. In fact, Honecker lifted not only the conceptual framework but even the wording of the Principal Task from

8 Günter Schabowski, *Der Absturz* (Berlin, 1991), pp. 144–5.
9 Leonid Brezhnev, *Report of the CPSU Central Committee to the 24th Congress of the Communist Party of the Soviet Union* (Moscow, 1971), pp. 49–50, 61–2.

Stalin's 1952 treatise, *Economic Problems of Socialism in the USSR*.[10] The return to a more orthodox line regarding production is illustrated by the first major economic decision Honecker took. At the fourth plenum of the ZK on 16–17 December, 1971, he authorized the nationalization of the remaining private firms in the GDR, most of which were small firms in the consumer sector.[11]

Nevertheless, Brezhnev's – and therefore Honecker's – emphasis on consumerism was truly novel. Under Ulbricht, the SED had sought to channel popular discontent with the paucity of key consumer items by tightening the rhetorical connection between current sacrifices and the future of a morally pristine prosperity, inventing such slogans as "The way we work today is the way we'll live tomorrow" (*Wie wir heute arbeiten, werden wir morgen leben*). In contrast, Honecker renounced future utopias in favor of present plenty, proclaiming an era of "real-existing socialism." The new First Secretary promised "a different, a new approach to the direction, planning, and organization of the supply of the population," averring that the economy was "a means to an end, a means for the ever-improving satisfaction of the growing material and cultural needs of working people."[12] Although he did not repudiate the Stalinist emphasis on extensive growth or the priority given to heavy industry, Honecker sought to restore the link, emphasized by Marx, between production and consumption. In this manner, he deftly implied that Ulbricht had presided over a confusion of means over ends in which the political goal of economic growth had become uncoupled from the social end of serving the people. Referring to conflicts between producing and distributing bureaucracies, he called on retailers

---

10 Hans-Hermann Hertle, "Die Diskussion der ökonomischen Krisen in der Führungsspitze der SED," in Theo Pirker, M. Rainer Lepsius, Rainer Weinert, and Hans-Hermann Hertle (eds.), *Der Plan als Befehl und Fiktion* (Opladen, 1995), p. 309.

11 Between February and July 1972, some 10,213 firms employing over 580,000 workers were nationalized. In contrast to the confiscations of the 1940s and 1950s, however, private owners were compensated for the forced sale of their property (Maria Haendcke-Hoppe, "Die Vergesellschaftungsaktion im Frühjahr 1972," *Deutschland Archiv* 6 [1973], pp. 37–41; Maria Haendcke-Hoppe-Arndt, *Die Hauptabteilung XVIII: Volkswirtschaft*, in Siegfried Suckut, Clemens Vollnhals, Walter Süß, and Roger Engelmann [eds.], *Anatomie der Staatssicherheit: Geschichte, Struktur und Methoden. MfS-Handbuch*, Teil III/10 [Berlin, 1997], pp. 61–2; Monika Kaiser, *1972 Knockout für den Mittelstand: Zum Wirken von SED, CDU, LDPD, und NDPD für die Verstaatlichung der Klein- und Mittelbetriebe* [East Berlin, 1990]; Kopstein, *The Politics of Economic Decline*, pp. 77–8).

12 Erich Honecker, "Bericht des Zentralkomitees der Sozialistischen Einheitspartei Deutschlands an den VIII. Parteitag der SED," in *Protokoll der Verhandlungen des VIII. Parteitages der Sozialistischen Einheitspartei Deutschlands* (East Berlin, 1971), p. 62. A central aspect of the Principal Task consisted of creating more residential housing. Between 1976 and 1980, Honecker promised to spend 50 billion East German marks constructing 550,000 new housing units and renovating 200,000 old units (ibid., p. 65).

and wholesalers to "represent the needs of the populace more vigorously against the forces of production" and warned "we cannot tolerate ambivalence regarding this subject, its neglect as a 'secondary task' anywhere."[13] In line with Leninist predictions regarding socialist efficiency, Honecker maintained that "a meaningful increase in labor productivity and the effectiveness of labor throughout the whole economy" would pay for his rather ambitious program.[14] In addition to this theoretically inevitable increase in productivity, Honecker calculated that short-term increases in living standards, from housing to consumer goods, would motivate workers and spur long-term gains in labor productivity. Later that year, he made a giddy promise to the second plenum of the ZK that "the domestic market will no longer be the stepchild of our economic upswing. That will be noticeable in a few months."[15]

It is difficult to underestimate the consequences of this shift in policy. In asserting the primacy of consumption over production, Honecker broke with the economic paradigm that had governed East Germany until his rule. The new policy endeavored to make some material concessions to consumer demand without completely abandoning the Marxist-Leninist critique of consumerism that served to legitimate the planned economy or repudiating the Stalinist template for economic growth. Yet this uneasy compromise between political interest and socialist ideology ultimately foundered on its own internal contradictions and the constraints of East Germany's productive capacity; Honecker's new approach to consumerism might have curried popular favor, but it also laid bare the material limitations of the planned economy. East German industry was unable to deliver on Honecker's modest consumer promises, much less catch up to its capitalist rival. At the same time, the SED's shift in focus inevitably raised popular expectations, which were directed at the state's ability to supply consumer goods. The socialist state's limited ability to produce consumer goods and distribute them evenly, however, invited unfavorable comparisons with West Germany. In fact, by shifting popular attention from future postulates to present perfection, Honecker had opened the door to criticism of the real-existing here and now. In turn, the material limitations of the planned economy exposed

---

13 Ibid., pp. 65–6. See also Doris Cornelsen, "Die Wirtschaft der DDR in der Honecker-Ära," in Glaeßner (ed.), *Die DDR in der Ära Honecker*, pp. 357–9.
14 Honecker, "Bericht des Zentralkomitees," p. 66. Lenin's claim that socialism would distinguish itself from capitalism through higher labor productivity is most clearly expressed in V. I. Lenin, "A Great Beginning: Heroism of the Workers of the Rear. 'Communist Subbotniks,'" in *Collected Works*, vol. 29, p. 427.
15 Cited in Joachim Nawrocki, "Verfehlte Wirtshaftspolitik belastet DDR-Wirtschaft," *Deutschland Archiv* 11 (1971), p. 1121.

its ideological inconsistencies. The partial satisfaction of East German consumer demand, for example, necessitated abandoning Marxist-Leninist distinctions between legitimate consumer needs and ethically dubious desires for social status. Stripped of its most potent argument against consumer plenty, however, the SED was unable to make East Germans experience the chronic shortages of consumer goods characteristic of planned economies in a positive light. Arguably, fading memories of Nazi tyranny, coupled with the advent of a generation born too late to identify with the SED's antifascist appeals, necessitated some kind of shift in the SED's approach to governance. Honecker's Principal Task, however, undermined the delicate balance between the theoretical framework and practical basis of socialist power.

Ironically, one of Honecker's most powerful arguments against Ulbricht was his accusation that Ulbricht's reforms had forced the GDR into debt. During the power struggle between the two men, Honecker pilloried Ulbricht for "driving the GDR to the brink of a catastrophe" and castigated him for "playing into the hands of the Federal Republic" and allowing it "to gain a foothold in the GDR."[16] By the late 1970s, however, Honecker's own policies had involved West Germany in the finances of East Germany to an unprecedented degree. Table 1 portrays the regime's internal calculations of its debt to the West through 1980.[17]

16 SAPMO-BA, DY30, JIV 2/2A 3196, "Zur Korrektur der Wirtschaftspolitik Walter Ulbrichts auf der 14. Tagung des Zentralkomitees der SED 1970," p. 3. For more on East German economic policy under Honecker, see Kopstein, *The Politics of Economic Decline*, pp. 73–105; Maier, *Dissolution*, pp. 59–107. For an East German account, see Schürer, *Gewagt und Verloren*, pp. 119–20; Schürer, "Die Wirtschafts-und Sozialpolitik der DDR," in Dietmar Keller, Hans Modrow, and Herbert Wolf (eds.), *Ansichten zur Geschichte der DDR*, vol. 3 (Bonn and Berlin, 1994), pp. 131–71.

17 This book employs East German statistics as indications of economic trends used by party leaders to set policy, rather than as accurate assessments of real economic performance. There are methodological and political reasons for this. First, the communist approach to data collection distorted results. Because economic planning emphasized quantitative measurements over qualitative values, for example, and denigrated money as a unit of accounting, retrospective calculations of relative prices are difficult. Moreover, the ubiquitous subsidies granted to producers, which are peculiar to the East German case, frustrate attempts to identify real costs. Second, political pressure to whitewash poor performance, which existed at every level of the reporting process, often rendered the data unreliable. In the worst cases, the economic content of statistical information was subordinated to politics. Thus, the SED routinely falsified statistics with a view to convincing a skeptical public of the economic effectiveness of its policies, while economic leaders sought to deceive their colleagues in the Politburo. Economic Secretary Günter Mittag, for example, manipulated various statistics in an effort to increase his political influence by shaping decision making at the highest levels of the party. See BArchB, DN1, VS 13/90, Nr. 7, Staatliche Zentralverwaltung für Statistik, "Zu Grundproblemen bei der Durchführung der Wirtschafts- und Sozialpolitik in den Jahren 1986 bis 1989," 7.11.89; Burghard Ciesla, "Hinter den Zahlen. Zur Wirtschaftsstatistik und Wirtschaftsberichterstattung in der DDR," in Alf Lüdtke and Peter Becker (eds.), *Akten. Eingaben. Schaufenster: Die DDR und ihre Texte. Erkundungen zur Herrschaft und Alltag* (Berlin, 1997); Kopstein, *The Politics of Economic Decline*, pp. 132–6. See also the discussion in Chapter 4.

Table 1. *East German Trade Imbalances with the West, 1970–1980 (in billions of DM)*

	Internal East German Figures[a]		Post-Unification Western Figures[b]	
Year	*Net Annual Trade Deficit*	*Net Debt to the West*	*Net Annual Trade Deficit*	*Net Debt to the West*
1970	No data	−2.0	No data	No data
1971		−2.6	No data	No data
1972	Total trade deficits	−3.4	No data	No data
1973	1971–5 =	−5.3	No data	No data
1974	DM −8.9 billion	−7.8	No data	No data
1975		−10.7	−2.755	−8.863
1976	−3.8	−14.8	−4.069	−13.148
1977	−3.1	−17.9	−3.869	−16.525
1978	−2.4	−21.2	−2.85	−19.008
1979	−2.7	−25.1	−3.699	−21.486
1980	No data	−27.9	−2.764	−23.637

[a] *Sources:* BArchB, DE1, 56323, Mittag and Schürer to Honecker, 14.3.77, p. 408; SAPMO–BA, DY30, JIV 4/94, "Vorlage für das Politbüro, Betreff: Information über die Entwicklung der Zahlungsbilanz und der Außenwirtschaftsbeziehungen bis Ende Dezember 1979," p. 2; BArchB, DE1, 56296, Gerhard Schürer, "Zusammengefaßte Einschätzung zum Entwurf des Fünfjahrplanes 1976–1980," 6.10.76, p. 9; BStU, Arbeitsbereich Mittag, Nr. 58, "Zu den ausgewählten Problemen bei der Durchführung der Beschlüsse des XI. Parteitages der SED zur ökonomischen Entwicklung der DDR," Anlage 3, "Entwicklung des Saldos aus Forderungen und Verbindlichkeiten gegenüber dem Nichtsozialistischen Wirtschaftsgebiet im Zeitraum 1970 bis 1989," p. 37. Note: Alternate figures for the cumulative debt to the West ($1 billion for 1970, DM 13.6 billion for 1977, DM 16.4 billion for 1978, and DM 19.0 billion for 1979) result from differing calculations of conversion rates between the two German currencies (BArchB, DE1, 56323, Staatliche Plankommission, "Stand und Probleme der Ausarbeitung der staatlichen Aufgaben für das Jahr 1979," 16.5.79, p. 5; BArchB, DE1, 56323, "Betreff: b. Stand der Zahlungsbilanz der DDR gegenüber dem nichtsozialistischen Wirtschaftsgebiet 1978 und 1979 sowie erforderliche Maßnahmen," 1.2.79, pp. 2, 4). The hard-currency deficit does not include the Swing credits permitted the GDR under the Four Powers Agreement.
[b] *Source:* Deutsche Bundesbank (ed.), *Zahlungsbilanz der ehemaligen DDR, 1975 bis 1989* (Frankfurt/ Main, 1999), pp. 49, 50, 60.

According to East German figures, the GDR's foreign debt under Ulbricht had risen to an unprecedented $1 billion by 1970, which caused great consternation in the ranks of the party leadership. Just ten years later, however, the debt had jumped to $11 billion and would reach $20.6 billion by 1989. During Honecker's first five years in power, East German trade deficits with the West totaled nearly DM 8.9 billion.[18] Between 1971 and

18 BArchB, DE1, 56323, "Zu den Ursachen der Verpflichtungen der DDR gegenüber der NSW," p. 1; BArchB, DE1, 56296, Schürer, "Zusammengefaßte Einschätzung zum Entwurf des Fünfjahrplanes 1976–1980," 6.10.76, p. 9; BArchB, DE1, 56320, VK 12. Tagung, 17–18.11.89, p 143. Schalck argues that the debt under Ulbricht was actually about $2 billion (Pirker et al., *Der Plan*, p. 169).

1980, the GDR imported DM 21 billion more than it exported.[19] Honecker had dug a hole from which the GDR would never emerge.

Because the GDR was importing more than it exported, it was forced to take out loans to cover its trade deficits, which only increased its net foreign indebtedness. In 1976, one of Honecker's senior economic advisors, State Planning Commissioner Gerhard Schürer, presented a gloomy account of the GDR's future. He warned that interest payments alone on the trade deficits would amount to DM 10 billion between 1976 and 1980. Merely servicing the debt for 1980, he calculated, would cost 50 percent of the growth in national income planned for that year.[20] The danger was that the GDR's exports would not raise enough Western money to meet even the interest payments on its growing debts to the West. As Schürer remarked, "the basic question for the GDR is not the amount of credits and debts, but the deficit of [Western] cash."[21] For 1977, Schürer anticipated that the GDR would end up DM 2.1 billion short, requiring the country to take out even more loans just to cover interest payments on the money it had previously borrowed.[22] By 1980, the State Planning Commissioner continued, "the current amount of the debt will no longer permit the GDR to pay all of the interest and capital burdens it has incurred out of its own hard-currency revenues even with extraordinary increases in exports. All of the interest payments together amount to two-thirds of the export revenues in convertible currency earned in one year." Schürer concluded by noting that servicing the debt "restricts the opportunities for investment and consumption in the GDR to an increasing degree. If the capitalist banks cease providing loans to the GDR," he cautioned, "the GDR will default on its debts within a few months and no longer be able to import anything anymore."[23]

Schürer's dire warning must have filled his colleagues with dread. Despite their antipathy to money, the communist leadership well understood the political meaning of defaulting on Western loans. In return for restructuring the GDR's debt, capitalist creditors would pressure the SED to refocus

19 SAPMO-BA, DY30, JIV 2/2A/3252, Politbüro-Sitzung vom 31.10.89, Schürer, "Analyse der ökonomischen Lage der DDR mit Schlußfolgerungen," 30.10.89, p. 10.
20 BArchB, DE1, 56296, Schürer, "Zusammengefaßte Einschätzung," 6.10.76, p. 12.
21 BArchB, DE1, 56323, Mittag and Schürer to Honecker, 14.3.77, p. 411.
22 BArchB, DE1, 56296, Schürer, "Zusammengefaßte Einschätzung," 6.10.76, p. 13.
23 BArchB, DE1, 56323, "Konzeption zum Abbau der Höhe der Verbindlichkeiten der DDR gegenüber dem nichtsozialistischen Wirtschaftsgebiet vom 27.6.1980," pp. 1–2. The structure of East German debt to the West considerably weakened the GDR's position vis-à-vis its creditors because it consisted largely of short-term loans with high interest rates that could be called in quickly or not extended.

its economic priorities to better meet its foreign financial obligations. In addition to forcing a reduction in imports from the West, which had become vital to East German consumers, they would demand increased domestic savings to pay off the loans, resulting in a tangible decline in living standards. Imposing austerity measures to satisfy Western bankers was an unsettling prospect for a political elite whose raison d'être was hostility to capitalism.

To the SED's peculiarly embattled cast of mind, however, falling into the clutches of Western financial circles touched on two of its worst fears. First, the division of Germany had the potential to transform the slightest dependency on the West into a struggle for the GDR's survival. Sitting across a table from capitalists determined to put the financial vulnerability of a socialist state to political use would inspire fear in any communist. For East German communists, however, the prospect of asking clemency from West Germany, a hostile state openly dedicated to reunifying Germans under capitalist auspices, recalled just how precarious their position was as leaders of an unpopular dictatorship.

Second, Honecker and his colleagues feared that lowering living standards to pay off loans from the West would almost certainly provoke popular unrest. The uprising of 17 June 1953 had seared the correlation between austerity measures and political discontent into their memory. At the time, the party had blamed the insurrection on West German agents provocateurs. Behind closed doors, however, the SED leadership conceded that its economic policies – specifically, its reduction of wages for manual laborers – had triggered spontaneous walkouts by workers in East Berlin, which had quickly spread to the rest of East Germany.[24] It was of little consolation that SED leaders could depend on the intervention of Soviet tanks to end the insurrection, not least because it had been mounted by the very class the SED claimed to represent.

Years later, memories of 1953 continued to disrupt the SED leadership's ability to consider solutions to economic problems dispassionately. Many of the SED's leaders, including Honecker himself, had held positions of political responsibility during the uprising. When confronted with the need to impose austerity measures to hold down costs after 1953, the fear of provoking political rebellion stiffened their resistance to lowering wages

---

24 For all of its critical distance, Stefan Heym's narrative *5 Tage im Juni* (Frankfurt/Main, 1977) illustrates how difficult 1953 was for communists to understand. For general accounts of the insurrection, see Arnulf Baring, *Der 17. Juni 1953* (Stuttgart, 1983); Manfred Hagen, *DDR-Juni 1953* (Stuttgart, 1992). For a more economic orientation, see Kopstein, *The Politics of Economic Decline*. Torpey, *Intellectuals, Socialism, and Dissent* examines the lack of solidarity between workers and intellectuals during the uprising.

or raising food prices. The Polish experiences of 1970, 1976, and 1979, when increases in food prices provoked civil unrest, only confirmed the East German leadership in its belief that economic success, as measured by the pocketbooks of ordinary East Germans, determined the party's political survival.[25] As Schürer was to write after 1989, "since it had increased the price of sugar before 17 June 1953, the political leadership was so scared of raising the prices of basic necessities that no one accomplished a change" in policy.[26] Ironically, it was this very fear of the political consequences of parsimony that would lead Honecker to raise East German living standards artificially by borrowing money from West Germany, deflecting the present problem to an indefinite future.

Honecker's own sense of his position as leader of the SED, moreover, was shaped by an emphasis on political stability secured by economic prosperity. The conditions under which he came to power, for example, reinforced his willingness to keep living standards high at any cost. In December 1970, just months before Honecker ousted Ulbricht, there were riots in Poland triggered by increases in food prices. The unrest led to the replacement of the Polish leader Władysław Gomułka by Edward Gierek. Not only did popular resistance to austerity measures resonate powerfully with Honecker's experience of 1953, but the change in leadership raised concerns about whether Honecker would survive a similar debacle. From Honecker's perspective, there were powerful reasons to borrow time and money from the West to stave off hard economic choices.

This is not to argue that the GDR's economic problems were solely of Honecker's creation. As Schürer observed, many of the reasons for the GDR's dire financial straits were exogenous to the Principal Task. The GDR had experienced a few bad harvests, for example, forcing it to import more grain than usual at a cost of DM 3.8 billion between 1971 and 1978.[27] In addition, growth of domestic demand for products that the GDR had previously shipped overseas began to translate into a reduction of exports to the West. For example, East Germans began eating more meat in part because the SED had lowered standards regulating fat content: People were obliged to consume larger volumes to obtain the same amount of meat. At

---

25 Jan Kubik, *The Power of Symbols against the Symbols of Power: The Rise of Solidarity and the Fall of State Socialism in Poland* (University Park, Penn., 1994), pp. 17–29, 31–3; Slay, *The Polish Economy*, pp. 35–6, 43–4.

26 Schürer, *Gewagt und Verloren*, p. 75. See also Günter Mittag, *Um jeden Preis. Im Spannungsfeld zweier Systeme* (Berlin and Weimar, 1991), p. 68.

27 BArchB, DE1, 56323, "Betreff: b. Stand der Zahlungsbilanz der DDR gegenüber dem nichtsozialistischen Wirtschaftsgebiet 1978 und 1979 sowie erforderliche Maßnahmen," 1.2.79, p. 13. Bad harvests in the USSR in 1972 and 1974 increased pressure on world grain prices.

the same time, the poor supply, variety, and quality of fish drove many East Germans to eat more meat than they otherwise might have.[28] Publicizing increases in the consumption of meat proved a useful measure of affluence in the propaganda war with West Germany. But East German eating habits were also expensive. Because of the expansion of domestic demand, the GDR was forced to import meat between 1976 and 1980, which cost the country another DM 500,000.[29] As the Chairman of the District Council of Frankfurt an der Oder noted in 1984, "meat consumption is a political problem. That is, our expectations are oriented too much toward consumption. We have not quite overcome some phenomena, where meat and butter consumption were emphasized as a political asset in the struggle with the West."[30] Schürer also estimated that the dramatic jump in the price of natural resources (excluding oil) on international markets during the 1970s had cost the GDR an extra DM 3.1 billion between 1971 and 1978.[31] Despite the use of planning to achieve economic independence from the capitalist West, the resource-poor GDR found that it was not impervious to the surge in inflation that affected the rest of the industrialized world.

Nor was it Honecker's fault that the GDR's alliance with the Soviet Union could not shield it from price shocks like the oil crises.[32] Although the USSR had previously found it politically expedient to subsidize the energy and raw materials needs of its Comecon partners, this policy had become a financial burden by the mid-1970s. A series of poor agricultural performances forced the Soviet leadership to purchase grain on international markets, which meant that the USSR was forced to sell oil on international markets in return for the dollars necessary to pay for the grain. In 1976, the

28 SAPMO-BA, DY30, Vorläufige SED 31984, Ministerium für Handel und Versorgung, "Vorschläge zur Einflußnahme auf die Verbraucherentwicklung bei Fleisch und Wurstwaren," 4.8.88.
29 BArchB, DE1, 56323, Staatliche Plankommission, "Stand und Probleme der Ausarbeitung der staatlichen Aufgaben für das Jahr 1979," 16.5.79, p. 12; BArchB, DE1, 56296, "Ergänzung der Übersicht vom 10.8.1979," p. 298.
30 SAPMO-BA, DY30, Vorläufige SED 31984, Stellvertreter des Ministers, "Meinungsäußerungen von Vorsitzenden der Räte der Bezirke zu den Ursachen der Fleischversorgung," 26.3.84, p. 1.
31 BArchB, DE1, 56323, "Betreff: b. Stand der Zahlungsbilanz," 1.2.79, p. 13.
32 Ibid. Elsewhere, Schürer calculated that the cost of oil imports from the West rose from DM 1.2 billion in 1973 to 2 billion in 1977 (BArchB, DE1, 56323, Staatliche Plankommission, "Stand und Probleme," 16.5.79, p. 12). In the wake of the 1973 Arab–Israeli war, the price of crude oil in New York jumped from $3.40 a barrel on 17.10.73 to $12 by December. By the end of 1974, prices had risen to five times their 1972 levels. The Iranian revolution triggered the second oil crisis; by 1981, prices had soared by more than 300 percent to $34.50 a barrel. The third crisis, however, was deflationary. As a result of the Iran–Iraq war, oil prices had fallen by 1986 to less than one-half their 1981 levels (Sidney Pollard, *The International Economy since 1945* [London and New York, 1997], p. 108; Cornelsen, "Die Wirtschaft der DDR," pp. 358–9; Eric Owen Smith, *The German Economy* [London, 1994], p. 160).

Soviet Union decided to pass higher prices for oil and natural gas on to its allies, increasing the price of oil from 14 rubles per ton to 35 rubles and the price of natural gas from 14.25 rubles to 31 rubles per 1,000 cubic meters.[33] The extra cost to the GDR for the year 1976 alone ran to about DM 388 million. In the five years between 1976 and 1980, the State Planning Commission calculated that price increases had cost the GDR nearly DM 11.6 billion.[34]

When the Soviet Union unilaterally abrogated its 1968 agreement with the GDR on energy inputs, it also eliminated the main advantage of membership in Comecon: its ability to shield planned economies from price fluctuations and guarantee deliveries over the long term. No longer could the GDR depend on fixed prices in trade with its allies to protect it from the volatility of international markets.[35] More importantly, higher prices for Soviet raw materials translated into higher costs for East German industry. First, the GDR was obliged to export more capital goods and consumer products to the USSR to pay for the same amount of oil and natural gas. The GDR benefited from the fact that the price of Soviet oil was lower than the price on open markets. Nevertheless, higher oil prices fundamentally altered the GDR's terms of trade with the Soviet Union, spelling an end to the GDR's positive trade balance with the USSR. Second, increased exports to the USSR shifted valuable resources away from domestic use and export to the West.

The Soviet Union's inability to sustain the flow of low-cost natural resources to its trading partners presaged the end of the global division between capitalist and communist economic blocs. It also meant that capitalist money, which planned economies were forced to acquire to obtain the food, technology, and capital equipment they coveted, became the touchstone of communist economic strategies. As the integration of communist with capitalist markets proceeded apace, the Marxist-Leninist practice of separating trade with capitalist and socialist partners into hard and soft currency ledgers degenerated into a mere accounting trick. Dividing opposing economic orders into neat categories could not conceal the GDR's increasing dependence on the West. Worse still, this economic integration was disadvantageous for the Soviet bloc precisely because it occurred on capitalist

---

33 SAPMO-BA, DY30, Vorläufige SED 31970, Jarowinsky to Honecker, 26.6.75. The USSR had also chosen to use loans to cover its purchases of grain in 1975, tying the Soviet economy more closely to world markets (Smith, *The Planned Economies*, pp. 213–14).

34 Figures calculated using the GDR's internal exchange rate of 2 East German marks to 1 D-Mark (BArchB, DE1, 56296, "Ergänzung der Übersicht vom 10.8.1979," p. 298).

35 Smith, *The Planned Economies*, pp. 211–37.

Table 2. *Net and Per Capita Debt: GDR, Poland, and Romania, 1971–1979 (in millions of US dollars)*

	Poland		Romania		GDR	
Year	Net Debt	Per Capita Debt	Net Debt	Per Capita Debt	Net Debt	Per Capita Debt
1971	764	20	1,227	53	808	47
1975	7,381	194	2,449	107	4,350	259
1979	20,200	526	6,700	230	13,148	785

Sources: Deutsche Bundesbank (ed.), *Zahlungsbilanz der ehemaligen DDR*, p. 60; Smith, *The Planned Economies*, p. 226; Zloch-Christy, *Debt Problems of Eastern Europe*, pp. 35–6. East German debt figures have been converted using the internal rates set by the East German government. Population data for Poland and Romania are given according to Joseph Held, *Dictionary of Eastern European History since 1945* (Westport, Conn., 1994), p. 301; population for the GDR is taken from Staatliche Zentralverwaltung für Statistik (ed.), *Statistisches Jahrbuch der Deutschen Demokratischen Republik 1989* (East Berlin, 1989), p. 1.

terms. The international oil market, for example, used U.S. dollars as a unit of accounting. Thus, the GDR was forced to obtain American money to pay for any oil it needed in addition to Soviet imports. In addition, the socialist state's lack of integration into international monetary structures added to the GDR's considerable financial burdens. Because the East German mark was nonconvertible, and thus not traded against other currencies, the GDR was unable to profit from the dollar's significant loss of value during the 1970s. In contrast, West Germany, which also had to import almost all of its fuel, benefited greatly from having a strong currency: The D-Mark appreciated throughout the 1970s against the dollar, cushioning the impact of soaring oil prices on its economic growth.[36] Thus, the Marxist-Leninist ideological antipathy toward markets and money saddled Soviet-style regimes with a tremendous disadvantage in their burgeoning trade with the West.

It is also worth pointing out that the GDR under Honecker was not the only socialist state to expand trade with the West. Other communist regimes such as Poland and Romania, embarked on similar programs of export-led growth. Although most did not take on as much Western debt as the GDR, Poland and Romania were arguably in a worse position by the end of the 1970s. As Table 2 shows, most of the debt accumulated during the 1970s by these three countries was incurred in the four years between 1975 and

36 The cost of imported oil for the Federal Republic was eight times higher than in 1970, although prices had risen by 20 times (Smith, *The German Economy*, pp. 159–60). Of course, the GDR's exceptional relationship with the Federal Republic shielded it more from developments in international markets than other Comecon countries, since the bulk of its trade with the West was denominated in D-Marks rather than dollars.

1979, largely because of higher prices for natural resources and the purchase of capital goods. Capital expenditures financed with external funds were meant to enhance productive capacity and thereby generate a surplus that would help pay down these loans. By the end of the decade, Poland's net debt far exceeded net East German debt, which itself was double Romania's debt. On the other hand, East German per capita debt was far higher than that of either country.[37] What matters when estimating debt, however, is not a country's absolute or per capita liabilities. After all, central to a state's ability to repay foreign debt is its ability to earn export surpluses. In contrast to its Eastern European allies, the GDR enjoyed a reputation as the tenth largest economy in the world – something neither Poland nor Romania could boast. Unfortunately, the GDR's international standing was inflated by statistical manipulation, over which Honecker did indeed have control. Soft budget constraints might mitigate the consequences of falsification at home, but financial obligations to Western creditors involved hard budgetary constraints and thus accountability.

External factors such as the oil price saltations, together with the domestic liabilities of economic planning and competition with West Germany, contributed to the GDR's economic morass. But the real culprit responsible for generating debts during the 1970s was Honecker's Principal Task. His attempt to ingratiate himself with a recalcitrant citizenry necessitated domestic and foreign subsidies that weighed heavily on the country's productive capacities. According to State Planning Commissioner Schürer, most of the imports that had created the financial crisis went toward immediate consumption, crowding out necessary investment in the country's aging capital stock.[38] In addition, subsidies for consumer goods skyrocketed under Honecker. In 1970, Ulbricht's final year in power, they reached a peak of 8 billion East German marks. By the end of Honecker's rule, they had jumped to 58 billion.[39] Rather than investing in new technologies that might produce goods for domestic consumption as well as export, Honecker preferred to gratify East German consumer demand immediately. Moreover, Honecker had permitted wages and consumption to outpace productivity

---

37 The GDR's ratio of debt service payments to export earnings in hard currency rose from 18 percent in 1972 to 38 percent in 1977. Anything below 25 percent is considered safe (Zloch-Christy, *Debt Problems*, p. 41).

38 Schürer claimed that 55 percent of all imports between 1971 and 1989 went toward consumer perishable and nonperishable goods (BArchB, DE1, 56323, "Zu den Verpflichtungen der DDR gegenüber dem NSW," 17/18.11.89, p. 5).

39 Ibid., p. 3. See also the Stasi's assessment in BStU, Arbeitsbereich Mittig, Nr. 58, "Zu den ausgewählten Problemen bei der Durchführung der Beschlüsse des XI. Parteitages der SED zur ökonomischen Entwicklung der DDR," p. 2.

in the belief that better living standards would improve worker morale and result in long-term productivity gains. He was sorely disappointed. Not only did aggregate consumption as calculated by East German economists rise more quickly than national income, but it drastically outpaced investments.[40] The GDR was not simply living beyond its means. It was mortgaging its future to the West − eating oranges now and worrying about paying for them later.

SUBORDINATING ECONOMIC RATIONALITY TO POLITICAL CALCULATION

The efforts of the planning apparatus during the 1970s to reverse these trends failed. Honecker remained impervious to sound economic advice when it required political sacrifices, preferring sycophancy to the Cassandra-like predictions of the dismal science. In his effort to place political before economic concerns, Honecker was supported by the generational dynamics peculiar to the East German dictatorship. A pivotal confrontation between Honecker and two of his most prominent advisors in 1977 illustrates the way in which the SED's antifascist ideology shielded the General Secretary from having to make difficult decisions about finite resources. The clash also marks the end of an alliance that might have produced reform: It was the last time that Günter Mittag, Economic Secretary of the Central Committee, joined forces with State Planning Commissioner Gerhard Schürer to convince Honecker to implement much-needed policy changes.

Concerned by Honecker's denial of the economic constraints on his political behavior, Mittag and Schürer confronted him candidly about the dangers looming ahead for the GDR if the debt were not kept in check. In particular, they argued that the scarcity of hard currency confronting the GDR was the result of "years of excessive imports of commodities which, after their use in the GDR, do not contribute directly to increasing productivity and thereby to the source of their repayment."[41] Furious at their boldness, Honecker lambasted them − not for their economic analysis,

---

40 Net investment in the productive sector, which in Marxist-Leninist economic theory excluded the service, health, education, and entertainment sectors as well as all forms of administration, totaled 22.6 billion East German marks in 1970. It rose to 24.6 billion in 1975, but plummeted to 17.7 billion marks in 1984. By 1989, it had nominally regained the levels of spending from the Ulbricht period, rising to 23.5 billion, but was lower in real terms. In contrast, net investment in the nonproductive sector, which included everything from health care to cinemas, totaled 11.8 billion marks in 1970. It rose to 17.4 in 1975, and soared to 21.2 billion in 1981. After dipping slightly to 20.3 billion in 1984, it jumped to 23.5 billion East German marks in 1987 (BStU, Arbeitsbereich Mittig, Nr. 58, "Zu den ausgewählten Problemen," Anlage 2, p. 32).
41 BArchB, DE1, 56323, Mittag and Schürer to Honecker, 14.3.77, p. 410.

Figure 3. Erich Honecker after his reelection as General Secretary of the Politburo of the ZK of the SED at the Eleventh Party Congress in April 1986. (Courtesy of Bundesarchiv Koblenz, Bildarchiv, 183/1986/0421/044.)

but for their political foolhardiness. "We cannot simply change all of our policies overnight," the General Secretary remonstrated. "What has been suggested means deep cuts [in the standard of living]. We would have to go before the Central Committee and say: We did not foresee this or we lied to you."[42] In addition to the popular unrest austerity measures might provoke, Honecker was worried about being shown up before his political rivals.

The General Secretary then flatly denied his own responsibility for the GDR's financial morass, confounding economic fact with political theater. Pointing to the disparity between the party's own rhetoric and Mittag and Schürer's analysis, Honecker chose to uphold the legend of the party's infallibility in the face of clear evidence to the contrary. Indirectly accusing the two men of lying, Honecker countered that "the cause [of the debt] is not, as

42 BArchB, DE1, 56323, "Zum Material vom 14.3.1977," pp. 372.

you wrote, that more has been consumed since 1971 than produced. Then the resolutions of the Eighth Party Congress would be false, and those of the Ninth Party Congress, too."[43] Because Honecker's ouster of Ulbricht in 1971 had put an end to poor economic performance, and because the party was always right, Honecker's economic policy could not be wrong. In the rarified air of politics in Soviet-style regimes, personal ambitions and wishful thinking, buttressed by appeals to party discipline, held sway over economic exigency.

The vehemence of Honecker's reaction, remarkable for such a stolid man, and his implicit charge of insubordination cowed his two aides. According to Schürer, Honecker "was furious and red in the face."[44] Mittag beat a hasty retreat. Seeking to assuage Honecker, Mittag attributed the altercation to the language he and Schürer had used rather than to a conflict over policy. This willingness to sacrifice principle to politics was very much in keeping with Mittag's previous behavior. In the face of Soviet and East German opposition to his own economic reforms in the 1960s, for example, Mittag had unceremoniously deserted the NES. When it had become clear that Ulbricht's position was no longer tenable, moreover, he joined Honecker's palace coup.[45]

Even in a political environment that rewarded unscrupulous behavior, however, opportunism sometimes met with resistance. In mid-1972, Mittag was stripped of his position as Economic Secretary and demoted to the position of Deputy Chairman of the Council of Ministers until 1976. In a play on the meaning of Mittag's name, this period was often referred to sarcastically by East German wags as the *Mittagspause* – the "lunch break." In part, his demotion derived from the political debts Honecker had incurred while ousting Ulbricht, which the new First Secretary paid off through patronage.[46] But Mittag was also a deeply unpopular man. In particular, his surly manner, sharp tongue, and penchant for publicly humiliating colleagues aroused widespread loathing among other SED leaders. If

---

43 Ibid. According to Hertle, Honecker added that "in [your] proposal it ends up looking as if the policy after Ulbricht was wrong, as if Ulbricht incurred no debts and Honecker creates debts" (Hertle, "Die Diskussion," p. 315).

44 Interview, Schürer, Berlin, 19.4.95.   45 Grieder, *The East German Leadership*, p. 190.

46 Mittag's demotion formed part of Honecker's attack at the 8th Plenum in October 1973 on the technocrats installed by Ulbricht, which he capped by removing Walter Halbritter, a major advocate of reform under Ulbricht, from the Politburo. According to Heinz Klopfer, Honecker permitted Mittag to intervene in economic affairs beginning in 1974; around 1976, when Willi Stoph became Chairman of the Council of Ministers, Honecker gave Mittag greater latitude as a method of containing Stoph's influence (interview, Klopfer, Berlin, 4.10.95).

Figure 4. Economic Secretary Günter Mittag at the Erfurt district party delegates' conference in May 1971. (Courtesy of Bundesarchiv Koblenz, Bildarchiv, 183/K0516/0009/001.)

his sadism and tendency to view discussion as insubordination instilled fear in his inferiors, Mittag's toadyism in Honecker's presence inspired sheer hatred.[47]

Nevertheless, Mittag's managerial talents were considerable. His keen mind, administrative skills, and sheer ruthlessness soon placed him at the center of economic policy making once again. The ineptitude of his main competitors – including the incompetent Werner Krolikowski, who briefly replaced Mittag as Economic Secretary, and the ineffectual Horst Sindermann, who fleetingly replaced Willi Stoph as head of the Council of Ministers – only drew attention to his energy and effectiveness. Indeed,

---

47 Examples of Mittag's viciousness include the public demotion of the general director of VEB Kombinat Zweirad in 1984/5; an attack on Construction Minister Wolfgang Junker in the Central Committee because he dared to speak of bottlenecks in the production of cement; the excruciatingly negative public evaluations of Machine Tooling and Construction Minister Rudi Georgi's work; the attacks on Hans Modrow in December 1984; and Mittag's nasty treatment of his colleagues during a meeting regarding the value of the East German mark in late 1988. This portrait of Mittag is culled from meetings of the Council of Ministers, the Economic Commission, and the Politburo and corroborated by nearly every East German functionary I interviewed. The various memoirs written by SED politicians place too much blame on Mittag but confirm their hatred of his person. See Egon Krenz, *Wenn Mauern fallen. Die friedliche Revolution: Vorgeschichte-Ablauf-Auswirkungen* (Vienna, 1990), pp. 78–9; Erhard Meyer, "Der Bereich Günter Mittag: Das wirtschaftspolitische Machtzentrum," in Hans Modrow (ed.), *Das Große Haus: Insider berichten aus dem ZK der SED* (Berlin, 1994); the various interviews in Pirker et al., *Der Plan*; Schabowski, *Der Absturz*, pp. 227–8.

Mittag's seemingly inexhaustible capacity for hard work won him grudging respect from his colleagues. Even after his legs had been amputated below the knees because of diabetes, for example, he refused to miss public rituals, such as factory visits and political parades, although long hours walking on his prosthetic limbs caused him excruciating pain.

By the mid-1970s, Mittag had completed his transformation from late convert to Honecker's cause to Honecker's key economic aide. His formal restoration came in 1976, when Honecker reshuffled his government to consolidate his power. Seizing upon their obvious incompetence, Honecker demoted Krolikowski and Sindermann and returned Mittag to the post of Economic Secretary. Honecker then moved his one-time rival Stoph back to his old position as head of the Council of Ministers, freeing Honecker to assume chairmanship of the Council of State. Honecker also changed his formal title from First Secretary to the Stalinist moniker "General Secretary" to emphasize his preeminence.

Within a few more years, Mittag's remarkable combination of political skill, prodigious work, uninhibited sycophancy, and relentless mendacity would make him Honecker's most trusted confidante and the second most powerful man in the GDR. In 1977, however, he had yet to consolidate his position with Honecker. Confronted with the General Secretary's truculent disregard for judicious counsel, Mittag chose to abandon economic wisdom in favor of political ambition. As Mittag understood only too well, political success in Honecker's GDR was not contingent on economic prudence, but rather on personal access to the General Secretary.

In contrast to Mittag, Schürer was sincerely dismayed by Honecker's anger. Evidently bewildered, he felt it necessary to reiterate his personal loyalty to the General Secretary. Like Mittag, Schürer owed his position to Ulbricht. In contrast to Mittag, however, he had become increasingly alarmed by Ulbricht's economic experimentation and defected early on to Honecker's camp – even daring to attack Ulbricht openly during at least one high-level meeting.[48] Once in power, Honecker rewarded Schürer by retaining him as State Planning Commissioner and promoting him to candidate membership in the Politburo.[49] Worried that his criticism of Honecker's

---

[48] Interview, Schürer, Berlin, 19.4.95; Grieder, *The East German Leadership*, pp. 165–70. See also Schürer's letter to Stoph expressing distaste for Ulbricht's leadership from 13.11.70 in Matthias Judt (ed.), *DDR-Geschichte in Dokumenten: Beschlüsse, Berichte, interne Materialien und Alltagszeugnis* (Berlin, 1997), pp. 136–7.

[49] Schürer argues that Honecker refused to promote him to full membership because he chose to speak his mind too frequently. It is worth noting, however, that planning commissioners were seldom promoted to Politburo membership in Soviet-style regimes (interview, Schürer, Berlin, 19.4.95).

economic leadership appeared disloyal, Schürer was at pains to reiterate his fealty to Honecker in the most effusive terms. Recalling his gratitude to Honecker for doing away with Ulbricht's economic adventurism, Schürer confessed that "I am deeply disturbed and moved that the report we handed in created such an impression. . . . How could someone like me, how could we at the State Planning Commission – who are deeply grateful to you, Erich, because you have made it possible to work out real plans – formulate personal attacks on you and the agreed-upon policy line. We are ready to correct our formulations." Despite his intentions, Schürer's flattery betrayed his real concern. In his embarrassed rush to placate the General Secretary, Schürer nevertheless insisted on the need to formulate "real plans" – a reference to Ulbricht's unrealistic projects that could be easily applied to Honecker's policies. To emphasize his loyalty to Honecker, Schürer dropped his objections to the General Secretary's strategy. Yet he remained troubled by an economic policy that threatened the future of socialism in Germany.

The readiness of Mittag and Schürer to retract their opposition to Honecker's spendthrift ways reflects an impulse to conformity that was encouraged by the dictatorship. Both men arrived at a similarly craven willingness to withdraw their warnings, but they did so because of key differences in personality: Where Mittag was unscrupulously opportunistic, Schürer was doggedly loyal. These different character traits were not simply personal qualities, however. Rather, Mittag's pragmatic submission to political authority and Schürer's frequent retreat from political conflict into the world of technical expertise are consistent with the generational dynamics peculiar to post-1945 Germany. As many scholars have observed, the powerful legacy of National Socialism shaped an entire generation's approach to politics. Mittag's lack of loyalty to principle, for example, recalls Helmut Schelsky's famous description of the "skeptical generation."[50] Born between 1930 and 1940, the members of this generation were too young to have held positions of responsibility under the Nazis. Their experience of the Third Reich's collapse and the material privations that afflicted Germany during and just after World War II encouraged a deep-seated aversion to all-encompassing ideologies and a preference for pragmatic solutions to political

---

50 Helmut Schelsky, *Die skeptische Generation: Eine Soziologie der deutschen Jugend* (Düsseldorf, 1957). For Heinz Bude, the core group of this generation is the *Flakhelfer*, or the young men born between 1926 and 1930 drafted at the end of the war to stave off Germany's impending defeat (Heinz Bude, *Deutsche Karrieren: Lebenskonstruktionen sozialer Aufsteiger aus der Flakhelfer-Generation* [Frankfurt/Main, 1987], p. 51). See also Lutz Niethammer, Alexander von Plato, and Dorothee Wierling (eds.), *Die volkseigene Erfahrung* (Berlin, 1991); Lutz Niethammer, "Das Volk der DDR und die Revolution," in Charles Schüddekopf (ed.), *Wir sind das Volk!* (Reinbek, 1990), pp. 251–78.

problems. Men like Mittag, who was born in 1934, embraced Marxism-Leninism not because of its theoretical claims or revolutionary allure, but because it offered them moral absolution and social mobility. As Catherine Epstein has observed, "in return for loyalty to the new order, the SED essentially absolved these young people of their Hitler Youth pasts."[51] In addition, the SED offered them unique possibilities for professional advancement immediately after the war. The twin promises of historical exoneration and career opportunity fostered a strong sense of loyalty to the GDR.

Like Mittag, Schürer benefited from the extraordinary social mobility the SED offered. He belongs to the group of younger communists promoted by Ulbricht during the 1960s because of their technical expertise, which included Mittag, the economist Otto Reinhold, and the Politbüro member Werner Jarowinsky, who was responsible for consumer policy.[52] In contrast to Mittag, however, Schürer was too old to have been a member of the skeptical generation. Born in 1921, he served for six years in the Wehrmacht. Schürer's guilt over his youthful sympathy for National Socialism deeply influenced his approach to politics in the GDR.[53] His remorse made him especially vulnerable to the antifascist legends built around men of Honecker's generation. To compensate for the fact that the SED had come to power by coercive means, the party mythologized the communist struggle against the Nazis and heroized its murdered leader, Ernst Thälmann. Mediated by antifascism, the SED's philosophical anticapitalism proved an exceptionally reliable instrument of political integration in East Germany, helping to reconcile social groups outside the party with the state and cultivate an uncritical fealty to the SED leadership in party members.[54]

Honecker also cleverly harnessed the history of his own life to consolidate his position within the SED. Like Ulbricht, Honecker employed the fact that he was an Old Communist – one of the men and women who had joined the communist party before Hitler's takeover in 1933 – to forge a

---

51 Catherine Epstein, *The Last Revolutionaries: German Communists and Their Century* (Cambridge, Mass. and London, 2003), p. 228.
52 Since 1989, Schürer has sought to salvage his reputation by resurrecting the grand German tradition of the nonpartisan expert to argue – unconvincingly – that he was not a politician but rather an "accountant" (interview, Schürer, Berlin, 19.4.95; Schürer, *Gewagt und Verloren*; Schürer, "Die Wirtschafts- und Sozialpolitik der DDR").
53 Interview, Schürer, Berlin, 19.4.95 and 20.6.95.
54 As Vladimir Tismaneanu has observed, "for the whole SED elite, the GDR was conceivable only as an anti-fascist, socialist alternative to the Federal Republic" (Tismaneanu, *Reinventing Politics*, p. 210).

scarce commodity: revolutionary authenticity. But where Ulbricht had spent the Nazi period in Moscow, Honecker spent it incarcerated in a Nazi jail in Berlin. The heroism associated with his captivity infused Honecker's biography with far more charisma than Ulbricht had ever possessed. Forty years after Honecker's arrest, it continued to enhance his political authority in a culture constantly reminded of the genocidal evil of Nazism. Possession of this revolutionary authenticity had an almost talismanic effect on those who coveted it. Despite Honecker's unimposing physical appearance and reedy voice, the authority of his biography imbued his person with a charismatic aura in the eyes of many party members. Thus, Schürer's excessive submission to Honecker was not simply a function of political expedience or blind obedience. It was also an expression of an entire generation's approach to politics.

The use of the past to subjugate the future worked effectively against men like Schürer who were complicit at some level in National Socialist atrocities – who did not, in West German Chancellor Helmut Kohl's words, enjoy "the mercy of a late birth." The aura of revolutionary heroism surrounding Honecker's biography, coupled with the loyalty he commanded as General Secretary of the party, rendered dissent from his policies difficult and contemplation of his removal nearly impossible. The charisma of his biography thus silenced the most prominent voice of economic prudence, forcing technical expertise to conform to political ideology. Throughout Honecker's rule, ideology rather than material constraints would define the contours of political authority.[55]

Nevertheless, Schürer was one of the few SED leaders who exhibited a modicum of independence throughout the 1970s and 1980s, an exceptional quality in an otherwise quiescent Politburo. Although his actions can hardly be described as opposition, Schürer did periodically attempt to remind Honecker of the financial constraints on the GDR's behavior.[56] On a structural level, Schürer's episodic recalcitrance illustrates the tension between the economic and charismatic forms of authority characteristic of modern dictatorships. In his pathbreaking work on the transmission of political authority, Max Weber argued that the challenge for revolutionary parties after seizing power involves maintaining their élan by domesticating it. This they do through "the routinization of charisma" – by harnessing the

---

55 This is also Kopstein's conclusion (Kopstein, *The Politics of Economic Decline*, p. 111).
56 His first warning to Honecker came in 1972 (interview, Schürer, Berlin, 19.4.95; Schürer, "Die Wirtschafts- und Sozialpolitik der DDR," p. 151; Schabowski, *Der Absturz*, pp. 121–2). His most important attempt to force Honecker to accept limits on spending is discussed in Chapter 4.

romance of the revolution and charisma of the revolutionary to the more mundane tasks of postrevolutionary rule.[57] Institutionalizing an intangible quality such as charisma, however, necessitates reconciling the extraordinary characteristics that define charismatic leadership with the ordinary material constraints at work in an industrial society. Honecker's attempts to consolidate his authority within the SED by emphasizing the charismatic roots of his claim to power stood in stark opposition to Schürer's insistence on the economic limitations to that power. Honecker's heated resistance to Schürer's reasoned objections to the Principal Task, as well as Honecker's relative lack of interest in (and knowledge of) economic affairs, was neither entirely irrational nor simply ignorant, as some have implied.[58] It was also an understandable reaction against the instrumental rationality underpinning the economic sphere, which threatened to rob Honecker of the charisma on which his power was based.

Of course, Honecker did not rely solely on the power of ideology to consolidate his position. His political talents included an impressive understanding of institutions, which he used to undercut his rivals. Through administrative duplication and elision, Honecker undermined party organizations that might be used as platforms for alternatives to his leadership. With the assistance of a few close advisors, for example, Honecker quickly succeeded in bypassing the ZK's jurisdiction in such key areas as foreign policy, economics, and internal security, creating alternate administrative paths tied to his person. By inflating the number of members and alternates, moreover, Honecker promoted his political allies while simultaneously devaluing membership in the ZK. In 1950, the ZK had 81 members and candidates, compared with 222 in 1989.[59] He also undermined its political relevance by reducing the frequency and content of its meetings from three or four to two highly choreographed annual events, marked by carefully orchestrated protestations of fealty to Honecker's person and policies. Where his predecessor had at least permitted a modicum of debate and used ZK plenums to signal shifts in official policy, Honecker transformed what was supposed to be a deliberative body into a group of aging yes-men (plus a few token yes-women) – except, that is, for its final meetings in 1989, when the spontaneity of popular unrest overwhelmed the SED's narcissistic

57 Max Weber, *The Theory of Social and Economic Organization*, trans. A. M. Henderson and Talcott Parsons (New York, 1947), p. 372.
58 Hans-Hermann Hertle, "Staatsbankrott: Der ökonomische Untergang des SED-Staates," *Deutschland Archiv* 10 (1992), pp. 1019–30.
59 Herbst et al., *Die SED*, p. 526. In 1986, the average age was sixty-four. There were only twenty-seven female members and candidates.

complacency, interrupting its ritualistic self-affirmation with the threat of political insignificance.[60]

The General Secretary also offered up a series of nominal reforms aimed at appeasing senior leaders who might object to his policies. Behind this façade, however, Honecker continued to consolidate his power at the expense of economic rationality. Even the most important economic reform Honecker undertook, which is discussed below, served the purpose of tightening central control over the periphery rather than addressing the core problem of money and its economic meaning (or, in the vocabulary of capitalist economics, financial incentives and their allocational function). In this manner, Honecker managed to stave off the pressure for real change through cosmetic concessions.

In the face of his charismatic leadership and political skills, objections to Honecker's prodigality languished, while authoritarian structures rewarded economic irrationality. The reservations his senior advisors did articulate, moreover, simply went unheeded. Indeed, despite increasingly frequent and urgent decrees mandating drastic reductions in the foreign debt, things only got worse. As early as 1973, a special committee was established to keep the Politburo apprised every month of the parlous state of the country's balance of payments deficit. When the situation failed to improve, the committee began sending detailed reports on a weekly basis to Mittag and Willi Stoph, head of the Council of Ministers. There is no evidence, however, that they did anything to reduce the deficits.

This is not to imply that Honecker was insensitive to political discourse as an instrument of governance. At the Ninth Party Congress in 1976, for example, Honecker indulged in a rhetorical attempt to emphasize a necessary balance between production and consumption. To great fanfare, he renamed the Principal Task, expanding a rather simple motto to the unwieldy slogan "The Principal Task in its Unity of Economic and Social Policy," which was mercifully abbreviated to "The Unity of Economic and Social Policy."[61] Needless to say, this rather awkward change in wording did little to redress the hard-currency shortage. Equally fruitless was the "intensification campaign" (*Intensivisierungskampagne*) Honecker introduced, which aimed at creating efficiencies by applying the GDR's technical expertise to the manufacturing process. In the absence of real incentives for

---

60 Hans-Hermann Hertle and Gerd-Rüdiger Stephan (eds.), *Das Ende der SED: die letzten Tage des Zentralkomitees* (Berlin, 1997).

61 Erich Honecker, "Bericht des Zentralkomitees der Sozialistischen Einheitspartei Deutschlands an den IX. Parteitag der SED," in *Protokoll der Verhandlungen des IX. Parteitages der Sozialistischen Einheitspartei Deutschlands* (East Berlin, 1976), vol. 1, p. 62 ff.

enterprises to adopt new technologies, however, Honecker's plan remained mere exhortation.[62]

The only structural reforms that Honecker undertook, moreover, did little to augment the GDR's productive capacity. In 1976, he approved a plan by Economic Secretary Günter Mittag for a general revaluation of industrial prices. Recalculating the value of the GDR's industrial base was intended to reveal costs, especially for exports to the West, while permitting a more accurate assessment of the age of factory equipment. Since these recalculations had no bearing on the incentives with which enterprises were confronted, they naturally failed to alter their behavior.[63]

More significantly, Honecker authorized Mittag to reduce administrative costs and tighten central control over the production process by restructuring the chain of command between the industrial ministries and the factory floors. Until 1977, ministerial directives were put into practice by a second tier of management called the Association of People's Enterprises (Vereinigung Volkseigener Betriebe, or VVB). Responsible for a given sector of industry, the VVB instructed East German factories on fulfilling the plan. Starting in 1977, Mittag stripped away this extra layer of management, concentrating factories instead in combines, or large trusts that answered directly to the relevant ministries and ZK departments.[64] Most significantly, the switch streamlined management by vertically integrating research and development, production, and distribution channels in the hands of one economic agent, the general director of the combine.[65] Thus, the automobile industry was now integrated into one combine, which was dubbed the People's

62 As the Planning Directive presented by the SED leadership at the Ninth Party Congress in May 1976 put it, "the intensification of social production has become the decisive link in the [GDR's] further development" ("Direktive des IX. Parteitages der SED zum Fünfjahrplan für die Entwicklung der Volkswirtschaft der DDR in den Jahren 1976–1980," in *Protokoll der Verhandlungen des IX. Parteitages*, vol. 2, p. 310).

63 Prices were recalculated again in 1984 using new cost bases and including a nominal profit. In 1986, increases in the price of equipment were used to make production more expensive and costs more visible (SAPMO-BA, DY30, Vorläufige SED 34623, Amt für Preise, "Liste der Preisänderungskoeffizienten für Erzeugnisse und Leistungen, deren Industrie- bzw. Erzeugnispreise am 1. January 1986 geändert werden," no date). In addition, prices for nonessential consumer goods were recalculated in 1979 (Cornelsen, "Die Wirtschaft der DDR," pp. 362–4).

64 Some combine structures had existed since 1967. The restructuring continued into 1981, especially in the district-run food-processing sector (SAPMO-BA, DY30, Vorläufige SED 30054, Ehrensperger to Mittag, 8.4.81 and 12.5.81, and Abteilung Planung und Finanzen and Abteilung Leicht-, Lebensmittel- und Bezirksgeleitete Industrie to Mittag, "Bericht über die Prüfung der von den Bezirksleitungen der SED erarbeiteten Vorschläge zur Bildung von Kombinaten in der bezirksgeleiteten Industrie und die erreichten Ergebnisse," 8.4.81).

65 An official interpretation of the economic efficiencies gained from the restructuring can be found in Willi Kunz et al., *Umfassende Intensivierung – sozialistische ökonomische Integration – Kombinat* (East Berlin, 1988). A defense of the combines written by Mittag's aides can be found in Claus Krömke and Gerd Friedrich, *Kombinate: Rückgrat sozialistischer Planwirtschaft* (East Berlin, 1987).

Own Enterprise Industrial Association for Automotive Construction of the GDR Combine Personal Automotive Transport (Volkseigener Betrieb Industrieverband Fahrzeugbau der DDR Kombinat Personenkraftwagen, or IFA Combine). Although the ungainly name hardly suggests a more rational structure, the IFA Combine was designed to bring the entire automotive industry under one roof, linking manufacturers of car parts, motors, chassis, and bodies with car assembly, car design, car distribution, and automotive research. In addition, the combine benefited from the production-oriented position of its general director, who simultaneously served as the director of a key enterprise (*Stammbetrieb*) central to the combine's mission. By the end of the process, the GDR's economic structure consisted of 129 centrally directed combines comprising 6,480 enterprises.[66]

Although Mittag generally worked to tighten the center's control over economic activity, the creation of the combines implied a certain amount of decentralization. In contrast to the VVB directors, for example, the combine management controlled negotiations over planning targets with the ministry, managed production, including the right to merge production facilities, and directed the overall use of resources, including the funds used to pay workers and construct social or production facilities. In addition, the Foreign Trade Enterprises (*Außenhandelsbetriebe*, or AHB) were now integrated into the production process, rather than being simply answerable to the Ministry for Foreign Trade. Theoretically, inserting the AHBs into the combine structure forced the combine management to be more responsive to the needs of exporters, while making the AHBs more responsible for fulfilling the requirements of the plan. Not only did the combines win a degree of autonomy from the ministries, but they often circumvented Mittag's attempts to keep them on a short leash. At the annual convention for general directors in Leipzig, for example, Mittag tried to force his managers to make higher pledges than the plan required. In response to this pressure, the general directors factored Mittag's demands into their assessments of what they could produce, lowballing their commitments when the plan was set and then increasing them later in Leipzig.[67] If anything, Mittag's

---

66 In addition, there were 143 combines run by the districts, mostly involved with food processing and retailing, as well as another forty-four combines in the construction, transport, and agricultural sectors (Haendcke-Hoppe-Arndt, *Die Hauptabteilung XVIII*, pp. 72–3). According to Cornelsen, 132 of the East German combines comprised between twenty and forty enterprises and employed an average of 20,000 workers. Of the district-led combines, ninety-six averaged 2,000 employees (Cornelsen, "Die Wirtschaft der DDR," pp. 360–2). See also Kurt Erdmann and Manfred Melzer, "Die neue Kombinatsverordnung der DDR," *Deutschland Archiv* 13 (1980), pp. 929–44.

67 Interview, Jacob and Sachs, Chemnitz, 26.2.96; Bryson and Melzer, *The End of the East German Economy*, pp. 5–7, 29–31.

reorganization of East German industry had allied management more closely with the factory's interests, rather than those of the center.

However rational this reorganization of production was intended to be, it created new incentives for irrational behavior. At the factory level, the individual enterprises comprising the combine did not share the same interests or motivations as their general director. At times, this could result in squabbles over resources and outright insubordination, as the example of the automobile combine, discussed in Chapter 5, demonstrates. There is evidence, moreover, that the division of administrative guidance between the combines and the Ministry for Foreign Trade created conflicting goals for the AHBs. The combines responded to ministerial directives by drowning them in paperwork.[68] And while the new structure enhanced the bargaining position of the combines against their ministries, they were ultimately vulnerable to Mittag's increasing control over the ZK. The party's control over foreign trade, and Mittag's control over the party, meant that the combines were increasingly starved for capital, as the following chapters illustrate. Finally, whatever benefits were gained through economies of scale and streamlining management were offset by the combines' size, which made them slow to react to external stimuli. As a prominent East German economic historian remarked ruefully in 1990, "combines are the epitome today of monopoly structures and immobility."[69]

Not only did Mittag's managerial reorganization fall short of real reform, but it also substituted more direct party control for ministerial administration while introducing new opportunities for bureaucratic conflict. Paradoxically, the economic ineffectiveness of the combines attracted substantial political support. As Jeffrey Kopstein has noted, managers and economists supported Mittag's move precisely because they believed the combines would constitute a counterweight to the planning apparatus and the ministries.[70] Most communists, moreover, had a weakness for gigantism – for big and showy projects intended to create economies of scale, such as the engineered steel town of Eisenhüttenstadt. In contrast to Mittag's unpopular attempts at reform through decentralization during the 1960s, then, the creation of the combines attracted the support of the economic elite and party leadership

---

68 Haendcke-Hoppe-Arndt, *Die Hauptabteilung XVIII*, pp. 93–4.
69 Jörg Roesler, *Zwischen Plan und Markt: Die Wirtschaftsreform in der DDR zwischen 1963–1970* (Freiburg and Berlin, 1990), p. 13.
70 Kopstein suggests that the formation of the combines changed little economically, except for the creation of the prestigious position of general director, who functioned as a captain of socialist industry (Kopstein, *The Politics of Economic Decline*, pp. 95–8). I would argue that the structure of incentives did shift toward a more effective production process, but was offset by Mittag's increased ability to intervene in factory affairs.

while increasing central control over economic affairs. In this manner, Mittag enhanced his own position.

Neither Honecker's rhetoric nor Mittag's reorganization addressed the flaws in the production and distribution of East German goods, however. Without active money to provide an inducement to cost efficiency, East German industry failed to boost productivity or reduce wastefulness. Between 1976 and 1980, for example, production glitches alone cost the GDR around DM 3 billion worth of exportable products.[71] Aside from difficulties associated with production, moreover, ideological blinders hobbled the distribution of East German goods. In particular, Marxist-Leninist strictures on marketing hindered effective salesmanship. The GDR's marketing tactics were ill-informed, its quality control notoriously poor, the time-to-market for its products of long duration, and its service agreements entirely inadequate to the task.[72] The party's control over foreign trade, moreover, ought to have resulted in rapid reactions to shifts in customer preference and technological change. In fact, however, the split between producing and exporting bureaucracies and the gigantism of economic actors ensured that East German producers responded poorly to signals in Western markets.

No matter how effective Honecker's cosmetic reforms were in neutralizing potential opposition to the "Unity of Economic and Social Policy," they could not stave off the growing material constraints on his room for maneuver. The large volume of imports from the West continued to dwarf the GDR's exports, stimulating an increasingly unscrupulous quest for capitalist money. The success of political charisma over economic rationality made Honecker's position within the SED nearly unassailable, but his sway over the party nearly bankrupted the GDR in the process. To ward off insolvency and Honecker's treatment of the Western debt as a soft budget constraint, the planning apparatus found itself in the unenviable position of having to invent increasingly draconian methods of economizing: That is, East Germany's economic leaders responded to Honecker's irrational denial of the material limitations on his power with stopgap measures that undermined socialism in the long term. The increasingly irrational quality of economic policy in the GDR was reflected in two contradictory impulses, which were united by the single goal of reducing the debt.

---

71 BArchB, DE1, 56296, "Ergänzung der Übersicht vom 10.8.1979," p. 296.
72 BArchB, DE1, 56285, Klopfer, "Persönliche Notizen aus einer Beratung beim Mitglied des Politbüros und Sekretär des ZK der SED, Genossen Günter Mittag," 10.11.88, p. 11; BArchB, DE1, 56318, "Zur Frage, was erforderlich ist, damit eine Mark der DDR auch eine Valutamark wert ist," 8.9.88, p. 4; SAPMO-BA, DY30, Vorläufige SED 31970, Jarowinsky to Honecker, 26.6.75, p. 12.

On the one hand, planners such as Schürer proposed economically sound but politically unfeasible projects aimed at decreasing socialist dependence on the West. On the other hand, Mittag expanded cooperation with the West, paradoxically, to reduce the GDR's dependence on Western capital. In both cases, the GDR found itself compromising its political independence from West Germany to rescue what economic autonomy it still enjoyed.

THE TYRANNY OF DEBT

With mounting debt but without substantial reform, the planning apparatus was desperate to reduce costs by the late 1970s. It adopted a variety of strategies to balance the GDR's trade accounts, including trimming imports of key capital goods, fostering import substitution, seeking out licensing agreements, and encouraging rather adventurous attempts at technological innovation. Many of the belt-tightening measures advocated by the planners failed to gain the necessary political support, at times for good reason. Indeed, some of their cost-reduction strategies illustrate the more ridiculous aspects of the proscriptive abstinence inherent in Marxist-Leninist consumer ideology. In 1977, for example, dramatic increases in the price of coffee and cocoa on international markets threatened to add an extra DM 400 million–500 million to the GDR's bills. In response, Schürer recommended reducing the amount of coffee made available to the public by 80 percent. Brimming with pride, Schürer announced in support of his proposal that "the State Planning Commission has not been drinking coffee for a long time, and it is all right, we are still alive" – as if the rest of the population would be as eager to forego such simple pleasures.[73]

As the Politburo member Albert Norden pointed out, slashing coffee supplies entailed grave political risks. "The implementation of the measures contained in the draft will not meet with understanding," he warned, but instead "trigger great dissatisfaction." Norden conceded that "we are of course compelled to draw conclusions from the foreign economic situation. Without drastic hard-currency savings it will not work. And that must no doubt include the consumption sector." But "*which* items are cut or reduced," he admonished, "is in my opinion a political issue of the first order."[74] Like many other proposals put forward to save Western money,

---

73 BArchB, DE1, 56348, "Interne Beratung mit E. Honecker z. Schrb. 14.3.77," p. 113. East German coffee was often mixed with chicory to extend supplies.

74 SAPMO-BA, DY30, IV 2, 2.028/20, Norden to Honecker, 28.6.77, pp. 62–3.

Schürer's recommendation met with rejection because it neglected the political consequences of the reduction in living standards it entailed.

The planning apparatus also embarked on misguided attempts to engineer substitutes for imported items. In 1980, for example, scientists at the Central Institute for Nutrition at Potsdam-Rehbrücke patented a method of candying unripe tomatoes as an ersatz for sugar extracted from fruit, which is used in baked goods and sweets. According to the Workers and Peasants Inspectorate, DM 3 million could be saved annually by using this process and foregoing fruit imports from Greece. The main problem was that the Central Economic Association for Fruit, Vegetables, and Potatoes possessed neither the machines required to produce the sugar substitute nor the adequate storage facilities to hold the green tomatoes during the fermentation process – aside from serious questions about the surrogate sugar's taste.[75]

More effective, if rather desperate, were plans to sell off the GDR's cultural treasures, from works of art to the city of Weimar's cobblestones, as well as the country's gold reserves and weapons stockpiles.[76] Under Honecker, the party displayed a ruthless determination to monetize sectors of the economy traditionally insulated from cost concerns. The party put a price on the East German education system, for example, training students who had been rejected by West German medical schools in return for hard currency.[77] It even sold blood donated by East Germans to Western health officials.[78] The SED leadership also pursued more dubious revenue streams, such as hawking Western goods to East Germans for hard currency in the Intershops, appropriating the funds of Christian religious institutions, prostituting East German women, and selling political prisoners to the Federal Republic.[79]

---

75 SAPMO-BA, DY30, Vorläufige SED 34603, Komitee der ABI, "Information über die Kontrolle zur Verminderung von NSW-Importen durch beschleunigte Produkteinführung der Spitzenleistung 'Verarbeitung von grünen Tomaten zu Dickzuckerfrüchten zur Substitution von Zitronat'," 1.6.82.

76 BArchB, DE1, 56349, Anlage Nr. 8 zum Protokoll Nr. 50 vom 28.11.72, "Vorschläge zur Lösung von Problemen der Zahlungsbilanz," p. 336, authorizing the sale of DM 50 million worth of art objects, antiquities, and arts and crafts. See also Honecker's revealing comment that "I assume that we are not hoarding for a state of war" approving the sale of weapons from emergency reserves, as well as his green light for the sale of gold reserves (BArchB, DE1, 56348, "Beratung beim Generalsekretär des Zentralkomitees der SED, Genossen Erich Honecker, zur weiteren Durchführung des Planes 1977 und zur Zusammenarbeit des Volkswirtschaftsplanes 1978 am 2. Juni 1977," 2.6.77, p. 166). Honecker approved a large weapons deal during the crisis of 1982 (Haendcke-Hoppe-Arndt, *Die Hauptabteilung XVIII*, p. 77; BArchB, DE1, 56323, "Betreff: b. Stand der Zahlungsbilanz," 1.2.79, p. 12).

77 The GDR charged DM 25,000–35,000 a year for a five-year program (BStU, ZAIG 14614, pp. 11–13, 26–7; *Der Spiegel* 8 [1988], pp. 92–4). Bulgaria provided similar services for Greek students.

78 BStU, ZAIG 14614, p. 75.

79 *Der Spiegel* 33 (1978), pp. 30–1; Uta Falck, *VEB Bordell. Geschichte der Prostitution in der DDR* (Berlin, 1998). The GDR earned nearly DM 3.5 billion for the freedom of nearly 34,000 political

Even where the party leadership had reconciled itself to the necessity of importing consumer goods from the West, it invented ways to reduce that dependency. One important method of reducing payment in hard currency consisted of licensing Western capital goods and technology. Ideally, licensing involved a form of barter that benefited both actors. The Western firm profited from the socialist factory's cheap but skilled labor, while the Eastern enterprise obtained the machines and equipment it required to manufacture key commodities.[80] In 1984, for example, Volkswagen AG delivered an assembly line for the production of four-stroke motor engines to the GDR in return for the East German promise to deliver 100,000 motors worth DM 500 million over a three-year period. Little money was directly involved in the deal.[81] From the SED's perspective, moneyless exchanges such as the arrangement with Volkswagen promised to modernize East German industry without sapping hard-currency reserves while appealing to the ideological preferences of economic planners.

In practice, however, licensing agreements highlighted the gap between capitalist and socialist approaches to economic exchange, not to mention the difference in performance. The different principles at work are illustrated by the example of the GDR's ten-year contract with the U.S.-based multinational corporation Pepsi-Cola. The Pepsi case also underscores a central irony of the GDR's dependence on the West: The size of the GDR's current account deficit forced East German officials to place principal before principles, which undermined the anticapitalist goals of the socialist state.

In 1974, Pepsi agreed to install a modern bottling facility in the Baltic port of Rostock. In return, the GDR committed itself to purchase a specified

<hr>

prisoners and 220,000 people wanting to emigrate to the Federal Republic by exploiting the one-sided permeability of the Berlin Wall. Most of this money – DM 3.2 billion – came during Honecker's watch. The going rate for political prisoners in the early 1970s was DM 40,000 a person, but jumped to DM 95,847 in 1977. The GDR earned DM 4,500 for reuniting a family. Although the West German Protestant churches initially footed the bill, the sums quickly exceeded their capacity to pay, and the West German government stepped in (Gerhard Besier, *Der SED-Staat und die Kirche 1969-1990. Die Vision vom "Dritten Weg"* [Berlin and Frankfurt/Main, 1995], pp. 542–7; Timothy Garton Ash, *In Europe's Name: Germany and the Divided Continent* [New York, 1993], pp. 141–6, 154; Armin Volze, book review, *Deutschland Archiv* 25:6 [1992], p. 651; Armin Volze, "Geld und Politik in den innerdeutschen Beziehungen," *Deutschland Archiv* 23:3 [1990], p. 385; Armin Volze, "Kirchliche Transferleistungen in die DDR," *Deutschland Archiv* 24 [1991], pp. 59–66).

80 Although these kinds of deals had been fashionable in the 1950s and the early 1960s, the Berlin Wall placed serious obstacles in their way. According to one Western observer, licensing agreements became frequent again starting in 1975, about the time of Mittag's return to power as Economic Secretary (*Süddeutsche Zeitung*, 2.9.78). On licensing agreements in Eastern Europe, see Smith, *The Planned Economies*, pp. 215–20.

81 What little money did change hands came frequently in the form of long-term loans, which provided much-needed relief for the GDR's tight debt structure (BArchB, DE1, 56323, "Betreff: b. Stand der Zahlungsbilanz," 1.2.79, p. 16). For more on the Volkswagen deal, see Chapter 5.

amount of Pepsi concentrate annually over a ten-year period. The attraction of the deal for Pepsi did not center on the GDR's purchase of the concentrate. The amount of hard currency involved was relatively small – a total of $3.1 million over ten years in payment for 8,240 units of Pepsi concentrate.[82] Rather than immediate profits, Pepsi was after market share, in the East as well as the West. By having its product bottled in a cheap currency area, Pepsi aimed to reduce manufacturing costs, which would make its soft drink less expensive. Pepsi could then pass these savings on to consumers in the West and, by putting downward price pressure on competitors like Coca-Cola, make inroads into its rivals' customer base. In the East, by contrast, Pepsi looked to boost product recognition among socialist consumers, hoping that the SED's willingness to market Pepsi domestically would hook East Germans on the soft drink. To this end, Pepsi asked the GDR to keep rival Western beverages off its shelves, thereby giving Pepsi a virtual lock on the top end of the emerging East German soft-drink market.[83]

In contrast to Pepsi's emphasis on market share, the SED was focused on making money. To ensure that the GDR turned a profit, Mittag placed his protégé Alexander Schalck-Golodkowski in charge of negotiations with Pepsi. Schalck, who was an aggressive advocate of expanding trade with the West, found licensing agreements attractive precisely because the GDR obtained new capital stock from the West without having to pay for it in capitalist currency. But Schalck also believed that the GDR could make a go of bottling Pepsi for export to the West through arbitrage – by exploiting the difference in value between the dollar and the East German mark. Finally, he anticipated that manufacturing Pepsi for sale domestically would produce sizeable returns at home. Schalck appeared unconcerned, however, by a basic contradiction in his plan, which called for the socialist state to hawk a capitalist soft drink – the epitome of Western commercialism – to East Germans. Ever the profit-oriented communist, Schalck did not worry that selling Pepsi might seem hypocritical in East German eyes. Indeed, he regarded the opportunity to market Pepsi at home as politically beneficial because providing East German consumers with a high-quality soft drink might make them less restive.[84] What distinguished Pepsi from its East

---

82 The bottling plant, which was valued at $2.88 million, could produce 40 million units annually. One unit of concentrate produced 102.18 hectoliters of Pepsi-Cola (BArchB, DL2, VA 579, Vorsitzender des Wirtschaftsrats des Bezirks Rostock, "Verhandlungskonzeption über die weiteren Vertragsbeziehung mit der Pepsico, Inc.," 31.3.78, p. 123, "Pepsi-Cola," no date, p. 174, and Schalck to Mittag, 18.8.88, p. 3).

83 BArchB, DL2, VA 579, Dämmrich, Forum, "Vermerk (intern) über die Verhandlung mit Pepsi Cola, Wien am 14.01.1982," 4.2.82, p. 59.

84 BArchB, DL2, VA 579, "Vermerk zum Gestattungsvorhaben Pepsi-Cola," 30.11.76, p. 187.

German partners, then, was not the matter of money itself, but rather how they set about earning it.

Unfortunately for Pepsi, the East Germans proved to be difficult business associates, not the least because they did not feel themselves to be constrained by their contractual obligations. According to the agreement, for example, Pepsi retained the right to undertake on-site inspections once a month to verify that the bottling plant in Rostock kept to Pepsi's standards. In particular, the VEB Rostocker Brauerei was obligated to use water that met Pepsi's specifications to produce the soft drink. Because the quality of the water strongly affected the taste of the beverage, and because the GDR was a notorious polluter, Pepsi had cause for concern. Despite their contractual obligations, however, the East German authorities failed to comply with the agreement, inventing various excuses to keep Pepsi's inspectors from entering the country. More seriously, Pepsi officials soon discovered that the GDR was using the new factory to bottle beer instead of Pepsi because it brought in more Western money.[85] To their chagrin, Pepsi's managers were learning that entering into agreements with a communist state made enforcing contracts difficult.

Even getting a straight answer out of East Berlin was tricky. In May 1976, Herbert Ley, who was Vice President of Pepsi's Vienna-based international operations, wrote to his East German counterparts expressing surprise at their assurances that production was proceeding smoothly. "I've been receiving a growing number of letters to my office," Ley wrote, "from citizens of the GDR and foreign tourists visiting your country who express their astonishment that it is extremely difficult to find Pepsi even once in a while."[86] Ley's information was excellent. A year and a half into the deal, nearly half of the 2,575 units of concentrate that the GDR had agreed to purchase between 1974 and 1976 was in storage, unbottled and undisturbed.[87] For all intents and purposes, the East Germans had abandoned the manufacture of Pepsi.

After repeated prompting from Ley, Schalck's aides finally conceded that they had halted production of Pepsi because it was simply not profitable. Bewildered, Pepsi officials suggested that perhaps the GDR had not

---

85 BArchB, DL2, VA 579, "Bottling Appointment Contract (Gestattungsvertrag)," no date, p. 133 "Verhandlungsdirektive mit dem Pepsi-Cola-Konzern," no date, p. 117, "Aktenvermerk über der Betriebsbesuch der Fa. Pepsi-Cola am 13.6.1978 in Rostock," p. 100, Ley and Gunka to Steinert and Asbeck, 14.1.76, p. 216, and "Protokoll der Verhandlungen über Pepsi-Cola in Rostock am 6.6.75," 9.6.75, p. 233. There is some evidence suggesting that Schalck tried to moderate the bottling of beer (BArchB, DL2, VA 579, Schalck to Wange, 13.6.75, pp. 225–6).
86 BArchB, DL2, VA 579, Ley to Asbeck, 5.7.76, p. 199.
87 BArchB, DL2, VA 579, "Vermerk zum Gestattungsvorhaben Pepsi-Cola," 30.11.76, p. 188.

understood how to price the beverage correctly. According to their calculations, the GDR should have earned DM 0.41 per bottle on exported Pepsi, DM 0.59 on each bottle of Pepsi sold in the Intershops, and 0.53 East German marks per bottle sold in Ostmark retail shops.[88]

Superficially, the evidence corroborated Pepsi's price-oriented explanation of the problem. In the hopes that Pepsi would become a high-end alternative to domestic soft drinks such as Margon and Club Cola, Schalck had priced Pepsi at 1 East German mark. But that made Pepsi very expensive compared to East German soft drinks, which cost only 0.35 Ostmark. This price structure suppressed demand for Pepsi, as East Germans substituted the cheaper homemade beverage for the expensive Western drink. To stimulate East German demand for Pepsi, Schalck cut the price of Pepsi to match the domestic brands. Even at the lower price, however, Pepsi failed to catch on. For once, East Germans preferred a socialist consumer good to the capitalist commodities Schalck was pushing. If that political miscalculation was worrisome, cutting the price to 0.35 marks created a financial headache, since the GDR was now selling Pepsi on the domestic market at a loss of 0.12 marks.[89] Confronted with this kind of math, Schalck halted production. It seemed as if Pepsi's managers were right: East German planners did not understand the domestic market well enough to develop a competitive pricing environment.

But faulty pricing was not the reason for the GDR's failure to profit from Pepsi. After all, the domestic market was not the main reason Schalck had agreed to the deal; the prospect of obtaining new bottling facilities and earning hard currency by exporting Pepsi to Austria and West Germany was. What Schalck had not anticipated were the problems that always plagued economic planners: production bottlenecks. In a classic case of failed complementarity, VEB Rostock Brauerei found it impossible to obtain enough bottles and cases that met Pepsi's approval. Without bottles or containers to ship them in, the factory could hardly make the drink for export.[90] Of course, Schalck could have requisitioned or even purchased more glass production capacity and packaging facilities. But the last thing he wanted was to siphon off more of East Germany's overextended glass manufacturing capacity or to allocate more hard currency for a project intended to save money. Instead, he turned to Poland, which luckily had a licensing contract with

---

88 BArchB, DL2, VA 579, "Concentrate Purchases," no date, pp. 46–9.
89 BArchB, DL2, VA 579, Schalck to Mittag, 18.8.88, p. 3.
90 BArchB, DL2, VA 579, "Information zum Gestattungsvorhaben 'Pepsi-Cola'," no date, p. 184, and Steinert, "Vermerk über eine Verhandlung mit der Fa. Pepsi-Cola am 11.3.1980," 11.3.80, pp. 79–80.

Pepsi to produce Pepsi bottles. The Poles realized that their socialist neighbors were now entirely dependent on them for the production of Pepsi. Rather than demonstrating solidarity with their East German allies, however, the GDR's Polish suppliers raised their prices.[91] In response, the GDR simply reduced its purchases of bottles, transforming a pricing problem into one of complementarity.

Unable to make a go of bottling Pepsi for sale at home or abroad, East German officials began whittling away at their contractual obligations. Pepsi had never enjoyed much leverage over its communist partners, but transferring ownership of the factory to the East Germans in 1979 removed the last constraint on their behavior. In May 1979, Schalck's aides suggested that the GDR reduce its purchases of Pepsi concentrate and use its own bottles instead of those required by Pepsi. Pepsi countered by reminding the GDR of its legal commitments. In response, the GDR simply reneged on its obligations.[92]

The conflict with the GDR, in addition to a dispute with Pepsi's Polish partners, cost Ley his job. His successor Robert Pagnucco tried to retreat from the mess without entirely losing face. He insisted that the GDR pay for the final three years of the contract, which came to $1.2 million for 3,090 units of concentrate. If the GDR refused to comply, Pagnucco threatened, Pepsi would take the GDR to court in Vienna.[93] While a lawsuit in the capitalist West could hardly have been enforced against a sovereign socialist state, open confrontation might have seriously damaged the GDR's future prospects for business deals with Western partners. To avoid negative publicity, the GDR agreed to pay a mere $300,000, or one-quarter of what it owed.[94] The decision to settle with Pepsi was eased, moreover, by the fact that Coca-Cola announced that it was interested in cutting a deal with the GDR.[95]

---

91 BArchB, DL2, VA 579, Schalck to Mittag, 18.8.88, p. 3.
92 BArchB, DL2, VA 579, Dämmrich, Forum, "Vermerk (intern)," 4.2.82, p. 59, "Hinweise für das Gespräch mit Gen. Dr. Wange am 4.5.1979," 4.5.79, p. 89, Steinert, "Vermerk über eine Verhandlung," p. 79, Steinert, "Telefonat mit Gen. Dr. Wange am 18.3.1980," 19.3.80, p. 7, and "Telefonat – Gen. Sroke, BD Brauerei Rostock," 10.4.81, p. 64.
93 BArchB, DL2, VA 579, Panse, "Bericht über die Dienstreise nach Wien in der Zeit vom 6.12. bis 8.12.1982," 14.12.82, p. 26, and Politzer to Steinert, 5.8.82, p. 56.
94 BArchB, DL2, VA 579, Panse, "Bericht über die Dienstreise," 14.12.82, pp. 29, 30, Panse telex to Pagnucco, 21.12.82, p. 10, and Briksa to Wange, 7.12.82, p. 7.
95 BArchB, DL2, VA 579, Ziegler, SGD Import, Forum HG, "Vermerk über die Verhandlung mit der Firma Pepsi Cola am 5.1.1983," 10.1.83, p. 21. According to Ziegler, Coke was well informed about the conflict with Pepsi. Although no licensing agreement resulted from these negotiations, Coke contacted the GDR again in 1989 with a business proposition (BArchB, DL2, VA 579, R. Lerche, "Information für Genossen Seidel," 17.4.89, p. 258). After Honecker's ouster, however, Schalck's assistants argued against the deal (BArchB, DL2, VA 579, Bleßing, "Information für Genossen Dr. Schalck zum Vorschlag des Coca-Cola-Konzerns," 3.11.89, p. 258).

In the end, the GDR had obtained a state-of-the-art bottling facility without paying much for it. In addition, a rival capitalist firm, propelled by the search for new markets, was prepared to take Pepsi's place. Nevertheless, the strategy of giving capitalists enough rope to hang themselves had its limits. Eventually, Western firms would realize that the GDR could outmaneuver them by selectively fulfilling its contractual agreements. More important, the success of the licensing agreements hinged upon the East German ability to manufacture commodities that were suitable for import substitution or export to the West. Merely integrating Western technology into the poorly organized East German production process was not sufficient to ensure the project's success. In the case of Pepsi, for example, a lack of complementarity undermined the GDR's efforts to export the soft drink to the West and capitalize on the difference between the two currencies. The shortage of bottles also informed a domestic pricing policy that led East Germans to avoid drinking Pepsi. Production problems often drove East German officials to renege on their contractual obligations, which is why they cut corners, bottled beer instead of Pepsi, and ultimately refused to adhere to the agreement. In fact, the vast majority of East German attempts to import capital goods via licensing agreements ended up costing the GDR more than if it had purchased them outright.[96]

Even more important than the financial consequences of licensing agreements were the political ramifications of increasing East German contacts with capitalist firms. After all, these kinds of barter arrangements involved more than a simple exchange of technology or even of the ideas embodied by that technology. Licensing agreements brought Western experts to the GDR to install equipment and train their East German counterparts, increasing contact between the emissaries of capitalism and the citizens of the socialist state. In at least one case, the encounter between capitalism and socialism also entailed the exchange of sex for money. According to the East German secret police (Stasi), French engineers working on a project in Eisenhüttenstadt used their money to tempt local women into prostitution. Despite the Stasi's own use of prostitution for political and financial gain, its agents seized upon the chance to cast Mittag's encouragement of trade

---

96 As of 31 December 1979, some fifty-three projects involving licensing agreements had cost the GDR DM 7.502 billion plus another 10.928 billion in interest, while generating a mere DM 1.138 billion in exports. Over 50 percent of these projects involved West German partners (BArchB, DC20, 5272, p. 35, cited in Wilfriede Otto, *Erich Mielke–Biographie: Aufstieg und Fall eines Tschekisten* [Berlin, 2000], p. 420, fn. 264 and 265; BStU, MfS BKK [KoKo] 601, Captain Kühlmann interview of IMS "Adolf Matuschka," and "Einschätzung zum Messegeschehen im Bereich Forum," 19.3.87, p. 6; *Der Spiegel* 11 [1978], pp. 37–8). For a more successful instance, see the 1978 licensing agreement with the West German shoe manufacturer Salamander AG, which was extended several times (BStU, AG BKK, 1182).

with the West in the worst light.[97] Not satisfied with demonstrating the corrupting influence of capitalism on social relations, the report drew a lurid portrait of young girls willing to debauch themselves for ridiculously small sums of Western money. The Stasi observed indignantly that East German "school girls offer themselves for five DM at the discos." Worse still, capitalist money had edged out less attractive socialist money, and with it, socialist men: "These girls will only get involved with foreigners who have access to hard currency, while foreign workers from socialist countries are entirely uninteresting to them. Due to this phenomenon, the number of cases of venereal disease in this area is supposed to have risen greatly."[98] The Stasi conflated money with masculinity to object forcefully to the security risks posed by capitalists fraternizing with East Germans. Suffused with anger over the hierarchy of commercial and sexual congress disclosed by the preferences of East German women, the report suggested that sexual contact, and therefore the commercial contact that had made it possible, was both physically unclean and a social threat.

Both the Pepsi and prostitution cases highlight the layers of meaning that had become associated with money in the GDR by the late 1970s. Trade with the West upset the carefully managed relation between economic and ethical values embodied by socialist currency. As the Stasi's objections to contact with the West suggest, the GDR was prostituting itself to Western imperialists in return for capitalist money. By compromising its moral principles for Western cash, the socialist state had opened the door to contamination with the moral bankruptcy of the capitalist world. The spy agency's conflation of money with sex was apt because it played on the distinctions between "hard" and "soft" currencies, imagining the disparity as emasculating the GDR.

Socialist autarky, strengthened by the protective hand of the Soviet Union, would have been more preferable to the GDR's leadership than the threat of contact with the corrupt West. But the planned economy's failure to generate technological and managerial innovations made the GDR, like the rest of the socialist world, dependent on their capitalist enemies. Honecker, who had come to power on a program of putting an end to Ulbricht's experiments, did not look to reform as a way of ending the GDR's intellectual debt

---

97 Many in the ranks of the secret police and the SED leadership were deeply suspicious of expanding trade relations with the West, a policy they correctly identified with Mittag. In a 1986 meeting, Mittag noted the resistance of party leaders to licensing agreements (BArchB, DE1, VA 56287, Klopfer, "Persönliche Niederschrift über die Beratung beim Mitglied des Politbüros und Sekretär des Zentralkomitees der SED, Genossen Dr. Günter Mittag am 17.1.1986," 20.1.86, p. 320).

98 BStU, MfS HA II/6, Nr. 1584, "Information," 18.9.78, p. 2.

to capitalism. Instead, Honecker sought political stability through massive social expenditures, relying on Western financing to foot the bill. The General Secretary never took seriously the hard budget constraints imposed on the GDR by its debt to the West, not the least because he was accustomed to the planned economy's disregard for money. Neither inflationary developments on world markets, nor the Soviet Union's reduction of subsidies to its allies, nor the rapid growth of East German debt could convince Honecker otherwise. Instead, he continued to subordinate economic rationality to political calculation, deeming himself beyond accountability.

Instead of planning for economic development, he simply subordinated economic constraints to his short-term political needs, borrowing from the West what he could not find at home. Exiling the tensions inherent in the Principal Task to the West and to the future, however, only exacerbated the tensions between socialist ideology and material reality. Introducing capitalist commodities into the socialist economy, such as Levis jeans and Volkswagen cars, was tantamount to acknowledging the preeminence of Western goods and the social relations under which they had been manufactured. More important, no lasting provisions were made to ensure that the GDR could pay for these consumer goods. Instead, Honecker trusted Leninist theory, economic adventurism, and the financial scheming of talented but unscrupulous men such as Mittag and Schalck-Golodkowski to provide stopgap measures and somehow keep the GDR afloat. None of these measures provided real solutions to the GDR's problems. Instead of righting the confusion of means and ends that Honecker alleged had dominated the GDR under Ulbricht, the Principal Task launched a spiral of economic profligacy that indebted the GDR beyond its means. Rather than seeking reform from within to end this dependency, moreover, Honecker increased the GDR's reliance on Western financing to pay for his massive social expenditures. The growing asymmetry of economic power between socialism and capitalism expressed itself most concretely in monetary terms. Not only did capitalist money become the medium of exchange between the East and West, as it had between East German women and French men, but the East German debt also became a painful measure of socialist dependence on capitalism.

Back in 1973, Schürer's office had warned Honecker that his policies would lead to a loss of socialist autonomy. Prophetically, the State Planning Commission observed that "although the party and government of the GDR continuously pay great attention to these problems [of growing dependency on the West], it must be noted that the danger of a relationship of dependence of the GDR's economy on the Federal Republic continues to be underestimated."[99] But Honecker preferred the cravenness of Günter Mittag to the bland, yet persistent voice of economic reason personified by Schürer. The General Secretary's unwillingness to curtail this dependency soon endangered the GDR's economic future. Exacerbated by rising trade deficits, the need to obtain hard currency ate away at the East German mark's value. By the late 1980s, the depreciation of the Ostmark – its increasing softness – would become both a target of popular complaint and a vehicle for the unification of the two German states. In both cases, the softness of socialist money yielded to the firmness of the West German mark.

Nevertheless, it is well to remember that the failures of the East German economy and its currency in the 1970s did not exclusively derive from redistribution of resources toward consumption. The GDR's mounting debt resulted in no small part from factors, such as price increases for grain and energy, beyond the SED's control. Nor was economic planning, with its repudiation of money as an active conduit of information, conducive to boosting East German exports to the West. The confusion of means and ends inherent in Marxist-Leninist economic practice was aggravated by the systemic competition between capitalism and communism; the sign of this confusion was the tremendous debt to the West.

The Ostmark's softness also reflected Honecker's profligacy – his unwillingness to accept constraints on his power to decide social policy. His cavalier attitude toward economic policy, his willful neglect of the GDR's financial health, and his refusal to listen to the counsel of his economic aides permitted the debt to spin out of control. Because it eventually represented a hard budget constraint, however, the debt to the West severely constricted the SED's policy choices. Even the Soviets tried to drive this point home to Honecker. In 1979, Brezhnev warned the assembled members of the East German Politburo that "one can only consume what one has produced. After all, none of us wants to live at the expense of others or declare bankruptcy."[100] But Honecker refused to respond to the GDR's increasingly unfavorable terms of trade with the West by imposing austerity measures, which might have eased the GDR's current account and balance of payments

---

99 BArchB, DE1, 56296, "Einschätzung des Standes der Außenhandelsbeziehungen der DDR mit der BRD sowie mit Westberlin," 12.1.73, p. 4.
100 BArchB, DE1, 56296, "Stenografische Niederschrift der Zusammenkunft des Generalsekretärs des ZK der SED und Vorsitzenden des Staatsrates der DDR, Genossen Erich Honecker, so wie der weiteren Mitglieder und Kandidaten des Politbüros des ZK der SED mit dem Generalsekretär des ZK der KPdSU und Vorsitzenden des Präsidiums des Obersten Sowjets der UdSSR, Genossen Leonid Iljitsch Breschnew, sowie den anderen Mitgliedern der sowjetischen Partei- und Regierungsdelegation am Donnerstag, dem 4. Oktober, 1979, im Amtssitz des Staatsrates der Deutschen Demokratischen Republik," p. 23.

problems. Rather than choose the politically unsavory alternative of reducing the population's living standards to cut costs, he continued to believe that Günter Mittag, his right-hand man, would find a less painful solution to the GDR's financial dilemma. Ironically, depending on Mittag – the type of sycophantic intriguer who thrives in authoritarian regimes – to deliver the GDR from the West involved the very kind of prostitution the Stasi decried.

3

Parsimony and the Prince

Crisis and Stability, 1980–1985

Here is an infallible rule: a prince who is not himself wise cannot be well advised, unless he happens to put himself in the hands of one individual who looks after all his affairs and is an extremely shrewd man. In this case, he may well be given good advice, but he would not last long because the man who governs for him would soon deprive him of his state.[1]

By the late 1970s, it had become clear that Honecker's "Unity of Economic and Social Policy" had failed. His attempt to purchase political quiescence at home by borrowing abroad only worked as long as the GDR could honor its debts. Without much-needed capital investments, however, East German industry was increasingly unable to earn hard currency on international markets. The growing weight of their financial obligations to the "class enemy" soon confronted Honecker and his colleagues with an unpleasant choice: introduce austerity measures to reduce the debt, or default and permit capitalist creditors to intervene in the GDR's domestic affairs. In either case, the SED risked provoking the very unrest Honecker's policies were designed to preempt.

Beginning in 1979, a series of external shocks further constrained the SED leadership's room for maneuver. The second oil crisis, which began at the end of 1979, the Soviet Union's decision to slash oil deliveries to its allies, civil conflict in Poland, where price increases in 1980 triggered widespread and organized opposition to communist rule, Poland and Romania's suspension of debt payments in 1981, and a liquidity crunch in the West all threatened the GDR's ability to service its debts. By 1982, a full-fledged financial crisis threatened to rob the GDR of its fiscal sovereignty. Now more than ever, the SED's actions were dictated by money – and capitalist money at that.

1 Niccolò Machiavelli, *The Prince* (Middlesex, [1514] 1983), p. 127.

104

Rather than surrender to economic reality, however, Honecker preferred to pursue the illusory possibility of preserving his "Unity of Economic and Social Policy" while simultaneously reducing the debt. To square this circle, he turned to his trusted advisor, Economic Secretary Günter Mittag. Mittag's strategy for reconciling these incompatible policy goals consisted of embarking on a program of economic adventurism. In the language of liberal economic theory, he was gambling for resurrection – investing in high-risk schemes in the hopes of securing the GDR's survival. The centerpiece of Mittag's response to Honecker's excessive spending was parsimony, or a program of drastic economizing in production, rather than in consumption, by running down and selling off East German assets. By generating hard-currency revenues immediately, Mittag hoped to postpone the day of reckoning with Honecker's policies. To achieve savings on such a grand scale, however, Mittag ended up monetizing the planned economy: He introduced the logic of the profit motive, and with it a ruthless frugality, into the planned economy to earn more Western cash on international markets. Where he could not sell East German products, Mittag adopted a mercilessly penny-pinching attitude, starving East German industry of much-needed capital imports in the rush to prevent insolvency. During the early 1980s, his efforts to commoditize the planned economy in order to rescue it reached absurd heights, including a scheme to convert the economy back to coal in a quest to save oil for sale to the West.

Between 1981 and 1986, Mittag's strategy produced impressive successes, earning large trade surpluses. But his parsimony could hardly counteract Honecker's profligacy. Despite Mittag's best efforts, the GDR experienced a liquidity crisis in 1982 and nearly defaulted on its debts. To rescue the socialist state from its financial plight, Mittag turned to capitalism. He persuaded Honecker to exploit the GDR's special relationship with the FRG and link politics with money. In return for relaxing restrictions on contact between the two Germanys, the FRG agreed to loan the GDR nearly DM 2 billion.

The decision to rely on the West was to have far-reaching and unintended consequences for the socialist state. The infusion of Western cash blunted the imminent danger of insolvency. But it only postponed the more grave threat to the GDR's stability, which stemmed from the contradiction between Mittag's parsimony and Honecker's profligacy. Worse still, Honecker treated short-term debt relief as a serious substitute for genuine reform. Ironically, the West German decision to bail out the GDR, which was aimed at averting the possibility of violent conflict such as that experienced by Poland, helped convince Honecker that he need not reconsider his subordination of economics to politics. In the meantime, Mittag's strategy of squeezing the planned economy to earn hard currency exposed the GDR to grave economic risks. Not only did his oil-for-coal scheme eventually backfire, but selling off East German assets intensified bottlenecks and shortages, all of which greatly hindered the SED's ability to direct production. By the late 1980s, the deterioration of East Germany's capital stock would lead to the very decline in living standards Honecker sought to prevent.

If this policy incoherence was disastrous for the East German economy, it also had a ruinous effect on the sources of communist political power. Despite his shrewdness, Mittag's export-oriented cost–cutting measures undermined the socialist state's legitimacy because they set capitalist principal against communist principle: That is, the political imperative of staving off insolvency deepened the very reversal of means and ends that socialist ideology promised to rectify. Far from constraining the role of money in the lives of East Germans, Mittag subordinated all economic activity to the goal of earning capitalist currency. The regime's ideologically suspect forays into capitalist commerce, moreover, widened the discrepancy between the moral vision of socialist ideology and the political practice of East German communism. In addition, Mittag's efforts to free the GDR from its debt to the West by becoming more dependent on West Germany only emphasized the superiority of the capitalist model – a point that was not lost on the population. Most importantly, the administrative disorder that flowed from the competing priorities of SED policy, which combined profligacy with parsimony to ill effect, weakened the SED's ability to govern a restive populace. Mittag's relentless subordination of local concerns to the center's export priorities undermined the bureaucratic underpinnings of communist control by provoking popular discontent and alienating rank–and–file SED members.

The structural shortcomings of economic planning together with adverse developments on international commodity and capital markets certainly reduced the options available to communist rulers in Europe during the 1970s. Even so, Honecker neither ruled wisely nor allowed himself to be well advised. Rather than choosing the path of reform, Honecker handed over responsibility to an extremely shrewd man who would help deprive him of his state.

THE SECOND OIL CRISIS

The second oil crisis of 1979–80 and its effect on Comecon dealt a serious blow to Honecker's strategy of muddling through. Skyrocketing oil prices forced the General Secretary of the SED to confess at the eleventh plenum of the ZK in December 1979 that the GDR now found itself in a "new situation."[2] By 1981, the price of oil was twenty times higher on world markets than in 1970, peaking at $34.50 a barrel.[3] At the Tenth Party Congress in April 1981, Honecker responded to the new strains on the GDR's hard-currency resources by demanding "an increase in economic performance like never before."[4] In keeping with the voluntarist spirit of communism, however, he refused to pair exhortation with action. Not six months later, just as SED leaders were struggling to adapt to these new circumstances, the Soviets informed the SED leadership of their intention to reduce deliveries of oil and other natural resources to Comecon members.

The SED leadership was particularly taken aback by the USSR's timing. The Polish state's attempt to reduce its foreign debt by raising food prices encountered widespread resistance, but popular unrest in Poland, triggered by austerity measures aimed at pruning back Poland's Western debt, served as an unpleasant reminder to the SED leadership of its own vulnerabilities.[5] The fear that Polish unrest might spread to the GDR was accompanied by anxieties over West German intentions. In turn, the concern that the Federal Republic might exploit internal strife in the GDR to reunite Germany under the aegis of capitalism heightened the SED's feeling that it required Soviet protection. As State Planning Commissioner Gerhard Schürer complained to his Soviet interlocutors, "at our front door we have imperialism with its propaganda on three television channels. And now we have the counterrevolution in Poland at our backs."[6] Honecker rebuked Soviet leader Leonid Brezhnev, claiming that the reductions "would bury the cornerstone of the German Democratic Republic's existence."[7]

---

2 *Neues Deutschland*, 14.12.79, cited in Haendcke-Hoppe-Arndt, *Die Hauptabteilung XVIII*, p. 73.

3 Smith, *The German Economy*, p. 160; Cornelsen, "Die Wirtschaft der DDR," pp. 358–9; Schürer, "Die Wirtschafts- und Sozialpolitik der DDR," p. 159.

4 *Neues Deutschland*, 12.4.81, cited in Haendcke-Hoppe-Arndt, *Die Hauptabteilung XVIII*, p. 74.

5 During a Politburo meeting on 2 December 1980, Honecker compared the Polish crisis to the GDR's situation in 1953. In a meeting with Soviet bloc leaders a few days later, he once again made use of the comparison to explain his position regarding Solidarity, even bringing it up privately with Polish leader Stanisław Kania (SAPMO-BA, DY30, JIV 2/2A 2366; SAPMO-BA, DY30, JIV, 2/2A 2368; BStU, ZAIG, 5382, p. 6, cited in Otto, *Erich Mielke*, pp. 429–30). According to Politburo member Werner Krolikowski, Stasi chief Erich Mielke told Willi Stoph, Chairman of the Council of Ministers, that "the events in Poland have paralyzed [Honecker] with shock" ("Notiz von Werner Krolikowski über ein Gespräch zwischen Willi Stoph und Erich Mielke am 13. November 1980," in Peter Przybylski, *Tatort Politbüro. Die Akte Honecker* [Reinbek, 1992], p. 346). Mittag also links the strikes in Poland to memories of the East German uprising in 1953 (Mittag, *Um jeden Preis*, p. 68).

6 BArchB, DE1, 56296, "Niederschrift über die Beratung der Genossen Schürer und Baibakow am 15.9.1981," 16.9.81, pp. 1–11.

7 SAPMO-BA, DY30, JIV 2/2A/2422. Honecker's reaction to the USSR's announcement was reportedly one of barely controlled rage (Günter Sieber, "Ustinov tobte, Gorbatschow schwieg," in Brigitte Zimmermann and Hans-Dieter Schütt [eds.], *Ohnmacht: DDR Funktionäre sagen aus* [Berlin, 1992], pp. 217–34; Hertle, "Die Diskussion," pp. 321–2).

Notwithstanding vehement East German protests, the Soviets proceeded with their plans. Starting in October 1981, they cut oil shipments by 2.1 million tons a year to 17 million tons. They also raised their prices. A barrel of oil had cost the GDR 13.28 rubles in 1970, but by 1980 the price had jumped to 70.74 rubles and would soar to 168.18 rubles in 1985.[8] Between 1975 and 1985 – the two five-year plans spanning the second oil crisis – price increases of raw materials from the Soviet Union cost the GDR a staggering 31.425 billion rubles extra, or about DM 51.79 billion.[9] During the five years between 1980 and 1985 alone, the GDR paid 155 percent more for its imports from the Soviet Union.[10]

In 1987, the USSR did grant the GDR concessions on the prices of oil, natural gas, and various metals worth 2 billion East German marks – in line with developments on international markets.[11] Nevertheless, Honecker claimed in a 1989 meeting with his top advisors that increases in oil and grain prices, as well as in the prices of other natural resources, would end up costing the GDR over 200 billion East German marks between 1985 and 1990 – or DM 71.43 billion according to the GDR's internal exchange rate.[12] Because of the oil crisis, the GDR was forced to export more valuable technology to the USSR for less oil. Exporting more machines to the USSR, however, meant exporting fewer machines to the West, and exporting fewer machines to the West meant less hard-currency earnings to service the debt – especially since they generated the greatest profits.[13] It also meant that the GDR increasingly looked like a developing country in its trade with the

---

8 BArchB, DE1, 56285, "Zum Umrechnungsverhältnis der Mark," p. 4.
9 The costs are given as 145 billion East German marks (BArchB, DE1, 56296, "Ergebnis der Übersicht vom 10.8.1979, Zusammenfassung der Belastungen 1976–1980," p. 298). To arrive at a hard-currency figure, I used the party's own internal, nonmarket exchange rate between the nonconvertible East German mark and the West German mark, which averaged about M 2.8: DM 1 for this period. The black market rate during this period averaged M 4.8: DM 1, which lowers the figure to DM 30.2 billion. Whatever the calculation, the result illustrates the extent to which the terms of trade for the GDR had deteriorated.
10 BArchB, DE1, 56348, "Zum Einfluß der Preisentwicklung auf die Entwicklung des Außenhandels zwischen der DDR und der UdSSR," no date, pp. 42–3. Charles Maier suggests that the Soviet oil shipments helped subsidize the East German economy, at least until the price of oil declined in the mid-1980s (Maier, *Dissolution*, pp. 63–4). In contrast, Bryson and Melzer argue that the GDR's increased trade of machine tools in return for oil made the oil more expensive for the GDR, especially since those producer goods could have been sold to the West for hard currency (Bryson and Melzer, *The End of the East German Economy*, pp. 61, 76).
11 SAPMO-BA, DY30, JIV 2/2/2206, "Anlage 1, Bericht über die Ergebnisse der Verhandlungen zum Abschluß der Protokolle über die gegenseitige Warenlieferungen im Jahre 1987 a) mit der UdSSR b) mit anderen sozialistischen Ländern," no date, p. 63.
12 BArchB, DE1, 56285, Klopfer, "Persönliche Notizen über die Beratung beim Generalsekretär des ZK der SED und Vorsitzenden des Staatsrats der DDR, Genossen Erich Honecker," 16.5.89, pp. 15–16.
13 See, for example, Mittag's discussion of machine tools in BArchB, DE1, 56285, Klopfer, "Persönliche Notizen aus einer Beratung," 10.11.88, pp. 2, 5.

West, exchanging natural resources and low-tech, labor-intensive products for high-tech and consumer goods.[14] In the East as in the West, the GDR of 1980 suffered from a trade formula – paying more for less – that did not bode well for the future.

BETWEEN FRUGALITY AND FRAUD

Honecker's response to the GDR's deteriorating economic position was shaped by developments in the Soviet bloc. For the second time, the USSR had demonstrated that it could no longer fully insulate the GDR from capitalist markets. The unwillingness of the Soviet Union to continue bankrolling the SED reinforced Honecker and Mittag's reliance on trade with the West to solve the economic challenges confronting the GDR. A prominent feature of Cold War politics during the 1980s – the rapprochement between the Federal Republic and the GDR – thus had its origins in the GDR's abdication of its economic autonomy.

In addition to the end of Soviet largesse, the "counterrevolution" in Poland helped determine the GDR's economic orientation. The rebellion against communist rule in Poland stoked Honecker's fear that the austerity measures required to return the GDR to solvency would prove a greater threat to communist power because they would provoke popular resistance. To avoid an East German version of Polish unrest, Honecker sought to increase exports. This he hoped to accomplish by tightening central control over East German producers and starving them of much-needed capital imports. He entrusted his Economic Secretary, Günter Mittag, with the impossible task of reducing the debt without affecting living standards, furnishing him with discretionary powers that transformed him into Honecker's most important paladin. Given his economic expertise and experience, Mittag must have known that Honecker's unwillingness to defer to the material constraints on his political power was foolhardy. But Mittag's knack for political survival and taste for power overwhelmed whatever misgivings about Honecker's profligacy he might have had. Instead of protesting, he accepted that Honecker's "Unity of Economic and Social Policy" was a sacred cow. Although he knew it had to end in disaster, Mittag nevertheless set about generating the hard-currency revenue necessary to keep the GDR solvent in the short run.

---

14 The GDR's behavior followed Heckscher-Ohlin-Samuelson lines: "Countries tend to export goods that are intensive in the factors with which the countries are abundantly supplied," and labor was cheaper in the GDR than the FRG (Paul R. Krugman and Maurice Obstfeld, *International Economics: Theory and Policy* [Glenview, Ill., 1988], p. 87).

For a time, Mittag's program of slashing imports and boosting exports was successful. Between 1981 and 1986, the GDR posted trade surpluses with the West, which first slowed and then reversed the accumulation of debt.[15] Mittag's success, however, derived primarily from harnessing economic planning to the logic of capitalism: That is, Mittag reintroduced the profit motive into the GDR through his emphasis on parsimony and trade with the West. He used central direction to disseminate capitalist parameters of production, obliging enterprises, for example, to estimate how profitable new projects would be in terms of foreign exchange. He also created planning indicators linked to foreign trade, increasing their number in 1984–85 to 214 from 156.[16]

To some extent, the changes Mittag effected made it appear as if he had returned to NES, when he had advocated the use of financial incentives to boost production. Mittag began to permit enterprises to partake in profits. One late example involved giving producers hard currency in the amount of 1 percent of the value of their exports to the USSR, as well as extra incentives for trade with Yugoslavia and China. In contrast to his advocacy of reform under Ulbricht, however, Mittag studiously avoided any real overhaul of economic planning.[17]

This desperate attempt to improve the planned economy without engaging in systemic reform only contributed to the policy confusion unfolding under Mittag's guidance. Mittag's reluctance to implement real change no doubt stemmed from his experience with economic reform during the 1960s, which had sparked widespread opposition within the party. Many high-ranking party officials deplored NES because it entailed granting decision-making powers to factory managers. While a devolution of power from the center to the factories might have improved their performance, decentralization also constituted a threat to the SED's political preeminence. By the 1980s, an era of even tighter resources and older plant, the reforms most likely to improve East German productivity were also the most certain to provoke resistance within the party leadership, even among those who sought alternatives to Honecker's spendthrift ways. More

15 The GDR posted trade surpluses from 1981 to 1985 worth a total of $8 billion (BArchB, DE1, 56320, Schürer, "Zur Höhe der Verpflichtungen der DDR gegenüber dem Nichtsozialistischen Wirtschaftsgebiet und zu ihren Ursachen," 17–18.11.89, p. 143).
16 SAPMO-BA, DY30, Vorläufige SED 30075, "Vorlage für das Politbüro des ZK der SED, Betr. Maßnahmen zur weiteren Verkollkommnung der Leitung, Planung und wirtschaftliche Rechnungsführung"; Bryson and Melzer, *The End of the East German Economy*, pp. 37–8; Cornelsen, "Die Wirtschaft der DDR," p. 370.
17 SAPMO-BA, DY30 IV 2/2.039/73, "Politbürositzung vom 9. Mai 1989," pp. 9–10; Cornelsen, "Die Wirtschaft der DDR," p. 360.

importantly, Honecker's conservative approach to economic policy and his refusal to countenance any deviation from the "Unity for Economic and Social Policy" ruled out fundamental reform. In particular, reorganizing the structure of incentives that shaped the production process to generate greater efficiency would have entailed significant reductions in subsidies for consumer goods – a measure Honecker vehemently opposed.

Rather than espouse reform, Mittag tugged and pulled at the levers of economic production and made use of the vast powers concentrated in the center to improve the GDR's financial position. To squeeze savings out of the planned economy, Mittag actively limited the purchase of Western machines, making exceptions only when production had ground to a halt because decrepit equipment finally ceased to function. The majority of improvements Mittag did make to the GDR's industrial base went toward the more efficient manufacture of items for domestic production in an attempt to extend the life of Honecker's Principal Task. His key tool for modernizing the East German economy, for example, consisted of signing licensing agreements with West German companies. Yet, nearly all of the projects Mittag entered into during the 1980s, from an automobile engine deal with Volkswagen to a shoe contract with Salamander, entailed the production of nonexportable consumer goods. In this manner, Mittag satisfied the political imperative of safeguarding the consumer guidelines enshrined in Honecker's "Unity of Economic and Social Policy." He did so, however, only at the expense of neglecting the exporting industries capable of improving the GDR's terms of trade.

Mittag also took measures to reduce the costs of East German trade with the West. Some actions appealed as much ideologically as they did financially. For example, Mittag eliminated capitalist middlemen in export deals with noncapitalist countries. In 1983, the GDR agreed to conduct business directly with Algeria, rather than through the mediation of Chase Manhattan Bank in New York.[18] The GDR saved the hard-currency commissions charged by Western banks while presumably instilling greater confidence in trade with partners in developing countries. Yet the measure did little to make the actual merchandise on offer more attractive, which was the real problem.

Nor did many of his economizing measures produce clear-cut benefits. To cut corners, for example, he adopted the dangerous precedent of dipping

18 SAPMO–BA, DY30, Vorläufige SED 36639, Sektor Außenhandel, "Information über die Erhöhung der Zahlungssicherheit beim Abschluß und der Realisierung von NSW-Exportverträgen und zur Senkung überfälliger Forderungen (Material für die Sektorenleiterberatung am 26.10.1983)," 24.10.83, p. 6.

into the GDR's emergency stockpiles. In October 1982, this practice nearly brought life in the socialist state to a halt, leaving it with only four days' worth of gasoline and diesel fuel, and no reserves of grain and various metals.[19] In the spring of 1988, Honecker took Mittag's frugality to a reckless extreme. He demanded that the Minister of Health take the supplies of medication, bandages, and medical equipment that had been set aside for military emergencies and use them to alleviate current shortages. After all, the General Secretary reasoned, "the GDR will not exist after a war anyway."[20] As the GDR's financial needs grew, Honecker and Mittag turned increasingly to a ruthless form of parsimony that functioned like capitalist money in reverse, spreading a cynical disdain for East German citizens in its wake by placing economic over ethical cost.

The most significant example of Mittag's parsimonious method of earning foreign currency – his response to the oil crisis – illustrates the risks of opportunistic cost cutting. To minimize the GDR's exposure to international oil markets, Mittag converted the East German economy to lignite where he could and slashed oil use where he could not. Domestic oil use dropped precipitously, substantially reducing the GDR's reliance on imports from the West to supplement deliveries from the USSR.[21]

But Mittag's ultimate goal was not the frugal utilization of scarce resources. Rather, he had arrived at an ingenious scheme to profit from the differences between socialist barter and capitalist currency. Most likely influenced by the Romanian attempt to sell petroleum products to the West during the 1970s, he forced through a draconian cutback in oil usage by 6 million tons annually, on top of the Soviet reductions, so that he could sell the 6 million tons of oil on international markets for Western currency.[22] As long as oil prices in the West remained high, the GDR could make a tidy hard-currency profit on Soviet oil, which it purchased from the USSR via barter arrangements. As had Romania, Mittag also invested in petrochemical equipment so that the GDR could exploit its main comparative

19 BStU, ZAIG, 04810, Mielke, "auf der zentralen Dienstkonferenz zu ausgewählten Fragen politisch-operativer Arbeit der Kreisdienststellen und deren Führung und Leitung," 11.10.82, cited in Haendcke-Hoppe-Arndt, *Die Hauptabteilung XVIII*, p. 79.
20 BArchB, DE1, 55384, Klopfer, "Persönliche Niederschrift über die Beratung im Politbüro des ZK der SED am 19.4.1988," 19.4.88, p. 2.
21 Oil use in the GDR fell from 18 million tons in 1978 to 11 million tons annually in the early 1980s (Cornelsen, "Die Wirtschaft der DDR," p. 365).
22 Schürer, "Die Wirtschafts- und Sozialpolitik der DDR," p. 159. Because of Romania's partial integration in the Soviet bloc, it received no Soviet oil. Ceauşescu embarked on a policy of selling petrochemical equipment to oil-producing countries, a strategy that met with success until the oil crises set in. To make up for the shortfall in fuel supplies, Ceauşescu slashed oil use and turned to lignite.

advantage – cheap labor – and its nonconvertible currency to manufacture oil products and reap even greater hard-currency profits. The Western money the GDR earned from the oil held the debt at bay. Straddling the planned economies of the Soviet bloc, where products rather than money mattered, and the market economies of the West, where money regulated economic activity, Honecker's GDR played the two competing forms of economic organization off against each other to great profit.

Mittag's lignite-for-oil scheme was undeniably shrewd. But it also created new problems. Starving the domestic economy of resources to generate revenue abroad subordinated the East German infrastructure to the immediate goal of debt reduction, which had lasting and deleterious consequences for living standards. The regime's complete indifference to environmental concerns, for example, sanctioned ruthless strip mining, scarring vast areas in the south. The high level of impurities in East German lignite, moreover, and the SED's lack of investment in emissions reduction technology filled the East German air with record levels of sulfur dioxide, exposing the population to grave health risks.[23]

Nor did conversion of the energy sector from oil to coal proceed smoothly, as the GDR encountered problems in the generation of electricity. In response, Mittag conscripted worn-out fixed capital to produce more energy, bringing moribund plants in Böhlen and Espenhain back on line even though they had been shut down because they were completely outdated and inefficient.[24] Inevitably, the shift back to older technologies reduced economic efficiency. Because large portions of the East German railway system had been neglected and some rail even sold off to West Germany for hard currency, the transport sector was forced to ship the coal in inefficient, gasoline-burning trucks.[25] As Schürer would

23 Just after 1989, some former employees at the State Planning Commission claimed that sulfur dioxide levels in the GDR were the highest in Europe (Kusch et al., *Schlußbilanz – DDR*, pp. 36–7). As Monika Maron's novel *Flugasche* recounts, pollution took a heavy toll on the physical and mental health of East Germans (Monika Maron, *Flugasche* [Frankfurt/Main, 1981]).
24 Hertle, "Die Diskussion," p. 325. For an example of old factories kept on line despite generating intense pollution, see BArchB, DE1, 56285, Klopfer, "Persönliche Notizen über die Beratung des Präsidiums des Ministerrats am 7.7.1988," 8.7.88. For more on environmental pollution in the GDR, see Hannsjörg F. Buck, "Umweltpolitik und Umweltbelastung," in Eberhard Kuhrt (ed.), *Am Ende des realen Sozialismus (2): Die Wirtschaftliche und ökologische Situation der DDR in den achtziger Jahren* (Opladen, 1996).
25 BArchB, DE1, 56285, Staatssekretär der Staatlichen Plankommission, "Persönliche Niederschrift über die Beratung mit dem Minister für Verkehrswesen zu den staatlichen Aufgaben 1988," 26.2.87; Cornelsen, "Die Wirtschaft der DDR," p. 368; Haendcke-Hoppe-Arndt, "Außenwirtschaft und innerdeutscher Handel," in Kuhrt, *Am Ende des realen Sozialismus (2)*, p. 58; Rosemarie Schneider, "Das Verkehrswesen unter besonderer Berücksichtigung der Eisenbahn," in Kuhrt, *Am Ende des realen Sozialismus (2)*, pp. 179, 185, 209.

Figure 5. The regent and his retinue. Günter Mittag (bottom right) at an economic conference in Berlin on 29 September 1983. (Courtesy of Bundesarchiv Koblenz, Bildarchiv, 183/1983/0929/028.)

remark later, "more energy and often more oil was consumed than would have been necessary had oil-burning facilities continued to operate, not to mention the costs of technical equipment and the consequences for the environment."[26] Mittag's studied neglect of the East German infrastructure, as well as his narrow focus on exports, led to imbalances and bottlenecks that eventually cost more than they returned. This confusion of ends and means gradually undermined the GDR's primary goal of economic survival.

In the short run, however, Mittag looked clever indeed. The considerable profits the GDR earned initially distracted from the economy's longer-term problems and concealed the risky premise on which Mittag's scheme was based: that the price of oil would remain high. In his defense, there was little reason for anyone in the East or the West to anticipate any further change to the pricing environment – any more so than there had been in 1973 or 1979. Once again, conflict in the Middle East took economic planners by surprise. In 1980, a war broke out between Iraq and Iran that eventually led

26 Schürer, "Die Wirtschafts- und Sozialpolitik der DDR," p. 159. The GDR also experienced difficulties delivering heating during the harsh winter of 1983/84 (BStU, ZAIG 3327, "Information über einige Probleme im Zusammenhang mit der Energieversorgung im Winterhalbjahr 1983/4," 15.11.83).

to a dramatic decline in worldwide oil prices, as both countries increased their oil production to replenish their weapons arsenals. By 1986, the price of a barrel of oil had fallen to $15.35, or less than half of its 1981 level.[27] Between 1986 and 1989, the decline in oil prices cost the GDR about $2.5 billion.[28]

Nevertheless, Mittag's initial success in substituting lignite for oil had far-reaching consequences. In particular, it encouraged Mittag to overestimate the GDR's ability to save Western money through alternative energy sources. Many of the research projects he funded were inspired by a fetishization of technological solutions to the GDR's financial quandary, but few of them produced economically feasible results. Some schemes, such as using coal to produce synthetic petroleum, methanol, and other fuels, required horrendous investments of people and resources. At one point, he had 1,000 scientists and 750 million East German marks working on these designs. Another pet project sought to extract 1 million tons of gasoline from coal. It required 22 billion East German marks in investments, yet promised profits of only 0.146 billion West German marks.[29]

In addition, Mittag began relying on manipulations of the difference between capitalist and socialist money to improve the GDR's balance of payments, despite the confusion of ends and means it entailed. As with his oil strategy, Mittag took advantage of the nonconvertibility of the East German mark to liquidate East German assets. Aside from selling off the inherited artifacts of German cultural heritage, such as art objects and cobblestones, Mittag peddled merchandise the socialist state had manufactured, from weapons to political dissidents.[30] The SED had always argued with varying degrees of plausibility that ensuring the GDR's political survival legitimated sponsoring war and curtailing personal freedoms. Selling weapons and people for profit, however, smacked of a hypocrisy that

27 Smith, *The German Economy*, p. 160.
28 BArchB, DE1, 56320, Schürer, "Zur Höhe der Verpflichtungen," p. 143. Because other exports had stagnated, hard-currency profits began to evaporate; for the three years between 1986 and 1988, the GDR posted a trade surplus of only DM 1 billion. According to Schürer, debt service alone, which cost DM 13 billion between 1986 and 1988, once again outstripped export earnings (SAPMO-BA, DY30, JIV 2/2A/3252, Politbüro-Sitzung vom 31.10.89, Schürer, "Analyse der ökonomischen Lage," 30.10.89, p. 10).
29 BArchB, DE1, 56318, "Zur ökonomischen Wirksamkeit von Wissenschaft und Technologie," no date, pp. 1–3.
30 The payments made by the West German government in return for the freedom of political prisoners included shipments intended for the East German population. However, the average East German never saw these products, which Mittag and Schalck immediately sold back to capitalist entrepreneurs. In 1982, these reexports earned the GDR DM 412 million (BArchB, DE1, 56276, Staatliche Plankommission, "Zahlungsbilanz zum Entwurf der staatlichen Aufgaben 1983," 12.11.82, p. 6; Haendcke-Hoppe-Arndt, "Außenwirtschaft und innerdeutscher Handel," p. 60).

even the most gifted Marxist–Leninist rhetoricians were hard pressed to justify.

More lucrative were Mittag's attempts to cash in on West German nationalism. The political ambiguities that structured German–German relations to the GDR's advantage are perhaps best illustrated by the so-called Swing credits. This particular financial instrument was a curiosity of German national division, part of the larger set of agreements between the Federal Republic and the GDR that institutionalized financial relations between two hostile political systems. The FRG's refusal to formally recognize the other German state, which extended to such institutions as the East German mark, necessitated certain provisions for the reality of German–German trade. For their part, SED leaders were tormented by Cold War caricatures, worrying that revanchist West German tycoons holding vast quantities of socialist money might use their financial leverage to bring about unification.

The equivalency established between the capitalist and socialist currencies was necessarily the result of a political understanding – the 1951 Berlin Agreement – rather than a market valuation.[31] Even the SED leadership admitted internally that the East German mark was never worth a full D-Mark.[32] But the party nevertheless demanded parity for symbolic reasons. In part, the SED's insistence on parity was aimed at shoring up support for the Ostmark at home. The suggestion that socialist money was worth as much as capitalist currency, and the Federal Republic's acceptance of this interpretation, provided political support for the value of the East German mark.[33] Encouraging East Germans to think of the two currencies as equivalent, moreover, reinforced the perception that prices in the GDR were lower and more stable than in the FRG. Thus, the SED's assertion of equivalence helped bolster its political legitimacy and create the illusion that the purchasing power of the East German mark was equivalent to the D-Mark's.

By the 1980s, however, the propaganda value of monetary parity had been eclipsed by the financial advantages the GDR enjoyed because of the agreement. As we shall see, the SED's own policies, such as the expansion of the

31 The 1951 Berlin Agreement regulated trade through the use of a notational currency, the "accounting unit" (*Verrechnungseinheit*), which functioned as a buffer between the two circulating currencies. Using the accounting unit, the two central banks acted as clearinghouses for German–German trade. Central to the Agreement's success was the GDR's demand that the formula for calculating the "accounting unit" make 1 East German mark equivalent to 1 West German mark. There is indirect evidence that the "accounting unit" fell into disuse during the 1980s (BStU, MfS BKK [KoKo] 601, Captain Kühlmann interview of IMS "Adolf Matuschka," and "Einschätzung zum Messegeschehen im Bereich Forum," 19.3.87).
32 BArchB, DE1, 56318, "Zur Frage, was erforderlich ist," 8.9.88, p. 3.
33 BArchB, DL2, 659, "Warum ist das Kursverhältnis der Mark zur DM nicht 1:1," 9.1.87, p. 133.

Intershop retail stores, demonstrated to East Germans that the D-Mark was more valuable than the Ostmark. Nevertheless, representatives of the socialist state found it expedient to insist on equivalency between the two currencies because parity improved the GDR's terms of trade with the FRG. Given the long-term appreciation of the DM against other convertible currencies, the GDR's ability to demand payment on a 1:1 basis substantially increased the value of the transfer payments made by West German governments, which are discussed below.[34] The Berlin Agreement provided the GDR with access, limited at first but substantial by the 1980s, to the D-Mark and its remarkable record of strengthening value against other major currencies.

In addition to regulating the monetary conditions of intra-German commerce, the Berlin Agreement provided for the creation of "Swing" credits, or short-term intergovernmental loans that were free of interest and, of course, denominated in accounting units. In other words, the Swing credits constituted a revolving loan aimed at stabilizing, and therefore encouraging, trade between the two countries. Until the 1970s, the Swing credits were not a particularly important aspect of German–German relations. Honecker's shopping spree in the West, however, increased the volume of trade and therefore the GDR's use of the loans.[35] By the late 1970s, Mittag was also using the Swing credits to improve the GDR's credit rating and procure more commercial loans on better terms. In fact, he adopted methods of manipulating finances befitting a capitalist tycoon. Despite its pressing need for hard currency, the GDR refrained from utilizing the credit in its full scope, which had the effect of promoting the illusion that the GDR did not in fact require so much Western cash.[36] Because the Swing credits were one of the few reliable sources of information regarding the GDR's intake of hard currency, careful use of these loans succeeded in increasing the socialist state's creditworthiness with private financial institutions in the West. Foregoing such an attractive source of credit, Mittag hoped, might

34 Although the DM was revalued against the dollar three times under the Bretton Woods system before 1971, some observers argue that it remained historically undervalued, thereby contributing to West Germany's export-led growth (Smith, *The German Economy*, pp. 167–8). The D-Mark continued to appreciate against the dollar after the collapse of Bretton Woods, rising from 3.22 marks to the dollar in 1971 to 1.69 in 1989 (Figure 10, Chapter 4).

35 Between 1970 and 1989, the equivalent of DM 100 billion worth of goods and services were exchanged between the Federal Republic and the GDR. This sum does not include transactions instigated by private individuals, such as West German purchases of visas or of consumer goods for friends and family through Schalck's Genex mail-order retailer, which amounted to DM 24 billion between 1975 and 1988 (Volze, "Geld und Politik," pp. 383–4).

36 The GDR used about 80 percent of the available credits in the early 1980s, but managed to discipline itself and use only 31 percent in 1984, 29 percent in 1985, and 22 percent in 1986 (Hertle, "Die Diskussion," p. 331).

lead the Bundesbank and other West German institutions to believe that the GDR did not require so great an influx of Western capital, since only the largest commercial transactions were reported to the West German government.[37] In all of these ways, the GDR benefited financially from its special relationship with the Federal Republic.[38]

Whereas the Swing credits had become an important source of financing for the GDR by the 1980s, their political significance to the Federal Republic overshadowed their financial import. The Bundesbank was not enamored of the credits because they had an expansionary effect on the West German money supply. During the 1970s, the Social Democratic Chancellors Willy Brandt and Helmut Schmidt used them to pry political concessions from the SED, freeing up the circulation of people in return for an increased circulation of money.[39]

The critics of *Ostpolitik*, or détente in its West German form, objected strenuously to the link between financial aid and political freedom because it entailed the de facto recognition of the GDR and thus the acceptance of the division of Germany. Despite conservative opposition to *Ostpolitik*, however, Helmut Kohl, the Christian Democrat who became chancellor in October 1982, did not overturn his predecessors' policies. Instead, he supported the new policy of *Verflechtung* crafted by the long-serving liberal Foreign Minister Hans-Dietrich Genscher, which sought to "weave" the two Germanys together by increasing contacts between the FRG and the GDR. Rather than using the D-Mark to force political liberalization as the SPD had, the new conservative-liberal coalition sought to change the status quo by supporting it.

In fact, the Kohl government's argument that financial concessions would "undermine the SED regime without destabilizing it" resonated with the

---

37 Interview, Dieter von Würzen, State Secretary, West German Economics Ministry (1979–95), Bonn, 26.3.96; and Schürer, Berlin, 19.4.95. According to von Würzen, the Swing credits functioned as a signal to commercial banks regarding the GDR's current account.

38 In addition, the peculiar economic arrangement attending the division of Germany gave the GDR a "back door" to trade with European Community members.

39 Interview, von Würzen, Bonn, 26.3.96; and Karl-Otto Pöhl, State Secretary, West German Finance Ministry (1972–77), Bundesbank Vice President (1977–79), Bundesbank President (1979–92), Frankfurt am Main, 17.6.96. The Swing credits could be extended only with the approval of the FRG. The first extension, which occurred on 6.12.68, maintained the existing level of credits. The extension of 12.12.74, however, increased the maximum amount to 850 million accounting units in return for the GDR relaxing travel restrictions. On 18.6.82, the Schmidt government extended the Swing agreement, but reduced the maximum amount available to the GDR to 600 million. In return, the GDR agreed not to prosecute former East German citizens who had fled and permitted West Berliners on a one-day pass to East Berlin to remain until 2 A.M. On 5.7.85, the Kohl government extended the Swing agreement and raised the maximum level to 850 million accounting units – a major concession to the GDR.

Figure 6. Erich Honecker, General Secretary of the SED, visits Helmut Kohl, West German Chancellor, in Bonn, September 1987. (Courtesy of Bundesarchiv Koblenz, Bildarchiv, 183/1987/0907/017.)

"magnet theory," a CDU policy dating from the Adenauer era. The magnet theory held that the pull of West German prosperity would eventually reunify the two Germanys. Despite the failure of Adenauer's policy and Brandt's successful introduction of *Ostpolitik*, the magnet theory remained attractive to many Christian Democrats, and this facilitated their acceptance of *Verflechtung*. In the end, both *Ostpolitik* and *Verflechtung* helped make German unification possible, though not in the way that their adherents or detractors anticipated. As we shall see, providing material assistance to the GDR – even in exchange for such morally dubious deals as purchasing the liberty of political prisoners – furnished Honecker with a substitute for genuine reform, one that gradually undermined the political legitimacy of communism.

In the meantime, Honecker and Mittag proved adept at exploiting West German concern for East German citizens, translating national sentiment into hard cash. For example, they convinced the West German Protestant churches to underwrite the needs of their East German brethren, including building church offices and providing retirement benefits for ministers, to the tune of DM 1.42 billion between 1957 and 1990. With help from the churches, Honecker and Mittag also convinced the West German government to foot the bill for the renovation of architectural landmarks such as the Berlin Cathedral, which had served as the court church for the Hohenzollern family.[40]

Despite his official position of demarcation (*Abgrenzung*) against the West, the hallmark of Honecker's German–German policy was the link between Western money and political liberalization.[41] Beginning with the Transportation Treaty (*Verkehrsvertrag*) of 1972, Honecker assented to this trade-off between politics and economics. Out of this agreement grew the "lump-sum payments" (*Pauschale*), which commenced in 1976. Nominally, this direct transfer of funds consisted of compensation to the GDR for wear and tear on its infrastructure resulting from the influx of Western visitors, from road use to visa processing. Theoretically, the Federal Republic consented to pay for its citizens' improved access to the GDR. In reality, however, most of this money went toward purchasing political concessions.[42] The leaders of both German states recognized that the payments were born of the East German need for hard currency and the West German desire to increase contacts between the two Germanys in the hopes of alleviating the plight of ordinary East Germans and slowly subverting the communist regime.

By the 1980s, the direct transfer of West German money in return for relaxations in border restrictions had become a major source of income

40 Besier, *Der SED-Staat und die Kirche*, pp. 511–47; Armin Boyens, "'Den Gegner irgendwo festhalten': 'Transfergeschäfte' der Evangelischen Kirchen in Deutschland mit der DDR-Regierung 1957–1990," *Kirchliche Zeitgeschichte* 6 (1993), pp. 379–426; Volze, "Geld und Politik," p. 385.
41 Weber, *Geschichte der DDR*, p. 458.
42 Important exceptions include the post and rail agreements, which appear to have functioned the way they do between most countries. Because most mail deliveries went from West to East Germany, the West German postal service paid their East German counterparts 200 million accounting units a year for services they performed. For similar reasons, the East German rail system paid out more to the West German train service (Volze, "Geld und Politik," p. 384).

for the GDR. The transportation payments, for example, totaled DM 8.3 billion between 1972 and 1989;[43] the annual number of West German tourists reached 6 million in 1988.[44] The Federal Republic agreed to pay another DM 2.4 billion between 1975 and 1989 to build highways between Berlin and other destinations, such as Hamburg.[45] In every case, the various hard-currency payments benefited the GDR financially because the services rendered for them – when services were in fact rendered – were denominated in East German marks.

In addition to eliciting transfer payments from West German governments, the SED exploited its control over the border to coerce money from individual West Germans. Most notoriously, the party exploited national divisions to compel Westerners visiting the GDR to exchange a fixed amount of money at unfavorable rates for every day they stayed.[46] But the GDR also engaged in more common forms of income-earning harassment. Like the police in some American states, the People's Police set up road traps for Western drivers, then levied harsh penalties for traffic violations.[47] The most lucrative source of Western money, however, consisted of the Intershops, the hard-currency retailers that dominated the East German retail landscape by the 1980s. As Chapter 6 demonstrates, Schalck, with Mittag's encouragement, copied Western sales techniques, bringing both capitalist practices and capitalist goods to most East German households.[48]

In fact, the GDR's increasingly desperate financial situation removed whatever inhibitions Mittag might have had about using fraud to stimulate

---

43 Volze, "Geld und Politik," p. 384. The *Transitpauschale* totaled DM 400 million annually from 1976 to 1979, rising to DM 520 million from 1980 to 1989. In the 1980s, the *Pauschale* included DM 268 million in compensations for road use, 162 million for the sales tax on the transport of goods through the GDR (*Steuerausgleichsabgabe*), which was calculated by using the West German rates, 94 million in fees for processing visas, and 1 million in miscellaneous charges (SAPMO-BA, DY30, Vorläufige SED 42021, Schalck to Mittag, "Vorlage, Konzeption zur Neufestsetzung der Transitpauschale und der Pauschale für Personenkraftfahrzeuge der BRD und Westberlins im Wechsel- und Transitverkehr in dritten Staaten," 4.3.88, pp. 17–19).

44 Schürer estimated that a total of 30–35 million people visited in 1988, and a total of 1.5 million trucks transported 17 million tons of goods through the GDR (BArchB, DE1, 56323, no date, p. 576).

45 Volze, "Geld und Politik," p. 384.

46 According to Schürer, the GDR earned DM 360 million a year on compulsory exchange and visa processing for West Germans and other tourists (BArchB, DE1, 56323, p. 576). For West Germans, the fee was 25 marks at a rate of DM 1 to 1 Ostmark for most of the 1980s. For more on the methods the GDR used to earn hard currency off of West Germans, see Chapter 6.

47 The Interior Minister, Friedrich Dickel, had perfected these methods by the 1980s, averaging about DM 9.5 million a year (SAPMO-BA, DY30, IV 2/2.039/191, Dickel to Krenz, 20.4.87, p. 52). The author was twice the victim of this kind of chicanery.

48 By 1982, the Intershops constituted the single largest source of annual hard-currency revenue, bringing in DM 545 million compared to DM 520 million for the *Transitpauschale* (see Chapter 6).

frugality. Together with Schalck, for example, Mittag set in place what was in essence an elaborate shell game aimed at hoodwinking Western lending agencies into granting the GDR more favorable credit conditions. By moving cash around from bank to bank, they sought to create the illusion that the GDR was more solvent than it was.[49] As we have seen, Mittag also studiously avoided overuse of the Swing credits to conceal the GDR's hard-currency needs from West German eyes.[50]

By and large, however, Westerners were not deceived by Mittag and Schalck's schemes. Although accurate estimations of the GDR's productive capacities were hard to come by, the Bank for International Settlements in Basel provided reliable information on major loans made to the GDR.[51] In addition, West German politicians were well apprised of the GDR's need for hard currency. Successive West German governments might not have known the exact size of East German debt, but they readily identified the GDR's thirst for hard currency as a sign of financial weakness. Former Bundesbank President Karl-Otto Pöhl, for example, reported that the importance of hard currency to the GDR became clear to him in 1973, when Schalck began haggling with him over what Pöhl termed the "ludicrously small" sum of DM 25 million.[52] The importance of West German money to the East German economy entered the public domain in 1978, when the West German central bank reported that it could not meet its money supply target because of an outflow of D-Marks into the portfolios of individual East Germans.[53]

---

49 First, Mittag and Schalck used a variety of accounting tricks to make it appear as if the GDR had large capital assets at its disposal. For example, they misrepresented the cash flow from Schalck's hard-currency operations, which amounted to over DM 2 billion annually, as a kind of revolving credit, disguised long-term loans as cash revenue and redeposited them with different banks, and used money that foreigners had deposited with the GDR to improve the GDR's creditworthiness in the eyes of Western lenders (SAPMO-BA, DY30, Vorläufige SED 41757, Schürer, "Information zur Gesamtheit des Außenhandels sowie der Forderungen und Verbindlichkeiten der DDR," no date, pp. 6–7). Second, the two men established credit with a variety of banks, rather than using one bank as a clearinghouse for issuing and receiving payment in Western countries (ibid., p. 6; Przybylski, *Tatort Politbüro*, pp. 357–8, 372–80). Their machinations met with a measure of success, inducing some Western banks to extend larger loans to the GDR at better conditions on the basis of the large volumes of cash passing through East German accounts (SAPMO-BA, DY30, Vorläufige SED 36639, "Arbeitsübersetzung aus 'Rynki Zagraniczne' vom 23.11.1982, 'DDR überwindet Schulden'," 24.11.82, pp. 1–2).
50 The exception was DM 770 million in 1982 (BArchB, DE1, 56276, "Zahlungsbilanz," 12.11.82, p. 4).
51 BArchB, DE1, 56320, Schürer, "Zur Höhe der Verpflichtungen," p. 144.
52 Interview, Pöhl, Frankfurt am Main, 17.6.96. At the time, Pöhl was State Secretary in the West German Finance Ministry.
53 Erwin Sell and H. Jörg Thieme, "Nebenwährungen bei zentraler Planung des Wirtschaftsprozesses," in Alfred Schüller and Ulrich Wagner (eds.), *Außenwirtschaftspolitik und Stabilisierung von Wirtschaftssystemen* (Stuttgart and New York, 1980), p. 137.

Table 3. *East German Trade Imbalances with the West, 1980–1989 (in billions of DM)*[a]

Year	Internal East German Figures[b] Cumulative Debt to West	Western Figures[c] Annual Trade Surplus/Deficit	Annual Hard-Currency Surplus/Deficit	Cumulative Debt to West
1980	−27.9	−2.764	+3.582	−23.637
1981	−29.0	+0.372	+0.714	−23.134
1982	−27.3	+3.178	−2.866	−25.146
1983	−28.9	+2.447	−2.231	−22.339
1984	−27.2	+3.216	−5.634	−18.348
1985	−25.9	+3.026	−3.595	−15.480
1986	−28.7	+0.128	+1.072	−16.162
1987	−31.9	−1.918	+0.602	−16.209
1988	−34.6	−2.905	+2.391	−17.048
1989	−38.9	−2.874	+3.050	−19.887

[a] One *Valutamark* was the notational equivalent of one West German mark. Current account figures do not include the Swing credits.

[b] *Source:* BArchB, DE1, 56276, "Anlage zum Vorschlag zur Fertigstellung des Entwurfes des Volkswirtschaftsplanes 1983," 12.11.82, Anlage 4, "Hauptkennziffer der Zahlungsbilanz Nichtsozialistiches Wirtschaftsgebiet," pp. 16–17; SAPMO-BA, DY30, JIV 2/2A/3039, "Vorlage für das Politbüro, Information über die Entwicklung der Zahlungsbilanz und der Außenwirtschaftsbeziehungen bis Ende Mai 1987," 7.7.87, p. 1; SAPMO-BA, Vorläufige SED 41757, Schürer, "Information zur Gesamtheit des Außenhandels," no date, p. 1; and BStU, Arbeitsbereich Mittig, Nr. 58, "Zu den ausgewählten Problemen," Anlage 3, p. 37.

[c] *Source:* Deutsche Bundesbank (ed.), *Zahlungsbilanz der ehemaligen DDR, 1975 bis 1989*, pp. 49, 50, 60.

The real target of Mittag's deception was not capitalist financiers, however, but the members of his own party. During the crisis of 1982, Mittag began to intervene in the representation of the GDR's liabilities, squelching reports on the abatement of the debt made possible by the export drive and petroleum receipts.[54] He also failed to inform the Politburo of various parafiscal earnings, such as the revenue from Schalck's profitable hard-currency operations, which amounted to some DM 2 billion annually during the 1980s.[55] By 1989, Mittag's chicanery had inflated official representations of the debt by nearly 50 percent, or some DM 19 billion. Even the GDR's famed spy agency fell for Mittag's falsifications.[56]

54 Armin Volze, "Ein großer Bluff," *Deutschland Archiv* 29:5 (1996), p. 703.
55 Mittag used old-fashioned accounting tricks, including transferring debt to future budgets and creating a parafiscal "strategic and operative hard-currency reserve" – an emergency fund totaling DM 1 billion that did not appear in Schürer's budget (SAPMO–BA, DY30, Vorläufige SED 41757, Schürer, "Information zur Gesamtheit des Außenhandels," no date, pp. 4, 6).
56 BStU, Arbeitsbereich Mittig, Nr. 58, "Zu den ausgewählten Problemen," Anlage 2, p. 36.

Mittag used reports of an excessively large debt to focus attention and resources on paying it down. Even though his deceptions were aimed at improving his position in the ruling elite, they were to have their greatest impact on ordinary East Germans. Indeed, Mittag's statistical hyperbole helped determine the course of the East German revolution. In the aftermath of the October 1989 palace coup against Honecker, the new political leadership under Egon Krenz labored to distance itself from the "old regime." Krenz's credibility with the party rank and file, as well as his legitimacy in the eyes of the broader population, depended on his ability to create the perception that Honecker and Mittag had conspired together to mismanage the economy, then lied about it. In this manner, Krenz hoped to justify his removal of Honecker and suppress the memory of his own culpability as a member of Honecker's inner circle. One of the first measures Krenz took was to authorize Schürer, whose consistent criticism of Honecker's economic policies helped him survive the change in leadership, to undertake an unvarnished analysis of the GDR's economic position. Working under the pressure of time and revolutionary developments, the new leadership announced in November that the GDR's net debt totaled a dramatic DM 38.5 billion, far more than the actual DM 19.89 billion it owed.[57] In the end, Honecker's successors were unable to convince party members at the grassroots level, much less the East German population, that they had no connection to Mittag's fraudulent management of the economy. In fact, Krenz and Schürer were unable to offer much more than cosmetic changes to the dictatorship because they shared the same assumptions as Mittag regarding the necessity of deception rather than transparency in governance.

In this manner, the old SED leadership managed to pass the burden of Mittag's statistical legacy on to the reformist Modrow government, which took over shortly after the Berlin Wall collapsed. Despite his political savvy, Modrow was unable to prevent the majority of East Germans from concluding that the future of the GDR had been jeopardized by its poor financial health. As the GDR's economic prospects appeared to recede under a cloud of discouraging statistics, more and more East Germans began to leave the GDR for the FRG, while those who remained behind clamored for rapid unification with West Germany as the only realistic solution

57 Günter Ehrensperger, chair, Department of Planning and Finance at the ZK, Tenth Plenum of the ZK, 8–10 November 1989 (Hertle and Stephan, *Das Ende der SED*, p. 365; SAPMO-BA, DY30, IV 2/1/711). In his otherwise alarmist report, Schürer accurately estimated the GDR's gross debt to the West at 49 billion Valutamarks (SAPMO-BA, DY30, JIV 2/2A/3252, Schürer, "Analyse der ökonomischen Lage," 30.10.89, p. 6; Deutsche Bundesbank [ed.], *Zahlungsbilanz der ehemaligen DDR*, p. 59).

to the GDR's financial woes. Because the GDR's debt appeared insurmountable, Mittag's fraud made any alternative to rapid unification with the Federal Republic seem impossibly optimistic. Not only did his statistical chicanery discredit economic experimentation, such as talk of a "third way" between the immediate imposition of West German capitalism and the preservation of Honecker's neo-Stalinism, but the inflated debt made even the short-term retention of economic, and therefore political, sovereignty appear inadvisable.

Ironically, however, the GDR was not in as dire a position as politicians and the populace believed. Had the majority of East Germans, whose activism determined the political direction of the revolution from October 1989 to March 1990, known the more prosaic truth about the GDR's large but not insuperable debt burden, perhaps they would not have perceived rapid monetary union with the Federal Republic as the only available option. Perhaps they would have been prepared instead to contemplate a slower transition to unification that would have improved their bargaining position in negotiations with the Federal Republic over the terms of unification. The perversion of socialist ideals by the SED under Honecker had undercut the legitimacy of socialism in East Germany. It had also prepared the ground for the elimination of the actual currency of socialism – and with it the socialist state.

THE CRISIS OF 1982

As these examples indicate, Mittag's approach to the GDR's financial crisis was based on an extraordinarily risky combination of parsimony and guile that, for lack of a viable alternative, commoditized the planned economy by exposing it to the logic of the profit motive. Aside from how the savings were put to use, the difficulty with Mittag's extreme frugality was the administrative chaos it generated. Although Soviet-style economic planning was premised on increased rationality in the allocation of resources in the long run, what Reinhard Bendix described as the "simultaneous maximization of conflicting goals" that derived from the discrepancy between Marxist-Leninist theory and practice necessitated short-term irrationalities in the form of ad hoc deviations from the plan.[58] But Mittag's attempt to squeeze ever more export revenue from the East German economy aggravated the

---

58 Reinhard Bendix, "The Cultural and Political Setting of Economic Rationality in Western and Eastern Europe," in Gregory Grossman (ed.), *Value and Plan: Economic Calculation and Organization in Eastern Europe* (Berkeley and Los Angeles, Calif., 1960), p. 258.

subordination of ends to means inherent in the planned economy. Increasingly, the confusion of means and ends inspired by Mittag's parsimony required the imposition of central coercion to restore equilibrium.

By the early 1980s, the trade-off between long- and short-term goals expressed itself in the increasing cannibalization of the East German industrial base, since a substantial portion of exports to the West came at the expense of the GDR's future productive capacities: That is, the long-term goal of economic growth through investment fell victim to the immediate exigency of debt reduction. In 1981, for example, the Minister for Electrical and Electronic Engineering suggested exporting DM 80 million worth of rolled steel produced by VEB Kombinat Carl Zeiss Jena to the West. Because rolled steel was key to the GDR's machine tool industry, however, exporting it to the West necessarily reduced the production of machine tools for domestic consumption and foreign export.[59] As was so often the case, Mittag's preference for short-term fixes exacerbated long-term obstacles to economic growth.

More important than the economic irrationality generated by Mittag's inversion of means and ends, however, was the administrative disarray it caused. By 1982, Mittag's attempts to offset Honecker's profligacy through a plan of domestic parsimony had spawned bureaucratic turmoil that further undermined the SED's vanishing authority. Just as large-scale exports began to relieve external pressures on the GDR, upheaval in the agricultural sector aggravated the precarious internal imbalance of conflicting claims on resources, creating a shortage of meat. The crisis began with Mittag's order that more meat, and especially pork, be exported to West Germany.[60] His intervention set off a chain of calamities that were linked causally by the bane of economic planning – complementarity. To obtain additional quantities of meat for export, Mittag demanded both higher production and reductions in the supply of meat for the East German population. His export drive could only come at the expense of the average East German's diet – a dangerous proposition since it courted popular disfavor in a manner reminiscent of the Polish communist party's travails. This subordination of consumerism to economic imperatives, unusual under Honecker's stewardship, had to be

59 BArchB, DE1, 56287, Klopfer, "Persönliche Meinung zur Ausarbeitung des Fünfjahrplanes 1981–1985 and des Jahreswirtschaftsplanes 1982." The General Director of IFA Kombinat Personalwagen ordered the Automobilwerk Eisenach to lower car production to 35,000 automobiles from the 62,000 planned because of the shortage of rolled steel (BArchB, DE1, 52687, Klopfer, "Persönliche Niederschrift," 22.11.82, p. 216).

60 In addition to earning hard currency, selling meat to West Germans was politically significant, since much of the meat was delivered to friends of Bavarian Minister-President Franz Josef Strauß, who would be instrumental in securing large credits for the GDR.

handled carefully. To avoid potential political fallout, Mittag combined a minor reduction in meat provisions with a major shift in the structure of the supply, substituting poultry for exportable pork and beef.[61]

The pressure placed on the supply of meat available to East Germans might have been marginal had Mittag and his aides taken note of conditions in the meat processing industry. But they had not. For years, animal husbandry in the GDR had suffered from serious neglect. In 1982, it collapsed. A critical decline of standards in fodder, stalls, animal care, hygiene, and veterinary support made the GDR's livestock population vulnerable to disease. During the first three months of 1982 alone, a total of 774,100 hogs died – an ecological calamity of catastrophic proportions. Aside from the sheer number of dead animals, the age structure of the losses gave great cause for concern: The youngest animals were hit the hardest.[62]

At fault was the inadequate supply of fodder and poor care provided to the animals. Malnutrition, along with mass breeding in unsanitary conditions, weakened the pigs while exposing them to a greater incidence of disease. In mid-March, the district party leader of Magdeburg, Kurt Tiedke, cabled Honecker to report that "despite vaccinations, diseases of epidemic proportions appeared in hog stocks" because of malnutrition.[63] Never one to suffer the circulation of bad news, Mittag had Tiedke replaced as First Secretary of Magdeburg by Werner Eberlein, one of Mittag's allies.

If the loss of animal life due to neglect was catastrophic, Mittag's meddlesome demands for higher exports exacted an additional toll on the surviving animal population. Werner Walde, district party leader of Cottbus, reported that the district had about 80,000 tons of fodder less for the period between November 1981 and May 1982 than in the same period a year earlier. As a result, the district's livestock had lost a great deal of weight: Cows were averaging 459 kilos in 1982 compared with 483 in 1981, while hogs had slipped from 122 to an average 113 kilos.[64] Without enough to eat, the pigs and cows that survived such poor conditions weighed less at slaughter than was usual. Some districts, such as Frankfurt an der Oder, Schwerin,

---

61 SAPMO-BA, DY30, Vorläufige SED 31986, "Information zur Versorgung mit Fleisch und Wurstwaren," 17.5.82, pp. 1–2.

62 The bulk of the losses, or 58.5 percent, consisted of piglets. The mortality rate for young hogs also jumped, rising by 18.4 percent between the first quarter of 1982 and the same period in 1981. Worse still for the future of the East German pork industry, 28.2 percent more sows had died (SAPMO-BA, DY30, Vorläufige SED 31986, "Tierverluste in den sozialistischen Landwirtschaftsgebieten im Zeitraum 1.1. bis 30.4. DDR insgesamt," no date).

63 SAPMO-BA, DY30, Vorläufige SED 31984, Tiedke cable to Honecker, p. 5, and Chemnitzer cable to Honecker, 17.5.82, pp. 2, 6; SAPMO-BA, DY30, Vorläufige SED 31986, Weber cable to Honecker, 17.5.82, p. 4.

64 SAPMO-BA, DY30, Vorläufige SED 31984, Walde cable to Honecker, 17.5.82, p. 1.

Magdeburg, and Karl-Marx-Stadt, were unable to meet the revised quotas because their animals were undernourished. Other districts sacrificed the future to fulfill the plan in the present. Cottbus, for example, produced 599 tons more meat in the first quarter of 1982 than in the same period in the previous year. Because its livestock was underweight, however, the district could fulfill the new production quotas only by decimating its animal population.[65]

The decline in livestock numbers, the smaller size of surviving animals, and the inability of some districts to meet production quotas quickly placed tremendous strains on the GDR's ability to feed its citizens. As early as March 1982, some district party leaders began reporting shortfalls of meat; many predicted serious shortages by summer.[66] Beset by popular criticism, local officials responded to declining supplies by trying to curb demand through bureaucratic means. Honecker and Mittag, however, actively discouraged "administrative" solutions to the imbalance between supply and demand, such as rationing. As always, dispelling a shortage took a backseat to fears that strong measures might communicate the extent of the SED's mismanagement and trigger panic purchases.[67]

Enjoined from disciplining demand, local leaders tried to regulate supply. Specifically, they tinkered with meat provisions in the hopes of compelling an adjustment of demand to supply. Thus, local stores began offering less attractive pork parts, such as pork knees, pork tails, and innards, to compensate for the dearth of pork and beef. They also made more poultry and eggs available. Restaurants and factory cafeterias followed suit, completely removing pork and beef from their menus and offering poultry instead.[68] By forcing East Germans to substitute one food for another, local party officials hoped to reestablish equilibrium between supply and demand.

Unfortunately for the SED, however, East Germans refused to comply with such authoritarian solutions to the shortage, preferring not to eat chicken in lieu of pork. Instead, the SED was confronted with widescale

---

65 Ibid.; SAPMO-BA, DY30, Vorläufige SED 31984, Chemnitzer cable to Honecker, 17.5.82, p. 3.

66 SAPMO-BA, DY30, Vorläufige SED 31986, Abteilung Handel, Versorgung und Außenhandel, "Bemerkungen in den Parteiinformationen zur Fleischversorgung," 30.3.82, pp. 1–2.

67 SAPMO-BA, DY30, Vorläufige SED 31986, Weber cable to Honecker, 17.5.82, pp. 3–4.

68 Suhl substituted meat for poultry and eggs. Cottbus made up for shortfalls of meat by making 180 tons or 38.6 percent more poultry available to the population. SAPMO-BA, DY30, Vorläufige SED 31984, Walde to Honecker, 16.5.82, p. 1, and Walde cable to Honecker, 17.5.82, p. 2; SAPMO-BA, DY30, Vorläufige SED 31986, Weber cable to Honecker, 17.5.82, p. 6, and "Welche Maßnahmen wurden bisher zum korrektiven Einsatz von Fleisch eingeleitet," no date, pp. 1–3. For a discussion of forced substitution in Soviet-style economies, see Kornai, *The Socialist System*, pp. 233–40.

hoarding as Easter approached.[69] To make matters worse, East Germans began to binge on what pork or beef they could find just as meat production plunged to new lows. By early May, some regions were reporting that meat provisions had fallen by 40 percent. By the middle of May, many districts were entirely unable to supply the population with meat. Distraught party officials in Erfurt reported long lines, while Schwerin related that meat had not been available in stores since the end of April.[70]

Just when it seemed that things could get no worse, the problem of complementarity conspired to destabilize the GDR further. As the meat crisis was easing, East Germans were confronted with a shortage of milk products, especially butter.[71] The campaign to export meat, coupled with the greater incidence of disease, had thinned out the number of milk cows.[72] The little milk that was produced went sour waiting to be processed. Aging equipment at factories such as the euphemistically named VEB Always Good Stavenhagen (VEB Immergut Stavenhagen) broke down, forcing workers to leave the milk standing. Of the remaining milk that was successfully processed, much went to waste when milk cartons were crushed and the labels incorrectly affixed by defective equipment.[73] Local butter producers reacted to the shortfalls in milk production by reducing the amount of fat in the butter they made. While this solution permitted them to fulfill the physical quantities prescribed by the plan, East German consumers simply refused to buy butter with a low fat content. As with the meat shortage, their unwillingness to comply with this form of enforced substitution led to hoarding, thereby aggravating already acute shortages.

The meager food supply quickly affected worker productivity in sectors unrelated to food production. Local officials throughout East Germany observed widespread grumbling and, more seriously, "political discussions," which was the party's euphemism for open displays of politicized

69 SAPMO-BA, DY30, Vorläufige SED 31984, Modrow cable to Honecker, 17.5.82, p. 2. In response to the fear of shortages, people would often purchase large amounts of foodstuffs they thought they might not see again for a while and go on eating binges.

70 SAPMO-BA, DY30, Vorläufige SED 31986, "Zur Information Fleisch," 11.5.82, p. 8, and "Information zur Versorgung mit Fleisch und Wurstwaren," 17.5.82, p. 3.

71 Declining production of milk, and therefore of the milk fat necessary to make butter, resulted in butter shortfalls totaling 237,000 tons in August, 296,000 tons in September, and widening to between 440,000 and 480,000 tons by November (SAPMO-BA, DY30, Vorläufige SED 31986, "Einschätzung der Versorgung mit Butter/Nahrungsfetten zum Zeitpunkt der Beschlußfassung 10.8.1982," 14.10.82, p. 1; BArchB, DE1, 56276, Abteilung Planung und Finanzen, "Stellungnahme zur Vorlage für das Politbüro der SED 'Maßnahmen zur Sicherung der Versorgung der Bevölkerung mit Fleisch, Butter und Eiern im IV. Quartal 1982,'" 12.11.82, p. 5).

72 SAPMO-BA, DY30, Vorläufige SED 31986, "Tierverluste," no date.

73 SAPMO-BA, DY30, Vorläufige SED 31986, Ministerium für Handel und Versorgung, "Information zu ausgewählten Erzeugnissen," Anlage 6, "Qualitätsprobleme," 20.9.82, pp. 1–2.

discontent.[74] The district party leadership of Karl-Marx-Stadt, moreover, reported that women were leaving the workplace to shop for meat.[75] That workers felt it necessary to leave the factories to purchase food was serious enough, but news that women were walking out en masse underlined the gravity of the shortage.

Women occupied a key position in the GDR, straddling both production and consumption. In contrast to the middle-class vision of women as housewives that prevailed in the Federal Republic, the emancipation of women constituted a significant Marxist-Leninist political goal.[76] Rather than consigning women to their traditional domestic role, East German communists interpreted women's liberation as providing for equal access to the workplace. The SED's commitment to women's rights also conveniently dovetailed with its economic goal of increased industrial output. In an economy so hungry for labor, expanding the labor force by adding female workers helped stimulate economic growth.

Despite its progressive rhetoric, however, the SED spent little time and fewer resources relaxing the social constraints on women. The party encouraged women to pursue careers outside the house, but it did little to help them achieve professional parity with men. Not only did the SED fail to use the considerable power of the state it controlled to promote women to key administrative positions, but the upper ranks of the party remained effectively closed to women. There was only one female member of the Council of State, Margot Honecker, and her competence was often denigrated by reference to the flagrant nepotism by which she had secured the job, since she was the General Secretary's wife. Between 1971 and 1989, moreover,

74 In March, some districts and counties reported "negative commentaries" (SAPMO-BA, DY30, Vorläufige SED 31986, Abteilung Handel, Versorgung und Außenhandel, "Bemerkungen in den Parteiinformationen zur Fleischversorgung," 30.3.82, pp. 1–2). By May, almost every district reported grumbling among ordinary East Germans (SAPMO-BA, DY30, Vorläufige SED 31984 and 31986).
75 SAPMO-BA, DY30, Vorläufige SED 31986, Weber cable to Honecker, 17.5.82, pp. 2–3. On the other hand, Cottbus reported that "there are no signs of worker dissatisfaction with supply in the factories" (SAPMO-BA, DY30, Vorläufige SED 31984, Walde to Honecker, 17.5.82, p. 2).
76 On West German consumer ideals, see Michael Wildt, *Am Beginn der 'Konsumgesellschaft'. Mangelerfahrung, Lebenshaltung, Wohlstandshoffnung in Westdeutschland in den fünfziger Jahren* (Hamburg, 1994). On the discrepancy between the official rhetoric of women's emancipation and changes in work and family patterns, see Donna Harsch, "Society, the State, and Abortion in East Germany 1950–1972," *American Historical Review* 107 (February 1997), pp. 53–84; Gisela Helwig, "Staat und Familie in der DDR," in Glaeßner, *Die DDR in der Ära Honecker*, pp. 466–80; Christian Lemke, "Frauen, Technik und Fortschritt: Zur Bedeutung neuer Technologien für die Berufssituation von Frauen in der DDR," in Glaeßner, *Die DDR in der Ära Honecker*, pp. 481–98; Katherine Pence, "Labours of Consumption: Gendered Consumers in Post-War East and West German Reconstruction," in Lynn Abrams and Elizabeth Harvey (eds.), *Gender Relations in German History: Power, Agency and Experience from the Sixteenth to the Twentieth Century* (London, 1996), pp. 211–38; Katherine Pence, "'You as a Woman Will Understand': Consumption, Gender and the Relationship between State and Citizenry in the GDR's Crisis of 17 June 1953," *German History* 19 (2001), pp. 218–52.

Figure 7. The prince and his paladins. The Politburo greets Erich Honecker on his 65th birthday on 25 August 1977. From right to left: Hermann Axen, Werner Walde (behind Axen), Erich Mückenberger, Konrad Naumann, Margarete Müller, Werner Felfe, Gerhard Grüneberg, Joachim Herrman, Horst Sindermann, Werner Lamberz, Friedrich Ebert, Günter Mittag, Erich Honecker, Alfred Neumann (behind Honecker), Ingeburg Lange, Willi Stoph, Egon Krenz (behind Stoph), Werner Krolikowski, Albert Norden, Heinz Hoffmann, Horst Dohlus (behind Hoffmann), Kurt Hager, Paul Verner, Harry Tisch (behind Verner), Gerhard Schürer, Erich Mielke, Werner Jarowinsky, Günther Kleiber. (Courtesy of Bundesarchiv Koblenz, Bildarchiv, 183/S0825/0032.)

thirty-nine people sat on the Politburo at one time or another (in 1989 there were twenty-six), but only two were women, Inge Lange and Margarete Müller. Neither were full members, and both were marginalized figures.

Most importantly, the party failed to disrupt the gendered distribution of roles in East German families. Instead, the structures and symbols of everyday life in the GDR reinforced the traditional position of women as primary caretakers. East German women thus found themselves in the unenviable position of working outside of the home at full-time yet subaltern jobs while running the household, often with little assistance from their male partners in the work of shopping, preparing meals, or caring for children. Forced to choose between arrhythmic schedules in the workplace and the chance to obtain food for their families, it is no wonder that women chose to put their homes first.[77]

77 For a sense of the problems confronting women in their dual role as consumers and producers, see the anonymous letter to Honecker from 21.5.85 in SAPMO-BA, DY30, Vorläufige SED 41852.

Thus, food shortages represented a political danger to the SED because politically frustrated East German consumers might vent their displeasure at the party's economic management, and an economic threat because work stoppages resulting from discontinuities in food supplies, which party officials were powerless to prevent, only made the situation worse. Worker absenteeism was a chronic problem for planned economies; in 1987, the State Planning Commission estimated it cost the GDR 256 hours of work time a year per worker, compared to 134 hours for West German workers, 64 hours for American workers, and 35 hours for Japanese workers. Of course, these figures were politically skewed to make the GDR look better, since they did not distinguish sick leave, which is publicly funded in the FRG, from playing hooky.[78] The walkout by women in the spring of 1982, however, threatened to disrupt life in East German homes as well as in the factories.

In a letter from 17 May 1982, Cottbus party leader Werner Walde tried to impress upon Honecker how grave the crisis was. Trying to relieve the shortages of perishable goods such as meat by reducing supplies, he argued, created more political trouble than it was worth. Instead, he tried to convince Honecker that parsimony directed at "luxury" goods, such as consumer durables, rather than basic necessities, would find more support among ordinary East Germans. Saving money by slashing the supply of consumer durable goods, Walde declared, "would be better understood by the population than meat exports, about which there is much discussion."[79] His carefully constructed warnings fell on deaf ears. Honecker and Mittag refused to ease the crisis by scaling back meat exports. The prospect of earning Western cash overshadowed domestic hardship.

The center's attempts to solve macroeconomic problems without regard for the concerns of the periphery tied the hands of local party leaders, creating a new source of administrative confusion. The centralization of decision-making power facilitated the party's ability to react quickly to crises. But the rigidly hierarchical transmission of power under Honecker only magnified the policy confusion emanating from Berlin, as the center neglected local concerns until they became emergencies, then reversed course to correct them. In this manner, Mittag's continued pressure on the food-processing industry weakened the SED's control over the economy, transforming shortage into crisis. The center's injunction against regulating

78 BArchB, DE1, 56756, Wenzel, "Zum Stand und zur Entwicklung der Arbeitsproduktivität der DDR im internationalen Vergleich," p. 209; BArchB, DE1, 56323, "Rentabilität des Exportes der DDR," no date, p. 585.
79 SAPMO-BA, DY30, Vorläufige SED 31984, Walde to Honecker, 17.5.82, p. 5.

demand, moreover, deprived party officials at the periphery of the most effective means of reacting to the crisis. Local leaders could combat the shortages only with a combination of public disinformation and party discipline – or as Werner Walde put it, "through daily operative guidance and control and clever economizing and argumentation."[80]

Honecker and Mittag's increasing reliance on central control, supported by discursive manipulation in the face of disappearing resources, invited popular forms of disobedience. It also discredited the leadership with the party rank-and-file. During the 1982 crisis, signs of unrest among ordinary party members grew; by May, there were unmistakeable signs of resentment among low-level party representatives against the SED leadership's management of the meat crisis.[81] To some extent, their low morale resulted from the impossible task of justifying the party line to nonparty members. Local disagreement with, or incomprehension of, the center's instructions was by no means a new phenomenon. Because the primary function of local party representatives was to reconcile the populace with SED policy through ideological direction, their proximity to the concerns of ordinary East Germans had often led them to criticize Berlin in the past.[82] Moreover, the frustration felt by rank-and-file SED members at the leadership's unresponsiveness to their concerns was a recurring by-product of dictatorial rule.

By the 1980s, however, the atmosphere of foreign and domestic crisis, the increasing rigidity of the structures that transmitted the dictatorship, and Honecker's own unwillingness to countenance critical analysis left local leaders little room to convey their dissatisfaction with the leadership's decisions. The center's shackles on local governance, tightened by the material constraints deriving from the external debt, increasingly deprived district and county officials of the means with which to manage the crisis. Without the administrative powers to resolve economic imbalances, leaders at the periphery could meet breakdowns in material culture only with exhortations. Rhetoric, however, was a poor substitute for the real goods people longed for. Potsdam district leader Günther Jahn's pitiful boast to Honecker that "we are diligently working on reducing the rest [of the problems caused by the crisis] with political responsibility and healthy common sense" illustrates just how poorly exaggeration concealed the party's near helplessness.[83] Like other goods, responsibility and common sense were in short supply in the East Germany of 1982.

80 SAPMO-BA, DY30, Vorläufige SED 31984, Walde to Honecker, 16.5.82, p. 4.
81 SAPMO-BA, DY30, Vorläufige SED 31986, Weber cable to Honecker, 17.5.82, p. 3.
82 See, for example, the account in Fulbrook, *Anatomy of a Dictatorship*, pp. 62–77.
83 SAPMO-BA, DY30, Vorläufige SED 31984, Jahn to Honecker, 17.5.82, pp. 1–2.

Some party officials dared to identify the conflicting administrative signals as emanating from the top leadership. In a frank conversation, Gerhard Müller, the party leader in Erfurt, remarked to Heinz Klopfer, Schürer's deputy at the State Planning Commission, that "we had the impression in the last few months that we have lots of ministries, but no Council of Ministers." Because local officials had little say over the direction of economic policy, they were powerless to disentangle the competing impulses at work during the export drive. Müller also asserted that Mittag's drive to increase central control at the expense of the periphery had achieved the opposite of his ends. By cutting local leaders out of the loop, Müller avowed, "district and county party organizations are basically sidelined in economic questions. We received the directives [from the Politburo], and much of what transpired in practice contradicted these directives."[84] The crisis of 1982 exacerbated the confusion of ends and means characteristic of Soviet-style economies, conflating production with consumption, organizing supply against demand, and unleashing bureaucratic competition for scarce resources.

Even Stasi chief Erich Mielke expressed concern over the political fallout from the economic crisis. At a top-level meeting, Mielke argued that the shortages of consumer goods stemming from the export drive and the import reductions constituted risks to the internal stability of the GDR. Simply put, he did not believe the greater danger to the SED's hold on power emanated from the East German population. Instead, Mielke feared for the morale of communist party members, who might "resign or capitulate in the face of complicated tasks."[85] However misplaced and cynical his concern for the party over the population was, Mielke articulated the main danger created by economic mismanagement in an authoritarian regime – the erosion of ideological legitimacy attending a tangible deterioration in the state's ability to alleviate material distress. After all, if the SED could no longer rely on the lower ranks to carry out orders, quelling an uprising would prove impossible. Mielke had put his finger on a key problem that the SED would confront in 1989.

What forced Mittag to relent on his export drive was the fear of political insurrection. By October 1982, SED leaders had become concerned that the short supply of key foodstuffs would weigh on holiday celebrations.[86]

84 BArchB, DE1, 56287, Klopfer, "Persönliche Niederschrift," 22.11.82, pp. 216–17.
85 BStU, ZAIG, 04810, Mielke, "auf der zentralen Dienstkonferenz," 11.10.82, pp. 78–9.
86 SAPMO-BA, DY30, JIV 2/2A/2516, Arbeitsprotokoll Nr. 42, Politbürositzung vom 20.10.82, "Vorlage für das Politbüro des Zentralkomitees der SED, Betreff: Information über die Versorgung der Bevölkerung im IV. Quartal 1982 in ausgewählten Einzelpositionen und festtagstypischen Erzeugnissen," 19.10.82, pp. 1–3, and Anlage 1, Ministerium für Handel und Versorgung, "Information über die Versorgung der Bevölkerung im IV. Quartal 1982 in ausgewählten Einzelpositionen und festtagstypischen Erzeugnissen."

Honecker had always placed a high priority on making key perishable goods available over Christmas as a method of placating restive East German consumers. Memories of the sequence of events in Poland a year earlier, moreover, only intensified the East German leadership's anxieties. In the run-up to the winter holidays in 1981, opposition to the Polish communist party had deepened. Communist strongman Wojciech Jaruselzki reacted to the increased willingness of the population to voice its discontent by declaring martial law on 13 December 1981. At such a sensitive time of year, with its emphasis on family celebration around mealtimes, the SED could ill afford to arouse the population's ire.

In late October 1982, the Politburo finally relented, agreeing to relieve the pressure by slowing the export drive somewhat.[87] The leadership's concessions, however, were slow to take effect. According to Western sources, November saw severe shortages of a variety of perishable goods. In Dresden, there were no potatoes, Erfurt had not seen coffee for weeks, and the villages of Mecklenburg had run out of toilet paper.[88] In response, the Department of Planning and Finance at the ZK, which was one of Mittag's main organs for transmitting his power, authorized a "variety of measures [that] are necessary for supplying the population" with consumer goods.[89] It yielded to reductions of exports of crucial foodstuffs in short supply, such as eggs. Reacting to the continued shortage of butter, the department also agreed to make butter that was originally intended for export to the West available for domestic consumption – but only because SED leaders could find no Western customers to purchase it. In a reaction characteristic of functionaries used to dealing with shortages, moreover, planners tried to stretch the volume of butter by dilution, demanding that producers water down 3,200 tons to create 3,800 tons of lower-quality butter for East German tables.[90] Although rather belated, the department also made concessions to the meat-processing industry. It lowered export targets for 1983 and authorized increased fodder imports from the West.

As the crisis of 1982 demonstrates, the centralization of power in the GDR enabled Mittag to force the priorities of Berlin onto regional SED leaders. The economic imperatives of the center, however, soon collided with the administrative requirements of the periphery, as Mittag's attempts

87 BArchB, DE1, 56287, Klopfer, "Persönliche Niederschrift," 22.11.82, p. 217.
88 *Die Welt*, 22.11.82, in BArchB, DE1, 56287, p. 218.
89 BArchB, DE1, 56276, Abteilung Planung und Finanzen, "Stellungnahme zur Vorlage," 12.11.82, p. 1.
90 SAPMO-BA, DY30, Vorläufige SED 31986, "Einschätzung der Versorgung mit Butter/Nahrungsfetten zum Zeitpunkt der Beschlußfassung 10.8.1982," 14.10.82, pp. 1–3, and Ministerium für Handel und Versorgung, "Einschätzung zur Lage in der Versorgung mit Butter," 14.10.82, p. 3.

to harness socialist production to the goal of earning Western money contradicted local leaders' priority of feeding the population. Mittag's ability to
dictate economic priorities to local managers transformed the already ten-
uous balance between supply and demand into acute shortages. Moreover,
his policies fueled the anxieties of local officials over popular reactions to the
SED's mismanagement of the economy, eroding support among rank-and-
file members for the leadership's goals. But it was the financial imbalance
between parsimony and prodigality that would shake the East German communist party to its foundations in 1982.

BETWEEN PARSIMONY AND PROFLIGACY

If the food shortages of 1982 seriously weakened the SED leadership's standing with party members and the population, its consumer policies nearly
bankrupted the GDR. Despite generating a trade surplus in 1982, the GDR
was suddenly overwhelmed by the financial liabilities it had incurred from
years of trade deficits. After all was said and done, Mittag still came up
DM 2.6 billion short on interest and principal payments: That is, the GDR
had earned more than enough money to pay for what it imported during
the current year, but not enough to service its debts from previous years.[91]
Worse still, the actual structure of the debt posed an immediate threat to the
GDR's solvency. The SED had managed its financial affairs so poorly that
by 1982 the enormous sum of DM 13.8 billion, or 55 percent of the total
debt, consisted of short-term loans.[92] The problem with short-term loans
was not simply that they cost the GDR more, but also that they had to be
rolled over.

Thanks to the GDR's socialist allies, the prospects for convincing Western
creditors to renew these loans looked bleak. In the fall of 1981, Poland
defaulted on its debts. A few months later, Romania followed suit. In both
cases, the balance-of-payments problems that brought on the financial crisis
originated in overestimations of how much capital these planned economies
could gainfully absorb, of their ability to repay the loans through exports, and
of their ability to withstand external shocks such as natural disasters and rising prices for raw materials. During the 1970s, for example, Poland pursued
an import-led growth policy aimed at making Polish industry more competitive on world markets. To stimulate labor productivity, the communist
party raised living standards by purchasing Western consumer goods on

91 Deutsche Bundesbank (ed.), *Zahlungsbilanz der ehemaligen DDR*, p. 49.
92 BArchB, DE1, 56276, Staatliche Plankommission, "Zahlungsbilanz," 12.11.82, p. 6.

credit, much as the GDR did. Despite extensive capital investments, however, demand for Polish manufactured goods remained low. Through poor management, overinvestment, and rising fuel prices, the communist party squandered billions of dollars. By 1979, Western sources estimated Poland's net foreign debt at about $20 billion. Measured in per capita terms, Poland's debt was much lower than the GDR's. Because Poland could not earn money on Western markets, however, 92 percent of its exports in 1979 went toward servicing the debt.[93]

To improve Poland's balance of payments, communist party leader Edward Gierek proposed raising prices for basic foodstuffs. However economically sound his measures were, they met with political resistance, triggering popular protests and Gierek's ouster. By 1981, Poland was unable to pay the interest on its debts. Forced to declare insolvency that October, Poland began negotiations with its Western creditors to reschedule its debt payments. Not two months later, however, the party declared martial law. Led by the United States, the West responded to the use of violence to quell protests by breaking off negotiations, rejecting Poland's application for membership in the International Monetary Fund, and applying trade sanctions against Polish goods. Poland was forced to reorient its economic activity toward the USSR, which helped stabilize the economy but did not make Poland more competitive on world markets.

In contrast to Poland and the GDR, Romania's Western imports consisted almost entirely of capital goods. Romanian dictator Nicolae Ceaușescu's overinvestment in the domestic oil industry not only indebted Romania to the West, but paradoxically created a shortage of petroleum products in Eastern Europe's only oil-rich country. Like other communist leaders, moreover, Ceaușescu failed to allow for contingencies such as inclement weather or earthquakes like the one in 1977. By 1981, Romania's net debt to Western bankers amounted to $10.2 billion. Measured in per capita terms, Romania's debt was more modest than Poland's or the GDR's. The poor quality of Romanian manufactured goods, however, meant that exporting its way out of the debt crisis was impossible.[94]

---

93 On the financial crisis in Poland, see Simatupang, *The Polish Economic Crisis*; Slay, *The Polish Economy*; Smith, *The Planned Economies*; Zloch-Christy, *Debt Problems*, pp. 41, 74–6, 105–13. In 1979, Polish net per capita debt was $526 million per person versus $785 million for the GDR (Table 2, Chapter 2).

94 For more on the causes of Romania's insolvency, see Dennis Deletant, "New Evidence on Romania and the Warsaw Pact, 1955–1989," in *Cold War History Project*, e-Dossier No. 6; Shafir, *Romania*; Smith, *The Planned Economies*, pp. 229–30; Zloch-Christy, *Debt Problems*, pp. 80–3. Because Moscow did not deliver subsidized oil to Bucharest, Romania's vulnerability to price saltations was magnified. The net per capita debt in 1981 was $440 million.

Relying on his brutal security apparatus, Ceauşescu extracted savings to repay the loans by imposing dramatic price increases and shocking reductions of basic foodstuffs, heat, and electricity starting in 1979. In 1981, he went further, cutting off street lighting, limiting heating in offices to a maximum of 57 degrees Fahrenheit, prohibiting the use of vacuum cleaners and refrigerators, reintroducing bread rationing, preventing peasants from purchasing food outside their villages, and restricting cooking to evening hours only. When even these extreme measures failed to ease the crisis, Ceauşescu suspended payments later that year. Romania eventually concluded an agreement with the Paris Club in July 1982. Only a few weeks later, however, it requested a rescheduling.[95]

The financial crises in Poland and Romania, as well as those countries' use of political violence to resolve economic problems, aggravated the GDR's liquidity problems. The higher risk introduced by the Polish and Romanian insolvencies led Western financial markets to discount loans to Soviet bloc states at higher rates. The Polish declaration of martial law, moreover, politicized lending to the Soviet bloc. Lending money to a state engaged in brutally repressing its own people smacked of the worst kind of hypocrisy.

To make matters worse, Western capital markets were immersed in a severe liquidity crunch, making credit harder to obtain. The crunch was chiefly the result of substantial hikes in the U.S. Federal Reserve's interest rates, which were aimed at quelling double-digit inflation rates. During the 1970s, the failure of Keynesian methods of managing aggregate demand to resolve contemporaneous supply and demand pressures (stagflation) contributed to the increased acceptance of monetarism, an economic theory that links developments in price levels almost exclusively to the evolution of money supply. As early as 1975, for example, the West German central bank embraced monetarist policies, such as money-supply targets. But the turning point for capital markets came in the summer of 1979, when Paul Volcker was appointed Chairman of the U.S. Federal Reserve by Democratic President Jimmy Carter. That autumn, Volcker pushed through a series of measures designed to attack inflation by reducing the U.S. money supply. By 1982, the Fed's hawkish anti-inflationary stance had pushed interest rates to historically high levels and sent the U.S. economy into a recession.[96]

95 Deletant, "New Evidence on Romania"; Shafir, *Romania*, pp. 117–18; Zloch-Christy, *Debt Problems*, pp. 113–15. Romania suspended payments once again in July 1986.
96 Peter A. Johnson, *The Government of Money: Monetarism in Germany and the United States* (Ithaca, N.Y., and London, 1998); Karl Kaltenthaler, *Germany and the Politics of Europe's Money* (Durham, N.C., and London, 1998); Smith, *The German Economy*, pp. 139–94; W. R. Smyser, *The German Economy: Colossus at the Crossroads* (New York, 1992), pp. 203–36.

Even the GDR felt the effects of the ensuing credit crunch. In the first six months of 1982 alone, foreign investors called in 40 percent of their short-term deposits with the GDR because they could get better returns on the money in the United States.[97] The combination of the perceived risk associated with lending to communist states, political pressure not to lend to the Soviet bloc, and a tight-money policy meant that money was not only more difficult to secure, but that the GDR had to pay higher interest rates to borrow it.[98]

Given their ideological hostility to money, however, the SED's leaders did not see it this way. From the anticapitalist perspective of the East German Politburo, the triumph of monetarism in the West represented yet another attempt by the international bourgeoisie to use money to oppress the working class. The revision of the GDR's credit rating following the insolvency of Poland and Romania seemed to East German Marxist-Leninists nothing less than a gratuitous expression of imperialist animosity toward socialism. Mixing military with monetary metaphors, the SED depicted the GDR as a victim of "the economic boycott of capitalist countries" resulting from "the continuously sharpening economic war of the imperialist countries" against socialism.[99] Without a firm understanding of the meaning of money to explain why credit had dried up, the SED leadership fell back on the polemics of class warfare. Indeed, it seems as if the party could make rising interest rates and tougher borrowing conditions coherent only if they were depicted as an organized and malicious attempt to withhold much-needed funds from the GDR.

Political shifts in West Germany also contributed to financial uncertainties. On 2 October 1982, economic stagnation, as well as passionate disagreement over the stationing of U.S. cruise missiles on West German soil, toppled

---

97 BArchB, DE1, 56323, "Dokumente über Beschlüsse zur Zahlungsfähigkeit der DDR gegenüber dem NSW," 5.5.89, "Vorlage für das Politbüro des ZK der SED 'Weitere Maßnahmen zur Durchführung der außerwirtschaftlichen Aufgaben der DDR in den Jahren 1982 und 1983' vom 17.8.1982," p. 3.

98 Given the amount of hard currency the GDR required, the State Planning Commission estimated that each percentage point of interest cost the GDR DM 112.5 million. But the liquidity crunch made it more difficult to obtain long-term loans, which were a more stable source of funds even though they initially carried higher interest rates. The State Planning Commission reported that loans with a term of at least 360 days would reduce the GDR's cash deficit by DM 900 million. But expensive money was still money; the State Planning Commission worried that the GDR would obtain DM 1.9 billion less in credits in 1983 than in 1982 (BArchB, DE1, 56276, Staatliche Plankommission, "Zahlungsbilanz," 12.11.82, pp. 6–7; BArchB, DE1, 56318, "Eine Bemerkung zu der Frage, warum 1 Mark der DDR im Ausweis des Devisenerlöses nur 25 Valutapfennige wert ist," 30.8.88, p. 3).

99 BArchB, DE1, 56323, "Anlage zum Vorschlag zur Fertigstellung des Entwurfes des Volkswirtschafts-planes, Zahlungsbilanz zum Entwurf der Staatlichen Auflage," 12.11.82, p. 1; BArchB, DE1, 56276, Staatliche Plankommission, "Vorschlag zur Fertigstellung des Entwurfs des Volkswirtschaftsplanes 1983," 12.11.82, p. 21.

the left–liberal coalition led by Helmut Schmidt in the Federal Republic's first constructive vote of no confidence. Given the vociferous opposition to communism of the new Christian Democratic chancellor, Helmut Kohl, the direction of relations between the two Germanys appeared uncertain. U.S. President Ronald Reagan's aggressive anti-Soviet stance, moreover, created a climate of confrontation that did not augur well for German–German relations. It took several months for Honecker and Kohl to establish the contours of their relationship, which ultimately resembled that of the Brandt and Schmidt governments.

By 1982, the GDR was confronted with even higher debt payments and less goodwill from the international financial community. In addition, the conditions attached by Western producers to trade with communist states had hardened. In particular, the GDR obtained fewer commercial credits for its imports, forcing the socialist state to pay in cash for a larger portion of its imports. Unable to secure new loans to prevent insolvency, confronted with foreign pressure and domestic turmoil, the GDR teetered on the brink of collapse.[100]

What saved the GDR from defaulting was West German capitalism. In perhaps the most ironic twist in the GDR's history, the staunchly anticommunist center-right coalition in West Germany rescued Honecker and Mittag from the consequences of their bungling. In fact, the Kohl government proved even more generous than its Social Democratic predecessors. On 29 June 1983, Bavarian Minister-President Franz Josef Strauß, who had made a career out of his vitriolic anticommunism, helped the GDR secure loans worth DM 1 billion at excellent terms. The first loan was followed by another DM 950 million in 1984.[101] The money could not have come at a better time for the East German state. Mittag's pork exports, which were directed by Schalck to a Munich-based company whose owners were close friends of Strauß, had proven lucrative in unforeseen ways.

In return for such an unprecedented amount of money, the West Germans demanded political concessions. Honecker agreed to minor relaxations in

---

100 The State Planning Commission estimated that during the course of 1983 the GDR had to pay DM 16.9 billion in principal and 4 billion in interest, and anticipated a cash deficit of DM 6.1 billion. Moreover, Schürer was told that Schalck would make no contribution in 1983 from his KoKo operations (Schalck most likely contributed, but off the books to which Schürer had access). The result was that during some months of 1983, such as August and September, the GDR was essentially insolvent (BArchB, DE1, 56323, "Vorlage für das Politbüro des ZK der SED vom 17.8.1982," p. 3; BArchB, DE1, 56276, "Zahlungsbilanz," 12.11.82, p. 6). Zloch-Christy argues that the GDR's problem was one of illiquidity, rather than insolvency (Zloch-Christy, *Debt Problems*, pp. 78–80).

101 The smaller amount of the second loan was intended to deflect public attention from the Kohl government's support of the GDR.

Figure 8. Business as usual. KoKo chief Alexander Schalck–Golodkowski (third from left) and Economic Secretary Günter Mittag (fourth from left) with Bavarian Minister-President Franz Josef Strauß (center) and SED leader Erich Honecker (right) at the Spring Fair in Leipzig, 1987. West German Finance Minister Theo Waigel is standing behind Strauß. (Courtesy of Bundesarchiv Koblenz, Bildarchiv, 183/1990/0226/301.)

travel arrangements for West Germans and promised to facilitate family reunions.[102] In 1984, the GDR also emended the regulations restricting the visits of retired East Germans to the West.[103] These liberalizations translated into concrete results, easing the plight of many German families. More importantly, they signaled the SED's willingness to continue opening up the border in return for money at a time when East–West relations were quite strained. Even more dramatically, however, Honecker yielded to intense West German pressure to dismantle the tripwire weapons that lined the border with West Germany. The symbolic importance of this gesture is hard to underestimate. On the one hand, demilitarizing the German–German border abated tensions just as the two superpowers were engaged in a highly

102 The GDR dropped the minimum exchange requirements for children fourteen and under, eased regulations regarding marriage between East Germans and "foreigners," and agreed to reunite families more swiftly. It also agreed to drop some of the restrictions on sending gift packages (Garton Ash, *In Europe's Name*, pp. 155–6; Hertle, "Die Diskussion," pp. 327–9).
103 Starting on 1 August 1984, the GDR permitted East German retirees to stay for up to sixty days in the West and broadened the categories of legitimate reasons for travel to the Federal Republic to include visiting friends as well as family.

confrontational arms race. On the other hand, reducing the deadliness of the Wall even by a small amount spoke to the deep-seated aversion felt by many Germans toward the most frightening aspect of national division. Because of the SED's concessions, the new center-right coalition was able to sell the social democratic policy of *Ostpolitik* to a skeptical West German public.

But what Kohl and Strauß were really trying to buy was a continuation of détente with the GDR. Strauß, who was well informed about East Germany's financial distress, worried that insolvency might turn the GDR away from the West and toward its Comecon partners, as had transpired with Poland. In fact, during the negotiations Schalck had attempted to blackmail Strauß along precisely these lines. He threatened to put an end to good relations with West Germany, telling Strauß that "we will close the doors" if the Federal Republic did not help alleviate the situation.[104] The consequences of East German insolvency, moreover, distressed West German politicians, especially in light of Poland's declaration of martial law and Romania's imposition of extreme austerity measures. Despite his ideological antipathy to the SED, Strauß insisted that the Federal Republic provide massive financial assistance to the GDR to stabilize it now, rather than watch as the SED used political violence to stabilize it later. West German money, he argued, would help Honecker pursue a policy of détente even if the Federal Republic were to decide to station short-range U.S. cruise missiles on West German soil, as it would do in 1984.[105]

Although Strauß eventually found political backing for the loans, it came at a price. Continued resistance to *Ostpolitik* on his right led some Bavarian opponents of *Ostpolitik* to leave the CSU and form a radical right-wing party, the Republikaner. Nevertheless, the loans allowed the new West German government to claim a victory in German–German relations and consolidate its domestic position ahead of new elections. The domestic political benefits that accrued to the CDU/CSU, often overlooked by political historians, were considerable.[106]

Nevertheless, the concessions that Honecker granted were more symbolic than substantial. Contrary to the arguments of Timothy Garton Ash, the SED had in reality done little to loosen the constraints on congress between

---

104 Schalck, "Niederschrift über das geführte Gespräch zwischen dem Vorsitzenden der CSU, F. J. Strauß, dem Staatsminister im Bundeskanzleramt, Jenninger, und Genossen Schalck am 5.6.1983 in Spöck/Chiemsee," 6.6.83, cited in Hertle, "Die Diskussion," p. 327.

105 The original NATO decision to balance the Soviet Union's upgraded missiles was taken on 12.12.79. The West German parliament voted to accept the U.S. missiles with 286 votes for and 225 against on 22.11.83.

106 See, for example, Garton Ash, *In Europe's Name*, pp. 152–7.

the two Germanys.[107] The new travel ordinances, for example, amounted to minor steps in the direction of liberalization. They were overshadowed by Honecker's agreement with Helmut Schmidt the previous year to permit former East German citizens to travel to the GDR without fear of reprisal in return for extending the Swing agreement. In contrast, Honecker's refusal to lower the minimum amount of hard currency West Germans were obliged to exchange when visiting the GDR diminished the travel relaxations he did grant the Kohl government.[108] And although Honecker removed the automatic firing mechanisms, he continued to instruct the border patrols to use deadly force against people trying to escape.[109] At most, Kohl and Strauß had purchased the momentary goodwill of a hostile government during a tense time, along with the promise of future liberalizations. In this sense, the loans truly were "cash against hope," to borrow a slogan from the time.[110]

If the loans amounted to an investment in the future of détente, however, it was their unintended – rather than the intended – consequences that were to have the greatest impact on the prospects for German unification. On the surface, it appeared as if the staunchly anticommunist Strauß had secured the financial autonomy of communism in Germany. Not only had West German aid staved off the immediate threat of insolvency, but it also stabilized the GDR's financial situation, since the West German government's willingness to back the loans encouraged Western bankers to resume lending to the GDR. The loans certainly contributed to the thaw in German–German relations, but they did so by shoring up the SED and pushing an eventual

107 Garton Ash does note that the German–German agreements were lopsided, but he also implies that the CDU "had secured valuable concessions" (ibid., p. 155). Yet the more important travel concession, which permitted pensioners to visit the West starting on 15.2.82, came before the Strauß credits. Moreover, the 1983 Postal Treaty, which the GDR agreed to as a quid pro quo for an increase in the lump-sum payments made by the FRG, had the most significant impact on the SED's political authority. But neither side anticipated the treaty's consequences. As I argue in Chapter 5, it permitted West Germans to send more gifts and money to relatives and friends, which permitted Schalck to expand the Intershops. The result was the increased influence of West German currency and consumer goods in the GDR to the detriment of socialist currency and consumer goods.

108 Just after the West German parliamentary elections of October 1980, the GDR nearly doubled the minimum amount, raising it from DM 13 to DM 25. The number of West Germans traveling to the GDR fell precipitously. In return for Kohl's largesse, Honecker made two minor concessions: relaxing the rule for children under fourteen in September 1983 and reducing the sum for pensioners in July 1984.

109 Many East Germans, bent on escaping the GDR, continued to risk – and lose – their lives trying to reach the Federal Republic. Perhaps the most infamous case after 1982 was Chris Gueffroy, who bled to death at the Wall on 6.2.89 after having been wounded by East German border guards, who then denied him medical assistance.

110 The slogan was first used against SPD Chancellor Helmut Schmidt by CDU leader Rainer Barzel in 1980, then thrown back in Kohl's face by the Social Democrat Hans Apel in 1985 (Garton Ash, *In Europe's Name*, pp. 155, 514).

unification into the indistinct future. On this interpretation, the timely Strauß credits had secured the GDR's future, not undermined it. As the economic historian Armin Volze writes, "if the GDR had been forced to default on its international debts without the billion mark credits – which is not very likely – then granting the credits would perhaps be a political mistake from today's vantage point."[111]

In fact, however, Strauß's intervention actually facilitated German uni-fication, albeit in a complicated and indirect way. The reason involves the legacy of Honecker's profligacy to the revolution of 1989. By rescuing the GDR from the political consequences of the SED's economic policy in 1983, Strauß salvaged Honecker's career. Had the GDR defaulted, or even come close, Honecker would have been shunted aside by his colleagues, as Gierek had been in Poland. Although Strauß could hardly have foreseen, much less intended it, Honecker's place at the helm of the GDR was key to the collapse of socialism in East Germany. His disastrous economic policies – along with his opposition to Soviet reforms later on – thoroughly discredited socialism with the population and the party itself.

As things began to go from bad to worse for the SED, especially after the fall of the Wall, talk turned from reforming the GDR to its abolition. If the refusal of Soviet troops to intervene militarily ultimately doomed the SED, it did not necessarily doom the GDR. Had the party successfully cultivated a loyalty to the second German state, perhaps East Germans might have seriously considered an independent GDR on the lines of Austria. Of course, much credit for ending the SED's dictatorship belongs to Soviet leader Mikhail Gorbachev. His refusal to prop up the Soviet Union's satellite states in 1989 made it impossible for the SED to continue its rule through the use of force. But the SED itself had trained East Germans to look westward. Having failed to construct a genuine alternative to capitalism and Western consumerism, East German communism relied increasingly on West Germany to sustain itself. Given the SED's own promotion of Western merchandise and money, it is not surprising that East Germans decided to go to the source, rather than stick with a bad copy of what they had learned to value, or tarry with the incoherent and untried alternatives offered by the civil rights movement.

The end of Honecker's rule would no doubt have strengthened the GDR. The candidate replacing Honecker would have enjoyed a mandate to rein in Honecker's profligate consumer policies. Most likely, the new General

---

111 Volze, "Geld und Politik," p. 387. Garton Ash mentions the problem without drawing a conclusion (Garton Ash, *In Europe's Name*, pp. 156–7).

Secretary would belong to the generation of Old Communists before power was handed over to a younger generation, similar to the compromise that brought Gorbachev to power in 1985. One can easily imagine Willi Stoph, for example, placing the blame for a series of austerity measures on profit-seeking capitalists as a way of deflecting popular criticism. This new SED leader would move quickly to dismiss Honecker's henchman, the unpopular Günter Mittag, and put an end to the more suspect ventures he encouraged. A new East German leadership, moreover, might well have resolved some of the economic causes of the financial crisis, channeling more money into investment than consumption. By distancing himself from Honecker and Mittag, the new General Secretary might have rallied the party – and perhaps even mobilized a degree of support in the general population – for measures aimed at restoring the socialist state's solvency.

This is not to argue that a new leadership could have addressed the failure of economic planning to replenish East Germany's industrial base or satisfy East German consumer demand. Even a reinvigorated SED leadership could hardly have averted the GDR's collapse, which had its roots not only in economic mismanagement, but also in the political coercion necessary to maintain the SED's rule. But the SED leadership might have entered the pivotal year of 1989 with less debt on its record. And this alone might have prevented the complete and thorough discrediting of socialism that convinced most East Germans in 1989 that their immediate future lay with West Germany.

As it was, Strauß extracted Honecker, Mittag, and Schalck from a protracted crisis, postponing the final financial reckoning for the "Unity of Economic and Social Policy" for another five years. Paradoxically, this respite strengthened Honecker's hand in the Politburo. The pressure on the ruling clique to reconsider its indifference to money matters dissipated, and with it the willingness to confront the General Secretary and his policies. A stronger Honecker, moreover, meant a continuation of the SED's contradictory economic policies – Mittag's parsimony as a countervailing force to Honecker's profligacy – and the attendant growth of popular discontent.

In addition, the Strauß credits bound the GDR more solidly to West Germany, a conundrum that posed a considerable challenge to East German socialism. The alleviation of the financial crisis by an entrenched enemy of the GDR such as Strauß reinforced Honecker's disdain for the economic constraints on his power. This financial deus ex machina encouraged Honecker to believe that the economic chaos he had generated was not a serious threat to the GDR's sovereignty. Honecker appeared to conceive of the GDR's economy as one large East German enterprise; the West German loans simply made it easier to imagine that the debt to the West was a soft, rather than a hard, budget constraint. And even if money did impinge on his political plans, this too was a small matter. If the USSR did not step into the breach to rescue the GDR, West Germany would.

For many in the SED leadership, 1982 was a turning point. As the GDR's chief statistician for twenty-seven years, Arno Donda was one of the few people privy to the unmanipulated reality of the GDR's economic difficulties. Looking back at the crisis of 1982, Donda commented that "it was quite clear, on the basis of all the material known to me at the time, . . . that we were heading for economic collapse. But the so-called Strauß-credit and the following agreements . . . managed to allay these fears to a considerable extent."[112] Through little effort of its own, the SED had purchased a respite from the threat of insolvency through West German financial largesse.

Even before concern about the debt resumed in 1986, however, it was clear that the unstable mixture of parsimony and profligacy encouraged by Honecker had transformed the dictatorship of the proletariat, with its utopian vision of a moneyless society, into a dictatorial welfare state, where principal, not principle, determined state policy and the contours of everyday life. Unwilling to countenance reform from within, Honecker purchased a brief improvement in East German living standards in the early 1970s by importing it from the West. In doing so, however, he abandoned the goal of economic autarky that had guided economic planning under Ulbricht. By the early 1980s, the GDR's reliance on Western cash endangered even this modest improvement in living standards. In his analysis of the financial crisis that triggered the French Revolution, Alexis de Tocqueville observed that the ancien régime's "desire to make money out of everything" hindered its ability to exercise power, so that "its greed frustrated its ambition."[113] Similarly, Mittag's attempts to rescue socialism by selling off the Berlin Wall bit by bit only hastened the demise of the GDR.

During the crisis year of 1982, an acute meat shortage followed by a dearth of milk and butter shook East German society while the state teetered on a financial precipice. Rather than encouraging reform, however, these economic shocks only reinforced Honecker's unwillingness to reconsider his policies. Even after the financial crisis had been averted, Honecker refused to respond to the GDR's increasingly disadvantageous terms of trade with a

112 Arno Donda in *Ohnmacht. DDR-Funktionäre sagen aus* (Berlin, 1992), p. 37, cited in Fulbrook, *Anatomy of a Dictatorship*, p. 37.
113 Alexis de Tocqueville, *The Ancien Regime and the French Revolution*, trans. Stuart Gilbert (New York, 1983), p. 109.

series of austerity measures that might have improved the GDR's current-account and balance-of-payments problems. To protect his program of purchasing political support with economic prosperity, he turned to his acolyte, Günter Mittag. Mittag responded by implementing a strict regime of frugality aimed at extracting savings from the East German industrial base. His narrow focus on debt reduction, however, undermined the GDR's prospects for future economic growth.

More importantly, Mittag's parsimonious approach to the economy squandered what little political capital the SED possessed. As the meat crisis of 1982 illustrates, his attempt to tighten central control over available resources to maximize East German exports to the West offered no relief to East German producers or consumers. Rather, it intensifed the shortages afflicting the planned economy, which aroused popular ire. The administrative confusion stemming from the competing priorities at the core of SED policy, moreover, weakened the ability of local party officials to address those shortages. Ultimately, the contradictory imperatives at the heart of Honecker's economic policy obliged him to reverse the strategy by which he had previously governed, but not before they had deprived the party leadership of its authority with rank-and-file members. By 1982, he could no longer afford to subordinate economics to politics.

After 1982, finance increasingly dictated Honecker's political agenda, as the GDR was forced to rely on capitalist money, capitalist methods, and even capitalist states to stave off bankruptcy. By 1983, Honecker no longer had any compunction about turning to West German anticommunists to stabilize the GDR. For his part, Mittag had few qualms whatsoever, as long as he remained in power. In fact, Mittag's own ambitions now led him to seek closer relations with capitalists even though he had lambasted Ulbricht's chumminess with West Germany in 1971 and loudly demanded an "ever increasing economic, political, and ideological separation" of the GDR from the West.[114]

Even West German financial assistance could not rescue the GDR from its economic quandary, however. Without real gains in productivity, prompted by structural reform, foreign loans could neither postpone economic decline nor shield East Germans from a reduction in living standards. In the hopes of prolonging the stay of execution and augmenting his own power, Mittag resorted to fraud to conceal the GDR's predicament. Although his duplicity and frugality stabilized the GDR in the near term, they contributed greatly to the erosion of the SED's political legitimacy in the long term. During the

114 Grieder, *The East German Leadership*, p. 181.

revolution of 1989, Mittag's mendacity would convince East Germans that the GDR, and the socialism on which it rested, had no future. Honecker's refusal to listen to prudent counsel, as well as his willingness to entrust the GDR's economic future to the most devious of advisors, illustrates the durability of Machiavelli's "infallible rule."

4

The Currency of Decline

The Dis-Integration of the East German Economy, 1986–1989

> Money provides an extremely effective technique for despotism, as a means for incorporating the most remote areas into its rule that, in a barter economy, always tend to separate and become autonomous.[1]

In mid-1988, a shortage of meat once again threatened to destabilize the GDR. Against a background of economic decline and increasingly frequent shortages, the SED leadership sought to avert popular anger over its economic mismanagement.[2] Fearful that a new crisis might galvanize the population against the party, Honecker told the Politburo that "we cannot allow the creation of any problems whatsoever in the area of supply." Otherwise, "the supply of consumer goods will become the population's main question. They will say, what use are computer chips when we need to guarantee a stable supply of consumer goods."[3] Mindful of the calamity of 1982, when the party's mismanagement transformed meat shortages into a serious crisis, the Ministry for Trade and Supply counseled against any bureaucratic curtailment of supply in the hopes of dampening demand. "The experiences collected in 1982," it warned, "confirm that every administrative restriction on consumption, such as issuing limits for stores, rationing for customers, concentrating provisions on the weekend, meat-free days in restaurants, and visible measures aimed at economizing supplies, . . . will lead to political discussions and frenetic hoarding behavior, which will quickly leap from meat and sausage products to other basic necessities. Instead of a decline in

---

1 Simmel, *Philosophie des Geldes*, p. 378.
2 SAPMO-BA, DY30, Vorläufige SED 31984, Ministerium für Handel und Versorgung, "Vorschläge zur Einflußnahme auf die Verbrauchsentwicklung bei Fleisch und Wurstwaren," 4.8.88, p. 1.
3 BArchB, DE1, 55384, Klopfer, "Persönliche Notizen über die Beratung im Politbüro des ZK der SED am 20.12.1988," 20.12.88, p. 2.

consumption, an uncontrolled increase in demand will set in, promoted by the fact that 37 percent of all households have freezers."[4] Following this advice, the Politburo tried to forestall a run on meat supplies by increasing the quantity of meat available. To do so, it reduced agricultural exports by DM 60 million and urged meat processors, retailers, and restaurants to make greater use of pork tails, entrails, and heads.[5]

As was so often the case, however, the SED's short-term solutions to long-term problems were mismatched. For starters, the causes of the meat shortfall in 1988-89 were the opposite of those at work during the crisis of 1982, when malnourishment had decimated animal populations. The East German animal husbandry sector had learned its lesson well, embarking on a successful campaign to fatten up its cattle. By 1989, the average weight of East German hogs had jumped to 151 kilos from 1982's low of 113. But this tremendous gain in weight also had significant drawbacks. The party's campaign to fatten up East German pigs simultaneously reduced the quality of the meat because the hogs added body fat rather than muscle tissue. Because of its unusually high fat content, many East Germans refused to buy the pork on offer.[6]

Not much meat was on offer, however. The animal husbandry sector's fat years coincided with the food processing industry's thin years, as Mittag's decision to curtail investment in the GDR's factories had created a dearth of functioning machines. Of the seventy-six abattoirs operating in the GDR, forty-four were run down and worn out. East German health inspectors lobbied to have these forty-four slaughterhouses closed on the grounds that they represented a serious risk to public health. Given the GDR's lax enforcement of health and safety standards, these abattoirs must have been in terrible shape. But the political imperative of making at least a show of providing consumers with meat, together with the shortage of capital equipment, outweighed other concerns. The party overruled the inspectors and ordered the unsanitary, run-down slaughterhouses to continue production.[7]

4 SAPMO-BA, DY30, Vorläufige SED 31984, Ministerium für Handel und Versorgung, "Vorschläge zur Einflußnahme auf die Verbrauchsentwicklung bei Fleisch und Wurstwaren," 4.8.88, p. 1.
5 Together with a halt to the "unprofitable" butter exports, this measure was expected to save the GDR around 500 million East German marks worth of subsidies (SAPMO-BA, DY30, IV 2/2.039.64, Politburo meeting from 16.8.88, pp. 28–9; SAPMO-BA, DY30, IV 2/2 039/268, "Bericht zu den Ergebnissen der Tätigkeit der in den Bezirken und Kreisen eingesetzten Arbeitsgruppen zur Verbesserung der Versorgung der Bevölkerung mit Fleisch und Wurstwaren, Obst und Gemüse sowie Getränken," no date, p. 142).
6 SAPMO-BA, DY30, IV 2/2 039/268, "Bericht zu den Ergebnissen," no date, p. 142; SAPMO-BA, DY30, Vorläufige SED 31984, cable from Walde to Honecker, 17.5.82, p. 1.
7 SAPMO-BA, DY30, IV 2/2 039/268, "Bericht zu den Ergebnissen," no date, p. 141.

The hogs that were slaughtered, moreover, could not always be delivered because the transport sector possessed few refrigerated trucks and railroad cars that still functioned. When pig carcasses were delivered, the poorly outfitted meat-processing sector, with its worn-out equipment, was over-matched by their corpulence. Because of a shortage of "trained experts," the meat processors often delivered whole carcasses rather than the smaller, more manageable portions stipulated by regulation.[8] That placed the onus of carving the meat on workers at the meat counters in retail stores, a job that was not particularly attractive to begin with. The sales staff was called upon to carve the meat into individual portions, a task considerably complicated by a shortage of knives and slicing machines. Without the necessary equipment, the sales staff was forced to work after business hours, and particularly on weekends, when they could prepack the meat without having to attend to customers.[9] Nor were they well compensated for what was dirty and back-breaking work under the best of conditions.[10] Their low pay resulted from a confluence of Marxist-Leninist ideology and working-class traditions, which privileged production over services, and the traditional distribution of labor along gender lines, which ensured that the sales staff was overwhelmingly female.[11] Despite the SED's progressive rhetoric, the labor of women was simply not valued by the regime as equivalent to that of men. Management claimed, for example, that this work was especially tough on women, who were not up to the "great amount of counting in their heads" required by the job.[12] Once again, the relation of money

8 At the VEB Fleischkombinat Leipzig, over 45 percent of the fixed capital was no longer functional. In the combine's main factory, 70 percent of the machines and 50 percent of the buildings that housed them were worn out. Nor were there enough forklifts or packing machines to go around. In the district of Neubrandenburg, moreover, deliveries had been reduced by half (ibid., pp. 139, 142–3). Whole carcasses were often delivered without being quartered or otherwise prepared, and many portions weighed more than 40 kilos (SAPMO-BA, DY30, Vorläufige SED 31984, Generaldirektion des volkseigenen Einzelhandels [HO], "Bericht über die Untersuchung der Frage 'Warum wollen die Verkäuferinnen nicht am Fleischstand arbeiten,'" 22.9.89, p. 2, and "Ursachen für die nicht ausreichende Sicherung des Arbeitsvermögens," no date, p. 1).
9 SAPMO-BA, DY30, IV 2/2 039/268, "Bericht zu den Ergebnissen," no date, p. 145; SAPMO-BA, DY30, Vorläufige SED 31984, Generaldirektion des volkseigenen Einzelhandels [HO], "Bericht über die Untersuchung der Frage," 22.9.89, p. 2, and VdK der DDR, "Operative Versorgungskontrolle zu Problemen der Fleischversorgung in der Hauptstadt der DDR, Berlin," 26.9.89, p. 1.
10 Meat-counter clerks earned between 850 and 920 marks a month, considerably less than the average monthly wage of 1,280 marks (SAPMO-BA, DY30, Vorläufige SED 31984, Generaldirektion des volkseigenen Einzelhandels [HO], "Bericht über die Untersuchung der Frage," 22.9.89, p. 2; Staatliche Zentralverwaltung der Statistik [ed.], *Statistisches Jahrbuch der Deutschen Demokratischen Republik 1989*, p. 129).
11 SAPMO-BA, DY30, Vorläufige SED 31984, "Ursachen," no date, p. 2.
12 SAPMO-BA, DY30, Vorläufige SED 31984, Generaldirektion des volkseigenen Einzelhandels (HO), "Bericht über die Untersuchung der Frage," 22.9.89, p. 2.

Figure 9. Working at the meat counter in the Pomeranian town of Siedenbolltin, north of Neubrandenburg, 1985. (Courtesy of Bundesarchiv Koblenz, Bildarchiv, 183/1985/ 0919/401.)

to production and gender combined to disclose the discrepancy between theory and practice in the socialist state.

The excessive physical burden associated with the work, the lack of equipment, long hours, low pay, and minimal status led to permanent understaffing, which only increased the workload of the employees who stayed on.[13] Saleswomen began to quit, leaving the trickle of meat that arrived

---

13 Given that the HO management limited its investigation to Berlin, which as a rule enjoyed a superior supply of consumer goods, it is safe to assume that the situation in the rest of the Republic was even worse (ibid., p. 1; SAPMO-BA, DY30, Vorläufige SED 31984, VdK der DDR, "Operative Versorgungskontrolle," 26.9.89, p. 1).

uncut, unpacked, and unsold. By mid–1989, meat counters in department and grocery stores were suffering from a shortage of workers, operating with 20–50 percent fewer employees than they required, as well as meat. The dearth of workers, together with the shortage of meat, forced stores to reduce their opening hours or close down entirely. In the town of Waß-mannsdorf in the district of Potsdam, for example, a community of 1,200 people, the local meat shop closed its doors for the entire month of July 1989.[14]

In an environment of such scarcity, incentives and opportunities for cor-ruption abounded. Employees often stole supplies from the workplace for use at home or sale on the black market, a problem endemic to Soviet-style economies.[15] In the GDR, however, working conditions in retail stores had deteriorated by the mid-1980s to the point where theft was perceived by workers as appropriate compensation for being overworked and under-paid. Employees of the Kaufhalle department store Datzberg in the city of Neubrandenburg, for example, stole 67,600 marks worth of material between October 1987 and April 1988 – double the thefts in previous years. Likewise, East German meat-counter clerks had no difficulty legitimating petty theft as a form of just recompense for their low pay and poor working conditions.[16] Most commonly, saleswomen saved the best cuts of meat for friends and family, paralleling the practice of misappropriation throughout the rest of the economy. Many also engaged in a form of profiteering, par-laying their structural position as distributors of scarce commodities into financial leverage over prospective customers. With increasing frequency, sales personnel hid choice pieces of meat and sold them at a personal profit to those customers willing to pay more.

The development of black markets represented a serious threat to the SED's grip on power. This form of petty theft saddled the primary

---

14 SAPMO-BA, DY30, Vorläufige SED 31984, Generaldirektion des volkseigenen Einzelhandels (HO), "Bericht über die Untersuchung der Frage," 22.9.89, p. 2. Turnover was so high that 127 clerks left Berlin meat counters during the first eight months of 1989 (SAPMO-BA, DY30, Vorläufige SED 31984, "Ursachen," no date, pp. 1–2). Out of 300 butchers in the Dresden district, 12 had completely shut down. Others turned to Vietnamese, Mozambican, and Polish migrant workers to fill the gap (SAPMO-BA, DY30, IV 2/2 039/268, "Bericht zu den Ergebnissen," no date, pp. 141, 145).

15 Istvan Gábor, "The Second Economy in Socialism: General Lessons of the Hungarian Experience," in János Timár (ed.), *Papers on Labour Economics* (Budapest, 1984); János Kenedi, *Do It Yourself: Hungary's Hidden Economy* (London, 1981). For East German examples, from paper tissues to soap, see SAPMO-BA, DY30, Vorläufige SED 41853, Komitee der ABI, Arbeitsgruppe für Organisation und Inspektion beim Ministerrat, Staatliche Finanzrevision, no date, p. 6; SAPMO-BA, DY30, Vorläufige SED 31984, Generaldirektion des volkseigenen Einzelhandels (HO), "Bericht über die Untersuchung der Frage," 22.9.89, p. 2.

16 SAPMO-BA, DY30, Vorläufige SED 41853, Komitee der ABI, Arbeitsgruppe für Organisation und Inspektion beim Ministerrat, Staatliche Finanzrevision, no date, p. 6; SAPMO-BA, DY30, Vorläufige SED 31984, Generaldirektion des volkseigenen Einzelhandels (HO), "Bericht über die Untersuchung der Frage," 22.9.89, p. 2.

Production

economy with higher costs of feeding the population, adding to the financial burdens shouldered by the socialist state. Because of the SED's paternalist approach to the economic welfare of the population, however, East Germans continued to hold the party responsible for the shortages, no matter how much they personally benefited from their participation in the black market. More importantly, these scarce commodities – often referred to as "bend-over goods" (*Bück-Dich-Waren*) because of the motion required by the clandestine, under-the-counter transaction – were distributed according to principles that contradicted socialist notions of exchange.[17] The shortages fostered the growth of a parallel economy that made use of informal distribution networks based on personal ties or capitalist principles. Driven by personal gain and the profit motive, this illegal trade made use of the very market mechanisms that East German socialism abhorred.

But the black, or secondary, market in scarce commodities did not simply pose an ideological threat to the planned economy.[18] It also undermined the value of the East German mark, reducing the power of the SED to direct commercial activity. The black market employed alternate media of exchange, from social connections to barterable goods and Western money, which stood in direct competition to socialist money. Not only did the principles embodied by these illegal currencies contradict the ideal of consumer egalitarianism advanced by the SED, but West German money also began to displace socialist money as an instrument of exchange in many other sectors of the economy. As a result, the black market accelerated the very process of social differentiation and materialism that the SED had devoted itself to eradicating, dividing those who had access to capitalist money from those who did not, and engendering avarice, envy, and the desire for social status where equality and solidarity should have reigned. The illegal trade in scarce commodities also diminished the SED's control over how resources were distributed, placing material constraints on the ability of planners to realize the social priorities of the center. Ironically, it was the SED's own

---

17 As one woman writing to complain about the chronic shortages remarked, "children's juices are shortage goods or 'bend-over goods'; without connections nothing works" (BArchB, DL1, 26395, petition from 13.10.89).

18 A "black" market arises when excess demand that is regulated by officially fixed prices induces sellers to ask prices that exceed legal limitations. In contrast, a "gray" market stems from an excess of supply. To protect producers, the state sets a minimum price, as is often the case with agricultural products. If the state price is too high to attract sufficient demand, producers will try to sell their merchandise at a lower price than legally permitted. The term "secondary" market deemphasizes the legal content of responses to excess supply or demand while emphasizing the interdependence between the "primary" or "official" market and the various responses to it, illegal though they may be. Given the importance of the state as an economic actor in Soviet-style regimes, I prefer to emphasize the costs associated with circumventing administrative forms of rationing.

mismanagement of the economy – its constant generation and exacerbation of shortages – that had created the black market in the first place.

For these reasons, serious shortages of long duration always had the potential of becoming a political issue. During most of 1988 and 1989, East German consumers were confronted with closed stores, overworked saleswomen, a scarcity of meat, and – when it could be found at all – a choice between fatty meat or better-quality meat obtainable only through extralegal means. In response to prodding from party leaders concerned about consumer dissatisfaction, the management of the retail trade combine Handelsorganisation (HO) launched a thorough investigation of the saleswomen. In the end, management proposed a solution designed to ease the labor shortage by restoring the primacy of the East German mark. Rather than call for the purchase of new equipment to improve working conditions, the managers recommended increasing wages and introducing bonuses for the saleswomen. For the first time in this sector, the socialist regime accepted market-based solutions to imbalances in supply and demand, using income incentives to ease shortages.[19]

Injecting more East German marks into the money supply did not, however, put an end to black market activities. In fact, the increasingly frequent shortages opened up new opportunities for forms of exchange that did not include socialist money. As the East German mark, unable to overcome the conditions of shortage, retreated into a partially effective medium of exchange, other media of exchange, from social connections to barterable goods and capitalist currency, achieved what socialist money could not. The fragmentation of the East German economy into socialist and capitalist (or administered and supply-and-demand driven) spheres of exchange paralleled the fractured unity of money in the GDR brought about by SED policy. The most important consequence was the inversion of Georg Simmel's postulate that money furthers economic and therefore political integration, thus providing despotic regimes with an important instrument of subjugation: The disaggregation of money in the GDR into an object of limited equivalency was accompanied by the separation out of economic realms no longer amenable to central control. Through its own actions, the East German dictatorship had crippled one of its most effective instruments of power and fostered the growth of autonomous social organizations. It had undermined the currency of socialism.

---

19 SAPMO-BA, DY30, Vorläufige SED 31984, Abteilung Handel, Versorgung und Außenhandel to Abteilung Parteiorgane, 21.8.89, p. 1, VdK der DDR, "Operative Versorgungskontrolle," 26.9.89, p. 2, and "Ursachen," no date, p. 2; Merkel, *Utopie und Bedürfnis*, pp. 191–4.

By the mid-1980s, acute shortages had become an important feature of life in the GDR, with little prospect of relief. Despite massive financial aid from West Germany, Honecker's consumer policies continued to devour resources that should have been earmarked for investment, while the planned economy continued to prove itself unable to innovate or increase labor productivity. After a brief improvement in the GDR's trading position, the socialist state was threatened with insolvency again in the late 1980s. Living standards began to fall. Honecker and Mittag responded by returning to the desperate measures of the early 1980s, subordinating socialist economic activity to the imperative of earning capitalist money. By monetizing commercial operations, however, Mittag's policies forced vast areas of the GDR's official economy, from the Intershops to the medical profession, to operate along market-oriented lines. In contrast to its humanist precepts, the SED actively subordinated the welfare of East Germans as individuals to the goal of amassing more hard currency.

PRODUCTION VERSUS PRODUCTIVITY

Despite the West German government's aid to the GDR and Mittag's clever attempts to prolong the respite it provided, the problems confronting the East German economy could not be solved by quick financial fixes. Honecker's refusal to cut spending on consumer goods, coupled with his willingness to cannibalize East German industry for immediate profit, worked for a time. Aided by high prices for petrochemical goods, the GDR posted trade surpluses from 1981 to 1986. Even to party leaders who were privy only to Mittag's misrepresentations, the threat of insolvency appeared to recede.

But the party could not control all aspects of commerce, despite its pretensions. As soon as oil prices fell in the wake of the Iran–Iraq War, the GDR's balance of payments turned negative once again.[20] Other exogenous factors, such as bad weather, continued to place great strain on the GDR's resources. The winter of 1986–87, for example, was so severe that Mittag had to call out the army to unload shipments of coal to heat the hard-hit towns of Magdeburg and Cottbus. In Leipzig, 100,000 people living in 35,000 houses had no heat in the dead of an unusually cold winter.[21]

---

20 Between 1986 and 1988, the GDR earned DM 4 billion less than anticipated because of falling prices (BArchB, DE1, 56317, Mittag to Honecker, no date, Anlage, "Übersicht über das Wirken ökonomischer Faktoren in der Volkswirtschaft der DDR seit Mitte der siebziger Jahre," p. 2; BStU, Arbeitsbereich Mittig, Nr. 58, "Zu den ausgewählten Problemen," p. 10).
21 SAPMO-BA, DY30, JIV 2/2/2215, Politbüro-Sitzung vom 21. April 1987, "Anlage Bericht und Vorschläge zur Sicherung der Entwicklung der Energiewirtschaft unter Berücksichtigung der Schluß-

Despite bad luck with prices for natural resources and the weather, however, most of the GDR's problems were homemade. Because Mittag had channeled the slim revenues the GDR earned into reducing the debt and placating East German consumers, little investment flowed back into the GDR's industrial base. By the mid-1980s, production was hobbled by a dearth of new and efficient fixed capital. As a proportion of the plan, the investment rate for the "productive" sector stood at 16.1 percent of budgeted expenditures in 1970, but had fallen to 9.9 percent by 1989. Even more discouraging, investments in production were completely outstripped by investments in the "nonproductive" sector, rising only 22 percent for the period between 1970 and 1989, compared to 200 percent for consumer goods and services. The SED had also run down the GDR's social infrastructure. Honecker's pet housing project, for example, consumed most of the resources directed toward improving living standards, to the detriment of health care and other goods and services.[22]

The State Planning Commission bewailed the tilt away from investment in economically "useful" purposes. Taking the East German school system to task, it lamented that "the educational structure does not sufficiently correspond to that of an industrial society with a primary orientation toward productive goals. Too many historians, psychologists, lawyers, and art historians are being educated."[23] The production–oriented mentality inspired by central planning converged with the antipathy toward cultural criticism promoted by an authoritarian state to depict the craft of symbolic analysis as frivolous. Except as apologists for the SED's rule, historians were not wanted.

Honecker's prodigality in the social sphere, paired with Mittag's parsimony in the industrial sphere, combined to throttle investment in the GDR's industrial base. Without new technology, however, efforts to maintain, much less increase, productivity rates could not succeed. On the one hand, the East German workplace was undermechanized. As late as 1987, for example, 40.4 percent of East German jobs still relied on manual labor.[24] On the other hand, the machines that were integrated into the production process broke down constantly from age and overuse. Perhaps the single most

folgerungen aus dem Winter 1986/87"; SAPMO-BA, DY30, IV 2/2.039/83, "Sitzung des Sekretariats des ZK vom 19.8.87," p. 139; Bryson and Melzer, *The End of the East German Economy*, p. 22.

22 SAPMO-BA, DY30, JIV 2/2A/3252, Schürer, "Analyse der ökonomischen Lage," 30.10.89, p. 5.

23 BArchB, DE1, 56318, "Es sollte eine Überprüfung der Entwicklung der Investitionen," no date, p. 2.

24 This was a marginal improvement over the 41.4 percent registered in 1980 (BArchB, DE1, 56756, Wenzel, "Zum Stand," p. 207).

important factor contributing to the inefficiency of East German industry was the age of its fixed capital. By 1989, only 27 percent of all equipment in the East German manufacturing, mining, and energy sectors was five years old or less, compared to 35 percent of all machines in West Germany. Particularly telling was the prominence of obsolescent machines in the GDR: Fully half of all East German plant was more than ten years old, compared to only 35 percent for the Federal Republic.[25] According to its own calculations, the number of worn-out machines still in use rose from 47.1 percent in 1975 to 53.8 percent in 1988.[26]

An important indication of the pressing need for renewal of the GDR's capital stock was the increasing frequency and gravity of industrial accidents, mechanical failures, and factory fires. In the mid-1980s, the Stasi, which was consistently critical of Mittag's leadership, reported that costly accidents and failures were on the rise. By the end of the decade, a combination of age, overuse, and relaxed safety standards had taken its toll on East German manufacturing.[27]

The impediments to production augmented local resistance to economic steering from the center. To give but one example, factory directors in the Leipzig district balked at the center's proposed production increases during negotiations over the plan in June 1987. Refusal to participate in the political theater created around bargaining over planning targets was no small event in the economic life of the GDR, especially in light of the center's growing financial desperation.[28] In their defense, factory managers notified their superiors that old and run-down machines as well as the lack of investment made contemplating increased production impossible. They also complained that the lack of complementarity forced much of the machinery that did function to remain idle. In a report to Berlin, the Leipzig party leadership related that managers frequently mentioned "the lack of spare parts, which leads to underuse of basic equipment and to increasing difficulties. Thus,

25 BStU, Arbeitsbereich Mittig, Nr. 58, "Zu den ausgewählten Problemen," pp. 16–17, and Anlage 5, p. 42; *Neues Deutschland*, 11.1.90; Bryson and Melzer, *The End of the East German Economy*, p. 87; Kusch et al., *Schlußbilanz*, p. 56.

26 Likewise, the amount of moribund equipment in the construction sector rose from 49 to 67 percent, in the transportation sector from 48.4 to 52.1 percent, and in the agricultural, forestry, and food-processing sectors from 50.2 to 61.3 percent (BArchB, DE1, 55384, Klopfer, "Persönliche Notizen über ein Gespräch beim Mitglied des Politbüros und Sekretär des ZK der SED, Genossen Dr. Mittag," 23.11.88, p. 6; BStU, Arbeitsbereich Mittig, Nr. 58, "Zu den ausgewählten Problemen," pp. 12–13).

27 Between April 1984 and April 1985, the Stasi recorded eight accidents and fires causing 15 million East German marks in damage. In the following twelve months, the number of industrial mishaps doubled, nearly quadrupling the damages. These losses doubled again in 1986, with accidents and fires causing 134 million marks worth of damage, then soared to 508 million in 1987 (Haendcke-Hoppe-Arndt, *Die Hauptabteilung XVIII*, pp. 96–7).

28 See the discussion of planning negotiations as political ritual in Kopstein, *The Politics of Economic Decline*, pp. 131–72.

the sanitation department of the city of Leipzig cannot utilize a portion of its equipment."[29] But for the lack of spare parts, the garbage in the GDR's second largest city could not be collected.

The GDR's creaking infrastructure created yet another obstacle to the effective use of scarce resources. The Workers' and Peasants' Inspectorate, which was responsible for monitoring the state apparatus, reported in 1988 that barely half of the warehouses in the GDR met the regime's rather loosely defined construction standards. The other 45 percent had holes in the roof through which rain dripped onto foodstuffs, consumer goods, and machinery and ruined them.[30] Nor did factories possess the tools to store their wares correctly. The government estimated in 1988 that the GDR had only 28 percent of the forklifts that its industry required.[31]

The East German distribution network fared little better. In a desperate plea for resources, Transport Minister Otto Arndt warned in 1987 that the East German rail system serviced only 80 percent of destinations, that the main lines were operating entirely without spare parts, and that breakdowns necessitated speed restrictions at over 1,000 junctions. Nor was the trucking industry able to take up the slack. In the district of Magdeburg alone, for example, 283 out of 399 trucks were more than ten years old. Arndt complained that streets in the GDR had fallen into disrepair, with only one-third of regional roads open to traffic.[32] In fact, the maintenance of public space had deteriorated so much that the Workers' and Peasants' Inspectorate felt impelled in 1988 to investigate the state of sanitation in the GDR. After checking the toilets in over 10,000 stores and 6,000 restaurants, it classified more than half as substandard. The worst cases involved restaurant facilities in which fecal matter had not been removed for years.[33]

---

29 SAPMO-BA, DY30, Vorläufige SED 40080, SED-Bezirksleitung Leipzig, "Information über die Führung der Plandiskussion zum Volkswirtschaftsplan 1988 und der eingehenden Beratung seiner Ziele und Aufgaben mit den Werktätigen im Bezirk Leipzig," 22.6.87, pp. 2–3.

30 SAPMO-BA, DY30, Vorläufige SED 41853, Komitee der ABI, Arbeitsgruppe für Organisation und Inspektion beim Ministerrat, Staatliche Finanzrevision, no date, Anlage 1, p. 5. Other problems included high humidity and aging storage space, some of which was from the fifteenth century.

31 SAPMO-BA, DY30, Vorläufige SED 41853, Komitee der ABI, Arbeitsgruppe für Organisation und Inspektion beim Ministerrat, Staatliche Finanzrevision, no date, Anlage 1, p. 5, and Komitee der ABI, Inspektion Chemische Industrie, 12.7.88, p. 3. The forklift problem was so severe that it was discussed at a Politbüro meeting on 2.2.88 (SAPMO-BA, DY30, IV 2/2.039/58, p. 6) and again during the revolution of 1989 by the ZK (SAPMO-BA, DY30, IV 2/1/710, 2. Beratungstag, 9.11.89, p. 115).

32 BArchB, DE1, 56285, Staatssekretär der Staatlichen Plankommission, "Persönliche Niederschrift über die Beratung mit dem Minister für Verkehrswesen zu den staatlichen Aufgaben 1988," 26.2.87, p. 3; SAPMO-BA, DY30, IV 2/2 039/268, "Bericht zu den Ergebnissen," no date, pp. 142–8.

33 SAPMO-BA, DY30, Vorläufige SED 41853, Komitee der ABI, Inspektion Handel und Versorgung, "Bericht über Ergebnisse der Massenkontrolle zur Durchsetzung von Ordnung, Sauberkeit und Hygiene in gesellschaftlichen Einrichtungen des Territoriums – Bereich Handel und Versorgung," 24.5.88.

The decrepit infrastructure often conspired with production bottlenecks to bring work to a complete standstill. In a 1988 meeting, Finance Minister Ernst Höfner observed that the rapid deterioration of the East German industrial base had led to "an ever-increasing portion of working time consumed by breakdowns" of machines. Indeed, factory idleness resulting from production bottlenecks and the lack of complementarity continued to rise throughout the 1980s.[34] Material problems, moreover, were compounded by poorly conceived service and distribution schedules. Insulated against costs and customers, enterprises focused on production, not delivery. Without financial incentives, only observational discipline through such supervisory agencies as the Workers' and Peasants' Inspectorate could reduce delays in delivery. After a series of spot checks in 1988, for example, the Inspectorate observed that truck drivers completed their deliveries hours before their shifts ended, then sat around idly. Often they could not complete their assigned deliveries because of the arbitrary closing times of stores, which had little incentive to load and unload deliveries. In the first seven months of 1988, the Inspectorate estimated that 353 million marks worth of consumer goods failed to reach stores because of delivery delays and contractual abrogations.[35]

The planned economy's emphasis on production volume, moreover, resulted in indifference to quality as long as the assigned volume of production was met. This so-called tonnage ideology, a key feature of Stalinist economies, proved extraordinarily wasteful. In 1988, for example, the Workers' and Peasants' Inspectorate reported that around 23,000 color televisions, or about 8.2 percent of the units manufactured annually in the GDR, had to be returned to the factory because they were defective. Worse still, some 40 percent of the television sets that finally made it out of the store required repairs.[36]

---

34 BArchB, DE1, 55384, Klopfer, "Persönliche Notizen über die Beratung beim amtierenden Vorsitzenden des Ministerrates am 25.10.1988," 25.10.88, p. 7; BArchB, DE1, 56756, Wenzel, "Zum Stand," p. 209.

35 SAPMO-BA, DY30, Vorläufige SED 41853, Komitee der ABI, Inspektion Handel und Versorgung, "Bericht zur Kontrolle 'Effektiver Einsatz des Transportraumes im Territorium zur Sicherung des Warenumschlages bei Frischwaren und ausgewählten Industriewaren,'" 25.07.88, p. 3, and Komitee der ABI, Arbeitsgruppe für Organisation und Inspektion beim Ministerrat, Staatliche Finanzrevision, no date, p. 6.

36 SAPMO-BA, DY30, Vorläufige SED 41853, Komitee der ABI, Arbeitsgruppe für Organisation und Inspektion beim Ministerrat, Staatliche Finanzrevision, no date, Anlage 6, "Zur Überprüfung der Bestände im Zentralen Warenkontor Technik, Kulturwaren und Sportartikel," p. 2, and "Bemerkungen zum 'Bericht zur Arbeit mit den Warenbeständen im Konsumgüterbinnenhandel,'" p. 8; SAPMO-BA, DY30, Vorläufige SED 41850, "Information über einige Probleme aus dem Monatsbericht des Genossen Schumann, Bezirksleitung Leipzig," no date, p. 7.

Despite Mittag's efforts to husband scarce resources, the SED's elimination of money in the production sector rendered East German industry indifferent to cost concerns. By its own measure, for example, the GDR used energy less efficiently than any country in the world except for the United States and Canada. Despite having one-third of the population and far less industrial output, the GDR consumed 30 percent more energy than did West Germany. Focused on meeting planning targets rather than pleasing their customers, moreover, East German exporters neglected quality controls. In January 1982 alone, for example, defects in manufacturing and packaging cost the GDR DM 220 million.[37]

The deterioration of machines, the constant interruption of production due to bottlenecks, and arrhythmic work schedules weighed heavily on working conditions. Long periods of inactivity punctuated by "storming," or the practice of meeting production deadlines by deploying all available labor around the clock, loosened worker identification with factory production.[38] The constant shortage of consumer goods, moreover, helped justify the decision of employees to leave the workplace and stand in line for the commodities they desired. Because the East German mark did not suffice to overcome these shortages, factory managers could do little to influence workers. As a result, worker absenteeism became common, rising drastically between 1984 and 1987. Because of no-shows, the GDR lost 256 hours a year per employee in 1987 – compared to 134 in the Federal Republic, 142 in France, 64 in the United States, and 35 in Japan – at an estimated cost of 500 million East German marks. By 1989, unexcused absences had climbed to an average of six hours a week per worker.[39] Despite the SED's slogan "Work Time Is Performance Time" (*Arbeitszeit ist Leistungszeit*), moreover, employees who stayed on the job often did not work. As Willi Stoph, Chairman of the Council of Ministers, exclaimed in exasperation in 1988, "people really have to work during working hours."[40]

---

37 BArchB, DE1, 56285, Klopfer, "Persönliche Niederschrift über die Beratung der Wirtschaftskommission beim Politbüro am 9. Januar 1989," 10.1.89, pp. 18–19; BArchB, DE1, 56287, Klopfer, "Niederschrift über die Beratung des Ministerrates am 11. Februar 1982 zur Erfüllung des Volkswirtschaftsplanes 1982 – Monat Januar," 11.2.82, p. 251.

38 For more on the practice of storming, see Kopstein, *The Politics of Economic Decline*, p. 229, fn. 26. For more on the incentives to hoard labor, see Kornai, *The Socialist System*, pp. 223–4.

39 BArchB, DE1, 56756, Wenzel, "Zum Stand," p. 209; BArchB, DE1, 56285, "Zum Umrechnungsverhältnis der Mark," no date, p. 7; BArchB, DE1, 55384, Klopfer, "Persönliche Notizen über eine Beratung im Politbüro des ZK der SED am 14.2.1989," 14.2.89, p. 8.

40 BArchB, DE1, 56285, "Arbeitsniederschrift über eine Beratung beim Generalsekretär des ZK der SED, Genossen Erich Honecker, zu den Materialien des Entwurfs der staatlichen Aufgaben 1989," 6.9.88, p. 3; SAPMO-BA, DY30, Vorläufige SED 41852, letter to Honecker from 21.5.85.

Table 4. *Comparative Productivity Rates: SED Estimates*
as of 1989 (GDR = 100)

Country	Productivity Rate
United States	157
France	142
Federal Republic	139
Canada	135
Great Britain	105
GDR	100
Italy	98
Czechoslovakia	84
USSR	79
Hungary	66
Poland	53

Source: BArchB, DE1, 56323, "Rentabilität des Exportes der
DDR," no date, p. 585.

No matter how one measured it, East German productivity was declining, in comparison both to its previous accomplishments and to the West.
In the 1970s, Honecker's aides estimated East German productivity at 70
percent of West German productivity. By 1980, they calculated that this
figure had dropped to 57 percent, although it appeared to recover to about
61 percent by 1987.[41] After the palace coup against Honecker in October
1989, State Planning Commissioner Gerhard Schürer offered a more accurate estimate, revealing that worker productivity in the GDR came to about
40 percent of West German levels.[42] Contemporary Western estimates were
a bit more generous, placing East German productivity at 50 percent of West
German levels.[43] Even if the GDR compared poorly to its West German
competitor, the SED's economic experts believed that it fared well against
its socialist allies. As Table 4 illustrates, they reckoned that East German
productivity was higher than other Soviet bloc states', nearly on par with
Great Britain and Italy, but significantly lower than France, West Germany,

41 BArchB, DE1, 56318, "Eine Bemerkung zu der Frage," 30.8.88, p. 2; BArchB, DE1, 56285, "Zum
   Umrechnungsverhältnis der Mark," no date, p. 6.
42 SAPMO-BA, DY30, JIV 2/2A/3252, Politbüro-Sitzung vom 31.10.89, Schürer, "Analyse der
   ökonomischen Lage," 30.10.89, p. 4; BArchB, DN1, VS 13/90, Nr. 7, Staatliche Zentralverwaltung
   für Statistik, "Zu Grundproblemen bei der Durchführung der Wirtschafts- und Sozialpolitik in den
   Jahren 1986 bis 1989," 7.11.89; *Neues Deutschland*, 11.1.90.
43 The German Institute for Economics in Berlin and the Institute for World Economy in Kiel overestimated East German productivity at 50 percent of West German levels (*Handelsblatt*, 8.2.90; Bryson
   and Melzer, *The End of the East German Economy*, pp. 87, 98).

and the United States. The notion that East German productivity was on par with British levels is incongruous, despite decades of neglect of Great Britain's infrastructure. But the growing gap with other industrial powers gave party officials little cause for celebration.

By the late 1980s, the planned economy's indifference to money had become an expensive liability on international markets. Declining East German productivity translated into deteriorating terms of trade for the GDR.[44] According to the SED's own calculations, the planned economy's export profitability fell precipitously during the 1980s. Finance Minister Höfner estimated that the GDR earned more than 10 billion East German marks less in 1987 for the same amount of goods they had sold to the West in 1985. East German enterprises, he calculated, required 10.2 marks to earn one U.S. dollar, far more than under Ulbricht.[45] Although some durable goods continued to find markets, other East German merchandise had become unprofitable as profit margins were squeezed by the declining efficiency of East German capital equipment.[46] By 1989, the GDR was earning 20 West German pfennigs for every Ostmark worth of goods it exported to the West.[47]

It is worth noting, however, that representations of comparative productivity and costs suffer from incommensurable differences in economic organization between the East and West. Most significantly, the SED's political imperatives saddled East German producers with tremendous social responsibilities not shared by their Western counterparts, which made life a little easier for workers but increased unit costs considerably. As the SED's economic experts phrased it, "industrial prices in the GDR reflect first of all domestic costs, which also include extensive social expenditures that are not an element of costs under capitalist conditions."[48] For example, the SED

---

44 According to economists at the State Planning Commission, the FRG benefited from improving terms of trade between 1971 and 1987 by some $152 billion, while the GDR lost about $22 billion from unfavorable terms of trade (Kusch et al., *Schlußbilanz*, p. 52).
45 BArchB, DN1, VS 13/90, Höfner, Nr. 1, "Analyse der Entwicklung der Zuschüsse des Staatshaushaltes für den Export in das sozialistische und nichtsozialistische Wirtschaftsgebiet," 6.3.87, pp. 3–14.
46 In 1988, for example, offset printers, which were one of the GDR's most successful export items, earned DM 1 for every 0.60 East German marks worth of value put into them, while transistors earned DM 1 for every 17.28 marks (BArchB, DE1, 56285, "Zum Umrechnungsverhältnis der Mark," no date, p. 8). These figures do not reflect the subsidies enjoyed by manufacturers on producer goods.
47 BArchB, DE1, 56285, Klopfer, "Persönliche Notizen über die Beratung beim Generalsekretär," 16.5.89, p. 47.
48 BArchB, DE1, 56318, "Zur Frage, was erforderlich ist," 8.9.88, p. 2.

located a variety of social services at the factory, from health and child-care services to grocery stores and festival halls. Socialist enterprises, such as the VEB Berliner Glühlampenwerk "Rosa Luxemburg" and the VEB Schwermaschinenbau "S.M. Kirow" Leipzig, underwrote such basic conveniences as lunch and vacations for their workers.[49] The Berliner Glühlampenwerk, for example, spent 1,961 marks annually per employee on its cafeteria and 511 marks on each worker's vacation, compared to 379 and 383 marks, respectively, for the Kirow. Under Honecker, factories expanded benefits to workers, offering time off to do housework, paid leaves to women nearing the end of pregnancy, and a sabbatical of one year for new mothers to stay at home with their babies.

Yet the social obligations of the enterprises toward their workers did not end with generous time off or social services. The Berliner Glühlampenwerk, for example, maintained a factory school and an academy, employing eighty-two people who were paid a total of 1.8 million marks a year. For its part, the Kirow built and maintained a cultural center and a restaurant, which became important fixtures for the local community, frequented not just by workers, but also by other Leipzig residents. Yet the state did not reimburse the Kirow for the 364,000 marks a year it cost to run the center and the restaurant. Instead, these "cultural" expenditures were factored into the costs of production.

Social services also took their toll on the structure of the workforce, adding more white collar workers to factory payrolls. Some 7.4 percent of the workers at the Berliner Glühlampenwerk, for example, were employed solely for the purpose of putting on "cultural and social" events, compared to 3.4 percent at the Kirow. For every manager, moreover, the Berliner Glühlampenwerk employed 3.45 workers on the production line, while the Kirow employed 2.10 workers per manager.[50] In fact, 16.1 percent of all employees in East German industry were managers.[51]

However much the broad array of social services offered by East German factories weighed on their productivity rates, the soft budget constraints under which they labored encouraged an indifference to costs. The primary goal of socialist enterprises was to fulfill the plan; few troubled

---

49 The following account is derived from BArchB, DE1, 56318, Ministerium der Finanzen, "Information über Untersuchungsergebnisse zur Kostenentstehung in 4 ausgewählten Betrieben für das Jahr 1987," 23.9.88, pp. 1–6.
50 The VEB Druckmaschinenwerke Leipzig had an even worse ratio, employing 1.86 workers in production for each manager (ibid., p. 2).
51 BArchB, DE1, 56285, "Zum Umrechnungsverhältnis der Mark," no date, p. 8.

themselves about expenses, whether they were related to production or not. The Berliner Glühlampenwerk, for example, had no compunction whatsoever about wasting money. In fact, the money it lost through the assessment of penalties for production delays, stallage, and defective inventory came to 28.5 million East German marks in 1987 – more than five times what the factory paid its workers.[52] "Some people act as if our money is worth nothing," grumbled Honecker in 1988.[53]

As the GDR's industrial base began to crumble, Mittag began to see the social obligations of East German factories as an impediment to economic efficiency. Frustrated by reports of falling productivity, he called for cost accounting to render the difference between manufacturing and welfare transparent – a rather bold move, even for a politician who advocated the monetization of the socialist economy. "We should really evaluate how the social components affect the factories," Mittag blurted out during a meeting with other economic leaders in 1988. "Otherwise, one can arrive at false comparisons of increases in productivity." Although the Economic Secretary fell shy of proposing a reduction in the provision of social welfare through factories, he did seek to uncouple production from social services by arguing for the frugal use of resources. During the meeting, Mittag cast the entire system into doubt, observing that "we must decide if we want it to continue this way or not. . . . Perhaps the costs are not even distributed appropriately? We are really distorting the entire cost structure? . . . And we stick the enterprises with everything."[54] As always, however, Mittag was more concerned about the representation of costs, rather than the costs themselves, because they could be manipulated to reflect his stewardship of the economy in a positive light. Predictably, nothing came of this surprisingly frank discussion.

The passivity of money, or its inability to shape the parameters of production, encouraged East German manufacturers to neglect the financial conditions of trade with the West. During the 1980s, the cost of sales for exportable goods skyrocketed: That is, in addition to the domestic expenses of production, which were denominated in East German marks, the hard-currency costs of obtaining customers for East German products rose during

---

52 BArchB, DE1, 56318, Ministerium der Finanzen, "Information über Untersuchungsergebnisse zur Kostenentstehung," 23.9.88, p. 6.
53 BArchB, DE1, 55384, Klopfer, "Persönliche Notizen über eine Beratung von Mitgliedern der Parteiführung," 22.11.88, p. 5.
54 BArchB, DE1, 56285, Klopfer, "Persönliche Notizen aus einer Beratung," 10.11.88, p. 5.

the 1980s,[55] outpacing increases in the volume of exports.[56] In 1981, for example, the Department of Trade, Supply, and Foreign Trade at the ZK calculated that on average the GDR spent DM 15.93 on marketing for every DM 1,000 worth of products they sold, or 1.6 percent of hard-currency revenues. By 1985, this figure had more than doubled, rising to DM 36.26 per DM 1,000 generated, or 3.6 percent. Thus, the Carl Zeiss Jena combine, which produced everything from computers to binoculars, spent 23.4 percent of its revenues on selling its products, while the Fortschritt Landmaschinen combine, which primarily sold agricultural equipment, spent 10 percent.[57]

The lack of financial constraints led East German producers to ignore the requirements of their Western clients, which often led them to incur large penalties for late deliveries and product defects. In 1983, for example, the GDR was forced to pay DM 105 million in penalties for breaches of contract, DM 125.3 million in interest fines for late shipments, 45 million East German marks in compensation for damages incurred to their partners, and over DM 30 million in other costs related to shipment problems. In 1989, the General Director of the Household Appliances combine expressed trepidation about traveling to France, normally a sought-after perquisite, because he was ashamed of his combine's shipment delays. As the GDR lost market share in the West, moreover, East German enterprises became desperate to retain customers, making it easier for Western commercial partners to wrest contractual concessions from them.[58]

55 Miscellaneous costs, such as commissions paid to sales staff and Western middlemen, rose from DM 256.7 million in 1981 to nearly 300 million in 1984, or nearly 60 percent of total marketing costs (SAPMO-BA, DY30, Vorläufige SED 36639, "Referat für eine Sonderberatung mit den Hauptbuchhaltern der Außenhandelsbetreibe/Dienstleistungsbetriebe," 18.10.81, p. 2; SAPMO-BA, DY30, Vorläufige SED 36640, Abteilung Handel, Versorgung und Außenhandel, "Entwicklung der Zirkulationskosten NSW in Valuta nach Außenhandelsbetrieben und Ländern," 17.4.85, p. 5). East German industry also incurred sizeable travel costs, despite remarkably restrictive policies on travel to the West. In 1984, for example, the socialist state spent a stunning DM 70 million on business trips for factory directors and sales staff. Finally, transportation costs were increased by security measures at the border. In 1981, these costs alone came to DM 2.93 billion (SAPMO-BA, DY30, Vorläufige SED 36640, Sektor Außenhandel, "Einschätzungen zur Entwicklung der Kosten im Jahre 1983 im Außenhandel und Maßnahmen zur weiteren Kostensenkung," 28.2.84, p. 4).

56 SAPMO-BA, DY30, Vorläufige SED 36640, Sektor Außenhandel, "Einschätzungen zur Entwicklung der Kosten," 28.2.84, p. 2.

57 SAPMO-BA, DY30, Vorläufige SED 36640, Sektor Außenhandel, "Information über die Entwicklung der Kosten im Außenhandel im Jahre 1982," 28.3.83, p. 2, and Abteilung Handel, Versorgung und Außenhandel, "Entwicklung der Zirkulationskosten," 17.4.85, p. 6.

58 SAPMO-BA, DY30, Vorläufige SED 36640, Abteilung Handel, Versorgung und Außenhandel, "Entwicklung der Zirkulationskosten," 17.4.85, p. 5; BArchB, DE1, 56285, Klopfer, "Persönliche Notizen über die Beratung beim Generalsekretär," 16.5.89, p. 17; SAPMO-BA, DY30, Vorläufige SED 36639, Sektor Außenhandel, "Information über die Entwicklung der Zahlungsbedingungen," 6.5.85, Abteilung Finanzökonomie, "Struktur und Entwicklung der Zahlungsbedingungen

THE SECONDARY MARKET

Arguably, the most significant indicator of the GDR's industrial decline was pecuniary. Despite the SED's antipathy toward money, the GDR's shortage of hard currency focused the party leadership's attention on the depreciation of the *Mark der DDR*. The ideological and practical politics of money in the GDR, however, made obtaining an accurate measure of the East German mark's value difficult. Like the money issued by most countries in the world, the East German mark was a nonconvertible currency. That is, the Ostmark was legal tender inside the GDR, but had no official value outside the GDR. The decision to construct a currency without any international value stemmed in part from an ideological hostility toward capitalism that abhorred money as a necessary evil, but found capital markets particularly objectionable.[59]

But a purely domestic currency also offered the communist party practical advantages. Nonconvertible money functioned as a buffer against integration with world markets, most of which were organized along capitalist principles. In addition, maintaining a nonconvertible currency freed the GDR from the costs of supporting it on international markets. Without capital markets to influence the price of money, for example, East Germans were not called upon to make the social sacrifices associated with tight money policies, such as unemployment, which ran counter to the basic tenets of economic planning. And without economic slowdowns induced by reductions in the money supply, the SED's social program was easier to achieve. Finally, a nonconvertible currency relieved the state of costly interventions on international markets to defend its currency against speculators. Thus, protection against the international division of labor embodied in capitalist markets provided the SED with greater control over economic affairs at home.

Despite the ideological prohibitions on comparing socialist with capitalist money, the empirical reality of trade with the West made it necessary for East German economists to inquire about the GDR's terms of trade. Rather than rely on black market rates, the party devised its own method of estimating how much it cost the GDR to sell its products on international markets. Officially, the SED perpetuated the political myth that 1 Ostmark

---

und Zahlungssicherheiten," and Sektor Außenhandel, "Information über die Erhöhung der Zahlungssicherheit," 24.10.83.

59 The idea of using money to protect domestic society from foreign influence goes back at least to Thomas More, who argues that money would not be necessary at home, but that foreign trade necessitated by the need for raw materials and national defense would make it expedient to use money abroad (More, *Utopia*, pp. 49–52).

was equivalent to 1 Westmark. For internal accounting purposes, however, the SED constructed a notational currency, the Valutamark, which permitted planners and factory managers to "reflect the relation between foreign currencies and the domestic cost of exports accurately."[60]

Although the SED officially insisted that "in no case is the Valutamark equivalent to a mark of the Federal Republic of Germany," Honecker's aides conceded that it "is practically equivalent to 1 DM."[61] To bridge the gap between the Valutamark and the Ostmark, communist financial experts devised a formula that consisted of adding a directional coefficient (Riko) to the Valutamark. The Riko, in turn, expressed the domestic cost to the GDR of its exports to hard-currency countries. As Honecker's economic advisors put it, the fixed rate between the Valutamark and the East German mark "is the average of official exchange rate relations between the *Mark der DDR* and currencies of the main capitalist countries. A comparison can be made to the so-called European currency, the so-called ECU."[62]

In other words, this convenient financial fiction permitted East German economists to assess how market forces valued socialist commodities and currency without contradicting the political myths about East German autonomy from Western trade.[63] Figure 10 traces the East German mark's loss of value over time as measured by exports to the West and consumer demand on the black market. By any calculation, it is clear that the East German mark declined sharply in strength against the West German mark during the 1980s. A comparison of the two German currencies against the dollar throws into relief just how striking the depreciation of the Ostmark was. Whereas the West German mark consistently gained ground against

---

60 BArchB, DE1, 56318, "Zur Frage, was erforderlich ist," 8.9.88, p. 2. As the State Planning Commission noted, "the Valutamark does not exist as a concrete currency of any country" (BArchB, DE1, 56318, "Eine Bemerkung zu der Frage," 30.8.88, p. 1).

61 BArchB, DE1, 56318, "Eine Bemerkung zu der Frage," 30.8.88, p. 1; BArchB, DE1, 56285, "Zum Umrechnungsverhältnis der Mark," no date, p. 2.

62 BArchB, DE1, 56318, "Eine Bemerkung zu der Frage," 30.8.88, p. 1.

63 In contrast to trade with nonsocialist countries, trade with Comecon members was denominated in a supranational notational currency, the transferable ruble. Exchange rates were nominally agreed upon bilaterally, though the Soviet Union clearly wielded the most influence. Despite higher East German productivity levels, the *Mark der DDR* was clearly undervalued against most other currencies, just as the DM was historically undervalued by its Western partners. In the 1980s, for example, the Soviets refused to increase the valuation of the transferable ruble against the East German mark from 7.5 to 6 East German marks. The reason was simple: At 7.5 marks to the transfer ruble, the GDR was forced to spend 320 million marks more on its annual obligation to provide room and board for the Soviet troops stationed on East German territory (BArchB, DN1, VS 13/90, letter to Mittag from 13.4.82, pp. 2–3, and Nr. 12, Groche, "Information über die Wirkung des Umrechnungsverhältnisses der Mark der DDR zum transferablen Rubel auf die wirtschaftliche Rechnungsführung," no date, pp. 1–3).

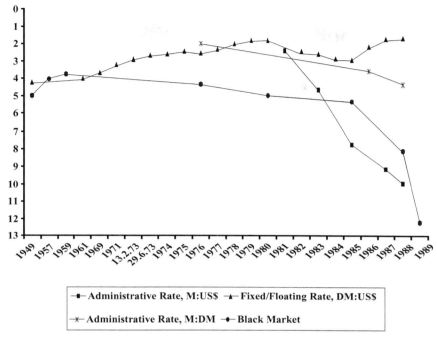

Figure 10. Value of the East German mark against the DM and US $, 1949–1989. *Sources:* SAPMO, DY30, 3702, "Die Entwicklung des Wechselstubengeschäfts und des Wechselstubenkurses," pp. 233–4; BStU, HA XVIII, 6166, p. 7; BStU, Arbeitsbereich Mittig, Nr. 58, "Zu den ausgewählten Problemen," pp. 21, 24; BArchB, DE1 56756, Schalck-Golodkowsky and König, "Zur Entwicklung des Kurses der Mark der DDR zu kapitalistischen Währungen seit 1989," no date, pp. 172–3, and Anhang 3; BArchB, DE1 56318, "Zur Frage, was erforderlich ist," 8.9.88, p. 3; and BArchB, DN1. VS 13/90, Nr. 6, Nickel and Kaminsky, "Einschätzung zur Stabilität," 26.10.89, p. 15.

the U.S. dollar, the SED's own calculations showed that the East German mark fell precipitously against the dollar.

Similarly, the domestic purchasing power of the Ostmark, which the regime constantly lauded as a measure of consumer access to high living standards, deteriorated rapidly in the 1980s. Like other Marxist-Leninist regimes, the GDR held prices of basic consumer goods stable.[64] In the

---

64 The East German claim regarding price stability rested on a rather dubious formality: Nominal prices rose modestly if at all, but the subsidies required to maintain price stability rose rapidly (BArchB, DN10, 2285, Abteilung Grundfonds, Staatsbank der DDR, "Argumentationsmaterial Wie ist die Kaufkraft der Mark der DDR einzuschätzen," 21.11.89, p. 2).

German context, where memories of the inflations of the 1920s and 1940s and the hardships they created were still very much alive, price stability resonated politically. Despite infrequent price increases, however, inflation did exist in the GDR, stimulated by shortages and Honecker's priming of the pump.

Some of the inflation experienced by the GDR was open inflation, or price pressures that were reflected in official statistics. Using a basket of goods of its own devising, for example, the Ministry of Finance conceded in 1989 that its calculations "registered a slightly downward trend of the purchasing power of the *Mark der DDR* against the DM."[65] This "downward trend" derived from the expansion of the GDR's monetary base for political purposes: Honecker pursued a strategy of creating the perception of prosperity by raising East German wages beyond what the East German economy could bear.[66] As Figures 11 and 12 demonstrate, the growth of East German wages outpaced the gains made in productivity as well as the amount of goods purchased by East Germans.[67] In addition, chronic shortages forced people to save their money, leading to an inflationary overhang of about 6 billion marks by 1988.[68] According to the Staatsbank, open inflation ran to a shocking 16.5 percent annually for the period between 1975 and 1988.[69]

The most important indications of inflation in the GDR, however, can be culled only from indirect evidence.[70] The ideological strictures on price increases prevented supply and demand from finding equilibrium through higher prices. Instead, the SED attempted to discipline excess demand through rationing and the enforced substitution of one good for another.

65 BArchB, DN1, VS 13/90, Nr. 2, Lebig, "Ergebnis des Kaufkraftvergleichs zwischen der Mark der DDR und der DM der BRD auf dem Gebiet des Bevölkerungsverbrauchs für das Jahr 1988," 13.7.89.
66 Ironically, the inflationary consequences of the pay increases were aggravated by financial incentives intended to raise productivity. Overtime pay skyrocketed as factory idleness resulting from production bottlenecks, the lack of complementarity, and worker absenteeism forced managers to make up delays by hoarding labor and creating more shifts (BArchB, DE1, 56756, Wenzel, "Zum Stand," no date, p. 213).
67 The greatest deterioration took place between 1985 and 1987, when the ratio of labor productivity to the average wage fell from 2.21 to 0.81 (BArchB, DE1, 56285, "Zum Umrechnungsverhältnis der Mark," no date, p. 7).
68 Savings on deposit for East German private individuals rose from 99.7 billion East German marks in 1980 to 141.8 billion in 1987. In 1989, moreover, the population was paid 5 billion East German marks in interest, more than the planned increase in consumer goods manufactured for the year (BStU, Arbeitsbereich Mittig, Nr. 58, "Zu den ausgewählten Problemen," Anlage 7, p. 43; BArchB, DE1, 55384, Klopfer, "Persönliche Notizen über ein Gespräch," 23.11.88).
69 BArchB, DN10, 2285, Abteilung Grundfonds, Staatsbank der DDR, "Argumentationsmaterial," 21.11.89, p. 2.
70 František Pindák, "Inflation under Central Planning," *Jahrbuch der Wirtschaft Osteuropas* 10:2 (1983), p. 96.

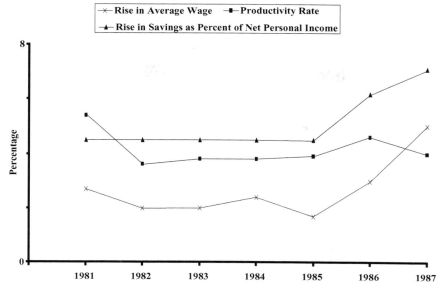

Figure 11. Open inflation in the GDR, 1981–1987, measured in terms of productivity. *Source:* BStU, Arbeitsbereich Mittig, Nr. 58, "Zu den ausgewählten Problemen," p. 19.

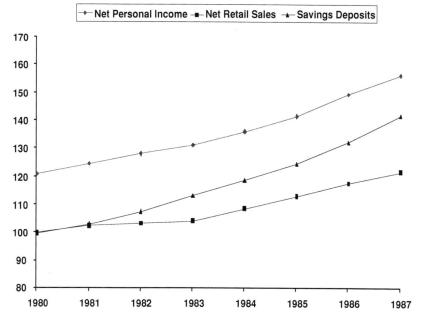

Figure 12. Open inflation in the GDR, 1980–1987, measured in terms of purchasing power (1980 = 100). *Source:* BStU, Arbeitsbereich Mittig, Nr. 58, "Zu den ausgewählten Problemen," p. 18, and Anlage 7, p. 43.

171

The party was able to divert some demand into savings accounts, where it took the form of future claims on production. But the intensity of demand also overwhelmed legal restrictions on trade, leading to black markets. Some of this illegal trade functioned via barter, a terribly inefficient form of exchange. Berliners, for example, traded schnapps and potatoes for smoked eel from the Baltic region. Sometimes, too, proximity to power functioned as currency. Not only could local or central party officials obtain scarce commodities based on their connections, but ties of kinship or friendship with the person standing behind the counter could help procure the desired commodity.

Perhaps most important was embezzlement. The misappropriation of supplies from the workplace, for example, had long functioned in the GDR as a third paycheck after wages and benefits. In the 1980s, however, petty theft blossomed. By 1987, theft of public property accounted for 25 percent of all crimes committed, with the value of losses increasing by 65 million East German marks over 1986.[71] Encouraged by management's lackadaisical attitude, for example, employees at the VEB Backwarenkombinat Cottbus regularly stole bread for family and friends.[72] Similarly, workers in the service sector "stole" their own labor, moonlighting at considerable personal profit. Even factory managers were making off with public assets, inventing such scams as underreporting production in order to pocket the excess or embezzling loans from the Staatsbank.[73] By 1989, participation in black market trade had become so widespread as to elicit the helpless demand from Politburo member Willi Stoph that "income from work must return to being the most important source of income for the employee."[74]

The most sought-after currency and commodities, however, came from West Germany. In fact, the Stasi estimated that at least 50 percent of the merchandise on the black market in 1987 was not available for purchase in the GDR, even through the Intershops.[75] After the construction of the Berlin

---

71 SAPMO-BA, DY30, IV 2/2.039/60, "Politbüro-Sitzung vom 19.4.1988," pp. 43–5.
72 One truck driver stole 300 loaves of bread by using a fake delivery slip, while another stole 104 loaves and 600 rolls outright. Moreover, the Party Control Commission estimated that the enterprise sold around 20,600 loaves of bread a month as "rubbish" to collective farms to use as fodder, or enough to feed 4,000 people a month in Cottbus (SAPMO-BA, Vorläufige SED 35986, ZPKK to Mittag, 5.6.86, SED Kreisleitung Cottbus-Stadt, Kreisparteikontrollkommission, "Bericht zur Untersuchung der KPKK in der GO VEB Backwarenkombinat Cottbus," 27.2.86, and Bezirksparteikontrollkommission, "Information an den Kandidaten des Politbüros und 1. Sekretär der Bezirksleitung SED Cottbus, Genossen Werner Walde," no date).
73 SAPMO-BA, DY30, IV 2/2.039/60, "Politbüro-Sitzung vom 19.4.1988," pp. 43–5.
74 BArchB, DE1, 56285, Klopfer, "Persönliche Notizen über die Beratung beim Generalsekretär," 16.5.89, p. 13.
75 BStU, HA XVIII, 6166, "Hinweise zu einigen bedeutsamen Problemen des Schmuggels und der Spekulation mit Waren, Gegenständen und Zahlungsmitteln," 1987, p. 12.

Wall in 1961, it is remarkable that anything illegal found its way into or out of the GDR. But Honecker understood early on that the Wall itself was a fungible asset, that he could trade political liberalization for hard currency. Starting with the Transportation Treaty of 1972, Honecker began permitting West Germans to travel to the GDR in return for financial concessions. The East German black market received a tremendous boost in 1983, moreover, when the threat of bankruptcy led Honecker to allow some categories of East Germans to travel to the West in exchange for West German loans. By the time of the revolution in 1989, some 8 million East Germans were visiting West Germany a year, while around 35 million Westerners traveled to the GDR, of whom around 6 million were West Germans.[76] The expanded contact brought new opportunities for commercial exchange, which was driven by pent-up East German demand for consumer goods. As the Staatsbank conceded in late 1989, the discrepancy between the money in East German pockets and the shortage of commodities "contributed to marks illegally flowing out" of the country.[77]

The GDR's shortage of hard currency also encouraged Honecker to use the Intershops to attract Western cash from East German citizens, as Chapter 6 argues. In the wake of the further relaxation of travel restrictions in 1983, Honecker authorized an aggressive drive to increase the presence of Intershops as a response to the flourishing black market and the socialist state's need for hard currency. Honecker's efforts to profit from the large volume of capitalist money being brought into the GDR had the important, if unintended, consequence of encouraging illicit trade denominated in the currency of the class enemy: That is, the Intershops, which functioned as outposts of Western consumerism on socialist soil, provided material support for the black markets by promoting the use of capitalist money and merchandise. The hard-currency stores even served as sales points for some black market trade.

As a result of relaxed travel restrictions and the increased presence of the Intershops, the black market flourished during the 1980s. East Germans, such as the pensioners who were allowed to visit the West starting in August 1984, looked to increase their stock of West German marks so they could purchase more Western consumer goods on their shopping sprees.[78]

---

76 BArchB, DE1, VA 56323, pp. 576, 628; SAPMO-BA, DY30, JIV 2/2A/3252, "Welchen Nutzen haben wir alle aus dem Intershophandel," p. 1; SAPMO-BA, DY30, IV 2/2.039/307, Abteilung Sicherheitsfragen, "Information und Schlußfolgerung zur Durchführung des Beschlusses des Politbüros vom 9.11.1988," 28.2.89, Anlage, p. 129.

77 BArchB, DN10, 2285, Abteilung Grundfonds, Staatsbank der DDR, "Argumentationsmaterial," 21.11.89, p. 2.

78 BStU, HA XVIII, 6166, "Hinweise," 1987, pp. 17–18.

Conversely, Western tourists, including Allied soldiers, exchanged West German for East German marks so they could buy goods that the socialist state subsidized, from bread and alcoholic beverages to sheet music and books. In addition, West Germans brought their money to the GDR in the form of gifts and gratuities. As a result, the exchange counters in West Berlin and Frankfurt am Main did a surprisingly robust business in East German marks. Despite the fact that the use of the Ostmark outside of the GDR was not authorized by the regime, the volume of East German cash in circulation abroad was astonishingly high. East German estimates at the end of 1989 put the amount at 300 million–350 million Ostmarks in West Germany and another 150 million–200 million in socialist countries.[79] All in all, ordinary East German citizens smuggled around 800 million marks out of the GDR during 1988.[80]

Soon the black market was large enough to warrant the Staatsbank taking countermeasures against counterfeiting – not of East German marks, but of West German marks.[81] Once counterfeit notes left the black market and entered official circulation through the Intershops, the GDR could not use them to pay down its debt, but was stuck with worthless notes not recognized by the West German central bank. Some of the bad notes were no more than photocopies of West German bills.[82] Others were convincing enough to force customs and central bank officials to acquaint themselves with the niceties of West German numismatics. So as to elude the more well-informed and vigilant functionaries in Berlin, East Germans often tried to pass off counterfeit bills in the provinces. Although most of the traffic in counterfeit notes involved small sums, some East German citizens were clearly involved in large-scale organized crime.[83] The growing allure

79 BArchB, DN1, VS 13/90, Nr. 6, Nickel and Kaminsky, "Einschätzung zur Stabilität," 26.10.89, pp. 14–15; BStU, Arbeitsbereich Mittig, Nr. 58, "Zu den ausgewählten Problemen," p. 24. Before the construction of the Berlin Wall in 1961, around 500,000 East German marks changed hands daily for an annual volume approaching 182.5 million marks. Aside from the exchange outlets of Western banks, Berlin enjoyed a lively street market for currency, located mostly at Bahnhof Zoo and Sachsendamm. Demand for both currencies was facilitated by the integration of the city's economy, since people could live in one part of the divided city and work in the other (*Grenzgänger*). The West Berlin municipal government created a floor for exchange rates by permitting East Germans to pay for some goods and services, such as tickets to the cinema, in East German marks at the rate of DM 1 to 5 East German marks. Although the market was illegal in the eyes of West as well as East Berlin officials, it was tolerated by the West (Hoernung, *Zwischen den Fronten*, pp. 37, 50–3, 97).
80 Given the high level of smuggling activity by diplomats, it is likely that these estimates of East German marks in circulation are conservative (BArchB, DN1, VS 13/90, Nr. 6, Nickel and Kaminsky, "Einschätzung zur Stabilität," 26.10.89, pp. 14–15).
81 BArchB, DN10, 3285, Abteilung Emissionsverwaltung Staatsbank, Falschgeldunterlagen BRD, 1970–90, and letter from Deutsche Außenhandelsbank AG, 12.8.77.
82 BArchB, DN10, 3285, "Protokoll über Falschgeld," 8.2.89.
83 In 1987, for example, the Stasi arrested two East German citizens who had stashed large sums of money in their houses: $200 worth of real American notes and DM 20,300, of which DM 18,100

of Western money spurred corruption even among central bank officials. During the 1980s, a number of Staatsbank employees were caught stealing foreign currency.[84]

In 1987, the Ministry for State Security (MfS) noted with alarm that the relaxed travel restrictions had made the GDR more vulnerable to smuggling.[85] The illegal export and import of goods through the GDR was greatly facilitated by the fact that some groups crossed East German borders easily. Foreign diplomats, for example, exploited their immunity to profit from exchanging East for West German money. Although representatives of Western European countries such as Britain were involved in currency smuggling, diplomats from developing countries, especially from African and Arab nations, were the most egregious offenders. The diplomats smuggled Western commodities, especially electronic goods such as video recorders and quartz watches, into the GDR and smuggled either cultural treasures, such as paintings and musical instruments, or financial assets, such as gold or East German money, back out.[86]

The GDR's openness to the East also spurred trade on the black market. The shortages of consumer goods endemic to Comecon countries, coupled with the lack of travel restrictions, created markets for socialist currencies, sending Poles to East German shops in search of chocolate and lingerie, East Germans in search of Czechoslovakian videotapes for their VCRs, Czechs and Slovaks in search of East German shoes, children's clothes, and wallpaper, and so on.[87] In addition, a brisk trade flourished in precious metals because the price paid by the East German state, coupled with the East German mark's relative strength against the Czechoslovakian crown and Polish zloty, brought in a tidy profit for the sale of gold and silver.[88] The

was fake (BArchB, DN10, 3285, Böttcher, Abteilungsleiter Emission, "Genosse Kaminsky zur Information," 13.11.87, Böttcher to Klotz, Staatsanwaltschaft des Bezirkes Halle/Saale, 13.11.87, Kaminsky to Ehrensperger, 17.11.87, and Kaminsky to Möbius, 17.11.87). See also BStU, MfS BKK (KoKo) 601, Panse to Schalck, "Jahresanalyse über die im Zeitraum vom 1. Dezember 1984 bis 30. Dezember 1985 gemeldeten Vorkommnisse im Bereich des IS-Einzelhandels," 27.12.85, p. 17.

84 BArchB, DN10, 2909, Abteilung Innenrevision, "Information Nr. 2/1990 über Hauptkenntnisse aus der Untersuchung besonderer Vorkommnisse im Jahre 1989," 7.12.89, pp. 3, 6.

85 BStU, HA XVIII, 6166, "Hinweise," 1987.

86 Ibid., p. 2. See also Peter Kaiser, Norbert Moc, and Heinz-Peter Zierholz, *Heisse Ware: Spektakuläre Fälle der DDR-Zollfahndung* (Berlin, 1997).

87 SAPMO-BA, DY30, IV 2/2.039/204, Abteilung für Sicherheitsfragen, "Information über Ergebnisse der Zollkontrolle und Feststellungsbearbeitung im paß- und visafreien Reiseverkehr an der Staatsgrenze zur CSSR im Jahre 1983," 3.2.84, p. 5; BArchB, DL2, VA 612. For more on the problem of consumer tourism, see Jonathan R. Zatlin, "Polnische Wirtschaft, deutsche Ordnung? Der Umgang mit den Polen in der DDR unter Honecker," in Christian T. Müller and Patrice G. Poutrus (eds.), *Ankunft-Alltag-Ausreise. Migration und interkulturelle Begegnungen in der DDR-Gesellschaft* (Cologne and Weimar, 2005), pp. 295–315.

88 SAPMO-BA, DY30, IV 2/2.039/204, Abteilung für Sicherheitsfragen, "Information über Ergebnisse der Zollkontrolle und Feststellungsbearbeitung im paß- und visafreien Reiseverkehr an der

Soviet troops stationed in the GDR also engaged in large-scale smuggling operations. In late 1989, for example, East German officials estimated that Soviet citizens had illegally moved more than 1.225 million pairs of shoes out of the GDR. Nor did all of the trade in contraband consist of Western money or various consumer goods. Because of its border with West Germany, the GDR functioned as a transit corridor for drug trafficking. Some East Germans also traveled to Czechoslovakia to meet with West Germans during the 1980s and tried to smuggle "antisocialist printed matter" into the GDR.[89]

The East German authorities were most concerned by the movement of East German products to Poland. Naturally, most of the contraband consisted of consumer goods that were relatively plentiful in the GDR but scarce in Poland. As the East German customs police put it, "differences in the market, supply, and prices and the potential for profit associated with them" fueled the trade. The consumer goods desired by Poles, however, were also commodities that the GDR either subsidized or imported from the West.[90] Their migration from East German stores to illegal Polish markets constituted an expensive drain on the GDR's dwindling reserves. In 1988, the Security Department of the Central Committee estimated Polish smuggling operations cost the GDR 300–400 million East German marks a year.[91]

The Polish case is instructive because it demonstrates the ability of central planning to shape social policy along xenophobic lines. The SED's decision to subsidize goods rather than people transformed every sale from an exchange that enriched all participants to a fiscal burden that impoverished the state. In a letter to Honecker, for example, Mittag described the "losses of

Staatsgrenze zur CSSR," 3.2.84, p. 7, and Abteilung für Sicherheitsfragen, "Information über Ergebnisse der Zollkontrolle und Feststellungsbearbeitung im Reiseverkehr über die Staatsgrenze zur VR Polen im Jahre 1983," 3.2.84, p. 15.

89 SAPMO-BA, DY30, IV 2/2.039/204, Hauptverwaltung, Abteilung Rechenzentrum, "Information zur Ausfuhr von Schuhwaren durch Bürger der UdSSR," 18.11.89, pp. 200–2, Abteilung für Sicherheitsfragen, "Information über Ergebnisse der zollrechtlichen Bestimmungen im Reiseverkehr an den Staatsgrenzen zur BRD und zu Berlin (West) im Jahre 1983," 22.2.84, p. 7, and Abteilung für Sicherheitsfragen, "Information über Ergebnisse der Zollkontrolle und Feststellungsbearbeitung im paß- und visafreien Reiseverkehr an der Staatsgrenze zur CSSR," 3.2.84, p. 5.

90 SAPMO-BA, DY30, IV 2/2.039/204, Zollverwaltung der DDR, "Information zur Änderung von Zollbestimmungen der Volksrepublik Polen," 1.6.88, p. 84, and Leiter der Zollverwaltung der DDR, "Entwicklungen und Tendenzen der Zollkriminalität, Erkenntnisse und Schlußfolgerungen aus der Untersuchung und Verfolgung von Zoll- und Devisenstraftaten," 1988, p. 122; Zatlin, "Polnische Wirtschaft, deutsche Ordnung."

91 SAPMO-BA, DY30, IV 2/2.039/204, Abteilung für Sicherheitsfragen, "Information zu ausgewählten Problemen der Zollkriminalität," 29.9.88, p. 142, and Zollverwaltung der DDR, "Information zur Änderung von Zollbestimmungen der Volksrepublik Polen," 1.6.88, p. 84.

commodities because of visitors and tourists," along with the black market in currency, as costing the GDR 1.1 billion East German marks a year.[92] Of course, foreigners were not responsible for the enforced underconsumption characteristic of Soviet-style regimes – the SED was. But Marxist–Leninist ideology encouraged East Germans to believe they were because it cast market transactions as a zero-sum game in which one party can gain only at the expense of the other. The official censure of market solutions to resource allocation provided convenient political cover for economic planners, who could employ this misidentification of shortage with trade to mobilize popular xenophobia and distract from their economic bungling.[93] Despite the SED's official condemnation of racism, its internationalist impulses took a backseat to bureaucratic calculation.

Likewise, the security apparatus mixed xenophobia with anticapitalism to distract attention from its failure to avert criminal activity and to lobby against Honecker and Mittag's decision to open up the GDR to increased contact with the capitalist West. In one report, for example, the Stasi warned darkly of large criminal organizations that "are partially integrated into internationally constituted groups and are overwhelmingly initiated and directed from West Berlin or the Federal Republic of Germany." Building on old anti-Semitic stereotypes, the Stasi lumped Soviet Jews who had emigrated to the West together with capitalists, whom they perceived as criminals. The "misuse of the GDR as a transit nation" between the East and West, the security forces claimed, was dominated by "established smuggling rings in West Berlin in which a number of former Soviet citizens of Jewish nationality are integrated." The Stasi reinforced its representation of Jews as disloyal to the USSR and to socialism by linking their ethnic background to their involvement in criminal conspiracies aimed at undermining the East German economy.[94]

From the Stasi's point of view, however, international conspiracies were less objectionable than organized groups operating within reach of the police. To explain how a large ring numbering more than fifty-seven people had successfully smuggled quartz watches into the GDR from West Berlin over a period of years, for example, the security apparatus harnessed a politically explosive mix of xenophobia and economic envy. Its report deliberately

---

92 BArchB, DE1, 56317, Mittag to Honecker, no date, Anlage, "Übersicht über das Wirken ökonomischer Faktoren," p. 2.

93 For more on economic sources of anti-Polish sentiment, see Zatlin, "Polnische Wirtschaft, deutsche Ordnung."

94 BStU, HA XVIII, 6166, "Hinweise," 1987, pp. 3, 8, 9.

highlighted the criminals' ethnic background, describing them as a "band of Gypsies" rather than as the Polish and Czechoslovakian citizens they were.[95] In emphasizing the criminals' ethnicity, the Stasi deployed an old notion that the loyalty of the Romany, or Gypsies, to their host nations was trumped by stronger ethnic ties. As with the Jews, the report preferred to explain smuggling by linking it to ethnicity rather than consumer demand.

These aspersions about the "rootlessness" of the Romany, however only masked the concerns of the MfS about the effectiveness of its disciplinary observation of a recalcitrant population: That is, the Stasi made use of racial markers to render perceived threats to the security of the GDR visible. Barely controlled indignation over the Romany's invisibility, for example, fills the Stasi's complaint that the smugglers "were able to remain in the GDR for long periods of time by misusing travel regulations [between the GDR and Poland] that do not require passports and visas and by violating the mandatory registration requirements with the People's Police and earned their living exclusively through criminal activities."[96] Once again, the security apparatus's strong xenophobic streak, which was reinforced by its mission to protect the GDR from the capitalist menace lurking beyond the Wall, led it to cast international contact as harmful to the GDR. In particular, the Romany embodied the secret police's fear that its ability to observe the population with impunity might be curtailed.

Despite the Stasi's paranoid musings on ethnicity, the burgeoning black market did constitute a serious challenge to the SED's power. The mere existence of illegal trade attested to the planned economy's inability to meet the demands of East German consumers, which successfully scaled the heights of the Berlin Wall. But the black market posed less of a security threat than it undermined the SED's political legitimacy by weakening the party's control over commercial activity. After all, the black market functioned as a site of alternative value systems in competition with the regime. The prices asked by suppliers revealed a system of value based on personal gain that contradicted the socialist virtue of the common good. The secondary market may have distributed currency and commodities efficiently, moreover, but it also created new social divisions in East German society, privileging people by virtue of their social position rather than by virtue of their work. More importantly, the black market rewarded the very people most likely to disrespect the socialist state, to engage in petty theft, to abuse their connections, and to maintain contact with friends and family in the West.

95 Ibid., p. 6.   96 Ibid.

If the economic mode of exchange contradicted the egalitarian ideals of the SED, many of the objects exchanged, from West German money to American blue jeans and Japanese Walkmen, embodied social relations the communist party had publicly committed itself to eradicating. Nowhere was the allure of Western consumerism and the repudiation of the socialist approach to consumer needs more evident than in the demand for the West-mark, which had displaced the Ostmark in large sectors of the economy. The East German mark's retreat into a state of partial exchangeability was not merely symbolic, but placed material constraints on the SED's power. The East German communist party soon experienced the unraveling of money as an instrument of central control. The black market, and the East German desires it expressed, shattered the singularity of money in the GDR, fragmenting one unified medium of exchange into two major currencies. The resulting disintegration of the East German monetary regime constrained the SED's control over economic life. Money no longer served as an effective instrument of despotism; the periphery was no longer fully under central control, and capitalist money and merchandise were busy interrupting the circulation of socialist power.

While the black markets for consumer goods posed a variety of threats to the SED's control over the East German population, the growth of secondary markets for producers threatened to undermine the SED's control over production as well as consumption, replacing central planning with market forces. Saddled with obsolete and worn-out equipment, East German enterprises were increasingly unable to meet their planning targets. Scarce resources and production bottlenecks fostered the growth of secondary markets for producer goods. By the late 1980s, capitalist currencies began to find their way into official contracts between socialist enterprises. Sometimes the use of capitalist currency occurred with official sanction. Mittag took several measures aimed at boosting exports, for example, that permitted enterprises to retain a portion of the hard currency they earned.[97] There were also signs that commercial transactions between socialist countries increasingly relied on payment in Western money to conclude deals.[98]

By the 1980s, a black market among producers had taken root, driven by shortages of such key goods as concrete and steel. The competition for resources, coupled with pressure from the center to overfulfill the plan, helped contribute to the development of informal (and illegal) markets for

97 Bryson and Melzer, *The End of the East German Economy*, p. 39; BArchB, DE1, 55384, Klopfer, "Persönliche Notizen über eine Beratung von Mitgliedern der Parteiführung," 22.11.89, p. 4.
98 BArchB, DL2, 860, Forum, "Vermerk über Möglichkeiten der Verwertung der im Brief vom 17.11.1988 angebotenen Rubelbestände," 2.12.88.

producer goods. Payment was made through either barterable goods or hard currency. For example, the IFA-Kombinat Personenkraftwagen, which manufactured automobiles and light trucks, clandestinely produced about 10,000 cars and light trucks beyond the 200,000 set by the plan. The relative scarcity of cars and trucks added to their value, which enabled the combine's directors to trade them for commodities, such as rolled steel, that the combine needed to achieve its planning targets. Peter Jacob, the former Economic Director of the combine, described such barter transactions as a quid pro quo: "If you build a hall for me, I'll give you a few transport vehicles."[99] Some East German enterprises also engaged directly in large black market operations. Because of the shortage of computer diskettes – the waiting period ran to 12 months – retailers were willing to purchase them from smugglers for resale to factories, combines, research institutes, and even ministries.[100] By the end of the 1980s, the secondary market for producer goods had grown so much that some enterprises even began printing catalogs containing the products they were willing to trade.[101] Those enterprises with access to hard currency, moreover, began using it to purchase the semifinished goods they required from the West. Others turned to Mittag's minion, Alexander Schalck-Golodkowski, for hard currency. Schalck operated just like a capitalist bank, issuing loans at market-oriented interest rates. As Christian Scholwin, the Deputy Minister for General Machine, Agricultural Machine, and Automotive Construction (ALF), observed, "if you were friends with Schalck, you got" the machines you needed.[102]

While these secondary markets for producer goods may have been more efficient in distributing resources, they posed similar challenges to the planned economy as the illegal trade in consumer goods. Not only did the introduction of market forces belie the ideological underpinnings of the planned economy, but transactions conducted on black markets violated East German law. More importantly, they occurred outside the control of the planners – even if highly placed officials sometimes looked the other way precisely because the secondary markets solved the problem of shortages more effectively than the primary market.[103] As a Central Committee report from 1983 observed, the growth of this parallel market interfered with the social priorities of the regime while creating an area of the domestic economy

---

99 Interview, Jacob and Sachs, Chemnitz, 26.2.96; and Christian Scholwin, Deputy Minister for General Machine, Agricultural Machine, and Automotive Construction (1978–88), Berlin, 23.11.95.
100 BStU, HA XVIII, 6166, "Hinweise," 1987, p. 12.
101 Interview, Jacob and Sachs, Chemnitz, 26.2.96; and Scholwin, Berlin, 23.11.95.
102 Interview, Scholwin, Berlin, 23.11.95.		103 Ibid.; interview, Klopfer, Berlin, 4.10.95

that resembled capitalism.[104] The shortcomings of the planned economy, exacerbated by Honecker's spendthrift social programs and Mittag's ruthless frugality, soon placed the GDR's future into the invisible hands of market forces. Not only did the GDR have to contend with its dependence on capitalist financiers, but the growth of capitalist trade inside the GDR severely curtailed the SED's power.

MITTAG'S RESPONSE

Despite falling productivity rates, the resurgent balance-of-payments deficit, and expanding black markets, Honecker continued to avoid undertaking the reforms necessary to stabilize the East German economy. For his part, Mittag chose to preserve his power by avoiding a break with Honecker rather than to remedy the GDR's ills by cutting expenditures on social programs and modernizing industry. In fact, he redoubled his efforts to force savings by starving factories of capital and exporting as much as possible to the West. The result was the thorough-going monetization of the socialist economy, often at the expense of ordinary East Germans.

While insufficient in the long run, some of Mittag's stopgap solutions briefly alleviated specific problems. One example was his attempt to add more workers to the labor pool. The GDR's declining productivity rates and increasingly worn-out capital stock aggravated the labor shortage in an economy that already hoarded labor. One rich source of labor was women, to whom the GDR had turned in the 1950s and 1960s. Another important source, especially during crises, was the army, which Mittag put to work more and more frequently as time went on. In the 1980s, Mittag traveled the same route as the Federal Republic had in the 1960s, importing contract workers – cheap labor from developing countries – to satisfy the needs of East German producers. The official rhetoric of socialist internationalism described labor relations between developed and developing countries as an exchange aimed at a transfer of skills and knowledge. In reality, however, the relationship between the GDR and such socialist allies as Cuba, Vietnam, and Mozambique was colonial and exploitative. Although the East German authorities claimed that they were training these foreign employees and equipping them with skills they could take home, most of them were employed as manual laborers. The GDR profited from their labor, paying them very little and providing appallingly cheap housing. This arrangement

---

104 SAPMO-BA, DY30, Vorläufige SED 36639, Sektor Außenhandel, "Zu Fragen der Valutarechnung," 2.8.83, p. 2.

permitted the GDR to throw unskilled labor into the production breach to replace defective machinery and repay its socialist ally with products of its own making. As East Germany ran down its capital stock, the number of foreign employees rose. In 1981, only 24,098 foreigners worked in the East German economy. By 1989, however, the number had soared to 93,562.[105]

As always, Mittag sought to stimulate economic growth by tightening the center's control over the periphery's scope for decision making. As Peter Jacob and Wolfgang Sachs, top managers in the automobile industry, remarked, "once the shortages worsened, the center wrested more control for itself."[106] To stimulate unit production, for example, Mittag increased the reporting responsibilities of manufacturing enterprises, compelling them to communicate their performance every ten days and, in some cases such as the automobile industry, every day. Mittag's attempts to gain more control over life on the factory floor, however, were disrupted by the gap between accounting and accountability. Daily statistics describing unit production in industries such as the automobile sector invited manipulation. Obliging managers to report within smaller timeframes, for example, disclosed little about the progress made on the production line. After all, making a car could not be measured in one-day rhythms.[107]

Although he consistently opposed long-term investments in capital equipment to boost production, Mittag did make some attempts to modernize East Germany's industrial base. Aside from emergency purchases of key machines, however, nearly all of Mittag's projects involved improvements in the production of goods for domestic consumption, not producer goods. The major exceptions that did constitute upgrades of East German manufacturing were plagued by bad management decisions, cost overruns, technological obsolescence, and construction delays costing billions of marks.[108]

By far the most prominent development plan was Mittag's project to facilitate the GDR's entry into the digital age. As Charles S. Maier has pointed out, the decision to invest heavily in computer technology entailed "a race between computers and collapse."[109] The integration of digital processors in the production process provided the GDR with two different

---

105 Sandra Gruner-Domić, "Zur Geschichte der Arbeitskräftemigration in die DDR. Die bilateralen Verträge zur Beschäftigung ausländischer Arbeiter (1961–1989)," *Internationale wissenschaftliche Korrespondenz zur Geschichte der deutschen Arbeiterbewegung* 2 (1996), p. 229.

106 Interview, Jacob and Sachs, Chemnitz, 26.2.96.

107 Ibid. The daily reports were one of the first things that Schürer recommended for elimination after Honecker and Mittag were ousted in 1989 (SAPMO-BA, DY30, JIV 2/2A/3252, Schürer, Beil, Schalck, Höfner, and Donda, "Analyse der ökonomischen Lage," 30.10.89, point 9).

108 BStU, Arbeitsbereich Mittig, Nr. 58, "Zu den ausgewählten Problemen," Anlage 5, pp. 39–41.

109 Maier, *Dissolution*, p. 73.

opportunities to improve its economic position. On the one hand, for-eign sales of electronic processing equipment promised the GDR a new source of hard-currency revenue, reducing the threat of insolvency just as it returned with renewed vigor. On the other hand, domestic integration of computers throughout the East German economy held out the prospect of dramatic gains in productivity. Raising productivity rates was the key not only to reversing the decline of the GDR's competitiveness on international markets, but also to reducing the costs of Honecker's social welfare system.

As always, political considerations shaped economic decisions. The large-scale investments authorized by Honecker and Mittag illustrate the fetishiza-tion of technology characteristic of Marxism-Leninism. Both the modernist elements of communist ideology and the link established by Lenin between productivity and systemic competition with capitalism encouraged an offi-cial obsession with technological achievement. In the GDR, this fascination with technical innovation reached a highpoint with Ulbricht's cybernetics program. The sheer size of Mittag's computer project, moreover, was in keeping with the Stalinist tradition of embarking on projects whose gargan-tuan scope reflected the volume-oriented production parameters empha-sized by the planned economy as much as it did a need for prestigious victories.[110] At a time when the Soviet Union under Gorbachev was prov-ing to be a difficult partner economically and politically, the GDR's status as the only Comecon country able to mass-produce memory chips was a source of immense gratification to the SED leadership.

The exaggerated sense of self-importance and self-sufficiency Honecker derived from the achievements of the East German high-tech sector also had its roots in a well-founded anxiety over the GDR's economic future. Given East Germany's falling productivity rates and the unfavorable shift in its trade structure, the fear of being left behind by Western innovation inspired a desperate trust in the "scientific-technological revolution."[111] The structural deficiencies of the planned economy, however, impeded sci-entific development, hobbled production, and held back the adoption of new technologies.[112] East German scientists and engineers could not on their own have designed memory chips or the technology to produce them. To some extent, technological progress in socialist countries had stagnated

110 By 1988, the GDR had sunk 14 billion East German marks into manufacturing and another 14 billion into researching computer electronics, not counting several billion West German marks worth of hard currency (Hertle, "Die Diskussion," pp. 335–6).
111 For an official statement regarding the scientific-technological revolution under Honecker's "Unity of Economic and Social Policy," see Harry Nick, *Wissenschaftlich-technische Revolution – historischer Platz – Entwicklungsetappen – soziales Wesen* (East Berlin, 1983).
112 Stokes argues that in the 1950s, the failure to innovate was a problem of integrating scientific discovery into production (Stokes, *Constructing Socialism*, p. 49).

because the incentives to hoard labor outweighed incentives to innovate and produce labor-saving devices. In addition, the plan forced enterprises to continue with failed projects, while soft budgets made it unclear where areas of specialization lay.[113] Nor could the GDR, with its antipathy toward money, match the structural incentives created by capitalist financial instruments, from venture capital to stock options, which fostered creative growth in places like America's Silicon Valley.

To bridge the technological gap, Honecker's GDR once again turned to the West. However, the Western decision to control the dissemination of technology through the Committee for Coordinating East-West Trade (CoCom) made the purchase of Western computer products difficult. To overcome this obstacle to their plans, Mittag and Schalck employed bribery and deception: What they could not invent or buy legally, they purchased clandestinely or stole outright. And socialists could always count on the help of capitalists who placed profit margins above appeals to national security. With the assistance of the Japanese corporation Toshiba, for example, the GDR circumvented CoCom's embargo. In return for DM 25 million, the GDR secretly concluded a deal to manufacture its own 256-kilobyte memory chips. Toshiba turned out to be an excellent business partner, delivering products and customer service with remarkable eagerness. When the CIA became suspicious of Toshiba, however, the Japanese company demanded that the East Germans destroy all evidence of the deal, including the chip designs. Under the watchful eyes of Toshiba's representatives, the East Germans complied. But Schalck had tricked the Japanese: The designs destroyed by the East Germans were merely copies that he had fashioned for this ruse. Thanks to Schalck's deception, the GDR was still in possession of the original templates.[114]

Acquiring the technology, even by illegal and duplicitous means, however, was not the same thing as manufacturing the 256-kilobyte microchip. Bottlenecks characteristic of the planned economy delayed and disrupted mass production.[115] Similarly, mass production of 16-bit microprocessors took place about 4.5 years after West Germany took up manufacturing

---

113 Bruce Kogut and Udo Zander, "Did Socialism Fail to Innovate? A Natural Experiment of the Two Zeiss Companies," *American Sociological Review* 45 (April 2000), pp. 169–90.

114 BStU, MfS AIM, 10823/91, Teil II, Band 3, Ronneberger to Schalck and Nendel, "Information," 10.2.88, pp. 97–8; Klaus Krakat, "Probleme der DDR-Industrie im letzten Fünfjahrplanzeitraum," in Kuhrt, *Am Ende des realen Sozialismus (2)*, pp. 161–2; Przybylski, *Tatort Politbüro*, p. 128. Toshiba was the first company to produce 256-KB chips, which were the most advanced at the time.

115 At the GDR's unveiling of its 1-MB chip, for example, the Soviet leader Mikhail Gorbachev asked when mass production would begin. Embarrassed, the East Germans quickly ushered him away (Kopstein, *The Politics of Economic Decline*, p. 101).

them and 7.5 years after their introduction in the United States; it was not until 1989 that the GDR was able to produce a 32-bit processor – one based on information stolen from the U.S. corporation Intel.[116]

Even more discouraging, the costs of production were astronomical. A single 256-kilobyte microchip cost more than 566 East German marks to make – and that was not even counting the various hidden subsidies embedded in the manufacturing process. To encourage domestic adoption of the new technology, the party offered the chips to East German producers at a discounted price of 17 marks. But even this heavily subsidized price compared poorly with the going rate in the European Community for similar chips, which fluctuated between DM 5 and 15. And, as always, questions about product reliability and quality control hung like Damocles' sword over East German merchandise.[117] In addition, the increasing specialization and flexibility offered by computer-assisted machines accelerated the trend away from standardized products toward customized manufacturing. As Maier has observed, if the GDR encountered difficulties with Fordist production techniques, it was unclear how it would match the post-Fordist, flexible production techniques of American, Japanese, and Taiwanese manufacturers to gain market share.[118] The tribulations of the GDR's computer industry illustrate just how far the planned economies of Eastern Europe and the Soviet Union lagged behind the capitalist West.

Of course, the GDR did not have to compete directly with Western manufacturers. Instead, Mittag could have used the technology to modernize the East German economy. Despite the party's rhetorical encouragement and subsidies, however, the integration of computer equipment into the production and service sectors proceeded haphazardly.[119] Without hard budget constraints, East German factories had little incentive to lower costs by raising productivity. But even when the East German economy did make use of computers, it did not always reduce costs. Merely printing out a list of the export contracts secured by East German foreign trade enterprises, for example, required two hours and cost 2,000 East German marks.[120] In addition to these considerable economic impediments, the culture of East German production posed a significant obstacle to computerization. The SED's financial experts, for example, complained that it took 900 kilos

116 Krakat, "Probleme der DDR-Industrie," pp. 162–3; Hertle, "Die Diskussion," pp. 335–6.
117 BArchB, DE1, 56318, "Eine Bemerkung zu der Frage," 30.8.88, p. 3; Schabowski, *Der Absturz*, p. 126; Hertle, "Die Diskussion," pp. 332–6; Maier, *Dissolution*, pp. 73–6.
118 Maier, *Dissolution*, p. 75.
119 BStU, Arbeitsbereich Mittig, Nr. 58, "Zu den ausgewählten Problemen," pp. 12–13; Kusch et al., *Schlußbilanz*, p. 48.
120 SAPMO-BA, DY30, Vorläufige SED 36639, Sektor Außenhandel, "Information für Genossen Weiß, Analyse der Entwicklung der Zahlungsbedingungen 1981," 5.2.82.

of material to make a product weighing just 1.5 grams. The advantages of miniaturization were not clear to planners, who operated in a production regime that valued size and volume. The security apparatus, moreover, was bound to raise political objections to the widespread use of computers, which would permit the rapid dissemination of alternatives to official ideology.

In evaluating the Honecker period, Maier argues that the failures of the East German economy did not inhere in the principles that organized production in the GDR, but were the result of political decisions and of Honecker's leadership in particular.[121] As Maier reminds us, any discussion of the planned economy's shortcomings cannot ignore the crises of inflation, unemployment, and government debt experienced by market economies during the 1970s and 1980s. The difficulty with Maier's argument, however, lies in his attempt to separate socialist production methods from the political repression necessary to maintain them. Absent the application of political force, the East German dictatorship offered little ideological or material reason for the population to acquiesce in its rule during the 1980s. The GDR's debt to the West reflected the planned economy's inherent inability to renew its industrial base, but it also flowed from Honecker's attempt to govern an industrial society by force.

In the meantime, the resurgence of the debt problem necessitated that the GDR export anything and everything that it could. Once again, Mittag appeared to reach back to the reforms of the 1960s over which he had presided to find solutions to the GDR's economic ills. At a secretive meeting with the GDR's key economic leaders in late 1988, he concluded that "we must make profits so that we can hold to the party's basic position" on the economy.[122] In order to save the socialist patient, it was necessary to kill it. Warning that "we must link our planning and balancing more closely with the monetary system," Mittag even entertained suggestions about furnishing monetary policy with enough autonomy to stimulate exporting enterprises to reduce costs.[123] The immediate need for hard currency, however, impelled Mittag to undertake a series of essentially Pyrrhic victories, exporting goods even if they cost more to produce than they could be sold for. In 1989, for example, Schalck arranged for 3,400 tons of butter to be sold in the West for DM 9.4 million. Using the SED's internal exchange rate, this translates into revenue of around 41.4 million East German marks. But it cost

121 Maier, *Dissolution*, p. 79 ff.
122 BArchB, DE1, 56285, Klopfer, "Persönliche Notizen über eine Beratung," 7.12.88, p. 9.
123 Ibid., p. 12.

75.5 million East German marks to make the butter, resulting in a net loss of 34.1 million marks.[124]

Most importantly, financial desperation deepened the contradictions between the SED's economic imperatives and its official profession of respect for its citizens. In at least one case, for example, the prospect of throwing away hard-currency assets convinced East German leaders to sell East Germans spoiled food. In June 1985, the food-processing plant VEB OGIS Zeitz imported 41 tons of tomato concentrate from Greece worth 750 million East German marks.[125] The concentrate was to be turned into tomato paste for the local population of Zeitz, a small town in the Halle district. Production bottlenecks, however, forced OGIS Zeitz to delay production for ten months. In the meantime, the factory placed the tomato concentrate in a storage facility. Given the poor state of warehouses and refrigerating equipment in the GDR, storing perishable goods was a risky endeavor. Undeterred, OGIS Zeitz began production in late April 1986, turning 8 tons of concentrate into 15.2 tons of bottled tomato paste. During a routine check, however, the Halle District Hygiene Inspectorate and Institute found that the stored goods had begun to rot. Nearly 45 percent of the imported concentrate was "entirely spoiled," it reported. The remaining 55 percent, which had begun to ferment, contained yeast and mold. The Inspectorate observed that it had a "sour to bitter taste" and an "impure aftertaste."

Because the spoiled concentrate had been purchased using scarce Western currency, the incident quickly attracted the Politburo's attention. The party leadership expressed alarm at OGIS Zeitz's readiness to sell East German citizens spoiled tomato paste. To deter similar behavior, the ZK recommended charging the plant manager for "the crudest infractions against the most elementary rules of order, discipline, and sanitation."[126] Nevertheless, the SED leadership was reluctant simply to throw the tomatoes away, since they had been imported from the West. Instead, it ordered OGIS Zeitz to cover up the sour taste caused by fermentation by adding sugar and turn the concentrate into ketchup. As a sop to consumers, party officials declared

124 BArchB, DE1, 56285, Klopfer, "Niederschrift über die Beratung im Politbüro des ZK der SED am 15.9.88," p. 2; BArchB, DE1, 55382, Schalck to Mittag, 23.1.89, p. 1. One post-1989 estimate put the cost to the GDR of exporting a ton of butter at a net 20,000 East German marks (Hoover Institution Archives, *Protokolle der Beratungen des Runden Tisches*, Vorlage Nr. 11/17, session 11, Grüne Partei, "Anfrage an die Regierung," 5.2.90).
125 The following story is based on SAPMO-BA, DY30, Vorläufige SED 41850, Böhme to Jarowinsky, 12.6.86, Pöschel to Mittag, 23.5.86, Briksa to Jarowinsky, 5.6.86, Weiß to Pöschel, 9.6.86, Diwisch, Bezirks-Hygieneinspektion und -Institut, Rat des Bezirks Halle, 23.5.86, and Götze, Fachabteilung Nahrungsgüter, Fachgebiet Obst- und Gemüseerzeugnisse, Amt für Mess- und Standardisierungswesen, 26.5.86.
126 SAPMO-BA, DY30, Vorläufige SED 41850, Pöschel to Mittag, 23.5.86, p. 1.

the ketchup unfit for sale in stores and ordered that it be offered only in restaurants and cafeterias. Where the SED's confusion of ends and means had previously been restricted to ill-advised economic measures, financial desperation now convinced the party to serve up spoiled food.

Eventually, the corrupting influence of fiscal necessity spread to areas of life commonly considered ethically sacrosanct, such as medicine. The rapacity of the East German economic apparatus, fueled by the GDR's need to remain financially sovereign, induced it to conclude increasingly dubious compromises on public health. In 1988, for example, the GDR agreed to permit Hoechst AG, one of the largest West German pharmaceutical companies, to conduct tests of a new medication for high blood pressure called Ramipril.[127] Hoechst approached East German authorities for a variety of reasons, including the shared language, common culture, excellent medical training of East German physicians, and low cost of conducting a study in a cheap currency area. The most important reason for turning to the GDR, however, was the discretion afforded by a dictatorship. Hoechst had been prevented from conducting double-blind studies in the Federal Republic because West German authorities believed testing the drug constituted a danger to human life. In contrast, the SED was willing to trade public health for capitalist money: In return for DM 500,000, it agreed to make East German subjects available for the study.

The economic experts who supported the agreement were well aware of the risks that testing Ramipril entailed. Hoechst wanted to use patients in an "already advanced stage of illness" for a double-blind study in which half the patients would receive the test drug and the other half a placebo. As the Stasi was quick to point out, "the attending physician does not know according to this scheme what he or she is actually giving the patient. If a patient who is that sick then receives a placebo, that is, an absolutely ineffective product, it can lead to an acute health risk including death. And the physician has no idea what is happening, and so cannot react (if that is at all still possible and death has not yet occurred)." Appalled by the deal, one member of the East German medical community sought to win concessions for the patients during the negotiations with Hoechst. When that failed, he protested unsuccessfully against the agreement itself. Worried that "the contract will be based on a one-sided consideration of the money," he

127 Ramipril is now widely used to combat heart disease (Salim Yusuf, Peter Sleight, Janice Pogue, Jackie Bosch, Richard Davies, and Gilles Dagenais, "Effects of an Angiotensin-Converting-Enzyme Inhibitor, Ramipril, on Cardiovascular Events in High-Risk Patients," in *New England Journal of Medicine* 342 [2000], pp. 145–53). The following information is drawn from BStU, ZAIG, 14614, Hauptabteilung XX/3, "Bericht. Medikamententestung in der DDR," 18.2.88, pp. 23–4.

sought assistance from the secret police against the Ministry of Health and the economic apparatus. The Stasi agreed to help – less because of ethical questions raised by the double-blind study than for security reasons. If news of the test leaked, the Stasi reasoned, it could "be used for negative political activities against the GDR." In addition, the GDR's business partners might attempt "to blackmail the GDR." Bureaucratic rivalry also shaped the Stasi's response. Differences over policies and personalities that pitted the Stasi's economic analysts against Schalck and Mittag were easily disguised as security concerns.

Whatever the motivating force behind the Stasi's protests, this incident and others like it complicate arguments that seek to reduce life in the GDR to the coercive excesses of its secret police.[128] Often enough, representatives of the SED's economic apparatus were capable of an even greater disregard for human life in the pursuit of money than the most cynical Stasi officers. In May 1989, for example, the economic section of the MfS, the Hauptabteilung XVIII (HA XVIII), rejected Schalck's proposal to transport West German garbage from Hamburg to the rubbish heap that had been created in Schöneiche (outside East Berlin) for just this purpose. The Stasi officers argued that fifty garbage trucks driving through the Republic every day would alarm the local populace because of the environmental implications. The potential for political destabilization, the Stasi complained, was not worth the DM 6 million Schalck hoped to earn.[129] The Stasi's sensitivity to the political costs of becoming West Germany's garbage dump provided some counterweight to Schalck's subordination of morality to money. But no East German authority voiced concern for the health risks.

OPPOSITION WITHIN THE PARTY

If declining productivity and the renewed threat of insolvency reduced the Politburo's political room for maneuver, the increasing inability of the planned economy to deliver the high living standards it promised eroded solidarity within the SED ranks. Honecker and Mittag's increasing reliance on the West transformed differences of opinion over economic policy into serious political rifts. Two indistinct groups gradually coalesced in the

---

128 For a discussion of this tendency, see Catherine Epstein, "The Stasi: New Research on the East German Ministry of State Security," in *Kritika: Explorations in Russian and Eurasian History* 5 (2004), pp. 321–48.

129 BStU, ZA, HA XVIII, 5748, Schalck to Mielke, 3.5.89, and HA XVIII, "Stellungnahme zum beabsichtigten Abschluß eines zusätzlichen kommerziellen Vertrages zur Abnahme von Hausmüll aus Hamburg und dessen Verbringung auf die Deponie Schöneiche/Zossen/Potsdam," pp. 11–14, cited in Haendcke-Hoppe-Arndt, *Die Hauptabteilung XVIII*, p. 115.

Politburo in opposition to Honecker and Mittag, one based at the Ministry for State Security and one among economic leaders. Fueling this dissent was the person of Mittag, who had long attracted the ire of his colleagues. His close association with Honecker, autocratic behavior toward his peers, and penchant for deception caused many party members to resent his growing influence. "It was a creepy relationship to many of us in the Politburo," commented Honecker's longtime heir apparent, Egon Krenz, after 1989. "The General Secretary, himself no learned economist, trusted Mittag's political-economic calculations blindly.... [T]oward the end of his time in office, [Honecker] rejected all reminders to rein in his Economic Secretary – most likely out of fear of a rude awakening."[130]

By 1980, the economic desk at the MfS had become the most outspoken center of opposition to Mittag and his policies. Shortly before the Tenth Party Congress in 1981, Colonel Horst Roigk of HA XVIII put together a report at Stasi chief Erich Mielke's request on the state of the East German economy. Roigk attacked the SED's economic program, assailing Mittag and Schalck by name. To some extent, Roigk's censure of the SED's economic policy was motivated by his distaste for Schalck, who had replaced him as head of KoKo. Nevertheless, placing Mittag and his crony Schalck at the center of the GDR's economic difficulties did not lie far from the truth of the matter.

The status-conscious Mielke, however, was indignant that Roigk had dared to rebuke the Economic Secretary of the Central Committee. The Minister for State Security ordered the report destroyed, severely reprimanded Roigk, and forced two of Roigk's colleagues to repudiate their "arrogance" for having criticized Mittag.[131] Mielke then solicited the opinion of the head of the economic desk, Major General Alfred Kleine, on the well-being of the East German economy. Although he obviously sympathized with Roigk's concerns, Kleine was more discreet in his approach and refrained from direct criticism of Mittag. The result was more devastating than Roigk's vitriol. In particular, Kleine's report singled out a deliberative body called the Economic Commission of the Politburo that Mittag had created to bypass the Council of Ministers for creating "a second system of governance."

Despite his anger at the temerity of his underlings, Mielke worried that Mittag and Honecker were indeed running the economy into the ground. The security chief found the GDR's increasing reliance on the West rather than on the Soviet Union to resolve its trade imbalances particularly

---

130 Krenz, *Wenn Mauern fallen*, p. 78.
131 The following is based on Haendcke-Hoppe-Arndt, *Die Hauptabteilung XVIII*, pp. 75–6.

disturbing. His concern over Mittag's Western orientation was shared by Politburo member Werner Krolikowski, who had been replaced by Mittag after his undistinguished tenure as Economic Secretary from 1973 to 1976. In late 1980, Mielke and Krolikowski met secretly – no small accomplishment in the paranoid climate of the Politburo – to fume over Honecker's "gravitation to the West," which Krolikowski lambasted as "the worst kind of opportunism."[132]

In December 1980, Mielke approached Willi Stoph, the Chairman of the Council of Ministers, to sound him out on his views. Stoph's stature among senior party leaders as a longtime Politburo member was enhanced by his effectiveness as an administrator, although he had slowed down by the 1980s because of his advanced age.[133] In 1971, Stoph had joined forces with Honecker against Ulbricht, but he chafed under Honecker's autocratic leadership and was periodically beset by bouts of inconclusive rebelliousness. As the head of the Council of Ministers, moreover, Stoph must have been rankled by Mittag's accumulation of power and circumvention of the Council's jurisdiction over economic affairs. Discouraged by the economic mess Honecker's "Unity of Economic and Social Policy" was creating, Stoph dared to articulate his misgivings openly in April 1980. After Schürer had issued yet another of his warnings regarding the GDR's financial health during a Politburo meeting, Stoph leapt to his defense. Affronted by Stoph's display of opposition, Honecker interrupted him, claiming that Stoph's objections were "just holding us up." In a comment aimed at discrediting Stoph and Schürer, Honecker tried to reassure other Politburo members by asserting that "a year ago some comrades were saying that we would go bankrupt now. There can be no talk of that [now]."[134] Stoph waited nine years to repay this humiliation, when he would deliver the first blow against Honecker during the palace coup of October 1989.

While these criticisms of Honecker and Mittag's economic leadership were well founded, looking to the USSR for the GDR's economic future, as this "pro-Soviet faction" did, nonetheless involved an optimistic assessment of that country's capacities.[135] In his self-serving memoirs, Mittag disparages

---

132 Przybylski, *Tatort Politbüro*, pp. 341, 348; Otto, *Erich Mielke*, p. 426.

133 M. Rainer Lepsius, "Handlungsräume und Rationalitätskriterien," in Pirker et al. (eds.), *Der Plan als Befehl und Fiktion*, pp. 353–4; interview, Scholwin, Berlin, 23.11.95.

134 BArchB, DC20, 5272, pp. 174–83, cited in Otto, *Erich Mielke*, pp. 421–2; interview, Klopfer, Berlin, 4.10.95.

135 In the early 1980s, "pro-Soviet" meant a fealty to Moscow mediated by the generational experience of Soviet assistance in the creation of the GDR. Good ties to Moscow were indispensable to political success, and Stoph had excellent ties to various Soviet institutions and personalities. By the time *perestroika* was under way in the late 1980s, however, a different pro-Soviet faction had emerged.

Figure 13. Erich Honecker at the Eleventh Party Congress in April 1986, looking on as his rival Willi Stoph (left), Chairman of the Council of Ministers, shakes hands with Soviet leader Mikhail Gorbachev (middle). State Planning Commissioner Gerhard Schürer is applauding at the top, second from the right. (Courtesy of Bundesarchiv Koblenz, Bildarchiv, 183/1986/0419/062.)

several members of this group for opposing his reliance on trade with the West. In particular, he criticizes Stoph and Krolikowski for "having the illusion that the GDR could get international know-how from Comecon."[136] There is no question that some, such as Mielke and Krolikowski, trusted too much to the Soviet Union to subsidize the GDR.[137] Nevertheless, their objections to Honecker's prodigality and Mittag's parsimony were shared by many key players in the economic community. Schürer's chief deputy, the versatile Heinz Klopfer, for example, was troubled enough by Mittag's

Where the older generation was disturbed by Gorbachev's reforms, which contradicted their vision of the USSR's role, a younger generation of SED leaders felt that the East German economy could benefit from harnessing market forces, however vaguely defined (interview, Klaus Höpcke, Deputy Minister of Culture [1973–89], Erfurt, 24.2.96; Christa Luft, Chancellor, Hochschule für Ökonomie [1988–9], Economics Minister [December 1989–March 1990], Berlin, 18.3.96; and Hans Modrow, Dresden District Party Leader [1973–89], Central Committee member [1967–89], Chairman, Council of Ministers [November 1989–March 1990], Berlin, 16.4.96; Hertle, *Der Fall der Mauer*, pp. 124–7).

136 Mittag, *Um jeden Preis*, pp. 39–40.
137 Schürer relates that when he shared his alarm with Mielke in 1989 regarding the GDR's insolvency, Mielke responded with startling aplomb, intoning serenely, "don't worry Gerhard, [the Soviets] won't leave us in the lurch" (Schürer, *Gewagt und Verloren*, p. 147).

aggressive economizing that he submitted a strongly worded protest in late 1981.[138] Even Mittag's most important aide-de-camp, Günter Ehrensperger, showed signs of disaffection. In 1985, for example, he told his staff at the Department of Planning and Finance that Mittag vastly overestimated the GDR's economic strength.[139]

Nevertheless, the repeated economic crises provoked by Honecker's social expenditures and Mittag's ruthless frugality could not overcome the mental taboos regarding sustained criticism of Mittag, since attacking Mittag was equivalent to attacking the General Secretary. On the one hand, Honecker's charismatic authority paralyzed the willingness of younger leaders, such as Schürer and Krenz, to act against him. On the other hand, forming alliances was hampered by the Stalinist proscription on faction building. The paranoid climate of the Politburo, moreover, erected a variety of informal prohibitions that prevented clandestine meetings among leaders.[140]

In 1982, it briefly seemed as if objections to Honecker and Mittag's economic leadership might establish a stable alliance against the General Secretary. As the prospect of insolvency and the experience of massive shortages shook the GDR, Honecker found it impossible to continue proscribing debate over economic policy in the Politburo by banishing it to a variety of less meaningful committees. But the danger to the GDR from the capitalists encouraged party leaders to close ranks. And while the "pro-Soviet faction" may have been appalled by the GDR's willingness to make use of West German financial support, the successful resolution of the immediate threat of insolvency engendered a relief that dampened criticism of Honecker and Mittag.

More important than the concerted attacks issued by the economic desk at the MfS against Mittag, and more effective than the episodic qualms of Stoph, Mielke, and Krolikowski, was the open challenge raised by State Planning Commissioner Gerhard Schürer to Honecker's spendthrift ways.

138 BArchB, DE1, VA 56287, "Persönliche Meinung zur Ausarbeitung des Fünfjahrplanes 1981–1985 und des Jahresvolkswirtschaftsplanes 1982," 21.8.81.
139 Peter Przybylski, *Tatort Politbüro. Band 2: Honecker, Mittag und Schalck-Golodkowski* (Berlin, 1992), p. 377.
140 Even walks together in the park at Wandlitz, the settlement outside Berlin where Politburo members lived, were highly discouraged (interview, Schürer, Berlin, 20.5.95). By 1989, however, the GDR's economic deterioration helped some Politburo members, led by Stoph, to overcome their inhibitions and meet clandestinely (BStU, MfS HA XX, 6529, "Vermerk," 6.6.89, pp. 328–30). At the same time, Honecker's skills as an effective intriguer and talented manipulator of people and institutions should not be underestimated. As Rainer Lepsius writes, "Stoph was no match for Honecker, nor Krolikowski a match for Mittag" (Lepsius, "Handlungsräume und Rationalitätskriterien," p. 354).

Since the pivotal confrontation between Schürer, Mittag, and Honecker in 1977, Mittag had ceased to articulate any criticism of Honecker's "Unity of Economic and Social Policy." Schürer, however, continued to express his reservations about the growing domestic and foreign debts. Throughout the 1980s, the State Planning Commission produced numerous reports warning that the debt to the West would bankrupt the GDR. Schürer and his assistants consistently implied that reduced expenditure on consumption and increased investment in the infrastructure formed the only guarantees against insolvency.

By 1987, however, Schürer believed that a fundamental alteration in economic strategy was required to preserve the GDR's autonomy. After working with his aides for six months compiling information and soliciting proposals, Schürer put together a proposal calling for drastic reductions in the subsidies for consumers that were at the core of Honecker's economic policies.[141] In addition, Schürer called for an end to industrial subsidies for costly programs that were unprofitable, such as the vast computerization project. Instead, he proposed to set aside the unsuccessful efforts to achieve economic autarky and integrate the GDR into the global economy. "Our conclusion," he wrote, "must be that every project, however important it is, be confronted with the hard economic conditions of the world market. The decisive question has become not only what, but above all at what cost and profit something is produced."[142] The savings, Schürer believed, would go some way toward restoring the balance between production and consumption. Although his overarching concern was to make ends meet, Schürer did not entirely neglect the social consequences of price increases. To navigate between financial exigency and political reality, he grounded his choices in Marxist-Leninist categories, arguing for a pricing system that reflected the differences between "necessary" and "unnecessary" consumer goods.

Drawing on his previous experiences with Honecker, Schürer refrained from criticizing the General Secretary's policies directly or proposing fundamental reforms to the planned economy. Nevertheless, Schürer presented Honecker with a stark choice between a balanced budget and a continuation of his catastrophic prodigality. The question was how to deliver a potentially

---

141 BArchB, DE1, VA 56319. Price subsidies rose from 7.9 million marks in Ulbricht's last year to 17.2 billion in 1980 and 58.4 billion in 1988, with foodstuffs and consumer goods taking up the lion's share of expenses (BArchB, DE1, VA 56323, "Preisstützungen Bevölkerung [Subventionen]," p. 540).

142 BArchB, DE1, 56285, Gerhard Schürer, "Überlegungen zur weiteren Arbeit am Volkswirtschaftsplanes 1989 und darüber hinaus," 26.4.88, p. 3.

explosive recommendation in a way that would facilitate its implementation. Going directly to the Politburo with a proposal to dismantle the subsidies that were at the heart of Honecker's economic program was not a promising avenue, since it would have signaled open revolt against the General Secretary. Nor could he count on Mittag's help to approach Honecker, as he had done in 1977; Mittag's craven realization of Honecker's ideas was part of the problem. Instead, Schürer decided to circumvent Mittag and appeal personally to Honecker.

Any noticeable deviation from the General Secretary's policy required a modicum of personal courage, especially given the conformist atmosphere Honecker cultivated. Moreover, the experience of 1977, when the General Secretary had reacted with fury to a rather modest savings proposal, was demonstration enough that he was not amenable to rational discussion of his policies. Indeed, Honecker's negative reaction to Schürer's proposals was entirely predictable. Instead of keeping Schürer's paper private, he passed it on to his attack dog, Günter Mittag. It is hard to understand why Schürer thought he could bypass Mittag, since Schürer's critique of Honecker was also a critique of Mittag. Still, once in Mittag's hands, Schürer's proposals might have died a death of neglect, locked away in Mittag's desk until they could be produced to increase Mittag's power. But Willi Stoph got hold of the paper. Stoph, who sympathized with Schürer's recommendations and welcomed any opportunity to tweak Honecker and Mittag, distributed Schürer's paper to the Politburo and Council of Ministers. Stoph's action did not simply force a discussion of Schürer's proposals, it also transformed Schürer's "private" suggestion into a "public" question. Schürer's worries over the GDR's economic future were transformed into a referendum on Honecker's power.

But Schürer had not intended his proposals to be the object of conflict, nor had he canvassed other SED leaders for their support. Without allies, he stood no chance of initiating a policy debate. At the next Politburo meeting, Honecker defended his policies first by proxy, as was his wont. Mittag, who was clearly piqued by Schürer's audacity, submitted a detailed thirty-five-page rebuttal of Schürer's thirteen-page proposal. After insinuating that Schürer's proposals were both impractical and disloyal, he counterattacked by demanding that the State Planning Commission undertake an exact analysis of the subsidies for every economic entity in the GDR – effectively banishing Schürer's proposed reforms to the drudgery of busywork.

In the midst of this carefully orchestrated attack, however, something unusual happened: Stoph leapt to Schürer's defense. Taking aim at Honecker, he sought to force a change in policy by invoking the principle of collective leadership. The GDR's economic situation, Stoph declared, "is no longer tolerable for any of us."[143] To ward off criticism that he was insensitive to the political repercussions of economic decisions, Stoph agreed with Honecker that "the living standards that prevail in the GDR must at the least be maintained, and naturally we must realize the residential housing program." Then Stoph went on the offensive. He implied that Honecker had been disloyal to the party by straying from its economic program, and he demanded that the debt problem be taken seriously: "But we stood up at the Eighth Party Congress with the explanation that we can only consume what we have produced. Thus, we cannot live beyond our means."

In contrast to the long and devastating criticism of Schürer's proposals made by Mittag and Stoph's more pointed remarks, Honecker's response was laconic. He began by saying that "in my opinion, comrade Mittag is correct on all points," thereby dispensing with Schürer's proposals. Honecker then rounded on Stoph. Responding in his characteristically cavalier manner to calls for debt reduction, Honecker dismissed Stoph's charge that his actions had contradicted his policies by noting that responsibility for failing to reduce the debt was collective. "Nothing," declared the General Secretary, "has come of cutting the debt in half, as the Politburo directed. The opposite has come to pass. So the signatures [on the directive] are not valid." Rather than blame the Politburo, however, Honecker shrewdly absolved his colleagues for the failure to reduce the debt. Instead, he shifted the blame onto technical experts who had advocated money-losing projects, slyly reminding his colleagues that "these proposals were made by experts because none of us can judge them comprehensively." By ridiculing the fallability of technical expertise, moreover, Honecker had thoroughly discredited Schürer, whose only authority rested on his economic proficiency. Once again, Honecker's political authority had triumphed over economic rationality.

Schürer's humiliation was complete. He was not demoted, although Mittag would take pleasure in making caustic references to his audacity in the following months. Nor did he resign. To some extent, Schürer's failure to stand up for his principles is but one more manifestation of the communist belief that the party (and therefore the General Secretary of the party) is always right, and that there is no life outside the party. Schürer also seems to have believed that he could accomplish some of his goals by staying on.[144]

143 The following is based on BArchB, DE1, 56285, Politburo meeting on 10.5.88.
144 BArchB, DE1, 56320, Gerhard Schürer, "Rede bei der Parteiaktivtagung der Parteiorganisation der SPK," 14.11.89, pp. 152–5; interview, Schürer, Berlin, 19.4.95 and 20.5.95.

But like most politicians, Schürer was loathe to surrender power until it was taken from him.

Ironically, the next few months saw Honecker and Mittag accept many of the State Planning Commissioner's proposals piecemeal, without acknowledging they were doing so. Even the Politburo member Günter Kleiber, who was closely allied with Honecker, argued that "we must let [expenditures for] social needs stagnate, or even reduce them."[145] By the fall, Schürer enjoyed the support of many of the GDR's leaders for reducing subsidies.[146] Eventually Mittag agreed to a cutback in subsidies for consumer goods, although he would countenance it only on his own terms. For the first time, moreover, Honecker seemed to understand just how dangerous defaulting was and agreed to reduce the bloated military budget.[147] As the economic historian Rainer Karlsch has noted, "at a time when postponing the bankruptcy of the state was paramount, even the military lost influence in the political calculations of the SED leadership."[148]

But these measures were too little too late. Right after he had helped depose Honecker in October 1989, Schürer told the Politburo that the GDR would default on its debts, if not in 1990, then in 1991. Merely servicing the debt (which he calculated would rise to DM 57 billion) would cost DM 8 billion. Under the best conditions, however, the GDR would post a trade surplus of only DM 0.5 billion. To make ends meet, the GDR would have to reduce consumption – including politically sensitive consumer goods – by the horrendous figure of 25 to 30 percent. Honecker's nightmare scenario of a political insurrection sparked by sharp declines in living standards had finally materialized – and through his own handiwork.[149]

---

145 At the same meeting, Kurt Hager acknowledged that "we are living beyond our means, that there is too much purchasing power." He was immediately interrupted by Honecker, who bellowed, "that is totally incorrect. All of these calculations are false!" (BArchB, DE1, 56285, Klopfer, "Persönliche Notizen über die Beratung beim Generalsekretär," 16.5.89, pp. 20, 32).

146 Most important was a meeting in October 1988 convened by Stoph to which Mittag was not invited (BArchB, DE1, 56285, Klopfer, "Persönliche Notizen über die Beratung beim amtierenden Vorsitzenden des Ministerrates am 25.10.1988," 25.10.88; BArchB, DN1, VS 13/90, Nr. 4, Höfner, Halbritter, and Kaminsky, "Analyse der finanziellen Umverteilungsprozesse, die sich über den Staatshaushalt und das Kreditsystem vollziehen," 22.8.89).

147 BArchB, DE1, 55384, Klopfer, "Persönliche Notizen über eine Beratung von Mitgliedern der Parteiführung," 22.1.89, pp. 1–2, 12.

148 Rainer Karlsch, "'Ein Buch mit sieben Siegeln.' Die Schattenhaushalte für den Militär- und Sicherheitsbereich in der DDR und ihre wirtschaftliche Bedeutung," in Wolfram Fischer, Uwe Müller, and Frank Zschaler (eds.), *Wirtschaft im Umbruch. Strukturveränderungen und Wirtschaftspolitik im 19. und 20. Jahrhundert. Festschrift für Lothar Baar zum 65. Geburtstag* (St. Katharinen, 1997), p. 306.

149 Honecker anticipated that the GDR would earn enough hard currency to cover 35 percent of the necessary interest payments, while 65 percent could be covered only by taking on new debt. That meant that the GDR had a debt-to-export ratio of 150 percent, far above the limit of 25 percent most lenders deemed creditworthy (SAPMO-BA, DY30, JIV 2/2A/3252, Politbüro-Sitzung vom 31.10.89, and Schürer, "Analyse der ökonomischen Lage," 30.10.89, pp. 5, 11).

The second half of Erich Honecker's rule saw a rapid deterioration in the GDR's economic position. Although some exogenous factors contributed to the erosion of the GDR's productive capacities, most of the problems afflicting the East German economy were self-made. The GDR's economic ailments were not merely the product of the fiscal exigencies of failed autarky or confused attempts to adjust the strictures of ideology to power-oriented practice. Honecker's attempt to consolidate his political power after removing Ulbricht created a developmental path that ultimately bankrupted the GDR. By the time that Mikhail Gorbachev visited the GDR during its fortieth-anniversary celebration in October 1989, this bankruptcy had taken on moral as well as material form.

Although it was formally committed to vitiating social alienation, the SED under Honecker ruthlessly commodified the planned economy in an attempt to rescue it. The most obvious sign of the declining authority of socialism, however, was not the regime's foray into capitalist commerce, but the burgeoning black market in consumer and producer goods. The increasing shortages of consumer goods, aggravated by Mittag's neglect of East German industry and his ruthless monetization of the East German economy, undermined the planned economy. Consumer demand circumvented legal restrictions on travel and trade, as ordinary East Germans imported vast quantities of Western money and merchandise. This vibrant yet illicit market loosened the grip of the communist party over economic life, displaced the currency of Marxism-Leninism, and sapped the ideological appeal of socialism.

The fragmentation of the East German economy into socialist and capitalist spheres – into sectors based on Ostmark and Westmark – reflected the disjunctions between Marxist-Leninist theory and Honecker's power-oriented practice. Whereas shortages of goods, rather than a shortage of money, had previously characterized life in the GDR, by the early 1980s the East German workforce found itself in the extraordinary position of having to work for money, rather than have money work for it. Worse still, the SED's drive to earn hard currency at all costs meant that East Germans found themselves working for capitalist rather than socialist money. Not only were the fruits of their labor shipped to the West to offset the debts, but ordinary workers were increasingly unable to purchase the consumer goods they desired with East German marks, while the burgeoning black market worked best with West German money. For East Germans hoping to use D-Marks to facilitate a purchase on the black market at home or traveling to West Germany, the declining strength of the East German mark relative to the West German mark was a sobering reminder of the declining value of their own money and the work they had done to earn it. Even the SED leadership was forced to realize that "the feeling for money has been partially lost."[150] Despite Honecker's political skills, the contradictions inherent in his economic policies eventually goaded his colleagues into acting against him. Their action, however, came too late to undo the damage he had done.

150 BArchB, DE1, 56285, "Arbeitsniederschrift über eine Beratung," 6.9.88, p. 17, comment by Mittag.

PART II

Consumption

5

The Vehicle of Desire

The Trabant, the Wartburg, and the Discipline of Demand

The basis of bureaucratic rule is the poverty of society in objects of consumption, with the resulting struggle of each against all. When there is enough goods in a store the purchasers are compelled to stand in line. When the lines are very long, it is necessary to appoint a policeman to keep order. Such is the starting-point of the power of the Soviet bureaucracy. It "knows" who is to get something and who has to wait.[1]

In early June 1989, shortly before East Germans began pouring into Hungary, Czechoslovakia, and Poland in search of an exit from the GDR, the Stasi put together a report for the SED leadership on popular attitudes toward the economy. Like many reports written during the last year of the GDR's existence, this one noted with alarm the increasing inclination of the East German population to link economic performance, as measured by the supply of consumer products, to questions of political legitimacy. The quantity and quality of consumer goods in the GDR, the report claimed, "is increasingly becoming the basic criterion for the assessment of the attractiveness of socialism in comparison to capitalism." The report went on to warn that the political stability of the GDR risked becoming dependent upon the availability of one consumer good, the automobile. "Many citizens," the Stasi wrote, "view the solution of the automobile problem as a measure of the success of the GDR's economic policies."[2]

Clearly, other glaring deficits in East German society in addition to the shortages of consumer goods contributed to the general political unrest that overwhelmed the SED in the autumn of 1989. On the one hand, the ubiquitous abrogations of civil rights permitted the harassment of critics of

1 Leon Trotsky, cited in Isaac Deutscher, *Stalin* (London, 1949), p. 339.
2 SAPMO-BA, DY30, IV 2/2039/268, "Hinweise auf beachtenswerte Aspekte der Reaktion der Bevölkerung zur Um- und Durchsetzung der ökonomischen Strategie der SED," 6.6.89, pp. 78, 80.

the regime, such as those protesting for the right to free speech in January 1988. On the other, the party's hollow promises of democratic representation found cynical expression in fixed electoral outcomes, such as the rigged communal elections of May 1989. These political deficits, together with the economic deficiencies, transformed the GDR into a society wracked by an overabundance of shortcomings. In fact, it was this very plenitude of wants that finally did the GDR in once the protective hand of the Soviet Union was removed.

The growth of popular discontent with the regime's economic failings throughout the 1980s was fueled by the politicization of the economic sphere. Consumer shortages, but especially the inadequate number of automobiles, engendered a variety of criticisms of the SED, from written reproaches in petitions to economic behavior criminalized by the party. The longer people were forced to wait for whatever item they desired, moreover, the more likely their grievances were to become programmatic censures of the regime. The SED coped with such criticism primarily through a combination of formalized neglect and disciplinary observation, ranging from attempts to influence people's desires rhetorically to the creation of registration systems aimed at rendering these desires visible and therefore more manageable.

Despite the warnings of the Stasi, the planning apparatus, and technocrats at the ZK, however, the leadership of the SED was unable to do the one thing that might have dampened popular discontent: make more consumer goods available, and more cars in particular. Instead, the quantitative and qualitative inadequacies of the SED's economic strategies found their concrete expression in the Trabant and the Wartburg, the two domestically produced automobiles. The Trabant's plastic body, for example, was a creative response to a shortage of sheet metal, presented to the public as a statement of modern design.[3] To the population, however, which referred to the Trabant as the "cardboard racecar" (*Rennpappe*), the dangerously pliable body was an excellent example of the SED's botched attempts to meet consumer needs. Even by Soviet bloc standards, the Trabant did not live up to the modernist promise of its name (Satellite), which had been bestowed on the car in honor of the Soviet Union's technological triumph, the *Sputnik* satellite.[4] But popular expectations in East Germany regarding the quality

---

3 Franz Meißner, chief of Research and Design at VEB Sachsenring in Zwickau, 1960s, *Der Tagesspiegel*, 7.7.97; Peter Kirchberg, *Horch, Audi, DKW, IFA: 80 Jahre Geschichte der Autos aus Zwickau* (Berlin, 1991), pp. 180–2.
4 The differences between the National Socialist "People's Car" (*Volkswagen*) and the Socialist Unity Party's "Satellite" merit an analysis of modernist utopias that falls outside the confines of this chapter.

of consumer goods were largely shaped by perceptions of Western abundance culled from West German television and radio. Thus, the quality of the Trabant was the butt of many a bitter joke, such as the following: "How do you double the value of a Trabant? Fill it up with gas." The perceived contrast between Western plenty and Eastern penury, combined with insufficient quality, politicized discontent; desire intensified by its frustration ultimately drove the East German population to insurrection.

The paucity of key consumer items plagued the East German regime from the start, leading the SED under Ulbricht to tighten the rhetorical connection between current sacrifices and the future of a morally pristine prosperity. With Honecker's assumption of power in 1971, however, the GDR entered the phase of "real-existing socialism," a slogan reflecting the new policy of shifting resources to meet consumer demands. As we saw in the preceding chapters, Honecker did not invent a new model of Marxist-Leninist consumerism, but instead committed the SED to an immediate improvement of the array and caliber of goods available to East German consumers. By renouncing future utopias in favor of present plenty, however, Honecker simultaneously opened the door to criticism of the real-existing here and now.

The relative squalor of that socialist present, moreover, was derived directly from the SED's subordination of the economy to the moral objective of social equity. The ex ante elevation of political aims over economic practice laid the foundations for an economic regime designed to eradicate poverty, guarantee full employment, and provide everyone with basic foodstuffs at little cost, while "overcom[ing] outdated consumption and living habits as well as restrain[ing] the influence of bourgeois consumption ideologies."[5] Yet the planned economy proved incapable of producing and distributing consumer goods in the quantity and quality desired by the population. The resulting economy of shortages generated widespread dissatisfaction, which became a political threat to the party not merely because of material discontent, but also because of the moral shortcomings of a regime that incessantly asserted its ethical superiority over its capitalist neighbor.

It should be noted, however, that this Nazi celebration of private transportation and consumerism entailed an egalitarianism of a different sort than did the SED's prescriptive abstinence – one built on a racial community that excluded, exploited, and eventually exterminated non-Aryans. On the Volkswagen, see Wolfgang König, *Volkswagen, Volksempfänger, Volksgemeinschaft: "Volksprodukte" im Dritten Reich: vom Scheitern einer nationalsozialistischen Konsumgesellschaft* (Paderborn, 2004), pp. 17–18, 20–1, 151–91; Hans Mommsen and Manfred Geiger, *Das Volkswagenwerk und seine Arbeiter im Dritten Reich* (Düsseldorf, 1996), pp. 53–70, 179–202; Overy, *War and Economy in the Third Reich*, ch. 2.

5 BArchB, DL1, 23780, Institut für Marktforschung, "Prognose der Entwicklung des Konsumgüterverbrauchs," 1973, p. 3.

The SED's philippics against capitalist exploitation and its paeans to the virtues of socialist production methods were belied by the deficiencies of overcentralization and by the diminishing sense of social equity the shortages created. Whatever camaraderie of deprivation people might have experienced just after the Second World War evaporated when they saw the privileges enjoyed by party members and those who had relatives in the West. In fact, the discrepancy between material privation and verbal excess only succeeded in further arousing popular loathing and consumer appetite. Under these conditions, the Trabant became a symbol of the shortcomings of the SED's economic policies and the concomitant political lack of the freedom to travel. With its plastic body and two-stroke engine, it came to epitomize the regime of want created by the failure of the Marxist-Leninist moral economy.

The "automobile problem" to which the Stasi rather obliquely referred in 1989 was in reality nothing less than the paucity of cars manufactured, although the tendency of the SED to conflate cause with effect led the Stasi to focus on the consumer behavior induced by the shortage of cars rather than on the production levels responsible for the shortage. According to official statistics, which were often slanted to represent the reporting authority in the best possible light, the roughly 17 million East Germans seem to have had at their disposal the largest number of cars in Eastern Europe, with a total of just under 3.6 million automobiles registered to private persons as of October 1988.[6] The majority of these cars were Trabants, but there was a goodly portion of Wartburgs, as well as Soviet Ladas, Moskvitches, Zaporozhets, and Volgas, Czechoslovak Škodas, Romanian Dacias, and Polski Fiats. There were even some Western makes, including Volkswagens, Citroëns, Mazdas, and Volvos.[7]

Yet in comparison to its West German neighbor, which was the standard of measurement for most East Germans, these accomplishments looked far more modest.[8] The Federal Republic dwarfed the GDR in the ratio of automobiles to the population: In 1988, the last full calendar year before the Berlin Wall came down, there was one car for every two West Germans

---

6 SAPMO-BA, DY30, Vorläufige SED 38644, Ministerium des Innern, "Lageeinschätzung zum spekulativen Handel mit gebrauchten PKW," no date, p. 1; Philip J. Bryson, *The Consumer under Socialist Planning* (New York, 1984), p. 112.

7 SAPMO-BA, DY30, Vorläufige SED 38644, Ministerium des Innern, "Lageeinschätzung," no date, Anlage 1.

8 Of course, automobile production and consumption is not necessarily a mark of progress. The GDR placed great emphasis on its public transportation network, which was both inexpensive and convenient. Even so, the East German rail system compared poorly with its West German counterpart by the 1980s.

compared to one car for every four-and-a-half East Germans. According to internal GDR figures, some 50 percent of East German households owned cars in the late 1980s.[9] A more realistic estimation lies probably under 40 percent, but either way it compares poorly to the rough figure of over 70 percent for West Germany.[10] The main reason for this disparity was the low level of production, which by the late 1980s had stagnated at just under 220,000 annually. Car production for the Federal Republic in 1988 totaled 3.98 million, or nearly 20 times annual East German production.[11]

Worse still, not all of the cars manufactured in the GDR were made available for domestic consumption. This was less because of international demand for the Trabant and the Wartburg, which was quite limited.[12] Rather, the political constraints of economic cooperation with the Soviet bloc promoted an inequitable trade structure for the transportation sector, requiring that the GDR export more than it imported.[13] The plan for the year 1989, for example, foresaw the retention of about two-thirds of the automobiles actually produced for domestic consumption. Even when we add the 21,513 imported cars to this sum – for the most part Soviet Ladas and Czechoslovak Škodas – the total number of cars the SED planned to

9 SAPMO-BA, DY30, IV 2/2039/191, Ministerium des Innern, HA Verkehrspolizei, "Information über den Bestand und bemerkenswerte Tendenzen der Entwicklung in der DDR zugelassener Fahrzeuge (Stand 30.9.1986)," 6.4.87, p. 1.
10 SAPMO-BA, DY30, Vorläufige SED 38644, "Zur Situation bei der Versorgung mit Pkw" (no date), p. 1. A comparison of car ownership per household is problematic. Not only did statisticians in each country define "household" differently, but the structure of each society was different, not the least because of the shortage of residential housing in East Germany and the larger number of single adults living alone in the Federal Republic. Even if this figure overestimates car ownership per household, moreover, it is likely that the proportion of East German households in possession of a car increased during the 1980s. Unfortunately, the FRG does not provide statistics on the number of cars held by households. These figures were estimated by comparing the total number of units registered in the country (30.26 million) to the number of households as defined by the government, which excluded people with incomes over 25,000 marks a month and people living in *Gemeinschaftsunterkünfte* (24.69 million), and again to the figures for households reported as owning cars (16.75 million), as reported in Statistisches Bundesamt (ed.), *Statistisches Jahrbuch der Bundesrepublik Deutschland für 1989* (Stuttgart, 1990), pp. 275, 471.
11 BArchB, DE1, 55382, Vorlage für das Sekretariat des ZK, "Zur grundsätzlichen Veränderung der Situation bei der Versorgung der Bevölkerung mit Service- und Instandhaltungsleistungen für Personenkraftwagen," 1987, p. 8; Statistisches Bundesamt (ed.), *Statistisches Jahrbuch der BRD für 1989*, p. 185.
12 Between 1959 and 1973, the years when the Trabant was the least outmoded, about 30,000 were exported to capitalist countries, including a paltry 900 to the FRG (Matthias Röcke, *Die Trabi-Story. Der Dauerbrenner aus Zwickau* [Schindellegi, Switzerland, 1998], p. 17).
13 This is in contrast to the earlier claim by Thomas Weymar that the GDR sought to compensate for the domestic shortage of motor vehicles with imports (Thomas Weymar, "Das Auto – Statussymbol auch im Sozialismus. Soziale und politische Folgeprobleme des Individualverkehrs in der DDR," *Deutschland Archiv* 3 [1977], p. 273).

Table 5. *Automobile Production in East Germany, 1938–1989*

Year	Total Cars Produced[a]	Number of Cars Exported[b]	Number of Cars Imported[c]	Number Made Available to Population[d]
1938	57,485	No data	No data	No data
1946	1,439	No data	No data	No data
1951	11,092	No data	No data	No data
1956	28,145	No data	No data	No data
1961	69,562	No data	No data	No data
1966	106,460	No data	No data	No data
1971	134,265	No data	No data	108,500
1976	163,970	(Total of 353,129	(Total of 371,919	155,500
1978	170,697	exported 1976–80)	imported 1976–80)	160,200
1979	171,345			129,000
1980	176,761			136,600
1981	180,233	(Total of 338,519	(Total of 144,875	123,000
1982	182,930	exported 1981–85)	imported 1981–85)	121,600
1983	188,300			120,800
1984	202,000			131,100
1985	210,370			139,100
1986	217,931	73,338	24,238	147,900
1987	217,936	72,913	23,803	146,700
1988	218,045	69,689	18,163	147,910
1989	216,969	56,080	21,700	150,100

[a] *Sources: Statistische Jahrbücher der DDR.* Figures for 1938 are for Eastern Germany only (Peter Kirchberg, "Die Geschichte der Automobilindustrie in Sachsen," *Archiv und Wirtschaft: Zeitschrift für das Archivwesen der Wirtschaft* 25:4 [1992], p. 140).

[b] *Sources:* SAPMO-BA, DY30, Vorläufige SED 38644, Weiß to Jarowinsky, "Übersicht zum PKW-Export der DDR," Anlage 1, 20.4.89, and "Information zum Stand der Durchführung der festgelegten SW-Exporte und Importe bei Pkw im Jahre 1989," 2.5.89. Figures include exports to socialist as well as nonsocialist countries.

[c] *Source:* SAPMO-BA, DY30, Vorläufige SED 38644, Weiß to Jarowinsky, 20.4.89, "Übersicht zum PKW-Export der DDR," Anlage 2. Figures include imports from socialist and nonsocialist countries, excluding 50 VW Golfs that were imported between 1987 and 1989.

[d] *Sources:* SAPMO-BA, DY30, Vorläufige SED 38644, Abteilung Handel, Versorgung und Außenhandel, "Bemerkungen zur Vorlage," 15.8.88, and "Warenbereitstellung von PKW in 1000 Stück," no date; SAPMO-BA, DY30, Vorläufige SED 41852, "Zu den gegenwärtig gültigen Verkaufspreisen für PKW," 4.6.85, and "Die Bereitstellung PKW für Bevölkerung im Zeitraum 1971 bis 1985"; SAPMO-BA, DY30, IV 2/2.039/70, "Politbüro-Sitzung vom 14. Februar 1989," p. 26. These figures are likely to include imports. Figures for 1988 and 1989 are planning targets, not concrete figures.

make available to the populace amounted to a mere 168,093, far less than total domestic production.[14]

The wave of automobile purchases soon after German monetary union in July 1990 provides ample evidence of the pent-up desire for automobiles in the GDR. Nor were SED leaders unaware of the growing demand. Tens of thousands of letters written annually by East German citizens to factory managers and state and party officials attest to the population's desire to own a car. Some party leaders even linked the shortfall of automobiles to the erosion of political support for the party among key social groups. In 1988, for example, Gerhard Briksa, the Minister of Trade and Supply, wrote to Politburo member Willi Stoph that "making a larger number of cars available to the population would permit us to react to growing criticism from broad groups of the population about long waits... and help motivate employees and especially groups such as physicians, teachers, and the technical intelligentsia to higher levels of performance."[15]

"WE MAKE THE TRABANT AS CHEAP AS IT LOOKS"[16]

Why, then, did the party not decide to produce more automobiles, especially given the political headaches the shortage caused? The most important factors included economic overcentralization, which starved the industry of capital, and insufficient standardization, which undermined the rational management of scarce resources. In addition, production fell prey to a political rivalry that was occasioned by the geographic dispersal of factories. This political division was embodied in the SED's decision to produce two different cars, the Trabant and the Wartburg. In the absence of one single, standardized automobile, East Germans enjoyed greater choice, but at the expense of higher production levels. More important than these material constraints, however, was the SED's ideological suspicion of automobiles. Not only was the party wary of the individual mobility that accompanied automobile culture, but it was also deeply mistrustful of the social status conferred by owning a car.

Some authors have suggested that Soviet occupation policy negatively influenced the development of the East German automobile industry. The USSR, they note, decided early on that the GDR should concentrate its

14 SAPMO-BA, DY30, IV 2/2039/70, "Politbüro-Sitzung vom 14. Februar 1989," p. 26; SAPMO-BA, DY30, Vorläufige SED 38644, Abteilung Handel, Versorgung und Außenhandel, "Bemerkung zur Vorlage 'Beschlußvorlage zur Bestätigung des Verbraucherpreises für den Pkw Wartburg mit 4-Takt-Otto Motor,'" 15.8.88, p. 1.
15 SAPMO-BA, DY30, Vorläufige SED 41792, Briksa to Stoph, 27.6.88, p. 4.
16 "Wir machen den Trabant so billig, wie er aussieht." I am grateful to Volker Lange for this joke.

efforts on producing light trucks rather than cars.[17] Yet Soviet influence was hardly responsible for the technological lag or the impediments to production that plagued the GDR's automobile industry. The main drag on East German automotive design during the 1950s, for example consisted of brain drain – a flight of engineers to the West, lured by the promise of better living standards.[18] Nor is it clear that making trucks for the Red Army constituted a developmental cul-de-sac, since the demand-pull stimulated the production of engines and chassis.

More important were chronic problems in the production process, problems characteristic of the planned economy. Obsolete and worn-out machines, poor and outmoded designs, and the ubiquitous presence of metal dust, which abraded delicate machines and soft human tissue alike, contributed to production losses. The structure of East German manufacturing, moreover, created significant obstacles to the integration of new technologies, from its overcentralization and top-heavy management to its inability to offer clear incentives to workers to increase productivity.

In this context, it is worth pointing out just how problematic post–1989 claims are that the East German automobile industry was technologically more advanced than West Germany's. Even in the unlikely event that the prototypes constructed by East German engineers did anticipate Western designs, the problem East German industry faced was one of production, not conception. It is one thing to construct an automobile for test purposes, but quite another to mass produce it. And the GDR never really mastered large-scale production techniques.

The myth of superior East German design, moreover, was spread by East German engineers concerned to shift responsibility for the poor quality of and long waits for the Trabant and Wartburg onto politicians, who allegedly placed their careers before the technological demands of the nation.[19] Many East Germans disappointed by the course of German unification have eagerly taken up this tale of a sophisticated automotive technology relegated to the scrapheap by narrow-minded communist leaders. The belief that East German industry did not founder on its engineering but rather on a lack of

---

17 In January 1946, the Soviet Military Administration (SMAD) took over the BMW works in Eisenach. Rather than dismantle them, SMAD created SAG Awto-Velo (later VEB Automobilwerke Eisenach) and used the factory to produce a small number of BMWs. In contrast, the SMAD dismantled much of the old Horch and Audi factories and shipped them back to the Soviet Union. With what was left, SMAD had the factories produce light vans (Kirchberg, "Die Geschichte," pp. 142–4; Kirchberg, *Horch, Audi, DKW, IFA*, pp. 170–6; Röcke, *Die Trabi-Story*, pp. 15–16).

18 Interview, Jacob and Sachs, Chemnitz, 26.2.96; and Scholwin, Berlin, 23.11.95.

19 See, for example, the improbable assertions of Werner Lang, head of the Construction Department at VEB Sachsenring Zwickau from 1958 to 1983, that the P603 prototype from 1969 would have given the GDR "a technological lead of two years over international competitors" (*Berliner Zeitung*, 7.11.97; see also *Quick*, 15.2.90, and *Die Zeit*, 26.4.96).

political insight may help compensate for a sense of loss and even inferiority, feelings that have been reinforced by the near-complete West German domination of the unified German economy. But it is not supported by the facts. The SED's last-ditch attempt to modernize automobile production, for example, was a costly failure. It swallowed over 11 billion East German marks during the 1980s, yet was plagued by expensive disappointments, from breakdowns at the new foundry that was supposed to produce steel for engines to the constant problems encountered in the production of carburetors.[20] Perhaps most embarrassing, however, was the ill-advised licensing agreement with Volkswagen that Economic Secretary Günter Mittag concluded in 1984. In return for an assembly line for producing four-stroke Otto motors, the East German automobile industry agreed to deliver DM 500 million worth of motors over several years. Although lauded by Mittag and West German Chancellor Helmut Kohl as an example of German–German cooperation, the deal was a disaster for the GDR.[21] Not only was the plant delivered by VW worn out, but the East Germans proved incapable of delivering the motors in compensation for the equipment.[22] In addition, production shortfalls and poor working conditions weighed heavily on labor morale. As a result, the number of workers leaving VEB Automobilwerke Sachsenring Zwickau's body production unit jumped from 13 percent of the factory's workforce in 1985 to 35 percent in 1988.[23] For all of its braggadocio regarding socialist production methods, the GDR never really mastered mass production techniques. By the 1980s, when Japanese manufacturing models were revolutionizing automobile production, the GDR was still mired in unsuccessful attempts to make a go of its socialist version of Fordism.[24]

---

20 BArchB, DE1, 56309, "Information zur Motorenkonzeption für die Pkw 'Wartburg' und 'Trabant' und zur Erhöhung der Produktion," 26.11.87; BStU, Arbeitsbereich Mittig, Nr. 58, "Zu den ausgewählten Problemen," Anlage 5, pp. 39–41; SAPMO-BA, DY30, Vorläufige SED 41772, Scholwin, "Information über eingeleitete Maßnahmen zur Stabilisierung der Lage im VEB Metallgußwerk Leipzig," 4.12.87; SAPMO-BA, DY30, Vorläufige SED 35650, "Ersatzteile für PKW Wartburg"; BArchB, DN10, 1533, correspondence regarding carburetors and ignition systems.

21 SAPMO-BA, DY30, JIV 2/2A/2644, "Niederschrift über das Gespräch Günter Mittags mit Helmut Kohl in Bonn am 6. April 1984," cited in Detlev Nakath and Gerd-Rüdiger Stephan (eds.), *Von Hubertusstock nach Bonn. Eine dokumentierte Geschichte der deutsch-deutschen Beziehungen auf höchster Ebene, 1980–1987* (Berlin, 1995), p. 181.

22 SAPMO-BA, DY30, Vorläufige SED 41850, "Information über einige Probleme aus dem Monatsbericht des Genossen Schumann, Bezirksleitung Leipzig," no date, p. 7; BArchB, DE1, 55382, Vorlage für das Sekretariat des ZK, "Zur grundsätzlichen Veränderung der Situation"; BArchB, DE1, 56309, Staatliche Plankommission, "Information zur Motorenkonzeption," 26.11.87.

23 BArchB, DE1, 56309, Staatliche Plankommission, "Standpunkt zu dem Material des Betriebsdirektors des VEB Automobilwerke Zwickau," 24.11.88, pp. 183–6; Hipp, VEB Sachsenring Automobilwerke Zwickau, "Standpunkt zu Rundrichtungen der weiteren Entwicklung der Trabant-Produktion," 18.10.88, pp. 191–5.

24 For more on production problems in the East German automobile industry, see Werner Abelshauser, "Two Kinds of Fordism: On the Differing Roles of Industry in the Development of the Two German States," in Haruhito Shiomi and Kazuo Wada (eds.), *Fordism Transformed: The Development of*

More fateful for the East German automotive sector was the political map that the SED superimposed on the geographical distribution of production in Saxony, which institutionalized economic irrationalities in the production process. In 1938, Saxony accounted for about 30 percent of total German automobile production and 25 percent of sales, with the most important factories located at the Horch and Audi works in Zwickau and the BMW plant in Eisenach.[25] Perhaps with an eye to brand recognition and worker loyalties, the SED decided in 1949 not to unify production under one management, thus preserving industrial continuities with capitalist and fascist Germany. Whatever the case, the communist party's political division of the country into geographical districts had the unintended consequence of reinforcing the old capitalist rivalry between Horch and BMW because it placed the Zwickau works under the jurisdiction of the district party leadership of Karl-Marx-Stadt and the Eisenach works under the Erfurt party leadership.[26] This freed politicians, who were loath to surrender their command over resources as prestigious and valuable as cars, to pursue local rivalries by meddling in the management of production.

A second chance to reorganize the motor vehicle industry along rational lines opened up in 1977. Mittag's plan to streamline management structures by introducing combines offered an unusual opportunity to place the two centers of automobile production under the same direction. After some deliberation, he placed control of the new automobile combine in the hands of the Barkas works in Karl-Marx-Stadt. Formally, this decision ended the conflict by subordinating Wartburg factory managers and the Erfurt district leadership to the Trabant and Karl-Marx-Stadt. In reality, however, the new managerial structure was riven by continued territorial rivalries and political frictions, which Mittag eagerly exploited for his own purposes. Driven by his political ambitions, Mittag not only resisted consolidating automobile production geographically, but he actively undercut Karl-Marx-Stadt's dominance of the industry by promoting a political ally, Gerhard Müller, to the position of district party leader in Erfurt. With Mittag's support, Müller was free to pursue his rivalry with Siegfried Lorenz, district party leader of Karl-Marx-Stadt.[27] The two district party leaderships fought proxy

---

Production Methods in the Automobile Industry (Oxford, 1995), pp. 269–96. I find the term "Fordism" misleading in the communist context, since economic planning completely ignored the demand side of Fordism's equation.

25 Kirchberg, "Die Geschichte," p. 140.

26 Ibid., pp. 142–4; Kirchberg, *Horch, Audi, DKW, IFA*, pp. 170–6; Röcke, *Die Trabi-Story*, pp. 15–17.

27 Müller was Erfurt district leader from 1981 to 1989, and candidate Politburo member from 1985 to 1989. He did not shy away from using his connection to Mittag to increase Eisenach's autonomy from Karl-Marx-Stadt and acquire new fixed capital (SAPMO-BA, DY30, Vorläufige SED 38527,

wars through their factory managers, often over the distribution of scarce resources. As a result, an economically irrational competition continued to shape automobile production in the GDR. By the mid-1980s, tensions between Müller and Lorenz were so serious that they began to erode the chain of industrial command. Backed by Müller, for example, the director of the VEB Automobilwerke Eisenach was openly insubordinate toward the combine's general director on numerous occasions.[28]

Magnified by local particularism, these personal antagonisms thwarted more rational solutions to production shortages in the automobile industry. The most production-oriented approach entailed merging the two plants and constructing a standardized car (*Einheitsauto*). Many in the planning apparatus believed that manufacturing just one automobile rather than two models would be more economical and make better use of the GDR's limited resources. After all, making the Trabant as well as the Wartburg required two different production standards for two different motors, chassis, and bodies. Manufacturing two different cars also split production forces and reduced economies of scale, while duplicating many processes and positions. The main obstacle to producing one standardized car was the two district party leaders, who refused to surrender control over resources, especially when those assets conveyed so much prestige and power.[29] Mittag encouraged this competition, even when it made no economic sense. His decision to upgrade the Wartburg before the Trabant, for example, was predicated less on producing large numbers of modern cars for the East German population than on advancing his protégé Müller.

The convergence of divided power and fragmented production created an important anomaly in the SED's direction of the economy: The automobile sector became one of the few East German consumer industries that offered more than one brand of the same product. For ideological reasons, the SED endeavored more often than not to manufacture only one consumer good in a particular category. According to Marxist-Leninist theory, capitalist producers require a measure of deception to stimulate demand and focus therefore on variety of design without regard for difference in

Müller to Mittag, 8.8.86, Blessing to Mittag, 3.9.86, and Mittag to Müller, no date). Lorenz, who belonged to the group of "reformers" who would depose Honecker, was Karl-Marx-Stadt district leader from 1976 to 1989, candidate Politburo member in 1985, and full Politburo member from 1986 to 1989.

28 SAPMO-BA, DY30, Vorläufige SED 35649, Fehr to Voigt, "Aufgabenstellung aus der Problembe-ratung am 27.2.1985 (M 29) im VEB AWE," 24.4.85; interview, Klopfer, Berlin, 4.10.95; Scholwin, Berlin, 23.11.95; and Jacob and Sachs, Chemnitz, 26.2.96.

29 Interview, Schürer, Berlin, 20.5.95; Klopfer, Berlin, 4.10.95; Scholwin, Berlin, 23.11.95; and Jacob and Sachs, Chemnitz, 26.2.96.

function. In contrast, the liberation from monetary constraints allegedly freed socialist production to emphasize transparency, uniting function with form. In fact, East German design sought to integrate the Bauhaus tradition into a Soviet-style "realism," making use of sparse lines to convey the industrial process embodied in the artifact in a way that was unencumbered by the distasteful aspects of Western commercialism. The resulting "aesthetic stringency" of East German design complemented the modest selection of available commodities and appealed to many Germans, in the GDR as well as in the FRG, who mistrusted the commercialism of the West.[30] By the time Honecker had assumed power, however, the radical edge of East German design had given way to bald imitation of West German products, impoverished in conception as well as execution. For most East Germans, the resulting monotony of design and paucity of choice, from televisions to tampons, lent the socialist state a grayness that made its West German neighbor seem that much more colorful. Whatever increased sense of freedom East German consumers may have enjoyed because they could choose between the Trabant and the Wartburg was thus undercut by the drabness of the options and, more importantly, the shortage of cars.

The planning apparatus' efforts to rationalize production were not only stymied by political quarrels at home. The SED leadership's mistrust of its communist allies also doomed international attempts to forge cooperative ventures aimed at manufacturing more cars more cheaply. In the early 1970s, for example, a deal was worked out between IFA and the Škoda works in Slovakia to modernize outmoded technology and increase automobile production in the GDR and Czechoslovakia. The agreement foresaw a division of labor that combined Czechoslovak motor technology with East German car design. The proposal eventually met with the East German Politburo's rejection, however, because it required each side to surrender technology to the other and cooperate in an atmosphere of suspicion and autarky. More modest proposals foundered on Honecker's reservations in 1974 and again in 1979.[31]

CONSTRUCTING CONSUMERISM

In the end, however, the underproduction of automobiles in the GDR was not determined by material constraints, the idiosyncrasies of central

30 Georg C. Bertsch, Ernst Hedler, and Matthias Dietz, *Schönes Einheits-Design − Stunning Eastern Design − Savoir Eviter le Design* (Cologne, 1994), p. 21.
31 BArchB, DE1, 56309, "Information zum Motorenkonzeption," 26.11.87, p. 205; Röcke, *Die Trabi-Story*, pp. 86–8; interview, Klopfer, Berlin, 4.10.95; Scholwin, Berlin, 23.11.95; and Jacob and Sachs, Chemnitz, 26.2.96.

planning, political divisions, or the lack of cooperation in the Soviet bloc. Instead, Marxist–Leninist theory combined with German working-class traditions to determine how resources were apportioned for production. The production of consumer goods in the GDR was largely organized by the epistemological distinction made by the SED between "real" and "false" needs. As discussed in Chapter 1, the East German communist party argued that the pursuit of money drives capitalists to seek out new markets, manipulate established ones, and maximize profits by manufacturing commodities whose form obscures their function. Through catchy advertising and colorful packaging, producers stimulate desires, which they then market to consumers as needs. In the party's turgid formulation, capitalism generates "a mass manipulation aimed above all at steering people toward the material needs of a so-called increase in living standards, as well as the misuse of the advertising industry to suggest needs for new goods or services."[32] The SED linked these desires to the form of social alienation that Marx termed commodity fetishism, or the false ascription to inanimate objects of the power to satisfy human needs. The production relations of capitalism alienate human needs, the SED argued, transforming them into "needs [that] are deformed, manipulated, and in part artificially manufactured to suggest illusions to working people about their real situation in society."[33] In this manner, the SED presented "false" needs, from "the desire to gain status through consumption, to vanity, sensationalism, sexuality, etc." as constituent elements of capitalism.[34]

By portraying desire as an ethically dubious need to enhance individual identity by buying into the social hierarchies often attached to consumer goods, the party tapped into a tradition of anticapitalist thought that had deep roots in Germany on the right as well as on the left. The denigration of desire enabled the party to portray certain kinds of consumer demand as illegitimate while appealing to working-class resentments of the status hierarchies mediated by the ostentatious acquisition of commodities. For Honecker's generation, critiques of bourgeois and aristocratic patterns of consumption as extravagant, and therefore useless and socially divisive, coexisted alongside

---

32 *Ökonomisches Lexikon A-G* (East Berlin, 1978), p. 291. In socialism, advertisement was not an instrument aimed at commodifying the world, but rather a tool of enlightenment – "part of the total work of educating the public" that could be harnessed to "eliminate false ideas and errors." In the GDR, advertisement was supposed to be "objective and truthful, and arouse attention and interest [but it] must be rational and effective" (Hans Borchert [ed.], *Lexikon der Wirtschaft: Industrie* [East Berlin, 1970], p. 866). For more on advertising in the GDR, see Pamela Swett, S. Jonathan Wiesen, and Jonathan R. Zatlin (eds.), *Selling Modernity: Advertising and Public Relations in Modern German History* (Durham, N.C., in press).
33 Seeger (ed.), *Lexikon der Wirtschaft: Volkswirtschaftsplanung*, pp. 86–7.
34 *Ökonomisches Lexikon A-G*, p. 285.

the colonization of working-class taste by bourgeois custom.[35] Without the means to buy into the latest fashionable trend or the social currency to obtain access to sought-after products, workers were consigned to the bottom of a status hierarchy driven by the unequal distribution of wealth. For the gerontocracy that dominated Honecker's Politburo, it was easy to view West Germany as offering the same elite model of consumerism. After all, Ludwig Erhard, the most vigorous proponent of the West German social market economy, made expanded access to consumer goods contingent on an initial phase of exclusivity, when wealthy individuals willing to pay a premium could enjoy new and expensive commodities.[36] Working-class hostility to and envy of a consumer culture restricted to the upper and middle classes reinforced the communist party's theoretical reservations about social desire, producing a powerful critique of Western commercialism.

Linking desire to commodity fetishism, moreover, provided the party with an important argument in its struggle against Western criticism of the planned economy. By deploying the distinction between real and false needs, for example, it can be argued that the notion of "consumer sovereignty" overstates the significance of political liberty by neglecting economic constraints on individual freedom. In phrases such as "the customer is king," market economies celebrate limitations on the power of producers to shape the framework within which economic exchange takes place. From the socialist vantage point, however, apologists for capitalism confuse consumers' subjective experience of power with the actual power they wield. If capitalist consumers are busily attempting to gratify alienated needs through the purchase of commodities, then the freedom of choice they experience during commercial transactions must also be alienated. Because it overestimates consumer autonomy, moreover, the concept of consumer sovereignty obscures the central role played by governments and corporations in constructing consumption and consumer goods to which commodity fetishism draws attention. Nor is it clear that choice is equivalent to freedom. In contrast, the SED presented state intervention in the economy as a necessary guarantee against the dissemination of false needs and choices.

Aside from mobilizing hostility toward West Germany, the SED's distinction between false and real needs permitted the party to articulate a theoretical alternative to the capitalist model of consumption. In contrast to "the manipulated petit-bourgeois acquisitiveness and greed [that reigns]

---

35 For the French, British, and American examples, see Gary Cross, *Time and Money: The Making of Consumer Culture* (London and New York, 1993).
36 Wildt, *Am Beginn der 'Konsumgesellschaft,'* pp. 9–10.

in capitalism," the SED maintained, the public ownership of the means of production under socialism makes possible the conditions under which real needs can develop and become autonomous.[37] As we saw in Chapter 1, the SED asserted that organizing production according to egalitarian precepts, rather than market mechanisms, provided a means of rationally allocating resources aimed at satisfying real needs. In a 1973 report on the practical implications of Honecker's economic policy, the Leipzig Institute for Market Research explained that "rational standards of consumption [would] overcome obsolete consumer lifestyles and habits as well as suppress the influence of bourgeois ideologies of consumption."[38] By attending to real needs, Honecker's economic program would contribute toward "the harmonious development of socialist society under the leadership of the working class and simultaneously toward an increasingly perfect formation of socialist personalities."

In order to ensure the elimination of commodity fetishism, as well as the status hierarchies accompanying the inequitable ownership of consumer products, the SED under Honecker pursued a redistribution of income intended to level access to consumer goods. Raising incomes would, in turn, raise individual consumption among workers commensurate with "the leading position of the working class in [socialist] society." In addition, the party was engaged in "the systematic and planned direction of and influence on the use of consumer goods" by setting "rational consumer standards" – a euphemism for its division of consumer goods into the necessary, which included goods and services deemed basic to existence such as bread and rent, and the nonnecessary, which included consumer durables such as televisions and cars. To realize these political priorities, Honecker subsidized the "basic necessities" of life while pursuing a strategy of underproduction and high prices aimed at restraining demand for consumer durables. On such an ethical scale, cars appeared as a luxury and thus enjoyed a low priority in the apportioning of funds for production and distribution. As Honecker reminded his colleagues in 1988, the regime built three million residential housing units for the population, "but it was never promised that every family must have a car by 1990."[39]

Despite its proscription of desire, however, the planned economy failed to devise a viable alternative to the Western model of consumerism.

---

37 Ehlert et al., *Wörterbuch der Ökonomie: Sozialismus*, pp. 485–6.
38 This and the following quotes taken from BArchB, DL1, 23780, Institut für Marktforschung, "Prognose der Entwicklung des Konsumgüterverbrauchs," 1973, pp. 3, 1, 5.
39 BArchB, DE1, 56285, Klopfer, "Persönliche Notizen über die Beratung der Wirtschaftskommission des Politbüros beim ZK der SED vom 17.10.1988," 17.10.88, p. 7.

Rather than inventing a new model of socialist consumerism, the SED was content to sell need to East Germans as if it were desire. The result was a "dictatorship over needs," in which the bureaucracy became the ultimate arbiter of what the East German population should consume.[40] Had the SED matched its theoretical austerity with a similarly modest policy, the party might have managed the gap between need and desire – and between the socialist East and the capitalist West – with more success. By offering East Germans the hope of improvement in their living standards, however, Honecker had raised expectations about the GDR's productive capacities that were unrealistic and invited direct comparisons between socialism and capitalism. Honecker's consumer policy would soon embroil the regime in a contradiction between the utopian ends of socialist society and the real-existing means of the socialist state.

Ideological antipathy toward individual autonomy sporadically mobilized attacks against the car as a luxury symbolic of false needs. The state's need to keep a dissatisfied population in check, epitomized by the Berlin Wall, made SED leaders suspicious of private travel and provided little incentive for the party to satisfy the desire for individual mobility as represented by the automobile. At one point in the 1970s, for example, there were plans to stop producing cars altogether.[41] Nor were significant efforts made to manage the extreme shortage of parking space, which intensified in the late 1980s as the number of cars increased.[42] According to one Western newspaper, the going rate for a parking space in the late 1970s was 8,000 East German marks a year – far more than the cost of renting an apartment for an entire year and almost the cost of a new Trabant.[43] Most often, the bias against individual transportation exhausted itself in arguments regarding the ethical superiority of collective travel. Calls for an end to the production of automobiles and for the privileging of public transportation seem to have been restricted to specific institutions, such as the Ministry of Transportation, which had little influence over the allocation of resources. The planning apparatus was less concerned with such arguments.[44]

Despite mounting demand, the regime did little to accelerate the pace of motorization in the GDR. Instead, the SED established strong disincentives

40 Ferenc Feher, Agnes Heller, and Gyorgy Markus, *Dictatorship over Needs* (Oxford, 1983).
41 The party briefly entertained plans to terminate production by 1975 (Weymar, "Das Auto," pp. 278–9).
42 Interview, Bernd Ohliger and Ulrich Wittek, Mila Fahrschule, Berlin, 26.1.96; BArchB, DL2, 930, Eule/VSA, Vermerk, 4.3.88.
43 BArchB, DL2, 995, unidentified Western newspaper from early September 1978. Of course, renting a parking space was illegal.
44 Otto Arndt, "Aktuelle Aufgaben des sozialistischen Verkehrswesens bei der Lösung der Hauptaufgabe der Wirtschaft," in *Wissenschaft und Technik im Transport- und Nachrichtenwesen 1* (East Berlin, 1975), p. 18, cited in Weymar, "Das Auto," p. 279 ff.; interview, Klopfer, Berlin, 4.10.95.

to obtaining cars through prohibitive pricing structures and long delivery delays due to low production levels. The party also decided to discourage purchases by renouncing the use of installment plans, which are used in market economies to make consumer goods more accessible to the less wealthy. As a central bank official put it, "there will be no deviation from the basic principle that no credits will be given for such luxury items."[45] The balance of payments deficit created by Honecker's policy of subsidizing goods rather than people, moreover, introduced a fiscal factor into the equation. Subsidizing goods rather than people benefits individuals with higher incomes, who pay the same prices for products as those with lower disposable incomes. Such a policy only reinforces existing social differentiation while encouraging waste by distorting pricing systems. Because bread was so cheap, for example, it was widely used as animal fodder, especially for pigs.[46]

Increasingly, the SED found itself confronted by the dilemma of having to export more in order to pay for the increasing cost of the subsidies for basic needs. Consequently, the party encouraged the growth of sectors, such as heavy industry and microelectronics, which it believed to have the greatest export potential. Where possible, consumer goods of sufficient quality and value – such as washing machines and furniture – were exported rather than made available to the domestic market to reduce the crushing foreign debt. Little was invested in the Trabant and Wartburg because they were not considered exportable or as having an exportable future in the West.

Ironically, the party leadership's ideological distaste for producing cars blocked an important avenue toward economic modernization. Investment in the automobile sector would have entailed an admittedly expensive but much-needed renewal of the capital stock in many related industries. Arguably, the party's decision not to produce cars suitable for sale on Western markets – and its disastrous attempt to play catch-up in the mid-1980s – robbed the GDR of a potentially large source of hard-currency revenue.[47]

---

45 BArchB, DN10, 1583, Abteilung Sparkassen, "Eingabenanalysen 2. Halbjahr 1984," 30.1.85, p. 1. For a discussion of the genesis of this policy in the early 1950s, see Merkel, *Utopie und Bedürfnis*, pp. 116–19.

46 SAPMO-BA, DY30, Vorläufige SED 35986, ZPKK to Mittag, 5.6.86, and SED Kreisleitung Cottbus-Stadt, Kreisparteikontrollkommission, "Bericht zur Untersuchung der KPKK in der GO VEB Backwarenkombinat Cottbus," 27.2.86, p. 3; SAPMO-BA, DY30, Vorläufige SED 31984, Hauptabteilung Preise, 28.3.84; SAPMO-BA, DY30, IV/2/2039/268, "Analyse der Leserbriefe zum Artikel 'Sozialpolitik, Preise und Subventionen' von Prof. Dr. Otto Reinhold" *Neues Deutschland*, 14 Februar 1989," no date, p. 64.

47 The automobile combine made parts for foreign car producers, especially the French. In 1985, for example, the IFA Combine PKW produced 5,900 cardan shafts worth DM 1.1 million for Citroën (BArchB, DN10, 1533, Sektor IFA-Kombinat PKW, Industriebankfilial Maschinenbau Karl-Marx-Stadt to Trommler, Staatsbank, 29.3.85). I am thankful to Dave Luckso for explaining what cardan shafts are.

A modest, well-designed car aimed at the lower end of Western markets, aided by the GDR's exemption from tariffs levied by the European Community, might have proven quite remunerative for the GDR. A marketing strategy that took advantage of the German reputation for higher-quality goods, coupled with a vision of consumer egalitarianism that emphasized the unity of functionality and form, might have carved out a market segment much larger than the Czechoslovak Škoda or Yugoslav Yugo ever gained. Given the SED's ideological prejudice against automobiles, however, party leaders never seriously entertained hitching the East German economy to a successful automotive industry. In fact, when Mittag finally agreed to invest in the automotive sector, he complained bitterly that "thirty or forty investment projects have grown out of one single project. Everyone wants to modernize" by participating in plans to update the engine.[48]

The relative lack of importance the SED attached to automobile manufacture is illustrated by the small number actually produced. The near-complete neglect of the cars' design and engineering and the pricing structure devised for them also testify to the low priority placed on developing technologies in this sector. The antecedents of the Trabant, which were assembled in the old Horch plant in Zwickau, were three-cylinder, two-stroke engines with 28 horsepower and front-wheel drive. The Trabant itself, with its plastic body, was introduced in 1958, and by the time the GDR began mass production, it had a two-cylinder, two-stroke engine with front-wheel drive, but only 23 horsepower. Although already outmoded, the engine was upgraded to 26 horsepower in 1964. Except for minor cosmetic changes, however, no major improvements were made to the car for the next twenty-five years. In fact, the SED invested only 730 million marks in the Trabant between 1970 and 1987, even though Trabant sales remitted 5.5 billion East German marks to the state budget during the same period.[49]

The Trabant finally underwent its first major upgrade in 1989, when it was outfitted with a four-stroke engine with technology purchased from Volkswagen. The SED declined, however, to update the car's design. As Figure 15 illustrates, the new Trabant retained outmoded features, including the same rounded headlights that had been out of style in the West for years, a flat hood, and a lackluster grill. It is no wonder that the State Planning

---

48 BArchB, DE1, 56287, Klopfer, "Persönliche Niederschrift über die Beratung beim Mitglied des Politbüros und Sekretär des Zentralkomitees der SED, Genossen Dr. Günter Mittag am 13.6.86," 16.6.86, p. 452.

49 SAPMO-BA, DY30, Vorläufige SED 38644, "Zur technischen Entwicklung der Zwickauer Automobile," no date; BArchB, DE1, 56309, Staatliche Plankommission, "Standpunkt zu dem Material," 24.11.88, p. 184; Kirchberg, "Die Geschichte," pp. 140–4.

Figure 14. The Trabant 601 in 1975. The caption boasted that "the car has won itself a worthy spot in the assortment of cars on offer domestically and in socialist countries." (Courtesy of Bundesarchiv Koblenz, Bildarchiv, 183/PO619/306.)

Commission concurred with the Sachsenring factory director's analysis that "the Trabant 601 is an 'outmoded' product, despite constant measures to continue its development."[50] Similarly, the Barkas van received a new motor, but retained a design that recalled the utopian optimism of the GDR's early years. By the late 1980s, the van's exterior seemed stranded in time, a poor cousin of the popular VW bus it appeared to imitate.

The Wartburg was based on a BMW motor, originally a six-cylinder, four-stroke engine with 45 horsepower. It went on line in 1956 with a

50 Ibid., p. 183.

Figure 15. A catalog touting the Trabant 1.1, which appeared with a four-stroke engine beginning in 1989. (Courtesy of the author.)

Figure 16. The Barkas 1000 light van in 1989. (Courtesy of the author.)

three-cylinder, two-stroke engine and 37 horsepower; in 1966, the body was remodeled and the horsepower increased to 45. Over the next two decades, it underwent only minor improvements.[51] In 1988, the Wartburg was modernized. Its two-stroke engine was replaced with a four-stroke engine, and the car was furnished with a more contemporary external design sporting newer lines and more fashionable square headlights.

The party's belated and ill-considered decision to invest in the automobile industry during the 1980s is emblematic of the Marxist-Leninist approach to consumerism. By the time Mittag finally authorized improvements to the Trabant, the Wartburg, and the Barkas minivan, the SED had surrendered nearly all of the socialist ideals embodied by previous car designs. Rather than placing its productionist precepts or egalitarian values on display, the party entirely neglected the Trabant's design. The new Wartburg model, moreover, seemed oddly derivative of its Western counterparts. The party could argue, of course, that its denigration of design avoided the pitfalls of emphasizing form over function and reflected instead a more appropriate engagement with the car's purpose. The problem was that its efforts to improve the functionality of the cars were wholly unconvincing. The technical improvements made to the Trabant and the Wartburg compared unfavorably

51 SAPMO-BA, DY30, Vorläufige SED 38644, "Zur technischen Entwicklung der Eisenacher Automobile," no date.

Figure 17. The Wartburg 311 in 1964, photographed beneath Wartburg Castle in Eisenach, where Martin Luther lived. (Courtesy of SAPMO/BA, Bildarchiv, 32/96N.)

to the powerful motors and emphasis on personal comfort churned out by West German producers on a regular basis. Nor did the new engines significantly reduce the foul-smelling pollution belched out by the East German cars. The SED failed to provide a serious alternative to the Western approach to consumerism, offering instead "new" cars that looked and functioned like inferior versions of capitalist cars. The cars' homeliness underlines the growing theoretical and practical dependency of East German socialism on capitalist approaches to production and consumption at a time when the

Figure 18. The Wartburg 1.3 in 1988. The original caption states with a whiff of disbelief that "the manufacturer puts the car's highest speed at 135 km/h." (Courtesy of Bundesarchiv Koblenz, Bildarchiv, 183/1990/0404/423.)

legitimacy of socialism as an alternative to capitalism was increasingly being called into question.

As with most consumer goods the SED had decided were nonessential, the price structure of automobiles reflected an attempt to provide a powerful disincentive to those wishing to purchase them. Because they were not subsidized, cars were very expensive for most East Germans.[52] In 1989, the average monthly income was around 800 marks. A roll cost 5 pfennigs and a haircut 1.90 East German marks, but the cheapest two-stroke Trabant cost 12,000 marks. The cheapest version of the last Wartburg with its four-stroke engine cost 30,200 marks.[53] Worse still, these prices did not include such things as the spare tire or the piece of plastic covering the area between the

52 This is despite the fact that automotive producers received subsidies that amounted to significant financial support (BArchB, DE1, VA 56319, Halbritter, "Ausgewählte Beispiele subventionierter Industriewaren, die dem Grundbedarf zuzurechnen sind," 2.10.87, p. 1).

53 SAPMO-BA, DY30, IV 2/2039/268, "Analyse der Leserbriefe," no date, p. 66; Armin Volze, "Die Devisengeschäfte der DDR: Genex und Intershop," *Deutschland Archiv* 24:11 (1991), p. 1146; SAPMO-BA, DY30, Vorläufige SED 41775/1, Blessing to Mittag, 26.4.89, p. 5; SAPMO-BA, DY30, IV 2/2039/64, Politbüro-Sitzung vom 16.8.88, p. 21.

back seat and the trunk, which were considered "extras."[54] To add insult to injury, moreover, the cars were delivered without gas to remote locations. In Berlin, for example, people had to trudge out to Karlshorst with a gas can filled with enough gas to get back to the city. These high prices reflected the high production costs of an economy hobbled by aging fixed capital and a predilection for labor-intensive manufacturing methods. They also provided a convenient way for the party to recoup some of the money lost in subsidizing basic needs such as bread.

In fact, this was an important reason that the party decided to make as many cars as it did. By the 1980s, financial calculations had made manufacturing ideologically problematic consumer goods such as cars more appealing. As we saw in Chapter 4, Honecker's strategy of placating the population by increasing wages and salaries created strong inflationary pressures. The fiscal problem caused by too much money chasing goods that were too cheap was exacerbated by the general shortage of durable goods, making those commodities more valuable because of their scarcity and therefore more desirable than their actual utility might warrant. The SED could not overlook this problem, and producing cars was one method of soaking up the extra cash it was throwing at its citizens.[55]

Another reason to manufacture cars was that automobile production enjoyed great prestige in Soviet-style economies – despite Marxist-Leninist denunciations of commodity fetishism. Party leaders and factory managers, for example, had a personal interest in protecting the automotive industry, since their positions entitled them to such perks as access to a state-owned car, with all of the convenience and social status that came with it.[56] But this question of personal prestige was also linked to larger questions of East German identity in a European context. Over time, the GDR's national identity, particularly among SED members, became contingent on garnering prestige in the Soviet bloc through far-flung industrial projects such as automobile or computer chip production. Similarly, the systemic competition with the Federal Republic placed the GDR in the impossible situation

---

54 In the early 1980s, cars were comparatively cheaper. A basic Trabant cost 8,050 East German marks in 1985. Adding 2,678 worth of "extras" and 428.35 in registration, licensing, and insurance fees, brought the total to 11,156.35 marks. Likewise, a 1985 Wartburg cost 17,950 marks plus another 3,495 for "extras" (not including such luxuries as a radio) and 823.55 in registration, licensing, and insurance fees, bringing the total to 22,268.55 marks (SAPMO-BA, DY30, Vorläufige SED 41852).

55 In 1973, the Institute for Market Research in Leipzig estimated that automobile purchases, maintenance, and accessories – about 80 billion marks – would absorb about 10 percent of the population's income (BArchB, DL1, 23780, Institut für Marktforschung, "Die Entwicklung des PKW-Bedarfs der Bevölkerung bis 1990," 1973, pp. 20–1).

56 For information on pay scales, see SAPMO-BA, DY30, IV 2/2.039/80, "Sitzung vom 28.3.85," pp. 16–17, 32–4; for examples of car allotments for factory managers, see BArchB, DG7, 1153.

of trying to furnish its population with at least some consumer items, even though the number and often the excellence of those goods ended up eliciting anger rather than mollifying disgruntled East German consumers. Thus, the economic consequences of the SED's social policies, as well as its own desire for power and prestige, forced an irrational course of action upon the party that stood in stark contrast to the more rational elements of its social criticism.

ALLOCATING NEED

Once the decision was made to manufacture automobiles, the problem remained of how to determine the appropriate level of production. The suppression of market mechanisms – specifically, the refusal to allow measures such as supply and demand an independent status – closed off one of the most reliable methods of gathering information about the extent of "need" in the automotive sector.[57] Unwilling to abandon motor vehicle production to the vagaries of the market, the SED devised a bureaucratic system of numeric oversight to cope with the mounting demand for cars. The registration system established by the planning apparatus sought to make the needs of the population, as defined by the party, transparent to planners in the form of mathematical divisions in time. Upon turning eighteen, every citizen of the GDR was permitted to place an order for an automobile with the local IFA Distribution enterprise, a subsidiary of the IFA combine. In return, would-be consumers received a slip of paper recording the date of their order. Planners seem to have believed they could employ the registration system to inhibit the desire for a commodity whose production did not conform to their political priorities while simultaneously channeling the backed-up demand for cars resulting from low production levels into an orderly but delayed gratification. Once visible to the party, people's desires could be kept in line and the order in that line enforced.

Needless to say, this strategy did not come close to solving the basic problem, which was one of production rather than registration. In fact, the registration system degenerated into little more than a glorified queue, which continued to lengthen as production fell behind ever-increasing demand. In 1989, the IFA combine was just beginning to deliver Trabants to people who had ordered them in 1976. People who had ordered a Wartburg,

---

57 The party relied greatly on researching consumer needs by evaluating direct contact with the customer through the sales staff, although it admitted that such a method "is limited in its meaningfulness" (Bley, *Lexikon der Wirtschaft. Arbeit*, p. 135). See also Merkel, *Utopie und Bedürfnis*, pp. 133–53.

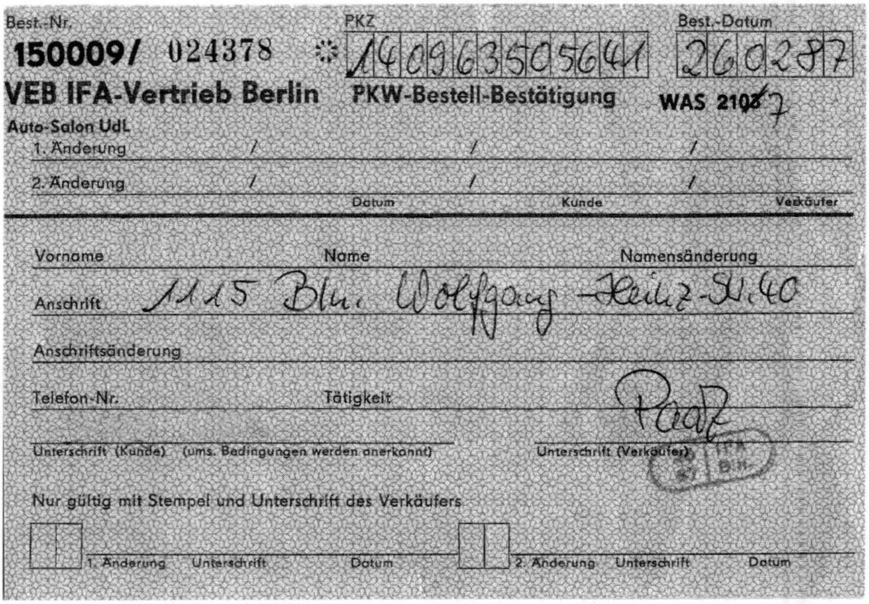
Best.-Nr. PKZ Best.-Datum
150009/ 024378 140963505641 260287
VEB IFA-Vertrieb Berlin PKW-Bestell-Bestätigung WAS 2107
Auto-Salon UdL
1. Änderung / / /
2. Änderung / / /
Datum Kunde Verkäufer
Vorname Name Namensänderung
Anschrift 1115 Bln. Wolfgang-Heinz-Str. 40
Anschriftsänderung
Telefon-Nr. Tätigkeit
Unterschrift (Kunde) (ums. Bedingungen werden anerkannt) Unterschrift (Verkäufer)
Nur gültig mit Stempel und Unterschrift des Verkäufers
1. Änderung Unterschrift Datum 2. Änderung Unterschrift Datum

Figure 19. Order slip for a Lada 2107 from 1987. (Courtesy of the author.)

which was somewhat more desirable than the Trabant because its body was actually made of metal, had to wait a bit longer – an average of sixteen years depending on where one lived. The waiting time for Ladas and Škodas, which had better motors, was eighteen years. As of April 1989, the IFA combine had registered a total of 6.2 million orders for cars. In other words, for each person who received an automobile there were forty-three still waiting for a car.[58] In a state that supposedly prized leisure time over the commodification of life, the long delays and time-consuming activities associated with waiting in line only embittered consumers against the SED's mismanagement.[59]

Far from exerting negative pressure on demand, the registration system had the opposite of its intended effect. First, it not only failed to provide an effective substitute for market mechanisms, but – as the planners themselves admitted – even introduced inaccuracies into the collection of data. Because

58 SAPMO-BA, DY30, Vorläufige SED 41775/1, Blessing to Mittag, 26.4.89, p. 4.

59 Distribution also posed a problem for the SED. Despite the shortage, new Trabants stood exposed to the weather for an average of ten months after they had been assembled for want of the proper storage facilities. The result was serious damage to the cars' engines, which forced the producer to offer deep discounts on the cars affected (BArchB, DN10, 1533, Landmann to Voigt, 29.11.85).

of the shortage of automobiles and the long waiting periods, there was an incentive for everyone to order cars even if they had no immediate use for them, which meant that demand as recorded by registration was inflated.[60] Unfortunately, planners had no means of establishing precisely how large this variable was. Neither could registration in the aggregate capture the qualitative aspects of consumer demand: The mass of orders disclosed nothing about consumer preferences because there were no alternatives to the cars people were waiting for anyhow.

Most problematic for a party that tirelessly trumpeted its ability to dispense social justice, however, was the way that lining up encouraged social inequities. The Department of Mechanical Engineering and Metallurgy at the ZK, for example, concluded that "with the current ordering system, the financial, health, or territorial situation of the person ordering the car is not taken into account."[61] In practice, however, these factors did play a major role. Berlin and the two party districts where production was located, Erfurt and Karl-Marx-Stadt, enjoyed shorter waiting periods – about two years shorter on average – than other districts, a fact that did not escape the attention of the population.[62] The superior provisioning of Berlin relative to other cities and towns had always been a focal point for popular dissatisfaction in the highly centralized GDR. Honecker's decision to utilize Berlin as a propaganda tool and transform the Eastern half of the divided city into a "Window onto the East" (*Schaufenster des Ostens*), however, turned disaffection into outright resentment. The short supply of cars also intensified traditional tensions between town and country. Because the East German retail network only extended thin roots into more remote areas, people living in small villages were forced to travel to do their shopping. Without a car, consumption often turned into an arduous expedition.[63]

In addition, differences in demography created new social cleavages. Larger families, for example, enjoyed an advantage because grandparents were able to pass the order forms on to their grandchildren, thereby cutting down the waiting periods substantially. The Department of Mechanical Engineering and Metallurgy estimated that "many families can buy a new automobile for themselves inside of six to eight years, while young families and those registering for the first time are affected by the long

---

60 SAPMO-BA, DY30, Vorläufige SED 41775/1, Blessing to Mittag, 26.4.89, p. 4.
61 Ibid.
62 SAPMO-BA, DY30, Vorläufige SED 38644, Ministerium des Innern, "Lageeinschätzung," no date, Anlage 2.
63 See, for example, the petitions in BArchB, DG7, VA–1813. For more on tensions between town and country under Ulbricht, see Merkel, *Utopie und Bedürfnis*, pp. 199–202.

waiting periods" — as if a six- to eight-year delay did not constitute waiting.[64] And while the SED prided itself on "social" solutions to economic problems, it had no institutional method of ensuring that the handicapped, frail, or ill had access to the decided improvement in the quality of their lives made possible by the automobile. Instead, those who were left behind were forced to throw themselves on the mercy of East German bureaucrats.

As might be expected, the protracted wait led to various forms of jumping the line, most of which were illegal. To reduce the lag between ordering and purchasing a car, for example, people began to trade the registration slips, simply ignoring the fact that they were not transferable. The closer to delivery the car came, the more the slip gained in value, rather like a bond. The hitch was that neither the party nor the producer of the cars profited from the slips, which sold in the 1980s for anywhere from 2,000 to 40,000 East German marks, depending on their due date and the make of car.[65] Buying registration slips was akin to buying time, moving one closer to the object of desire, even though the slip did not comprise the purchase of the object to which it referred since the price of the car itself was not included. Nevertheless, these black market transactions illustrate people's ability to appropriate government regulation aimed at making their behavior transparent and so easier to control.

The thriving black market for used cars was even more problematic for the SED because it threatened the party's control over economic behavior and challenged the Marxist-Leninist conceptualization of just prices. The SED measured the value of a brand-new product within a moral hierarchy that replaced market-driven price structures with notions of social utility. Officially, the prices of used goods were determined in relation to their cost when sold as new, but reduced by the so-called current value (*Zeitwert*) to reflect wear and tear. By this measure, prices for used cars could not exceed their sticker prices. Conditions under which used items were sold at rates in excess of their sticker price suggested that pricing mechanisms independent of the SED's theories were at work — pricing mechanisms that restored capitalist relations of profit and social alienation. It is no wonder, then, that the SED labeled the black market for used cars in the GDR "speculative" and accused people engaged in it of leading "a parasitic way of life."[66] The party's vilification of attempts to satiate desire did little,

64 SAPMO-BA, DY30, Vorläufige SED 41775/1, Blessing to Mittag, 26.4.89, p. 4.
65 Ibid.; SAPMO-BA, DY30, Vorläufige SED 38644, Ministerium des Innern, "Zur Situation bei der Versorgung mit Pkw," no date, p. 3; interview, Ohliger and Wittek, Berlin, 26.1.96.
66 SAPMO-BA, DY30, Vorläufige SED 38644, Ministerium des Innern, "Lageeinschätzung," no date, p. 2.

Figure 20. "You must have forgotten to roll the windows all the way up last night!" (Courtesy of *Eulenspiegel* 51 [1988], p. 7.)

however, to change the fact that a goodly portion of the population was engaged in economic behavior that ran counter to the SED's moral precepts. In fact, it even seems to have elicited mild ridicule in the form of open jokes about how widespread black market practices were. The procedure for soliciting offers for a used car, for example, was to park at a location that was known for this practice, such as the Blankenburgstraße, the Pettkofer-straße, or Grünau in Berlin.[67] The seller then placed a piece of paper on the driver's seat with a number scrawled on it to encourage offers, and rolled the driver's window down so that people could toss their offers in. As the cartoon from the officially sanctioned satirical magazine *Eulenspiegel* illustrates, the number of bids tossed into the car by prospective buyers was often overwhelming.

Of course, the party did not content itself with mere invective, but also sought to inhibit practices out of line with its definition of ethical economic conduct by outlawing them. According to paragraph 173 of the GDR's penal code, for example, speculation could be punished with fines or a prison

67 BArchB, DL2, 995, unidentified Western newspaper from early September 1978. The car markets in the Blankenburgstraße and Grünau were tolerated until 1987, when they became too conspicuous and the People's Police began to crack down on them (interview, Ohliger and Wittek, Berlin, 26.1.96).

sentence of up to two years, and in "serious cases" eight years.[68] Dealing in used cars on the black market became quite a serious business: Those who were caught were prosecuted to the fullest extent of the law. Yet the penalties constituted no deterrent against the demand for cars. According to a report from 1989, the East German police caught three men working separately who had no other jobs except dealing in used cars. Together, they had sold an astounding 127 cars for profits totaling 940,000 East German marks. More impressive than the size of their profits are the circumstances under which they were earned. Not only did these wheeler-dealers have to find a place to park the cars they were selling without attracting official attention, but they had to spend their profits without becoming too conspicuous in a society in which modesty remained the norm.

Illegal trade was not restricted to full-time used-car dealers, however. Even people in professions that nominally enjoyed the trust of the regime were active in the market. Between 1979 and 1982, for example, a teacher sold forty-nine cars for a profit of 99,480 marks. When he was caught, he was trying to sell sixteen cars and one trailer.[69] The harsh prosecution of used-car kings was aimed at making examples of the most visible infractions and deflecting criticism of the party by exciting indignation at wealthy racketeers. At the same time, the party was aware that it could not employ the police to discipline the economic behavior created by its production system.[70] In fact, by the early 1980s the planning apparatus was prepared to look the other way and tolerate the parallel economy because it provided partial solutions to problems beyond the purview of the plan.[71] Once again, the desires of ordinary citizens not only thwarted the SED's attempt to regulate the nature of economic interaction, but forced the party to incorporate the very market mechanisms it deplored into the official economy.

Because criminalization was largely ineffective and even undesirable, the government introduced a mandatory "sales obligation" (*Anbietungspflicht*) in 1966 to monitor the trade in used cars. This system required those wanting to sell their cars to offer them at the official prices for used cars to the IFA Distribution enterprise, which delivered them to the People's Own

68 SAPMO-BA, DY30, Vorläufige SED 41775/1, "Überlegungen zur weitestgehenden Unterbindung der Spekulation mit gebrauchten bzw. neuen Kraftfahrzeugen," no date, p. 1; BArchB, DL2, 995, unidentified Western newspaper from early September 1978.
69 SAPMO-BA, DY30, Vorläufige SED 38644, Ministerium des Innern, "Lageeinschätzung," no date, Anlage 5.
70 Ibid., p. 2.
71 Government tolerance was especially in evidence for the black market in spare parts, where barter reigned and money was rarely in use (interview, Ohliger and Wittek, Berlin, 26.1.96; and Klopfer, Berlin, 4.10.95).

Enterprise Mechanical Engineering Retail, which then resold them to the public. The demand for cars was high enough, however, to motivate people to circumvent the *Anbietungspflicht* by selling the car directly to the buyer and simply neglecting to reregister it under the new owner's name. The Ministry of the Interior calculated that only 20 percent of all cars that changed hands in 1972 were resold legally. In 1975, the government revoked the *Anbietungspflicht*, not the least because it had become difficult for the police to trace the car owners.[72] Neither did the introduction of a clause into sales contracts prohibiting resale before a three-year period prove enforceable.[73] And even if such bureaucratic solutions had proven effective in curbing the sale of automobiles, they would have done little to frustrate the robust trade in spare parts or the practice of demanding hard currency or Western wares, such as coffee, in return for repairs.

In the meantime, the black market continued to thrive. By the summer of 1989, the party noted that used Trabants were going for nearly twice the official price of a new one, Wartburgs for nearly three times. Used Ladas, which cost 28,500 Ostmarks brand new, were selling for 80,000, and used Volkswagen Golfs for up to 150,000.[74] The discrepancy between official and illegal prices ensured that the black market would remain the locus of two problems for the SED. First, it intensified the very social divisions the party was devoted to eliminating by creating two classes of people: those who had access to large amounts of cash or, better yet, Western currency, and those who did not. Second, the black market functioned as an alternate system of valuation, in direct competition with the value system based on moral hierarchies that the GDR tried to impose on its citizens. This is not to argue that the two systems were mutually exclusive; many East Germans emphasized their belief in a morally just price in the letters they wrote to communist officials, which demonstrates the extent to which Marxist-Leninist ideas were internalized by the population. Nevertheless, the desire for cars and the shortages that sharpened it produced the opposite of the SED's explicit goal: The car quickly became a vehicle for social differentiation, as limited access led people to attach social status to possessing it. A peculiarly materialistic mentality developed, in which social station was measured in terms of visible wealth – "If you have something, you are something" (*Haste was, biste was*), as the popular saying went. The fact, for example, that people advertising in newspapers for potential spouses sometimes included a list of

72 SAPMO-BA, DY30, Vorläufige SED 38644, Ministerium des Innern, "Lageeinschätzung," no date, Anlage 5, p. 3.
73 SAPMO-BA, DY30, IV 2/2039/170, petition from 1.11.89.
74 SAPMO-BA, DY30, Vorläufige SED 41775/1, Blessing to Mittag, 26.4.89, p. 5.

their material possessions, and their cars in particular, made a mockery of the SED's insistence on separating sexual from economic desire.[75] Nor is it surprising that most of those using material possessions to attract a mate were men, since the SED had done little to challenge the gendered role distribution found in capitalist households despite its emancipatory rhetoric.

Worse still, the party itself actively partook in practices that encouraged social differentiation. Driven by its debt problems, the SED established the Geschenkdienst und Kleinexport GmbH (Genex), a mail-order retailer designed to earn hard currency that is discussed at length in Chapter 6. People who had relatives in the West could ask them to purchase a Trabant from Genex, which cost 9,000 West German marks in 1989. Even more unpopular were the Intershops. In 1975, the Intershops began selling Western cars, such as Fiats, Renaults, and BMWs.[76] The only people who could afford them, however, were those with relatives in the Federal Republic, artists who sold their work in the West, or those involved in the black market; even retired persons willing to commute and perform manual labor in West Berlin hardly had access to that kind of cash. Like Genex, the Intershops offered most East Germans little hope of satisfying their desires. On the contrary, Genex and the Intershops were nothing less than officially sanctioned forms of the same social discrimination carried out by the high prices on the black market. They generated a two-class, two-currency system, a kind of line jumping for capitalists and their relatives. These social divisions were greatly resented precisely because of the stark contrast between the SED's egalitarian claims and the social hierarchies its policies created, a disjunction that rested on equally distributed desire but institutionally rationed gratification.

OBJECTS OF DESIRE

Both the registration system and the *Anbietungspflicht* were characterized by an attempt to make people's behavior transparent by creating contractual

---

75 "Heiratet man ein Auto?" *Abendzeitung,* 22.6.71, cited in Weymar, "Das Auto," p. 286, fn. 129. In 1988, the SED banned "references to ownership or wealth" in the lonely-hearts section of newspapers and magazines (SAPMO-BA, DY30, J IV 2/3/4177, Anlage Nr. 7, p. 65).

76 BStU, MfS BKK (KoKo) 819, *HAZ,* 28.1.89, *Der Tagesspiegel,* 21.2.87, 17.9.88, and 18.2.89, and *Die Welt am Sonntag,* 14.5.89, pp. 1–2, 4–5, 16; Andreas Herbst, Winfried Ranke, and Jürgen Winkler, *So funktionierte die DDR Band 1. Lexikon der Organisationen und Institutionen* (Reinbek, 1994), p. 328; Weymar, "Das Auto," pp. 284–5; Armin Volze, "Die Devisengeschäfte," p. 1156. According to one Western newspaper, the most popular gifts from Genex were spark plugs (DM 24 for a pack of twenty-four), rpm displays (DM 39), and warning lights (BStU, MfS BKK [KoKo] 819, unnamed West German newspaper, 15.3.86, p. 10).

conditions between the state and the consumer. In this manner, planners sought to curtail agreements worked out between individuals, which in the party's eyes smacked of an autonomy inconsistent with Marxist–Leninist economic morality and a threat to its power. Whatever contractual features the registration slips and the *Anbietungspflicht* might have exemplified, however, were undermined by the SED's insistence on dictating the terms of the agreement. To counteract possible resistance to the authoritarian aspects of this and other arrangements, the party encouraged people to air their grievances in a formal procedure that was presented as a dialogue between the people and official institutions. Private persons were invited to address "citizens' petitions" (*Eingaben der Bürger*) directly to party and state organs or the individuals representing them, ostensibly because the party welcomed working people's suggestions about how to improve working conditions and living standards. The primary purpose of the petition system, however, lay in checking political fallout from consumer discontent and preventing individuals with similar complaints from organizing themselves. As Chapter 7 demonstrates, the system had a distinctly authoritarian cast, harking back to the right of subjects to plead their cases personally before the sovereign, and is revealing of the regime's penchant for hierarchy and discipline. The prompt answers given by impersonal institutions to the hundreds of thousands of complaints written each year by individuals sought to deflect discontent by imparting a feeling of personal involvement that was intended to compensate for the experience of material want.

Nevertheless, the right to petition was not merely a cynical attempt to render serious criticism harmless. Not only did the petitions provide valuable clues about the extent and nature of dissatisfaction with the SED's policies, but the party also viewed them as important indicators of its performance. The Department of Trade, Supply, and Foreign Trade at the ZK, for example, reduced the complaints contained in the petitions crossing its desks to a series of categories, employing rises and falls in the quantity of petitions to assess its progress in attending to gaps in the provision of goods. As with the automobile registration system, the attempt to represent desire in purely rational terms implied an overvaluation of quantitative analysis that slighted qualitative arguments. The content of the complaints was reduced to the receipt of the petition itself, which meant that the grounds of the complaints retreated behind composite numbers and failed to contribute to an evaluation of their origins. The Ministry for Trade and Supply, for example, reported to the Politburo that it had received 2,364 petitions containing 3,195 problems in 1987, amounting to an increase of 128 petitions and 246 problems over the previous year, and then broke them down into further numerical categories. The ministry warned that there had been a "continuing trend since 1983 of an increase in petitions and problems mentioned in the petitions," but hazarded no guess as to why this might be the case.[77] The affinity for statistical representations of qualitative arguments reflects the inability of the planning apparatus to generate systemic criticism of production or distribution methods. In internal communications, this ideological prohibition took the form of planners dissolving individual consumers into group categories. The inverse occurred when planners represented production and distribution externally to the individual author of a petition. The planning apparatus treated each person ad hoc, as an individual case removed from a group context, even if the complaint echoed thousands that had preceded it. The complaints expressed by individual consumers were reduced to their singularity, which allowed planners to reject criticism in a ritualized manner, since the desires of one consumer could hardly form the basis of the entire plan.

For their part, consumers did not treat the petition system as a form of ritualized dialogue, but as an opportunity to demand adherence to a contractual obligation. Whether complaining about the long lines to buy automobiles, the scarcity of spare parts, or the impossibility of getting anything repaired, people pointed to the disparity between the SED's public rhetoric and actual practice. While the terms of discourse used by petitioners and planners were similar in that both sides emphasized the promises made by a paternalist state to a subject population, there was no consensus about the problems or how to solve them. Petitioners demonstrated an admirable virtuosity in exploiting socialist argumentation to express their desires and improve their material situation. One person who demanded that the manufacturer undertake touch-up repairs on a newly delivered automobile, for example, justified his case by quoting from Articles 21 and 103 of the GDR's constitution. He argued that the manufacturer's refusal to respond to his suggestions abrogated his constitutional right to "codetermination and participation (*Mitbestimmung und Mitgestaltung*) in the affairs of government, which the socialist state defined as "a high moral duty for every citizen."[78] Another man quoted the People's Parliament and the Politburo as promising an increase in automobile production and tried to hold them to it. "The need for car bodies can

---

77 SAPMO-BA, DY30, Vorläufige SED 37988, Briksa to Jarowinsky, "Bericht über die Schwerpunkte der im Jahre 1987 an das MHV gerichteten Eingaben," no date, p. 2; similar reports in SAPMO-BA, DY30, Vorläufige SED 37987 and 37988.
78 BArchB, DG7, VA-1813, petition from 14.10.89; Article 103 of the GDR's 1974 constitution.

be recorded and planned," he wrote, turning the party's slogan regarding socialism's responsibility to the individual against the SED.[79]

Much of the criticism of the SED's economic policies focused on the feeling that prices were unjust. The IFA Distribution enterprise, for example, mistakenly delivered a car to the elderly man above, then demanded the car back as well as compensation for the extent to which it had been used. Enraged at the system of fiscal valuation revealed by the bill, the man fumed that "above all, I am very angry that the car was estimated at 1,000 marks lower after only being driven 315 kilometers. That means, in other words, that after only 9,450 kilometers the value of the car equals zero." He had been saving up to buy a Wartburg for years, he noted, which cost 22,000 marks when he registered for it. "Now, the car suddenly costs 31,000 marks, that is, 9,000 marks more. The new price is entirely unjustified, but the state pricing structure must really be right if a roll costs 5 pfennigs."[80] Another man, exasperated by the time he had invested in searching for spare tires, depicted the hardships imposed by the shortage economy in scathing terms. "Even a long unpaid vacation did not lead to success," he wrote. "In March of 1980, I wasted my time almost every day for three weeks showing up in vain at the IFA parts shop in the Friedrichstraße from six a.m. until it opened, only to be told each time: 'We're out.' . . . It is certainly not asking too much of me when I expect from the state that I can purchase commodities for my hard-earned money that measure up to my expectations, which really are not set so very high."[81] Yet another petitioner dispensed with arguments altogether and demanded that "whoever set this price [for a spare part] should be brought up on charges."[82]

Other petitions addressed imbalances in the distribution system based on residency, from rural versus urban tensions to territorial deviations in automobile allotments. In an open letter to the party leadership, for example, petitioners from the village of Großdeuben complained that the rural population was discriminated against right off the bat, since the small number of shops in rural areas made owning a car indispensable for buying food and other provisions.[83] Another person assailed the fact that some party districts received priority. Reminding the SED of its egalitarian ideals, she maintained that "those who do not live in Berlin should also have the

79 SAPMO-BA, DY30, IV 2/2039/153, petition from 18.1.87, p. 272.
80 Ibid.
81 BArchB, DG7, VA-616, petition from 23.7.80.
82 BArchB, DG7, VA-616, petition from 17.6.80.
83 BArchB, DL1, 26395, open letter, Großdeuben, 3.11.89.

opportunity of buying . . . a car." As with many petitioners, she also measured East German against West German consumer products. A hint of jealousy crept into her comment that "the GDR's automotive industry is not going to make a car similar to the [Volkswagen] Golf in the coming five-year plan either. That is regrettable and disappointing, since the retirement of the Trabant is long overdue."[84]

The responses of the party and state to petitioners consisted in the main of ritualized invocations of laws or references to tight resources. One woman from Rühlsdorf demanded an answer to "why the prices for automobiles are so high that no one can come up with the cash. For which part of the population are you producing these cars? Where is the normal citizen supposed to get this kind of money? If he or she doesn't come from a rich family with wealthy relatives in the West?"[85] The Ministry of Trade and Supply responded with the requisite justifications of the pricing structure, in which fiscal concerns were subordinated to moral postulates. "We hope that you understand," the Ministry wrote, "that cars cannot as a rule receive subsidies since the material and financial conditions do not exist. In fact, products of such high value should contribute to state revenues in order to pay for subsidies in other areas, which is certainly in your interest."[86]

There are some cases of people, mostly connected to the party or the mass organizations in its service, whose problems received more attention than a form letter. The man who quoted the SED's humanistic pretensions back at it, for example, was allotted a new car body by Egon Krenz's office – most likely because he was a SED member.[87] More clear was the case of Gerhard Bauer, a highly decorated soldier in the National People's Army. In a letter to Heinz Klopfer, the Deputy Chairman of the State Planning Commission and Chairman of the Working Group on Automobiles, Bauer appealed to Klopfer's sense of party solidarity. Bauer emphasized his life of service to the party, which began in 1947 and had continued past his retirement with his work for the Workers' and Peasants' Inspectorate. Clearly sympathetic to the man's desires, Klopfer asked that a car be delivered to him.[88]

In fact, the SED often used automobiles as rewards for service to the party. The Deputy Minister for ALF, Christian Scholwin, managed a reserve of around 1,000 cars for just this purpose. Scholwin used these automobiles to appease petitioners throughout the year. Sometimes cars were used to

84 BArchB, DG7, VA-616, petition from 14.7.80.
85 BArchB, DL1, 26395, petition from 13.10.89.
86 BArchB, DL1, 26395, Fischer to Döffinger, 16.11.89.
87 SAPMO-BA, DY30, IV 2/2039/153, petition from 18.1.87, pp. 272–3, 279.
88 BArchB, DE1, 55120, Bauer to Klopfer, 17.11.88, and Greß to Freyer, 29.12.88.

sweeten difficult party assignments. At other times, cars were used to appease artists and intellectuals loyal to the regime, especially if their work earned money in capitalist countries. Sometimes, too, senior party leaders strove to help people on their staff who were ill or handicapped.[89]

The use of cars as a form of currency did not stop at politically motivated bribery, however. Outright nepotism was also common, with leading party officials and their families enjoying important privileges.[90] In 1982, for example, Minister for Mining, Metallurgy, and Potash Kurt Singhuber wrote to Günther Kleiber, Minister for ALF, on ministerial stationery asking that his son Bernd receive a Trabant.[91] Even friends could sometimes drive away with cars, as long as they were chummy enough with the right people.[92] In fact, the number of high-profile interventions by senior party leaders on behalf of family and friends is astonishing. Nor were SED officials above helping themselves to material rewards. The hard-working Klopfer, whose prodigious memory played a key role in keeping the economy running smoothly, wrote to Kleiber in late 1982 asking for a new washing machine.[93]

Although modest by Western standards, party-based perquisites, political privilege, and outright nepotism earned the SED leadership a reputation for corruption. Proximity to the regime constituted a new kind of currency: Those who were well-connected – or as the East Germans called it, "Vitamin C for connections" (*Vitamin B für Beziehungen*) – could cash in on their political ties and move to the head of the line. Such real and imagined social inequities were the target of much sarcasm.[94] One man, for example, delivered a stinging indictment of the SED elite's fondness for Swedish automobiles, fulminating against the "honorable comrade Volvo drivers."[95] What better method of calling attention to the disjunction between communist ideal and East German reality than to remind the SED leadership that its preference for capitalist cars not only contradicted its egalitarian rhetoric,

89 See, for example, BArchB, DG7, 1153, Krenz to Kleiber, no date, Müller to Scholwin, 22.6.82, Kuhrig to Kleiber, 22.6.82, Kretschmer to Lietz, 10.12.82, Manfred Gerlach to Kleiber, 18.3.82, and Schabowski to Kleiber, 8.9.82; interview, Scholwin, Berlin, 23.11.95.

90 This is in contrast to my earlier claim that such instances were rare (Jonathan R. Zatlin, "The Vehicle of Desire: The Trabant, the Wartburg, and the End of the GDR," *German History* 15:3 [1997], p. 378).

91 BArchB, DG7, 1153, Singhuber to Kleiber, 17.12.82. This file contains many requests made by senior leaders, including Horst Sindermann and Kurt Rätz, an aide to Politburo member Kurt Hager.

92 BArchB, DG7, 1153, Sakowski to Kleiber, 2.12.82, and Seeger to Kleiber, 9.12.82.

93 BArchB, DG7, 1153, Klopfer to Kleiber, 13.12.82.

94 BArchB, DG7, VA-616, petition from 7.2.87.

95 BArchB, DG7, VA-2718, petition from 8.11.89.

but also constituted a vote of no confidence in the domestic automobile industry?

The petitions regarding cars, and, for that matter, other aspects of life in the GDR, chronicle with endless variation the way in which people's needs were not met by policies that claimed to do just that. The long lines turned those needs, whether real or otherwise, into longings, and the hypocrisy of the moral regime in which they lived transformed these desires into political as well as economic demand. Popular anger over what were perceived as unjust economic conditions was clearly on the increase during the 1980s. By the time the Stasi warned the SED leadership in June 1989 about popular frustration over the shortage of cars, solving the "automobile problem" was no longer possible. The demand for cars was projected by the regime itself to outstrip production wildly in the coming years because of the continued deterioration of capital stock. The Department of Mechanical Engineering and Metallurgy estimated that people ordering cars in 1989 would receive them forty years later. The director of the Department noted that "the drastic rise in the waiting period is meeting with growing incomprehension and increasing criticism from the population."[96] Overwhelmed by the intensity of popular demand and the unresponsiveness of his superiors, he suffered a nervous breakdown soon after filing this report. Six months later, televised images of Trabants chugging through the Brandenburg Gate served to point out the way in which frustration with the excessive economic shortages had become the vehicle of pent-up political demands.

Because of its theory of real and false needs, the SED was unable to perceive the threat to its legitimacy inherent in the political discontent arising from shortages of consumer goods. The party viewed desire as an expression of the social alienation it sought to eliminate – as a socially mediated wish to acquire status via material objects – thereby reducing it to a "false" need that could not and should not be satisfied. By contrast, the party justified its power by reference to the truth of the moral claim that it alone was capable of distinguishing real needs from desires. The plan was the means by which this truth, and thereby the party's power, was socially reproduced. In assuming it could know and plan for society's needs a priori, however, the SED made an epistemological blunder that excited its didactic inclinations and induced it to treat people as if they were unable to decide for themselves what their needs were. Both the SED's claims about truth

---

96 SAPMO-BA, DY30, Vorläufige SED 41775/1, Blessing to Mittag, 26.4.89, p. 4; interview, Gunther Beobach, Deputy Chief, Department of Agitation and Propaganda at the ZK (late 1980s), Berlin, 4.5.96; and Scholwin, Berlin, 23.11.95.

and its concomitant disregard for individual autonomy were carried over into the plan, which committed it to an authoritarian response toward any unplanned behavior.

The plan, however, simultaneously ensured the creation of conditions that flouted the SED's moral claims to power. The epistemological short-comings deriving from the distinction between real and false needs, for example, translated into real economic shortages. Confident that it could simply edit out socially counterproductive behavior, the party refused to devote sufficient resources to the manufacture of goods it deemed "bad." Yet in deciding to produce some automobiles, whether to keep up with the Federal Republic or the Soviet Union, the SED laid the foundations for precisely those social inequalities it loudly proclaimed it had abolished. The resulting shortage of cars transformed whatever "need" there might have been for them into a desire, as value was attached to that which was scarce. Thus, the social hierarchies created by the shortages derived not simply from owning a car, which in the GDR symbolized individual mobility and there-fore relative autonomy; social status also emanated from the access to power that enabled some to circumvent the lines. Even SED officials were led to agree that the sight of the car in the GDR generated desire for it, whether it was the Trabant or images of a Volkswagen Golf on West German televi-sion.[97] Just how elusive the satisfaction of that desire was, however, was felt all the more keenly when people saw the relative ease with which highly placed bureaucrats and those with access to Western currency could acquire the objects of their desire. The real and unequal distribution of cars led to a growing frustration with the SED's rhetorical insistence on the importance of socialist egalitarianism.

At the same time, the SED's authoritarian response to behavior for which it had not planned was shaped by its sensitivity to the relation between vision and discipline. The party's ideological criticism of desire, coupled with its aversion to permitting individual agents to interact without state mediation in the economic sphere, led it to respond to the lack of cars and the shortages of parts and patience by trying to keep an eye on consumers and keep them in line. But the strategy of observational discipline failed, forcing the party to turn a blind eye to practices that flouted its economic power. On the one hand, East Germans subverted the attempt to regulate their behavior, as with the registration system, and entered into contractual agreements with

---

97 The Workers' and Peasants' Inspectorate, for example, argued that "a model on display and therefore on offer arouses need, and the insufficient satisfaction of this need leads to anger" (SAPMO-BA, DY30, Vorläufige SED 41853, Komitee der ABI, "Bericht über die Kontrolle zur Sicherung eines hohen Niveaus in der gastronomischen Versorgung der Bevölkerung," 8.8.89).

each other that circumvented the state, while the SED was forced to tolerate this behavior because it helped bridge gaps in production. The alternative ethical and financial value systems exhibited by the black market reflected the way in which consumer desires had shifted from mere economic to political demand, but the party perceived the threat to its power too late. On the other hand, the petitions prompted people to view the SED as the patron of the individual, which encouraged them to hold the party personally responsible for their unfulfilled desires. Yet the criticisms of the party's moral legitimacy expressed in the petitions failed to turn the party's watchful eye back upon itself.

The SED's response to the problem of "consumer sovereignty" illustrates the failure of Marxism–Leninism to provide a politically stable solution to the challenge of consumer desire. If the effectiveness of capitalism lies in its ability to manufacture desire and sell it as need, thereby deflecting much systemic criticism into the activity of consuming the objects of desire, then the ineffectiveness of the planned economy lay in its understanding of desire in terms of need. The SED produced shortages that led to an inflation of desire, and it was the accrual of desire, symbolized by the long waits for scarce goods, that helped undermine the socialist value system financially as well as morally.

6

Consuming Ideology

The Intershops, Genex, and Retail Trade under Honecker

> But the citizens of the GDR wanted the GDR to be turned into an Intershop overnight.[1]

As in other communist countries, consumer culture in the GDR had always been characterized by the discrepancy between the model of socialist consumerism projected by the regime and the shortages of goods generated by the planned economy. After Honecker's takeover, however, this disjunction between justifying ideology and power-oriented practice deepened, until it overwhelmed both the party's ability to govern and its political legitimacy. The political exigency of staving off insolvency spawned a series of fiscal solutions to the problem, the most important of which was the decision to expand the Intershops' sphere of activities.

Making the Intershops an integral part of the party's domestic retail strategy, however, introduced new social conflicts into East German society that belied the egalitarianism of the SED's consumer ideology. These new rifts in the social fabric of the GDR, moreover, did not manifest themselves in traditional Marxist-Leninist categories of analysis, which were based on an individual's relation to the means of production, the cultural capital implicit in their social background, and their political loyalty to the Workers' and Peasants' State. Instead, social conflict under Honecker came to be defined by German rather than class divisions, by accidents of birth rather than any labors of socialist love – in short, by access to West German currency and the nimbus of Western lifestyle surrounding it. The party's ideological resourcefulness, moreover, proved inadequate to the task of explaining away this new distribution of privilege.

---

1 Lothar de Maizière (interview, Berlin, 8.5.96).

243

The SED's aggressive expansion of the Intershops also slighted the GDR's actual achievements while encouraging an orientation toward the West. The model of consumption on display in the Intershops, for example, offered East Germans the very same social fantasies that the SED officially condemned as commodity fetishism. Marx had expressed the hope that technical innovations such as the sewing machine would bring the exchange value of merchandise such as clothing into line with the value of its material content and labor, thereby eliminating "the murderous, meaningless caprices of fashion."[2] Yet the Intershops emphasized variety and trendiness, offering fifteen different types of jeans and forty different kinds of leather jackets and dresses – items enormously popular with East German consumers. Despite the SED's scorn for the capitalist practice of embellishing an item with frills that do not improve upon its use value, the socialist retail chain even sold fashionable door handles.

The Intershop business model increasingly resembled that of its capitalist counterparts. The failure of socialism to devise a genuine alternative to the attractions of Western consumerism reduced the retailer to imitating market trends in Western societies. Toward the end of the 1980s, for example, Intershop managers were compelled to acknowledge the growing relevance of convenience in food preparation as a category of consumption and sold some twenty-five different types of instant soups and various kinds of frozen pizzas.[3] The Intershops also adopted capitalist business practices, from arbitrage to manipulative price setting.

Thus, the Intershops helped delegitimize socialism by introducing new social conflicts that belied the GDR's claim to egalitarianism, by contradicting the SED's censure of commodity fetishism, and by adopting the business techniques of the class enemy. But the Intershops were not merely emblematic of the failures of East German economic and consumer policy; they also taught East Germans to believe that the power to overcome scarcity resided in the West German mark. Denominating social justice in the coin of capitalism, however, undermined the value of the East German mark – and by extension the economic order backing it. And it was this fetishization of West German money that would convince East Germans to abandon the GDR for the prospect of German unification under Western auspices.

2 Marx, *Capital*, vol. 35, p. 482.
3 SAPMO-BA, DY30, Vorläufige SED 42023, "Information über das aktuelle Angebot in den Intershops im Interhotel 'Metropol,' der Eitelstraße am Bahnhof Lichtenberg (Kaufhallentyp) und im Flachbau des Bahnhofs Friedrichstraße," no date, pp. 2–3. See also Rainer Gries, "'Help Yourself!' The History and Theory of Self Service in West and East Germany," in Swett et al., *Selling Modernity*.

THE INTERSHOPS

Much like the Soviet *Beriozka*, the Czechoslovak *Tuzex*, the Polish *Pewex*, and the Bulgarian *Corecom*, the East German Intershops were initially designed to offer Western or Western-quality goods exclusively to Western tourists as a way of supplementing the GDR's hard-currency receipts. Because it was illegal for them to possess Western currency, East German citizens were not allowed to shop in the hard-currency stores.[4] During the Ulbricht period, moreover, the Intershops maintained a modest public presence and contributed comparatively little to state coffers, like the stores in other Comecon countries. At first, their operations were confined to supplying provisions and equipment to Western sailors temporarily disembarking in the port cities of Wismar, Rostock, and Stralsund. The unanticipated success of the first hard-currency store, which opened on 1 August 1955 in Rostock, prompted the extension of operations to the GDR's airports.[5] After the construction of the Berlin Wall in 1961, the Intershops experienced a mild expansion, as the SED hastened to exploit its control over the circulation of ideas and people between the two Germanys. Wherever Western visitors were to be found, the regime set up Intershops – from border crossings, such as the Friedrichstraße in Berlin (beginning on 26 February 1962), to annual fairs, such as those held in Leipzig (beginning with the autumn fair in 1962).[6]

Once Honecker assumed power in 1971, however, the similarities between the Intershops and the hard-currency shops in other socialist countries ended. When the regime's convertible-currency requirements began to soar in the 1970s, the SED vastly enlarged the role of hard-currency retailing. Not only did the SED increase the number of stores, but it opened them to ordinary East Germans for the first time. By the mid-1970s, Honecker's policies had transformed the Intershops from a modest chain of duty-free shops into a major supplier of luxury goods to East Germans.

The institutional foundations for Honecker's expansion of the hard-currency sector were laid during the Ulbricht period. On the

---

4 BArchB, DL2, 1005, "Analyse der Entwicklung des Intershophandels im Jahre 1976," p. 4; SAPMO-BA, DY30, Vorläufige SED 42023, "Standpunkt zur ADN-Information über den 'Beschluß des Ministerrates der UdSSR über Maßnahmen zur grundlegenden Vervollkommnung des Intershopssystems,'" p. 8.

5 BArchB, L1, 3077, "Protokoll vom 17.8.1954," p. 37, cited in Katrin Böske, "Abwesend anwesend: Eine kleine Geschichte des Intershops," in Neue Gesellschaft für bildende Kunst (ed.), *Wunderwirtschaft: DDR-Konsumkultur in den 60er Jahren* (Cologne, Weimar, and Vienna, 1996), p. 215; BArchB, DL2, 993, Schalck to Sölle, 23.8.76; Volze, "Die Devisengeschäfte," p. 1150.

6 Böske, "Abwesend anwesend," pp. 216–17; Council of Ministers decree, "Gründung spezieller Einrichtungen für den Valutaverkehr auf dem Gebiet der DDR," 4.1.62.

recommendation of Alexander Schalck-Golodkowski, at the time a minor party official involved in exporting machines to the West, the SED consolidated the management of its various hard-currency operations in 1961 by unifying its various businesses under the jurisdiction of the Commercial Coordination Area (Bereich Kommerzielle Koordinierung, or KoKo). The decision placed control of KoKo's efforts to secure Western cash, from the companies run by the secret police to the Intershops, in the hands of Horst Roigk. As a Stasi agent whose previous job included overseeing the transfer of money from West German churches to their East German counterparts, Roigk seemed the perfect candidate for a position requiring experience with the financial and political division of Germany. A few months later, however, the SED leadership removed Roigk and placed Schalck in charge of KoKo.

Schalck's appointment to a seemingly insignificant post heralded a sea change in the East German economy. He succeeded in turning a niche business into the largest single provider of hard currency, but only by transforming its customer base from an exclusively Western to a predominantly Eastern clientele.[7] In the process, however, his hard-currency imperium, which operated on market principles, encroached on the system of production and distribution enshrined in the plan. Like Mittag, Schalck was gambling for resurrection — hoping that capitalist money would rescue the socialist state. Indeed, by making himself indispensable to Mittag, Schalck accumulated broad powers. In part, Schalck's burgeoning power resulted from the unique manner in which the party's macroeconomic concerns and the state's administration of resources were unified in his person. But his undeniable managerial talents as well as his adroit use of his Stasi connections played an important role in enhancing his growing clout. Stasi chief Mielke had fired Roigk and promoted Schalck in the mistaken belief that Schalck's status as a Stasi agent would strengthen his influence over the GDR's foreign trade policy.[8] Instead, Schalck used his connection to Mittag to free himself of police supervision, then fend off challenges to his power from party and state officials. By the mid-1980s, the premium Honecker

---

7 After 1982, Intershop revenue was the GDR's largest single source of hard currency. In that year, the Intershops brought in DM 545 million compared to 520 million earned from the *Transitpauschale*, or the lump-sum payments made by the FRG to the GDR (see the discussion of the *Pauschale* in Chapter 3 and the Intershop figures in Table 6).

8 Although placing KoKo under the direction of Schalck may have been prompted by his obvious and considerable talents, Mielke and the security agents responsible for monitoring the economy hoped that he would make ties between the Stasi and the Ministry of Foreign and Intra-German Trade "even stronger than before" (Heinz Volpert, "Vorschlag zur Einstellung eines Offiziers im besonderen Einsatz," 8.9.66, cited in Haendcke-Hoppe-Arndt, *Die Hauptabteilung XVIII*, p. 45).

had put on financial subterfuge at the expense of economic prudence catapulted Schalck into a position of nearly unrivaled power. Like Mittag and Honecker, Schalck would become one of socialism's gravediggers.

The first major shift in policy toward the hard-currency sector came as Honecker was easing Ulbricht out.[9] In July 1970, Schalck, along with the Minister of Finance, Siegfried Böhm, and the Deputy Minister of Finance, Herta König, proposed a plan for "a rapid increase of hard-currency revenues in Intershop trade." The plan called for opening new stores, but also for selling more GDR products in them.[10] Given the condition of scarcity that dominated many sectors of the planned economy, making already scarce goods less available for domestic consumption was not without political risks. To ensure that shifting resources from the domestic market to the Intershops did not create new shortages or deepen existing ones, the plan awarded the Ministry of Trade and Supply the right to veto Intershop purchases of commodities manufactured in the GDR. Authorizing the state to preside over the circulation of consumer goods according to the party's guidelines was standard procedure in the GDR. From the party's point of view, such a distribution of roles possessed the virtue of saddling individual ministers with the blame should their management of scarce resources provoke popular resentment, but allowing the party to take credit should state institutions successfully navigate the Scylla of shortage and the Charybdis of distribution.[11] Of course, granting the state nominal control over supply and trade did not mean that the SED actually respected the state's jurisdiction. As always, the party's economic priorities – in this case its increasingly desperate search for hard currency – took precedence over the state's mission to manage the provisioning of consumer goods in a rational manner. In the end, the latitude granted to him by Mittag, coupled with his pivotal role as a supplier to key institutions, ensured that Schalck could override the objections of state functionaries regarding the export of scarce consumer

---

9 For more on the cooperation between Schalck and Heinz Volpert, who invented the SED's practice of selling political prisoners for hard currency, as well as the larger rivalries that eventually thrust trade with the West to the forefront of the GDR's policies, see Armin Volze and Johannes L. Kuppe, "Doktor Schalck. Analyse einer Geheimdissertation," *Deutschland Archiv* 26:6 (1993), pp. 641–57.

10 BArchB, DN1, VS 3\89, Nr. 12, Böhm, "Beschluß zur schnelleren Steigerung der Valutaeinnahmen im Intershop-Handel der DDR," 17.7.70, pp. 4, 6–7. Despite Armin Volze's claim to the contrary, products of domestic origin, including liquor, glass, porcelain, and some automobile parts, were sold in the Intershops (BArchB, DL1, 930; *Süddeutsche Zeitung*, 31.10.89; Volze, "Die Devisengeschäfte," p. 1151).

11 According to Christian Scholwin, state officials often felt frustrated by the party's constant interventions, as well as its tendency to take credit for successes and blame the state for failures (interview, Scholwin, Berlin, 23.11.95). The tendency of highly placed functionaries to identify more strongly with the state than the party, despite their fidelity to the SED, does not compare with the Soviet Union, where the line between party and state was nearly invisible.

goods: East German products that sold well in the West, such as furniture, were simply removed from domestic circulation.[12]

In addition to paying lip service to the concerns of domestic consumers, Schalck, Böhm, and König also proposed breaking with previous practice and restructuring the Intershops' procurement system along capitalist lines to make it more efficient. Because the Intershops were able to undercut West German retailers, they enjoyed large profit margins even under Ulbricht. On such items as cigarettes and alcohol, for example, the state-run retail chain could sell at prices attractive to consumers yet still enjoy high profit margins compared to their West German competitors, who were required by the West German state to pay relatively high customs duties as well as sin and value-added taxes. Because of this comparative advantage, the Intershops' profitability vastly exceeded the achievements of the GDR's exporting industries.[13] The main reason the Intershops' costs were so low, however, stemmed from their unique geographical position. The stores parlayed their advantage of location into a monetary edge: They received payment in Western money, but could requite their already low expenses, such as sales and transportation costs, in East German marks, without diminishing the profit they had earned in hard currency. Nor did the Intershops have much in the way of advertising expenses. Sensitive to the potential for envy and dissatisfaction the hard-currency stores might provoke, the regime kept signs of their existence down to a minimum.[14]

Most importantly, the proposal made by Schalck, Böhm, and König fundamentally altered the planned economy by introducing capitalist business techniques. To improve the retail chain's performance, the plan introduced a profit-sharing scheme. If any of the various institutions cooperating with or providing space for the Intershop organization overfulfilled their part of the plan, they could keep 20 percent of the extra hard-currency revenues as a "material incentive." Likewise, East German manufacturers were promised the right to disburse as they saw fit 20 percent of the profits earned from their products, a strategy aimed at providing them with greater motivation to manufacture and deliver consumer goods to the Intershops.[15] Given the

12 See, for example, SAPMO-BA, DY 30, Vorläufige SED 37988, Ministerium für Handel und Versorgung, "Information über die Schwerpunkte der im Monat Mai 1987 an das MHV gerichteten Eingaben," p. 7.
13 SAPMO-BA, DY30, Vorläufige SED 42023, "Information zum Artikel in der 'Morgenpost' vom 13.11.1981," p. 20; BArchB, DN1, VS 3/89, Nr. 12, Böhm, "Beschluß," 17.7.70, p. 8.
14 Ibid.; SAPMO-BA, DY30, Vorläufige SED 42023, Anlage 1, "Grundsätze der Planung, Leitung und Durchführung des Intershopraumes," no date, p. 46.
15 BArchB, DN1, VS 3\89, Nr. 12, Böhm, "Beschluß," 17.7.70, pp. 6–7; Pirker et al., *Der Plan*, pp. 146, 158. The retail organizations eligible for the profit-sharing plan included the HO, which was the largest retailer, the official hotel chain (*Interhotel*), the restaurants and snackbars run on passenger trains by *Mitropa*, the ship suppliers (*Schiffsversorgung*), and the state travel agency (*Reisebüro der DDR*).

party's monopoly over foreign trade, which often collided with the need of producers to import machines and equipment from the West, such access to capitalist currency must have been attractive to factory managers.

This is not to imply that the adoption of profit-oriented business practices in one area of the East German economy sufficed to overcome the structural disincentives to efficiency and cost effectiveness that inhered in the rest of the economy. Because meeting planning targets rather than making a profit was still paramount, pecuniary incentives did not translate into a stimulus to production. The Interhotel Association, which supervised the Intershops found at the GDR's hotels, complained in 1976, for example, that the VEB Boizenberger Fliesenwerke, which produced decorative tiles, was an unreliable partner. Its management suggested that the Intershops shift to a Western supplier, adding weight to its recommendation with a reference to the concern that "the gaps in the domestic assortment of tiles represent a political problem."[16] Clearly, a few profit-sharing schemes could not reconcile the divergent interests of producers and distributors as long as soft budget constraints allowed them to ignore costs.

Despite Schalck's efforts, moreover, there were signs that the SED's antipathy to money encouraged purchasing and pricing practices disadvantageous to the GDR. The West German magazine *Der Spiegel*, for example, maintained that the Intershops often overpaid their Western partners. In addition, the Intershop management appears to have been slow to respond to price movements in West Germany. Despite the SED's control over the flow of information, informal networks helped East as well as West Germans adjust quickly to differences in prices between West German retailers and the Intershops.[17] Finally, Intershop prices, which were denominated in West German marks, were not sufficiently coordinated with the fixed exchange rates set by the East German government. In the late 1970s, for example, one Western newspaper noted that the DM-to-dollar exchange rate in the Intershops amounted to 3.66:1, or less than the official rate set by the East German state. For this reason, the paper concluded, "it is worthwhile for West German travelers to undertake a bit of currency speculation" and convert their D-Marks to dollars so they could purchase more in the Intershops.[18] Although designed to prop up the socialist system, the introduction

16 BArchB, DL2, 1005, Vereinigung Interhotel, Bereich Valutawirtschaft, "Jahresanalyse 1976 – Intershopeinzelhandel," 28.12.76, p. 13.
17 Ibid.; BArchB, DL2, 992, Panse, "Strategiekonzeption," 2.11.84, pp. 4, 14; *Der Spiegel* 34 (1988), pp. 37–8.
18 BArchB, DL2, 995, unidentified Western newspaper, no date.

of capitalist financial incentives was emblematic of the confusion of means and ends at the heart of East German socialism under Honecker – financial expediency at the expense of ideological orthodoxy.

TRADING ON DIVISIONS

Honecker's decision to expand the sphere of Intershop activities was reinforced throughout the 1970s by West German *Ostpolitik*. The relaxation of travel restrictions for West Germans agreed upon in the 1972 Transportation Treaty led to a level of Western tourism unprecedented for a Soviet bloc country.[19] The SED was ambivalent about the growing number of Western visitors, coveting their wealth but fearing the influence of their ideas. The party's first response to renewed contact with the West, for example, combined an attempt to decrease the flow of visitors with an effort to profit from those Westerners still willing to visit the GDR. On 15 November 1973, the socialist state doubled the amount of hard currency Western travelers were required to exchange, raising the minimum from DM 10 to 20 per day. As a result, the number of West Germans (excluding West Berliners) visiting the GDR fell for the first time in years, from 2.28 million in 1973 to 1.9 million in 1974. Eventually, West German negotiators succeeded in convincing the SED to lower the obligatory amount to DM 13 (DM 6.50 for West Berliners) starting on 20 December 1974. The effect was immediate. In 1975, the number of West German visitors jumped by one-third to 3.1 million.[20] The sheer number of Westerners passing through the GDR, then, justified an expansion of the Intershops as an instrument of monetary policy.

Naturally, the West German visitors brought with them West German currency, increasing the circulation of West German marks in East German hands. As Schalck explained, "based on the development of international travel, visitor, and tourist traffic, and especially the existing ties of family and friendship between citizens of the GDR and the Federal Republic and West Berlin, which are not comparable to other countries, a portion of GDR citizens has also come into possession of convertible currency."[21] In fact, the

19 The new treaty authorized travel by West Germans for private, but also for commercial, purposes, religious or cultural reasons, and sports events – all subject to the approval of East German officials. The treaty also provided for East German travel to the Federal Republic in "urgent family matters' – a loose formulation designed to invite bureaucratic intervention. In addition, the SED agreed to facilitate gift-giving by dropping customs duties on West German care packages. See the discussion in Chapter 3.

20 Zimmerman, *DDR Handbuch*, vol. 1, pp. 296, 634, and vol. 2, p. 1451.

21 SAPMO-BA, DY30, Vorläufige SED 42023, "Standpunkt zur ADN-Information," p. 8. Schalck was only partially right – Polish citizens also received Western money from family and friends living

main source of Western currency consisted of gifts from family and friends. In a 1976 analysis of its customer base, for example, the Intershop management concluded that the relaxation of restrictions on sending mail between the two Germanys had sparked a shift in gift-giving behavior among West Germans, who now preferred to send money rather than care packages.[22] Similarly, East Germans came into hard currency by inheriting property abroad.[23] Others acquired D-Marks by living or traveling outside the GDR. For example, the small minority of East Germans working abroad, including diplomats and construction workers on the Siberian oil pipeline, received a portion of their wages in hard currency, either to blunt the temptations of living in the midst of Western opulence or to make their arduous working conditions in the East more attractive.[24] During the 1980s, moreover, the gradual relaxation of travel restrictions for pensioners also increased the amount of DM in circulation in the GDR. Finally, one of the socially most significant sources of Western money consisted of what the regime termed the "unjust retention" of gratuities by workers in the service sector, such as waiters.[25]

Whether obtained through legal or illegal means, capitalist currency stimulated the growth of black markets, as East Germans used Western money to purchase goods and services they could not acquire with socialist money. As we have seen, trade on the black market, which had existed since the GDR's inception, represented a challenge to the party's power because it took place beyond the purview of the plan and embodied an alternate system of values in competition with the planned economy. Black market trade denominated in Western money, however, also threatened the stability of the East

abroad. But he was right about what counted, since Poland built more hard-currency stores, but earned far less money on them than the GDR. According to *Die Welt*, there were 650 Pewex stores in Poland as of 1983, with sales totaling $261 million (BArchB, DL2, 995, *Die Welt*, 11.9.84). A comparison of hard-currency stores in Soviet-style economies, which could not be undertaken here, would shed light on their different approaches to debt financing, public access to the West, and the structure of privilege in socialist economies.

22 BArchB, DL2, 1005, Vereinigung Interhotel, Bereich Valutawirtschaft, "Jahresanalyse 1976," 28.12.76, p. 4.

23 Before 1974, East Germans were not allowed to hold Western currency. Even afterwards, however, most East Germans left their property in the West because the GDR maintained predatory regulations regarding the transfer of Western assets to East German citizens (SAPMO-BA, DY30, Vorläufige SED 42023, "Standpunkt zur ADN-Information," p. 10; Franka Schneider, "'Jedem nach dem Wohnsitz seiner Tante'. Die Genex Geschenkdienst GmbH," in Neue Gesellschaft für bildende Kunst [ed.], *Wunderwirtschaft*, pp. 225–6).

24 According to *Der Spiegel*, 6,000 East Germans were working on the pipeline in 1985 (*Der Spiegel* 41 [1985], p. 140).

25 BArchB, DL2, 1005, Vereinigung Interhotel, Bereich Valutawirtschaft, "Jahresanalyse 1976," 28.12.76, p. 4. Some Western money also found its way into the pockets of East Germans via prostitution.

German mark. The party recognized that administrative measures could not adequately protect the East German currency, whose weakness derived from the shortage economy, Honecker's inflationary policies, and the division of Germany. Eventually the regime decided to defuse the threat by decriminalizing the possession of foreign currency starting on 1 February 1974.[26] Permitting East Germans to hold West German currency legally aimed at reducing the scope of black market trade denominated in Western money by moving it into the Intershops, which now opened their doors to East Germans. The law unlocked a new and important source of hard-currency revenue for the Intershops, even convincing many East German holders of West German assets to transfer their property to the GDR.

Despite the measure's obvious success, Schalck's coworkers preferred to view the shift of assets as a sign of capitalism's inferiority. The Interhotel management, for example, argued that the regulation had encouraged "a partial liquidation of hard-currency accounts in the FRG . . . because of the Western economic crisis."[27] The inflation experienced by the West in the wake of the oil crises may well have encouraged East Germans to liquidate their assets, but the fact that they were no longer obliged to exchange their Western holdings for East German money clearly constituted the greater incentive. More importantly, the new law transformed the Intershops' customer base from an exclusively Western clientele to a solidly East German one. By 1976, 85 percent of Intershop revenue came from East German customers; the Interhotel Association reported that 80 percent of its customers, in both the hotel Intershops and the hotel rooms, were East Germans.[28] Unsurprisingly, turnover and revenue skyrocketed after 1974. Sales soared from 286 million West German marks in 1974 to 829 million in 1980, reaching 1.16 billion in the abbreviated year of 1989. The Intershop management attributed this growth in sales to a broader distribution of Western money as well as an increase in the total number of customers. Because it straddled East and West, moreover, the divided city of Berlin remained a central component of the Intershops' success, accounting for a "considerable portion" of Intershop revenues.[29]

26 Devisengesetz vom 19.12.73, *Gesetzesblätter der DDR* I (1973), p. 574 ff.
27 BArchB, DL2, 1005, "Analyse der Entwicklung," p. 4, and Vereinigung Interhotel, Bereich Valutawirtschaft, "Jahresanalyse 1976," 28.12.76, p. 4.
28 BArchB, DL2, 1005, "Analyse der Entwicklung," p. 4, and Vereinigung Interhotel, Bereich Valutawirtschaft, "Jahresanalyse 1976," 28.12.76, p. 3.
29 SAPMO-BA, DY30, 42023, Briksa to Schalck, 10.4.85, p. 36, and "Information zur Erfüllung der Aufgaben auf dem Gebiet des Intershophandels im Jahre 1981," p. 21. Significantly, the value of the average purchase remained stable over time (BArchB, DL2, 1005, "Analyse der Entwicklung," p. 4).

Table 6. *Intershop Sales and Revenue, 1962–1989*[a] *(in millions of DM)*

Year	Turnover	Revenue
1962	1.119	No data
1970	100	No data
1971	170	No data
1972	243	No data
1973	277	No data
1974	286	No data
1975	464	No data
1976	556	435
1977	705	No data
1978	896	No data
1979	774	466
1980	820	480
1981	806	489
1982	896	545
1983	920	580
1984	989	646
1985	1,044	677
1986	1,076	705
1987	1,105	717
1988	1,123	685
1989	1,162	585

[a] *Sources:* SAPMO-BA, DY30, Vorläufige SED 42023, various reports; BArchB, DL2, 992, Panse, "Geschäftsbericht 1989," 2.2.90, p. 14; BArchB, DL2, 1005, "Analyse der Entwicklung," p. 4, and Panse, "Analyse zu ausgewählten Problemen des Intershophandels," 22.1.87, p. 2; Böske, "Abwesend anwesend," p. 218; Herbst et al. (eds.), *So funktionierte die DDR*, p. 434; Volze, "Die Devisengeschäfte," pp. 1150, 1155. These figures include the Interhotels and Intertank gas stations, but not Genex or other convertible-currency businesses.

Expanding the Intershop chain helped ease the GDR's external obligations by bringing in more hard currency. But it also created new domestic burdens. Opening the Intershops to East Germans invited attacks on the value of the Ostmark by encouraging trade in Westmark.[30] The black market in West German marks flourished, for example, because the zone in which hard currency was useful grew with every new Intershop added to the East German retail landscape. The Interhotel management noted with alarm in 1976 that "the argument is constantly overheard that people first

30 BArchB, DL2, 1005, "Analyse der Entwicklung," p. 4, and Vereinigung Interhotel, Bereich Valutawirtschaft, "Jahresanalyse 1976," 28.12.76, p. 3.

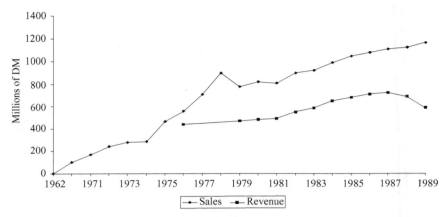

Figure 21. Intershop sales and revenue, 1962–1989. *Sources:* SAPMO–BA, DY30, Vorläufige SED 42023, various reports; BArchB, DL2, 992, Panse, "Geschäftsbericht 1989," 2.2.90, p. 14; BArchB, DL2, 1005, "Analyse der Entwicklung," p. 4, and Panse, "Analyse zu ausgewählten Problemen des Intershophandels," 22.1.87, p. 2; Böske, "Abwesend anwesend," p. 218; Herbst et al. (eds.), *So funktionierte die DDR*, p. 434; Volze, "Die Devisengeschäfte," pp. 1150, 1155. These figures include the Interhotels and Intertank gas stations, but not Genex or other convertible-currency businesses.

have to 'acquire' the money."[31] In addition to the black market in currency, many East Germans purchased electronic appliances from the Intershops, then resold them on the street.[32] East German demand for D-Marks expanded at such a pace that even West German officials took notice. In 1978, the Bundesbank declared that the massive expansion of the West German money supply was due not simply to inflationary pressures, but also to a dramatic influx of West German marks into the portfolios of East German individuals.[33]

Not only had the market for D-Marks grown, but the Intershops had become a site of capitalist business practices on socialist soil. While the regime struggled to differentiate morally between legal trade inside the Intershops and illegal transactions outside their doors, these distinctions appeared arbitrary to most East Germans. In fact, the division between the Intershops and the black market, between Westmark and Ostmark, and between capitalism and socialism reflected a growing split in the East German economy.

31 BArchB, DL2, 1005, Vereinigung Interhotel, Bereich Valutawirtschaft, "Jahresanalyse 1976," 28.12.76, p. 3.
32 In 1985 and 1986, the East German police uncovered 623 cases of smuggling and "speculation," which the Stasi estimated cost the GDR 199.6 million marks (BStU, MfS HA XVIII, 6166, "Hinweise," 1987, pp. 4, 11, 13).
33 Sell and Thieme, "Nebenwährungen," p. 137.

The SED was unable to reconcile its ideological aspirations – a society free of the social alienation represented by money and merchandise – with the practical exigencies of governing an industrial society by force. The party's attempts to manage the needs of consumers by turning to the West introduced commodities that had been produced outside the planned economy according to a system of valuation antithetical to socialism. Worse, the appearance of new and high-quality goods on the East German market, combined with the officially sanctioned method of distributing them via access to West German currency, only engendered the very same commodity fetishism, including social envy and the desire for status, that the SED publicly vituperated. Honecker's need for hard currency and the retail policy he countenanced as a solution to it threatened to upend the principles on which the communist party legitimated its rule.

In April 1979, the regime sought to remedy this by emending the currency law to constrain illegal trade in Western money. The new regulations compelled East German citizens to exchange their foreign currency in return for checks, called Forum checks after the Forum retail enterprise that oversaw the Intershops. They also increased the penalties for violations of the state's monopoly over hard-currency transactions.[34] The new law promised "to concentrate the previously uncontrolled circulation of freely convertible currency by GDR citizens in banking institutions and thereby use it to directly strengthen the performance of the economy." More to the point, the regime hoped that forcing East Germans to surrender their Western money and accept Forum checks in return would "constrict the area of speculative trade in convertible currency and directly combat the ideology of 'the existence of two currencies in the GDR' propagated by the imperialist mass media."[35]

Whatever the propaganda value of the Forum checks, the real advantage of the new currency law did not lie in shoring up the East German mark by disrupting the black market. Rather, the checks increased the regime's hard-currency revenues by functioning as an instrument of credit. East German citizens were obliged to exchange their foreign currency for Forum checks immediately, but were free to use the checks when they desired, whereas the state benefited at once by exploiting the time lag between the enforced deposit of funds and their redemption at Intershops for consumer goods. In 1981, for example, Schalck reported that DM 110 million in cash had

---

34 Änderungsgesetz vom 28.6.79, in *Gesetzesblätter der DDR* I (1979), p. 147f. The Soviet analogue was *Vneshposyltorg* checks; the Czechoslovakian version, *Tuzex-Koruna*.
35 SAPMO-BA, DY30, Vorläufige SED 42023, "Standpunkt zur ADN-Information," p. 8.

been deposited with the East German central bank since 1979 in return for Forum checks that had not yet been redeemed for the purchase of goods in the Intershops.[36]

Creating what was in effect an intermediary currency, however, did little to prop up confidence in the East German mark or make West German money less attractive. Although Forum congratulated itself that the population treated the checks "as equivalent to [Western] cash and sav[ed] them, too," the fact that East Germans accepted the Forum checks at all was less a confirmation of the regime's success in trying to influence the market for Western currency than evidence of the central role played by hard currencies in the East German economy.[37] In fact, many people continued to keep some West German marks on hand even though it was illegal because hard currency was particularly useful for obtaining increasingly scarce goods and services not offered in the Intershops. Nor did the sales staff enforce the law vigorously. Intershop clerks often failed to verify if customers paying in currency instead of Forum checks were foreigners and not East German citizens, most likely because earning Western money trumped legal concerns.[38] Instead of reducing the significance of Western money and all that it symbolized, the Intershops not only stimulated its use, but made the extent of its circulation more apparent. The Ostmark's loss of value against the Westmark was cause enough for financial concern. Once the regime gave its official blessing to a two-currency economy, however, the gradual depreciation of the socialist currency acquired a political dimension, in much the same way that the party leadership's public preference for Volvos devalued the domestic automobile industry.

Conceding the Intershops such a large role in the retail sector, moreover, encouraged the very social stratification that the SED was officially devoted to eradicating. Once again, proximity to the West, which the party desperately tried to keep at arm's length, proved the determining factor. Most of those blessed with West German money owed their access to it to ties of family or friendship. This automatically excluded most party members, who were obliged to cut off all contact with the Federal Republic. As one petitioner noted bitterly in a letter to Forum, "in the interests of our sons, we were required to break off the loose contacts to the West. Now I cannot really revive them [just] to obtain Western money."[39] The only East Germans with access to Western money by virtue of their vocation

---

36 SAPMO-BA, DY30, Vorläufige SED 42023, "Information zur Erfüllung der Aufgaben," p. 21.
37 SAPMO-BA, DY30, Vorläufige SED 42023, "Standpunkt zur ADN-Information," p. 8, and Schalck and Kaminsky, no date, p. 16.
38 Böske, "Abwesend anwesend," p. 221.   39 BArchB, DL2, 930, petition from 15.5.89.

were those in the service sector who received gratuities from Westerners, such as waiters in restaurants.[40] Rather than rewarding people loyal to the regime, then, or targeting the working class, the Intershop system privileged the very people with the least sympathy for the GDR. As officials in Leipzig reported in 1977, "a large number of citizens, particularly those who do not possess Western currency, still exhibit a lack of comprehension and rejection of the system of the Intershop stores. Numerous citizens claim that . . . those citizens with ties to citizens of the Federal Republic can obtain a higher standard of living for themselves, but are often exactly the same citizens who perform no socially useful work and do not demonstrate a progressive attitude to our state."[41] These privileges seemed particularly unfair in a country whose economic organization was supposedly founded on the premise of social equality and a rational distribution of wealth.

The corrosive social effects of the Intershops were closely linked to the social value attached to Western money, and to the Deutsche Mark in particular. This value was not restricted to the potential represented by the currency to purchase high-quality commodities, or even the prestige attached to these products because of their scarcity or Western origin. Rather, the West German mark was imbued with the nimbus of an alternative value system in direct competition, ideologically and monetarily, with the GDR. On the one hand, official sanction of trade denominated in hard currency was tantamount to legitimizing capitalist relations in the GDR. On the other hand, embracing Western economic institutions such as the Westmark reinforced the popular tendency to look to the West, rather than the East. Despite the objections of orthodox Marxist-Leninists, the SED's decision to tap domestic sources of hard currency encouraged a stronger orientation toward Western commodities and Western money. For example, East Germans adorned their bathrooms with empty Western cosmetics bottles, venerated "violins," as West German 20-mark notes were known because of the violin on the reverse, and eagerly sought "blue tiles," slang for the blue-colored DM 100 note. Ironically, the SED's own economic practices were eroding the ethical and financial ground on which the model of socialist consumerism stood.

The proliferation of meaning that accompanied the increased circulation of Western consumer goods because of the Intershops reflected this irony.

40 BArchB, DL2, 1005, "Analyse der Entwicklung," p. 4. Exceptions included East German diplomatic personnel and highly placed functionaries traveling to the West.
41 SAPMO-BA, DY6, Vorläufige 1761, Stadtausschuß Leipzig, "Informationsbericht über Meinungen, Argumente und Fragen der Bürger," 18.11.77, pp. 3–4.

The Western provenance of the cosmetic bottles, for example, hinted at a mystical realm of abundance just beyond the Wall that enclosed the GDR, conferring status on the householder by implying access to that fabled world of goods. The ornamental function of the make-up bottles also suggested a strange inversion of plenty over penury: The Western packaging, emptied of its contents, advertised an association with capitalist consumerism. Drained of their "useful" meaning, the bottles functioned as metonyms for the capitalist system that produced them. Precisely because they were physically empty, moreover, the bottles represented a curious reversal of the SED's productionist hierarchy, which privileged use value over exchange value, functionality over fashion, and need over desire. Through its own efforts, the SED had fragmented the unity of the planned economy, permitting an influx of capitalist currency and commodities to vie with socialist money and merchandise.

Perhaps even more telling was the language used by ordinary East Germans to describe the social processes that stood behind the function of West German money in the GDR. In contrast to the cosmetic bottles, the names given to the D-Mark notes by East Germans reflected the way in which the shortage economy had reduced money to objects. That is, the fragmentation of money in the GDR into monies had deprived these currencies of their properties as universal equivalents and transformed them into partially exchangeable goods with their own limited zones of acceptability. People did not use only East and West German marks to mediate exchange, but also certain scarce commodities. Instead of brewing West German coffee such as Jakobs Krönung, for example, East Germans left the package unopened and circulated it like money.

Because it was so difficult to obtain yet so useful, capitalist currency took on the very fetishistic qualities that Marx denounced so vehemently. The particular fascination with the Deutsche Mark revolved around the ability attributed to it by the regime as well as the populace to resolve a variety of practical problems. The broad powers ascribed to Western money because of its ability to overcome adversity are aptly satirized in the following East German joke. "Question: What does the repairman say when he arrives? Answer: What Forum does your problem take? (*Forum geht's denn?*)"[42] The joke substitutes the name of the Intershop parent company (*Forum*) for the German interrogative "what" (*Worum*), with which it rhymes. Not only does it poke fun at the capacity of hard currency to extract necessary

---

42 Wagner, *DDR-Witze*, p. 95. See also the variation in BStU, MfS BKK (KoKo) 819, *HAZ*, 28.1.89, p. 4.

services from repairmen, but the joke also highlights the power of service providers in an industrial economy that suffered from chronic shortages of parts and labor. The discrepancy between these material shortcomings and the regime's promises, of which there were no shortage, invited this sort of mockery. What should have given Honecker pause, however, was less the criticism itself; the population circulated jokes in defiance of the regime, just as it did with Western money and merchandise. The real danger to the SED lay in the concrete solutions to their problems that East Germans perceived in the GDR's West German rival.

THE ECONOMY WITHIN THE ECONOMY

Given both its real and perceived value, obtaining Western money constituted a significant social temptation, greatly affecting the behavior of people in close contact with it. Even minor injustices, such as the unequal distribution of hard-currency tips among workers' collectives, excited strong passions.[43] The attraction exerted by convertible currency gradually diminished social inhibitions against theft. Even in Schalck's imperium, which vetted employees for political reliability, graft and corruption were widespread. Clerks and managers confiscated tips given to other workers, falsified prices and inventory reports, and stole goods and money outright.[44] The attraction of Western money was so powerful that security officials were forced to depart from their habitual repertoire of repression and blend moral suasion with material blandishment to prevent hard-currency theft. In one case, for example, the police rewarded employees at the Hotel Stadt Frankfurt an der Oder for ratting out their colleagues. Despite the Stasi's redoubled efforts, however, Intershop employees embezzled ever larger amounts of Western money and products as the 1980s wore on.[45]

More ominously, not even Schalck's satraps were protected from the temptations of the West. Despite their supposed ideological probity, some

---

43 BArchB, DL2, 930, petition from 15.11.88, and Generaldirektor der Mitropa, SGD für Intershophandel, "Vermerk über eine Aussprache," 6.1.89; BArchB, DE1, VA 56323, "Anfrage: Gehalt in Valuta. Zu Einkaufsberechtigungen und Trinkgeldern," no date, p. 634; *Der Spiegel* 41 (1985), p. 134.
44 BStU, MfS BKK (KoKo) 601, Panse to Schalck, "Jahresanalyse über die im Zeitraum vom 1. Dezember 1984 bis 30. Dezember 1985 gemeldeten Vorkommnisse im Bereich des IS-Einzelhandels," 27.12.85, pp. 15–19; BStU, MfS HA XVIII, 8804, "Information zu Straftaten im Intershopeinzelhandel," 9.5.83, and Kleine, "Maßnahmen zur Kriminalitätsvorbeugungen im Intershopeinzelhandel," 10.5.83; SAPMO-BA, DY30, Vorläufige SED 42023, "Information über die Durchführung eines Strafprozesses," no date, pp. 88–9.
45 SAPMO-BA, DY30, Vorläufige SED 42023, Schalck to Mittag, 9.2.83, p. 87, and "Information über die Durchführung eines Strafprozesses," no date, pp. 88–9; BStU, MfS BKK (KoKo) 601, Panse to Schalck, "Jahresanalyse," 27.12.85, pp. 15–19.

of his closest aides decided to "Test the West," as a West German cigarette slogan advised. In one particularly embarrassing incident, Günter Asbeck, the head of the import-export firm Asimex, defected to the West in 1981. In 1983, moreover, Horst Schuster, General Director of Kunst und Antiquitäten GmbH (Schalck's conduit for the sale of East German cultural treasures to the West), absconded with the help of the West German spy agency. Ironically, Schalck turned Schuster's defection to his advantage, arguing successfully that the best way to prevent such embarrassments in the future was to place jurisdiction for policing KoKo in his hands, since he was a Stasi officer anyhow. Of course, permitting Schalck to supervise himself was rather like letting the fox guard the chicken coop: Eliminating Stasi oversight of his activities did not end graft, corruption, and defection, but it did remove the last check on his power.[46]

Despite the party's decision to harness the allure that capitalist commodities held for East Germans to pay down the GDR's debt to the West, the SED leadership was not insensitive to the potential for political discontent represented by the Intershops. At the beginning of the first wave of Intershop expansion, for example, Schalck had warned Horst Sölle, the Minister for Foreign Trade, that building more stores "cannot merely be viewed as the solution to an economic problem." The Intershops, Schalck declared, were "an extraordinarily important political question," and he advised the party to monitor popular reaction to the new stores closely.[47]

Continual surveillance of the population was consistent with the SED's predilection for observational discipline as a mode of governance. But Schalck's call for vigilance also reflected the party's concern that those who benefited from its retail policies were not always its most loyal. In 1958, for example, the Ministry of Finance noted with alarm that the West German Catholic Church had inquired if it could purchase fifty cars for delivery to its East German members. "In our opinion," ministry officials cautioned, "it is not politically viable to motorize the Church so that it can reach isolated areas quickly and potentially increase its influence with the population in the countryside."[48]

Policing people, however, forced the party to expend considerable human and financial resources. Because hard currency was a socially explosive issue, key party officials, including Schalck and Mittag, found it necessary to

46 SAPMO-BA, DY30, Vorläufige SED 42023, Schalck to Mittag, no date, p. 23, and "Zur Pressemitteilung aus der 'Berliner Morgenpost' vom 15.01.1982," p. 91; BStU, MfS HA XVIII, 8804, "Information zu Straftaten," 9.5.83, pp. 4–5, and Kleine, "Maßnahmen," 10.5.83, p. 6; Haendcke-Hoppe-Arndt, *Die Hauptabteilung XVIII*, pp. 89–91; Chapter 4.
47 BArchB, DL2, 992, Schalck to Sölle, 26.8.70.
48 BArchB, DN1, 11480, Ministerium der Finanzen, 30.7.58, cited in Schneider, "Jedem nach dem Wohnsitz," p. 228.

become involved in sorting out specific grievances. Seemingly minor cases, such as a complaint by an Intershop employee regarding the inequitable distribution of hard-currency tips, unleashed a flurry of official activity. To resolve the issue, the employee was called in for a meeting with five government representatives, a tactic clearly intended to intimidate the petitioner into withdrawing his complaint.[49] However effective it might have been in the short term, the high priority given to deflecting resentments often led to an inefficient use of managers' time. Schalck and Mittag spent a fair amount of energy evaluating specific complaints regarding the Intershops rather than attending to the larger policy problems they were charged with solving.[50]

In addition to defusing individual grievances, the SED endeavored to avoid arousing too much attention by reducing the general population's contact with the Intershops where possible. Among other stratagems, Schalck tried to direct the expansion of new Intershop stores, whose numbers jumped from 270 to 416 between 1970 and 1986, at Westerners.[51] In 1977, for example, Intershops were opened near the garbage dumps at Ketzin and Schöneiche to target West Berlin garbage men transporting Western rubbish to the East. These shops – as well as a small snack stand at Ketzin run by the railroad restaurateur Mitropa – did a brisk business because they formulated their prices with attention to their location but also to their working-class clientele, cleverly offering alcohol, cigarettes, and sweets at prices below the going rates at other Intershops.[52] In addition, Schalck took some pains to avoid arousing envy by reducing the public profile of the Intershops. Aside from keeping advertising down to a minimum, he recommended that repairs to the Intershop in East Berlin's Friedrichstraße be undertaken by West German, rather than East German, construction workers, despite the higher costs. More importantly, Schalck also made certain that local party leaders, retail managers, and experts on consumption were involved in decisions to open new stores. As he explained to Mittag in 1985, involving local officials in discussions about new stores had prevented a rise in the number of popular complaints about the Intershops.[53]

---

49 BArchB, DL2, 930, petition from 15.11.88, and Generaldirektor der Mitropa, SGD für Intershophandel, "Vermerk," 6.1.89.
50 See the petitions in BArchB, DL2, 930.
51 SAPMO-BA, DY30, Vorläufige SED 42023, "Maßnahmen zur Sicherung der Entwicklung des Intershophandels in den Jahren 1984 und 1985," Anlage 3, 11.4.85, and Schalck, "Information zu den Ergebnissen des Intershophandels im Jahre 1986," 12.12.86; Volze, "Die Devisengeschäfte," pp. 1150–1.
52 SAPMO-BA, DY30, Vorläufige SED 42023, "Information zum Artikel in der 'Morgenpost' vom 13.11.1981," p. 20.
53 SAPMO-BA, DY30, Vorläufige SED 42023, Schalck to Mittag, 11.4.85, p. 73, Schalck, "Information," 7.11.84, pp. 84–5, and Schalck, "Information," 26.3.85, p. 77.

Nevertheless, the Intershops remained unpopular enough to generate visible expressions of discontent in an otherwise tightly controlled society. In early 1978, for example, some East Germans attempted to buy goods with Ostmarks in the Intershop in Pirna, near Dresden, but were rebuffed by the sales staff. To assuage tensions, the store was closed.[54] This story dovetails with the report of a Western observer who witnessed two young East German men try to pay for a large variety of Western goods with Russian rubles in an Intershop in Jena in 1983. The seriousness of the prank was not lost on the saleswoman, who chased them out of the store.[55] By the mid-1980s, envy and resentment were running high. People communicated their anger in increasingly violent terms, smashing store windows and protesting in front of the shops. Reports began appearing in the Western press about revenge taken on East Germans who benefited materially from their Western connections. In one instance, a house was smeared with tar in retaliation for the owner's perceived privileges.[56]

This is not to imply that the Intershops had created a loyal constituency, much less successfully transferred a positive identification from the retailer to the socialist state. On the contrary, the retail chain often alienated its customer base. One source of frustration, for example, stemmed from the Forum checks. The smallest denomination of the checks was 50 pfennigs, but list prices rarely came to an even mark or 50 pfennigs. The mathematical discrepancy between the acceptable medium of payment and amount necessary to engage in a successful transaction was designed to benefit the regime, which could earn a few extra pennies by requiring exact change.

This kind of pettifoggery aroused the ire of many East Germans, especially those who possessed Western currency in small amounts. One woman, for example, accused the Intershop management of nickel-and-diming its customers. She had purchased a knitting magazine for DM 2.20. Because East German citizens were not permitted to pay in Western currency, but only with Forum checks, the Intershop sales staff refused to let her pay the 20 pfennigs in West German coins. Not only was the woman forced to pay with a check, but the sales representatives refused to give her the remaining 30 pfennigs. The only way for her to get her money's worth was to forego the transaction entirely or purchase the knitting magazine as well as

---

54 BStU, MfS BKK (KoKo) 601, Panse to Schalck, "Jahresanalyse," 27.12.85, p. 17; *Die Welt*, 28.6.78; *Der Spiegel* 33 (1978), pp. 30–1; *Der Tagesspiegel*, 5.9.78; Herbst et al., *So funktionierte die DDR*, pp. 434–5.
55 I am indebted to John Connelly for this story.
56 BStU, MfS BKK (KoKo) 601, Panse to Schalck, "Jahresanalyse," 27.12.85, pp. 17, 19; BStU, MfS BKK (KoKo) 819, *HAZ*, 28.1.89, p. 4.

something worth 30 pfennigs. In the end, the woman felt compelled to buy two chocolate bars she did not want. In a letter to Intershop management, she argued that their methods were unsocialist: "I have been in the retail sector for many years, and I can't get my customers to buy inexpensive products just to increase my sales. That would be criminal and equal to capitalist sales practices." When her petition failed to produce the desired response, the woman hurled calumnies at the regime, comparing her sense of disenfranchisement to the exclusionary tactics of the "Third Reich." "It is scandalous," she claimed, "that a third currency was introduced only for us citizens of the GDR and one is treated like a third-class person in your retail institutions. Such practices were the norm only under the Nazis, when Jews and non-Aryans were denied entry to certain businesses."[57]

The woman's attempt to equate her plight with that of the victims of National Socialist atrocities is empirically wrong and morally suspect, but it was politically effective. By invoking the Nazis in a letter to representatives of the antifascist state, she had employed a sure-fire method of attracting attention to her grievance in an environment unfriendly to customers. However questionable the analogy was, moreover, it highlights just how demeaning the experience of shopping in the GDR often was. Indeed, her comparison between the hierarchies of currency and people under two German dictatorships captures at once the absurdity of the GDR's monetary regime and its humiliating effect on the majority of the population. Even party members began to question the Intershops' single-minded focus on earning convertible currency, arguing that management's approach was needlessly rigid, especially when compared to that used in other Soviet bloc countries.[58]

Meanwhile, the capitalist goods sold by the Intershops created all sorts of headaches for the regime. When the warrantees expired on West German durable goods, for example, East Germans had to pay for service and repairs in D-Marks, a serious burden for many unhappy customers. In addition, Intershop managers often neglected to order spare parts and refills. Most likely, management was fixated on one-off sales of big-ticket items, rather than return sales, as a method of increasing revenue. This tactic often translated into a problem of complementarity, which only increased customer dissatisfaction. For example, the retail chain carried the popular fountain pens made by the West German firm Pelikan, but no nibs.[59] This tiny part hardly seems significant. But Pelikan pens were very popular in the

57 BArchB, DL2, 930, petitions from 5.3.89, pp. 1–2, and 27.3.89, p. 2.
58 BArchB, DL2, 930, petition from 3.4.89, p. 1, and Steger, 8.5.89.
59 BArchB, DL2, 930, especially the petition from 13.2.89; BArchB, DL2, 1005, Vereinigung Interhotel, Bereich Valutawirtschaft, "Jahresanalyse 1976," 28.12.76, p. 12.

GDR because they were a sign of access to the West – to the quality of its products as well as its freedom of thought. Lothar de Maizière, who would become the first (and last) freely elected leader of the GDR in March 1990, recounted an incident in which a young boy at his daughter's school broke seventeen fountain pens out of envy and rage. De Maizière purchased a new one for his daughter and one for the boy "so that there was finally peace."[60] It is not surprising that the plethora of complaints about the absence of spare parts and poor service prompted a study by the Workers' and Peasants' Inspectorate, which was unsparing in its criticism of the Intershops.[61]

Next to people who had little or no access to Western currency, the largest group of protesters against the Intershops appears to have been women. Despite the regime's officially articulated goal of gender equality, women in the GDR were expected not only to contribute to economic growth by working, but also to assume the traditional roles of wife and mother. Because East German women cooked, cleaned, and cared for their families, they – rather than men – also tended to do the household shopping. And because of the chronic shortages of basic consumer goods, from children's clothes to food, women were the group most affected by Honecker's retail stratagems. It is not surprising, then, that the majority of the written complaints regarding retail trade – and against the Intershop system – came from women.

The SED, however, did not perceive these gender divisions as problematic. As with other divisions among East Germans, the fault lines between men and women in the GDR were not intelligible to a leadership steeped in the traditional categories of class conflict. Instead, the social tensions created by the SED's inadequate response to the planned economy's shortcomings remained invisible to the party elite, which preferred to locate the causes of social strife in popular misapprehensions and bureaucratic rivalries. As a result, the party approached social stratification based on gender or ties to the West as an intellectual chimera best offset by improved propaganda or minor adjustments to the implementation of party directives.

Just how inadequate such an approach had become by the 1980s is evinced by popular anger over the second wave of Intershop expansion launched by Schalck in 1983. Striving to provide a more permanent solution to the GDR's voracious need for Western currency, he worked out a plan with the Politburo's support that envisioned yet another dramatic expansion of

---

60 Interview, de Maizière, Berlin, 8.5.96.
61 BArchB, DL2, 930, Funke, Komitee der ABI, "Vermerk Generelle Probleme der Reklamationsbearbeitung bei Käufen im Intershop," 29.6.89.

his hard-currency imperium. In particular, Schalck proposed raising the Intershops' contribution to the GDR's balance of payments to a whopping 35 percent between 1985 and 1990. He hoped to achieve this surge in revenue primarily by building even more stores and expanding existing sales space.[62] The results were impressive. Between 1983 and 1986 alone, Schalck added more than 100 stores, raising the total number of Intershop retail outlets to 416, with 46,200 square meters of floor space. During the same period, the total floor space available for selling products rose by 215 percent, from 13,100 to 28,000 square meters.[63]

The increased visibility of the hard-currency stores provoked popular unrest. In November 1984, the opening of a new Intershop in Dresden occasioned loud protests, which Schalck euphemistically described as "discussions." In contrast to Schalck, however, the local party leadership took these "discussions" quite seriously. Under the guidance of Dresden party leader Hans Modrow, who would become Minister-President during the 1989 revolution, the district immediately took action to build more stores where East Germans could shop using the Ostmark.[64]

The upsurge in popular discontent prompted other local and district party leaders to balk at opening more Intershop stores. In 1985, the district party organization in Gera had the temerity to advise Schalck's aides that the Intershops should offer only products "that are also sold in comparable quality and sufficient quantity in domestic retail shops." In response, Schalck demanded that the Politburo remind the Gera party leadership "in the appropriate form" of its obligation to conform to party directives. By appealing to the Politburo's sense of its place atop the party hierarchy, Schalck successfully overrode the concern of local officials that the Intershops posed a serious threat to the party's power.[65]

Popular unrest and the anxieties of local leaders prompted officials at the center who were responsible for supplying the populace with consumer goods to resist plans to build more Intershops. In February 1985, Gerhard Briksa, Minister for Trade and Supply, and Hilmar Weiß, Director of the Department of Trade, Supply, and Foreign Trade at the ZK, met secretly to work out a plan aimed at isolating the Intershops and Schalck.

---

62 SAPMO–BA, DY30, Vorläufige SED 42023, "Maßnahmen," Anlage 3, 11.04.85, p. 69.
63 Ibid., pp. 81–2; SAPMO–BA, DY30, Vorläufige SED 42023, "Zur Versorgungsleistung von Inter-shop," 10.10.89, p. 4.
64 SAPMO–BA, DY30, Vorläufige SED 42023, "Information," 26.3.85, p. 77.
65 SAPMO–BA, DY30, Vorläufige SED 42023, Schalck to Mittag, 9.5.85, p. 32. A similar problem seems to have arisen in Rostock (SAPMO–BA, DY30, Vorläufige SED 42023, Schalck to Mittag, "Standpunkt zu den aufgeworfenen Problemen des Interhotels am Standort Rostock," 5.12.85, pp. 28–30).

By centralizing Intershop management and unifying it in Schalck's hands, Briksa and Weiß believed they could shield the Ministry of Trade and Supply, the ZK, and local leaders from association with the hard-currency stores. No longer integrated into the decision-making process, local officials would then be free to pursue their own interests – which often meant disrupting the construction of new stores. Briksa represented the plan to Schalck as a move toward a more efficient management structure, rather than an attempt to abandon the Intershops. To sweeten the deal, he appealed to Schalck's penchant for espionage. Consolidating the administration of the Intershops would, Briksa argued, preserve the clandestine nature of its operations by reducing the opportunity for leaks.[66]

Not surprisingly, Schalck vehemently objected. He correctly understood the plan as an attempt to place the burden for a highly unpopular policy squarely on his shoulders and fashion an institutional environment hostile to the hard-currency economy. In characteristic fashion, Schalck defended his position through the adroit application of his ties to the Stasi and judicious calls to party discipline. He spied on the plotters, receiving clandestine reports on high-level meetings between Weiß and Briksa's aides. In a particularly deft move, Schalck used his Stasi connections to alert Mittag to the fact that Werner Jarowinsky, the Politburo member in charge of domestic trade, knew nothing of the plan. In the byzantine world of communist intrigue, Schalck's report signaled to Mittag that he was free to act on Schalck's behalf without fear of alienating other party leaders.[67]

But Schalck was not satisfied with subtle hints. He pressed Mittag to move against the proposed changes. In a series of urgent letters in March and April, Schalck blended compelling arguments about management techniques with carefully calibrated sycophancy to coax Mittag into opposing Briksa's plan. He pointed to the political dangers inherent in permitting central and local officials to evade responsibility for establishing new stores. In particular, he castigated the Ministry of Trade and Supply and the Department of Trade, Supply, and Foreign Trade for their complacency, claiming that they "only feel themselves to be responsible for ensuring the provisioning of the population with basic necessities." Without their participation, however, "no county or district party leadership, no district or county council would feel responsible for executing the measures approved" by Honecker himself.

66 SAPMO-BA, DY30, Vorläufige SED 42023, Briksa to Schalck, 28.2.85, pp. 79–80, Briksa to Schalck, 10.4.85, p. 37, and Briksa, Jurich, and Merkel, "Gesondert zu entscheidenden Fragen," no date, pp. 81–2.
67 SAPMO-BA, DY30, Vorläufige SED 42023, Schalck to Mittag, 11.04.85, p. 34, and "Information," 26.03.85, p. 78.

The uncomfortable result, Schalck warned, would be a disturbing lack of accountability bordering on insubordination and the unsettling association of Intershop policy with the persons of Mittag and Honecker. With Briksa already prevaricating, the plan quickly collapsed.[68]

Once again, Schalck had won an institutional skirmish. Once again, the way was clear for the hard-currency sector to expand dramatically at the expense of the planned economy. By the mid-1980s, one could speak of KoKo as an economy within the economy. Yet Schalck was unable to translate his political triumph into a financial guarantee of economic success for the socialist state. Nor could his solution to the GDR's economic quandary overcome the social divisions created by the Intershops or satisfy the misgivings of party and state officials.

EASTERN ILLS AND WESTERN BILLS

Concerned by reports of discord, Honecker made a half-hearted attempt early on to cushion the social impact of the hard-currency stores. In a meeting with his economic advisors during the summer of 1977, Honecker stated that "I am against the expansion of the Intershop stores. We should reduce the program. Although 100 million Valutamarks comes out of it, we've got a big discussion" about them.[69] His resolve was strengthened by the disapproval of the Soviet Union, which correctly feared that the Intershops might form a bridge between West and East Germany.[70] In addition, some of the more ideologically committed, both inside and outside the party, were clearly distressed by the shops. The writer Wolfgang Harich, for example, told the *Kölner Stadtanzeiger* in 1978 that the Intershops legitimized Western consumerism and aroused ethically dubious desires. He set off the meritocratic justice of an ideal socialism, which rewarded everyone according to their accomplishments, against the effects of the Intershops in real-existing socialism, which rewarded "everyone according to the residence of their aunt" – that is, according to their access to West Germany.[71]

By the late 1970s, however, the Intershops had assumed a central role in the Republic's finances, far too central to justify reducing their contribution

68 SAPMO-BA, DY30, Vorläufige SED 42023, Schalck to Mittag, 11.04.85, p. 35, and Briksa to Schalck, 10.04.85, p. 37.
69 BArchB, DE1, 56348, "Beratung beim Generalsekretär des Zentralkomitees der SED," 2.6.77, p. 199.
70 BArchB, DL2, 995, *Die Welt am Sonntag*, 12.11.78; Volze, "Die Devisengeschäfte," p. 1152.
71 *Kölner Stadtanzeiger*, 13.5.78, cited in Volze, "Die Devisengeschäfte," p. 1152; BArchB, DL2, 995, *Süddeutsche Zeitung*, 5.9.78. Harich was playing on the Marxist slogan, taken from *Critique of the Gotha Programme*, which proclaims "from each according to his abilities, to each according to his needs."

to state coffers. Nor could the SED simply abolish the retail chain, since too many East Germans had come to rely on the shops as an indispensable link to the world of consumption beyond the Wall. Honecker's freedom of action was constrained by two divergent imperatives: the need to respect hard financial facts and the need to concede something to popular opinion.

To dispel some of the anger the stores had aroused, Honecker announced plans in 1977 to increase the number of Exquisit and Delikat stores. Although he promised that the Intershops "will not be among the permanent companions of socialism," he also acknowledged that "citizens who do not possess convertible currency are disadvantaged." The Exquisit and Delikat stores, Honecker declared, would be expanded "as competition to the Intershops. This competition is already quite tangible. It has guaranteed that those who do not possess hard currency can also purchase international products."[72] The Exquisit stores, which sold leather goods and clothing, had been created parallel to the expansion of the Intershops in 1962, but had languished in their shadow.[73] In contrast, the Delikat stores were created in 1976 in response to unrest over the expansion of the Intershop chain. Although the Exquisit stores mainly carried products of domestic provenance, the Delikat stores sold a variety of foodstuffs, from popular West German perishable goods, such as Jakobs Krönung coffee and Nutella chocolate spread, to high-quality East German products.[74]

As was often the case, the party found ways to profit financially from its social policies, and the Delikat and Exquisit stores were no exception. Although they failed to earn the regime any hard currency, the two chains did provide high rates of return on the West German marks used to fill their shelves. Between October 1977 and October 1978, for example, the Exquisit stores earned 5 East German marks for every West German mark they spent buying Western merchandise, well above the average rate East German manufacturers earned on international markets. The Delikat stores performed even better, soaking up 6.2 Ostmarks for every Deutsche Mark.[75] Given the rapid rise in wages that marked Honecker's tenure, moreover,

72 *Neues Deutschland*, 27.9.77; Politburo decree of 12.10.77.
73 SAPMO-BA, DY30, Vorläufige SED 38624/1, Generaldirektion, VE PHU Exquisit, "Versorgung der Bevölkerung mit Exquisiterzeugnissen," 6.9.72, pp. 1–3.
74 Berlin's premiere Exquisit shop (the "Madelaine" in the Schillingsstraße) sold expensive merchandise to the privileged few (SAPMO-BA, Vorläufige SED 38624/1, "Information über eine Beratung zum Stand der Rekonstruktion und den Sortimentsvorschlag der Exquisit-Verkaufseinrichtung 'Madelaine' am 6.12.85," pp. 2–3).
75 SAPMO-BA, DY30, Vorläufige SED 31970, "Bericht über die Erfüllung des Politbürobeschlusses vom 12.10.1977," 16.10.78, p. 3; BArchB, DE1, 56323, "Dokumente über Beschlüsse zur Zahlungsfähigkeit," 5.5.89, Anlage 1, 26.11.79, pp. 23–4.

these stores also performed the not insignificant function of reducing inflationary pressures by removing "excess" East German marks from circulation.

Using the Delikat and Exquisit stores to offset the Intershops did little to mollify East German consumers, however, who were infuriated by the steep prices. The stores' pricing tactics also fueled fears that cheaper goods might completely disappear from the shelves, not the least because the Delikat and Exquisit stores deepened the chasm between the cheap "basic necessities" and the more expensive "luxuries."[76] By the late 1980s, consumers were so enraged by these discrepancies that they openly questioned the purpose of the upscale East German shops. One person, for example, asked, "Why do the Delikat and Exquisit businesses really exist? To my mind, these goods belong in normal stores at normal or inexpensive prices."[77] Such arguments were by no means misplaced, since the Delikat and Exquisit stores occupied the same space as the Forum checks. On the one hand, they were intended to soak up extra Ostmarks that had found their way into East German pockets as a result of Honecker's inflationary wage policies. On the other hand, the Delikat and Exquisit shops were little more than politically (and monetarily) "correct" versions of the Intershops. The reproach of another consumer demonstrated that the new policy had done little to alleviate the contradictions characterizing the retail sector in the GDR. "We cannot contradict the calculation that capitalist society is a two-thirds society," the author quipped, referring to the SED's argument that West German affluence was based on the immiseration of one-third of its population. "But how do we manage our thirds? One-third Intershop, one-third Delikat and Exquisit, [and] one-third consumer goods that no one will buy."[78] Similarly, a joke that circulated in the 1980s skewered the glaring discrepancy between the regime's rhetorical gestures and its real-existing consumer policies by cleverly spoofing Marxist-Leninist dogma regarding socialism as an intermediate stage on the way to communism: "What is the phase of transition from socialism to communism called? Delikatism!"[79]

In response to these criticisms, the SED leadership sought to gloss over the fact that the Delikat and Exquisit shops could hardly be reconciled with the egalitarian principles of Marxism-Leninism. ZK representatives,

---

76 SAPMO-BA, DY6, Vorläufige 1761, Stadtausschuß Leipzig, "Informationsbericht," 18.11.77, p. 4.
77 BArchB, DL1, 26395, petition from 13.10.89.
78 SAPMO-BA, DY30, 039–324, Bezirkvorstand des VBK-DDR, Bezirk Schwerin, to Hager, no date, p. 20.
79 Reinhard Ulbrich, *Kleines Lexikon großer Ostprodukte* (Köthen/Anhalt, 1996), p. 20. Along the same lines, people poked fun at the party's penchant for acronyms: "What are the most important letters in the GDR? SED: S is for Shop, E is for Exquisit, and D is for Delikat" (Wagner, *DDR-Witze*, p. 101).

for example, flatly denied that the luxury stores "stand in contradiction to the policy of the Principal Task." To lend credence to their claims, they conjured up a variety of tangential, misleading, and specious points to distract from the social tensions exacerbated by the stores. The Delikat and Exquisit shops "help us better to meet real-existing needs," they alleged, adding that "quality has its price, after all." In a particularly audacious moment, party leaders contended that the SED's retail policy was the envy of the world. Pointing to "international standards," they boasted that "even foreign critics must admit" that the 8,000 Exquisit shops "do not have a bad assortment of goods." Policy makers also sought to dispel widespread concern over the high prices charged in the stores, only to drown in a tangle of contradictions. First they offered rather unconvincing denials that prices were too high, then backtracked to argue that charging higher prices for "luxury" goods was socially progressive and benefited the country as a whole. As if aware how untenable their position was, they concluded petulantly that "no one is obliged to shop in the Exquisit stores."[80]

In the mid-1980s, party leaders strove to assure themselves that the Delikat stores "further solidify the relationship of trust between the party, state, and people" – at best an implausible assertion.[81] But they could no longer overlook the social strife created by the luxury shops. Worried that the Delikat stores were becoming a source of tension between high and low wage earners, state and party representatives met in 1985 to discuss the future of retailing in the GDR. Their solution consisted of admonishing the retail chain "not only to see the constraints of fulfilling the plan, but also the political effects."[82] Mere exhortation, however, could hardly counteract a retail policy that contradicted the party's own principles.

Although the Intershops were the most visible sign of the SED's attempt to harness the political division of Germany for financial gain, they were not the only East German retail institution that hitched capitalist means to socialist ends. Parallel to the expansion of the Intershops after 1970, the party leadership widened the scope of the other hard-currency store: Genex. Although it too originally targeted a purely West German clientele, Genex was, in contrast to the Intershops, a mail-order retailer.[83] Through Genex, West

---

80 SAPMO-BA, Vorläufige SED 31970, "Zur Versorgung mit Exquisit- und Delikaterzeugnissen," no date, pp. 1–3.
81 SAPMO-BA, DY30, Vorläufige SED 31781, Abteilung Handel, Versorgung und Außenhandel, "Vermerk über die Beratung mit Genossen Dr. Jarowinsky, Genossen Dr. Weiß und Genossen Briksa am 1.7.1985," 2.7.85, p. 2.
82 Ibid.
83 Aside from Genex and the Intershops, the party authorized one other hard-currency retail organization, *Versina*, which sold alcohol and cigarettes to diplomats and journalists (SAPMO-BA, DY30, Vorläufige SED 42023, "Standpunkt zur ADN-Information," p. 8; BArchB, DL2, 999, letter from 1.1.72, p. 296, cited in Schneider, "Jedem nach dem Wohnsitz," p. 231).

Germans could provide their East German friends and relatives with some of the consumer products they enjoyed but were often obliged to do without, from good-quality coffee to washing machines. To West Germans concerned about their poorer cousins, Genex offered a palliative for consciences made uneasy by increasing affluence.

Like the Intershops, Genex had been created in the 1950s in response to the division of Germany. Officially, Genex's mission was to combat "the introduction of commodities for the purposes of speculation into the GDR through gift packages."[84] Its actual purpose, however, was to profit from the political divisions separating German families and friends. Once those divisions were rigidified by construction of the Berlin Wall, Genex's stranglehold over "speculation" began to pay off.

In contrast to the Intershops, Genex was slow to exploit its geographical advantage. Before 1961, the main advantage for West Germans of sending care packages through Genex was that it cost less. Because it operated from third countries such as Denmark and Switzerland, Genex circumvented the currency regulations governing commerce between the two Germanys. Genex also sidestepped the customs duties levied on packages shipped between the two countries and passed on a portion of the savings to its West German customers. Equally important, Genex promised a more reliable delivery than the alternative – private shipments sent via the post.[85]

Despite these advantages, Genex was unable to exploit much of its potential market during the 1950s. Like the rest of the GDR's economy, Genex's shipments suffered from the poor quality of East German production facilities, shoddy packaging, and an unreliable transport system. As a result, Genex customers often opened their packages only to find a mess. Coffee, sugar, and hot chocolate, for example, were often boxed up so carelessly that they leaked out of their poor-quality containers and mixed together inside the parcel. More often, however, Genex's irrational organization occasioned serious shipping delays that kept customers waiting for their packages. By the time that perishable goods such as butter, which remained a scarce good throughout the GDR's history, reached customers, they were frequently rancid. Despite several attempts to restructure responsibilities and jurisdictions, Genex was constantly behind in its contractual

---

84 "Verordnung über den Geschenkpaket- und päckchenverkehr auf dem Postwege mit Westdeutschland, Westberlin und dem Ausland," 5.8.54, cited in Schneider, "Jedem nach dem Wohnsitz," pp. 223–4.

85 Genex used two intermediaries in third countries. Jauerfood, which operated out of Copenhagen, specialized in food products. Customers could select from a variety of baskets, which by the 1980s mostly contained West German products popular with East Germans. In contrast, Palatinus, which operated out of Switzerland, sold consumer durable goods such as cars.

obligations. In 1960, for example, the mail-order retailer had a backlog of orders for $80,000 worth of consumer products that it was unable to deliver. These kinds of difficulties scared off West German customers, and sales suffered.[86]

Only after the construction of the Berlin Wall did Genex prosper. The success of the SED's attempt to control congress between the two Germanys extended to the postal service, making Genex the only method of sending care packages to loved ones. Consequently, the value of trade in gifts from the West to the East increased during the 1960s, rising to 1.5 million packages sent annually from West Germany to the GDR, including 300,000 delivered during the Christmas season alone. Genex soon began proving itself a highly lucrative endeavor. Not only could the party sell goods produced in the East German economy for West German marks, it obtained an exchange rate that by the 1970s ran to 4 East German marks to 1 West German mark. While this ratio was still a far cry from the GDR's official insistence on a rate of 1:1, Genex more nearly approximated parity than did most East German manufacturing industries exporting their goods to the West. Working out of Denmark and Switzerland, moreover, lowered the GDR's transaction costs because it cut West German financial institutions out of the transactions and permitted direct payment in D-Marks rather than in the "clearing units" used to navigate ideological and financial conflicts between the FRG and GDR. Finally, the mail-order business allowed the GDR to profit from the time lag between payment and delivery, since West German customers paid in the present for goods to be delivered to East Germans in the future.[87]

What spelled an end to Genex's good fortunes was Honecker's decision to partially dismantle the Wall in return for the West German state's largesse. Once the SED agreed to relax the proscription of mail delivery between the two Germanys and permit direct transfers of West German money to East German citizens in 1983, Genex's sales appear to have faltered. According to Western sources, Genex was earning DM 200 million annually by the mid-1980s, down from around DM 500–600 million after the construction of the Wall.[88] Political liberalization had cut deeply into Genex's source of

86 Schneider, "Jedem nach dem Wohnsitz," pp. 225–6.
87 Ibid., p. 223. The exchange rate, which was for consumer durable goods, was calculated on the basis of the Trabant comparison above and BArchB, DL2, 995, *Sender Freies Berlin* (SFB), broadcast at 7.05 p.m., 26.3.79. See also Chapter 3.
88 BArchB, DL2, 995, *Berliner Morgenpost*, 28.12.86; BStU, MfS BKK [KoKo] 819, Andrea Schmeltzer, *RIAS-TV* broadcast at 5:50 p.m., 1.9.88, p. 6, and *Zitty* 10 (1988), p. 8; Schneider, "Jedem nach dem Wohnsitz," p. 223.

income by making it possible for West Germans to bestow Western cash and commodities directly on their friends and relatives.

But it was not simply the lifting of restrictions on commerce between the two Germanys that threatened Genex's sales. Genex also suffered from the fact that East German consumers preferred capitalist to socialist products. Had they favored merchandise manufactured in their own economy over West German commodities, Genex would have received more business than it did, since West Germans would have been forced to go through Genex to purchase East German items. With its monopoly over German–German retail trade, Genex would have profited handsomely. A consumer culture attractive to broad sections of the East and even West German populace, moreover, would have also rendered socialism more appealing. A clearly stated preference for East over West German consumer goods would have bestowed credibility on the economic system that manufactured these commodities, and by extension the ideology behind it.

The fact was, however, that consumer goods produced in the GDR did not enjoy a positive image. Among other things, they suffered from a reputation for shoddy production, poor design, gross inattention to consumer preferences, and chronic scarcity. Nor could the planned economy transform its production failures into distributional successes without forfeiting a good measure of its political legitimacy; using scarcity as a selling point worked only if scarcity was an exceptional condition, with positive connotations. Marxism-Leninism, however, did not recognize the creation of any value that was not generated by labor and consumed as a use value. Thus, political and ideological concerns prevented East German manufacturers from using capitalist marketing techniques, such as branding or eye-catching advertisements, to stimulate demand for their products.[89] Even Genex, with its promise of shortening the often interminable wait for certain goods, could not compensate for the basic fact of consumer life in the GDR: the clear preference of East German consumers for capitalist socialist wares.

The development of car sales provides an excellent illustration of this dilemma. During the 1980s, Genex experienced difficulties selling its allotment of Eastern European and Soviet automobiles.[90] To some extent,

89 In one instance, the Department of Trade, Supply, and Foreign Trade reprimanded the Delikat management for transforming the firm's designation into a brand name and using it to move merchandise and increase sales. "Turning the term 'Delikat,' which is not only printed on the products, but also put on the stores, into a company designation was not foreseen," the Department complained (SAPMO-BA, DY30 Vorläufige SED 31781, Abteilung Handel, Versorgung und Außenhandel, "Delikat," no date).

90 BArchB, DE1, 55120, Staatliche Planungskommission to Ministerium für ALF, "Festlegungsprotokoll zur Verwendung von Fondsrückgaben der GENEX-GmbH," 29.1.88, and

socialist cars fared poorly because Genex asked too high a price for East German products. Genex charged DM 4,900 for the Trabant in 1977, for example, yet the regime was unable to sell the car to West Germans for the substantially lower price of DM 3,500.[91] A more compelling reason for the poor sales of East German cars, however, lay in their inability to compete with their more popular Western counterparts. Tacitly acknowledging this fact, Genex expanded its automobile line during the 1970s to include Western cars. By 1989, lucky East Germans could drive away in a VW Golf or Passat, a Ford Orion, a Fiat Uno, a Peugeot 309, or even a BMW 318i.[92] Although they were more expensive and difficult to acquire than East German, Czechoslovak, or Soviet cars, capitalist cars were far more desirable because of their superior design, greater power, better quality, enhanced reliability, and exceptional durability – not to mention the social prestige derived from their scarcity and connection to the West.

The partiality of East German consumers for Western wares forced Schalck and his aides to eliminate East German goods from Genex's catalog over time. Naturally, Genex's management tried to portray the popular rejection of East German products as a triumph of the SED's economic policies. Living standards in the GDR had reached such high levels, General Director Charles Dewey opined, that "the present assortment of goods does not satisfy the need of the citizens of the GDR for an elevated genre" of consumer products.[93] Rather than continue to focus on sugar and butter, he felt that Genex should respond to the "need" of East German consumers for "luxury" goods.

Dewey was correct on at least one count: Consumption patterns in the GDR had shifted away from an overwhelming focus on the basic necessities of life. By the mid-1970s, the social structure of East German society had stimulated a growing desire for a variety of consumer durable goods – a desire inflamed by West German television and radio programs that

"Festlegungsprotokoll zur Verwendung von Fondsrückgaben der GENEX-GmbH," 31.5.89, p. 1; SAPMO-BA, Vorläufige SED 41773, Abteilung Maschinenbau und Metallurgie, "Aufkommen und Verteilung von Personenkraftwagen und Nutzkraftwagen B 1000," 6.6.88, pp. 1–2.

91 Herbst et al., *So funktionierte die DDR*, p. 328; Weymar, "Das Auto," pp. 284–5. The prices of socialist cars remained relatively stable during the late 1980s. On the other hand, Genex surrendered its advantage of timely delivery during the late 1980s. According to one Western report from 1989, underproduction and high domestic demand led Genex to declare that it was unable to deliver the new four-stroke Wartburgs (BStU, MfS BKK [KoKo] 819, *HAZ*, 28.1.89, p. 4, and *Der Tagesspiegel*, 20.2.88, p. 14).

92 BStU, MfS BKK (KoKo) 819, *Die Welt am Sonntag*, 14.5.89, *Der Tagesspiegel*, 18.2.89, 21.2.87, and 17.9.88, and *HAZ*, 28.1.89, pp. 1–2, 4, 5, 16.

93 BArchB, DL2, 998, "Gedanken zur Erweiterung und Reorganisation des Valutageschenkdienstes," p. 13, cited in Schneider, "Jedem nach dem Wohnsitz," p. 227.

showcased seemingly endless permutations of sleek convenience and alluring designs. The point that Dewey concealed behind the word "elevated," however, was the word "Western," since most of these "elevated genres" consisted of durable goods manufactured in the West. To assuage concerns that an influx of capitalist commodities might exacerbate social frictions in the GDR, Dewey sought to portray Genex as politically more responsible than the Intershops. In contrast to the Intershops, Dewey observed that Genex constituted a more discreet point of sale "since sales do not take place in an open store, but are executed in principle in the form of mail-order transactions." In addition, Genex could provide the Stasi with valuable information about the clientele it served because "the legal possession of foreign currency can be traced through the reporting offices of these GDR citizens or through their bank of deposit."[94] Dewey's argument, as well as the GDR's insatiable need for Western cash, carried the day. By 1989, Genex's catalog came to 240 pages advertising 3,000 products. Only twenty-two pages were devoted to perishable goods such as food, detergents, and cosmetics. The rest was given over to toys, such as Barbie dolls; home electronics, including computers and musical instruments; kitchen appliances, including microwave ovens; and furniture, clothing, and jewelry.[95]

Despite Dewey's clever conflation of financial expedience with ideological consistency, however, Genex's decision to sell Western products constituted a politically embarrassing admission that the GDR could not manufacture consumer goods that East Germans needed, to say nothing of what they desired. In addition to this de facto repudiation of the planned economy, selling luxury goods contradicted the communist party's aim of eradicating commodity fetishism and the inequitable distribution of income and goods. If nothing else, Genex's strategy of replacing the Eastern wares in its catalog with more profitable high-end Western items meant that it had begun serving a highly privileged and very tiny group of East Germans. Predictably, the result was social envy. And whereas the public profile of Genex during the Ulbricht period was marginal, Genex's promotion of Western luxury goods under Honecker made it as notorious as the Intershops.[96] Perhaps most

---

94 BArchB, DL2, 999, "Begründung zum Beschluß," 10.8.66, p. 385, cited in Schneider, "Jedem nach dem Wohnsitz," p. 231.
95 BStU, MfS BKK (KoKo) 819, *Die Welt am Sonntag*, 14.5.89, and *HAZ*, 28.1.89, pp. 1, 3. Genex was the easiest method for East Germans with West German family or friends but without party or factory connections to obtain porcelain from the prestigious Meißen works. According to Schneider, catalogs could be obtained from Genex's offices in Copenhagen, Lucerne, and after 1965 in Zurich. They could also be found in the Intershops until 1977 (Schneider, "Jedem nach dem Wohnsitz," p. 225). The 1988 Genex catalog ran to 228 pages (BStU, MfS BKK [KoKo] 819, *HAZ*, 28.1.89, p. 4).
96 Schneider, "Jedem nach dem Wohnsitz," p. 232.

ironically, catering to East German consumer preferences was simply bad business. No matter how much the move into Western goods boosted the volume of sales, it reduced the net amount of hard currency Genex took in.

To reverse this trend, Schalck had Genex move into a niche market – shortage goods. Sensitive to pent-up demand in the service sector, Genex managers made it possible to obtain vouchers for tailors, carpenters, and building contractors. They also sold vacations, including trips to the "Caucasian Riviera" and "adventure tours" to Mongolia and North Korea. Generous West Germans could even supply their more discriminating relatives with swimming pools, sail- or motorboats, recreational vehicles, or weekend homes, known in the GDR by their Russian name, *dachas*. Apparently Genex even considered selling gravestones.[97]

The profit motive encouraged Genex's managers to exhibit an unusual degree of creativity – and to commodify as many of the GDR's assets as they could. Using capitalist marketing techniques, for example, Genex bundled car insurance with the cars it sold, offering the insurance on the principle that Westerners making the purchase for their loved ones might toss in a comparatively cheap related item. For a mere DM 750 extra, Genex also offered driver's education courses, for which East Germans normally waited as long as four years.[98] Not only did Genex help West Germans help their East German family and friends, but it helped East Germans do an end run around the system of rationing created by the planned economy, bringing consumer goods and services that were in short supply within their reach.

By the 1980s, the ingenuity of the Genex management, as well as its willingness to commodify any East German goods that might attract West German currency, had become the butt of many jokes. In one example, a man greets his friend and is astonished to hear about the latter's new career move: "What, you're getting your doctorate? Without a high-school diploma and at this age?" "No problem," comes the swift reply. "With Genex anything is possible."[99]

97 BArchB, DL2, 995, *Berliner Morgenpost*, 28.12.86, *HAZ*, 28.1.89, and *Die Welt am Sonntag*, 14.5.89, pp. 1, 4.
98 BArchB, DL2, 995, *Sender Freies Berlin* (SFB), broadcast at 7:05 p.m., 26.3.79; BStU, MfS BKK (KoKo) 819, *HAZ*, 28.1.89, and unidentifiable Western newspaper, 15.3.86, pp. 3, 10. According to Bernd Ohliger and Ulrich Wittek of the Mila Fahrschule in East Berlin, the wait for driver's ed courses was about four years in 1976 in the East German capital, but had fallen to two years by the late 1980s. In Cottbus, however, one had to wait six years, in Dresden five years (interview, Bernd Ohliger and Ulrich Wittek, Mila Fahrschule, Berlin, 26.1.96). There was only one car insurer (Kasko), and insurance was mandatory.
99 BArchB, DL2, 995, *Stuttgarter Zeitung*, no date; BStU, MfS BKK (KoKo) 819, *Frankfurter Rundschau*, 23.12.86, p. 11. Another joke employs the same premise for the Intershops: "Question to the Radio Yerevan: Can men bear children? Answer: In principle, no. But you should ask in an Intershop store first, since they can make anything possible for Western money" (Wagner, *DDR-Witze*, p. 64).

In addition to exploiting the demand created by shortages, Schalck tried to raise Genex's revenue by reducing costs. As with the Intershops, he transformed financial necessity into political advantage, saving valuable Western cash by skimping on advertising. Not incidentally, less advertising possessed the political advantage of reducing the mail-order retailer's public presence at home. Even Genex's headquarters, on the aptly named Wall Street (Mauerstraße) near Checkpoint Charlie, was a rather modest affair.[100] In addition, Schalck compressed the variety and quantity of Genex's catalog from five to one single but expansive brochure.[101] Of course, had Genex been confronted with competition, it might have been forced to increase the availability of its catalog. As it was, however, the socialist enterprise could rely on West German newspapers and word of mouth to disseminate information about its operations free of cost. Nor did the retailer make any attempt to convey important information regarding changes in hard–currency regulations. When Forum checks were introduced in 1979, for example, Genex and the Intershops simply relied on word of mouth to spread the news.[102]

Paradoxically, proximity to the West was bad for Schalck's business. The gradual relaxation of restrictions on commerce between the two Germanys undermined the monopoly enjoyed by the Intershops and Genex over the sale of capitalist commodities. As East Germans availed themselves of new ways of obtaining Western products, Intershop and Genex revenues stagnated.[103] In particular, the socialist state's participation in the hard–currency economy, together with its decision to facilitate intra-German commerce, provided the black market with lasting advantages over the official distribution system. Removing the constraints on German–German trade, for example, reduced the risks of being caught trading on secondary markets, dramatically lowering transaction costs on the black market. Thus, the continued growth of the Intershops and Genex did not founder on the Wall, but rather on its gradual disassembly. Similarly, it was neither the Stasi nor East German politics that ultimately constrained Schalck's power, but rather the very market forces that he had so ably harnessed.

100 BStU, MfS BKK (KoKo) 819, *Zitty* 10 (1988), p. 8. There were three other Genex information offices in the GDR, in Leipzig, Rostock, and Karl-Marx-Stadt.
101 BArchB, DL2, 995, *Deutschlandfunk*, broadcast at 6:05 a.m., 25.3.79. The 1979 catalog came to 180 pages, or three-fourths its 1989 size.
102 See BStU, MfS HA XVIII 8804, "Information zur Situation in den Intershopläden," 18.8.78, pp. 1–2.
103 Sales increased marginally in 1988, the last full year of division between the GDR and the FRG. Schalck attributed the rise to West German tourism in the wake of political liberalization, noting that it concealed a fall in the number of East German purchases. In fact, transactions conducted using Forum checks showed a decline in real terms (SAPMO-BA, DY30, Vorläufige SED 42023, "Information zu den Ergebnissen des Intershophandels im Jahre 1988," 16.12.88, p. 6).

Table 7. *Political Map of Intershop Trade: Sales and Revenue Growth Rates Correlated with Policy Events, 1971–1989*[a]

Year	Sales Growth in %	Revenue Growth in %	Event
1971	70	No data	Honecker assumes power
1972	42.97	No data	Transportation Treaty reducing travel restrictions
1973	13.99	No data	First oil crisis; minimum exchange amount for Westerners visiting the GDR raised; Mittag ousted as Economic Secretary
1974	3.25	No data	First extension of Swing Agreement, ceiling raised to DM 850 million; East Germans permitted to own Western currency
1975	62.24	No data	Minimum exchange amount lowered
1976	19.83	No data	Foreign debt increases dramatically; Mittag restored as Economic Secretary
1977	26.80	No data	Mittag and Schürer protest Honecker's economic policy; rumors circulate that the SED will abolish Intershops; expansion of Exquisit stores, creation of Delikat chain
1978	27.09	No data	
1979	−13.62	No data	Second oil crisis; Forum checks introduced
1980	5.94	3	Increase of minimum exchange amount
1981	−1.71	1.8	Martial law declared in Poland; Poland and Romania default on Western debt; Soviets cut oil shipments to GDR, raise price
1982	11.17	11.45	Second extension of Swing Agreement, ceiling lowered to DM 600 million; GDR nearly defaults on its debts; meat and dairy shortages; Helmut Kohl becomes Chancellor of FRG in October
1983	2.68	6.42	First Strauß credit, transit lump sum in return for dismantling of lethal traps along border, minor relaxation of travel restrictions and barriers to sending gift packages (enshrined in Postal Agreement); second wave of Intershop expansion
1984	7.50	8.25	Second Strauß credit; regulations for visits to West by pensioners relaxed
1985	5.56	4.80	Third extension of Swing Agreement, ceiling increased to DM 800 million
1986	3.07	4.14	Oil prices fall; GDR's balance of payments takes turn for worse
1987	2.70	1.70	
1988	1.63	−4.46	Capital mobility between two Germanys increased; Schürer's failed reform proposal; meat shortage
1989	3.47	−14.60	Travel restrictions eased in April; Honecker ousted on 18 October; Berlin Wall breached 9 November

[a] *Sources:* SAPMO-BA, DY30, Vorläufige SED 42023, various reports; BArchB, DL2, 992, Panse, "Geschäftsbericht 1989," 2.2.90, p. 14; BArchB, DL2, 1005, "Analyse der Entwicklung," p. 4, and Panse, "Analyse zu ausgewählten Problemen des Intershophandels," 22.1.87, p. 2; Böske, "Abwesend anwesend," p. 218; Herbst et al., *So funktionierte die DDR*, p. 434; Volze, "Die Devisengeschäfte," pp. 1150, 1155. These figures include the Interhotels and Intertank gas stations, but not Genex or other convertible-currency businesses.

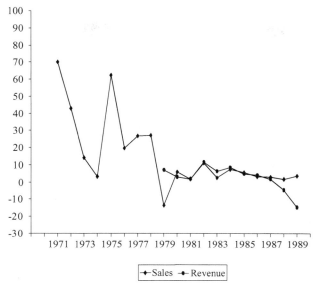

Figure 22. Intershop sales and revenue growth rates, 1971–1989. *Sources*: See Figure 21, p. 254.

In response, Schalck introduced a variety of new sales gimmicks, such as authorizing the Intershops to institute a delivery service. He also made use of the newest Western marketing techniques, such as adding special Intershop cars to trains traveling on East German territory, analogous to the duty-free carts found today on international flights. Once again, the retailers expanded their product line upwards, selling more and more products that could hardly be described as politically appropriate, such as Japanese motorcycles for DM 9,990 or chic blue toilet seats for DM 170. They even began to ignore the strictures of political alliances and add goods manufactured by capitalist countries that were otherwise anathema to the Soviet bloc, such as South Africa.[104]

But Schalck was well aware that quick financial fixes could not overcome long-term shifts in the political landscape. Rather than place all of his hopes of increasing the retailers' hard-currency revenue on cost reduction, distribution channels, or new product lines, Schalck embraced the GDR's growing ties to the Kohl government and tried to leverage them to improve the SED's access to West German cash. In particular, he sought to remove the remaining obstacles to capital mobility between the two Germanys in the

---

104 BArchB, DL2, 995, *Berliner Morgenpost*, 28.12.86; BArchB, DL2, 930, petition from Magdeburg, no date.

hopes of tapping the large reserves of East German assets in West Germany, which the Bundesbank estimated at between DM 2 and 3 billion.[105] In 1988, Schalck successfully concluded an agreement with the Kohl government that further reduced impediments to capital mobility.[106] Once again, obstacles to trade were removed by a curious convergence of East German avarice and West German anticommunism.

Despite the Kohl government's sometimes harsh expressions of anticommunism, the financial concessions it made were consistent with the SPD's *Ostpolitik*.[107] Like the Social Democratic chancellors Brandt and Schmidt, Kohl and his Free Democratic Foreign Minister Genscher were prepared to grant such large financial benefits to the GDR because they believed that the greater supply of Western consumer goods would alleviate the personal plight of many East Germans. The coalition government also supported these agreements because it perceived the circulation of West German products and money as a convenient advertisement for the material superiority of the social market economy. As the conservative *Bild Zeitung* proclaimed in 1986 – presciently, if prematurely – "the German Mark (West) has unified the nation."[108] Arguably, the residual attraction of the magnet theory, or the idea that West German economic success would ultimately pull the GDR into the FRG's orbit, led the Kohl government to exceed what even Social Democratic governments had been willing to offer the SED. In 1988, the Kohl government reversed longtime West German policy: Overcoming its concern that East German citizens might be coerced into delivering up their assets unto the SED, it agreed to ease the movement of capital between the two countries.[109]

In contrast to the 2 billion marks in credit that the Kohl government provided to the GDR in 1983 and 1984, however, increased capital mobility alone could not keep the GDR afloat. From the Stasi's point of view,

---

105 *Der Spiegel* 41 (1985), p. 131.
106 Most significantly, the treaty facilitated the access of East German holders of West German bank accounts to their money (BStU, MfS HA XVIII 10609, Mielke, "Erweiterung der Verfügungsmöglichkeiten über in der BRD bzw. Westberlin vorhandene Guthaben von DDR-Bürgern," 30.9.88, pp. 1–5). Among other concessions, the Kohl government dropped its limitations on West German gift giving to East Germans via the Intershops and Genex and permitted the establishment of Genex subsidiaries in Stuttgart and West Berlin (BStU, MfS BKK [KoKo] 819, *HAZ*, 28.1.89, pp. 3–4; *Der Spiegel* 41 [1985], p. 134). East Germans had about DM 300 million in 1988 on deposit with the Staatsbank (SAPMO-BA, DY30, Vorläufige 41757, Schürer, "Information zur Gesamtheit des Außenhandels," no date, pp. 7, 11).
107 Perhaps the most embarrassing example was Kohl's 1986 comparison of Soviet leader Mikhail Gorbachev to Nazi Propaganda Minister Joseph Goebbels.
108 BArchB, DL2, 995, *Bild Zeitung*, 7.3.86; interview, von Würzen, Bonn, 23.6.96.
109 BStU, MfS HA XVIII 10609, Mielke, "Erweiterung der Verfügungsmöglichkeiten," 30.9.88, p. 3; Volze and Kuppe, "Doktor Schalck," p. 650.

lowering barriers between the two Germanys actually imperiled the GDR's sovereignty. Mielke, for example, feared that the new regulations would permit the increased importation of electronic goods, from video recorders to computers, which might be used for "hostile-negative or speculative purposes." Improved ties to West Germany would result in the politically destabilizing proliferation of electronic media, whose ability to make information readily available at short notice was already proving increasingly difficult to control. For this reason, the use of photocopying machines in the GDR was carefully restricted. Nevertheless, Genex began selling them in 1988. The need for hard currency continued to take precedence over security concerns.[110]

Mielke also concluded that the new regulations would encourage economic chaos. The circle of people using the Forum checks, he feared, would expand and lead East Germans to use them as an alternative currency. During the previous year, the secret police had reported that greater numbers of Western consumer durable goods entering the East German market had caused an upsurge in black market activities.[111] Mielke surmised that the increased use and therefore value of the Forum checks would remove them from the Intershops, and thus the state's grasp. It might also pose a new threat to the East German mark, as bad money drove out the good. Previously the economic desk had been the center of resistance to Schalck, and therefore to Mittag and Honecker's economic policies. Now Mielke found himself in the awkward position of objecting to the SED's inversion of its short- and long-term economic aims.

SHARP CONTRADICTIONS

The contradictions between the SED's social and economic policies had long been the target of popular discontent, but by the late 1980s the Intershops were attracting the brunt of popular criticism. Some East Germans still sought to appeal to the regime's egalitarian sensibilities in the hopes that their grievances would be heard. One woman, for example, charged that "the GDR is a socialist state, in which privileges of certain people should be abolished. That is why I am indignant about the Intershops in this country. How can one obtain so-called Forum checks or other methods of payment in the GDR for Intershops, through good work in the factory or through

---

110 BStU, MfS HA XVIII 10609, Mielke, "Erweiterung der Verfügungsmöglichkeiten," 30.9.88, p. 4; BStU, MfS BKK (KoKo) 819, *Zitty* 10 (1988), p. 8.
111 BStU, MfS HA XVIII 10609, Mielke to duty officers, "Erweiterung der Verfügungsmöglichkeiten," 30.9.88, p. 4; BStU, MfS HA XVIII 6166, "Hinweise," 1987.

other means? . . . Is that not a sharp contradiction in this socialist society?"[112] Other writers directly questioned the contradictions created by the use of two currencies in one economy. Writing to the newspaper *Junge Welt*, for example, one man assailed the GDR's monetary regime, accusing it of being irrational. Why, he asked, do consumer goods produced by "the food and entertainment industry in the Federal Republic cost several times as much in the Delikat stores as the same products do in the Intershops when the exchange rate between the GDR mark and the DM of the Federal Republic is 1:1 according to the Staatsbank?"[113]

Other petitioners journeyed on to the next logical step. They inverted the relation between egalitarian ideology and divisive practice and demanded uniform access to West German money, and the Intershops along with it, as a right that should be accorded everyone in keeping with the regime's advocacy of social equality. Thus, one woman wrote Honecker to demand that "in the future, DM are to be part of monthly salaries" so that she might also have the opportunity to shop in the hard-currency stores.[114]

Similarly, jokes began circulating in the 1980s that poked fun at the SED's official explanations of the differences between capitalism and socialism. According to one joke, an East German pensioner is permitted to travel to West Germany, and when he returns, everyone wants to know what it was like. "Well," he says, "it's basically the same as here – you can get anything for West German marks." The joke derives its humor from its insinuation that ideological and social differences between East and West Germany have a common denominator – West German money. Another joke highlights the extent to which Western consumer ideals had become familiar because of the party's own practices. Have you heard the news, it begins. A People's Policeman ran into an Intershop the other day, jumped over the counter, and asked for political asylum.[115] Clearly, the distance between the Intershops and monetary union was narrowing.

What began as an attempt to modernize the retail sector in order to consolidate the rule of a new political leadership ended up intensifying the contradictions inherent in the GDR's approach to consumer sovereignty. The decision to expand the Intershop retail chain did help ease the financial crisis brought about by Honecker's policies. Where Ulbricht referred to the

---

112 BArchB, DL2, 930, petition from 4.2.88.   113 BArchB, DL2, 930, petition from 26.4.89.
114 BArchB, DN10, 931, Wünsch, Bezirksdirektion Erfurt, "Analyse über die Entwicklung der Eingaben," 23.12.88.
115 Reinhard Wagner, *DDR Witze Teil 2. Lieber von Sitte gemalt, als vom Sozialismus gezeichnet* (Berlin, 1997), pp. 93, 107.

Intershops in 1965 as "stopgaps" and a "necessary evil," Schalck argued in 1988 that "the revenues from the Intershops have reached such dimensions that we cannot do without this income in the interest of securing the balance of payments."[116] Genex's and the Intershops' greater role in the retail sector, however, also unleashed the demons of Western consumerism and national unity, creating social stratifications that could not be explained away by Marxist-Leninist ideology and further weakening traditional class-based identities. East Germans were tantalized by the glimpse of Western consumerism provided by Genex and the Intershops, which functioned as enclaves of capitalism on socialist soil yet were frustrated by the unequal access to it. Most importantly, both retail chains contributed to the gradual conflation in the public imagination of the egalitarian elements that characterized socialist consumerism with the panoply of abundance that distinguished its Western counterpart. By 1989, the party's preference for political expediency over ideological consistency had consumed both the GDR's financial strength and its political legitimacy, as some East Germans were permitted to consume what they could of the West, while the others were left with nothing to consume but the ideology itself.

But if Honecker's leadership encouraged the formation of ideological allegiances through economic practice, it was the SED's attempt to govern an industrial – and divided – nation by force that fostered the creation of political identities through money. The party claimed it had organized economic relations on the principle of egalitarianism. In the transition from capitalism to communism, the currency of socialism was supposed to function as a medium and symbol of these relations. The Ostmark, the SED hoped, would displace capitalist money and mores and distribute social equity in the place of social alienation. The intellectual debt of Marxism-Leninism to liberal economic theory, however, ensured the planned economy's inability to function without recourse to capitalist media of exchange. As we have seen in previous chapters, the SED failed to develop viable alternatives to the capitalist organization of industrial production, distribution, and consumption. Instead, the regime supplemented its coercive and inefficient variant of the market economy through market institutions, from importing fixed capital to establishing the Intershops and Genex. Thus, the party's response to the consumer desire manufactured by the GDR's industrial base consisted of abjuring the West German model while simultaneously promoting the circulation of West German money and merchandise.

---

116 Ulbricht at the Eighth Party Congress, cited in Haendcke-Hoppe-Arndt, *Die Hauptabteilung XVIII*, p. 43; SAPMO-BA, DY30, Vorläufige SED 42023, "Standpunkt zur ADN-Information," p. 8.

The consequences of such a contradictory approach were twofold. First, the proliferation of black markets, made necessary by the planned economy's shortcomings, actually limited the SED's ability to determine economic behavior. The party's instrumentalization of trade denominated in Western currency through the Intershops and Genex, as well as its attempt to restore its control over the medium of valuation through the use of Forum checks, created an economic zone that openly repudiated socialist ideals. The influx of Western currency and commodities weakened the SED's power over the contours of daily life in the GDR by expanding illegal trade denominated in convertible currencies. Rather than disseminating socialist economic practices, the black markets promoted trade practices whose contractual parameters eliminated the SED as a partner in the transactions while emphasizing the profit motive and commodity fetishism. Despite official pronouncements to the contrary, the party exercised only incomplete control over the economy – the very sphere of social life on which it based its claim to power.

By the 1980s, moreover, the official and unofficial hard-currency sectors had begun to encroach on the planned economy, arousing the opposition of the Stasi and the party and state officials in charge of supplying the public with consumer goods. The Stasi's belated attempts to restrain Schalck – a man who ironically began his career as their creature – were not mere expressions of the institutional rivalries or bureaucratic irrationalities characteristic of Soviet-style regimes. The vain efforts of Roigk and Kleine, but also Briksa and Weiß, to dislodge Schalck also illustrate the potency of the hard-currency economy in the GDR and the inexorable incursion of capitalist modes of exchange into the socialist economy.

Second, the rise of Schalck's economy within the economy heralded the demise of "real-existing" socialism in East Germany. Even had the hard-currency receipts obtained from KoKo's activities solved the GDR's balance-of-payments problems, which they could not, such a solution came at the expense of the socialist method of organizing economic affairs. Not only was the SED's macroeconomic response to systemic competition with the West bankrupting the GDR, but it threatened to ruin the monetary underpinnings of the planned economy. The SED's attempt to produce a coherent set of economic propositions whose interlocking premises would confer political authority on its authors was contradicted by the irrationality of the party's own policies. Similarly, the unity of the GDR's monetary regime was fragmented by the party's necessary toleration of, but also its active participation in, the hard-currency economy. This monetary division both refracted and reified the contradictions extant in the GDR. In fact, the great appeal of the West German mark, achieved at the expense of its East

German competitor, served as a metaphoric reminder of the central paradox of the planned economy: the SED's inability to introduce an economically coherent and socially attractive alternative to the social market economy. As a metonymy – the monetary part standing in for the capitalist whole – the West German mark and the East German demand for it were transfigured into a sign of things to come. The very reversal of cause and effect decried by Marx yet promoted by the SED had become the object of East German desire. Soon the Deutsche Mark itself would become the instrument of the material and moral reversal of the SED's fortunes.

7

Appealing to Authority

The Citizens' Petitions and the Rhetoric of Decline

To the Chairman of the Council of State, Comrade Erich Honecker, ... I hope very much that these lines reach you and are not processed by one of the numerous secretaries.[1]

The SED's economic policies, from its emphasis on heavy industry to its use of the Intershops to earn hard currency, generated social conflict, with the result that the party had to contend with intense resistance to its management of the economy.[2] Much of this resistance took the form of rejecting what the planned economy produced, although the Intershops did provoke sporadic demonstrations of popular anger. Many East Germans responded to the shortage of consumer goods by participating in the black market, where economic exchange was mediated by capitalist currency and shaped by the profit motive. When they could, they shopped in the hard-currency stores, where the socialist state promoted Western products. In both cases, East Germans went to great lengths to consume Western money and merchandise. By spurning the currency and commodities of socialism, however, East Germans were also rejecting the political value of socialism. Their preference for the economic products of the West also implied a preference for capitalist economic and political institutions. For reasons of economic expediency, the SED was no longer able or willing to disrupt the circulation of capitalist consumer goods and currency. Yet the party leadership

---

1 BArchB, DL1, 26252, petition from 2.8.89, p. 3.
2 By "resistance," I mean less the organized or active rejection of established authority on formally articulated grounds, but rather a willingness to contradict authority based on a personal interpretation of political events in the face of official attempts to control or influence that interpretation. For more on this problem, see Alf Lüdtke, *Eigen-Sinn: Fabrikalltag, Arbeitserfahrungen und Politik vom Kaiserreich bis in den Faschismus* (Hamburg, 1993); Ina Merkel, "Konsumkultur in der DDR: Über das Scheitern der Gegenmoderne auf dem Schlachtfeld des Konsums," *Mitteilungen aus der kulturwissenschaftlichen Forschung* 19 (1996), pp. 314–30.

was entirely unwilling to relinquish control over the circulation of ideas in the GDR.

Like other Marxist-Leninist parties, the SED could always rely on the threat of political violence to suppress open articulation of resistance to their policies. Ruling an industrial society by force, however, necessitated the use of a variety of mechanisms aimed at gathering information on potential opposition and preempting the expression of dissent. To this end, Soviet-style regimes established terror apparatuses to intimidate people as well as a simulacrum of civil society to co-opt them. This chapter examines the petition system in the GDR, which afforded individual citizens contact with the impersonal institutions of modern government in a manner designed to prevent the emergence of an autonomous public sphere that might challenge communist power.[3] East Germans made active use of the GDR's petition system to air their grievances. Their complaints provide a glimpse into the burdens of everyday life under Honecker's rule; their circulation renders legible types of economic activity otherwise ignored by official sources. In their uniquely obstreperous way, moreover, the petitions disclose the increasing link in popular imagination between economic prosperity and Western money. Likewise, the almost inflationary increase in the volume of letters during the 1980s mirrored the Ostmark's declining ability to command real resources.

In contrast to actively coercive institutions such as the secret police, the petition system in the GDR was designed to reconcile critics with the regime through a combination of authoritarian practice and the rhetoric of participatory democracy. During the 1980s, however, the ability of the petition system to control dissent seriously deteriorated. Party and state institutions registered a dramatic increase in the number of petitions as worsening shortages of consumer goods prompted more and more people to seek material improvement of their situation by appealing to authority. According to the SED, this growth in the volume of petitions was accompanied by increasingly direct indictments of the planned economy and of real-existing socialism. More and more people began appealing over the head of the SED to the

---

3 For more on petition systems in Soviet-style regimes, see Merle Fainsod, *Smolensk under Soviet Rule* (Cambridge, Mass., 1958); Sheila Fitzpatrick, "Supplicants and Citizens: Public Letter Writing in Soviet Russia in the 1930s," *Slavic Review* 55:1 (Spring 1996), pp. 78–105; Sheila Fitzpatrick and Robert Gellately (eds.), *Accusatory Practices* (Chicago and London, 1997); Nicholas Lampert, *Whistleblowing in the Soviet Union: Complaints and Abuses under State Socialism* (London, 1985); Oliver Werner, "'Politisch überzeugend, feinfühlig und vertrauensvoll'? Eingabenbearbeitung in der SED," in Heiner Timmermann (ed.), *Diktaturen in Europa im 20. Jahrhundert – der Fall DDR* (Berlin, 1996), pp. 461–79. For an apologetic account, see Felix Mühlberg, *Bürger, Bitten und Behörden: Geschichte der Eingabe in der DDR* (Berlin, 2004).

egalitarian values used by the party to legitimate its power. By arguing that the party's policies were leading to greater social differentiation rather than equality, petitioners sought to impeach the party's authority over the economy and induce it to bestow the commodity they desired. For its part, the SED understood the rhetorical reversal of the hierarchy it sought to formalize in the petition system as a sign of the declining legitimacy of its authority. The party leadership, however, was unable to act upon this understanding to shore up the regime. The collapse of the Berlin Wall, moreover, thoroughly undermined the SED's power to prevent the intrusion of the West German media into the East German revolution. As a result, West German organizations displaced and marginalized an emerging East German civil society, capping the revolution and securing the dependence of the East German population on the West German public sphere.

THE PETITIONS AND FORMAL LEGALITY

As in other communist countries, the petition system in the GDR was derived from predemocratic legal traditions guaranteeing subjects the right to appeal to the monarch in person for adjudication of a perceived injustice.[4] Drawing on absolutist practice, the SED presented the petitions as a private dialogue between individuals and the ruling elite. By insisting on the confidential character of the political opinions contained in the petitions, the SED could justify banning their publication to prevent people with similar grievances from organizing themselves. Similarly, the SED used direct-democratic arguments to assert a unity between citizen and state, much as enlightened despots had claimed to rule in the interest of all of their subjects.[5] Because the aims of the Workers' and Peasants' State and the interests of its citizens were supposedly identical, legal guarantees aimed at protecting individuals from violations of their rights by the state were unnecessary. Thus, the constitutionally guaranteed right to petition in the GDR was not a form of legal redress. Rather, it was an expression of "codetermination and participation" (*Mitbestimmung und Mitgestaltung*) in the affairs of government, a right guaranteed by the East German

---

4 On the other hand, the GDR was the only communist state to argue that unity of state and individual interests rendered the protection of civil liberties unnecessary. See Klaus-Jürgen Kuss. "Das Beschwerde- und Antragsrecht in der sowjetischen Verwaltungspraxis," *Recht in Ost und West* 28:3 (1984), p. 132.

5 Nazi Germany employed a similar discursive structure to encourage the ventilation of grievances, but it is unclear whether the Nazis created legal categories along similar lines. See John Connelly. "The Uses of Volksgemeinschaft: Letters to the NSDAP Kreisleitung Eisenach, 1939–1940," in Fitzpatrick and Gellately, *Accusatory Practices*.

constitution.[6] But the petition system in the GDR did not only serve to quell the emergence of a public sphere. It also provided the party leadership with an important instrument of surveillance. Like its absolutist predecessors, the SED employed the information contained in the petitions to observe popular discontent and monitor bureaucratic behavior.

Only in one key area did the SED break with absolutist practice. In addition to channeling discontent and stifling opposition to its rule, the East German communist party assigned the petition system a new purpose befitting the industrialized economy it administered: increasing economic efficiency by soliciting denunciations from citizens regarding the waste of resources. The structural inefficiencies of the East German economy, coupled with the debt burden of the 1980s, elevated the discovery of untapped resources and the campaign against waste to a source of significant savings. Given the party's reliance on discursive tools to govern the GDR, from its use of voluntarist rhetoric to mobilize workers to its use of planning indicators to structure production, it made sense that the SED would integrate yet another textually oriented method of observational discipline.

Ultimately, the party's attempt to consolidate its power through the use of a medium that it conceptualized as a confidential conversation between the ruler and the ruled failed. Despite the SED's claims about direct democracy, the petition system could not substitute for the rule of law, not the least because legal guarantees regarding the procedures for processing petitions could not be enforced. For the same reason, the petition system failed as an instrument of political control. Absent the threat of punitive action, East German bureaucrats simply ignored procedural regulations for handling the grievances contained in petitions. The SED's ideological justification of its rule, as well as the large number of agencies reporting on public opinion, led the SED under Honecker to underestimate the petition system as a source of information about the effectiveness of its rule.

In contrast to the SED's claims about the democratic value of petitions, the right to petition the sovereign to settle disputes was a relic of predemocratic administrative technique. Although it was a prominent feature of government in classical antiquity,[7] appealing to authority to mediate disagreements

---

6 The right to petition was guaranteed in the constitution of 1949 in Article 3 and in the constitutions of 1968 and 1974 in Article 103. The right to codetermination and participation was guaranteed in Article 3 in the 1949 constitution and Article 21 of the later constitutions. See also Wolfgang Weichelt, "Sozialistische Verfassung – Grundrechte – Rechtsstaatlichkeit," *Neue Justiz. Zeitschrift für sozialistische Recht- und Gesetzlichkeit* 43:11 (1989), pp. 438–41.

7 Johann Heinrich Kumpf, *Petitionsrecht und öffentliche Meinung im Entstehungsprozess der Paulskirchenverfassung 1848/9* (Frankfurt/Main, 1983), p. 35; Klaus Tenfelde and Helmuth Trischler (eds.), *Bis vor die Stufen des Throns: Bittschriften und Beschwerden von Bergarbeiten* (Munich, 1986), p. 11.

took on a new meaning with the development of modern bureaucracies under absolutist regimes. Generally, petitions to absolutist rulers fell into two broad categories distinguished by the kind of appeal they made about state power. Supplicants addressed complaints to the monarch about either the insufficient or the excessive intervention of state authorities in the form of petitions requesting the resolution of commercial disputes or seeking protection against administrative violations of individual rights. The first category of supplications, consisting largely of commercial complaints, was instrumental in accelerating the emergence of a rational legal code increasingly independent of the monarch's person. The complaints put forward in commercial petitions resulted from gaps in the law, since the case described was inadequately defined by existing legislation. The emergence of new technologies and forms of expression during the Industrial Revolution, for example, quickly outstripped existing legislation, opening the way for commercial partners to bring their dispute before the monarch for arbitration. The repetition of similar cases focused royal attention on those legal gaps, encouraging a resolution of the point in question and advancing the rationalization of the legal code.

The second category of petitions related more directly to the use of royal authority to curtail bureaucratic discretion and consisted largely of protests against the excesses of administrative authorities. Supplicants sought refuge in the sovereign's power to escape administrative sanction, appealing to the sovereign against his or her servants. Legal appeals to absolutist authority had the effect of strengthening the monarch administratively against the nascent bureaucracy. The information contained in these kinds of petitions provided the ruler with a direct source of information unmediated by bureaucratic channels, disclosing just how loyal those bureaucrats were. The petitions thus permitted the sovereign to monitor the activities of his or her servants and, if necessary, to discipline them. In this manner, the petitions provided the sovereign with partial compensation for the loss of power that the crown had ceded to the emerging bureaucracy.

But petitions did not only serve to shape the legal framework on which the rule of law and protection from arbitrary decisions taken by bureaucratic authorities was based. The petition was also a formidable tool in absolutist attempts to hinder the emergence of a public sphere – that is, a discursive forum outside the sovereign's sphere of influence in which private persons could form public relations. By presenting the right to petition as a private dialogue between individuals and the monarch, the monarch could more easily defuse potential challenges to the power of the crown. On the one hand, the absolutist claim that the monarch ruled in the interests of all of his or her subjects only obscured the monarch's real interests and the asymmetrical distribution of power between the ruler and the ruled. On the other hand, presenting this authoritarian understanding of discourse as a kind of benevolent paternalism helped to undercut potential political challenges to royal power. By casting the supplication as confidential, the sovereign could prevent social groups – and the bourgeoisie in particular – from organizing themselves. Allowing the publication of petitions, for example, would have permitted people with similar concerns to organize themselves around those interests. The concomitant flurry of discursive activity would have resulted in the constitution of a public sphere and entailed a loss in the monarch's power.

The growth of democratic institutions at the expense of absolutist regimes inevitably reduced the political significance of petitions. On the one hand, the gap between existing legislation and economic practice gradually diminished as new regulations addressed earlier complaints.[8] As the instrumental rationality at the core of capitalist exchange found a powerful guarantor in the increasing rationalization of the law, petitions began to lose their legal relevance. On the other hand, the introduction of individual rights as the centerpiece of liberal reform in Europe took on the function of restricting state power. Representative institutions, aided by civil associations and the press, gradually supplanted petitions as a method of monitoring bureaucratic abuse.

In Germany, the right to petition and to publish those petitions continued to be understood as an important source of democratic rule, as the Frankfurt and Weimar constitutions evince. Indeed, the infelicitous competition between direct-democratic and representative institutions in German legal thought bedeviled the Weimar Republic and was overcome only after 1945 in West Germany's "Basic Law" (*Grundgesetz*).[9] Although the Basic Law does guarantee the right to petition in Article 17, it excludes the possibility of oral complaints, reduces permissible petitions to a consultative role, and does not foresee using petitions as an independent method of resolving social conflicts or creating legislation. To this end, Article 17 stipulates that petitions should be addressed to parliament, rather than state institutions or the executive. In West German practice, individual petitions became less

---

8 Kumpf, "Petitionsrecht," p. 33.
9 For more on the conflicts between direct or plebiscitary and representative democracy, see Ernst Rudolf Huber, *Deutsche Verfassungsgeschichte seit 1789* (Stuttgart, 1969); Karl Dietrich Bracher, *Die Auflösung der Weimarer Republik* (Düsseldorf, 1984); Michael Stürmer, "Parliamentary Government in Weimar Germany, 1924–1929," in Anthony Nicholls and Erich Matthias (eds.), *German Democracy and the Triumph of Hitler* (London, 1971), pp. 59–78.

important than mass petitions, which are often used successfully by grassroots organizations to influence discussion in the press, monitor administrators, or exercise pressure on members of parliament. The public character of these petitions is key to their success.[10]

In the Federal Republic before unification, the use of the right to petition as a method of resolving conflict had become increasingly infrequent, indicating that the population no longer regarded petitions as the most important method of participating in government or of finding protection against the state. In 1989, for example, only 13,609 petitions were written to the responsible institution – the West German parliament. On the other hand, vestiges of absolutist practice survived in the custom of writing the chancellor, which thousands of West Germans did every year despite the lack of legal status accorded their letters. In addition, the parliamentary committee in charge of evaluating the letters regularly declared around 95 percent of all petitions resolved because more appropriate legal channels for action were available or because the behavior of the institution in question was determined to fall within legal guidelines.[11] In West Germany, then petitions provided little impulse for uncovering ambiguities in the law or even administrative improprieties. Both the parliament and the citizens it represented, moreover, had other means at their disposal to discipline bureaucrats and the institutions they served.

THE PETITION SYSTEM IN THE GDR

In contrast to West Germany, the right to petition played a central role in the GDR's economic and political life. The lack of coordinated accounting methods or centralized information gathering complicates any precise estimate of petition writing in the GDR, but the following examples illustrate the extent to which East Germans appealed to party and state leaders to take action against economic and bureaucratic institutions. During the 1980s, for example, East Germans addressed between 60,000 and 100,000 petitions annually to the Council of State. The Council of Ministers received comparatively fewer petitions; in 1986, for example, the number barely reached 15,000.[12] Instead, East Germans wrote directly to the ministries. During the

---

10 Wolfgang Graf Vitzthum, "Petitionsrecht," in Meinhard Schröder (ed.), *Ergänzbares Lexikon des Rechts. Ordner 2, Staats- und Verfassungsrecht* (Berlin, 1992), 5/530, p. 1.

11 Ibid., p. 5.

12 SAPMO-BA, DY30, JIV 4/184, "Beschluß über die Auswertung der Tagung des Staatsrates der DDR vom 23. März 1987," 10.4.87, Anlage, "Bericht über die an den Ministerrat im Jahre 1986 gerichteten Eingaben," p. 19.

summer of 1988, the Post Office received between 400 and 500 petitions every day complaining about the lack of telephone lines.[13] The number of petitions directed at the Ministry for ALF, in which people criticized the long waiting periods for cars, the poor quality of the automobiles, and the shortage of spare parts, ran to more than 30,000 a year during the 1980s.[14] Individual party leaders also received thousands of letters.[15] On local levels, as well, East Germans did not hesitate to air their grievances. In the parliamentary election year of 1984, for example, at least 146,709 petitions were addressed to local authorities.[16] East Germans also addressed enquiries and grievances to the various parties and mass organizations, newspapers, journals, magazines, radio, and television.[17] The total number of petitions written annually by East Germans during the 1980s and sent to various official institutions at the local and central level easily reached 500,000 – an astounding figure for a country of barely 17 million people.[18]

13 Waiting for a phone could take between ten and twenty years. The SED estimated that only 9.4 percent of East Germans had phone lines in 1985, lower than Bulgaria's 15.1 percent, the CSSR's 12.1 percent, and Yugoslavia's 9.9 percent. Western European countries averaged around 40 percent, with 41.9 percent for West Germany and 62.7 percent for Sweden (SAPMO-BA, DY30, IV 2/2.039.64, Politbürositzung vom 23.8.88, "2. Beschluß über Maßnahmen zur weiteren Entwicklung der Fernmeldeanlagen der Deutschen Post in der Hauptstadt der DDR," 23.8.88, pp. 53–4).

14 BArchB, DG7, 1559, Ministerum für ALF, "Bericht über die Eingabenarbeit im 1. Halbjahr 1980," 24.9.80, p. 1. The internal correspondence of the Ministry for ALF has been preserved in a fragmentary and haphazard manner, precluding a systematic sampling of the petitions or statistics regarding them. My research suggests, however, that the number of petitions rose dramatically during the 1980s in tandem with the increasing demand for cars. Even ministries uninvolved with the economy, such as the Ministry of Justice, received petitions about cars (see, for example, BArchB, DA5, 11437, Ministerium der Justiz, "Eingabenanalyse für das Jahr 1988," 7.2.88, pp. 1–2).

15 In the first six months of 1980, a total of 5,752 petitions were addressed to Honecker in his capacity as General Secretary of the SED. This number does not include the much larger number of petitions directed to Honecker in his capacity as Chairman of the Council of State, which fell under the jurisdiction of the Council (SAPMO-BA, DY30, JIV J/94, "Information über eingegangene Eingaben im 1. Halbjahr 1980," 15.8.80).

16 SAPMO-BA, DY30, JIV 4/13, "Bericht über die an den Ministerrat im Jahre 1984 gerichteten Eingaben," p. 43. People also wrote to parliament and communal institutions.

17 One television broadcast that dealt with legal issues, for example, received 27,053 letters in 1987, or 1,513 more than in 1986 (BArchB, DA5, 11437, Fernsehen der DDR, Chefredaktion Ratgeber, Senderreihe "Alles, was Recht ist," "Eingabenanalyse der Zuschauerpost 1987," 20.4.88, p. 1).

18 In the absence of centralized record keeping, it is difficult to confirm Inga Markovits's estimate of 750,000 petitions annually, or one petition for every twenty-three inhabitants (Inga Markovits, "Rechtsstaat oder Beschwerdestaat? Verwaltungsrechtsschutz in der DDR," *Recht in Ost und West* 31:5 [1987], p. 271.) A comparison with other Soviet bloc countries suggests that East Germans wrote more petitions a year than their neighbors. The number of petitions written by Bulgarians, for example, came to 250,000 in 1984, or one petition for every thirty-six inhabitants. Although Poland recorded 1,789,120 petitions in 1981, or one for every twenty-two people, this number includes letters written to the press. I have not included the number of petitions written to the East German media in my estimate, since the actual number is unclear (see Kuss, "Das Beschwerde- und Antragsrecht," pp. 131, 133). Felix Mühlberg provides no evidence for his claim that "at least two-thirds of all East German households composed a petition between 1949 and 1989" (Felix Mühlberg,

East Germans made heavy use of the right to petition because they possessed no other means of defending themselves from excesses committed by the party or state. The absence of due process in Soviet-style regimes enabled Marxist-Leninist parties to intervene at will in the daily affairs of their citizens and eliminate potential political competitors. Socialist states, moreover, relied on discursive means to compensate for and divert attention from their constant abrogation of civil rights. Like other communist parties, the SED argued that political freedoms are contingent on the economic organization of society. Subordinating civil to economic rights enabled the party to deride liberal guarantees of civil rights, such as those granted in Article 19 of the West German Basic Law, and portray the rule of law in liberal democracies as nothing more than an instrument of "class-based justice." By playing on the two meanings of the word *Bürger*, which means both citizen and bourgeois in German, the SED reinforced the notion that political liberty in the West is the liberty of the bourgeois. In this manner, the SED suggested that the legal framework underpinning Western democracies merely served the economic interests of the ruling class.

In contrast, the SED claimed that the ascendancy of the proletariat in the GDR guaranteed the necessary economic conditions for true political freedom, since "the historically constituted nature of the working class – the only class that has no special interests regarding society – expresses itself in the character of the socialist state."[19] Like absolutist rulers before them, the SED asserted an identity between citizens and their state on the basis of its allegedly democratic nature. The supposed ability of the Workers' and Peasants' State to act in the economic and political interest of all of its citizens meant that these citizens required no protection against state power. The mere existence of the socialist state objectively guaranteed their rights through the public ownership of property. This "unity" of the state and its citizens, moreover, expressed itself in the work of government, which was distinguished by its "participatory character" (*Mitgestaltungscharakter*).[20] Mobilizing the language of direct democracy, the party proclaimed that East German citizens enjoyed the constitutional right to "codetermination and participation" in the affairs of government. The right of cogovernance, however, came with responsibilities, including the "serious moral obligation" placed on East German citizens "to bring their concerns and suggestions"

"Konformismus oder Eigensinn? Eingaben als Quelle zur Erforschung der Alltagsgeschichte in der DDR," *Mitteilungen aus der kulturwissenschaftlichen Forschung* 19:37 [1996], p. 331).

19 *Wörterbuch zum sozialistischen Staat* (East Berlin, 1974), p. 299.

20 Weichelt, "Sozialistische Verfassung," pp. 438–41.

to the authorities.[21] The right to petition was a subcategory of the right to "codetermination and participation."[22] Officially, the right to petition was held up as "an important method of monitoring the strict adherence to socialist legality, in particular the basic rights of citizens, as well as the work of the state and economic apparatus."[23] Internally, however, the party was more frank about the use of petitions as a feedback mechanism to measure popular reception of state action. As a guide for employees of the Ministry for Trade and Supply phrased it, "the petitions are not simply the expression of the unmediated participation of working people in the exercise of state power and social control. They help tap unused resources, reflect the opinions and state of consciousness of the citizens, and are often an important sounding board for the correct evaluation of measures taken. Petitions are thus a source of current and reliable information." Because of its "great didactic content," the East German petition system promised to deepen popular acceptance of the regime by strengthening "the confidence of citizens in their state."[24]

In formal legal terms, then, East German constitutional law perpetuated the old conflict in Germany between direct and parliamentary democracy. In reality, however, the SED deployed a direct-democratic argument to justify disenfranchising the population. The party was less concerned about ensuring bureaucratic compliance with such ill-defined concepts as "codetermination and participation" than with neutralizing criticism and "mobilizing reserves to fulfill and overfulfill the state plans."[25] In fact, neither the constitution nor the legislation governing administrative procedure provided citizens with a means of securing their right to "codetermination and participation" against the various representative and administrative

---

21 Article 21, paragraph 3, 1968 and 1974 constitutions. Paragraph 2 of this article maintains that "the right to codetermination and participation is guaranteed by virtue of the fact that citizens can turn to societal, state, and economic organs and institutions with their concerns and suggestions." See also Weichelt, "Sozialistische Verfassung," pp. 439–40.

22 Hartmut Krüger, "Rechtsnatur und politische Funktion des 'Eingabenrechts' in der DDR," *Die Öffentliche Verwaltung* 30:12 (1977), p. 433. His view is shared by the *Wörterbuch zum sozialistischen Staat*, p. 86.

23 *Wörterbuch zum sozialistischen Staat*, p. 86. See also Manfred Cappallo et al., *Eingaben – Bürger gestalten Kommunalpolitik mit* (East Berlin, 1989); Werner Klemm and Manfred Naumann, *Zur Arbeit mit den Eingaben der Bürger* (East Berlin, 1977).

24 BArchB, DL1, 26252, "Richtlinie für die Arbeit mit den Eingaben," no date, pp. 1–2.

25 Rolf Opitz and Gerhard Schüßler, "Die Bearbeitung der Eingaben der Bevölkerung als Bestandteil der staatlichen Leitungstätigkeit," *Staat und Recht* 27:3 (1978), p. 220. The kernel of this interpretation already lies in article 10 of the Petition Law of 19.6.75 (*Gesetzesblätter der DDR* I [1975], p. 462). In fact, there are instances of whistle-blowing that reduced waste in the economy. See, for example, BArchB, DA5, 1454, "Kurzinformation über anonyme Zuschriften," no date, p. 58; BArchB, DE1, 55451, petition from 6.3.89.

organs. As one West German legal scholar has remarked, the constitution of the GDR did not provide "its citizens with any opportunity to collect information and participate in government, much less sanction their parliamentary representatives or the administrative authorities."[26] Given the largely formal character of the legal guarantees against excesses of the state, East Germans were unable to protect themselves from arbitrary decisions handed down by bureaucratic institutions. Nor did the Petition Law of 19 June 1975, which established guidelines for the treatment of petitions during Honecker's rule, provide any clear assurance that petitions would be processed.[27]

Because neglecting petitions carried no consequences, there was little incentive for local and central authorities to abide by the law. In fact, violation of the law was widespread, as numerous complaints from petitioners document.[28] For example, one petition addressed to Egon Krenz, the Politburo member who would depose Honecker in October 1989, lashed out at bureaucratic caprice and corruption. "I am quite astonished," the man commented acerbically, "that it is possible for a functionary to process a friend's petition within hours and, in violation of existing laws, turn a purely private view of the law into the official expression of an administrative agency."[29] Another East German criticized administrative attempts to discourage complaints, protesting that "it is really quite terrible when you have to run from one department to the next, when you are sent from one office to another, when documents are 'misplaced,' and people smile at you condescendingly [as if to say]: 'Some day they too will give up and resign themselves to their fate.'"[30]

---

26 Herwig Roggemann, *Die DDR-Verfassungen* (Berlin, 1976), p. 63. For more on the rule of law in the GDR, see Thomas Friedrich, "Aspekte der Verfassungentwicklung und der individuellen (Grund-) Rechtsposition in der DDR" in Kaelble et al., *Sozialgeschichte der DDR*; Karl König (ed.), *Verwaltungsstrukturen in der DDR* (Baden-Baden, 1991); Markovits, "Rechtsstaat oder Beschwerdestaat."

27 Although the law stipulated that the petitioner *should* receive an answer within the space of four weeks, it expressly offered administrators a method for extending that deadline indefinitely. The responsible authority was permitted to send a letter confirming that the petition had been received, rather than announcing a decision. The Petition Law also provided for disciplinary action to be taken against institutions that disregarded petitions. Because the kind and severity of the punishment was not specified, however, penalties were rarely assessed. See Article 7, paragraphs 2 and 3, Petition Law from 19.6.75, in *Gesetzesblätter der DDR* I (1975), p. 461. Most court cases involved divorce, labor, or criminal law (interview, de Maizière, Berlin, 8.5.96). However, there is at least one case of a citizen finding legal representation to pursue her rights against the car manufacturer. The letters written by her counsel in the matter, however, were treated by the Ministry for ALF as petitions (BArchB, DG7, VA-1813, correspondence from 26.5.89, 4.12.89, and letter to the *Deutsche Bauernzeitung* from 4.12.89).

28 See, for example, BArchB, DG7, VA-616 and VA-1813.

29 SAPMO-BA, DY30, IV 2/2.039.170, p. 82.

30 BArchB, DG7, VA-1813, petition from 6.11.89.

Senior officials were well aware of administrative irregularities. In 1982, for example, the Erfurt District Council conceded that some petitions contained "justified criticism of broken promises made by state authorities in Erfurt."[31] The Council of Ministers praised the work of the Erfurt Council, but reminded its representatives that "decisions regarding petitions must always be based on the relevant legislation."[32] In response to mounting popular criticism of bureaucratic caprice, moreover, the Council of State drew up guidelines in 1985 aimed at refining the procedures for processing petitions.[33] The lack of due process, however, frustrated the center's attempt to improve the petition system's responsiveness.

Even if a petition made its way successfully through the maze of administrative inertia and bureaucratic recalcitrance, the response often failed to satisfy the law. Sometimes state or party institutions decided explicitly to ignore petitions. In May 1989, for example, a man from the town of Höfchen expressed anger at the declining value of the East German mark. Officials at the Ministry for ALF, to which the petition had been addressed, agreed not to respond to the letter, despite their legal obligation to do so.[34] When they did not simply ignore petitions, the party and state often responded with perfunctory recapitulations of party policy or references to scarce resources.[35]

Bureaucratic disrespect for the laws governing the treatment of petitions derived in part from the proximity of public discourse to economic planning. The bulk of the petitions in the GDR consisted of economic grievances, ranging from complaints about the shortage of residential housing to the long wait to purchase automobiles. In particular, attempting to enforce warrantees on consumer goods proved difficult, since consumers had no means of holding manufacturers to their contractual agreements. Nor was there much incentive for state enterprises to acknowledge material defects in their products, given that the planned economy emphasized quantity, and not quality, of production. The monopoly enjoyed by most producers, moreover, did not furnish them with much motivation to cultivate good customer relations. In such a climate, insisting on one's constitutional rights had little impact. Nor did appealing to control mechanisms such as the Workers' and Peasants' Inspectorate, which was responsible for monitoring

---

31 SAPMO-BA, DY30, JIV 4/66, "Beschluß zum Bericht des Rates der Stadt Erfurt über die Durchführung des Eingabengesetzes vom 17. November 1983," Anlage 1, p. 15.

32 Ibid., Anlage 2, p. 23.

33 BArchB, DA5, 1460, Eichler to district councils, and "Empfehlungen des Staatsrates der Deutschen Demokratischen Republik."

34 BArchB, DG7, VA-1813, petition from 16.5.89.

35 See, for example, BArchB, DL1, 26395 and 26252, and the files of the Ministry for ALF.

the state apparatus, succeed in achieving the desired result.[36] At times, the contempt displayed by East German administrators for consumers bordered on the absurd. The experience of one woman to whom a defective automobile was delivered typifies the kind of bureaucratic chicanery encountered by thousands of East Germans. The Autohaus Dresden simply refused to deliver a new car that worked, despite the fact that it was legally obliged to provide her with a new automobile similar to the one she had ordered.[37]

If they could not invent a convincing reason for rejecting the case described in a petition, the responsible institution could always resort to implying that the petitioner had displayed an "antisocialist" attitude to justify its actions. An SED member working in the Ministry of Finance, for example, wrote at the end of 1988 to condemn the lax approach to tax fraud in the GDR. Displeased with his criticism, the party organization at the Ministry, which kept tabs on party members working there, sought to trivialize his arguments by impugning his character. It put together a description of his person that attested to "such character traits as self-importance and arrogance."[38] As evidence of his "political immaturity," moreover, the report noted that he had solicited bets with his colleagues that his criticisms would lead to his dismissal. The report then insinuated that he had a tendency toward speculation unbecoming in a financial expert. Having attacked the petitioner personally, the party organization proceeded to accuse him of a lack of confidence in socialist administration that bordered on disloyalty. The report willfully misinterpreted the petitioner's concern "that no one in the department has the courage to undertake a fundamental change in the prevailing regulations" as proof that he cast doubt on the personal integrity of his coworkers, then rebuked him for daring to question the disjunction between the letter of socialist law and the SED's more prosaic practice in the treatment of petitions.

What all of this had to do with tax fraud is unclear. Even had this financial official's political allegiance been questionable, impeaching his character did not refute his charge that tax evasion had become a problem for the socialist state. Treating petitioners with such a heavy hand, moreover, was hardly likely to uncover economic waste or placate a dissatisfied citizen, much less a disaffected party member. The fact that this party member had expressed his discontent through approved channels despite the expectation that his actions would elicit reprisals against his person demonstrates the extent to

---

36 See, for example, BArchB, DG7, VA-1813, petitions from 7.7.88 and 14.10.89.
37 BArchB, DG7, VA-1813, petition from 5.3.89.
38 The following account is based on SAPMO-BA, DY30, IV 2/2.039/155, SED-Betriebspartei-organisation im Ministerium der Finanzen, 18.2.88, pp. 87–9.

which a process of political delegitimization had penetrated the ranks of the party. In his case, the asymmetrical distribution of power enshrined in the petition system no longer functioned to deter criticism. His frank mistrust of the ZK's procedure for evaluating complaints signaled a shift from criticism aimed at improving the material circumstances of an individual or the collective toward skepticism about the petition system itself.

THE PETITION SYSTEM AS A POLITICAL OPPORTUNITY SPHERE

By the middle of the 1980s, the absence of restraints on bureaucratic caprice had undermined the effectiveness of the petition system in the GDR as a method of neutralizing popular discontent. This effect was reflected partly in a surge of petition writing, as people who had received unsatisfactory responses from local institutions rushed to appeal to the next highest authority.[39] In the decade after Honecker came to power, for example, the number of petitions addressed to the Council of State fluctuated between 41,000 and 62,000. In 1981, the number stood at 62,187, but by 1986 it had reached 74,983 and in 1989 jumped to 107,347. Not since the construction of the Berlin Wall had the Council of State received so many petitions.[40] Party institutions recorded a similar escalation in letter writing. The number of petitions processed by the Department of Trade, Supply, and Foreign Trade at the ZK, for example, rose by 60 percent between 1980 and 1987.[41] For the first time, moreover, complaints regarding the shortages of consumer goods increased more quickly than concerns over the shortage of housing space.[42]

The soaring number of letters of complaint had serious consequences for the administration of the authoritarian state. According to legal scholars

---

39 Some institutions, such as the Ministry of Justice and the state insurance company, did report declines in the number of petitions received (BArchB, DA5, 11437, Ministerium der Justiz, "Eingabenanalyse für das Jahr 1988," 7.2.88, pp. 1–2, and Generaldirektion, Staatliche Versicherung der DDR, "Analyse über die Arbeit mit den Eingaben der Bürger im Jahre 1987," 1.3.88, pp. 1–2).

40 *Neues Deutschland*, 9.12.66; BArchB, DA5, 627, Anlage 1, "Entwicklung der Eingaben zur Wohnungswirtschaft," p. 162a.

41 SAPMO-BA, DY30, Vorläufige SED 37987 and 37988.

42 BArchB, DA5, 11437, Komitee der ABI, "Bericht über die im Jahre 1988 an die Organe der Arbeiter- und Bauern-Inspektion gerichteten Eingaben," 27.1.89, p. 1. Werner Obst, an economic advisor to Willi Stoph during the 1960s, claims that the majority of complaints to the Council of State during the 1960s focused on the housing shortage, with complaints regarding the shortage of consumer goods running a distant third behind petitions to leave the GDR for West Germany (Obst, *DDR-Wirtschaft*, pp. 121–2). By the 1980s, complaints regarding housing directed to the Council of State continued to make up the largest single source of complaints, but the proportion of petitions expressing anger at the shortage of various consumer goods had increased dramatically. By the late 1980s, moreover, almost 50 percent of the complaints regarding consumer goods concerned automobiles (BArchB, DA5, 11426, "Bericht über den Hauptinhalt der an den Staatsrat gerichteten Eingaben der Bürger im 1. Halbjahr 1988," p. 5).

Table 8. *Written and Oral Petitions Addressed to the Council of State, 1961–1989*

Year	Number	Year	Number	Year	Number
1961	101,823	1971	No data	1981	62,187
1962	82,768	1972	No data	1982	64,237
1963	94,238	1973	40,494	1983	52,896
1964	91,612	1974	46,046	1984	62,009[a]
1965	81,344	1975	No data	1985	58,062
1966	74,055	1976	No data	1986	74,983
1967	70,184	1977	61,367[b]	1987	91,927
1968	68,364	1978	No data	1988	97,795
1969	67,055	1979	No data	1989	107,347
1970	62,681	1980	No data		

[a] This figure includes 1,200 collective petitions and 6,374 oral petitions – "the most in twenty years" (BArchB, DA5, 1566, "Bericht über den Hauptinhalt und die Bearbeitungsergebnisse der an den Staatsrat und seinen Vorsitzenden gerichteten Eingaben der Bürger im Jahre 1984," p. 1, and Anlage 1, p. 32).

[b] In 1977, the number of petitions written by women increased by 50 percent (BArchB, DA5, 9742, "Bericht über den Hauptinhalt," p. 1).

Sources: BArchB, DA5, 5999; BArchB, DA5, 5977, Kanzlei des Staatsrates, "Bericht über den Inhalt der an den Staatsrat gerichteten Eingaben," p. 3; BArchB, DA5, 5977, Kanzlei des Staatsrates, "Bericht über die Ergebnisse der Bearbeitung der Eingaben der Bürger durch die Kanzlei des Staatsrates im Jahre 1963;" BArchB, DA5, 958, "Bericht über den Hauptinhalt und die Bearbeitungsergebnisse der an den Staatsrat und seinen Vorsitzenden gerichteten Eingaben der Bürger im Jahre 1974," p. 73; BArchB, DA5, 9742, "Bericht über den Hauptinhalt der an den Staatsrat gerichteten Eingaben im Jahre 1977," p.1; BArchB, DA5, 11050, "Bericht über den Hauptinhalt und die Bearbeitung der im Jahre 1981 an den Staatsrat und seinen Vorsitzenden gerichteten Eingaben," p. 1; BArchB, DA5, 11069, "Bericht über den Hauptinhalt und die Bearbeitung der im Jahre 1981 an den Staatsrat gerichteten Eingaben der Bürger," p. 1; BArchB, DA5, 11088, "Bericht über den Hauptinhalt der an den Staatsrat gerichteten Eingaben der Bürger im Jahre 1983;" BArchB, DA5, 1566, Anlage 2, "Übersicht über Eingaben und Zuschriften im Jahr 1984," p. 34, and "Bericht über den Hauptinhalt und die Bearbeitungsergebnisse der an den Staatsrat und seinen Vorsitzenden gerichteten Eingaben der Bürger im Jahre 1988," Anlage 2, p. 99; BArchB, DA5, 1460, "Bericht über den Hauptinhalt und die Bearbeitungsergebnisse der an den Staatsrat und seinen Vorsitzenden gerichteten Eingaben der Bürger im Jahre 1984," p. 99; BArchB, DA5, 11419, "Bericht über den Hauptinhalt und die Bearbeitungsergebnisse der an den Staatsrat und seinen Vorsitzenden gerichteten Eingaben der Bürger im Jahre 1985," p. 1; BArchB, DA5, 12396, "Bericht über den Hauptinhalt und die Bearbeitungsergebnisse der an den Staatsrat gerichteten Eingaben der Bürger im Jahre 1986," 20.1.87, p. 1; BArchB, DA5, 1570, "Bericht über den Hauptinhalt und die Bearbeitungsergebnisse der an den Staatsrat und seinen Vorsitzenden gerichteten Eingaben der Bürger im Jahre 1988," p. 7; BArchB, DA5, 12400/7, "Bericht über die an den Staatsrat der DDR geichteten Eingaben der Bürger im Jahr 1989," 23.1.90, p.1. The calculations in Ina Merkel (ed.), *Wir sind doch nicht die Meckerecke der Nation! Briefe an das Fernsehen der DDR* (Berlin, 2000), p. 14, are inconsistent because they do not systematically include or exclude letters from foreigners or applications to leave the GDR, neither of which were classified as petitions by East German authorities.

at the University of Jena, the proliferation of complaints led to an increase in the amount of time that state agencies spent processing petitions.[43] The increased workload, moreover, did little to endear petitioners to administrators, which made satisfying aggrieved citizens more complicated. More importantly, the rising number of grievances forced functionaries to neglect their main tasks. Hans Modrow, the Dresden party boss who was to become the GDR's last communist leader, wrote after the revolution of 1989 that "some departments [of the ZK] spent up to one-half of their time processing petitions in the final years" of the GDR's existence.[44] The same was true at the local level. In late 1989, for example, the county council of Fürstenwalde near Frankfurt an der Oder complained to the Council of State that "processing the petitions sent to us entails an extra and considerable administrative burden. On top of this it is greatly time-consuming and expensive."[45]

As more petitions overwhelmed overworked bureaucrats, a vicious circle took shape: The greater willingness of East Germans to appeal to the party and state to improve their material position diminished the effectiveness of the petition system as an instrument of political control, while the inability to respond adequately to these complaints engendered new complaints. Ironically, this spiral negated the economic function of appeals that distinguished the communist from the absolutist petition system. Although the SED designed the petition system to improve economic efficiency via whistle-blowing, processing the rising number of petitions only added to the regime's administrative costs.

More importantly, however, the change in quantity was accompanied by a change in the quality of the petitions, as anger at the discrepancy between the party's ceaseless pronouncements of social equality and the experienced realities of privilege and the unequal distribution of wealth intensified during the 1980s. The camaraderie of deprivation experienced after the Second World War, as well as the willingness to sacrifice for a future socialist utopia, gave way with Erich Honecker's assumption of power in 1971 to the hope of greater consumer freedom. But the oil crises of the 1970s and the age of the GDR's capital stock forced the state to tighten its belt in the 1980s. The increasing inability of the regime to deliver on the economic promises it had made, coupled with its relentless mendacity, diminished whatever tolerance for economic mismanagement people still had.

43 Wolfgang Bernet, Axel Schöwe, and Richard Schüler, "Für eine effektivere Verwirklichung des Eingabenrechts!" *Neue Justiz. Zeitschrift für sozialistisches Recht und Gesetzlichkeit* 42:7 (1988), p. 283.
44 Otfrid Arnold and Hans Modrow, "Das Große Haus," in Modrow (ed.), *Das Große Haus*, pp. 61–2.
45 BArchB, DA5, 12400, Emmerich, Rat des Kreises Fürstenwalde, Bezirk Frankfurt an der Oder, to Abteilung Eingaben, Sektor III, Staatsrat, 17.11.89.

Because of its uncontested control over the productive forces of East German society, moreover, the party itself became the target of economic dissatisfaction. The SED sought to legitimate the socialist state's monopoly of the economy as the sole "seller of goods, employer, landlord, or service provider" by promising East Germans social justice.[46] As the planned economy manufactured increasing shortages of merchandise and morality, however, the state's paternalism became a liability for the SED. Criticisms of the supply of material goods began to take on political overtones. East Germans began to hold the state and the party that directed it responsible for their economic position. The SED, once a powerful authority to whom supplicants deferred for economic improvement of their lot, was degraded to the post of political errand boy. Instead of producing the "citizen-friendly government" that the SED constantly apostrophized, the dismissive behavior of administrators only manufactured more discontent.

The change in rhetorical strategies is most obvious when compared to letters from the Ulbricht period. Often petitions from the 1960s linked elliptical references to the discrepancy between economic promise and empirical reality with material remedies for malfeasance or scarcity. The authors presented their claim as supportive of the socialist state, suggesting that a quick solution to their predicament would improve not only their own well-being, but that of the collective as well. In 1966, for example, one woman wrote regarding her living situation that "these conditions influence our work negatively, since we often miss work because we are sick."[47] In general, the tenor of demands was more modest and respectful of the regime's material limitations. One man, for example, noted humbly that "of course, I realize that every citizen cannot immediately receive a modern apartment."[48] Finally, petitions from the 1960s usually contained formulaic statements regarding membership in the working class and a protestation of support for socialism, which was followed by a material claim on the state. Just after the adoption of a new constitution in 1968, for example, one man wrote to the Council of State saying that "I work in the VEB DBM as a metalworker. I work well, am a member of a socialist [workers'] brigade. Yesterday, my wife and I gladly said yes to the new constitution. But I also demand my right" to better housing.[49] Seldom did petitioners question the clemency of administrators by challenging their authority.

By the 1980s, however, the deterioration of the economy had effected a change in rhetorical strategies exhibited by petitioners. Rarely did letter

---

46 Markovits, "Rechtsstaat oder Beschwerdestaat," p. 265.
47 BArchB, DA5, 5986, petition from 10.8.66.   48 BArchB, DA5, 5986, petition from 14.11.66.
49 BArchB, DA5, 5985, petition from Döbeln.

writers simply state their class membership, list their rights, and hope for the best. Instead of throwing themselves on the mercy of indifferent functionaries, people began to contest bureaucratic authority. The shift from an attitude of supplication toward a more confrontational stance encompassed two main tactics. The most common approach was to combine socialist argumentation with the discursive structure of appeals to drive a wedge between socialism and the Socialist Unity Party. In this way, petitioners observed the rules of political decorum forced upon them by the regime while transforming the weakness of their position into a strength. One man, for example, turned a party slogan regarding socialism's responsibility to the individual against the SED: "It really is not in the spirit of the human being as the center of socialist society when I have to save up for years for a Trabant and then cannot use my car for more than a year because of a shortage of spare parts!"[50] Other writers focused on the disparity between the regime's official rhetoric and the experience of everyday life. One seized upon the contradiction between the SED's economic braggadocio and the shortage of consumer goods, remarking that "when I open the newspaper, I read about top products made by the GDR, such as light-conductor cables or answering machines. At the same time, I'm supposed to believe year after year that it is not possible to get a telephone line."[51]

Appealing to the authority of the ideas to which the SED nominally ascribed, however, also led to open disregard for the coercive etiquette of petition writing. One thoroughly annoyed elderly man assailed the discrepancy between party propaganda and empirical reality: "What is this for a miserable economic policy? How furious do you think I am about these conditions? When you read in the soc[ialist] press [about the] 'maximal satisfaction of the needs of the people and so on' and read on every page three times 'everything for the benefit of the people,' it makes me sick to my stomach."[52] Other petitioners employed sarcasm to underline the gap between the party's egalitarian promises and the ubiquity of privilege. As noted in Chapter 5, one man lambasted SED bigwigs, addressing them as "honorable comrade Volvo drivers."[53] A few petitioners dispensed with arguments altogether and demanded that those in positions of responsibility "be brought up on charges."[54] In their fury, some petitioners began making economic demands that constituted a complete rejection of the socialist state and all that it stood for. In an ominous sign of things to come, one

50 SAPMO, DY30, IV 2/2.039/153, petition from 18.1.87, p. 272.
51 SAPMO, DY30, IV 2/2.039/153, petition from 15.12.88, p. 21.
52 BArchB, DG7, VA-1813, petition from 1.11.89.
53 BArchB, DG7, VA-2718, petition from 8.11.89.
54 BArchB, DG7, VA-616, petition from 17.6.80.

elderly man denounced "the corruption and fraud blossoming in all walks of life. As a Christian, I do not want to be involved in this. The only way to remain honest is to obtain West German marks. At the black market rate of 1:13, my monthly salary is too small to change money. That is why I would like to apply for 50 percent of my salary to be paid out in DM. It is sad that people cannot purchase the basic necessities with their own currency."[55]

Money, and Western money in particular, increasingly became a symbol of social inequity. As we saw with the Intershops, some East Germans stopped protesting at the social injustices created by the party and began demanding instead that the socialist state provide equal access to West German money so they could secure the commodities they desired. After waiting five months for a repair to his car, for example, one man was told that it would take another three months to find the necessary part. Noting that the black market functioned more efficiently than bureaucratic pathways, he argued that the socialist state should simply provide him with the means to his end. "Since I do not possess the necessary connections and DM that would solve these problems really quickly," he wrote, "I turn to you," the People's Parliament.[56]

The second tactic increasingly employed by petitioners during the 1980s involved statements of conditional support for the regime that made the political legitimacy of the GDR subject to the availability of consumer goods. An elderly woman who had been waiting for a telephone line for years, for example, registered her concern "that the German Post sees the issue purely from the point of view of the shortage of telephone lines and fails to recognize that it diminishes the rule of law, deeply violates civil rights, and discredits the social system in the GDR."[57] Her emphasis on social justice had the effect of making the political legitimacy of the GDR contingent upon the receipt of material goods. Whether she took the claims of the socialist state seriously, or merely harnessed the ideological justifications of the dictatorship to her own ends, the formulation of her complaint demonstrates an impressive familiarity with the regime's arguments and a keen understanding of the SED's weaknesses.[58]

---

55 BArchB, DG7, VA-1813, petition from 16.5.89.

56 BArchB, DA5, 11428, "Auszüge aus Eingaben zu Fragen der Kraftfahrzeug-Ersatzteilversorgung," p. 3.

57 She received a telephone line, in part because she successfully argued that her advanced age made it absolutely necessary for her to rely on a telephone, and in part because the SED did make some attempt to redistribute the shortages according to social or political criteria. In addition, she sent her letter off at the beginning of the year, when the budget for telephone lines for petitioners had not yet been run down (SAPMO-BA, DY30, IV 2/2.039/154, petition from 6.2.89).

58 As early as 1975, Stoph, who was then Chairman of the Council of State, observed that "many of the petitions demonstrate that citizens know the decrees of the party and government quite well, much

Some petitions in the latter half of the 1980s equated political legitimacy with material goods in more drastic terms. One woman who was writing her dissertation quoted the regime against itself, declaring just before the rigged communal elections in May 1989 that "my trust in a citizen-friendly policy at the responsible institutions has evaporated during the nearly nine-month duration of this affair. That also detracts from my trust in the candidates standing in the communal elections."[59] Her thinly veiled refusal to participate in the political charade of East German elections was by no means an isolated incident.[60] The SED leadership in Frankfurt an der Oder, for example, was concerned enough about petitioners withholding their cooperation in communal affairs to order a "mass examination of the handling of petitions" before a session of communal representatives was to meet in late 1985.[61] In 1989, moreover, the Council of State reported that the number of petitioners who made cooperating in the ritualization of their political disenfranchisement dependent on the satisfaction of their material concerns had risen.[62] In unusually frank terms, it warned that "people declare their refusal to vote or their nonparticipation in the elections in the form of ultimatums if a solution to the advantage of the petitioner is not found before the elections take place. In numerous petitions, citizens refer to promises that were not kept in the parliamentary elections of 1986."[63] The petitions had become a political opportunity sphere, as East Germans bent an instrument of authoritarian control to their own purposes.

Even party members became disgusted by the contradictions in the society they were upholding, presaging the disintegration of the SED's

more precisely than they did before, and then measure the standards in these decrees critically with their own unmediated living and work experience" (BArchB, DA5, 960, "Sitzung des Staatsrates am 20. März 1975," p. 37).

59 BArchB, DG7, VA-1813, petition from 19.4.89.

60 The correlation between national elections and a rise in the number of petitions written was observed under Ulbricht as well (BArchB, DA5, 5981, Müller to Ritter, 18.5.65). During the 1960s, petitioners used similar arguments, though phrased less aggressively, to make the same linkage (see the petitions in BArchB, DA5, 5988). The difference is that the number of petitioners making the link declined the more the construction of the Wall receded into the past, whereas the number in the 1980s was on the rise.

61 BArchB, DA5, 11418, *Neuer Tag*, 28.10.85.

62 In comparison with the national elections of 1986, the Council of State reported an increase of petitions (BArchB, DA5, 1571, "Information zu Eingaben mit Bezug auf die Kommunalwahlen 1989," 20.2.89, p. 64). In addition, the Department for State and Legal Questions at the ZK reported that the number of petitions "increased by leaps and bounds" in years with national elections and party congresses, but noted that communal elections had not drawn a rise in appeals until 1984 (BArchB, DA5, 11437, Abteilung Staats- und Rechtsfragen, "Analyse der Eingaben an die Abteilung Staats- und Rechtsfragen im 2. Halbjahr 1988," pp. 1–2).

63 The Council then concluded with the dark assurance that "ultimatums in petitions will be dealt with in an appropriate fashion" (BArchB, DA5, 1571, "Information zu Eingaben mit Bezug auf die Kommunalwahlen 1989," 20.2.89, pp. 64–5).

legitimacy in its own ranks. A longtime party member and police officer, for example, was infuriated at the prospect of having to pay two and
a half times the official price for a new body for his car. "As an officer
and communist," he wrote, "I cannot very well go to the illegal market or
get ahold of hard currency in order to have my car repaired."[64] Similarly, a
city councilman from Dresden who had been a party man for twenty-seven
years complained bitterly about his inability to obtain spare parts to repair his
Lada. Incensed by the runaround he had received at the hands of the bureaucracy, he wrote that "the situation makes me indignant because I basically
confront this problem without protection and full rights, even though I am
politically and socially engaged and a comrade who is in addition severely
handicapped."[65]

To neutralize discontent more effectively, the party constantly reminded
local and central authorities to seek out personal conversations with the
petitioners.[66] In keeping with the authoritarian logic at the heart of the
petitions, the regime presented these meetings as an opportunity to put a
human face on an otherwise impersonal bureaucracy. In fact, however, the
confidential "conversation" deployed the asymmetry of power in a manner
designed to disarm the petitioner's challenge to authority. It only rehearsed
the trappings of dialogue, while several representatives of the Workers' and
Peasants' State worked in tandem to secure a written retraction of the petition, as we saw in the introduction.

The results of such conversations were sometimes disappointing for both
sides. In the 1980s, there were increasing signs that the regime's authoritarian approach to discourse elicited resistance and that East Germans were
becoming less inhibited about articulating their criticisms. The temptation
to reel off official policy without really discussing the grievance, or even
to coerce the petitioner into retracting his or her complaint, was difficult
for representatives of the state and party to resist. In February 1989, for
example, the party brought massive pressure to bear on one party member who had dared to attack the Intershops as a "right to inequality."
The hard-currency stores should be eliminated, she reasoned, because "the
scope, kind, and quality of commodities available in the Intershops discredits the significance of our own work for the party."[67] Her criticism
was reported to Schalck, who oversaw Intershop operations. Because she
was a party member, but also because money was a sensitive topic, Schalck

64 SAPMO-BA, DY30, IV 2/2.039/170, petition from 15.3.89.
65 BArchB, DG7, VA-1813, petition from 3.8.89, p. 2.
66 See SAPMO-BA, DY30, JIV 4/66, "Stellungnahme des Ministerrates zum Bericht des Rates des
   Bezirks Schwerin über die Durchführung des Eingabengesetzes," p. 27; Cappallo, *Eingaben*, p. 17.
67 BArchB, DL2, 930, petition from 27.11.88.

informed Mittag. Both men ordered Horst Steinert, a Forum manager and Stasi agent, to convince the woman to retract her criticisms in a personal conversation.[68]

But the meeting went awry. During the discussion, Steinert sought to counter the petitioner's objections with the usual arguments that the party's policy was above reproach. Surprisingly, the woman not only resisted Steinert's call to party discipline, but she also embarked on a sweeping attack on the SED's economic program. She quickly turned from the economic to the public sphere, castigating the party leadership for banning the Soviet journal *Sputnik*. Because *Sputnik* had published an article criticizing Stalin for the Great Purges, Honecker decided on 19 November 1988 to drop the journal from the postal delivery list, which was tantamount to withdrawing it from circulation. Although Honecker intended to stem the tide of *glasnost* emanating from Gorbachev's Soviet Union, his decision had the opposite effect, alienating many in the party from his policies.[69] As the report to Schalck rather euphemistically put it, this petitioner "was clearly not fully convinced by comrade Steinert's arguments" regarding the Intershops or *Sputnik*. Of course, a party member could be unconvinced of the wisdom of a specific policy yet still accept the party's authority. This particular party member, however, not only refused to hew to the party line, but she also transgressed against convention by treating the personal "conversation" as a real dialogue. Rather than register some form of compliance, however tepid, she "requested that the questions she had opened up be recorded in the report on the conversation."[70]

Schalck immediately advised Mittag of the woman's refusal to submit to party discipline. With Mittag's assent, he punished her by referring her case to the Central Party Control Commission, which was in charge of disciplining party members.[71] In addition to revealing the SED's increasingly harsh approach to criticism within its own ranks, this case illustrates the inefficiencies of authoritarian rule. Far from contributing to increased economic growth by eliminating the waste of resources, the petition system sometimes forced senior economic leaders to waste their time micromanaging political dissent.

Not infrequently, representatives of the party brought direct coercion to bear during face-to-face meetings.[72] One party member who criticized

---

68 BArchB, DL2, 930, Schalck to Mittag, 7.2.89.
69 Stephan, "Vom Mauerbau," pp. 92–3.
70 BArchB, DL2, 930, "Standpunkt des Genossen Steinert im Gespräch mit Genossin [G.] am 21.2.1989," and Steinert, "Ergänzung zum Vermerk vom 22.2.1989," 27.2.89.
71 BArchB, DL2, 930, Schalck to Mittag, 27.2.89, and Schalck to Müller, 27.2.89.
72 Sometimes this official delegation included a Stasi agent. See, for example, the aggressive request for a Stasi agent in BArchB, DL1, 26252, petition from 2.8.89, p. 3.

the inadequacies of the petition system deplored the practice of using personal conversations to pressure petitioners into retracting their complaints. Writing to Politburo member Kurt Hager, he reproached the SED for its "delaying tactics and attempts to wear petitioners down in the handling of petitions."[73] As an example of the intimidation employed by the party, he described how army officers had visited him in the hospital after he had written a previous petition. Unable to induce him to withdraw that petition, they threatened him outright. "In the end," he commented bitterly, "I was 'convinced' by reference to the fact that I was of course 'dependent on the doctors for further medical treatment.'"[74] In connection with his current petition, representatives from the Department for Security Questions at the ZK visited him. They concluded that he was mentally ill: "The absurdity of his letter, the way he argued in the conversation, as well as the fact that he currently has no job reinforces our assumption that the man is psychopathic, just as feared by the physicians."[75]

It is worth pointing out that the petitioner did give the security agents some reason to believe that his judgment was not entirely sound. In one letter, for example, he made use of the philosopher Martin Heidegger to imply that East Germans did not feel "at home" in the GDR. "The citizens of our homeland," he warned, "are 'lodged in homelessness' [*Heimatlosigkeit anwest*], to remain within Heidegger's language."[76] Although representatives of the East German security forces were unlikely to understand the philosophical grounds of the petitioner's critique, the mere mention of Heidegger's name was a red flag. After all, Heidegger's membership in the Nazi party rendered allusions to his work suspect in an antifascist state. This rather odd rhetorical tactic facilitated the SED officials' attempts to discredit the petitioner.

But rhetorical folly is not equivalent to mental illness. Even if the man's sanity was questionable, his letter contains a penetrating analysis of the petition system's failings. Accusing him of being psychopathic, however, not only discredited his person, but it also conveniently discredited the grounds of his complaint. The security agents were no longer obliged to explain the fact that a party member had the temerity to register a complaint about the petition system. Consigning the petitioner to the ranks of the insane,

---

73 SAPMO-BA, DY30, IV 2/2.039/153, petition from 21.09.88, p. 63–4.
74 Ibid., pp. 65–6.   75 Ibid., p. 78.
76 Ibid., p. 74. Heidegger's notion of *Anwesen* involves a temporality determined by presence. See Martin Heidegger, *Sein und Zeit* (Tübingen, [1927] 1993), pp. 25, 326; Heidegger, "The Age of the World Picture," in *The Question Concerning Technology and Other Essays*, trans. William Lovitt (New York, 1977).

however, did not change the fact that an SED member had made use of the petition system to challenge the petition system. Nor had the personal conversation favored by the SED as a method of deterring criticism successfully defused that challenge. In this instance, moreover, the petition system was unable to prevent the emergence of a metadiscourse – a discussion about the discussion. While the party could always use the threat of political violence to cow dissenters, it proved unable to deter the use of the right to petition to criticize the right to petition. Although constructed as a simulacrum of discourse, the petition system's use of discursive structures to legitimate the regime offered East Germans an opportunity to transform an instrument of control into an instrument for the articulation of dissent.

LIES, DAMNED LIES, AND PETITIONS

Despite its increasing inadequacies, the SED continued to praise its use of the petition system as an instrument of political control that employed persuasion to reconcile critics with the regime. The treatment of petitions was, according to official views, "extremely effective in strengthening the trust of citizens in their state [and] for continuing to develop an administrative style that is citizen-friendly."[77] Because the petitions were lauded as an expression of the right to "codetermination and participation," the use of this constitutional right could function as proof of the regime's ability to mobilize East Germans in support of the socialist state. In a daring bit of logic, local authorities, who enjoyed direct contact with the populace, portrayed the increase in letter writing not as an indication of popular discontent, but as proof of East German confidence in local administration to solve everyday problems. In their reports to the center, local agencies interpreted increases in the number of petitions they received as evidence of an increased legitimacy for the GDR in the areas under their territorial jurisdiction. Siegfried Lorenz, the district party leader of Karl-Marx-Stadt, acclaimed the 34,000 petitions that had been written to state institutions in his district during the course of 1983 as proof of the people's confidence in the state.[78] Similarly, the City Council of Stralsund hailed the increase in the number of petitions it had received during 1984 not as a sign of deepening disaffection, but

77 Opitz and Schüßler, "Die Bearbeitung der Eingaben," p. 220.
78 SAPMO-BA, DY30, IV 2/2.039/93, "Bericht der Bezirksleitung Karl-Marx-Stadt der SED an die Bezirksdelegiertenkonferenz am 11. und 12. Februar 1984," p. 48. In 1988, the East German legal journal *Neue Justiz* demanded that state authorities stop "counting nearly every matter of the citizens as a petition and demonstrating the efficacy and citizen-friendly nature of their work by reporting a high number of petitions" (Bernet et al., "Für eine effektivere Verwirklichung," p. 282).

rather as "an ever-increasing number of ideas and expressions of willingness to work actively" with local government.[79]

Local leaders also emphasized the fact that the majority of cases were decided in favor of petitioners – in stark contrast to West German practice – and interpreted this "success" as a measure of the "citizen-friendly" policies the regime pursued. In 1981, for example, the District Council of Schwerin reported that because of its guidance "decisions were reached in favor of the citizens' personal wishes in 87 percent of the petitions."[80] Despite the Schwerin Council's claims, this percentage did not signify an administrative policy of championing ordinary citizens.[81] Nor was it proof of mass participation in the work of government, much less acceptance of the SED's power. Rather, the large number of decisions granting petitioners their wishes reveals a lack of legal and institutional rationality in the GDR – the problem that produced the grievances in the first place. The lack of due process, moreover, made it possible for the regime to go unchallenged in its misrepresentation of itself as eliminating the asymmetry of power between East German citizens and the socialist state. Unperturbed, local leaders continued to utilize the number of petitions they received to win approval from the party leadership in Berlin.

In contrast to local authorities, central agencies such as the ZK and the ministries considered the number of petitions written as an indication of their ability to resolve institutional disagreements over the distribution of resources. Economic institutions in particular employed the letters of complaint to measure popular dissatisfaction with the supply of food and consumer goods. The attention to the quantity of supply and number of letters had the effect only of reinforcing the preference of economic planners for numerical arguments. As we saw with the complaints about the automobile shortage discussed in Chapter 5, the party's predilection for statistical representations of qualitative arguments made it difficult for the planning apparatus to generate systemic criticism of production or distribution methods. As Modrow put it, "in many cases, the task consisted of solving the problems of individual people, but not to analyze the reasons for the deplorable state of affairs."[82]

---

79 BArchB, DA5, 1455, "Bericht der Stadtverordnetenversammlung Stralsund über Erfahrungen bei der Kontrolle der Arbeit mit den Eingaben," 12.2.85, p. 25.

80 SAPMO-BA, DY30, JIV 4/66, "Bericht des Rates des Bezirkes Schwerin über die Durchführung des Eingabengesetzes," 12.5.82, p. 13.

81 As a report to the Council of State on a slew of petitions in 1985 regarding the freedom to travel noted, East Germans "view the decisions taken in their affairs as heartless and bureaucratic, and [believe] that their grounds for complaint are ignored" (BArchB, DA5, 11418, report on 214 travel-related petitions, no title, no date, p. 1).

82 Arnold and Modrow, "Das Große Haus," pp. 61–2.

The Department for State and Legal Questions at the ZK, for example, sedulously separated the grievances contained in the petitions into various categories, offering its superiors a multitude of numerical snapshots of dissent in the GDR. Like many other party and state organizations, moreover, the Department registered a constant increase in the number of complaints during the 1980s. In 1988, the Department recorded "the highest total number of petitions" it had ever received, an increase of 189 to 4,638, yet made no attempt to explain why.[83] To some extent, the exaggerated attention given to quantitative representations of political dissent at the expense of qualitative arguments was shaped by the party's emphasis on instrumental rationality. In the case of the petitions, however, the emphasis on counting the complaints rather than accounting for them also derived from a well-founded concern about job security. By the 1980s, Honecker's animosity toward the mildest form of criticism, as well as the notoriously captious Mittag's self-aggrandizement, made analytic evaluations a risky prospect. The ideological preference for quantitative over qualitative arguments, party discipline, and careerism inhibited any real engagement with the complaints brought to the attention of administrators.

While functionaries dissolved individual consumers into aggregate categories in correspondence with each other, they responded to individual petitioners as if each petition were unique. The planning apparatus, for example, treated the author of each petition as an individual case, even if the complaint echoed thousands that had preceded it. As with the right to appeal in absolutist regimes, the East German bureaucracy dealt with dissatisfied individuals in isolation. Such an approach reflected the fact that people with similar grievances were prevented from organizing concerted resistance to the regime's priorities. This enabled the state to project a personalized concern about the individual's welfare. The simulacrum of discourse, moreover, permitted planners to reject criticism in a ritualized manner, since the desires of one consumer could hardly form the basis of the entire plan.[84]

In fact, the reduction of individual concerns to statistical figures provided fertile ground for carrying out personal and institutional rivalries. Removed from their original context, the numbers could be harnessed to make nearly any argument. During one Politburo meeting, for example, Werner Jarowinsky, the ZK Secretary for Trade and Supply, used the absence of petitions to pander to Honecker. In response to a mild criticism of Honecker's economic program leveled by ideology chief Hager, Jarowinsky cited the fact

---

83 BArchB, DA5, 11437, Abteilung Staats- und Rechtsfragen, "Analyse der Eingaben," pp. 1–2. See also the "petition analyses" in SAPMO-BA, DY30, Vorläufige SED 37987 and 37988.
84 See the examples in BArchB, DL1, 26395.

that the General Secretary's price policies had not provoked a flurry of petition writing as evidence of Honecker's success.[85]

Where political rivals used the small number of petitions to score points in the Politburo, the increasing number of petitions was an effective weapon in the fight over the distribution of resources among the district party organizations. In 1987, for example, Hans-Joachim Böhme, the district party leader of Halle, tried to bring pressure to bear on the Ministry of Trade and Supply to deliver more food by informing the Politburo that "criticisms and petitions are on the increase in the population."[86] Jarowinsky, who was ultimately responsible for retail trade, responded by seizing upon the short supply of children's shoes to shift responsibility away from the distributing and onto the producing bureaucracy: "The high demand in the shops continues. One expression includes the numerous petitions written by the population as well as critical opinions expressed in the shops. Briksa [the Minister of Trade and Supply] reported the critical situation to the Council of Ministers, and the Supply Commission made the necessary changes on time. The repeated promises made by the Minister for Light Industry to carry out the tasks set out in the plan have not been kept."[87] As in capitalist countries, the use of statistics promoted various, and often contradictory, political causes. Stripped of their content, individual complaints were transformed into ciphers without valence. For this reason, the statistics could be exploited for any purpose. No authority was obliged to take responsibility for the grievances, yet everyone could use the petitions for their own ends.

THE CIRCULATION OF DECLINE

While the party and state used the petitions as indicators of their ability to resolve disputes over the distribution of tight resources, the East German populace received little benefit from them. Using the aggregate number of petitions to discover consumer needs and alleviate shortages failed to effect any change in the way the regime functioned, since the manufacture of commodities, as well as the production of social justice, could not be influenced by statistics. Not even the upsurge in petition writing, with

---

85 BArchB, DE1, 56317, Klopfer, "Persönliche Notizen über die Beratung beim Generalsekretär," 16.5.1989, p. 35. Jarowinsky's representation of the facts was hardly accurate.
86 SAPMO-BA, DY30, IV 2/2.039/268, "Auszüge aus den Berichten der Bezirksleitungen," 9.11.87, p. 6.
87 SAPMO-BA, DY30, Vorläufige SED 41852, Jarowinsky to Honecker, "Information zur Lage in der Versorgung mit Kinderhosen," 12.11.87, p. 1.

the excessive burdens it entailed, altered the party's ineffective attempts to improve social equality.

The change in the tenor of the petitions did not go unnoticed by the party. Jarowinsky warned at a Politburo meeting in late 1988 that "some questions [concerning consumer goods] are being put more aggressively, for example in petitions."[88] Although party and state institutions could always trot out statistics to demonstrate how the regime was solving problems of supply, the content of the letters showed the party leadership that the population was convinced of the opposite. In July 1989, the Department of Trade, Supply, and Foreign Trade reported that "criticisms and petitions [show] that the expectations and wishes of the population regarding the supply of goods are rising more quickly."[89] As East Germans began flowing into Hungary and Czechoslovakia to escape the GDR during the summer of 1989, the Council of Ministries observed that "the districts of Karl-Marx-Stadt, Halle, and Gera, as well as the capital, report an increase of petitions from the population. Statements critical of the supply situation are being coupled with the demand that, in the fortieth year of the GDR's existence, more stability in the supply of goods is to be expected."[90] Despite these and similar reports, the SED leadership was unable to halt the erosion of its legitimacy. In the meantime, the shortage of commodities, and the shortage of legality generated by the regime, led East Germans to link the frustration of their material desires with their political dissatisfaction.

By the end of 1988, the party's ability to quell the "aggressive" tone in the petitions had deteriorated. Mittag, for example, tried to ban the flurry of petitions written by construction workers at the atomic reactor *Nord*. Their complaints began as criticisms of the 1988 meat shortage, but quickly evolved into a programmatic censure of the regime itself. The letter-writing activity soon led to the workers organizing themselves and composing a mass petition. Mittag moved quickly to suppress this emerging public sphere, which represented a serious challenge to the SED's power. Despite his measures, however, the mass petition found its way into the hands of the West German press, demonstrating just how difficult it was for the SED to control the circulation of ideas, much less the circulation of commodities. In his report to the Politburo, Mittag complained that "the kinds of false ideologies that abounded there were terrible. They presented a political

---

88 SAPMO-BA, DY30, IV 2/2.039/64, Politbürositzung vom 30.8.88, p. 65.
89 SAPMO-BA, DY30, IV 2/2.039/266, Abteilung Handel, Versorgung und Außenhandel, "Information zur Lage in der Versorgung," 24.7.89, p. 186.
90 SAPMO-BA, DY30, IV 2/2.039/268, Instrukteurabteilung beim Vorsitzenden des Ministerrates, "Information über die Versorgung," 2.8.89, p. 108.

platform in their letters, saying that the party's policies had to be changed. That it was necessary for us to intervene is proven by the fact that the letter was printed in [the West German news magazine] *Der Spiegel* fourteen days later."[91]

It is worth noting that the presence of a critical mass media at the GDR's doorstep presented SED leaders with an intractable problem. Unlike any other Eastern European regime, the GDR could not effectively seal its borders from contact with the West. Despite construction of the Berlin Wall, East Germany was firmly bound to West Germany by the West German public sphere. Except for those living in the so-called valley of the clueless near Dresden, East Germans were able to receive West German television and radio and so "flee the country" (*Republikflucht begehen*) every night. Moreover, West German television shows such as "Kennzeichen D" performed precisely the same function that East German *samizdat*, or underground literature, would have.

Ironically, it is the influence of the West German public sphere, which ceaselessly broadcast its ideological animosity to the socialist state in the same language and with similar cultural references, that helps explain the comparative stability of SED rule until the mid-1980s. Most attempts to explain why organized opposition was so late in forming make use of Albert O. Hirschman's categories of "exit" and "voice" to explain how the Wall functioned to repress opposition to the SED's rule.[92] Hirschman describes the choices available to members of an organization when they dissent as consisting of leaving the organization (exit) or staying on to criticize it from within in the hopes of reforming it (voice). By constructing the Wall, the party leadership was able to close off the exit option and exercise greater control over the mobility of its population. As the gatekeeper, however, the SED could also use the exit option to weaken the voice option. The party granted artists and intellectuals the privilege of making work-related visits to the West, for example, to retain their loyalty. But the party's concession was double-edged, since it compromised the intelligentsia in the eyes of the majority of East Germans, who could not venture beyond the Wall. The SED could also decapitate opposition movements at will by exporting troublesome dissenters to West Germany, which was eager to integrate East German opposition figures for the public relations victory. Finally, the exit

91 BArchB, DE1, 56285, Klopfer, "Persönliche Niederschrift über die Beratung der Wirtschaftskommission beim Politbüro am 9. Januar 1989," 10.1.89, p. 4.
92 Albert O. Hirschman, *Exit, Voice, and Loyalty: Responses to Decline in Firms, Organizations, and States* (Cambridge, Mass., 1981); Hirschman, "Exit, Voice, and the Fate of the German Democratic Republic: An Essay in Conceptual History," *World Politics* 45 (1993), pp. 173–202.

option sowed disunity among opponents of the regime by dividing those who believed the GDR could be reformed from those who thought any cooperation futile.

Some historians also invoke the Wall to explain why organized opposition emerged so late in the GDR compared to other Soviet bloc countries.[93] The categories of exit and voice, however, do not really explain what was exceptional about the GDR. It is unclear, for example, that the Wall made it any easier for the GDR to deport "troublemakers" than it was for Poland to expatriate dissenters or the USSR to oscillate between internal and external exile of its dissidents. In fact, applying Hirschman's scheme to the GDR's situation appears to imply that the SED's use of the exit option would only increase discontent: No matter how many dissidents were exiled, the SED's authoritarianism would have simply generated new dissent. Nor is the exit option the only explanation for disunity among East German dissenters; resistance movements have always been plagued by disagreement over the most appropriate means of expressing opposition to dictatorship.

In fact, the explanatory power of exit and voice as analytic categories is based on the faulty premise that the SED fully controlled the GDR's access to the West. After all, exit and voice were not completely split off from each other. The intrusion of a capitalist public sphere into the socialist state undercut the need for East Germans to publish their own criticism of the regime.[94] Thus, when underground publishing activity finally did emerge around 1986 – much later than the illegal circulation of commodities – it did so in part because the West German public sphere did not speak to specifically East German concerns. In contrast, the main source of uncoordinated resistance to SED rule in East Germany consisted of the petition system, which underwent a slow transformation from a suppressed

93 Most authors date organized opposition in the GDR to the establishment of the Environmental Library in Berlin in 1986. One could, however, make a case for the Berlin Appeal, a petition written by the cleric Rainer Eppelmann and the Old Communist Robert Havemann in 1982 calling for nuclear disarmament (Eppelmann, *Wendewege* [Bonn, 1992], pp. 213–15.) According to Stephan Bickhardt, the Stasi tracked 2,500 people in the late 1980s that it believed were involved in "resistance activities" (Stephan Bickhardt, "Die Entwicklung der DDR-Opposition in den achtziger Jahren," in *Die Enquete-Kommission "Aufarbeitung von Geschichte und Folgen der SED-Diktatur in Deutschland" im Deutschen Bundestag*, vol. 7: *Widerstand, Opposition, Revolution* [Baden-Baden, 1995], part 1, p. 477).
94 John Torpey notes that "the dearth of independent publishing reflected the availability to the GDR's dissidents of the ersatz public sphere of the Federal Republic." Torpey, *Intellectuals, Socialism, and Dissent*, p. 97. In passing, Torpey mentions another reason that merits further investigation. He contends that the commitment to socialism common among many East German intellectuals entailed a concomitant belief that political freedoms were derived from the economic organization of society. This, he argues, "was the most important ideological factor delaying the emergence in East Germany of a truly oppositional movement for 'bourgeois' civil rights comparable to Czechoslovakia's Charter 77 and similar organizations in the other Soviet bloc countries" (ibid., p. 6).

forum for airing individual criticism into a public and increasingly organized voice.

At the heart of this emerging East German public sphere lay economic concerns. On the one hand, East German newspapers began printing letters to the editor that were critical of the SED's economic management. The *Berliner Zeitung*, for example, opened its pages to complaints about the shortages of consumer goods in late 1988.[95] On the other hand, the incidence of collective letter writing sparked by economic grievances was on the rise. During the summer of 1989, for example, the residents of the Gittersee area of Dresden protested against the party's economic policy in a mass petition. Mittag had ordered the construction of a silicon plant in this suburb, which aroused concern because of the pollution Gittersee residents feared it would cause. Many residents had written individual petitions before the communal elections in May 1989, but to no effect. To amplify their voice, the protestors began coordinating their efforts under the aegis of the church, the only semiautonomous institution in the GDR. In September 1989 – two weeks before the Synod of the Association of Protestant Churches in the GDR was to meet for a conference – the Lutheran bishop of Saxony sent a mass petition with 579 signatures to Honecker, citing the East German laws that the factory would violate and urging the General Secretary to intervene personally against the project.[96] Two days later, a high-level government delegation traveled to Dresden to meet with the bishop and convince him to cease agitating against the factory. Not only did the bishop refuse, but he requested that all further communication be undertaken in written form.[97] Clearly the SED was no longer in a position to proscribe ideas with impunity.

Events in October, however, thrust the controversy over the factory in Dresden into the background. On 18 October 1989, Egon Krenz ousted Honecker and Mittag with the support of the Politburo. With Honecker gone, a stream of letters written by party members, professional

---

95 See *Berliner Zeitung*, 20.9.88; SAPMO-BA, DY30, Vorläufige SED 41853, Komitee der ABI, "Bericht über Ergebnisse der Kontrolle zur Versorgung," 21.9.88, p. 4. Apparently, the *Lausitzer Rundschau* in Cottbus also began printing critical letters in the late summer.

96 BArchB, DA5, 12391, Evangelisch-Lutheranische Superintendenturen Dresden Mitte, Nord und West, "Gemeinschaftliche Eingabe an den Herrn Staatsratsvorsitzenden der DDR," 5.6.89; Reichenberg, "Vermerk für Genossen E. Honecker," 14.6.89. On the role of the Protestant churches in the revolution, see Erhart Neubert, *Eine Protestantische Revolution* (Osnabrück, 1990); Besier, *Der SED-Staat und die Kirche*.

97 BArchB, DA5, 12391, Löffler, Nendel, and Witteck, "Information über eine Aussprache mit dem Landesbischof der Evangelisch-Lutheranische Kirche Sachsens, Herrn Dr. Hempel," 7.9.89. For an SED analysis of the shift in attitudes among church leaders, see SAPMO, DY30, IV 2/2.029/87, Abteilung Parteiorgane, "Information über Atkivitäten staatlicher Organe und der Nationalen Front zur Vertiefung des Vertrauensverhältnisses zwischen Staat und Kirchen in der DDR," 2.9.89.

organizations, and whole villages overwhelmed central and local officials, proffering advice and making demands on the new General Secretary.[98] Realizing that the party had lost control of the petition system, Krenz moved quickly to prevent the right to appeal from turning into a public forum for discussing the absence of due process. In one of his first actions as the new General Secretary of the SED, Krenz established clear administrative guidelines for processing petitions and solicited "proposals for a decree."[99]

But his measures came too late. Open letters that no longer respected the proscription against publication made it impossible to force the genie back into the bottle. Just before the collapse of the Wall, for example, the town of Großdeuben near Leipzig sent an open letter to the Ministry for Trade and Supply complaining that even though the SED leadership had changed, the standard of living in Großdeuben had not. "Where," the letter demanded, "are the assortments of cheese, lettuce, yogurt, delicacies, diet brands, juices, fruits, vegetables, and much more? It is hard to believe, but we cannot even get newspapers and magazines."[100] A few weeks later, the citizens of Berka vor dem Hainich noted "the fear of the population that it might lose its hard-earned money" and requested that "our currency system be made like that of other countries."[101] Struggling to keep up with the revolution's momentum and retain a shred of legitimacy, local and regional newspapers, such as the *Leipziger Volkszeitung*, began publishing letters critical of the regime.[102] From there, it was a very small step to run articles detailing the economic mismanagement, privilege, and corruption that characterized the regime. At the same time, local authorities, who were increasingly unable to cope with their administrative burdens during the revolution, began refusing to process the petitions, which only reinforced the trend toward airing complaints in the media.[103] Gone was the SED's muzzle over public expression.

The collapse of the Berlin Wall on 9 November 1989 added a new element to the mixture by lifting the last restrictions on reporting by the West German press. The underfunded and underdeveloped East German

---

98 See, for example, the petitions and letters to Krenz just after he deposed Honecker in SAPMO–BA, DY30, JIV 2/2.039/323, JIV 2/2.039/324, and JIV 2/2.039/325.

99 SAPMO–BA, DY30, JIV 2/3/4455, Sitzung des Sekretariats des Politbüros am 25.10.89, p. 4.

100 BArchB, DL1, 26395, open letter from Großdeuben, 3.11.89.

101 BArchB, DA5, 12391, "Offener Brief der Bürger von Berka vor dem Hainich," 23.11.89, with 326 signatures, p. 2.

102 As noted above, the process of turning newspapers into venues for debate had started in late 1988, when the newspaper *Berliner Zeitung* began to open its pages to public critique.

103 BArchB, DA5, 12400, Emmerich to Abteilung Eingaben, Sektor III, Staatsrat, 17.11.89.

public sphere could not compete with the money and experience of the West German print and broadcast media. Yet the extension of the West German public sphere to the GDR did not simply retard the development of organized East German resistance to SED rule. It quickly marginalized, then entirely supplanted, an emerging circulation of ideas and commodities based on new forms of social relations that were springing up in the wake of communism's collapse. By the parliamentary elections of 18 March 1990, when East Germans voted to replace the Ostmark with the Westmark, East Germans were reading the West German press and watching West German television, while East German journalists struggled to remain relevant.

The SED's attempt to repress the public sphere through the petition system found its ideological legitimation in the Marxist-Leninist critique of liberal democratic institutions as insufficiently democratic. By portraying the right to petition as an instrument of direct democracy, the SED could argue that it formed an important counterweight to representative democratic institutions, such as parliament. In fact, however, the petition embodied the party's authoritarian approach to political dialogue. True to its absolutist origins, the petition system aimed at preventing people with similar interests from organizing themselves, deflecting popular discontent by introducing an allegedly personal note into an era of large and impersonal bureaucracies, and collecting information on public opinion and bureaucratic behavior at odds with the party leadership's policies.

Ironically, however, the very same lack of legality from which the petition system derived its ideological legitimacy hobbled its effectiveness as an instrument of political control. The party's ability to intervene with impunity in the distribution of resources constituted the most important source of its political power. Without clear and binding legal guidelines that could guarantee the application of legal sanctions to administrators who abrogated those guidelines, however, the petition system could not function as a reliable instrument for neutralizing political discontent. In addition, the reduction of the complaints to a series of statistics that were used to support nearly any bureaucratic or personal rivalry diminished the value of the petitions as a mechanism for reporting on the stability of the regime. At the same time, the SED possessed numerous reporting systems, from the secret police to the various mass organizations, which inundated the party leadership with insufficiently analyzed opinion on the regime's stability.[104]

104 According to Hans Modrow, district party leaders had to contend with an excess of low-quality reports that "were not sufficiently analyzed" (interview, Modrow, Berlin, 16.4.96).

In contrast to the absolutist system, moreover, the East German petition system was also supposed to increase the GDR's economic efficiency. As Jürgen Habermas has pointed out, the relation between the economy and the evolution of the public sphere is an important feature of emerging capitalist regimes, a relation that makes use of the Enlightenment ideals of intellectual transparency to support the economic interests of the bourgeoisie.[105] In contrast, the East German communist party made use of appeals to social justice to justify its control over the economy, which it sought to close off from change. Yet the level of industrialization in the GDR, as well as its engagement in systemic competition with the capitalist West, created connections between intellectual and material modes of exchange. In contrast to its absolutist forebears, moreover, the GDR found it more difficult to control the circulation of commodities and ideas. Not only did the SED, replete with organizations and associations the party had formed to preempt and manage public discourse, face a far more fragmented society than absolutist rulers, but it suppressed a public sphere that made use of new instruments of communication, such as the mass media, that were unknown to absolutist regimes. The GDR's task was rendered even more complicated, since its administration of its own airwaves was constantly interrupted by the intrusions of its capitalist competitor. Thus, the economic development of the GDR produced a political structure that the petition system could address inadequately at best.

The greatest weakness of the petition system in the GDR, however, was its textuality. Like the absolutist regimes that were gradually displaced by the growth of the public sphere, the GDR found itself entangled in a communicative aporia, using speech to restrict speech. The SED presented the petition system as a free discussion between ruler and ruled. It sought, however, to stifle resistance through the asymmetrical distribution of power between ruler and ruled and transform the East German petitioner from the teller of unpleasant tales into a tattletale. Ironically, however, the petition system's counterfeit communicative structure offered petitioners a platform to question the authority of the rulers. The deterioration of the planned economy during the 1980s, and the ensuing shortages of consumer goods, moved petitioners to use the rhetorical structure of the petition system to their own advantage. By appealing over the head of the party to the socialist ideals to which the SED officially subscribed, East German petitioners transformed an instrument of their political repression into a forum for

105 Jürgen Habermas, *The Structural Transformation of the Public Sphere: An Inquiry into a Category of Bourgeois Society* (Cambridge, Mass., 1991).

their concerns. By making use of a political institution in unforeseen ways, East Germans were able to transform their "audience" with the SED into the "roundtables" of the revolution. Suddenly, the "managed society" had become unmanageable.[106]

---

106 Alf Lüdtke first used the phrase *"durchherrschte Gesellschaft"* in his essay "'Helden der Arbeit' – Mühen beim Arbeiten. Zur mißmutigen Loyalität von Industriearbeitern in der DDR," in Kaelble et al., *Sozialgeschichte der DDR*, p. 188.

Epilogue

Revisiting Reunification

Our people want the social protection, the security, and the guarantee of jobs and education from us and the department stores from the FRG.[1]

"It is not people's consciousness that determines their existence," wrote Marx, "but their social existence that determines their consciousness."[2] This book has argued both with Marx that the material reality of "real-existing socialism" determined East German political culture, and against Marx that communist ideology gave East German material reality its shape. By insisting that ideas have an existence of their own, it has tried to show that the GDR collapsed for the same reasons the SED constructed it. To illustrate this point, it has traced East German history under Honecker by analyzing the economic function and cultural meaning of that most mysterious and impersonal of modern technologies – money.

By eliminating money as an agent of economic exchange, East German communists erroneously believed they could eliminate the economic scarcity and social injustice generated by capitalism and replace it with economic abundance and social harmony. Without money, the planned economy would abolish commodity fetishism, stamp out social hierarchies based on the acquisition of material goods, do away with the inequitable distribution of wealth, and eradicate economic and therefore political constraints on human freedom. This virtually moneyless society, organized around an allegedly rational allocation of resources, would shield East Germans from the vagaries of market forces, ensuring full employment, creating economic

---

1 Politburo member Harry Tisch (BArchB, DE1, 56285, "Arbeitsniederschrift über eine Beratung beim Generalsekretär," 6.9.88, p. 20).
2 My translation of Marx, *Zur Kritik der politischen Ökonomie*, p. 9 (Karl Marx, *A Contribution to the Critique of Political Economy*, in *Karl Marx and Friedrich Engels: Collected Works*, vol. 29 [Moscow, 1977], p. 263).

321

plenty through nonexploitative production relations, and fulfilling the material and spiritual needs of all of its citizens. Despite the SED's utopian aspirations, however, the partial elimination of money failed to free East Germans from economic need and social want. Instead, economic planning resulted in stagnating productivity, infrequent innovation, diminished efficiency, chronic waste, and frequent shortages, while Honecker's subordination of economics to politics and Mittag's unscrupulous frugality squandered what potential for growth remained.

As crucial as the shortcomings of economic planning were, however, the GDR did not fail in an absolute sense. Its economic decline was not comparable to the breakdowns that affected communist regimes in the developing world, such as the return to subsistence farming in Cambodia, the famine in Ethiopia, or the economic collapse in North Korea.[3] Nor was the tangible deterioration of living standards under Honecker as severe as the German experience during the Great Depression. And although the GDR became more dangerously dependent on the capitalist West than other Soviet-style regimes during the 1970s, it did not default on its debts, as did Poland and Romania.

Rather, the GDR failed in a relative sense because its actual performance matched neither the SED's exaggerated claims nor West German accomplishments. Like other communist regimes, the GDR collapsed because the party's loud insistence on the planned economy's unrivaled achievements became increasingly impossible to reconcile with the actual experience of material privation.[4] In fact, the SED's economic policies generated the very kinds of social inequities based on material and spiritual want for which it criticized the West. Under Honecker, the party even contributed to the commodification of East German life by adopting Western models of consumption and expanding the Intershops. Perhaps most paradoxically, socialist money, which was supposed to act as a conduit for social justice, had become a source of shortage and a symbol of disenfranchisement. By the 1980s, moreover, the glaring incommensurability between the SED's aims and its accomplishments had destroyed communist ideology as a political force. The equation of anticapitalism with antifascism that had proven particularly disabling to generations of older Germans was unable to convince younger Germans who had no direct experience of Nazi rule that economic privation was ennobling. To bolster its grip on power, the party was

3 Daniel Chirot, "What Happened in Eastern Europe in 1989," in Vladimir Tismaneanu (ed.), *The Revolutions of 1989* (London and New York, 1999), pp. 19–50, places the economic weakness of European communism in useful perspective.
4 Tismaneanu, *Reinventing Politics*, pp. 134–41.

increasingly forced to rely on the tools of its capitalist rivals, which only intensified the discrepancy between its daily recitation of socialist ideals and the reality of its political interests. Similar combinations of tangible economic decline and ideological hypocrisy helped delegitimize communism throughout the East.

What distinguished the GDR from other Soviet-style regimes was its peculiar status as a socialist state forced to compete in a divided national space with a powerful capitalist foe. When compared to the magnitude of West German successes, the relative failures of the East German planned economy loomed even larger. In real terms, the East German experience of economic shortage was certainly less acute than the Polish or Romanian experience. But the point of reference for East Germans was not Eastern Europe, but West Germany. As a result, the SED had to contend with an economic morass of its own making, as well as widespread rumors and televised reports of a vastly superior West German economy. The regime's persistently mendacious approach to the GDR's failures and the FRG's successes, however, delegitimized the socialist state while solidifying popular orientation toward West German society. The SED had not simply exhausted the sources of its political legitimacy. It had also created the material conditions for its own demise.

Under Honecker's leadership, the SED tried to consolidate its power by adopting a new approach to socialist consumerism. By trying to provide East Germans with modern residential housing and a continuous supply of quality consumer goods, Honecker sought to placate a recalcitrant population. Because the East German economy could not produce many of the most desirable commodities, however, the GDR was forced to import them in large quantities from the capitalist West. To finance these imports, the GDR borrowed money from its capitalist rivals. Meanwhile, the explosion in prices for natural resources during the 1970s, and for oil in particular, placed increasing burdens on East German productive capacities. In addition, the lack of technological innovation, which was rooted in the planned economy's denigration of money, increased the GDR's dependence on the West for a variety of capital and consumer goods.

Against the advice of his aides, Honecker continued to compensate for his massive social expenditures by expanding trade with the West. Rather than reducing the scope of his program or seeking reform from within, Honecker delegated the impossible task of continuing to import Western commodities without accruing more debt to his Economic Secretary, Günter Mittag. To reconcile Honecker's incompatible policy imperatives, Mittag monetized the planned economy, introducing the logic of the profit motive to enhance productivity and generate savings. Unable to reduce social expenditures, Mittag economized in the production sphere, starving East Germany's industrial base of much-needed capital, substituting energy sources, and selling off East German assets on Western markets. Between his parsimony and a large infusion of West German financial assistance, Mittag kept the GDR's creditors at bay for several years.

The long-term cost of Mittag's policies, however, overshadowed their short-term benefits. His narrow focus on debt reduction undermined the GDR's prospects for future economic growth. Nor did Mittag's frugality offer any relief to East German producers or consumers; instead, it intensified the shortages afflicting the planned economy. In addition, his attempt to tighten central control over available resources to maximize East German exports to the West created an administrative disarray that ultimately weakened the ability of local party officials to redress those shortages.

The increasingly frequent and severe shortages of consumer goods, moreover, undermined the planned economy materially and ideologically. The party's politically motivated underproduction of key consumer goods, such as cars, coupled with the deterioration of East German capital stock, could not keep pace with real consumer demand. Worse still, consumer expectations had been raised by the SED's irresponsible promises and exaggerated by tales of West German consumer plenty. By the 1980s, popular disappointment with the SED's consumer policies was transformed into political disaffection and economic disloyalty, as more and more East Germans turned to the burgeoning black market for consumer and producer goods – a development that had ironically been encouraged by the SED's own policies.

The growth of the black market, which operated according to a value system in contradiction to socialist ideals of exchange, posed an insurmountable challenge to the regime. On the one hand, the black market circumscribed the SED's ability to determine economic behavior. Growing numbers of East Germans were engaged in transactions that circumvented the socialist state, while the state was forced to tolerate this behavior because it helped overcome otherwise insuperable gaps in the supply of goods and services. On the other hand, the shadow economy undermined the value of the East German mark, itself a key instrument of state control over the economy. The black market employed alternate media of exchange, from social connections to barterable goods and Western money, all of which competed directly with socialist ideals and socialist money. The principles embodied by these illegal forms of currency contradicted the ideal of consumer egalitarianism advanced by the SED.

By the 1980s, West German money had displaced socialist money as a medium of exchange and store of value in many sectors of the economy. The flourishing black market, which thrived on the actual preferences of East Germans, accelerated the very process of social differentiation and materialism that the SED had devoted itself to eradicating, dividing those who had access to capitalist money from those who did not and engendering avarice, envy, and the desire for social status where equality and solidarity should have reigned. Through its own actions, the East German dictatorship had weakened an important symbol of its rule, socialist money, and fostered the growth of economic behavior in conflict with the party's professed ideals.

Most devastating, however, was the party's own involvement in capitalist trade. Honecker's decision to enlarge the scope of the Intershops opened up a large source of hard-currency revenue for the cash-starved GDR. Although it ostensibly served the socialist order, Alexander Schalck-Golodkowski's aggressive expansion of his hard-currency imperium, with its emphasis on cost accounting and profits, soon supplanted economic planning in many sectors. Schalck himself began acting as a broker of capital to East German industry, while the de facto legalization of Western currency in 1979 and the state sale of Western commodities encouraged consumers to behave in an antisocialist manner. Meanwhile, the expansion of the Intershops unleashed the twin demons of Western consumerism and national unity. The lure of superior capitalist consumer goods furthered a fixation on the world beyond the Wall while creating social divisions at home. These social divisions posed a serious threat to the SED's legitimacy because they weakened traditional class-based identities and because they could not be rationalized away by Marxist-Leninist ideology. In all of these ways, the socialist state's official sanction of Western money and merchandise devalued the currency of socialism in the eyes of the population.

As the citizens' petitions disclose, East German anger over these social divisions and the privileges underpinning them took an aggressive turn in the late 1980s. Frustration with the privilege and corruption created by the shortages peaked just as the capacity of the socialist state to neutralize discontent diminished. The party leadership was aware of the growing inclination of the populace to link economic performance to its moral claim to political leadership, but was unable to defuse the threat to its power. Honecker's consumer policies illustrate the failure of East German Marxism-Leninism to provide a politically stable solution to the challenge of "consumer sovereignty." The SED's inability to convince East Germans that the experience of shortage was ennobling left the party without a compelling argument against the intrusion of Western commercialism. The emergence of the petitions as a political opportunity sphere, moreover, was critical to the development of the East German revolution, just as their gradual marginal-ization by the West German media helped pave the way for German uni-fication. By 1989, the Ostmark's weak purchasing power had become both a target of popular complaint and a vehicle for the unification of the two German states. In both cases, the softness of socialist money yielded to the firmness of the West German mark.

Even as East Germans struggled to liberate themselves from the SED, however, the legacy of socialism continued to shape their perceptions. Forty years of communist rhetoric and the everyday experience of real-existing socialism, rather than any "natural" preference for capitalism, convinced East Germans to abdicate their monetary – and therefore political – sovereignty and embrace West German money and the political institutions that accom-panied it. Money, the object of the SED's utopian passions, unmade the GDR and then unified Germany.

Next to the Stasi, the East German mark was one of the most impor-tant targets of popular protest during 1989. The weakness of the socialist currency served as a compelling metaphor for all that was wrong with the GDR, providing demonstrators with an excellent opportunity to express their anger at the SED's hypocrisy and incompetence. Yet East Germans did not articulate their outrage at the party's arbitrary and inept rule in the categories of Western liberalism. Instead, the SED's attempt to subordinate economy to society had conditioned East Germans to frame economic prob-lems in moral terms. The lingering residue of Marxist-Leninist ideology was evident during the popular protests that began in the late summer of 1989. Triggered by Hungary's decision to open its border to the West, these mass demonstrations produced many slogans memorable for their epigrammatic criticisms of the communist regime.[5] At the heart of this abbreviated form lay an angry repudiation of communist clichés touting economic prosperity and social solidarity behind which the SED had concealed its shortcom-ings for forty years. Infuriated by the discrepancy between what the com-munist party preached and what it practiced, East German demonstrators denounced the regime's platitudes, inscribing parodies of socialist maxims

---

5 The Hungarian government took down the barbed-wire fence on its frontier with Austria on 2 May. By late August, some 150,000 East Germans had poured into Hungary in the hopes that the government would open the border. On 11 September, the Hungarian government opened its border with Austria, which "altered the balance of power between the regime and the population" (Hertle, *Der Fall der Mauer*, p. 109). For more on the Hungarian border, see ibid., pp. 91–109; Manfred Görtemaker, *Unifying Germany 1989–1990* (New York, 1994), pp. 57–71; Jarausch, *The Rush to Unity*, pp. 15–30; Maier, *Dissolution*, pp. 123–31; Philip Zelikow and Condoleeza Rice, *Germany Unified and Europe Transformed: A Study in Statecraft* (Cambridge, Mass., 1995), pp. 67–8.

on their own revolutionary posters. This revolutionary refrain derived its moral force from the very same authority on which the SED staked its own claim to legitimacy: the vision of social equality that animates the writings of Karl Marx. The protestors transformed the famous final sentence of *The Communist Manifesto*, for example, into a more pointed expression of that work's egalitarian spirit: "Privileged of the world, eliminate yourselves!" At the same time, they demanded fulfillment of the basic goal of Marxism – the right of workers to enjoy the fruits of their labor – in such catchphrases as "Hard money for hard work."[6] The revolutionaries also took aim at rumors of corruption among the ruling elite. Angered by allegations that Politburo members had embezzled West German money, for example, demonstrators in Leipzig sang "Where has all the hard currency gone?" to the tune of the American protest song "Where have all the flowers gone?"[7] By appealing to the ethical construction of economic life used by the party to legitimate its power, East German demonstrators sought to impeach the SED's authority.

Other slogans linked politics more directly to the economy, using money as shorthand for the shortcomings of "real-existing" socialism. As one of the more pithy mottoes put it, "Marx on the currency – Muck in the economy."[8] By equating Marx with material failure, the play on words asserted a causal link between Marxist(-Leninist) ideology and the GDR's economic woes, with money relating the theory to the practice of economic planning. Where the party had adorned the 100-Ostmark note with Marx's austere visage to confer moral authority on its control over the economy, the play on words coined in the streets suggested that the SED's willingness to back East German marks with Karl Marx was the cause of the country's economic decline. On a deeper level, the slogan sought to refute the inductive reasoning employed by the party to structure the economy. The pun embedded in the slogan challenged the legitimacy of an economic order whose ex ante elevation of moral over economic concerns paradoxically required political coercion to function, yet was unable to deliver the material well-being it promised.

In keeping with its authoritarian instincts, the SED's initial response to the voice of the revolution was to silence it. By late September, however, it had become clear that the protestors were no longer intimidated by beatings and arrests. By October, SED leaders were confronted with a choice between

---

6 Ewald Lang, *Wendehals und Stasilaus. Demo-Sprüche aus der DDR* (Munich, 1990), p. 164.
7 Timothy Garton Ash, *The Magic Lantern: The Revolution of '89 Witnessed in Warsaw, Budapest, Berlin and Prague* (New York, 1993), p. 70.
8 "Marx auf der Währung, Murks in der Wirtschaft," in mdv transparent (ed.), *"Wir sind das Volk." Aufbruch '89, Teil 1: Die Bewegung. September/Oktober 1989* (Halle and Leipzig, 1990), title page.

staging a massacre to quell the uprising (the so-called Chinese solution, referring to the slaughter of demonstrators in Tiananmen Square on 4 June 1989) and foreswearing violence. When Honecker signaled his readiness to deploy tanks against demonstrators in Leipzig on 9 October, his colleagues rebelled and deposed him.[9] Casting about for ways to stave off the dramatic decline in its political significance, the new leadership under Krenz quickly conceded the need for economic reform. Predictably, Schalck argued for remonetizing the economy to reinvigorate it.[10]

Struggling to counter the linguistic spontaneity of the street, Honecker's successors drew upon familiar associations of social justice with finance. To preempt calls for unification with West Germany, for example, the SED asked whether monetary union would mean "Equity for all or equities for a few?"[11] Given the failures of the planned economy, however, such word games made Krenz sound like Polonius, dispensing platitudes in a crisis.

The new leadership's incompetence and continued commitment to Marxism–Leninism immediately discredited it with East Germans. During October and November, Honecker's successors tried to disperse the demonstrators by easing travel restrictions, the very issue that was fueling the protests. Rather than staving off the party's loss of political relevance, however, Krenz's limited concessions only accentuated the major contradictions of the second German dictatorship – the lack of political liberty and economic prosperity – without pointing toward their resolution. But even as the SED was lurching toward a liberalism that would end with the dismantling of the Berlin Wall, millions of East Germans were insisting that the state had a moral obligation to intervene against market forces to preserve social solidarity. Despite their vehement rejection of communism, East Germans had come to accept some of the most illiberal features of economic planning.[12]

From the start, East German protestors demanded that the state remove the financial as well as the political obstacles to travel, echoing the SED's

---

9 Görtemaker, *Unifying Germany*, pp. 72–82; Hertle, *Der Fall der Mauer*, pp. 124–32; Jarausch, *The Rush to Unity*, pp. 53–9; Maier, *Dissolution*, pp. 143–7, 153–8.

10 BArchB, DN10, 3329, "Fernsehdiskussion AHA-aktuell: Offen gefragt – öffentlich geantwortet," 30.10.89, p. 10. Manfred von Ardenne, an inventor and economic advisor to Ulbricht, also demanded "the gradual return to money as a measure for achievement, for economic success or failure" – a call that resonated with the SED rank-and-file (SAPMO-BA, DY30, IV 2/2.039/325, von Ardenne to Krenz, 17.10.89, p. 2, and Gewerkschaftsgruppe KBC/SL-MAK des Forschungsinstituts für medizinische Diagnostik Dresden to Krenz, 23.10.89, p. 11).

11 "*Werte für alle oder Wertpapiere für wenige?*" (SAPMO-BA, DY30, JIV 2/2A/3262, Abteilung Propaganda, Vorlage "Themen für die Parteipresse," 22.11.89, p. 3).

12 For more on the influence of East German political culture on the revolution and its outcome, see Jonathan R. Zatlin, "Hard Marks and Soft Revolutionaries: The Economics of Entitlement and the Debate over German Unification, November 9, 1989–March 18, 1990," *German Politics and Society* 33 (Fall 1994), pp. 57–84.

claim that political liberty is contingent on economic freedom.[13] The SED had long sought to vitiate the attraction West German affluence held for East Germans by arguing that the financial inequalities characteristic of market economies resulted in a kind of economic unfreedom that rendered political freedoms meaningless. Under the shadow of the Wall, party officials eagerly pointed out that the political right to travel wherever one desires is practically rescinded if one does not possess enough money to take the trip.[14] But holding the communist state responsible for the gap in purchasing power between the East and West German marks was not merely a popular attempt to turn the SED's own arguments against it. The demand that the GDR subsidize travel to the FRG reveals the extent to which East Germans had accepted the premise that the state had a moral obligation to shield its citizens from the market and provide them with the financial means to exercise their legal rights. Popular experience with the GDR's fragmented monetary regime, moreover, had taught East Germans to associate basic needs with socialist money and "immoral" desires with West German money – and travel to the West was the avatar of forbidden desire.

In conversation with the West German liberal leader Wolfgang Mischnick on 25 October, Krenz acknowledged that the SED's authority was rapidly disintegrating. The party had to make significant concessions on the travel issue, he said, because "we want to avoid the impression that it is not a real solution."[15] On 6 November, the SED unveiled legislation that granted East Germans the right to travel to the West for the first time. But the party found it impossible to renounce its penchant for legalistic manipulation. To undercut the substance of its concession, the SED made obtaining the necessary travel documents subject to bureaucratic review, which would permit politically motivated delays. Even more importantly, the legislation explicitly rebuffed popular demands that the state subsidize East German tourism.[16] To its credit, the party leadership's refusal to bankroll East German jaunts to the West was grounded less in ideological than in financial concerns. After all, sponsoring private trips represented a significant financial burden,

13 Even reform communists agreed that the government should help East Germans realize their right to travel freely by providing them with DM 500 a year (Bohlener Treffen, "Für eine Vereinigte Linke," 13.10.89, in Zeno and Sabine Zimmerling [eds.], *Neue Chronik DDR*, Folge 1 [Berlin, 1990], p. 120).
14 See, for example, Klaus Gebauer and Hermann Wirsig et al. (eds.), *Studien- und Seminarhinweise für Teilnehmer und Propagandisten der Seminare zur politischen Ökonomie des Sozialismus und der ökonomischen Strategie der SED* (East Berlin, 1989), pp. 196–205, 208.
15 SAPMO-BA, DY30, IV 2/2.039/328, "Niederschrift über das Gespräch des Generalsekretärs des ZK der SED und Vorsitzenden des Staatsrates der DDR, Genossen Egon Krenz, mit dem Vorsitzenden der FDP-Fraktion im Bundestag, Wolfgang Mischnick, am 25. Oktober 1989," p. 20.
16 *Neues Deutschland*, 8.11.89; *Berliner Zeitung*, 6.11.89, in Zimmerling, *Neue Chronik*, Folge 1, p. 76.

which would have exacerbated the GDR's shortage of hard currency at a time when the SED's financial ineptitude was fueling political unrest. Krenz had come to power on a platform of economic prudence; in contrast to Honecker, he did not have the power to confuse economics with politics.

However fiscally responsible it might have been, the legislation's explicit exclusion of state subsidies was politically unpopular. The SED's refusal to take responsibility for the East German mark's lack of purchasing power unleashed a storm of protest. Large demonstrations erupted throughout the country; in Leipzig alone, some 500,000 marched against the new law.[17] Even loyal communists interpreted the paragraphs ruling out government subsidies for travel as an unnecessary slap in the face.[18] The next day, the forty-four member Council of Ministers publicly conceded that the proposed travel law was unsatisfactory and collectively resigned. On 8 November, the entire Politburo stepped down. Scrambling to make up for lost ground, a reconstituted Politburo offered yet another version of the travel law on 9 November. But SED leaders were unused to dealing with a media they did not control, and their garbled presentation of the revised regulations inadvertently brought down the Wall.[19] Krenz's ill-advised attempt to seize the political initiative had completely backfired, reinforcing instead the impression that the SED was incapable of meaningful reform while squandering the party's only real asset – the Berlin Wall – without receiving anything in return.

The collapse of the Wall removed the political obstacles to individual mobility, and with them the SED's ability to determine the revolution's direction. But the financial hurdles remained. From the protestors' perspective, the Ostmark was similar to the Wall in that its lack of convertibility and purchasing power represented yet another legacy of communist rule: an insuperable barrier to the satisfaction of pent-up consumer demand. From a liberal economic perspective, the Ostmark's weakness reflected the GDR's low productivity and the continued destruction of value by inefficient and wasteful enterprises. But the Ostmark also possessed advantages. With its weakness came a competitive advantage on international markets, since it effectively devalued East German labor costs on a comparative basis.

17 *Leipziger Volkszeitung*, 7.11.89.
18 See, for example, the article by Hans-Joachim Heintze, Institut für internationale Studien, and the interview with Claus-Dieter Knöfler, a member of the People's Parliament, in *Leipziger Volkszeitung*, 9.11.89.
19 Görtemaker, *Unifying Germany*, pp. 86–94; Hertle, *Der Fall der Mauer*, pp. 138–43; Jarausch, *The Rush to Unity*, pp. 22–3; Maier, *Dissolution*, pp. 160–3; Zelikow and Rice, *Germany Unified*, pp. 98–101.

For East Germans longing for the chance to see the forbidden fruits of capitalism firsthand, however, the socialist currency's lack of heft was a moral, not a financial, matter. As demand for West German marks soared, the informal exchange rate plummeted.[20] Calls for the state to compensate for the difference in value between the two currencies multiplied. A resident of Zwickau, for example, condemned the rate, warning that "we will not put up with an exchange rate of 1:10."[21] A man from a small town in Thuringia went further, introducing an egalitarian moment into the debate. "Western money for all citizens of the GDR or for none," he demanded. "Unlimited travel freedom for all GDR citizens to capitalist and socialist countries at affordable prices."[22] In addition to this grassroots pressure, leaders of the anticommunist opposition sought to coax the SED into creating an entitlement. Bärbel Bohley, one of the most prominent civil rights activists, reproached the SED with the observation that the legislation "should have contained a regulation on hard currency."[23] Ironically, the demands for state support and social equality were entirely in keeping with communist ideals and practices.

During the three weeks immediately after the Wall had been breached, the SED persisted doggedly in its rejection of public compensation for private travel. The party press warned against the "illusion that one decree will suffice to secure the unlimited financial means for travel," insisted on the "negative consequences of traveling," and compared exchanging money for travel to the West to throwing "hard-earned money into the fire."[24] In the meantime, the new government, which had been reorganized under the leadership of Dresden party chief Hans Modrow, was fighting a rearguard battle to rebuild the Wall by strengthening the border. It added more Stasi agents to crossing points to beef up border security, prevented foreigners from purchasing a variety of East German products, and slapped tariffs on selected consumer imports.[25] Without the threat of political violence

---

20 West German merchants, recognizing a potential windfall in the asymmetry between East German demand and West German supply, were willing to act as if the Ostmark were convertible. On 11 November, for example, the West Berlin department store C&A began accepting payment in Ostmark at a 10:1 rate, which had the unintended consequence of stabilizing the chaotic market for the Ostmark (mdv transparent [ed.], *"Wir sind das Volk." Hoffnung '89, Teil 2: Die Bewegung, Oktober/November 1989* [Halle and Leipzig, 1990], p. 90).

21 SAPMO-BA, DY16, Vorläufige 2751, Dumke, "Kurzbericht über die Teilnahme an einer Beratung des Kreisverbandes Zwickau-Land am 13.11.1989," 14.11.89, p. 5.

22 SAPMO-BA, DY16, Vorläufige 2755, letter from Eberhard W. Greiz, no date, p. 1.

23 *Berliner Zeitung*, 25/26.11.89, cited in mdv transparent (ed.), *"Wir sind das Volk." Ungeduld '89, Teil 3* (Halle and Leipzig, 1990), p. 49.

24 *Leipziger Volkszeitung*, 2.11.89, 23.11.89, and 24.11.89.

25 SAPMO-BA, DY30, JIV 2/2A//3262, Modrow, "Maßnahmen zur Abwehr von negativen Auswirkungen des Reiseverkehrs," 21.11.89, pp. 1–4, 6.

symbolized by the Wall, however, these measures hardly changed the basic fact that the SED no longer controlled the passage of people, products, and ideas between the two Germanys.

The sustained intensity of public outrage finally caused the SED to relent. On 30 November, the party introduced a new law that retroactively legalized the fall of the Wall and gave way on the financial issue. The new provisions guaranteed every East German the right to obtain a modest sum of West German marks at a fixed rate subsidized by the state. To finance the measure, however, the GDR was forced to turn to the Federal Republic, which agreed to furnish the DM 3.8 billion required to fund East German trips to West Germany in return for a commitment to democratic reform.[26] In keeping with the pattern established by Honecker, the GDR traded political liberalization for West German money.[27]

The SED's capitulation represents an important and often overlooked turning point in the revolution, understandably overshadowed by the drama attending the SED's unintentional dismantling of the Wall.[28] But as then–Bundesbank Vice President Helmut Schlesinger was to observe years later, "the travel regulation was the precursor of currency union," which was itself the prelude to unification.[29] The SED's agreement with the Kohl government pegged the Ostmark to the D-Mark at a fixed rate of 3:1. That was far better than the black market rate, but it was hardly the 1:1 parity on which the SED had publicly insisted since 1951. More importantly, it accurately reflected the gap in aggregate productivity between the two states.[30] In any

---

26 Although the GDR initially proposed the *Valutamark* rate of 4.4:1, the final regulation guaranteed adults DM 200 and children DM 100 a year at a rate of 3:1 (SAPMO-BA, DY30, IV 2/2.039/328, "Konzeption für ein Gespräch zwischen dem Generalsekretär des ZK der SED und Vorsitzenden des Staatsrates der DDR, Genossen Egon Krenz, und dem Bundeskanzler der BRD, Helmut Kohl," no date, pp. 40–6; BArchB, DN10, 2285, Staatsbank der DDR, "Information über die Entwicklung des Erwerbs von DM durch Bürger der DDR," 8.1.90, p. 2).

27 The Kohl government welcomed the arrangement because it gave the FRG political influence over the SED, permitted elimination of the so-called welcoming money (*Begrüßungsged*) extended to East Germans, and would result in a windfall for West German merchants, thereby expanding the state's tax revenue and securing a key constituency for the ruling coalition.

28 Despite his otherwise exhaustive praise for the Kohl government, Grosser has little to say about the arrangement (Grosser, *Das Wagnis*, p. 135). Neither do the more critical Maier or Hertle (Maier, *Dissolution*, pp. 161–95; Hertle, *Der Fall der Mauer*, pp. 159–60).

29 Interview, Helmut Schlesinger, Bundesbank Vice President (1980–91), President (1991–3), Berlin, 23.1.96. This was also the perception of the Round Table (Hoover Institution Archives, German Subject Collection, *Protokolle der Beratungen des Runden Tisch*, session 11, 5.2.90, Vorlage 11/22).

30 At the time, most Western analysts believed East German productivity and living standards were under half of West German levels (Deutsche Bundesbank [ed.], "Die Wirtschaftslage in der Bundesrepublik Deutschland im Herbst 1989," in Deutsche Bundesbank [ed.], *Monatsbericht der Deutschen Bundesbank* [Frankfurt/Main, December 1989], p. 15; "Reform der Wirtschaftsordnung in der DDR und die Aufgaben der Bundesrepublik," *Wochenbericht der DIW* 6 [1990]; *Handelsblatt*, 8.2.90; Helmut Schlesinger, *Das Handelsblatt*, 14.1.90; interview, Thilo Sarrazin, Director, National Currency Affairs

event, the fixed rate, together with the subsidy, mortgaged the GDR's fiscal future to West German political fortunes.

In deciding what should become of the GDR, however, the popular confusion of money with wealth turned out to be more important – and for East Germans more fateful – than the legacy of paternalism. Communist monetary theory, which held that money was the embodied form of labor, and communist economic policy, which had encouraged an equation between West German marks and consumer durable goods through its use of the Intershops and tolerance of black markets, had convinced East Germans that West German paper and coins not only had the power to command real resources but were in fact equivalent to wealth. In the chaotic aftermath of the Wall's collapse, this fundamental misapprehension about the meaning of money increasingly led East Germans to view a currency union with the FRG as the best solution to the challenges facing the GDR.

With West German assistance, the SED was able to stabilize the movement of capital, but neither state was prepared for the restoration of labor mobility. As Krenz confessed to a West German interlocutor, 9 November had unleashed "a return to circumstances before 1961," when some 3.5 million East Germans fled the political repression and economic mismanagement of communist rule for the relative safety and prosperity of the FRG.[31] Constructed under Honecker's supervision, the Wall had put an end to the politically embarrassing spectacle of East Germans "voting with their feet" against communism and to the labor exodus that seriously disrupted the East German economy. In the intervening years, however, Honecker had done little to create reasons for people to stay. During the revolutionary months of 1989, some 343,854 people deserted the GDR for West Germany. The

[Referat VII A1], Department for German–German Relations, West German Finance Ministry [1989–90], Berlin Senator for Finance [2002–present], Mainz, 13.6.96; Bryson and Melzer, *The End of the East German Economy*, p. 99). Later calculations put East German productivity at some 30 percent (George Akerlof, Andrew K. Rose, Janet L. Yellen, Helga Hessenius, Rudiger Dornbusch, and Manuel Guitian, "East Germany in from the Cold: The Economic Aftermath of Currency Union," *Brookings Papers on Economic Activity* 1 [1991], pp. 5–6; Rudiger Dornbusch, Holger Wolf, and Lewis Alexander, "Economic Transition in Eastern Germany," *Brookings Papers on Economic Activity* 1 [1992], p. 245; A. J. Hughes Hallett and Yue Ma, "East Germany, West Germany, and Their Mezzogiorno Problem: A Parable for European Economic Integration," *Economic Journal* 103 [March 1993], p. 417; Joachim Ragnitz, "Lagging Productivity in the East German Economy: Obstacles to Fast Convergence," in Michael Dauderstädt and Lothar Witte [eds.], *Cohesive Growth in the Enlarging Euroland* [Bonn, 2001], p. 94).

31 SAPMO-BA, DY30, JIV 2/2A/3262, "Bericht über das Gespräch mit dem Bundesminister für besondere Aufgaben und Chef des Bundeskanzleramtes der BRD, Rudolf Seiters, am 20. November 1989 in Berlin," 21.11.89, p. 16; Corey Ross, "Before the Wall: East Germans, Communist Authority, and the Mass Exodus to the West," *Historical Journal* 45:2 (2002), pp. 459–60; Kleßmann, *Zwei Staaten, eine Nation*, p. 558. The FRG's refusal to recognize the GDR and its treatment of East Germans as West German citizens facilitated migration.

pace of migration picked up in January 1990, when some 2,000 people were abandoning the GDR every day. This mass defection came as a political shock to both German governments, while the labor exodus once again threatened the East German economy. Within a short period of time, the GDR lost nearly 2.5 percent of its workforce, and most of these losses were concentrated in key economic sectors, including medicine, transportation, and construction. As in the 1950s, moreover, a disproportionate number of the people who packed up and left were young. Not only did they take with them the GDR's future, but they left behind an aging population, which further undermined the prospects for economic growth and stimulated more emigration.[32]

These East German refugees were not simply lured away by the wage differential between the GDR and FRG; they were also deserting the GDR. The possibility of a run on the Ostmark, the size of the foreign debt, and the SED's ambiguous commitment to democratic reform raised serious questions about the GDR's survival as an independent political entity. Even before the Wall collapsed, Krenz's advisors had warned that the West German mark was driving the Ostmark out of circulation.[33] After 9 November, however, the asymmetry between East German consumer demand and West German supply provoked a crisis of confidence in the Ostmark, no doubt intensified by memories of the two currency collapses in recent German history. Like many petitions sent to officials in November and December, an open letter from 326 residents of Berka vor dem Hainich emphasized "the population's fear of losing its hard-earned money."[34] In addition to their concern that the Ostmark might become worthless, many East Germans were disturbed by the social implications of the influx of D-Marks. One politician in Leipzig, for example, relayed popular fears that "social tensions between those who possess DM and those who do not will increase. Hard work, ethical values, and morality will fall victim to speculation in DM and corruption by ordinary people. Young people will continue to leave our country."[35] From this perspective, the only solution was to ensure social solidarity by importing the Deutsche Mark.

---

32 *Leipziger Volkszeitung*, 18.1.90 and 2.2.90; *Berliner Zeitung*, 6/7.1.90, in Zimmerling, *Neue Chronik DDR*, Folge 4/5, p. 31; Bryson and Melzer, *The End of the East German Economy*, p. 86. Although East Germans were speaking of unification just days after the Wall had been breached, it took the Kohl government three weeks to respond to events – and even then Kohl's "Ten Points" lagged behind the revolution's dynamic (Grosser, *Das Wagnis*, pp. 136–7; Stephen F. Szabo, *The Diplomacy of German Unification* [New York, 1992], pp. 38–40; Zelikow and Rice, *Germany Unified*, pp. 118–25).
33 BArchB, DN1 VS 13/90, Nr. 6, Nickel and Kaminsky, "Einschätzung," 26.10.89, p. 15.
34 BArchB, DA5, 12391, "Offener Brief der Bürger von Berka vor dem Hainich," 23.11.89, p. 2.
35 SAPMO-BA, DY16, Vorläufige 2764, Jahn, Stadtbezirksverband Leipzig-Nordost, 20.12.89, p. 1. See also the official representations of popular complaints in SAPMO-BA, DY30, IV 2/2.039/321, "Hinweise über die Reaktion der Bevölkerung," 24.11.89.

Nor did the magnitude of the GDR's financial obligations to the West assuage popular fears about the GDR's economic future. In an attempt to shore up the SED's credibility, the new leadership revealed in November that the GDR had accumulated financial liabilities to the West totaling DM 38.5 billion.[36] Ironically, Krenz hoped this disclosure would underscore his break with the SED's secretive past, but it only succeeded in passing Mittag's fraudulent accounting into the public record. As Chapter 3 argued, the announcement dramatically overstated the GDR's actual debt, which at DM 19.89 billion was only half of Mittag's figure. In fact, the East German economy was in better shape than Mittag's statistical ruse let on. Neither the inflated nor the actual debt levels were high enough to alarm the country's creditors. Despite work stoppages due to the ongoing demonstrations, moreover, exports were up. According to Doris Cornelsen, one of the most astute West German observers of the GDR, talk that the GDR might default was "nonsense" because the "GDR's debts are in no way immense."[37] But the damage had already been done; many East Germans were convinced that the GDR would never recover from what appeared to be an insurmountable financial hurdle.

If the SED's past performance weighed on the GDR's future prospects, the party's halting approach to democratic reform was even less reassuring. In December, for example, Modrow agreed to participate in roundtable discussions with the various opposition parties in an effort to stabilize the country. In mid-January, however, he foolishly attempted to reconstitute the Stasi. Fearing that a reinvigorated security apparatus would reestablish a police state, as it had after 1953, an angry crowd sacked Stasi headquarters in Berlin on 15 January. Nor did the party's confused approach to economic reform augur well. Under Krenz's short-lived leadership, the party refused to take responsibility for the economic morass, launching instead a xenophobic campaign against foreigners blaming them for shortages of consumer

---

36 SAPMO-BA, DY30, IV 2/1/711; Hertle, *Der Fall der Mauer*, pp. 143–9; Hertle and Stephan, *Das Ende der SED*, p. 365. In December 1989, the new Finance Minister and the President of the Staatsbank reported to the Modrow government that the net debt totaled $20.6 billion (BArchB, DN1, VS 13/90, Nr. 5, Nickel and Kaminsky, "Einschätzung," 15.12.89, p. 4).

37 *Leipziger Volkszeitung*, 21.2.90. It is worth pointing out, however, that the GDR's creditors had an implicit claim against West Germany. See Bryson and Melzer, *The End of the East German Economy*, pp. 89–90; Maier, *Dissolution*, pp. 229–31. In January 1990, the GDR ran a trade surplus with the West totaling $150 million. For the entire year, it posted a trade surplus with former Comecon countries totaling DM 11.9 billion (Hoover Institution Archives, German Subject Collection, *Protokolle der Beratungen des Runden Tisch*, Staatliche Zentralverwaltung für Statistik, "Mitteilung zur wirtschaftlichen und sozialen Entwicklung der DDR im Januar 1990," 13.2.90, p. 1; Deutsche Bundesbank [ed.], *Statistische Reihe für 1990*, pp. 56, 60). On the workdays lost, see BArchB, DE1, 56413, "Übersicht über den derzeitigen Stand," no date, p. 8. Of course, the GDR's economic position would deteriorate as it lost export markets in the East no matter what reforms were adopted.

goods.[38] If Krenz's allies still spoke of "a market-oriented planned economy," Modrow was more decisive about the need to eliminate subsidies and open the country to foreign investment. As late as March 1990, however, East German officials were still insisting that the only way to guarantee "social justice" was to limit Western participation in joint ventures with East German industry to minority stakes, even though it meant scaring off much-needed foreign capital.[39]

The contradictory signals sent by Modrow's government accelerated the collapse of central control over the economy, continuing a trend that had begun in the early 1980s. On 24 January, for example, the directors of the powerful IFA automobile combine failed to show up for a meeting in Berlin – an astonishing snub unthinkable only a few months earlier.[40] Similarly, East German retailers began refusing to accept mediocre goods from wholesalers, even though it meant violating the plan.[41] A similar erosion of communist authority was taking place inside enterprises. As a Staatsbank official warned East German leaders, "there is chaos in the factories right now. The authority of managers is in decline."[42]

Nor was there any serious alternative to the SED's policy confusion. Although civil rights leaders enjoyed widespread support in the revolution's early stages, they were soon marginalized by their insistence on a "third way" between communism and capitalism. The leaders of New Forum, for example, expressed continued skepticism about market economies, declaring in late November that "having liberated ourselves from the claws of Stalinism, we will not consider defecting with fluttering flags to the socially unjust two-thirds society of a Herr Kohl." The proclamation continued

---

38 SAPMO-BA, DY30, J IV 2/2A/3252, Arbeitsprotokolle, Politbürositzung vom 31.10.89, "Information zum Abkauf von Waren durch ausländische Bürger"; SAPMO-BA, DY IV, 2/2.039/266, "Zusammengefaßte Information über die Lage in der Volkswirtschaft," no date, p. 218; SAPMO-BA, DY30, IV 2/2.039/204, Hauptverwaltung Abteilung Rechenzentrum, "Information zur Ausfuhr von Schuhwaren," 18.11.89, p. 200; *Neues Deutschland*, 10.11.89 and 16.11.89. As the petitions from this period reveal, the campaign resonated with many East Germans (see, for example, BArchB, DQ3, 1804; Zatlin, "Deutsche Ordnung, Polnische Wirtschaft," pp. 313–14).

39 *Frankfurter Allgemeine Zeitung*, 7.11.89; BArchB, DE1, 56350, Grünheid to Romberg, 9.3.90, pp. 2, 4–5; interview, Modrow, Berlin, 6.4.96; interview, Luft, Berlin, 18.3.96; Grosser, *Das Wagnis*, pp. 117–27; Maier, *Dissolution*, pp. 228–9.

40 BArchB, DE1, 56413, Abteilung Materiell-Technische Sicherung der Produktion, Sektor Maschinenbau/Metallurgie, "Information über die Ergebnisse der Beratung über den Stand der Werkzeugversorgung 1990," 16.3.90, p. 29.

41 *Handelsblatt*, 4.1.90. By the summer, retailers were refusing outright to observe their contracts with East German wholesalers (BArchB, DL1, 26529, Herzer to Reider, 13.7.90; BArchB, DL1, 26560, Selex Handelsgesellschaft mbH to Reider, 30.7.90).

42 SAPMO-BA, DY16, Vorläufige 484, "Information über eine Beratung des stellvertretenden Präsidenten der Staatsbank der DDR, Kollegen Krause, mit Vertretern der NDPD, CDU, LDPD und DBD," no date.

Figure 23. West German Chancellor Helmut Kohl (left) and East German Prime Minister Lothar de Maizière (center) visit the European Parliament in Strasbourg on 16 May 1990 to seek approval for German unification. To the far left is West German Economics Minister Otto Graf von Lambsdorff, to the right Ireland's Prime Minister, Charles Haughey. (Courtesy of Rolf Heid/dpa/Landov.)

with a pun that equated the West German chancellor's name with the slang for cash in German: "We want to seize what is probably our last and certainly a unique opportunity to construct a just social order in which money [*Kohle*] is not the measure of all things."[43] Yet the substance of their proposals remained vague at a time when the majority of East Germans were wary of economic experimentation.

By January 1990, the GDR had been plunged into an existential crisis. The weakness of the socialist currency, the apparently intractable debt, the SED's intransigence, and the anticapitalist gestures of the opposition convinced increasing numbers of East Germans to take advantage of the open border and migrate westward. Those who remained also wanted a market economy. But stripping the GDR of the economic rationale that had set it apart from West German capitalism and had formed the basis of its identity

43 "Zum Wiedervereinigungsplan der pluralistischen Rechten," 28.11.89, in Julia Michaels (ed.), *Die ersten Texte des Neuen Forum* (East Berlin, 1990), p. 24. See also Jarausch, *The Rush to Unity*, pp. 77–94.

for forty years called the very existence of the "better Germany" into question. While the risks involved in reforming the planned economy seemed great, the political and economic institutions that had conferred prosperity on West Germans were there for the asking. In fact, unification with their wealthy neighbors promised to rescue East Germans from an almost certain reduction in their comparatively modest standard of living. In the climate of constant revelation that prevailed in December 1989 and January 1990, when newspaper headlines and television shows divulged new discrepancies every day between the party's lofty claims and the sobering realities of the GDR's economy, such a rescue seemed increasingly attractive.

Mirroring this development, the slogans protesting the SED's hypocrisy mutated into formulas demanding unification. Thus, the antiauthoritarian chant "We are the people" was swiftly replaced by the appeal to national solidarity "We are one people." In keeping with East German political culture, moreover, the crowds chose an economic path to political union. In a coda to the revolution, millions of East German demonstrators expressed their desire for political freedom in terms of West German money, chanting "If the D-Mark comes to us, we'll stay here/If not, we'll go to it over there." Their experience with enforced underconsumption and the GDR's confused monetary regime, together with the revolutionary chaos, had convinced them that possessing West German money meant acquiring West German wealth.

Although both East and West Germans are prone to forget it, unification was not imposed on the GDR by the FRG. Ordinary East Germans made unification inevitable by deploying the threat of continued migration and demanding integration with the FRG in continued demonstrations. On 5 February, the Kohl government reversed its previous position and offered East Germans what they wanted: the D-Mark. Kohl's about-face was undeniably brilliant, for it immediately changed the constellation of forces in both countries. Monetary union had originally been proposed by West German SPD leader Ingrid Matthias-Maier not as a stepping stone to unification, but rather as a "signal to stay" for East Germans.[44] By co-opting

---

44 Ingrid Matthias-Maier, "Signal zum Bleiben," *Die Zeit*, 19.1.90. Separately, Thilo Sarrazin, a Social Democrat working in the Finance Ministry, developed the plan for monetary union that Kohl would eventually adopt (interview, Sarrazin, Mainz, 13.6.96; Thilo Sarrazin, "Die Entstehung und Umsetzung des Konzepts der deutschen Wirtschafts-und Währungsunion," in Waigel and Schell, *Tage*, pp. 160–225; Grosser, *Das Wagnis*, pp. 151–73). A variety of alternatives to rapid monetary union were put forward between January, when discussion regarding the GDR's economic difficulties began in earnest, and 18 March, when parliamentary elections were held. Every proposal was forced to address two completely different problems. Not only did it have to compete with the exit option, but it also had to keep labor costs low enough to boost exports of East German products and attract

her proposal and transforming it into a plan for unification, Kohl stole the opposition's thunder in what was an election year for the FRG.[45] By agreeing to extend the D-Mark eastwards, Kohl successfully slowed the westward stream of refugees. By competing successfully with the "exit option," moreover, Kohl seized the political initiative from Modrow and the roundtable representatives, boosting the political fortunes of his East German allies in the process. Most importantly, however, Kohl undercut the East German government by withdrawing West German financial support until after parliamentary elections could be held.[46] West German largesse crowded out policy alternatives to rapid monetary union and diminished the GDR's freedom of maneuver by slicing through the sinews of statecraft.

The question, however, is not whether monetary union was good politics, but whether it was good economics.[47] Simply put, using monetary policy to constrain labor mobility placed the cart before the horse. From an economic perspective, the main incentive prompting East Germans to leave was the prospect of a more prosperous and secure future in the West. Monetary union provided political reassurance about the FRG's commitment to the East, but it could not by itself make East Germans wealthy. Nor

foreign investment to ease the transition from a planned to a market economy. Among the objections raised against the alternatives put forward was that it was impossible to reduce labor mobility yet keep East German labor cheap. In addition, it was charged that the GDR would never be able to export enough goods to help support the Ostmark, or, more generally, obtain the necessary amounts of hard currency to prop up the Ostmark. Finally, the plans that provided for West German financial support were attacked for endangering the stability of the West German mark and for inviting GDR governments to solve their problems through inflation. For the so-called Kronberger Kreis proposal, see *Süddeutsche Zeitung*, 31.1.90; for Hans D. Barbier's plan, see *Frankfurter Allgemeine Zeitung*, 2.2.90; for an East German plan, see Erwin Rohde, *Börsen-Zeitung*, 2.2.90; for Christa Luft's alternative, see *Handelsblatt*, 6.2.90; for Wolf Schäfer's plan, see *Die Zeit*, 8.2.90; for Klaus Wieners's plan, see *Börsen-Zeitung*, 9.2.90; for Lutz Hoffmann's plan, see *Frankfurter Allgemeine Zeitung*, 10.2.90; for the plan put forward by Steve H. Hanke and Alan A. Walters, see *Neue Züricher Zeitung*, 19.2.90).

45 The Kohl government's offer of monetary union usurped the Bundesbank's jurisdiction over monetary policy as guaranteed by Article 88 of the Basic Law. Capital markets interpreted the government's actions as undercutting the Bundesbank's independence, which not only sent interest rates higher but also forced the bank to act aggressively to prove that it remained in control of monetary policy (interview, Pöhl, Frankfurt am Main, 17.6.96; Schlesinger, Berlin, 23.1.96; Sarrazin, Mainz, 13.6.96; Hans Tietmeyer, State Secretary, West German Finance Ministry [1982–9], economic advisor to Chancellor Kohl on German unification [1989–90], Bundesbank Director [1990–3], Frankfurt am Main, 4.4.96; *Der Spiegel* 9 [1990]; *Berliner Zeitung*, 9.2.90, in Zimmerling, *Neue Chronik*, Folge 4/5, p. 171; Wolfgang Schäuble, *Der Vertrag: Wie ich über die deutsche Einheit verhandelte* [Munich, 1993], pp. 21–7; Manfred Schell, "Zusammenbruch mit Perspektive," in Theo Waigel and Manfred Schnell [eds.], *Tage, die Deutschland und die Welt veränderten: Vom Mauerfall zum Kaukasus – die deutsche Währungsunion* [Munich, 1994], p. 17).

46 Kohl withdrew the FRG's commitment to a DM 15 billion "solidarity payment" (Jarausch, *The Rush to Unity*, pp. 108–10; Zatlin, "Hard Marks Soft Revolutionaries," pp. 71–3).

47 As one commentator put it, "the concept of monetary union was not so much a masterpiece in an economic sense, but rather a master stroke in the political sphere" (Otto Singer, "Constructing the Economic Spectacle: The Role of Currency Union in the German Unification Process," *Journal of Economic Issues* 26:4 [December 1992], p. 1098).

was it clear what the economic advantages of monetary union were. On the one hand, the two countries hardly qualified as an optimum currency area, not the least because of the gap in labor productivity. At least according to Western monetary theory, unifying two economically disparate regions under one currency would require adjustment mechanisms such as labor mobility, relative wage flexibility, or large transfers of wealth.[48] Yet monetary union was offered as a low-cost method of stabilizing the labor market. On the other hand, replacing the cheap Ostmark with the D-Mark, which was one of the world's most valuable currencies, would vastly overvalue East German labor. As a result, East German goods would become uncompetitive on international markets overnight, necessitating a significant reduction in wages, which would trigger migration to West Germany, where higher productivity ensured higher wages, or force East German firms to fire workers, which would also prompt a labor exodus.[49]

For these reasons, a variety of West German economic experts argued for retaining the Ostmark, which they believed would provide the East German economy with an invaluable temporal and functional buffer against international competition and a method of raising its productivity.[50] Floating the Ostmark and allowing it to lose value on international markets would make East German exports attractive, making possible a more orderly adjustment to the international division of labor. The ensuing demand for East German products would increase economic activity, employment, and eventually productivity.[51] Once economic conditions in the GDR converged with those in the FRG, a common currency could be introduced without disruptive effect. Detlev Karsten Rohwedder, the Social Democrat who would oversee the sale of East German assets before his assassination in 1991 by the Red Army Faction, objected that "the foreign exchange rate is the only protection that the sick economy of the GDR

---

48 Robert A. Mundell, "A Theory of Optimum Currency Areas," *American Economic Review* 51 (November 1961), pp. 509–17.
49 As it turned out, the fear of unemployment was a greater factor in spurring out-migration than wage differentials (Akerlof et al., "East Germany in from the Cold," pp. 42–55).
50 See the comments of Bundesbank President Pöhl (*Leipziger Volkszeitung*, 25.1.90 and *Neue Zeit*, 7.2.90); Vice President Schlesinger (*Das Handelsblatt*, 14.1.90 and *Leipziger Volkszeitung*, 25.1.90); Dresdner Bank chief Wolfgang Röller (*Leipziger Volkszeitung*, 15.1.90); DIW chief Lutz Hoffmann (*Frankfurter Allgemeine Zeitung*, 6.2.90). See also the discussion in Bryson and Melzer, *The End of the East German Economy*, especially pp. 129–30; Grosser, *Das Wagnis*, pp. 153–8; Maier, *Dissolution*, pp. 233–5; and Zatlin, "Hard Marks, Soft Revolutionaries," pp. 68–9, 73.
51 Akerlof et al. argue that the benefits of retaining the Ostmark would have been undercut by inelastic demand for East German goods because of their poor quality and lack of conformity with Western standards, while the cost of improving working conditions and cleaning up pollution would have weighed on prices (Akerlof et al., "East Germany in from the Cold," p. 14).

has for a gradual convalescence."[52] Even when monetary union found support among economists, it was because the political message it would send to East Germans might stem labor migration. Thus, Cornelsen supported Kohl's plan because of "the political and psychological benefits and its meaning as a signal," all the while reiterating that it would not affect the gap in productivity between the two countries.[53]

If few Western economic experts confused monetary policy with labor productivity, key politicians believed that extending the D-Mark eastward would have the same impact on East Germany that its introduction in 1948 had on West Germany. Kohl's famous prediction of "flourishing landscapes," for example, was premised on the idea that the D-Mark would make possible an East German version of the West German "economic miracle."[54] Unfortunately, the analogy was without economic basis.[55] More puzzling is why Kohl advocated for the GDR what he refused to permit for the FRG. In negotiations with its partners in the European Community, Kohl and the Bundesbank had consistently maintained that a common currency could come about only at the end of a process of political and economic convergence.[56] In February 1990, the main point of convergence between the two German states involved the political utility of the D-Mark.

Yet it was not the calculations of West German actors that determined East German demand for the West German mark, but rather the intellectual and experiential legacy of communism. The surprising durability of communist ideas made itself known in a variety of ways, extending from the simple repetition of communist catchphrases, such as "the scientific-technical revolution," to more complicated ideas about money.[57] The run-up to the March parliamentary elections was suffused with anticapitalist gestures designed to reassure East German voters that the socially harmful consequences of free

---

52 *Frankfurter Allgemeine Zeitung*, 23.2.90.
53 *Frankfurter Allgemeine Zeitung*, 6.2.90. See also Maier, *Dissolution*, pp. 237–44.
54 Kohl first used the phrase on February 20 (Görtemaker, *Unifying Germany*, p. 124). See also the comments of West German Economics Minister Helmut Haussmann (ibid., p. 140).
55 In 1948, the DM replaced a currency that had been entirely devalued by excess money stock and was thoroughly rejected by the population (Manfred E. Streit, "German Monetary Union," in Deutsche Bundesbank [ed.], *Fifty Years of the Deutsche Mark*, pp. 640–3). The DM's relation to the "economic miracle" was indirect, since the currency's strength merely mirrored a very real story of economic success. More importantly, the GDR's starting point in 1989 was worse than the FRG's in 1948. Its labor was not as well adapted to market requirements, its plant in much worse shape, its production facilities often polluted beyond redemption, and many of its most enterprising citizens gone.
56 For more on the so-called coronation theory, see Barry Eichengreen and Charles Wyplosz, "The Unstable EMS," *Brookings Papers on Economic Activity* 1 (1993), pp. 51–143; Peter H. Loedel, *Deutsche Mark Politics: Germany in the European Monetary System* (London and Boulder, Colo., 1999), p. 164.
57 Hoover Institution Archives, German Subject Collection, Box 51, *Der Morgen. Zentralorgan der Liberal-Demokratischen Partei Deutschlands*, 12.12.89, p. 2.

trade could be mitigated by state intervention. In its final session before the elections, for example, the Round Table demanded that the right to work be constitutionally guaranteed.[58] Even the most consistent East German proponents of free markets emphasized that "people and nature should not be sacrificed to short-sighted economic interests."[59] In this manner, East German liberals sought to allay popular fears that West German manufacturers would pollute the environment as ruthlessly as East German factories had.

Most significantly, however, the election campaign revealed that East Germans across the political spectrum had come to believe the SED's claim that money embodied stored labor. The Round Table, which had initially greeted Kohl's offer of the DM with hostility, conceded that monetary union successfully addressed the problem of hard work seeking hard currency, observing that "thousands continue to leave our country every day [because] they want to earn 'real money.'"[60] Even the vigorously anticommunist right conflated labor with money. The Alliance for Germany, a coalition of conservative parties allied with the West German CDU, argued that the DM would restore to East Germans the prosperity that communism had stolen from them. As an election broadsheet for the Alliance put it, "socialism has cheated us out of the fruits of our labor for 40 years."[61] The Alliance's equation of socialism with theft turned the old communist claim that capitalism was a form of theft on its head. The idea that the SED had stolen East German wealth appealed to an angry electorate not the least because it placed responsibility for the GDR's underperformance squarely on the communist party. Similarly, the East German SPD argued that monetary union would guarantee East Germans "equal pay for equal work."[62] Borrowed from the women's liberation movement, this slogan neatly encapsulates the moral concerns driving the desire for the D-Mark. It spoke out against the sense of second-class citizenship from which many East Germans suffered while implying that East Germans had worked just as hard as West

---

58 The Round Table was also quick to explain that this constitutional right did not mean "the state guarantee of a job," a contradiction that reflects both the intellectual confusions and political divisions of the participants (Hoover Institution Archives, German Subject Collection, *Protokolle der Beratungen des Runden Tisch*, Ergebnisse des Runden Tisch, session 15, 3.3.90, paragraph 10, p. 21).

59 Hoover Institution Archives, German Subject Collection, Box 51, *Bund Freier Demokraten*, no date.

60 Hoover Institution Archives, German Subject Collection, *Protokolle der Beratungen des Runden Tisch*, Ergebnisse des Runden Tisch, session 11, 5.2.90, and SPD Vorlage 11/20.

61 SAPMO-BA, SgY, 20/5, "18. März: Allianz für Deutschland." See also Hoover Institution Archives, German Subject Collection, Box 51, *Ilmenau Kurier. Wahlzeitung der "Allianz für Deutschland"* and *DSU Kurier*.

62 *Leipziger Volkszeitung*, 13/14.1.90.

Germans but had been undercompensated. The unfortunate fact, however, was that East German labor was less valuable than West German labor.[63]

To this volatile mix of communist ideas about money and labor, rage against the SED, and a sense of social inferiority vis-à-vis West Germans, East Germans brought their own experience with the D-Mark in the GDR. The chaos of the GDR's fragmented monetary regime had taught East Germans to equate the West German mark with consumer goods they desired, convincing them in the process that West German money not only commanded real resources, but that it was itself a valuable resource. For all of these reasons, East Germans concluded that the currency of socialism had robbed them of the prosperity to which their hard work entitled them, and that acquiring the currency of capitalism was the same as aquiring that prosperity.

Encouraged by the irresponsible assurances of politicians like Kohl, East Germans expected that introducing the DM would not only stabilize the labor market, but also bestow West German wealth on them.[64] Hans D. Barbier, an editor at the conservative *Frankfurter Allgemeine Zeitung* who advocated floating the Ostmark, worried that East Germans mistakenly believed that West German money would confer West German wealth. "It would be catastrophic," he wrote, "if the mistake established itself with politicians and citizens of the GDR that the introduction of the D-Mark as a medium of exchange means the same thing as achieving the prosperity they hope for. Even this new money will not be pressed into anyone's hands without something in return. Prosperity is not handed out at the bank teller's window, but is earned on production lines and in offices."[65] To their chagrin, the millions of East Germans who purchased Western consumer durables, such as Renaults and used BMWs, with their newly obtained D-Marks were to discover that Barbier was correct. Without a job, they had no income, and without income, they could not afford those cars, which many were forced to unload at steep discounts during the early 1990s.

This is not to argue that the rapid currency union itself was a mistake. Even though it was a cumbersome method of addressing productivity differentials and labor mobility, monetary union prepared the way for an orderly

---

63 Zatlin, "Hard Marks, Soft Revolutionaries," p. 65.
64 Despite early predictions of an SPD victory, East Germans voted overwhelmingly for the Alliance because of its unequivocal advocacy of immediate monetary union, the West German SPD's opposition to monetary union, and the successful campaign to slander Social Democrats as communists. For more on the East German reception of Oskar Lafontaine, the SPD's chancellor candidate, see *Frankfurter Allgemeine Zeitung*, 24.2.90; for the East German SPD's support, see *Frankfurter Allgemeine Zeitung*, 25.1.90. See also Jarausch, *The Rush to Unity*, pp. 121–8; Maier, *Dissolution*, pp. 208–14.
65 *Frankfurter Allgemeine Zeitung*, 6.2.90.

unification of the two German states. In a climate of domestic turmoil and international uncertainty, Kohl's offer of the DM injected clarity and purpose into the East German debate over the GDR's future. It stabilized the labor market long enough to define a path to political union, beginning with elections on 18 March, the remarkably orderly currency substitution on 1 July, formal union on 3 October, and ending with all-German elections on 2 December. Monetary union also had the effect of shunting East German political actors aside, as the GDR's fiscal sovereignty was transferred to the FRG. Since the de Maizière government had only one purpose – to secure the DM at a 1:1 rate – it had no political leverage once it had discharged this duty. Even its last-minute use of illiberal trade policies to protect East German industry from a flood of West German imports could not change this fact.[66] Once monetary union went into effect, moreover, "the Bundesbank took over the government of the GDR."[67] Thus, monetary union completed the process begun by Honecker whereby the two states traded money for political liberalization. It is worth noting, too, that monetary union proved diplomatically indispensable, enabling the Kohl government in its negotiations with the Soviet Union and its Western allies to secure support for German unification by representing it as inevitable. For all of these reasons, the Kohl government was surely right to seize the opportunity to unify the two countries while it was possible and harness monetary policy to do so. After all, a slower approach, such as a confederation that would retain two currencies, might have been economically more advantageous for West Germans, since it would have reduced their transfer obligations, but was politically unacceptable to East Germans and carried substantial diplomatic risks.[68]

If monetary union was a necessary prelude to the political unification of the two Germanys, it failed to deliver a "second economic miracle," much less West German prosperity.[69] Instead, it exposed the struggling East German economy overnight to the rigors of international competition and a productivity gap with West Germany it has yet to overcome. Eastern German GDP contracted by more than 60 percent in the first two years after

66 BArchB, DL1, 26571, Pohl, Rieder, and Romberg, "Maßnahmen zur Förderung der Industrie und des Binnenhandels," 11.5.90, p. 2, and "Rededisposition zum Schutz des Binnenmarktes gegen Importe aus der BRD," no date, pp. 1, 5.
67 Interview, Pöhl, Frankfurt am Main, 17.6.96.
68 As Soviet Foreign Minister Eduard Shevardnadze reportedly told U.S. Secretary of State James Baker after Kohl's offer, unification will occur "and I'm not sure of any way to avoid it" (Zelikow and Rice, Germany Unified, p. 181); Theo Waigel, "Tage, die Deutschland und die Welt veränderten," in Waigel and Schnell, Tage, p. 26.
69 Baden-Württemberg Minister-President Lothar Späth (Frankfurter Allgemeine Zeitung, 4.2.90).

Figure 24. Overtaken but not caught up. (Courtesy of Bundesarchiv Koblenz, Bildarchiv, 183/1990/1023/015.)

unification.[70] The resulting collapse in output led firms to lay off workers, with unemployment in some regions rising to levels not seen since the Great Depression. The combination of real wage differentials and stubborn unemployment has provided little incentive for Easterners to remain in the five new *Bundesländer*. Far from providing them with lasting reasons to stay home, monetary union exacerbated the material legacy of communist rule and helped cement cultural divisions. As Antje Vollmer, a West German

70 Hans-Werner Sinn, "Germany's Economic Unification: An Assessment after Ten Years," *National Bureau of Economic Research*, Working Paper 7586 (Cambridge, Mass., 2000), p. 7.

Green, exclaimed in the parliamentary debate on the eve of monetary union, "the DM will come and all the problems will remain."[71]

As predicted, the D-Mark's introduction abruptly revalued eastern German labor, pricing it out of international markets. Products manufactured in eastern Germany were suddenly too expensive to compete with less expensive and better alternatives, while the cheaper currencies in neighboring countries, and especially Czechoslovakia, attracted more foreign investment. Even Western German firms, such as Volkswagen, preferred to invest in the Czech Republic than in Eastern Germany because of the currency differential.[72] It has been argued that Germany's mezzogiorno problem was created less by unifying the currencies than by unifying labor markets. Western German labor unions, concerned that lower wages in the eastern states might weaken their bargaining power, helped Easterners obtain higher wages than their productivity warranted.[73] But even if one argues that trade union policies rather than monetary union increased eastern wages beyond the ability of eastern firms to clear market prices, the point remains that the common currency both enabled and forced Western German unions to defend themselves against the prospect that labor migration and capital flight might reduce wages in the West.

Monetary union also saddled East German firms with crushingly large debts, which made it more difficult for them to compete against capitalist firms. Schlesinger, who was the Bundesbank's representative in the negotiations over monetary union, insisted that restoring hard budget constraints would have a salutary effect on East German enterprises. They should have debt, he affirmed in an interview later, "so that they learn how to use capital."[74] Aside from whether this kind of shock therapy was appropriate, the remark reveals the cultural gap at work in the West German approach to East German finances. In the planned economy, enterprise debt was entirely unrelated to the factory's economic production. Often debt stemmed from the social responsibilities the plan required of enterprises or was simply a meaningless accounting figure forced upon a factory by central authorities for the sake of quantitative symmetry. Debt might help teach Easterners about cost control, but saddling companies with crushing debts just when

71 *Frankfurter Allgemeine Zeitung*, 2.7.90.
72 According to Pöhl, it was the DM, rather than the nationalistic policies of the Treuhand, that scared off foreign investors (interview, Pöhl, Frankfurt am Main, 17.6.96).
73 Akerlof et al., "East Germany in from the Cold," pp. 60–3; Sinn, "Germany's Economic Unification," p. 20.
74 Schlesinger, Berlin, 23.1.96; Interview, Pöhl, Frankfurt am Main, 17.6.96; BArchB, DN10, 2285, Staatsbank der DDR, "Grundsätze und Modalitäten für eine Umstellung," 23.3.90, p. 9.

they were forced to scrounge for D-Marks to pay their employees every week pushed many into bankruptcy.

As a result, unemployment in Eastern Germany has persisted at stubbornly high rates. The aging of the population has complicated retraining efforts while the impressive modern infrastructure built at government expense has failed to attract investors.[75] The massive transfer of wealth from West to East has spared East Germans the material privations of their Eastern European neighbors. But the same West German welfare state that cushioned ordinary Easterners from the effects of mass unemployment in the short term has failed to bring long-term relief to Eastern Germany. Net financial transfers totaled about 75 billion Euros annually between 1990 and 2000, or between 5 and 6 percent of West German GDP; between 1991 and 2003, Western Germany had transferred some 1.25 trillion Euros to Eastern Germany.[76] In fact, "every third deutschmark spent in East Germany came from the West."[77] Yet more than half of these transfers were used for welfare payments, while only 12 percent were used to improve infrastructure. Most alarming, the transfers have acted to shield many firms from hard budget constraints, returning eastern business to old habits: Vast government subsidies have made the cost of capital negative, which has led firms to ignore labor productivity.[78]

Although extending the D-Mark eastwards slowed emigration at first, East Germans resumed their migration to the West as soon as the shock worked its way through the East German economy. From mid-1990 to the end of 1992, an estimated 1 million people left the former GDR permanently, amounting to a rate of nearly 2,000 a day. Between 1992 and 2002, another 521,000 people left for western Germany.[79] As in the 1950s, the flight of mostly younger people has created a vicious circle: As younger people leave, they deplete the local workforce, leaving behind an older population that is often unemployable and increasingly dependent on

---

75 Registered unemployment in eastern Germany amounted to 18.8 percent in 2000, more than twice the Western rate. If we add to this figure hidden unemployment resulting from forced early retirements, involuntary part-time work, make-work programs, and training schemes, the rate jumps to some 30 percent (Michael C. Burda and Jennifer Hunt, "From Reunification to Economic Integration: Productivity and the Labor Market in Eastern Germany," *Brookings Papers on Economic Activity* 2 [2001], p. 2).

76 Burda and Hunt, "From Reunification to Economic Integration," p. 11; Sinn, "Germany's Economic Unification," pp. 9–10; *Berliner Zeitung*, 07.04.04; *Der Spiegel* 15 (2004), p. 25.

77 Sinn, "Germany's Economic Unification," p. 6.

78 As Sinn puts it, "capital changed from being a factor of production to being an economic good" (ibid., pp. 14–16).

79 *Der Spiegel* 3 (1993), p. 52; Jan Priewe, "Zwischen Abkoppelung und Aufholen – Das schwache ostdeutsche Wachstumspotential," *WSI Mitteilungen* 12 (2002), p. 706.

government subsidies. As the real and perceived prospects of economic recovery shrink, more people decide to leave.

Nor does the German mezzogiorno show any signs of disappearing. Eastern German GDP has been growing at a slower rate than Western Germany's since 1996, and labor migration continues, albeit at a slower rate.[80] Far from reunifying Germans, moreover, Eastern German economic underperformance has exacerbated political differences and fueled cultural resentments. In the East, economic stagnation has enabled the political successors of the SED to speak for regional interests. Eastern Germans express anger at West German triumphalism and arrogance, but flee into the comfort of memory before the overwhelming influence of West German culture; the forgiving process of reminiscing transforms the camaraderie of deprivation that characterized the dictatorship into a cozy social solidarity that never was.[81] Although there is little support for a return to communist rule, the phenomenon of *Ostalgie*, or nostalgia for the (supposed) simplicity and (coerced) cohesion of the GDR, continues. Most ironically, Easterners have colluded in the commodification of communism, purchasing consumer goods, such as marmalade and *Rotkäppchen* champagne, which sport old socialist labels even though many of these products are now manufactured by western firms. In this manner, the communist presentation of "the people" as a harmonious and monolithic subject lives on in eastern memory. Similar regrets over unification have appeared in the West. Anger that years of financial sacrifice have brought such meager results has led to an outpouring of public anger directed at Easterners as well as former Chancellor Kohl for bringing them into the West German polity.[82] As it often does, economic scarcity breeds envy and discontent. In the East German case, cultural perceptions shaped by economic scarcity continue to trump economic logic and historical agency.

80 Sinn, "Germany's Economic Unification," pp. 9–10.
81 Jürgen Habermas, *The Past as Future*, trans. Max Pensky (Lincoln, Neb., 1994).
82 See, for example, the title cover of *Der Spiegel* 15 (2004), "1.25 Trillion Euros for What?" and the best-selling book by Gabor Steingart, *Deutschland, der Abstieg eines Superstars* (Munich, 2004).

Bibliography

I. PRIMARY SOURCES

A) Interviews

Gunther Beobach, Deputy Chief, Department of Agitation and Propaganda at the Central Committee (late 1980s): 4.5.96 in Berlin.

Klaus Höpcke, Deputy Minister of Culture (1973–89): 17.3.95 and 5.11.95 in Berlin; 24.2.96 in Erfurt.

Peter Jacob, Economic Director, IFA Combine (1980s): 26.2.96 in Chemnitz.

Heinz Klopfer, Deputy State Planning Commissioner (1963–66), State Secretary, State Planning Commission (1969–90), Central Committee candidate member (1976–89), Chairman of the Working Group on Automobiles (1980–89): 4.10.95 in Berlin.

Christa Luft, Chancellor, Hochschule für Ökonomie "Bruno Leuschner" (1988–9), Economics Minister (December 1989–March 1990): 18.3.96 in Berlin.

Lothar de Maizière, GDR Minister-President (March–December 1990): 8.5.96 in Berlin.

Hans Modrow, Dresden District Party Leader (1973–89), Central Committee member (1967–89), Chairman, Council of Ministers (November 1989–March 1990): 6.4.96 in Berlin.

Bernd Ohliger and Ulrich Wittek, driver's education teachers at the Mila Fahrschule, Berlin (1970s–1980s): 26.1.96 in Berlin.

Karl-Otto Pöhl, West German Finance Ministry (1972–77), Bundesbank Vice President (1977–9), Bundesbank President (1979–92): 17.6.96 in Frankfurt am Main.

Dietrich Rothe, FDGB chief, State Planning Commission (1970–5): 4.3.98 in Berlin.

Wolfgang Sachs, Director of Production and Planning, IFA Combine (1980s): 26.2.96 in Chemnitz.

Thilo Sarrazin, Director, National Currency Affairs (Referat VII A1), Department for German–German Relations, West German Finance Ministry (1989–90), Berlin Senator for Finance (2002–present): 13.6.96 in Mainz.

Helmut Schlesinger, Bundesbank Vice President (1980–91), Bundesbank President (1991–3): 23.1.96 in Berlin.

Christian Scholwin, Deputy Minister for General Machine, Agricultural Machine, and Automotive Construction (1978–88): 23.11.95 in Berlin.

Gerhard Schürer, State Planning Commissioner (1965–89), candidate member, Politburo (1973–89): 19.4.95 and 20.6.95 in Berlin.

Hans Tietmeyer, State Secretary, West German Finance Ministry (1982–9), economic advisor
  to Chancellor Kohl on German unification (1989–90), Bundesbank Director (1990–3),
  Bundesbank President (1993–99): 4.4.96 in Frankfurt am Main.
Dieter von Würzen, State Secretary, West German Economics Ministry (1979–95): 26.3.96
  in Bonn.

B) Unpublished Sources

Archives

Bundesarchiv Berlin (BArchB)

DA1   Volkskammer
DA5   Staatsrat der DDR
DC20   Ministerrat der DDR
DE1   Staatliche Plankommission
DG7   Ministerium für Allgemeinen Maschinen-, Landwirtschaftlichen Maschinen-,
          und Fahrzeugbau
DL1   Ministerium für Handel und Versorgung
DL2   Bereich Kommerzielle Koordinierung
DN1   Ministerium der Finanzen
DQ3   Ministerium für Arbeit und Löhne
DN10   Staatsbank der DDR

*Bundesbeauftragter für die Unterlagen des Staatssicherheitsdienstes der ehemaligen Deutschen
  Demokratischen Republik (BStU)*
Arbeitsbereich Mittig
Arbeitsgruppe Bereich Kommerzielle Koordinierung (AG BKK)
Hauptabteilung XVIII "Volkswirtschaft"
Zentrale Auswertungs- und Informationsgruppe (ZAIG)

Hoover Institution Archives
German Subject Collection

Konrad-Adenauer-Stiftung, Archiv für Christlich-Demokratische Politik

Stiftung Archiv der Parteien und Massenorganisationen in Bundesarchiv (SAPMO-BA)

DY 6   Nationale Front
DY 16   Nationaldemokratische Partei Deutschlands
DY 30   Sozialistische Einheitspartei Deutschlands

  Abteilung Forschung und technische Entwicklung
  Abteilung Handel, Versorgung und Außenhandel
  Abteilung Internationale Politik und Wirtschaft
  Abteilung Maschinenbau/Metallurgie
  Abteilung Parteiorgane
  Abteilung Planung und Finanzen
  Abteilung Sozialistische Wirtschaftsführung
  Akademie für Gesellschaftswissenschaften beim ZK der SED
  Arbeitsprotokolle des Politbüros
  Büro Honecker

Büro Jarowinsky
Büro Krenz
Büro Mittag
Informationen an den Ministerrat
Komitee der Arbeiter- und Bauern-Inspektion
Parteiorgane
Redaktion "Einheit"
Sekretariat des Politbüros
Sitzungen des Politbüros
Zentralinstitut für sozialistische Wirtschaftsführung

Dissertations
Schalck-Golodkowski, Alexander, and Heinz Volpert. "Zur Vermeldung ökonomischer Verluste und zur Erwirtschaftung zusätzlicher Devisen im Bereich Kommerzielle Koordinierung des Ministeriums für Außenwirtschaft der Deutschen Demokratischen Republik." Dissertation, Potsdam, 1970.

C) Published Sources

Periodicals
Berliner Zeitung
Börsen-Zeitung
Bunte
Eulenspiegel
Frankfurter Allgemeine Zeitung
Gesetzesblätter der DDR
Handelsblatt
Leipziger Volkszeitung
Neues Deutschland
New York Times
Quick
Der Spiegel
Süddeutsche Zeitung
Die Wirtschaft
Wochenbericht der DIW
Die Zeit

Books
Akademie der Wissenschaften der DDR, ed. *Zur aktiven Rolle der Finanzen*. East Berlin, 1980.
Akademie für Gesellschaftswissenschaften beim ZK der SED, ed. *Die Volkswirtschaft der DDR*. East Berlin, 1979.
Bernet, Wolfgang, Axel Schöwe, and Richard Schüler. "Für eine effektivere Verwirklichung des Eingabenrechts!" *Neue Justiz: Zeitschrift für sozialistisches Recht und Gesetzlichkeit* 42:7 (1988), pp. 282–4.
Bley, H., et al., eds. *Lexikon der Wirtschaft: Arbeit*. East Berlin, 1968.
Borchert, Hans, ed. *Lexikon der Wirtschaft: Industrie*. East Berlin, 1970.
Brecht, Bertolt. *The Threepenny Opera*.
Brezhnev, Leonid. *Report of the CPSU Central Committee to the 24th Congress of the Communist Party of the Soviet Union*. Moscow, 1971.

Cappallo, Manfred, et al., eds. *Eingaben – Bürger gestalten Kommunalpolitik mit.* East Berlin, 1989.

Cicero, Marcus Tullius. *Philippics*, trans. D. R. Shackleton Bailey. Chapel Hill, N.C., 1986.

Danek, Paul. "Der Warencharakter des Geldes." In Hannelore Riedel, ed., *Das Geld im gegenwärtigen Kapitalismus.* East Berlin, 1989, pp. 41–55.

"Direktive des IX. Parteitages der SED zum Fünfjahrplan für die Entwicklung der Volkswirtschaft der DDR in den Jahren 1976–1980." In *Protokoll der Verhandlungen des IX. Parteitages der Sozialistischen Einheitspartei Deutschlands*, vol. 2. East Berlin, 1976.

Ebert, Georg, Fred Matho, and Harry Milke. *Ökonomische Gesetze in der entwickelten sozialistischen Gesellschaft.* East Berlin, 1975.

Ehlert, Willi, Diethelm Hunstock, and Karlheinz Tannert, eds. *Geld und Kredit in der Deutschen Demokratischen Republik.* East Berlin, 1985.

———. *Geldzirkulation und Kredit in der sozialistischen Planwirtschaft.* East Berlin, 1976.

Ehlert, Willi, Heinz Joswig, Willi Luchterhand, and Karl-Heinz Stiemerling, eds. *Wörterbuch der Ökonomie Sozialismus.* East Berlin, 1984.

Gebauer, Klaus, Hermann Wirsig, et al., eds. *Studien- und Seminarhinweise für Teilnehmer und Propagandisten der Seminare zur politischen Ökonomie des Sozialismus und der ökonomischen Strategie der SED.* East Berlin, 1989.

Heym, Stefan. *5 Tage im Juni.* Frankfurt/Main, 1977.

Honecker, Erich. "Bericht des Zentralkomitees der Sozialistischen Einheitspartei Deutschlands an den VIII. Parteitag der SED." In *Protokoll der Verhandlungen des VIII. Parteitages der Sozialistischen Einheitspartei Deutschlands.* East Berlin, 1971.

———. "Bericht des Zentralkomitees der Sozialistischen Einheitspartei Deutschlands an den IX. Parteitag der SED." In *Protokoll der Verhandlungen des IX. Parteitages der Sozialistischen Einheitspartei Deutschlands*, vol. 1. East Berlin, 1976.

Judt, Matthias, ed. *DDR-Geschichte in Dokumenten: Beschlüsse, Berichte, interne Materialien und Alltagszeugnis.* Berlin, 1997.

Kautsky, Karl. *The Social Revolution*, trans. A. M. and May Wood Simons. Chicago, 1910.

Klemm, Werner, and Manfred Naumann. *Zur Arbeit mit den Eingaben der Bürger.* East Berlin, 1977.

Kohlmey, Gunther. *Das Geldsystem der Deutschen Demokratischen Republik.* East Berlin, 1956.

Kolbe, Uwe. *Hineingeboren: Gedichte 1975–1979.* East Berlin, 1980.

Koziolek, Helmut. "Schlußwort." In Akademie der Wissenschaften der DDR, ed., *Zur aktiven Rolle der Finanzen.* East Berlin, 1980.

Krömke, Claus, and Gerd Friedrich. *Kombinate. Rückgrat sozialistischer Planwirtschaft.* East Berlin, 1987.

Krüger, Hartmut. "Rechtsnatur und politische Funktion des 'Eingabenrechts' in der DDR." *Die Öffentliche Verwaltung* 30:12 (1977), pp. 432–7.

Kunz, Willi, et al. *Umfassende Intensivierung – sozialistische ökonomische Integration – Kombinat.* East Berlin, 1988.

Lang, Ewald. *Wendehals und Stasilaus. Demo-Sprüche aus der DDR.* Munich, 1990.

Lenin, Vladimir Ilyich. "Can the Bolsheviks Retain State Power?" In *Collected Works*, vol. 2. Moscow, 1964.

———. "First All-Russia Congress on Adult Education." In *Collected Works*, vol. 29. Moscow, 1965.

———. "Greetings to the Hungarian Workers." In *Collected Works*, vol. 29. Moscow, 1965.

———. "A Great Beginning: Heroism of the Workers of the Rear. 'Communist Subbotniks.'" In *Collected Works*, vol. 29. Moscow, 1965.

————. "Seventh Moscow Gubernia Conference of the Russian Communist Party, October 19–21, 1921." In *Collected Works*, vol. 33. Moscow, 1966.

Machiavelli, Niccolò. *The Prince* (1514). Middlesex, 1983.

Mandeville, Bernard. *A Fable of the Bees, or Private Vices, Publik Benefits*. London, 1714.

Maron, Monika. *Flugasche*. Frankfurt/Main, 1981.

Marx, Karl. *Capital*. In *Karl Marx and Friedrich Engels: Collected Works*, vols. 35, 36, and 37. New York, 1997.

————. *A Contribution to the Critique of Political Economy*. In *Karl Marx and Friedrich Engels: Collected Works*, vol. 29. Moscow, 1977.

————. "Critique of the Gotha Programme." In *Karl Marx and Friedrich Engels: Collected Works*, vol. 24. Moscow, 1989.

————. *Die Deutsche Ideologie*. In *Marx-Engels Werke*, vol. 3. East Berlin, 1983.

————. "Economic and Philosophical Manuscripts of 1844." In *Karl Marx and Friedrich Engels: Collected Works*, vol. 3. New York, 1975.

————. "Einleitung zu den 'Grundrissen der Kritik der politischen Ökonomie'." In *Marx-Engels Werke*, vol. 42. East Berlin, 1983.

————. *Das Kapital*. *Marx-Engels Werke*, vol. 23, 24, and 25. East Berlin, 1970.

————. Letter to Ludwig Kugelmann, 11 July 1868. In *Karl Marx and Friedrich Engels: Collected Works*, vol. 43. New York, 1988.

————. "Ökonomisch-Philosophische Manuskripte 1844." In *Marx-Engels Werke*. *Ergänzungsband Schriften bis 1844. Erster Teil-Karl Marx*. East Berlin, 1968.

————. "On the Jewish Question." In *Karl Marx and Friedrich Engels: Collected Works*, vol. 3. New York, 1975.

————. *The Poverty of Philosophy*. In *Karl Marx and Friedrich Engels: Collected Works*, vol. 6. New York, 1976.

————. "Zur Judenfrage." In *Marx-Engels Werke*, vol. 1. East Berlin, 1981.

————. *Zur Kritik der Politischen Ökonomie*. In *Marx-Engels Werke*, vol. 13. East Berlin, 1974.

More, Thomas. *Utopia. A New Translation. Backgrounds. Criticism*. New York and London, 1975.

Nakath, Detlev, and Gerd-Rüdiger Stephan, eds. *Von Hubertusstock nach Bonn. Eine dokumentierte Geschichte der deutsch-deutschen Beziehungen auf höchster Ebene, 1980–1987*. Berlin, 1995.

Nick, Harry. *Wissenschaftlich-techniche Revolution: historischer Platz – Entwicklungsetappen – soziales Wesen*. East Berlin, 1983.

Ökonomisches Lexikon A-G. East Berlin, 1978.

Opitz, Rolf, and Gerhard Schüßler. "Die Bearbeitung der Eingaben der Bevölkerung als Bestandteil der staatlichen Leitungstätigkeit." *Staat und Recht* 27:3 (1978), p. 220.

Proudhon, Pierre-Joseph. *Organisation du credit et de la circulation et solution du problème sociale*. In *Oeuvres complétes*, vol. VI. Paris, 1868.

Seeger, Horst, ed. *Lexikon der Wirtschaft: Volkswirtschaftsplanung*. East Berlin, 1980.

Simmel, Georg. *Philosophie des Geldes* (1900). Frankfurt/Main, 1989.

Smith, Adam. *Wealth of Nations* (1776). Amherst, N.Y., 1991.

Staatliche Zentralverwaltung für Statistik, ed. *Statistisches Jahrbuch der Deutschen Demokratischen Republik 1979*. East Berlin, 1980.

Staatliche Zentralverwaltung für Statistik, ed. *Statistisches Jahrbuch der Deutschen Demokratischen Republik 1989*. East Berlin, 1989.

Stalin, Joseph. *Economic Problems of Socialism in the USSR*. New York, 1952.

Statistisches Bundesamt, ed. *Statistisches Jahrbuch der Bundesrepublik Deutschland für 1989*. Stuttgart, 1990.

Tannert, Karlheinz, ed. *Geld, Kredit, Finanzen aus neuer Sicht*. East Berlin, 1990.
Trotsky, Leon. *Political Profiles*, trans. R. Chappell. London, 1972.
Ulbrich, Reinhard. *Kleines Lexikon großer Ostprodukte*. Köthen/Anhalt, 1996.
Wagner, Reinhard. *DDR-Witze: Walter schützt vor Torheit nicht, Erich währt am längsten*. Berlin, 1995.
————. *DDR Witze Teil 2. Lieber von Sitte gemalt, als vom Sozialismus gezeichnet*. Berlin, 1997.
Weichelt, Wolfgang. "Sozialistische Verfassung – Grundrechte – Rechtstaatlichkeit." *Neue Justiz. Zeitschrift für sozialistisches Recht und Gesetzlichkeit* 43:11 (1989), pp. 438–41.
Wörterbuch zum sozialistischen Staat. East Berlin, 1974.

Memoirs
Eppelmann, Rainer. *Wendewege*. Bonn, 1992.
Krenz, Egon. *Wenn Mauern fallen. Die friedliche Revolution: Vorgeschichte-Ablauf-Auswirkungen*. Vienna, 1990.
Krug, Manfred. *Abgehauen: Ein Mitschnitt und ein Tagebuch*. Düsseldorf, 1997.
Mittag, Günter. *Um jeden Preis: Im Spannungsfeld zweier Systeme*. Berlin and Weimar, 1991.
Schabowski, Günter. *Der Absturz*. Berlin, 1991.
Schäuble, Wolfgang. *Der Vertrag. Wie ich über die deutsche Einheit verhandelte*. Munich, 1993.
Schürer, Gerhard. *Gewagt und Verloren. Eine deutsche Biografie*. Frankfurt/Oder, 1996.

II. SECONDARY SOURCES

Abelshauser, Werner. "Two Kinds of Fordism: On the Differing Roles of Industry in the Development of the Two German States." In Haruhito Shiomi and Kazuo Wada, eds., *Fordism Transformed: The Development of Production Methods in the Automobile Industry*. Oxford, 1995, pp. 269–96.
Akerloff, George, Andrew K. Rose, Janet L. Yellen, Helga Hessenius, Rudiger Dornbusch, and Manuel Guitian. "East Germany in from the Cold: The Economic Aftermath of Currency Union." *Brookings Papers on Economic Activity* 1 (1991), pp. 1–105.
Arnold, Arnold Z. *Banks, Credit, and Money in Soviet Russia*. New York, 1937.
Arnold, Otfrid, and Hans Modrow. "Das Große Haus." In Hans Modrow, ed., *Das Große Haus. Insider berichten aus dem ZK der SED*. Berlin, 1994, pp. 11–70.
Avineri, Schlomo. *The Social and Political Thought of Karl Marx*. Cambridge, 1988.
Bahro, Rudolf. *The Alternative in Eastern Europe*. London, 1978.
Baring, Arnulf. *Der 17. Juni 1953*. Stuttgart, 1983.
Barkai, Avraham. *Nazi Economics: Ideology, Theory, and Policy*, trans. Ruth Hadass-Vashitz. New Haven, Conn., 1990.
Baylis, Thomas A. *The East German Elite and the Technocratic Intelligentsia*. Berkeley and Los Angeles, Calif., 1974.
Bendix, Reinhard. "The Cultural and Political Setting of Economic Rationality in Western and Eastern Europe." In Gregory Grossman, ed., *Value and Plan: Economic Calculation and Organization in Eastern Europe*. Berkeley and Los Angeles, Calif., 1960.
Berend, Ivan T. *The Hungarian Economic Reforms, 1953–1988*. Cambridge, 1990.
Bertsch, Georg C., Ernst Hedler, and Matthias Dietz. *Schönes Einheits-Design – Stunning Eastern Design – Savoir eviter le design*. Cologne, 1994.
Besier, Gerhard. *Der SED-Staat und die Kirche 1969–1990. Die Vision vom "Dritten Weg."* Berlin and Frankfurt/Main, 1995.

Bickhardt, Stephan. "Die Entwicklung der DDR-Opposition in den achtziger Jahren." In *Die Enquete-Kommission.* "*Aufarbeitung von Geschichte und Folgen der SED-Diktatur in Deutschland" im Deutschen Bundestag,* vol. 7, *Widerstand, Opposition, Revolution,* part 1. Baden-Baden, 1995.

Blaug, Mark. *Economic Theory in Retrospect.* Cambridge, 1996.

————. *Ricardian Economics: A Historical Study.* New Haven, Conn., 1958.

Blinder, Alan S. *Hard Heads, Soft Hearts: Tough-Minded Economics for a Just Society.* Reading, Mass., 1987.

Böske, Katrin. "Abwesend anwesend: Eine kleine Geschichte des Intershops." In Neue Gesellschaft für bildende Kunst, ed., *Wunderwirtschaft: DDR-Konsumkultur in den 60er Jahren.* Cologne, Weimar, and Vienna, 1996.

Boyens, Armin. "'Den Gegner irgendwo festhalten' – 'Transfergeschäfte' der Evangelischen Kirchen in Deutschland mit der DDR-Regierung 1957–1990." *Kirchliche Zeitgeschichte* 6 (1993), pp. 379–426.

Boyer, Christoph. "Sozialgeschichte der Arbeiterschaft und staatssozialistische Entwicklungspfade: konzeptionelle Überlegungen und eine Erklärungsskizze." In Peter Hübner, Christoph Kleßmann, and Klaus Tenfelde, eds., *Arbeiter im Staatssozialismus – Ideologischer Anspruch und soziale Wirklichkeit.* Cologne, Weimar, and Vienna, 2005, pp. 71–86.

Bracher, Karl Dietrich. *Die Auflösung der Weimarer Republik.* Düsseldorf, 1984.

Bryson, Phillip J. *The Consumer under Socialist Planning.* New York, 1984.

Bryson, Phillip J., and Manfred Melzer. *The End of the East German Economy: From Honecker to Reunification.* New York, 1991.

Buchheim, Christoph. "The Establishment of the Bank deutscher Länder and the West German Currency Reform." In Deutsche Bundesbank, ed., *Fifty Years of the Deutsche Mark: Central Bank and the Currency in Germany since 1948.* Oxford and New York, 1999, pp. 55–100.

————. "Kriegsfolgen und Wirtschaftswachstum in der SBZ/DDR." *Geschichte und Gesellschaft* 25 (1999), pp. 515–55.

Buck, Hannsjörg F. "Umweltpolitik und Umweltbelastung." In Eberhard Kuhrt, ed., *Am Ende des realen Sozialismus 2: Die wirtschaftliche und ökologische Situation der DDR in den achtziger Jahren.* Opladen, 1996, pp. 223–66.

Bude, Heinz. *Deutsche Karrieren: Lebenskonstruktionen sozialer Aufsteiger aus der Flakhelfer-Generation.* Frankfurt/Main, 1987.

Burda, Michael C., and Jennifer Hunt. "From Reunification to Economic Integration: Productivity and the Labor Market in Eastern Germany." *Brookings Papers on Economic Activity* 2 (2001), pp. 1–71.

Chirot, Daniel. "What Happened in Eastern Europe in 1989." In Vladimir Tismaneanu (ed.), *The Revolutions of 1989.* London and New York, 1999, pp. 19–50.

Ciesla, Burghard. "Hinter den Zahlen: Zur Wirtschaftsstatistik und Wirtschaftsberichterstattung in der DDR." In Alf Lüdtke and Peter Becker, eds., *Akten. Eingaben. Schaufenster. Die DDR und ihre Texte. Erkundungen zur Herrschaft und Alltag.* Berlin, 1997, pp. 39–55.

Connelly, John. *Captive University: The Sovietization of East German, Czech, and Polish Higher Education, 1945–1956.* Chapel Hill, N.C., 2000.

————. "The Uses of Volksgemeinschaft: Letters to the NSDAP Kreisleitung Eisenach, 1939–1940." In Sheila Fitzpatrick and Robert Gellately, eds., *Accusatory Practices.* Chicago and London, 1997, pp. 153–84.

Cornelsen, Doris. "Die Wirtschaft der DDR in der Honecker-Ära." In Gert-Joachim Glaeßner, ed., *Die DDR in der Ära Honecker: Politik. Kultur. Gesellschaft.* Opladen, 1988, pp. 357–70.

Cross, Gary. *Time and Money: The Making of Consumer Culture.* London and New York, 1993.

Dahrendorf, Ralf. *Der moderne soziale Konflikt. Essay zur Politik der Freiheit.* Stuttgart, 1992.

Davies, Glyn. *History of Money: From Ancient Times to the Present Day.* Cardiff, 2002.

De Brunhoff, Suzanne. *Marx on Money.* Paris, 1973.

Deletant, Dennis. "New Evidence on Romania and the Warsaw Pact, 1955–1989." *Cold War History Project,* e-Dossier No. 6.

Deutsche Bundesbank, ed. *Monatsbericht der Deutschen Bundesbank.* Frankfurt/Main, December 1989.

———. *Statistische Reihe für 1990.* Frankfurt/Main, 1990.

———. *Zahlungsbilanz der ehemaligen DDR, 1975 bis 1989.* Frankfurt/Main, 1999.

Deutscher, Isaac. *Stalin.* London, 1949.

Dodd, Nigel. *The Sociology of Money: Economics, Reason and Contemporary Society.* Cambridge, 1994.

Dornbusch, Rudiger, Holger Wolf, and Lewis Alexander. "Economic Transition in Eastern Germany." *Brookings Papers on Economic Activity* 1 (1992), pp. 235–72.

Eggertsson, Thráinn. *Economic Behavior and Institutions.* Cambridge, 1990.

Eichengreen, Barry, and Charles Wyplosz. "The Unstable EMS." *Brookings Papers on Economic Activity* 1 (1993), pp. 51–143.

Evans, Richard, and Dick Geary, eds. *The German Unemployed: Experiences and Consequences of Mass Unemployment from the Weimar Republic to the Third Reich.* London, 1987.

Epstein, Catherine. *The Last Revolutionaries: German Communists and Their Century.* Cambridge, Mass., and London, 2003.

———. "The Stasi: New Research on the East German Ministry of State Security." *Kritika: Explorations in Russian and Eurasian History* 5 (2004), pp. 321–48.

Erdmann, Kurt, and Manfred Melzer. "Die neue Kombinatsverordnung der DDR." *Deutschland Archiv* 13 (1980), pp. 929–44.

Fainsod, Merle. *Smolensk under Soviet Rule.* Cambridge, Mass., 1958.

Falck, Uta. *VEB Bordell. Geschichte der Prostitution in der DDR.* Berlin, 1998.

Feher, Ferenc, Agnes Heller, and Gyorgy Markus. *Dictatorship over Needs.* Oxford, 1983.

Feldman, Gerald D. *The Great Disorder: Politics, Economics, and Society in the German Inflation, 1914–1924.* New York and Oxford, 1993.

Fischer, Stanley. "Distinguished Lecture on Economics in Government: Exchange Rate Regimes: Is the Bipolar View Correct?" *Journal of Economic Perspectives* 15:2 (2001), pp. 3–24.

Fitzpatrick, Sheila. *Everyday Stalinism: Ordinary Life in Extraordinary Times. Soviet Russia in the 1930s.* New York, 1999.

———. "Supplicants and Citizens: Public Letter Writing in Soviet Russia in the 1930s." *Slavic Review* 55:1 (Spring 1996), pp. 78–105.

———, ed. *Stalinism: New Directions.* London and New York, 2000.

———, and Robert Gellately, eds. *Accusatory Practices.* Chicago and London, 1997.

Flechtheim, Ossip. *Die Kommunistische Partei Deutschlands in der Weimarer Republik.* Offenbach/Main, 1948.

Friedrich, Thomas. "Aspekte der Verfassungentwicklung und der individuellen (Grund-) Rechtsposition in der DDR." In Hartmut Kaelble, Jürgen Kocka, and Hartmut Zwahr, eds., *Sozialgeschichte der DDR.* Stuttgart, 1994, pp. 483–97.

Fulbrook, Mary. *Anatomy of a Dictatorship: Inside the GDR, 1949–1989.* Oxford, 1995.

Gábor, Istvan. "The Second Economy in Socialism: General Lessons of the Hungarian Experience." In János Timár, ed., *Papers on Labour Economics.* Budapest, 1984.

Garton Ash, Timothy. *In Europe's Name: Germany and the Divided Continent.* New York, 1993.

————. *The Magic Lantern: The Revolution of '89 Witnessed in Warsaw, Budapest, Berlin and Prague.* New York, 1993.

Görtemaker, Manfred. *Unifying Germany, 1989–1990.* New York, 1994.

Grieder, Peter. *The East German Leadership, 1946–1973: Conflict and Crisis.* Manchester and New York, 1999.

Grosser, Dieter, *Das Wagnis der Währungs-, Wirtschafts- und Sozialunion. Politische Zwänge im Konflikt mit ökonomischen Regeln.* Stuttgart, 1998.

Grossman, Gregory. "Gold and the Sword: Money in the Soviet Command Economy." In Henry Rosovsky, ed., *Industrialization in Two Systems: Essays in Honor of Alexander Gerschenkron.* New York, London, and Sydney, 1966, pp. 204–36.

————, ed. *Money and Plan: Financial Aspects of East European Economic Reform.* Berkeley and Los Angeles, Calif., 1968.

Gruner-Domić, Sandra. "Zur Geschichte der Arbeitskräfteemigration in die DDR. Die bilateralen Verträge zur Beschäftigung ausländischer Arbeiter 1961–1989." *Internationale wissenschaftliche Korrespondenz zur Geschichte der deutschen Arbeiterbewegung* 2 (1996), pp. 204–30.

Habermas, Jürgen. *The Past as Future*, trans. Max Pensky. Lincoln, Neb., 1994.

————. *The Structural Transformation of the Public Sphere: An Inquiry into a Category of Bourgeois Society.* Cambridge, Mass., 1991.

Haendcke-Hoppe, Maria. "Die Vergesellschaftungsaktion im Frühjahr 1972." *Deutschland Archiv* 6 (1973), pp. 37–41.

Haendcke-Hoppe-Arndt, Maria. "Die Hauptabteilung XVIII: Volkswirtschaft." In Siegfried Suckut, Clemens Vollnhals, Walter Süß, and Roger Engelmann, eds., *Anatomie der Staatssicherheit. Geschichte, Struktur und Methoden. MfS-Handbuch*, Teil II/10. Berlin, 1997.

Hagen, Manfred. *DDR – Juni 1953.* Stuttgart, 1992.

Hammond, Thomas T. "Leninist Authoritarianism before the Revolution." In Ernest J. Simmons, ed., *Continuity and Change in Russian and Soviet Thought.* Cambridge, Mass., 1955, pp. 144–56.

Harrison, Hope M. *Ulbricht and the Concrete "Rose": New Archival Evidence on the Dynamics of Soviet–East German Relations and the Berlin Crisis, 1958–1961.* Washington, D.C., 1993.

Harrison, John F. C. *Quest for the New Moral World: Robert Owen and the Owenites in Britain and America.* New York, 1969.

Harsch, Donna. "Society, the State, and Abortion in East Germany, 1950–1972." *American Historical Review* 107:1 (1997), pp. 53–84.

von Hayek, Friedrich. "Socialist Calculation: The Competitive Solution." *Economica* 7 (1940): pp. 125–49.

————. "The Use of Knowledge in Society." *American Economic Review* 35 (1945), pp. 519–30.

Heckscher, Eli F. *Mercantilism*, vol. 2. London and New York, 1955.

Heidegger, Martin. "The Age of the World Picture." In *The Question Concerning Technology and Other Essays*, trans. William Lovitt. New York, 1977.

————. *Sein und Zeit* (1927). Tübingen, 1993.

Held, Joseph. *Dictionary of Eastern European History since 1945.* Westport, Conn., 1994.

Heller, Agnes. *The Theory of Need in Marx.* Nottingham, 1976.

Helwig, Gisela. "Staat und Familie in der DDR." In Gert-Joachim Glaeßner, ed., *Die DDR in der Ära Honecker: Politik. Kultur. Gesellschaft.* Opladen, 1988, pp. 466–80.

Herbst, Andreas, Winfried Ranke, and Jürgen Winkler, eds. *So funktionierte die DDR, Band 1. Lexikon der Organisationen und Institutionen.* Reinbek, 1994.

————, Gerd-Rüdiger Stephan, and Jürgen Winkler, eds. *Die SED. Geschichte – Organisation – Politik. Ein Handbuch.* Berlin, 1997.

Herf, Jeffrey. *Divided Memory: The Nazi Past in the Two Germanys.* Cambridge, Mass., 1997.

Hertle, Hans-Hermann. "Die Diskussion der ökonomischen Krisen in der Führungsspitze der SED." In Theo Pirker, M. Rainer Lepsius, Rainer Weinert, and Hans-Hermann Hertle, eds., *Der Plan als Befehl und Fiktion. Wirtschaftsführung in der DDR.* Opladen, 1995, pp. 309–46.

————, and Gerd-Rüdiger Stephan, eds. *Das Ende der SED: die letzten Tage des Zentralkomitees.* Berlin, 1997.

————. *Der Fall der Mauer. Die unbeabsichtigte Selbstauflösung des SED-Staates.* Opladen, 1996.

————. "Staatsbankrott. Der ökonomische Untergang des SED-Staates." *Deutschland Archiv* 10 (1992), pp. 1019–30.

————. *Vor dem Bankrott der DDR. Dokumente des Politbüros des ZK der SED aus dem Jahre 1988 zum Scheitern der "Einheit von Wirtschafts- und Sozialpolitik."* Die Schürer-Mittag Kontroverse. Berliner Arbeitshefte und Berichte zur sozialwissenschaftlichen Forschung. Berlin, August 1991.

Hessler, Julie M. "Cultured Trade: The Stalinist Turn towards Consumerism." In Sheila Fitzpatrick, ed., *Stalinism: New Directions.* London and New York, 2000, pp. 182–209.

Hilgenberg, Dorothea. *Bedarfs- und Marktforschung in der DDR. Anspruch und Wirklichkeit.* Cologne, 1979.

Hirschman, Albert O. *Exit, Voice, and Loyalty: Responses to Decline in Firms, Organizations, and States.* Cambridge, Mass., 1981.

————. "Exit, Voice, and the Fate of the German Democratic Republic: An Essay in Conceptual History." *World Politics* 45 (1993), pp. 173–202.

————. *The Passions and the Interests: Political Arguments for Capitalism before Its Triumph.* Princeton, N.J., 1981.

Hoerning, Erika M. *Zwischen den Fronten. Berliner Grenzgänger und Grenzhändler 1948–1961.* Cologne, Weimar, and Vienna, 1992.

Huber, Ernst Rudolf. *Deutsche Verfassungsgeschichte seit 1789.* Stuttgart, 1969.

Hughes Hallett, A. J., and Yue Ma. "East Germany, West Germany, and Their Mezzogiorno Problem: A Parable for European Economic Integration." *Economic Journal* 103 (March 1993), pp. 416–28.

James, Harold. *The German Slump: Politics and Economics, 1924–1936.* Oxford, 1986.

Jarausch, Konrad. *The Rush to German Unity.* New York, 1994.

Johnson, Harry G. *Macroeconomics and Monetary Theory.* Chicago, 1977.

Johnson, Peter A. *The Government of Money: Monetarism in Germany and the United States.* Ithaca, N.Y., and London, 1998.

Johnson, Simon, and Peter Temin. "The Macroeconomics of NEP." *Economic History Review* 46 (November 1993), pp. 750–67.

Kaiser, Monika. *1972 Knockout für den Mittelstand. Zum Wirken von SED, CDU, LDPD, und NDPD für die Verstaatlichung der Klein- und Mittelbetriebe.* Berlin, 1990.

Kaiser, Peter, Norbert Moc, and Heinz-Peter Zierholz. *Heisse Ware: Spektakuläre Fälle der DDR-Zollfahndung.* Berlin, 1997.

Kaltenthaler, Karl. *Germany and the Politics of Europe's Money.* Durham, N.C., and London, 1998.

Karlsch, Rainer. *Allein bezahlt? Die Reparationsleistungen der SBZ/DDR 1945–53.* Berlin, 1993.

————. "'Ein Buch mit sieben Siegeln.' Die Schattenhaushalte für den Militär- und Sicherheitsbereich in der DDR und ihre wirtschaftliche Bedeutung." In Wolfram Fischer, Uwe Müller, and Frank Zschaler, eds., *Wirtschaft im Umbruch. Strukturveränderungen und Wirtschaftspolitik im 19. und 20. Jahrhundert. Festschrift für Lothar Baar zum 65. Geburtstag.* St. Katharinen, 1997, pp. 282–306.

Katzenellenbaum, S. S. *Russian Currency and Banking, 1914–1924.* London, 1925.

Kenedi, János. *Do It Yourself: Hungary's Hidden Economy.* London, 1981.

Kenyon, Timothy. *Utopian Communism and Political Thought in Early Modern England.* London, 1989.

Kirchberg, Peter. "Die Geschichte der Automobilindustrie in Sachsen." *Archiv und Wirtschaft - Zeitschrift für das Archivwesen der Wirtschaft* 25:4 (1992), pp. 138–48.

————. *Horch, Audi, DKW, IFA: 80 Jahre Geschichte der Autos aus Zwickau.* Berlin, 1991.

Kleßmann, Christoph. *Die doppelte Staatsgründung: deutsche Geschichte, 1945–1955.* Bonn, 1991.

————. *Zwei Staaten, eine Nation: Deutsche Geschichte 1955–1970.* Bonn, 1988.

Kogut, Bruce, and Udo Zander. "Did Socialism Fail to Innovate? A Natural Experiment of the Two Zeiss Companies." *American Sociological Review* 45:2 (2000), pp. 169–90.

Kolakowski, Leszek. *Main Currents of Marxism: Its Rise, Growth, and Dissolution,* vols. 1 and 2. Oxford, 1978.

König, Karl, ed. *Verwaltungsstrukturen in der DDR.* Baden-Baden, 1991.

König, Wolfgang. *Volkswagen, Volksempfänger, Volksgemeinschaft: "Volksprodukte" im Dritten Reich: vom Scheitern einer nationalsozialistischen Konsumgesellschaft.* Paderborn, 2004.

Kopstein, Jeffrey. *The Politics of Economic Decline in East Germany, 1945–1989.* Chapel Hill, N.C., and London, 1997.

Kornai, János. *The Socialist System: The Political Economy of Communism.* Princeton, N.J., 1992.

Krakat, Klaus. "Probleme der DDR-Industrie im letzten Fünfjahrplanzeitraum." In Eberhard Kuhrt, ed., *Am Ende des realen Sozialismus 2: Die wirtschaftliche und ökologische Situation der DDR in den achtziger Jahren.* Opladen, 1996, pp. 137–76.

Krugman, Paul R., and Maurice Obstfeld. *International Economics: Theory and Policy.* Glenview, Ill., 1988.

Kubik, Jan. *The Power of Symbols against the Symbols of Power: The Rise of Solidarity and the Fall of State Socialism in Poland.* University Park, Penn., 1994.

Kumpf, Johann Heinrich. *Petitionsrecht und öffentliche Meinung im Entstehungsprozess der Paulskirchenverfassung 1848/9.* Frankfurt/Main, 1983.

Kusch, Günter, Rolf Montag, Günter Specht, and Konrad Wetzker. *Schlußbilanz – DDR. Fazit einer verfehlten Wirtschafts- und Sozialpolitik.* Berlin, 1991.

Kuschpèta, O. *The Banking and Credit System of the USSR.* Leiden and Boston, 1978.

Kuss, Klaus-Jürgen. "Das Beschwerde- und Antragsrecht in der sowjetischen Verwaltungspraxis." *Recht in Ost und West* 28:3 (1984), pp. 128–41.

Lampert, Nicholas. *Whistleblowing in the Soviet Union: Complaints and Abuses under State Socialism.* London, 1985.

Lange, Oskar. "On the Economic Theory of Socialism, Part I." *Review of Economic Studies* 4 (1936), pp. 53–71.

Lavigne, Marie. *The Socialist Economies of the Soviet Union and Europe,* trans. T. G. Waywell. White Plains, N.Y., 1974.

Lepsius, M. Rainer. "Handlungsräume und Rationalitätskriterien." In Theo Pirker, M. Rainer Lepsius, Rainer Weinert, and Hans-Hermann Hertle, eds., *Der Plan als Befehl und Fiktion: Wirtschaftsführung in der DDR.* Opladen, 1995, pp. 347–62.

Lichtheim, George. *A Short History of Socialism.* New York, 1970.

Loedel, Peter H. *Deutsche Mark Politics: Germany in the European Monetary System.* London and Boulder, Colo., 1999.

Lüdtke, Alf. *Eigen-Sinn: Fabrikalltag, Arbeitserfahrungen und Politik vom Kaiserreich bis in den Faschismus.* Hamburg, 1993.

———. "'Helden der Arbeit' – Mühen beim Arbeiten. Zur mißmutigen Loyalität von Industriearbeitern in der DDR." In Hartmut Kaelble, Jürgen Kocka, and Hartmut Zwahr, eds., *Sozialgeschichte der DDR.* Stuttgart, 1994, pp. 188–213.

Ludz, Peter. *Parteielite im Wandel.* Opladen, 1969.

Maier, Charles S. *Dissolution: The Crisis of Communism and the End of East Germany.* Princeton, N.J., 1997.

Major, Patrick. "Going West: The Open Border and the Problem of *Republikflucht.*" In Patrick Major and Jonathan Osmond, eds., *The Workers' and Peasants' State: Communism and Society in East Germany under Ulbricht 1945–1971.* Manchester and New York, 2002, pp. 190–208.

Malycha, Andreas. "Von der Gründung 1945/46 bis zum Mauerbau 1961." In Andreas Herbst, Gerd-Rüdiger Stephan, and Jürgen Winkler, eds. *Die SED. Geschichte – Organisation – Politik. Ein Handbuch.* Berlin, 1997, pp. 1–55.

Markovits, Inga. "Rechtsstaat oder Beschwerdestaat? Verwaltungsrechtsschutz in der DDR." *Recht in Ost und West* 31:5 (1987), pp. 265–9.

mdv transparent, ed. *"Wir sind das Volk." Aufbruch '89, Teil 1: Die Bewegung.* September/Oktober 1989. Halle and Leipzig, 1990.

———. *"Wir sind das Volk." Hoffnung '89, Teil 2: Die Bewegung.* Oktober/November 1989. Halle and Leipzig, 1990.

———. *"Wir sind das Volk." Ungeduld '89, Teil 3.* Halle and Leipzig, 1990.

Merkel, Ina. "Konsumkultur in der DDR. Über das Scheitern der Gegenmoderne auf dem Schlachtfeld des Konsums." *Mitteilungen aus der kulturwissenschaftlichen Forschung* 19:37 (1996), pp. 314–30.

———. *Utopie und Bedürfnis. Die Geschichte der Konsumkultur in der DDR.* Cologne, Weimar, and Vienna, 1999.

———, ed. *Wir sind doch nicht die Meckerecke der Nation! Briefe an das Fernsehen der DDR.* Berlin, 2000.

Meuschel, Sigrid. *Legitimation und Parteiherrschaft. Zum Paradox von Stabilität und Revolution in der DDR, 1945–1989.* Frankfurt/Main, 1992.

Meyer, Erhard. "Der Bereich Günter Mittag. Das wirtschaftspolitische Machtzentrum." In Hans Modrow, ed., *Das Große Haus. Insider berichten aus dem ZK der SED.* Berlin, 1994, pp. 137–54.

Michaels, Julia, ed. *Die ersten Texte des Neuen Forum.* East Berlin, 1990.

von Mises, Ludwig. "Die Wirtschaftsrechnung im sozialistischen Gemeinwesen." *Archiv für Sozialwissenschaften und Sozialpolitik* 47 (1920), pp. 86–121.

Mohr, Heinrich. "'Das gebeutelte Hätschelkind'. Literatur und Literaten in der Ära Honecker." In Gert-Joachim Glaeßner, ed., *Die DDR in der Ära Honecker: Politik. Kultur. Gesellschaft.* Opladen, 1988.

Mommsen, Hans, and Manfred Geiger. *Das Volkswagenwerk und seine Arbeiter im Dritten Reich.* Düsseldorf, 1996.

Mühlberg, Felix. *Bürger, Bitten und Behörden. Geschichte der Eingabe in der DDR.* Berlin, 2004.

———. "Konformismus oder Eigensinn? Eingaben als Quelle zur Erforschung der Alltagsgeschichte in der DDR." *Mitteilungen aus der kulturwissenschaftlichen Forschung* 19:37 (1996), pp. 331–45.

Mundell, Robert A. "A Theory of Optimum Currency Areas." *American Economic Review* 51 (1961), pp. 509–17.

Naimark, Norman. *The Russians in Germany: A History of the Soviet Zone of Occupation, 1945–1949.* Cambridge, Mass., 1995.

Nawrocki, Joachim. "Verfehlte Wirtschaftspolitik belastet DDR-Wirtschaft." *Deutschland Archiv* 11 (1971), 1121–4.

Neebe, Reinhard. *Großindustrie, Staat und NSDAP 1930–1933: Paul Silverberg und der Reichsverband der Deutschen Industrie in der Krise der Weimarer Republik.* Göttingen, 1981.

Nelson, Anitra. *Marx's Concept of Money: The God of Commodities.* London and New York, 1999.

Neubert, Erhart. *Eine Protestantische Revolution.* Osnabrück, 1990.

Nicholls, Anthony James. *Freedom with Responsibility: The Social Market Economy in Germany, 1918–1963.* Oxford and New York, 1994.

Niethammer, Lutz. "Das Volk der DDR und die Revolution." In Charles Schüddekopf, ed., *Wir sind das Volk!* Reinbek, 1990, pp. 251–78.

———. Alexander von Plato, and Dorothee Wierling, eds. *Die volkseigene Erfahrung.* Berlin, 1991.

Nove, Alec. *An Economic History of the U.S.S.R.* London, 1989.

———. *The Economics of Feasible Socialism.* London, 1983.

Obst, Werner. *DDR-Wirtschaft. Modell und Wirklichkeit.* Hamburg, 1973.

Osokina, Elena. *Our Daily Bread: Socialist Distribution and the Art of Survival in Stalin's Russia, 1927–1941.* Armonk, N.Y., and London, 2001.

Otto, Wilfriede. *Erich Mielke – Biographie: Aufstieg und Fall eines Tschekisten.* Berlin, 2000.

Overy, Richard J. *War and Economy in the Third Reich.* Oxford, 1994.

Peebles, Gavin. *A Short History of Socialist Money.* Sydney, London, and Boston, 1991.

Pence, Katherine. "Labours of Consumption: Gendered Consumers in Post-War East and West German Reconstruction." In Lynn Abrams and Elizabeth Harvey, eds., *Gender Relations in German History: Power, Agency and Experience from the Sixteenth to the Twentieth Century.* London, 1996, pp. 211–38.

———. "'You as a Woman Will Understand': Consumption, Gender and the Relationship between State and Citizenry in the GDR's Crisis of 17 June 1953." *German History* 19 (2001), pp. 218–52.

Pindák, František. "Inflation under Central Planning." *Jahrbuch der Wirtschaft Osteuropas* 10:2 (1983), pp. 93–131.

Podewin, Norbert. *Walter Ulbricht: Eine neue Biographie.* Berlin, 1995.

Podmore, Frank. *Robert Owen: A Biography,* vol. 2. London, 1906.

Pollard, Sidney. *The International Economy since 1945.* London and New York, 1997.

Polyani, Karl. *The Great Transformation: The Political and Economic Origins of Our Time.* Boston, 2001.

Postoutenko, Kirill. "Die Geburt des Rubels aus dem Geist des Platonismus zur Entstehungsgeschichte des sowjetischen Geld- und Wertesystems." *Zeit-Räume Wiener Slawistischer Almanach* 49 (2003), pp. 75–91.

Poutrus, Patrice G. *Die Erfindung des Goldbroilers: Über den Zusammenhang zwischen Herrschaftssicherung und Konsumentwicklung in der DDR.* Weimar and Vienna, 2002.

Priewe, Jan. "Zwischen Abkoppelung und Aufholen – das schwache ostdeutsche Wachstumspotential." *WSI Mitteilungen* 12 (2002), pp. 706–13.

Przybylski, Peter. *Tatort Politbüro. Die Akte Honecker.* Reinbek, 1992.

———. *Tatort Politbüro. Band 2: Honecker, Mittag und Schalck-Golodkowski.* Berlin, 1992.

Ragnitz, Joachim. "Lagging Productivity in the East German Economy: Obstacles to Fast Convergence." In Michael Dauderstädt and Lothar Witte, eds., *Cohesive Growth in the Enlarging Euroland*. Bonn, 2001, pp. 94–105.

Riasanovsky, Nicholas V. *The Teaching of Charles Fourier*. Berkeley and Los Angeles, Calif., 1969.

Riese, Hajo. *Geld im Sozialismus: Zur theoretischen Fundierung von Konzeptionen des Sozialismus*. Regensburg, 1990.

Rittmann, Herbert. *Deutsche Geldgeschichte seit 1914*. Munich, 1986.

Roberts, Paul Craig, and Matthew A. Stephenson. *Marx's Theory of Exchange, Alienation and Crisis*. Stanford, Calif., 1973.

Röcke, Matthias. *Die Trabi-Story. Der Dauerbrenner aus Zwickau*. Schindellegi, Switzerland, 1998.

Roesler, Jörg. *Zwischen Plan und Markt: Die Wirtschaftsreform in der DDR zwischen 1963–1970*. Freiburg and Berlin, 1990.

Roggemann, Herwig. *Die DDR-Verfassungen*. Berlin, 1976.

Roll, Eric. *A History of Economic Thought*. London, 1992.

Ross, Corey. "Before the Wall: East Germans, Communist Authority, and the Mass Exodus to the West." *Historical Journal* 45:2 (2002), pp. 459–480.

Sarotte, M. E. *Dealing with the Devil: East Germany, Détente and Ostpolitik, 1969–1973*. Chapel Hill, N.C., 2001.

Sarrazin, Thilo. "Die Entstehung und Umsetzung des Konzepts der deutschen Wirtschafts- und Währungsunion." In Theo Waigel and Manfred Schnell, eds., *Tage, die Deutschland und die Welt veränderten. Vom Mauerfall zum Kaukasus – die deutsche Währungsunion*. Munich, 1994, pp. 160–225.

Schell, Manfred. "Zusammenbruch mit Perspektive." In Theo Waigel and Manfred Schell, eds., *Tage, die Deutschland und die Welt veränderten. Vom Mauerfall zum Kaukasus – die deutsche Währungsunion*. Munich, 1994, pp. 12–25.

Schelsky, Helmut. *Die skeptische Generation. Eine Soziologie der deutschen Jugend*. Düsseldorf, 1957.

Schneider, Franka. "'Jedem nach dem Wohnsitz seiner Tante'. Die Genex Geschenk- dienst GmbH." In Neue Gesellschaft für bildende Kunst, ed., *Wunderwirtschaft. DDR-Konsumkultur in den 60er Jahren*. Cologne, Weimar, and Vienna, 1996.

Schneider, Rosemarie. "Das Verkehrswesen unter besonderer Berücksichtigung der Eisenbahn." In Eberhard Kuhrt, ed., *Am Ende des realen Sozialismus 2: Die wirtschaftliche und ökologische Situation der DDR in den achtziger Jahren*. Opladen, 1996, pp. 171–222.

Schumpeter, Joseph A. *Das Wesen des Geldes*. Göttingen, 1970.

Schürer, Gerhard. "Die Wirtschafts- und Sozialpolitik der DDR." In Dietmar Keller, Hans Modrow, and Herbert Wolf, eds., *Ansichten zur Geschichte der DDR*, vol. 3. Bonn and Berlin, 1994, pp. 131–72.

Sell, Erwin, and H. Jörg Thieme. "Nebenwährungen bei zentraler Planung des Wirtschafts- prozesses." In Alfred Schüller and Ulrich Wagner, eds., *Außenwirtschaftspolitik und Stabilisierung von Wirtschaftssystemen*. Stuttgart and New York, 1980, pp. 127–42.

Shafir, Michael. *Romania: Politics, Economics, and Society*. London, 1985.

Sieber, Günter. "Ustinov tobte, Gorbatschow schwieg." In Brigitte Zimmermann and Hans- Dieter Schütt, eds., *Ohnmacht – DDR Funktionäre sagen aus*. Berlin, 1992, pp. 217–34.

Simatupang, Batara. *The Polish Economic Crisis: Background, Causes, Aftermath*. London, 1994.

Singer, Otto. "Constructing the Economic Spectacle: The Role of Currency Union in the German Unification Process." *Journal of Economic Issues* 4 (1992), pp. 1095–1115.

Sinn, Hans-Werner. "Germany's Economic Unification: An Assessment after Ten Years." *National Bureau of Economic Research*, Working Paper 7586. Cambridge, Mass., 2000.

Slay, Ben. *The Polish Economy: Crisis, Reform, and Transformation.* Princeton, N.J., 1994.

Smith, Alan H. *The Planned Economies of Eastern Europe.* New York, 1983.

Smith, Eric Owen. *The German Economy.* London, 1994.

Smyser, W. R. *The German Economy: Colossus at the Crossroads.* New York, 1992.

Staadt, Jochen. "Walter Ulbrichts letzter Machtkampf." *Deutschland Archiv* 29 (1996), pp. 686–700.

Stachura, Peter D., ed. *Unemployment and the Great Depression in Weimar Germany.* London, 1986.

Steiner, André. *Die DDR-Wirtschaftsreform der sechziger Jahre. Konflikt zwischen Effizienz- und Machtkalkül.* Berlin, 1999.

Steingart, Gabor. *Deutschland, der Abstieg eines Superstars.* Munich, 2004.

Stelkens, Jochen. "Machtwechsel in Ost-Berlin." *Vierteljahreshefte für Zeitgeschichte* 45 (1997), pp. 503–33.

Stephan, Gerd-Rüdiger. "Vom Mauerbau 1961 bis zur Wende 1989." In Andreas Herbst, Gerd-Rüdiger Stephan, and Jürgen Winkler, eds., *Die SED. Geschichte – Organisation – Politik. Ein Handbuch.* Berlin, 1997, pp. 56–100.

Stokes, Raymond G. *Constructing Socialism: Technology and Change in East Germany, 1945–1990.* Baltimore, Md., 2000.

Streit, Manfred E. "German Monetary Union." In Deutsche Bundesbank, ed., *Fifty Years of the Deutsche Mark: Central Bank and the Currency in Germany since 1948.* Oxford and New York, 1999, pp. 476–83.

Stürmer, Michael. "Parliamentary Government in Weimar Germany, 1924–1929." In Anthony Nicholls and Erich Matthias, eds., *German Democracy and the Triumph of Hitler.* London, 1971, pp. 59–78.

Swain, Nigel. *Hungary: The Rise and Fall of Feasible Socialism.* London and New York, 1992.

Swett, Pamela, S. Jonathan Wiesen, and Jonathan R. Zatlin, eds. *Selling Modernity: Advertising and Public Relations in Modern German History.* Durham, N.C., 2007.

Szabo, Stephen F. *The Diplomacy of German Unification.* New York, 1992.

Taylor, Keith. *The Political Ideas of the Utopian Socialists.* London, 1982.

Tenfelde, Klaus, and Helmuth Trischler, eds. *Bis vor die Stufen des Throns: Bittschriften und Beschwerden von Bergleuten im Zeitalter der Industrialisierung.* Munich, 1986.

Thieme, H. Jörg. "The Central Bank and Money in the GDR." In Deutsche Bundesbank, ed., *Fifty Years of the Deutsche Mark: Central Bank and the Currency in Germany since 1948.* Oxford and New York, 1999, pp. 575–617.

Thomas, Rüdiger. "Kulturpolitik und Künstlerbewußtsein seit dem VIII. Parteitag der SED." In Gert-Joachim Glaeßner, ed., *Die DDR in der Ära Honecker: Politik. Kultur. Gesellschaft.* Opladen, 1988.

Thompson, Edward Palmer. *The Making of the English Working Class.* New York, 1963.

Timm, Angelika. *Hammer, Zirkel, Davidstern: das gestörte Verhältnis der DDR zum Zionismus und Staat Israel.* Bonn, 1997.

Tismaneanu, Vladimir. *Reinventing Politics: Eastern Europe from Stalin to Havel.* New York, 1992.

de Tocqueville, Alexis. *The Ancien Regime and the French Revolution*, trans. Stuart Gilbert. New York, 1983.

Torpey, John C. *Intellectuals, Socialism, and Dissent: The East German Opposition and Its Legacy.* Minneapolis, Minn., and London, 1995.

Vitzthum, Wolfgang Graf. "Petitionsrecht." In Meinhard Schröder, ed., *Ergänzbares Lexikon des Rechts. Ordner 2, Staats- und Verfassungsrecht*. Berlin, 1992, pp. 1–6.

Volze, Armin. Book review. *Deutschland Archiv* 6 (1992), p. 651.

———. "Die Devisengeschäfte der DDR. Genex und Intershop." *Deutschland Archiv* 24:11 (1991), pp. 1145–59.

———. "Geld und Politik in den innerdeutschen Beziehungen." *Deutschland Archiv* 23:3 (1990), pp. 382–7.

———. "Ein großer Bluff?" *Deutschland Archiv* 29:5 (1996), pp. 701–13.

———. "Kirchliche Transferleistungen in die DDR." *Deutschland Archiv* 24 (1991), pp. 59–66.

———, and Johannes L. Kuppe. "Doktor Schalck. Analyse einer Geheimdissertation." *Deutschland Archiv* 26:6 (1993), pp. 641–57.

Waigel, Theo. "Tage, die Deutschland und die Welt veränderten." In Theo Waigel and Manfred Schnell, eds., *Tage, die Deutschland und die Welt veränderten. Vom Mauerfall zum Kaukasus – die deutsche Währungsunion*. Munich, 1994, pp. 26–56.

Weber, Hermann. *Geschichte der DDR*. Munich, 1989.

———. *Die Wandlungen des deutschen Kommunismus*, vol. 1. Frankfurt/Main, 1969.

Weber, Max. *The Theory of Social and Economic Organization*, trans. A. M. Henderson and Talcott Parsons. New York, 1947.

———. *Wirtschaft und Gesellschaft: Grundriß der verstehenden Soziologie*. Tübingen, 1972.

Werner, Oliver. "'Politisch überzeugend, feinfühlig und vertrauensvoll'? Eingabenbearbeitung in der SED." In Heiner Timmermann, ed., *Diktaturen in Europa im 20. Jahrhundert – der Fall DDR*. Berlin, 1996, pp. 461–79.

Weymar, Thomas. "Das Auto – Statussymbol auch im Sozialismus. Soziale und politische Folgeprobleme des Individualverkehrs in der DDR." *Deutschland Archiv* 3 (1977), pp. 271–86.

Wiesen, S. Jonathan. *West German Industry and the Challenge of the Nazi Past, 1945–1955*. Chapel Hill, N.C., 2001.

Wildt, Michael. *Am Beginn der 'Konsumgesellschaft'. Mangelerfahrung, Lebenshaltung, Wohlstandshoffnung in Westdeutschland in den fünfziger Jahren*. Hamburg, 1994.

Winkler, Heinrich A. *Der Weg in die Katastrophe: Arbeiter und Arbeiterbewegung in der Weimarer Repubik 1930 bis 1933*. Berlin, 1987.

Winkler, Jürgen. "Kulturpolitik." In Andreas Herbst, Gerd-Rüdiger Stephan, and Jürgen Winkler, eds., *Die SED. Geschichte – Organisation – Politik. Ein Handbuch*. Berlin, 1997.

Woodcock, George. *Pierre-Joseph Proudhon: A Biography*. Montreal and New York, 1987.

Woodruff, David Marshall. "The Making of Money: Media of Exchange and Politics in Post-Soviet Russia." PhD Dissertation, University of California at Berkeley, 1996.

———. *Money Unmade: Barter and the Fate of Russian Capitalism*. Ithaca, N.Y., 2000.

Yusuf, Salim, Peter Sleight, Janice Pogue, Jackie Bosch, Richard Davies, and Gilles Dagenais. "Effects of an Angiotensin-Converting-Enzyme Inhibitor, Ramipril, on Cardiovascular Events in High-Risk Patients." *New England Journal of Medicine 342* (2000), pp. 145–53.

Zatlin, Jonathan R. "Hard Marks and Soft Revolutionaries: The Economics of Entitlement and the Debate over German Unification, November 9, 1989–March 18, 1990." *German Politics and Society* 33 (Fall 1994), pp. 57–84.

———. "Polnische Wirtschaft, deutsche Ordnung? Der Umgang mit den Polen in der DDR unter Honecker." In Christian T. Müller and Patrice G. Poutrus, eds., *Ankunft-Alltag-Ausreise. Migration und interkulturelle Begegnungen in der DDR-Gesellschaft*. Cologne and Weimar, 2005.

Zelikow, Philip, and Condoleezza Rice. *Germany Unified and Europe Transformed: A Study in Statecraft.* Cambridge, Mass., 1995.

Zimmerling, Zeno, and Sabine Zimmerling, eds. *Neue Chronik DDR*, Folge 1 and Folge 4/5. Berlin, 1990.

Zimmermann, Hartmut, ed. *DDR Handbuch*, vols. 1 and 2. Cologne, 1985.

Zloch-Christy, Iliana. *Debt Problems of Eastern Europe.* Cambridge, 1987.

Zschaler, Frank. *Öffentliche Finanzen und Finanzpolitik in Berlin, 1945–1961.* Berlin and New York, 1995.

Index